THE
AFRICAN
AMERICAN
BOOK OF VALUES

EDITED WITH COMMENTARY BY

STEVEN BARBOZA

DOUBLEDAY
New York · London · Toronto · Sydney · Auckland

THE
AFRICAN
AMERICAN
BOOK OF VALUES

CLASSIC MORAL STORIES

PUBLISHED BY DOUBLEDAY
a division of Bantam Doubleday Dell Publishing Group, Inc.
1540 Broadway, New York, New York 10036

DOUBLEDAY and the portrayal of an anchor with a dolphin
are trademarks of Doubleday, a division of
Bantam Doubleday Dell Publishing Group, Inc.

Library of Congress Cataloging-in-Publication Data
Barboza, Steven.
The African American book of values : classic moral stories /
by Steven Barboza. — 1st ed.
p.   cm.
Includes index.
1. Afro-Americans—Conduct of life.
2. Social values—Unites States.   I. Title.
E185.86.B35   1998
170′.89′96073—dc21   97-25628
CIP

For all Americans, and especially for
Michael Crawford and Yvette Hawkins.

ACKNOWLEDGMENTS

I am deeply grateful to the many people who helped make this book a reality. First among them is Janet Hill, my editor, whose judgment, skill, creativity, and perseverance made a vital difference and put this book on the right track.

My agent, Denise Stinson, saved the project from certain abandonment in its early stages. Without her guidance, gentle prodding, and wise counsel, this book would not have made it to print.

Many others played an important role in shaping this book, among them the librarians of the Schomburg Center for Research in Black Culture, including the staff of the Manuscripts, Archives, and Rare Books Division—Diana Lachatanere, curator, Berlena Robinson, Andre Elizee, Paula Williams, and Aisha al-Adawiya; also Genette McLaurin, curator, and Betty Odabashian, and Sharon Howard, librarians in the Jean Blackwell Hutson General Research and Reference Division. They knew where to find examples of values, and I am indebted to them for their help.

Among others who assisted are Amir and Tamu Al-Islam, José Ananias, Langston and Lien Barboza, Allene Carter, Maureen Cullen, David Gerhan, George and Valentine Hill, Selena James, the Mark McClain family, Elvin Montgomery, Mayuri Reddy, Lt. Col. Guy Shields, Steve Vitoff, Darryl Williams, and Julie Youmans. I would also like to acknowledge the copy editing, design, and production staff at Doubleday for making this project a reality. I thank them all.

Finally, I wish to thank my wife, Regina Fe, for her infinite patience, loving kindness, understanding, selflessness, and friendship. She is the embodiment of what this book is all about.

Contents

THE BOOK OF SELF-MASTERY

SELF-DISCIPLINE

COURAGE

HONESTY

SELF-ESTEEM

CREATIVITY

FAITH

THE BOOK OF EMPATHY

FAMILY

COMMUNITY

LOVE

RESPECT

LOYALTY

SURVIVAL HUMOR

THE

AFRICAN
AMERICAN
BOOK OF VALUES

INTRODUCTION

Black Family Values

My mother's bedtime stories put me on my first solo flights in a world where misery transformed itself magically into good things and happiness. Borne by my imagination, I floated on a magic carpet that doubled as my bed, her words transporting me safely from the south end of town, occupied by colored folks like us, to places that might have been off-limits to African Americans by tradition if not by law.

I was the fourth of eight sons, so even though Mom only had an eighth grade education, by the time I came along she had had plenty of practice reading children's stories. She knew a trick or two about pirates' coves and Sherwood Forest hideouts and all the king's horses and all the king's men. And I was sure she could outwit giants in the sky, or chop down an overgrown beanstalk with the edge of her hand. The sound of her voice tucked me in, warmed me in winter, stirred up a dreamy breeze on raggedy hot summer nights, thrilled, soothed, and offered the sharpest contrast to the call of troubled streets.

Home was that old whaling port, New Bedford, Massachusetts, safe harbor at one time for Captain Ahab and other ancient mariners who chased whale blubber to the ends of the earth and returned from three-year odysseys bearing wondrous tales of mermaids or mean white whales. New Bedford had a marvelous legacy of salt water tales. But for all I knew, they might have remained a secret.

In my house, the library was meager—a feast for only the most imaginative child. My own books (mostly hand-me-downs) told of the usual assortment of childhood characters: bear families, wise owls, animals who walked and talked and blew houses down. Yet for all their remarkably human traits, not one of them could do the simplest thing of all: speak like a black person. And in those tales, not a soul lived in a neighborhood that bore any resemblance to my own. What's more, the only "people" in tales or fables that I knew were wooden-bodied, or white—except, that is, for a little boy named Sambo.

Sambo confounded me. Perhaps my confusion was the key to my fascination with him. During my youth, he was the only black character I had come across as a fan of fables. He was blacker than anybody I knew in real life, and he exhibited virtually no control over his world.

As his story goes, Sambo's mother, Black Mumbo, sews him a red jacket and trousers. His father, Black Jumbo, buys him an umbrella and purple shoes with crimson soles and linings. Dressed to kill, Sambo ventures into the jungle, where on separate occasions he confronts a different tiger who threatens to eat him alive. Sambo bargains for his life, giving each tiger an article of clothing. Then, wandering virtually naked through the jungle, Sambo hears growling and sees the tigers arguing among themselves as to which is the best dressed. They undress, bite each other's tail, and whirl around a palm tree. Sambo then reclaims his clothes and returns home. The tigers, meanwhile, whiz around the tree so fast that they melt into a stream of butter. Along comes old Black Jumbo, who scoops the butter into a brass pot and brings it home. Mumbo cooks hundreds of pancakes, using the tiger butter and milk and sugar and eggs. Then the family eats its heart out.

Looking back, I can easily vouch for the craziness behind the Sambo story.* The Sambo caricature was one of the first indirect attacks on my formative black self. The fable may have been related, in theme at least, to the shuck-'n'-jive acts of old minstrelsy troupes, popular diversions for whites who got their jollies from such stereotypic assaults.

Sambo's legacy as the spook who sat by the tree drove home a lesson I didn't come to grips with for many years: that the function of language, even seemingly innocent children's stories, is humanity's attempt to control and manipulate the universe by describing it, for the real power of words lies in how they shape ideas, unleash or bog down the imagination, stir emotions, and define reality. Forget Sambo or what his creator said about blacks; what had my own people said about themselves? What "manipulations" had they exercised over their own uni-

---

* The Sambo story was created in 1899 by Helen Bannerman, an Englishwoman. She wrote and illustrated it to entertain her two daughters while living in India, where, her American publisher reported, "black children abound and tigers are everyday affairs."

verse? What devils had they *exorcised* from America? Or Africa? And what about that illegitimate manchild of the jungle, Tarzan? How is it that I could identify with him, swinging in trees like a hyperactive monkey to escape bone-through-the-nose cannibals out to stuff him in a pot? Only that Commando of the Vines possessed enough man-size dignity and apely strength to master the "Dark Continent," which to me appeared in desperate need of taming.

I cannot blame my mother for a lack of sophistication in reading material. She and I were a captive audience. Bookstores and libraries and publishers offered us a minute repertoire from which to choose. Except for strange tales like Sambo's, my race was passed off as virtually fable-less in my hometown. So the three little bears versus the fiendish wolf had to suffice. And if I wanted to see a reflection of myself in fairy tales set outside of the animal kingdom, I had to mask my folks' humanity—my own humanity—in white skin in nearly every characterization that met my mind's eye before I drifted off to sleep. Still, something was always lacking, something black and kingly.

Decades later, I discovered that black tales abound. They're just what children need, a body of literature they can be proud of: Sambo-less imagery. Stories that entertain without sacrificing the humanity of black folks. Stories with an eye toward teaching moral lessons. Stories that let black children know they have as much right to inherit the earth as anyone. Stories that establish a healthy frame of reference for people who can—and do—exercise control over their universe.

The African American Book of Values is a compendium of "black values," which are quite simply the values of black folks. No secret here. As the title implies, this book is intended for use in the moral instruction of both children and adults, imparting lessons that involve codes of conduct, respectfulness, healthy and wholesome regard for oneself and one's community. This book can give children, families, teachers, and friends glimpses of values in action and provide moral examples that any reader can recognize.

More than ever, young people need to see evidence of morality in others around them and develop a knack for survival. In drugs and violence, youth today face more danger than their parents did. Black-on-black crime rates have reached a crisis point. Kids shoot one another in cold blood, and we've become so inured to armed pupils that to "solve" the problem we install metal detectors in schools. Homicide is the leading cause of death among black males between age fifteen and thirty-four, and it is reported that each year, more blacks die at the hands of other blacks than the total number of lynchings in Ku Klux Klan history. Part of the solutions to these problems may lie in exhorting black values.

Though the stories in this volume can inspire, this is not a book of inspiration; and while its contents may bear meditative worth, it is not a book of meditations. It *is* a book of guidance. To help children (and adults) develop upstanding habits and traits, we must explain why they're important to uphold, admire, and emulate. Literature has long been a tool for accomplishing this task.

The material here originates in the treasure trove of black experience—from the planting fields of pre–Civil War Mississippi to the bustling sidewalks of Harlem during the Renaissance, and from the corner beauty parlor to the local church. There is a rich library of material *by* black folks *about* black folks *for* black folks, and it is growing all the time.

In the following pages, you will find do-unto-others stories, cautionary tales on how to act right, stories on cooperative decision-making, domestic dramas, trickster stories. You will also find other forms of expression—folk songs, spirituals, and blues, for example.

The descendants of kidnapped Africans gave us many of our early spirituals, songs borne out of the hazards of life in America. The lyrics are cries for freedom, or testimonies of strength and resiliency. Spirituals and blues and ballads pit courage against prevailing circumstances, compassion and love against the inhumanity of man.

These songs are also a unique legacy. They may have been inspired by African rhythms and chants, but they're as un-African as a jazz band. "[The African's] mother did not sing 'Sometimes I Feel Like a Motherless Child,'" James Baldwin wrote, "and he has not, all his life long, ached for acceptance in a culture which pronounced straight hair and white skin the only acceptable beauty."

Some spirituals and folk songs report historical events. They honor heroes (bad men, too), tell sad love stories, express nostalgia and pain, or protest conditions. These songs are passed down through an oral tradition that continues to transform them, as singers reinvent the same tunes again and again.

Likewise, the narratives, stories and poems in this book span many generations, relaying the values and wisdom of countless Americans, reflecting many a raconteur's—or main character's—triumphs and tragedies in confronting human dilemmas. Taken together, the poetry and prose and songs of slaves and free blacks make for a deep reservoir of information on what African Americans value as a people.

THE WORLD APPARENTLY needs moral literature to entertain and imbue a sense of order and justice, right and wrong, good and bad. Morals essentially are social conventions established for the greater benefit of a people. As a river winds and bends its way into the sea, the morals of various groups of people flow into the vast body of world-class literature. No single race, ethnic group, or nationality can rightly claim a monopoly on the greatest moral stories. Each group displays its own special talent for painting morals in a new face, with a distinct personality; each nurtures and hones its moral values through unique forms of cultural expression.*

From their beginning in America, blacks were forced to abide by an ethical system that pronounced a cruel indifference to Africanity. Though black values regarding the family and community still evolved on Western soil, they did so on "the far side" of the racial fence. Blacks cultivated a hidden language, sometimes camouflaging thoughts and beliefs in song or in speech that remained unintelligible to whites. Whites joked about this jargon-filled "language." But blacks endured the derision and used the language to ridicule whites without provoking their wrath.

Throughout American history, society has color-coded its values, producing expectations that sometimes hinged on race. For example, what was considered fine and righteous behavior for a white boy in slave-holding Dixie might have gotten a black boy savagely beaten or killed for boldness; and while honesty has always been highly valued by

---

* "A particular people usually has its own particular set of skills for dealing with the economic and social necessities of life—and also its own particular set of values as to what are the higher and lower purposes of life," Thomas Sowell wrote in *Race and Culture, A World View.* "These sets of skills and values typically follow them wherever they go."

most societies, blacks escaping slavery via the Underground Railroad certainly should be excused for concealing the truth of their whereabouts. Blacks' values, then, had to be sociologically driven, defined or delineated vis-à-vis race.* Ultimately, survival depended on this.

Modern studies suggest a high degree of consensus on what are defined as family values in the United States: love, compassion, respect, responsibility. A new wave of moral literature has evolved to cater to Americans' perception that parents are failing to discipline their children and provide proper guidelines for ethical life in society. Black families and white families alike are the beneficiaries of this literature. It must be remembered, however, that the term *black family values* is ambiguous at best; it is used here for convenience's sake, for its descriptive capacity. There is no formal school of African American morality, and though the morals of African Americans may differ slightly from those of other groups, any difference exists mainly in expression only, not in substance.

Even so, the world's moral literature is richer for African Americans' contributions, which should be included in any treasury of great moral stories. Read any story or poem in this book and you will determine that the values it renders can apply equally to anyone, regardless of race or ethnicity.

As adults, we may be familiar with some of the material in this book. But for most children, the stories, poems, and other forms of expression will probably cover uncharted territory. Though taken directly from the black experience, some of the values included here have been ignored or forgotten. It is time to resurrect them and lend them a place of importance in schools, homes, and places of worship.

Like a plant, which needs sunlight, soil, and water to grow, values, too, must be shared, cultivated, protected. Children, after all, are not

---

* How should we define the Negro race? Gunnar Myrdal, in his landmark study *An American Dilemma*, published in 1944, attempted this definition: "The 'Negro race' is defined in America by the white people. It is defined in terms of parentage. Everybody having a *known* trace of Negro blood in his veins—no matter how far back it was acquired—is classified as a Negro. No amount of white ancestry, except one hundred per cent, will permit entrance to the white race. . . .

"The definition of the 'Negro race' is thus a social and conventional, not a biological concept. The social definition and not the biological facts actually determines the status of an individual and his place in interracial relations. . . . In modern biological or ethnological research 'race' as a scientific concept has lost sharpness of meaning, and the term is disappearing in sober writings."

natural-born moralists; they're not endowed with an innate ability to distinguish ethical values from despicableness. They must be taught, and adults have a hand in the lessons today, just as in the past.

During the first half of the twentieth century, moral lessons were a given in American schools. "Moral instruction," according to a 1914 *New York Times* article, "should be as systematic and as definite as a course in mathematics." But in the 1960s, after the U.S. Supreme Court ruled that making prayer and Bible study a part of the curriculum violated a person's constitutional rights, moral education fell out of favor in public schools.

Today, with mounting fears of violence and drug abuse, parents are taking up the banner for teaching values in school. Several mid-1990s surveys reported that more than 90 percent of American adults, black and white, want public schools to teach honesty, racial tolerance, belief in democracy, and the Golden Rule. These days, informed school district officials are wise enough to avoid imposing their own values on students. Instead, they inject only the most widely shared "core values" into the curriculum. In addition, school is underpinned by certain ground rules requiring children to respect authority and act considerate and civil toward others. Without this "hidden curriculum," learning would be handicapped. Meanwhile, a not-so-hidden "curriculum" exists in the home. a foundation of respect and love (or lack thereof) that affects—indeed, *becomes*—a child's value system.

In many ways, *The African American Book of Values* will help on both fronts—at home and at school. First, as an anthology, it serves as a useful aid in illustrating core values. Adults can use this book to entertain and enlighten youngsters.

Second, in this book children will find paradigms for moral reasoning. Black experience in America is brimming with morals that can help steer children down a "straight path" through either the 'hood or the backwoods, especially in times of senseless drive-by shootings and ferociously raunchy song lyrics, an era when many twist the words *nigga* and *bitch* into icons of love.

Next, learning about values is a lifelong process. Teaching children that they are the inheritors of a great treasury of values can serve to reimmerse adults in those same lessons, helping them to polish and refocus their ideals and principles, if need be. Adults, then, can derive as much benefit as children from this material; they don't need to use a child as an excuse to plunge in.

And finally, children will come to cherish these stories, poems, and songs, and through them develop a new appreciation for the culture that continues to shape their experiences.

This book will also challenge assumptions that American culture is monolithic. As Eric V. Copage points out in his book *Black Pearls:* "To be black in America is to be marked and differentiated like no other group in American society. . . . For centuries our skin color, hair texture, and facial features have marked us as a people held in bondage, and even after emancipation, we have been marked for rare virulence in ongoing discrimination." For many readers, these pages will offer a fresh perspective, one affirming positive black values.

IDEAS—BOTH GOOD ones and bad ones—drive history. Two have wreaked havoc and destruction across the centuries, leaving blood in their wake: that *black is evil,* and *white is good.** These concepts are ingrained in our national psyche and in much of the world's. The art and literature of Western civilization casts much of its symbolism in darkness versus the light. Scholars point out that the Scriptures do this, too, using *black* to convey wickedness, sin, evil, and ignorance. In one passage, Job cries out, "My skin is black," lending weight to his burden of sin by blackening it.

If the cloak of damnation is black, then the fate of African Americans must have been sealed long ago, so that now even the most assiduously well read and immaculately tailored blacks, incorrigible as they are presumed to be, must inevitably surrender to their assignments among the doomed, among society's most estranged and alienated members.

Of course, the brighter side of the equation is the "goodness of whiteness." In a society that holds white skin in the healthiest regard, white people are deemed "positive" to blacks' "negative"; whites stand

---

* In *The New World of Negro Americans,* Harold R. Isaacs writes that "history is clothed" with these concepts, which are in any dictionary—"white hope" . . . "whitewash" . . . "black arts" . . . "black-browed" . . . "blackhearted" . . . "blacklist" . . . "blackmail." Isaacs continues: "This raising of 'white' and debasement of 'black' has been marked deep on the minds of all through time and every 'white' person has more or less unconsciously imbibed it as nourishment for his self-esteem."

to gain when blacks lose; whites' self-esteem soars when blacks' plunges. This happens subconsciously for some; for others, the facts are incontestably clear.

America, ultimately, must bear responsibility for its own racial landscape, one in which racist films like *The Birth of a Nation* and characters like Bigger Thomas in Richard Wright's *Native Son* can be either real or imagined. For centuries white society held blacks in contempt, treating them as orphans, losers, and nobodies. In the face of such discrimination, Ralph Ellison's protagonist in *Invisible Man* goes so far as to declare himself invisible.* Critics contend that the real tragedy of this character was that he remained invisible to himself—and it is *this* invisibility, his own peculiar inability to spy himself in the mirror, that rendered him powerless, ineffectual, impotent. He must even convince himself of his own existence.†

The world inherited by young black children has quite a legacy of hatred and self-contempt and danger. How can we expect to raise models of morality in this setting? How can children ever hope to value mercy if they are continually subjected to peril? How can a child begin to understand respect and compassion if his or her closest friend is likely to wind up in a pool of blood, the victim of some youth's tragic need to take someone else's life in order to attest his own virility?

Perhaps the only possible answer is: through example.

This book is not meant to condemn or to lay blame; rather, it focuses on the strengths, versatility, and resiliency of blacks—historic figures and relative unknowns. I have focused chiefly on what is beautiful, strong, worth sharing. The nation has been deeply moved by great inspirers and compelling orators such as Frederick Douglass and Martin Luther King Jr., whose words are included in the following pages.

For the most part, the book contains little on politics; so people of every political persuasion, whether conservative, radical, or liberal, can take equal pleasure in its contents. You will not find discussions on

---

* He says: "I am invisible, understand, simply because people refuse to see me. . . . When they approach me they see only my surroundings, themselves, or figments of their imagination—indeed, everything and anything except me."

† "You ache with the need to convince yourself that you do exist in the real world, that you're a part of all the sound and anguish, and you strike out with your fists, you curse and you swear to make them recognize you. And, alas, it's seldom successful."

welfare, abortion, or affirmative action here. My objective has only been to help establish moral groundwork, the basis for good character. If we help children gain a foothold in the basics, we can reasonably expect them to develop the moral aptitude needed for grappling compassionately with delicate and challenging issues. It is probably more difficult, anyway, to establish a moral baseline than to tackle the day's political issues.

(Certain political realities are inescapable, of course, and are brought to bear whenever the word *black* is mentioned, whether linked to values, virtues, or vices. James Baldwin submitted, "Color is not a human or a personal reality; it is a political reality." If this is so, then breaking barriers and acting to gain equal rights for blacks can be construed as political—such as the lunch counter sit-ins in the early 1960s to desegregate Southern restaurants. The demonstrators still exhibited courage, so their trial by fire is included here.)

The values featured in this book are not the exclusive domain of any particular faith, either. Nor are they intended to promote indifferentism—the belief that all religions are equally valid—a notion that offends some people's sensibilities. Religion, I believe, is an entirely personal matter that should not be subject to the whims or compulsions of others.

Whether you are Baptist or Muslim, Republican or Democrat, a fan of Duke Ellington or Queen Latifah or both, this book can still apply to you and the children around you. It illustrates those noble values that can help dispel the debilitating sense of disability and nobodiness that has been imposed on black people for centuries.

A solid ethical system provides tools for self-mastery and empathy, two prime values from which most others stem. With these two basic clusters of values—those dealing with oneself (such as honesty and tenacity) and those shaping one's orientation toward others (such as compassion and loyalty)—a person can equip himself or herself to be a moral force in the community. Thus, I have used "self-mastery" and "empathy" as organizing principles for this book.

Humor, too, has played an important role in black survival. It has served as a shield against harsh realities, directed attention at the nation's racial ills, and brought joy. Thus, I considered it a value worth including.

I never intended this book to contain every moral black America has ever produced. No single volume could. Space was limited, and there was much to cover.

Though some stories might seem dated, they nevertheless relate values that are as vital today as they were yesterday. Other inclusions deal with slavery because the words of slaves may offer insights into our human condition today. Everyone can benefit from knowing certain harsh facts about American history, including slavery.

This is not a history book, however. Using either excerpts or complete text, I have included both fiction and fact, the stuff of legend as well as the "minutes of meetings." In some cases, the literal facts are bent to serve the moral ones. Lessons to be gleaned are what really counts.

So that this book will also benefit your child, read it aloud from cover to cover, or in whatever chapter order strikes you as good on a particular day. Use the table of contents to find entries that will prove helpful when a specific lesson is required. Or simply browse through the book as you would a favorite collection. Youth are invited to browse, too.

It is my hope that this work will provide a source of comfort, not necessarily admonition. It is a book meant to hearten, to give strength, not to sadden or to deflate. It is meant to appeal to our higher instincts; to jump-start us in our daily endeavors. Muhammad, the Prophet of Islam, once said, "Everyone starts his day and is a vendor of his soul, either freeing it or bringing about its ruin." I hope that both readers and listeners will end each day with a reading from these pages and awake as a "vendor" of the values instilled the night before.

—Steven Barboza

From the press . . . we have suffered much by being incorrectly represented . . . Our vices and our degradation are ever arrayed against us,
but our virtues are passed by unnoticed.

—John Russwurm,
Freedom's Journal,
March 16, 1827

THE BOOK OF
SELF-MASTERY

SELF-DISCIPLINE

Self-discipline is "home training" and then some. It is the ability to round out your own rough edges, correct your own raggedy ways, curb your own appetite for things or people that are bound to get you into a world of trouble or at least hot water.

And self-discipline is more than that. It is a talent for self-improvement—for presenting to the world your "new and improved" version: a person who can summon sheer willpower and self-control whenever the need arises. For most of us, doing this is no easy feat; it involves concentrated effort.

On the surface, self-discipline may appear to be no different for African Americans than for any other people. Self-control, we naturally assume, is self-control, regardless of race. Whether you're black or white, something like learning to read probably involves the same intense struggle to master the alphabet and phonetics.

Actually, history has proven otherwise. In slave-holding America, working harder, faster, and more profitably on behalf of whites was the status quo for slaves. But self-improvement for slaves' own sake? That was grounds for punishment. Blacks were expected to aspire to no more in life than hard, back-breaking labor for others. A black who could think for himself or herself and who could delve at will into the world's vast library of knowledge was for slave masters an invitation to trouble. Whites, then, merely had to attend school to learn to read, while blacks had to learn on the sly—an act of defiance and enormous courage, an expression of self-discipline that was considered highly subversive. After all, it was considered utterly outrageous—and criminal—for blacks to try to fulfill their human potential in a society that regarded them as merely three-fifths human.

Civil War and emancipation brought an end to this inhuman treatment, yet left blacks at the bottom of the social ladder. Learning to read no longer entailed hiding one's primer from Old Massa. Still, the climb up the social ladder was difficult and steep for most African Americans, particularly after centuries of neglect, degradation and racial practices that only served to undermine black self-respect and self-love. Blacks moved onward and upward, though, and are still climbing today.

This chapter includes stories that will inspire people who are seeking to improve themselves under ordinary or extraordinary circumstances. Surely, no one's schooling came harder than Frederick Douglass's reading lessons or Malcolm X's self-taught prison studies. Everyday situations are explored in a piece by Ralph Ellison that shows the wisdom of practicing diligently, even when the audience for your musicianship is nowhere to be seen. Here you will also find etiquette lessons as taught by black America's "Miss Manners," Charlotte Hawkins Brown, old folk rhymes with valuable advice, and Langston Hughes offers an amusing ten-point system on how *not* to write.

The basics in self-discipline are covered here, whether acquiring a new talent, polishing an old one, or simply resisting temptation to backslide. Habit is key, practice essential. And the more practicing you do, the much better your chances for success and self-improvement.

∽◈∾

The battles that count aren't the ones for gold medals. The struggles within yourself—the invisible, inevitable battles inside all of us—that's where it's at.

—*Jesse Owens*

∽◈∾

WRITING
FREDERICK DOUGLASS

In 1740, the American Colonies began enacting compulsory ignorance laws, prohibiting the teaching of slaves or free blacks. However, despite the risk of punishment and even disfigurement for learning to read, thousands of enslaved African Americans defied the laws. For the young Frederick Douglass, gaining an education was a form of rebellion. Born in 1818 on the eastern shore of Maryland, Douglass was raised by his grandmother on a plantation. He was then sent to a new master in Baltimore at age eight. At first, his new master's wife encouraged him to read and write, until her husband convinced her that "learning would spoil the best nigger." The following selection, taken from his autobiography, shows Douglass's resourcefulness and resolve to learn in a society that deemed black literacy dangerous.

The frequent hearing of my mistress reading the bible—for she often read aloud when her husband was absent—soon awakened my curiosity in respect to this *mystery* of reading, and roused in me the desire to learn. Having no fear of my kind mistress before my eyes, (she had then given me no reason to fear,) I frankly asked her to teach me to read; and, without hesitation, the dear woman began the task, and very soon, by her assistance, I was master of the alphabet, and could spell words of three or four letters. My mistress seemed almost as proud of my progress, as if I had been her own child; and, supposing that her husband would be as well pleased, she made no secret of what she was doing for me. Indeed, she exultingly told him of the aptness of her pupil, of her intention to persevere in teaching me, and of the duty which she felt it to teach me, at least to read *the bible*. Here arose the first cloud over my Baltimore prospects, the precursor of drenching rains and chilling blasts.

Master Hugh was amazed at the simplicity of his spouse, and, probably for the first time, he unfolded to her the true philosophy of slavery, and the peculiar rules necessary to be observed by masters and mistresses, in the management of their human chattels. Mr. Auld promptly forbade the continuance of her instruction; telling her, in the first place, that the thing itself was unlawful; that it was also unsafe, and could only lead to mischief. To use his own words, further, he said, "if you give a nigger an inch, he will take an ell;" "he should know nothing but the will of his master, and learn to obey it." "Learning would spoil the best nigger in the world;" "if you teach that nigger—speaking of myself— how to read the bible, there will be no keeping him;" "it would forever unfit him for the duties of a slave;" and "as to himself, learning would do him no good, but probably, a great deal of harm—making him disconsolate and unhappy." "If you learn him now to read, he'll want to know how to write; and, this accomplished, he'll be running away with himself." Such was the tenor of Master Hugh's oracular exposition of the true philosophy of training a human chattel; and it must be confessed that he very clearly comprehended the nature and the requirements of the relation of master and slave. His discourse was the first decidedly anti-slavery lecture to which it had been my lot to listen. Mrs. Auld evidently felt the force of his remarks; and, like an obedient wife, began to shape her course in the direction indicated by her husband. The effect of his words, *on me*, was neither slight nor transitory. His iron sentences—cold and harsh—sunk deep into my heart, and stirred up not only my feelings into a sort of rebellion, but awakened within me a slumbering train of vital thought. It was a new and special revelation, dispelling a painful mystery, against which my youthful understanding had struggled, and struggled in vain, to wit: the *white* man's power to perpetuate the enslavement of the *black* man. "Very well," thought I; "knowledge unfits a child to be a slave." I instinctively assented to the proposition; and from that moment I understood the direct pathway from slavery to freedom. This was just what I needed; and I got it at a time, and from a source, whence I least expected it. I was saddened at the thought of losing the assistance of my kind mistress; but the information, so instantly derived, to some extent compensated me for the loss I had sustained in this direction. Wise as Mr. Auld was, he evidently underrated my comprehension, and had little idea of the use to which I was capable of putting the impressive lesson he was giving to his wife. *He* wanted me to be *a slave;* I had already voted against that on the home plantation of Col. Lloyd. That which he most loved I most hated; and the very determination which he expressed to keep me in ignorance, only rendered me the more resolute in seeking intelligence. In learning to read, therefore, I am not sure that I do not owe quite as much to the opposition of my master, as to the kindly assistance of my amiable mistress. I acknowledge the benefit rendered me by the one, and by the other; believing, that but for my mistress, I might have grown up in ignorance. . . .

I lived in the family of Master Hugh, at Baltimore, seven years, during which time —as the almanac makers say of the weather—my condition was variable. The most interesting feature of my history here, was my learning to read and write, under somewhat marked disadvantages. In attaining this knowledge, I was compelled to resort to indirections by no means congenial to my nature, and which were really humiliating to me. My mistress—who, as the reader has already seen, had begun to teach me —was suddenly checked in her benevolent design, by the strong advice of her husband. In faithful compliance with this advice, the good lady had not only ceased to instruct me, herself, but had set her face as a flint against my learning to read by any means. It is due, however, to my mistress to say, that she did not adopt this course in all its stringency at the first. She either thought it unnecessary, or she lacked the depravity indispensable to shutting me up in mental darkness. It was, at least, necessary for her to have some training, and some hardening, in the exercise of the slaveholder's prerogative, to make her equal to forgetting my human nature and character, and to treating me as a thing destitute of a moral or an intellectual nature.

It is easy to see, that, in entering upon the duties of a slaveholder, some little experience is needed. Nature has done almost nothing to prepare men and women to be either slaves or slaveholders. Nothing but rigid training, long persisted in, can perfect the character of the one or the other. One cannot easily forget to love freedom; and it is as hard to cease to respect that natural love in our fellow creatures. On entering upon the career of a slaveholding mistress, Mrs. Auld was singularly deficient; nature, which fits nobody for such an office, had done less for her than any lady I had known. It was no easy matter to induce her to think and to feel that the curly-headed boy, who stood by her side, and even leaned on her lap; who was loved by little Tommy, and who loved little Tommy in turn; sustained to her only the relation of a chattel. I was *more* than that, and she felt me to be more than that. I could talk and sing; I could laugh and weep; I could reason and remember; I could love and hate. I was human, and she, dear lady, knew and felt me to be so. How could she, then, treat me as a brute, without a mighty struggle with all the noble powers of her own soul. That struggle came, and the will and power of the husband was victorious. Her noble soul was overthrown; but, he that overthrew it did not, himself, escape the consequences. He, not less than the other parties, was injured in his domestic peace by the fall.

When I went into their family, it was the abode of happiness and contentment. The mistress of the house was a model of affection and tenderness. Her fervent piety and watchful uprightness made it impossible to see her without thinking and feeling—*"that woman is a christian."* There was no sorrow nor suffering for which she had not a tear, and there was no innocent joy for which she had not a smile. She had bread for the hungry, clothes for the naked, and comfort for every mourner that came within her reach. Slavery soon proved its ability to divest her of these excellent qualities, and her home of its early happiness. Conscience cannot stand much violence. Once thoroughly broken down, *who* is he that can repair the damage? It may be broken toward the slave, on Sunday, and toward the master on Monday. It cannot endure such shocks. It must stand entire, or it does not stand at all. If my condition waxed bad, that of the family waxed not better. The first step, in the wrong direction, was the violence done to nature and to conscience, in arresting the benevolence that would have enlightened my young mind. In ceasing to instruct me, she must begin to justify herself *to* herself; and, once consenting to take sides in such a debate, she was riveted to her position. One needs very little knowledge of moral philosophy, to see *where* my mistress now landed. She finally became even more violent in her opposition to my learning to read, than was her husband himself. She was not satisfied with simply doing as *well* as her husband had commanded her, but seemed resolved to better his instruction. Nothing appeared to make my poor mistress—after her turning toward the downward path—more angry, than seeing me, seated in some nook or corner, quietly reading a book or a newspaper. I have had her rush at me, with the utmost fury, and snatch from my hand such newspaper or book, with something of the wrath and consternation which a traitor might be supposed to feel on being discovered in a plot by some danger- ous spy.

Mrs. Auld was an apt woman, and the advice of her husband, and her own experience, soon demonstrated, to her entire satisfaction, that edu- cation and slavery are incompatible with each other. When this convic- tion was thoroughly established, I was most narrowly watched in all my movements. If I remained in a separate room from the family for any considerable length of time, I was sure to be suspected of having a book, and was at once called upon to give an account of myself. All this, however, was entirely *too late*. The first, and never to be retraced, step had been taken. In teaching me the alphabet, in the days of her simplicity and kindness, my mistress had given me the *"inch,"* and now, no ordi- nary precaution could prevent me from taking the *"ell."*

Seized with a determination to learn to read, at any cost, I hit upon many expedients to accomplish the desired end. The plea which I mainly adopted, and the one by which I was most successful, was that of using my young white playmates, with whom I met in the street, as teachers. I used to carry, almost constantly, a copy of Webster's spelling book in my pocket; and, when sent on errands, or when play time was allowed me, I would step, with my young friends, aside, and take a lesson in spelling. I generally paid my *tuition fee* to the boys, with bread, which I also carried in my pocket. For a single biscuit, any of my hungry little comrades would give me a lesson more valuable to me than bread. Not every one, however, demanded this consideration, for there were those who took pleasure in teaching me, whenever I had a chance to be taught by them. I am strongly tempted to give the names of two or three of those little boys, as a slight testimonial of the gratitude and affection I bear them, but prudence forbids; not that it would injure me, but it might, possibly, embarrass them; for it is almost an unpardonable of- fense to do any thing, directly or indirectly, to promote a slave's freedom, in a slave state. It is enough to say, of my warm-hearted little play fellows, that they lived on Philpot street, very near Durgin & Bailey's shipyard.

LEARNING TO READ
FRANCES E. W. HARPER

In the years following the Civil War, four and a half million former slaves struggled to acquire "book learning." One journalist reported: "The whole colored population, of all sexes and ages, is repeating from morning to night, a-b, ab, e-b, eb; i-b, ib; c-a-t, cat; d-o-g, dog; c-u-p, cup." The following poem, by Frances E. W. Harper (1825–1911), tells of sixty-year-old Aunt Chloe's quest to read, reminding us that slaves placed great value on education.

> Very soon the Yankee teachers
>   Came down and set up school;
> But, oh! how the Rebs did hate it,—
>   It was agin' their rule.
>
> Our masters always tried to hide
>   Book learning from our eyes;
> Knowledge didn't agree with slavery—
>   'Twould make us all too wise.
>
> But some of us would try to steal
>   A little from the book,
> And put the words together,
>   And learn by hook or crook.
>
> I remember Uncle Caldwell,
>   Who took pot-liquor fat

And greased the pages of his book,
    And hid it in his hat.

And had his master ever seen
    The leaves upon his head,
He'd have thought them greasy papers,
    But nothing to be read.

And there was Mr. Turner's Ben,
    Who heard the children spell,
And picked the words right up by heart,
    And learned to read 'em well.

Well, the Northern folks kept sending
    The Yankee teachers down;
And they stood right up and helped us,
    Though Rebs did sneer and frown.

And, I longed to read my Bible,
    For precious words it said;
But when I begun to learn it,
    Folks just shook their heads,

And said there is no use trying,
    Oh! Chloe, you're too late;
But as I was rising sixty,
    I had no time to wait.

So I got a pair of glasses,
    And straight to work I went,
And never stopped till I could read
    The hymns and Testament.

Then I got a little cabin—
    A place to call my own—
And I felt as independent
    As the queen upon her throne.

❦

Education is our passport to the future, for tomorrow belongs to the people who prepare for it today.

—*Malcolm X*

❦

SELF-DETERMINATION
MALCOLM X

In the 1940s, when he was sent to prison, Malcolm X, then known as Malcolm Little, was a hoodlum who relied mainly on his highly developed "street wits" to survive. In prison, however, he changed dramatically—he read and studied, improving his knowledge of history, politics, and religion. He also set out to enlarge his vocabulary—from A to Z. It was his passion for self-disciplined learning that eventually helped transform him into a captivating public speaker and a formidable debater.

I became increasingly frustrated at not being able to express what I wanted to convey in letters that I wrote, especially those to Mr. Elijah Muhammad. In the street, I had been the most articulate hustler out there—I had commanded attention when I said something. But now, trying to write simple English, I not only wasn't articulate, I wasn't even functional. How would I sound writing in slang, the way I would *say* it, something such as "Look, daddy, let me pull your coat about a cat, Elijah Muhammad—"

Many who today hear me somewhere in person, or on television, or those who read something I've said, will think I went to school far beyond the eighth grade. This impression is due entirely to my prison studies.

It had really begun back in the Charlestown Prison, when Bimbi first made me feel envy of his stock of knowledge. Bimbi had always taken charge of any conversation he was in, and I had tried to emulate him. But every book I picked up had few sentences which didn't contain anywhere from one to nearly all of the words that might as well have been in Chinese. When I just skipped those words, of course, I really ended up with little idea of what the book said. So I had come to the Norfolk Prison Colony still going through only book-reading motions. Pretty soon, I would have quit even these motions, unless I had received the motivation that I did.

I saw that the best thing I could do was get hold of a dictionary—to study, to learn some words. I was lucky enough to reason also that I should try to improve my penmanship. It was sad. I couldn't even write in a straight line. It was both ideas together that moved me to request a dictionary along with some tablets and pencils from the Norfolk Prison Colony school.

I spent two days just riffling uncertainly through the dictionary's pages. I'd never realized so many words existed! I didn't know *which* words I needed to learn. Finally, just to start some kind of action, I began copying.

In my slow, painstaking, ragged handwriting, I copied into my tablet everything printed on that first page, down to the punctuation marks.

I believe it took me a day. Then, aloud, I read back, to myself, everything I'd written on the tablet. Over and over, aloud, to myself, I read my own handwriting.

I woke up the next morning, thinking about those words—immensely proud to realize that not only had I written so much at one time, but I'd written words that I never knew were in the world. Moreover, with a little effort, I also could remember what many of these words meant. I reviewed the words whose meanings I didn't remember.

I was so fascinated that I went on—I copied the dictionary's next page. And the same experience came when I studied that. With every succeeding page, I also learned of people and places and events from history. Actually the dictionary is like a miniature encyclopedia. Finally the dictionary's A section had filled a whole tablet—and I went on into the B's. That was the way I started copying what eventually became the entire dictionary.

I suppose it was inevitable that as my word-base broadened, I could for the first time pick up a book and read and now begin to understand what the book was saying. Anyone who has read a great deal can imagine the new world that opened. Let me tell you something: from then until I left that prison, in every free moment I had, if I was not reading in the library, I was reading on my bunk. You couldn't have gotten me out of books with a wedge. In fact, up to then, I never had been so truly free in my life.

MY SORT O' MAN
PAUL LAURENCE DUNBAR

Paul Laurence Dunbar (1872–1906), the son of former slaves, gained fame for his folksy Southern dialect poetry, with images of seemingly contented, accommodating Negroes. Often, hints of subversion were concealed in his plantation speech. In this poem Dunbar tells how to take the true measure of a person. No matter how high or humble one's birth, any man, woman, or child would do well to honor these insights.

I don't believe in ristercrats
   An' never did, you see;
The plain ol' homelike sorter folks
   Is good enough fur me.
O' course, I don't desire a man
   To be too tarnal rough,
But then I think all folks should know
   When they air nice enough.

Now, there is folks in this here world,
   From peasant up to king,
Who want to be so awful nice
   They overdo the thing.
That's jest the thing that makes me sick,
   An' quicker than a wink
I set it down that them same folks
   Ain't half so good's you think.

I like to see a man dress nice,
　In clothes becomin', too;
I like to see a woman fix
　As women orter do;
An' boys an' gals I like to see
　Look fresh an' young an' spry.—
We all must have our vanity
　An' pride before we die.

But I jedge no man by his clothes,—
　Nor gentleman nor tramp;
The man that wears the finest suit
　May be the biggest scamp,
An' he whose limbs are clad in rags
　That make a mournful sight,
In life's great battle may have proved
　A hero in the fight.

I don't believe in 'ristercrats;
　I like the honest tan
That lies upon the healthful cheek
　An' speaks the honest man;
I like to grasp the brawny hand
　That labor's lips have kissed,
For he who has not labored here
　Life's greatest pride has missed,—

The pride to feel that yo'r own strength
　Has cleaved fur you the way
To heights to which you were not born,
　But struggled day by day.
What though the thousands sneer an' scoff,
　An' scorn yo'r humble birth?
Kings are but subject; you are king
　By right o' royal worth.

The man who simply sits an' waits
    Fur good to come along,
Ain't worth the breath that one would take
    To tell him he is wrong.
Fur good ain't flowin' round this world
    Fur ev'ry fool to sup;
You've got to put yo'r see-ers on,
    An' go an' hunt it up.

Good goes with honesty, I say,
    To honor an' to bless;
To rich an' poor alike it brings
    A wealth o' happiness.
The 'ristercrats ain't got it all,
    Fur much to their su'prise,
That's one of earth's most blessed things
    They can't monopolize.

THE LITTLE MAN AT CHEHAW STATION
RALPH ELLISON

Before embarking on a career that eventually helped to shape modern concepts of "the great American novel," Ralph Ellison (1914–94) was drawn to music, specifically jazz. He played several brass instruments and got a scholarship to study music composition at the Tuskegee Institute in 1933. It was there that he developed a passion for literature. It was also at Tuskegee that he learned a valuable lesson. A person (in this case, a musician) must always strive to do his best. This story explains why.

It was at Tuskegee Institute during the mid-1930s that I was made aware of the little man behind the stove. At the time I was a trumpeter majoring in music and had aspirations of becoming a classical composer. As such, shortly before the little man came to my attention, I had outraged the faculty members who judged my monthly student's recital by substituting a certain skill of lips and fingers for the intelligent and artistic structuring of emotion that was demanded in performing the music assigned to me. Afterward, still dressed in my hired tuxedo, my ears burning from the harsh negatives of their criticism, I had sought solace in the basement studio of Hazel Harrison, a highly respected concert pianist and teacher. . . . It was not the first time that I had appealed to Miss Harrison's generosity of spirit, but today her reaction to my rather adolescent complaint was less than sympathetic.

"But, baby," she said, "in this country you must always prepare yourself to play your very best wherever you are, on all occasions."

"But everybody tells you that," I said.

"Yes," she said, "but there's more to it than you're usually told. Of course you've always been taught to *do* your best, *look* your best, *be* your best. You've been told such things all your life. But now you're becoming a musician, an artist, and when it comes to performing the classics in this country, there's something more involved."

Watching me closely, she paused. "Are you ready to listen?"

"Yes, ma'am."

"All right," she said, "you must *always* play your best, even if it's only in the waiting room at Chehaw Station, because in this country there'll always be a little man hidden behind the stove."

"A *what?*"

She nodded. "That's right," she said. "There'll always be the little man whom you don't expect, and he'll know the *music*, and the *tradition*, and the standards of *musicianship* required for whatever you set out to perform!"

Speechless, I stared at her. After the working-over I'd just received from the faculty, I was in no mood for joking. But no, Miss Harrison's face was quite serious. So what did she mean? Chehaw Station was a lonely whistle-stop where swift north- or southbound trains paused with haughty impatience to drop off or take on passengers; the point where, on homecoming weekends, special coaches crowded with festive visitors were cut loose, coupled to a waiting switch engine, and hauled to Tuskegee's railroad siding. I knew it well, and as I stood beside Miss Harrison's piano, visualizing the station, I told myself, *She has GOT to be kidding!*

For, in my view, the atmosphere of Chehaw's claustrophobic little waiting room was enough to discourage even a blind street musician from picking out blues on his guitar, no matter how tedious his wait for the train. . . . [And] Chehaw Station was the last place in the area where I would expect to encounter a connoisseur lying in wait to pounce upon some rash, unsuspecting musician. . . . Not a chance!

So as Miss Harrison watched to see the effect of her words, I said with a shrug, "Yes, ma'am."

She smiled, her prominent eyes a-twinkle. "I hope so," she said. "But if you don't just now, you will by the time you become an artist. So remember the little man behind the stove."

With that, seating herself at her piano, she began thumbing through a sheaf of scores—a signal that our discussion was ended.

So, I thought, *you ask for sympathy and you get a riddle. . . .*

THREE YEARS LATER, after having abandoned my hope of becoming a musician, I had just about forgotten Miss Harrison's mythical little man behind the stove. Then, in faraway New York, concrete evidence of his actual existence arose and blasted me like the heat from an internally combusted ton of coal.

As a member of the Federal Writers' Project, I was spending a clammy late-fall afternoon of freedom circulating a petition in support of some now long-forgotten social issue that I regarded as indispensable to the public good. I found myself inside a tenement building in San Juan Hill, a Negro district that disappeared with the coming of Lincoln Center. Starting on the top floor of the building, I had collected an acceptable number of signatures, and having descended from the ground floor to the basement level, was moving along the dimly lit hallway toward a door through which I could hear loud voices. They were male Afro-American voices, raised in violent argument. The language was profane, the style of speech a Southern idiomatic vernacular such as was spoken by formally uneducated Afro-American workingmen. . . .

The subject of their contention confounded all my assumptions regarding the correlation between educational levels, class, race, and the possession of conscious culture. Impossible as it seemed, these foul-mouthed black workingmen were locked in verbal combat over which of two celebrated Metropolitan Opera divas was the superior soprano!

I myself attended the opera only when I could raise the funds, and I knew full well that opera-going was far from the usual cultural pursuit of men identified with the linguistic style of such voices. And yet, confounding such facile logic, they were voicing (and loudly) a familiarity with the Met far greater than my own. In their graphic, irreverent, and vehement criticism they were describing not only the sopranos' acting abilities but were ridiculing the gestures with which each gave animation to her roles, and they shouted strong opinions as to the ranges of the divas' vocal equipment. Thus, with such a distortion of perspective being imposed upon me, I was challenged either to solve the mystery of their knowledge by entering into their midst or to leave the building with my sense of logic reduced forever to a level of college-trained absurdity.

So challenged, I knocked. I knocked out of curiosity, I knocked out of outrage. I knocked in fear and trembling. I knocked in anticipation of whatever insights—malicious or transcendent, I no longer cared which—I would discover beyond the door.

For a moment there was an abrupt and portentous silence; then came the sound of chair legs thumping dully upon the floor, followed by further silence. I knocked again, loudly, with an authority fired by an impatient and anxious urgency.

Again silence—until a gravel voice boomed an annoyed "Come in!"

Opening the door with an unsteady hand, I looked inside, and was even less prepared for the scene that met my eyes than for the content of their loudmouthed contention.

In a small, rank-smelling, lamplit room, four huge black men sat sprawled around a circular dining-room table, looking toward me with undisguised hostility. The sooty-chimneyed lamp glowed in the center of the bare oak table, casting its yellow light upon four water tumblers and a half-empty pint of whiskey. As the men straightened in their chairs I became aware of a fireplace with a coal fire glowing in its grate, and leaning against the ornate marble facing of its mantelpiece, I saw four enormous coal scoops.

"All right," one of the men said, rising to his feet. "What the hell can we do for *you?*"

"And we ain't buying nothing, buddy," one of the seated men added, his palm slapping the table.

Closing the door, I moved forward, holding my petition like a flag of truce before me, noting that the men wore faded blue overalls and jumper jackets, and becoming aware that while all were of dark complexion, their blackness was accentuated in the dim lamplight by the dust and grime of their profession.

"Come on, man, speak up," the man who had arisen said. "We ain't got all day."

"I'm sorry to interrupt," I said, "but I thought you might be interested in supporting my petition," and began hurriedly to explain.

"Say," one of the men said, "you look like one of them relief investigators. You're not out to jive us, are you?"

"Oh, no, sir," I said. "I happen to work on the Writers' Project . . ."

The standing man leaned toward me. "You on the Writers' Project?" he said, looking me up and down.

"That's right," I said. "I'm a writer."

"Now is that right?" he said. "How long you been writing?"

I hesitated. "About a year," I said.

He grinned, looking at the others. "Y'all hear that? Ol' Home-boy here has done up and jumped on the *gravy* train! Now that's pretty good. Pretty damn good! So what did you do before that?" he said.

"I studied music," I said, "at Tuskegee."

"Hey, now!" the standing man said. "They got a damn good choir down there. Y'all remember back when they opened Radio City? They had that fellow William L. Dawson for a director. Son, let's see that paper."

Relieved, I handed him the petition, watching him stretch it between his hardened hands. After a moment of soundlessly mouthing the words of its appeal, he gave me a skeptical look and turned to the others.

"What the hell," he said, "signing this piece of paper won't do no good, but since Home here's a musician, it won't do us no harm to help him out. Let's go along with him."

Fishing a blunt-pointed pencil from the bib of his overalls, he wrote his name and passed the petition to his friends, who followed suit.

This took some time, and as I watched the petition move from hand to hand, I could barely contain myself or control my need to unravel the mystery that had now become far more important than just getting their signatures on my petition.

"There you go," the last one said, extending the petition toward me. "Having our names on there don't mean a thing, but you got 'em."

"Thank you," I said. "Thank you very much."

They watched me with amused eyes, expecting me to leave, but, clearing my throat nervously, I stood in my tracks, too intrigued to leave and suddenly too embarrassed to ask my question.

"So what'er you waiting for?" one of them said. "You got what you came for. What else do you want?"

And then I blurted it out. "I'd like to ask you just one question," I said.

"Like what?" the standing one said.

"Like where on earth did you gentlemen learn so much about grand opera?"

For a moment he stared at me with parted lips; then, pounding the mantelpiece with his palm, he collapsed with a roar of laughter. As the laughter of the others erupted like a string of giant firecrackers I looked on with growing feelings of embarrassment and insult, trying to grasp the handle to what appeared to be an unfriendly joke. Finally, wiping coal-dust-stained tears from his cheeks, he interrupted his laughter long enough to initiate me into the mystery.

"Hell, son," he laughed, "we learn it down at the Met, that's where . . ."

"You learned it *where?*"

"At the Metropolitan Opera, just like I told you. Strip us fellows down and give us some costumes and we make about the finest damn bunch of Egyptians you ever seen. Hell, we been down there wearing leopard skins and carrying spears or waving things like palm leafs and ostrich-tail fans for *years!*"

Now, purged by the revelation, and with Hazel Harrison's voice echoing in my ears, it was my turn to roar with laughter. With a shock of recognition I joined them in appreciation of the hilarious American joke that centered on the incongruities of race, economic status, and culture. My sense of order restored, my appreciation of the arcane ways of American cultural possibility was vastly extended. The men were products of both past *and* present; were both coal heavers *and* Met extras; were both workingmen *and* opera buffs. Seen in the clear, pluralistic, melting-pot light of American cultural possibility there was no contradiction. The joke, the apparent contradiction, sprang from my attempting to see them by the light of social concepts that cast less illumination than an inert lump of coal. I was delighted, because during a moment when I least expected to encounter the little man behind the stove (Miss Harrison's vernacular music critic, as it were), I had stumbled upon four such men. Not behind the stove, it is true, but even more wondrously, they had materialized at an even more unexpected location: at the depth of the American social hierarchy and, of all possible hiding places, behind a coal pile. Where there's a melting pot there's smoke, and where there's smoke it is not simply optimistic to expect fire, it's imperative to watch for the phoenix's vernacular, but transcendent, rising.

THE TUG-OF-WAR BETWEEN THE ELEPHANT AND THE WHALE

During slavery, the trickster rabbit, popular in African American story-telling, outwitted bigger, stronger foes in the animal kingdom. His trickery symbolized a slave outsmarting the master and thus being released from the limitations imposed on other slaves. In this Louisiana folktale, the rabbit uses cunning to make up for a deficit in size and strength.

One day Compere Rabbit and Compere Bouki were making a trip together. When they reached the shore of a sea, they saw something that was so strange that they stopped to watch and listen. An elephant and a whale were talking.

The elephant said to the whale: "Compere Whale, since you are the largest and strongest around in the sea, and I am the largest and strongest on land, we rule over all beasts; and anyone who doesn't like it, we'll just have to kill, all right, compere?" "Yes, compere," agreed the whale. "You keep the land and I'll keep the sea, and between us we'll rule everyone."

"You hear that?" said Bouki. "Let's get going. We better not get caught listening in on their conversation." "Oh, I don't care," said Rabbit. "I know more tricks than they do. Just watch how I am going to fix them." "No," said Bouki, "I'm scared. I'm going." "Well, go if you can't have a little fun because you are scared of everything! Go ahead and leave, and quick because I'm sick and tired of you."

Compere Rabbit went to get a rope that was long and strong. Then he got his drum and hid it in the grass. He took one end of the rope, and went up to Elephant, complimenting him: "Sir, Compere Elephant, you who are so good and so strong, I wonder if you could do me a favor? You could help me a lot and save me from losing my money, too, if you would do me a favor." Elephant always enjoyed hearing such fine compliments, so he said: "Compere, what do you want? I am always ready to help my friends."

"Well," said Rabbit, "This cow of mine is stuck in the mud down on the coast, and I have tried and tried, but I'm just not strong enough to pull her out. I hope you can help me. If you could just take this rope in your trunk, I could tie it to the cow and you could pull her out. When you hear me beat the drum, if you will pull hard on the rope, we'll soon have her out of that mud." "That's all right," said Elephant. "I guarantee I'll pull the cow out, or the rope will break." So he tied the rope around the neck of Elephant.

Then Compere Rabbit took the other end of the rope and ran toward the sea. He went up to Whale and paid her some of the same compliments. He asked her if she wouldn't help him free up his cow that was stuck in the woods in a bayou. He was so convincing that no one could ever refuse him anything. So Whale took hold of the rope and said: "When I hear the drum beat, I'll pull." "Yes," said Rabbit; "begin pulling gently, and then harder and harder." "Don't you worry," said Whale; "I'll pull out the cow, even if the Devil is holding her." "That is good," said Rabbit. And he went off aways from both Whale and Elephant so they couldn't see him and began to beat on his drum.

The elephant began to pull so hard that the rope was stretched to the breaking point. Whale, on her side, was pulling and pulling, but she was losing ground and being pulled to the land because she didn't have any ground to plant herself on. When she saw that she was being pulled onto the land she beat her tail furiously and plunged headlong toward the depths of the sea. Now Elephant found himself being dragged into the sea. "What is happening? That cow must be really scared!" So he twisted the rope around his trunk and planted his feet so well that he was able to pull so hard that he pulled Whale onto the shore.

When he looked back he was astonished to see that his friend Whale was on the other end of the rope. "What is this? I thought I was pulling Compere Rabbit's cow," he said. "Rabbit told me the same thing," said Whale. "I think he must be playing a trick on us." "He'll pay for that," said Elephant, "if I ever catch him on land." "And if he comes near the sea, I'll get him," said Whale.

Hearing all this, Compere Rabbit said to Bouki: "It's getting pretty hot; I guess it's time for us to get out of here." "You see," said Bouki, "you are always getting us into trouble." "Oh, don't worry, I'm not through with them; you'll see how I'll fix them yet."

So they went away and after a while they separated. When Compere Rabbit arrived in the wood, he found a little dead deer. The dogs had worried the hair off its skin in many places, and when Rabbit skinned the deer and put it on his back, he looked just like a wounded deer.

He passed limping by Elephant, who said to him: "Poor little deer, how sick you look." "Oh, yes, I'm really suffering," he said sadly. "You see, Compere Rabbit poisoned me and put his curse on me, because I wanted to stop him from eating grass on land. Take care Mr. Elephant, Compere Rabbit has made a bargain with the Devil; he will be hard on you too, if you don't take care."

Now Elephant got frightened. He said, "Little deer, tell Compere Rabbit that I am still his friend. When you see him, send him my regards."

A little later the deer met Whale in the sea. "Poor little deer, why are you limping so? You seem sick today." "Oh yes, Compere Rabbit did that. Take care, Compere Whale, for Rabbit can poison anyone he wants because the Devil gave him the power to do so." The whale was frightened too, and said: "I don't want anything to do with Devil; send Compere Rabbit my regards when you see him again."

Now Rabbit met Bouki and he took off the deer's skin and they both laughed until their sides ached. "No matter who's the largest," Rabbit said, "I'm still the strongest—at least when I use my head!"

A "SQUARE"
ANDY RAZAF

Andy Razaf (1895–1973), one of Tin Pan Alley's greatest songwriters, wrote more than a thousand tunes. Razaf met Thomas "Fats" Waller in 1923. Together they formed a highly successful team, whose songs included "Ain't Misbehavin'," "Honeysuckle Rose," and "This Joint Is Jumping." Razaf was born Andreamentania Paul Razafinkeriefo in Washington, D.C. His mother was African American; his father, Henri, was a nephew of Queen Ranavalona III of Madagascar.

Besides songs, Razaf wrote poems.* Langston Hughes considered him a poet who was close to the people—a writer with a common man's sensibilities. Here Razaf considers a dilemma faced by so many young people: Should I care if I'm a square? Razaf's solution is enlightening.

Keep on being a "square," young man,
In the end you will find that it pays,
For it's the "cool" and "crazy cats"
Who live in a mental daze.

Think for yourself and don't follow the pack.
If you're wise you will not string along
With a hoodlum gang that breaks the law,
And feels that it's "smart" to do wrong.

---

* Most of the poems by Razaf that appear in this book are taken from his unpublished manuscript, *Poems for a Mixed-Up World*.

Keep on being a "square," young girl,
For a "solid chick" learns in time
That in being "hip," she is easy to trip,
And turn to a life of crime.

The juvenile halls and jails overflow
With the "cool, crazy cats," everywhere.
Very often they even wind up in "death row,"
While a "square" you will seldom find there.

So being a "square" more than pays these days.
You can walk with head high, without shame,
While the "cats" and "chicks" ruin their lives for "kicks,"
By defying the rules of life's game.

WE REAL COOL
GWENDOLYN BROOKS

Chicago poet Gwendolyn Brooks (b. 1917) was the first African American to be awarded the Pulitzer Prize.* Among the most visible poets in America, she was named poet laureate of Illinois in 1968. In the following poem, she warns that sometimes coolness can be downright deadly.

> *The Pool Players.*
> *Seven at the Golden Shovel.*

We real cool. We
Left school. We

* She won it in 1950 for her second book, *Annie Allen*, a collection of poems published in 1949.

Lurk late. We
Strike straight. We

Sing sin. We
Thin gin. We

Jazz June. We
Die soon.

⚭

No brain, no gain.

—*Motto of Get Ready, Inc.*

⚭

GET READY, INC.
DOUGLASS "JOCKO" HENDERSON

Douglass "Jocko" Henderson, a popular radio disk jockey during the rise of rhythm and blues, spread a musical, rap-style lesson among Philadelphia public school students: Live the drug-free life.

Jocko, Jocko, where have you been?
I helped bust a pusher.
Now I'm back again.

Don't feel guilty if you turn in a friend.
Let the cops know,
Be a good citizen, save some lives.
That's the way to go.

Now there's a pusher trying to hook you.
His name could be Jim.
Tell the cops he's dealing—drop a dime on him!

Don't let anybody know—you made the call.
You did a good deed, now you're standing tall.

You can't cope when it comes to dope.
No way is that being cool.
If you're dumb enough to be a dopey dope,
You're the world's biggest fool.

Now, if you don't want your life blown away,
When it comes to drugs—say, "No way!"

If you're using drugs—hey! You bit.
Your mind's been blown—you're out of it!

You'll rob, you'll steal, you'll even kill
To get those drugs, you need the dollar bill.

There's a tranquilizer called PCP.
It can knock out a horse so easy.
It was made for animals
To stop them in their tracks.
Take it from the Jock
These are cold stone facts.

PCP makes you crazy.
If you use it, how dumb can you be?
The question is, why you want to die?
If that's the way you want to go—bye, bye.

Then there's a deadly drug—ah, Cocaine.
Scientists discovered it to ease a pain.
Doctors prescribe it very carefully.
Without the right prescription, it's deadly.
Don't try Cocaine—take a tip from me.
It's a thrill—that can kill immediately.
It's not OK to light up a "J."
It can blow your mind for the rest of the day.

When you've had a "J"—your eyes are red.
You're half asleep—your brain is dead.

Some students light up before they go to class.
They nod—learn nothing—no way can they pass.
Education that they need has passed them by.
They have missed the boat—they are too high to try.

Now drugs are designed to destroy you.
You'll wake up one morning and you won't know what to do.
Your body is wrecked, your mind confused.
No way can you win—you've got to lose!

That junk can back up and damage the brain.
Many thousands of users have gone insane.
Think about it, just a moment or two.
Is this really, really, really what you want to do?
No way, Jose! Can you throw your life away?
Live the drug free life—it's so great that way!

Speed—could make you think you have wings.
You may try to fly—or do many dumb things.
Do yourself a big favor—pass it by.
You don't have wings—you just can't fly.
Speed confuses the mind,
It'll destroy you—it's just a matter of time.

Quaaludes and alcohol
Is the wrong way to have a ball.
Use them together, they can do you in.
Together they can be like poison.
They can put you in a coma for a long time,
Or take you away long before your time.

I knew a junky—his name was Ted.
Stayed high on drugs and now he's dead.
Mary—Reggie—Janie, and Tom

They thought it was hip to be turned on.
They took pills, shot needles—snorted "Coke" they bought.
They're all gone, I'm sorry to report.

You see, the big drug pushers don't care who they kill.
They're dealing for that dollar bill.
Ashes to ashes, dust to dust.
If drugs kill you—don't blame us.

You're a big fool if you drop out of school.
Don't even be late.
Forget about the drugs.
Hang in there—hang till you graduate.

❧

If it is to be, it's up to me.

—*Traditional*

❧

❧

HOME TRAINING *(hōm trān′ing) n. colloq., African American.* 1. The education, instruction, or discipline of a person in accepted mores or values. 2. Possessing behavior that is reflective of proper rearing. 3. Correct breeding. *Synonyms:* good manners; proper breeding; polite behavior. *Antonyms:* rude; impolite; without culture or refinement.
            —*From* Basic Black: Home Training for Modern Times
❧

TEACHING TABLE MANNERS

In this old folk rhyme, Uncle Bill passes on a lesson in etiquette.

Now whilst we's here 'round de table,
All you young ones git right still.

I wants to l'arn you some good manners,
So's you'll think o' Uncle Bill.

Cose we's gwineter 'scuse Merlindy,
Caze she's jes a baby yit.
But it's time you udder young ones
Wus a-l'arnin' a liddle bit.

I can 'member as a youngster,
Lak you youngsters is to-day;
How my mammy l'arnt me manners
In a 'culiar kind o' way.

One o' mammy's ole time 'quaintance.
(Ole Aunt Donie wus her name)
Come one night to see my mammy.
Mammy co'se 'pared fer de same.

Mammy got de sifter, Honey;
An' she tuck an' make up dough,
Which she tu'n into hot biscuits.
Den we all git smart, you know.

'Zerves an' biscuits on de table!
Honey, noways could I wait.
Ole Aunt Donie wus a good ole 'oman,
An' I jes had to pass my plate.

I soon swallered down dem biscuit,
E't 'em faster dan a shoat.
Dey wus a liddle tough an' knotty,
But I chawed 'em lak a goat.

"Pass de biscuits, please, Mam!
Please, Mam, fer I wants some mō'."
Lawd! You'd oughter seed my mammy
Frownin' up, jes "sorter so."

"Won't you pass de biscuit, please, Mam?"
I said wid a liddle fear.
Dere wus not but one mō' lef', Sir.
Mammy riz up out'n her chear.

W'en Aunt Donie lef' our house, Suh,
Mammy come lak bees an' ants,
Put my head down 'twixt her knees, Suh,
Almos' roll me out'n my pants.

She had a great big tough hick'ry,
An' it help till it convince.
Frum dat day clean down to dis one,
I'se had manners ev'r since.

DO THE RIGHT THINGS
CHARLOTTE HAWKINS BROWN

*Black America's "Miss Manners," Charlotte Hawkins Brown (1883–
1961), left an endearing legacy: her book,* The Correct Thing To Do—
To Say—To Wear, *published in 1941. With it, Dr. Brown (who founded
Palmer Memorial Institute in Sedalia, North Carolina) has educated
generations of black ladies and gents in the social graces. Nowadays,
many folks regard her rules of proper and polite conduct as quaint, but
passé. However, her pointers still spell the difference between rudeness and
courteousness. Here are some of her tips:*

AT HOME

Some of the thoughtful acts that help make home really a "Home Sweet
Home":

• Don't get up in the morning with a "grouch." Always greet each member of the family with a cheerful "good morning," and maintain a sunny disposition throughout the day.

• When you are going out, let someone know where you may be found and when you may be expected to return. You never can tell what will happen and you may be needed.

• Don't mistake a family bathroom for a private bath. Every other person has the same right to use it that you have.

• Don't save your table manners until company comes. You and your family are just as good and deserve just as much consideration as any of your friends or acquaintances.

• *Be saving*. Don't burn lights unnecessarily. Be sure that the hot water faucet is turned off. Don't leave the hose on too long in the back yard. Don't drive the automobile around the corner when you can walk. Don't turn the radio on in the morning and let it run all day. Don't leave the outside doors wide open when the furnace is going full blast.

• Remember that your parents have done more for you than anyone else in the world. Always accord them the greatest respect and attention under all circumstances.

• Respect each person's private property. Do not read mail, go into or borrow personal things without asking permission.

• Never permit any older members of the family to open a door if you are near it.

• Whatever else happens, in order to keep home happy, don't be a combatant. You may be smart and you may be the only one in the family that has a B.S., but the rest of the family may have been somewhere too and seen a few things and possess that most uncommon of all common things—common sense and discretion. Truly learned people are the last to parade their knowledge to the disparagement of those who are less advantaged.

AT MEALTIME

• Always arrive at a meal at the appointed time.

• Young men, draw back the chair for the girl or woman next to you, push it under her as she sits down and then take your seat.

• Keep up an interesting conversation in which all persons at the table are included.

• Avoid lounging. Keep your spine straight, your body poised a little forward and your mind occupied with the conversation you are helping to make pleasant.

• Keep elbows and arms off the table.*

• Never laugh at an accident or misfortune at the table.

• Avoid talking with food in the mouth.

• Keep lips closed while chewing and make as little noise as possible.

• Let your napkin lie, partly folded, across your lap while eating.

• Never drink from a saucer, and do not drink noisily from cup, glass, or spoon.

• Do not use the knife for conveying food to the mouth.

• Use a fork when eating vegetables and salad. If cutting the leaves of a salad is necessary, cut with the fork.

• At the conclusion of the meal, place the knife and fork across the back of the plate parallel to each other.

• Eat a little less of everything than you might. Shrink from the slightest appearance of greediness.

• When the hostess rises, young men, rise and draw back the chair of the girl or woman next to you as she rises and precedes you from the room.

THE EARMARKS OF A LADY

A lady:

• Passes behind people.

• Does not chew gum in public.

• Awaits her turn; never bruskly pushes ahead.

• Does not laugh at the mistakes or misfortunes of others.

• Is always well groomed, appropriately dressed, scrupulously clean in body and attire with hair carefully arranged.

---

* This is a safe rule for children, but may be altered by adults who know how to relax gracefully during the meal.

- Does not make advances for acquaintance of young men or go out of her way to attract their attention.
- Accepts courtesy of young men graciously.

THE EARMARKS OF A GENTLEMAN

A real gentleman:

- Maintains and exhibits a genuine respect for women.
- Is careful to call a person's name when addressing him, and to say "Thank you," "If you please," and "I beg your pardon" when they should be used.
- Avoids making an unnecessary "scene" under any circumstances.
- When he makes a mistake, admits his fault and seeks to rectify it if possible. He does not fashion alibis to cover his failings.
- Keeps himself well groomed and appropriately dressed at all times. Even if he is working he keeps as clean and neat as possible. The fireman's clothes don't have to look like the coal.
- Does not use profane language or tell questionable jokes.
- Lets no opportunity whatsoever escape for improving himself.

❦❧

Talk some, leave some.

—*Jamaica*

❦❧

SELF-CONTROL

This old-time folk rhyme is a recipe for controlling one's temper.

Befo' you says dat ugly word,
You stop an' count ten.

Den if you wants to say dat word,
Begin an' count again.

Don't have a tongue tied in de middle,
An' loose frum en' to en'.
You mus' think twice, den speak once;
Dat donkey cain't count ten.

SATCHEL'S SYSTEM
LEROY (SATCHEL) PAIGE

LeRoy "Satchel" Paige (1906–82), a near mythic figure in sports history, pitched his first professional baseball game in 1926 and his last in 1965. The Negro Baseball Leagues' biggest star attraction, Paige was famous for his windmill windup and hesitation pitch. He also became known as a great humorist. Here are his rules "for staying young," which, he said, "are mighty good for anybody."

- Avoid fried meats which angry up the blood.
- If your stomach disputes you, lie down and pacify it with cool thoughts.
- Keep the juices flowing by jangling around gently as you move.
- Go very light on the vices, such as carrying on in society—the social ramble ain't restful.
- Avoid running at all times.
- And don't look back. Something might be gaining on you.

MAN IN THE MIRROR
GORDON PARKS

Gordon Parks made a mark as a photographer, bestselling author, poet, filmmaker, painter, composer, and opera librettist. And he did it all in spite of humble beginnings. Born to cattle herders on the Kansas prairie in 1912, he was the youngest of fifteen children. What compelled him to create art was restlessness, energy, and a sheer doggedness to express himself. "I was born with a need to explore every tool shop of my mind," he explained in his autobiography. Here is an instructive discussion with "the man in the mirror" that helped put Parks on the road to success.

I don't pretend to be an authority on common sense. I speak from only seventy-seven years of experience—which tells you next to nothing. As a term it has been undefined fully for centuries, and will probably remain so for centuries to come. I like to think of it as wisdom, and I've learned not to confuse wisdom with intelligence. There is a difference.

No doubt it was wisdom that taught me that my most dangerous enemy could be myself. One morning, with shaving razor in hand, I had stared into the mirror and asked myself some rather bothersome questions. With hard eyes I stared back at myself and reeled off some disturbing facts, along with some advice: "You're approaching manhood and you dislike yourself. That's why you're interrogating me. *[Well, make up your mind to do something about it.]* You're so thin-skinned that the softest criticism rubs you raw. *[Accept criticism, man. It can't hurt, and it could be helpful.]* Envy of others' success hangs around your neck like a rope. *[That's stupid. Use their success to give you inspiration.]* You squander too much time on trivial things, always hurrying to nowhere, and in a rush to get there. *[Take your time, man. Think things out first, then go.]* You avoid questions about yourself that you find hard to answer. *[Figure things out. You just don't have the right answers. So admit to it.]* You talk rapid-fire just to be heard, and without having anything worthwhile to say. *[That's downright ego. Listen more. Keep your big mouth shut and keep your ears open. Your insecurity's showing.]* Well, enough for now. There's plenty left on the list for tomorrow. *[One last thing: Until you're sure of yourself, you won't be sure of anything. Think it over. See you tomorrow morning.]*"

I remember that session with the mirror so well because it forced me to take stock of myself. I was struggling for a positive image. But it was one thing to acknowledge my faults, and another thing to do something about them.

A MAN OF WORDS

An old folk rhyme about what it's like to be "all talk and no action."

A man o' words an' not o' deeds,
Is lak a gyarden full o' weeds.
   De weeds 'gin to grow
   Lak a gyarden full o' snow.
   De snow 'gin to fly
   Lak a eagle in de sky.
   De sky 'gin to roar
   Lak a hammer on yō' door.
   De door 'gin to crack
   Lak a hick'ry on yō' back.

   Yō' back 'gin to smart
   Lak a knife in yō' heart.
   Yō' heart 'gin to fail
   Lak a boat widout a sail.
   De boat 'gin to sink
   Lak a bottle full o' ink.
   Dat ink, it won't write
   Neider black nor white.
Dat man o' words an' not o' deeds,
Is lak a gyarden full o' weeds.

An idle mind is the devil's workshop.

—Traditional

THE WORD THE DEVIL MADE UP
ADAPTED FROM ZORA NEALE HURSTON

Ever wonder where the expression "unh-hunh" originated?

The Old Devil looked around Hell one day and saw that his place was short of help, so he thought he'd run up to Heaven and kidnap some angels to keep things running till he got reinforcements from Miami.

Well, he slipped up behind a great crowd of angels on the outskirts of Heaven and stuffed a couple of thousand in his mouth, a few hundred under each arm, and wrapped his tail around another thousand. And he darted off toward Hell.

When he was flying low over the earth looking for a place to land, a man looked up and saw the Devil and asked him, "Old Devil, I see you have a load of angels. Are you going back for more?"

Devil opened his mouth and told him, "Yeah," and all the little angels flew out of his mouth and went on back to Heaven. While he was trying to catch them, he lost all the others. So he had to go back after another load.

He was flying low again and the same man saw him and said, "Old Devil, I see you got another load of angels."

Devil nodded his head and mumbled, "unh hunh," and that's why we say it that way today.

OPPORTUNITY KNOCKS
CHUCK BERRY

With hit records like "Maybelline," recorded in 1955, the legendary Chuck Berry helped define the sound, style, and subject matter of rock 'n' roll. He became the first black rock 'n' roll star partly because he had the discipline that enabled him to take advantage of opportunities. Here's what he wrote about being prepared when opportunity knocks.

A man there was—of unusual gift—
who bore such a good honored name.
Life came to him—filled to the brim—
offering him both wealth and fame.
But turned he his head—in choosing instead—
to follow a leisurely trend,
Thinking that he—was never to be—
the genius he well could have been.

When opportunity—knocked at his door—
there came no compliance at all.
Long did it wait—with patience that fate—
would bring him to answer his call.
Day after day—time wasted away—
in pleasures he took as devout.
Intrigued with the thought—that fun, as he sought—
was what life was all about.

When opportunity—knocked once again—
it found his ideal still unbent.
Over and over—it knocked to uncover—
his talent from trivial content.
But gloried name—and chance for fame—
were lost from lack of will.
So as it went—his life was spent—
his genius unfulfilled.

NEW BLACK SCRIBE
TERRY MCMILLAN

A survey in 1996 found that African American readers purchase some 160 million books each year. Yet it wasn't until fairly recently that many mainstream publishers helped to nurture black literature. With their best-selling books, Terry McMillan (b. 1951) and a handful of other authors proved that there is a huge audience for stories about black characters. The success of these writers helped pave the way for others. But just how does a person become a writer? Here is McMillan's path to publishing.

As a child, I didn't know that African-American people wrote books. I grew up in a small town in northern Michigan, where the only books I came across were the Bible and required reading for school. I did not read for pleasure, and it wasn't until I was sixteen when I got a job shelving books at the public library that I got lost in a book. It was a biography of Louisa May Alcott. I was excited because I had not really read about poor white folks before; her father was so eccentric and idealistic that at the time I just thought he was crazy. I related to Louisa because she had to help support her family at a young age, which was what I was doing at the library.

Then one day I went to put a book away, and saw James Baldwin's face staring up at me. "Who in the world is this?" I wondered. I remember feeling embarrassed and did not read his book because I was too afraid. I couldn't imagine that he'd have anything better or different to say than Thomas Mann, Henry Thoreau, Ralph Waldo Emerson, Nathaniel Hawthorne, Ernest Hemingway, William Faulkner, etc. and a horde of other mostly white male writers that I'd been introduced to in Literature 101 in high school. I mean, not only had there not been any African American authors included in any of those textbooks, but I'd never been given a clue that if we did have anything important to say that somebody would actually publish it. Needless to say, I was not just naïve, but had not yet acquired an ounce of black pride. I never once questioned why there were no representative works by us in any of those textbooks. After all, I had never heard of any African American writers, and no one I knew hardly read *any* books.

And then things changed.

It wasn't until after Malcolm X had been assassinated that I found out who he was. I know I should be embarrassed about this, but I'm not. I read Alex Haley's biography of him and it literally changed my life. First and foremost, I realized that there was no reason to be ashamed of being black, that it was ridiculous. That we had a history, and much to be proud of. I began to notice how we had actually been treated as less than human; began to see our strength as a people whereas I'd only been made aware of our inferiorities. I started thinking about my role in the world and not just on my street. I started *thinking*. Thinking about things I'd never thought about before, and the thinking turned into questions. But I had more questions than answers.

So I went to college. When I looked through the catalog and saw a class called Afro-American Literature, I signed up and couldn't wait for the first day of class. Did *we* really have enough writers to warrant an entire class? I remember the textbook was called *Dark Symphony: Negro Literature in America* because I still have it. I couldn't believe the rush I felt over and over once I discovered Countee Cullen, Langston Hughes, Ann Petry, Zora Neale Hurston, Ralph Ellison, Jean Toomer, Richard Wright, and rediscovered and read James Baldwin, to name just a few. I'm surprised I didn't need glasses by the end of the semester. My world opened up. I accumulated and gained a totally new insight about, and perception of, our lives as "black" people, as if I had been an outsider and was finally let in. To discover that our lives held as much significance and importance as our white counterparts was more than gratifying, it was exhilarating. Not only had we lived diverse, interesting, provocative, and relentless lives, but during, through, and as a result of all these painful experiences, some folks had taken the time to write it down.

Not once, throughout my entire four years as an undergraduate did it occur to me that I might one day *be* a writer. I mean, these folks had genuine knowledge and insight. They also had a fascination with the truth. They had something to write about. Their work was bold, not flamboyant. They learned how to exploit the language so that readers would be affected by what they said and how they said it. And they had talent.

I never considered myself to be in possession of many of the above, and yet when I was twenty years old, the first man I fell in love with broke my heart. I was so devastated and felt so helpless that my reaction manifested itself in a poem. I did not sit down and say, "I'm going to write a poem about this." It was more like magic. I didn't even know I was writing a poem until I had written it. Afterward, I felt lighter, as if something had happened to lessen the pain. And when I read this "thing" I was shocked because I didn't know where the words came from. I was scared, to say the least, about what I had just experienced, because I didn't understand what had happened.

For the next few days, I read that poem over and over in disbelief because *I* had written it. One day, a colleague saw it lying on the kitchen table and read it. I was embarrassed and shocked when he said he liked it, then went on to tell me that he had just started a black literary magazine at the college and he wanted to publish it. Publish it? He was serious and it found its way onto a typeset page.

Seeing my name in print excited me. And from that point on, if a leaf moved on a tree, I wrote a poem about it. If a crack in the sidewalk glistened, surely there was a poem in that. Some of these verbose things actually got published in various campus newspapers that were obviously desperate to fill up space. I did not call myself a poet; I told people I wrote poems.

Years passed.

Those poems started turning into sentences and I started getting nervous. What the hell did I think I was doing? Writing these little go-nowhere vignettes. All these beginnings. And who did I think I was, trying to tell a story? And who cared? Even though I had no idea what I was doing, all I knew was that I was beginning to realize that a lot of things mattered to me, things disturbed me, things that I couldn't change. Writing became an outlet for my dissatisfactions, distaste, and my way of trying to make sense of what I saw happening around me. It was my way of trying to fix what I thought was broken. It later became the only way to explore personally what I didn't understand. The problem, however, was that I was writing more about ideas than people. Everything was so "large," and eventually I had to find a common denominator. I ended up asking myself what I really cared about: it was people, and particularly African-American people.

The whole idea of taking myself seriously as a writer was terrifying. I didn't know any writers. Didn't know how you knew if you "had" it or

not. Didn't know if I was or would ever be good enough. I didn't know
how you went about the business of writing, and besides, I sincerely
wanted to make a decent living. (I had read the horror stories of how so
few writers were able to live off of their writing alone, many having
lived like bohemians.) At first, I thought being a social worker was the
right thing to do, since I was bent on saving the world (I was an
idealistic twenty-two years old), but when I found I couldn't do it that
way, I had to figure out another way to make an impact on folks. A
positive impact. I ended up majoring in journalism because writing was
"easy" for me, but it didn't take long for me to learn that I did not like
answering the "who, what, when, where, and why" of anything. I
then—upon the urging of my mother and friends who had graduated
and gotten "normal" jobs—decided to try something that would still
allow me to "express myself" but was relatively safer, though still risky:
I went to film school. Of course what was inherent in my quest to find
my "spot" in the world was this whole notion of affecting people on
some grand scale. Malcolm and Martin caused me to think like this.
Writing for me, as it's turned out, is philanthropy. It didn't take years
for me to realize the impact that other writers' work had had on me, and
if I was going to write, I did not want to write inconsequential, mediocre
stories that didn't conjure up or arouse much in a reader. So I had to
start by exciting myself and paying special attention to what I cared
about, what mattered to me.

Film school didn't work out. Besides, I never could stop writing,
which ultimately forced me to stop fighting it. It took even longer to
realize that writing was not something you aspired to be, it was something you did because you had to.

HOW TO BE A BAD WRITER
(in Ten Easy Lessons)
LANGSTON HUGHES

Here is a list of to-do's for those intending to become virtually unread-able writers.

1. Use all the clichés possible, such as "He had a gleam in his eye," or "Her teeth were white as pearls."

2. If you are a Negro, try very hard to write with an eye dead on the white market—use modern stereotypes of older stereotypes—big burly Negroes, criminals, low-lifers, and prostitutes.

3. Put in a lot of profanity and as many pages as possible of near-pornography and you will be so modern you pre-date Pompei in your lonely crusade toward the best seller lists. By all means be misunder-stood, unappreciated, and ahead of your time in print and out, then you can be felt-sorry-for by your own self, if not the public.

4. Never characterize characters. Just name them and then let them go for themselves. Let all of them talk the same way. If the reader hasn't imagination enough to make something out of cardboard cut-outs, shame on him!

5. Write about China, Greece, Tibet, or the Argentine pampas—anyplace you've never seen and know nothing about. Never write about anything you know, your home town, or your home folks, or your-self.

6. Have nothing to say, but use a great many words, particularly high-sounding words, to say it.

7. If a playwright, put into your script a lot of hand-waving and spirituals, preferably the ones everybody has heard a thousand times from Marion Anderson to the Golden Gates.

8. If a poet, rhyme June with moon as often and in as many ways as possible. Also use *thee's* and *thou's* and *'tis* and *o'er*, and invert your sentences all the time. Never say, "The sun rose, bright and shining." But, rather, "Bright and shining rose the sun."

9. Pay no attention really to spelling or grammar or the neatness of the manuscript. And in writing letters, never sign your name so anyone

can read it. A rapid scrawl will better indicate how important and how busy you are.

10. Drink as much liquor as possible and always write under the influence of alcohol. When you can't afford alcohol yourself, or even if you can, drink on your friends, fans, and the general public.

If you are white, there are many more things I can advise in order to be a bad writer, but since this piece is for colored writers, there are some things I know a Negro just will not do, not even for writing's sake, so there is no use mentioning them.

❧

We all have ability. The difference is how we use it.

—Stevie Wonder

❧

COURAGE

ourage is the stuff of heroes (and of ordinary folks, too) who are brave enough to do the right thing in times of grave danger or looming adversity. It steeled the nerves of Harriet Tubman as she shuttled passengers on the Underground Railroad, warmed Matthew Henson's blood in the deep-freeze of the Arctic, and sat down on the bus with the tired and overworked Rosa Parks. Courage is among the finest of virtues. It has always made a difference in our lives, and it always will.

Ask the courageous what drives them, though, and many can only shrug. Most brave souls do not feel an overpowering urge for daredevilishness. Some maintain that their act was the only possible thing to do under the circumstances. We know better. Refusing to act is often an option. But idly sitting by is something the brave hardly ever consider. The courageous simply decide that a change is gonna come, and they will have to make the change themselves.

Fear still affects the courageous. For most of us, it is an overriding concern, a kind of disease that paralyzes the joints, bringing action to a crashing halt. The brave might sense their own fear at first, just like ordinary folks. But then they manage to cast it aside and take action anyway.

Sometimes instincts will drive a person to bravery. Being courageous, however, does not mean forsaking the ability to think clearly. The brave reason well, and their clarity of mind only serves to fortify their resolve, spurring them to new heights of human endeavor.

History is filled with profiles of African American courage. The stories of great black figures come to us down through the ages, detailing struggles to survive the savagery of slavery and the indignities of discrimination. Those who fled slavery exhibited a special brand of courage. Many walked hundreds of miles through forests, using the stars as their guide and putting their lives in the hands of strangers along the way. They hid from bounty hunters and others who sought rewards for capturing slaves. A number of "great escape" stories are included in this chapter.

In more recent times, black bravery has still figured prominently.

Behind enemy lines in World War II, Lieutenant Vernon Baker destroyed well-camouflaged enemy observation and machinegun posts and then led a patrol across a mine field, heading straight into heavy gunfire. Some years later, four North Carolina college students displayed remarkable courage just by sitting down at a segregated lunch counter and attempting to order coffee. These stories serve as inspiration for both children and adults.

But courage isn't limited to extraordinary exploits that are certain to go down in history. It is often exemplified in our everyday lives—when we overcome a fear of the dark, or conquer a fright of speaking before crowds, or publish writing that reveals our innermost thoughts and feelings, or finally learn to read after a lifetime of not knowing how.

Bravery *can* be cultivated—by example and by practice. When adults cope well with fear and danger, they set a good example. Remaining confident, perseverent and reasonable when facing daunting problems, hazards, or tasks also presents a portrait of courage. Finally, teaching children to confront situations head-on can help them understand that bravery is a very important skill to develop.

෨ᘒᔍ

Courage may be the most important of all virtues, because without it one cannot practice any other virtue with consistency.

—*Maya Angelou*

෨ᘒᔍ

CRISPUS ATTUCKS, FIRST BLOOD
JIM HASKINS

In the 1770s, African Americans were one fifth of the population of the colonies. Though some five thousand black patriots served in the Revolutionary War, only a handful have been identified in war documents and military rolls. Still, black patriots played a crucial role in founding this country. The first to fall in what became known as the Boston Massacre, Crispus Attucks was the first martyr, black or white, in the cause of American liberty.

Ran-away from his master *William Brown* of *Framingham*, on the 30th of Sept. last, a Molatto Fellow, about 27 Years of Age, named *Crispas*, 6 Feet two Inches high, short curl'd Hair, his Knees nearer together than common; had on a light colour'd Bearskin Coat, plain brown Fustian Jacket, or Brown all-Wool one, new Buckskin Breeches, blue YarnStockings, and a check'd woollenShirt.

Whoever shall take up said Runaway, and convey him to his abovesaid Master, shall have *ten Pounds*, old TenorReward, and all necessary Charges paid. And allMasters of Vessels and others, are hereby caution'd against concealing or carrying off saidServant on Penalty of the Law.

—Boston Gazette, *October 2, 1750*

In 1770 Crispus Attucks, a black man born a slave, was the first American to die in the cause of the American Revolution. As the advertisement shows, he had already declared his own independence twenty years earlier.

Little is known about Crispus's early life. He was born into slavery, probably in the colony of Massachusetts. It is said that his father was African, and if so then his father was brought to the colonies on a slave ship. Crispus's mother was said to be an Indian and was probably a descendant of John Attucks.

John Attucks was a member of the Natick Indian tribe, and the word *attuck* in the language of the Naticks means deer. John Attucks lived in the 1600s and converted to Christianity. But during an Indian uprising that came to be known as King Philip's War, he sided with his own people. He was executed by New England colonists for treason in 1676.

Crispus was born some fifty years after that. We do not know anything about his upbringing, only that by 1750 he was a slave who belonged to a William Brown of Framingham.

According to local legend in Framingham, Attucks was an expert trader of horses and cattle, and dealt with free white men all the time. He kept the money he made for himself and probably tried to buy his freedom from William Brown. But Brown would not sell him his freedom, perhaps because Crispus was too valuable to him. So Crispus ran away.

In spite of the ad, Crispus was never caught and sent back to his master. No one knows what he did for the next twenty years. More than likely, he spent those years as a sailor, working on cargo ships that sailed to and from the West Indies, and on whaling ships off the New England coast.

During those same twenty years, trouble had arisen between England and her far-off colonies on the eastern coast of North America. Citizens of the colonies resented having to buy nearly everything they needed from England and complained about the lack of free trade. The colonies also complained of having to pay taxes to the king when they had no say in their own government.

Citizens of the colony of Massachusetts, especially in Boston, the capital of the colony, were the most outspoken in their complaints about British tyranny. So restive was that colony that in 1768 the British king, George III, decided to send in troops to occupy Boston. The king's hope was that the troops would calm down Boston and also serve as a warning to other colonies not to make trouble.

Two regiments, totaling about 1,000 soldiers, from British posts in Canada sailed into Boston Harbor on six warships in the late fall of 1769. The first ever sent to the colonies in peacetime, the troops marched ashore and took over the Customs House on King Street (now State Street). They set up tents on Boston Common and proceeded to anger the local citizens by stopping and searching innocent people. What made the citizens even angrier was that the city of Boston and the colony of Massachusetts were ordered to pay for the board and lodging of the very troops that had been sent to occupy their city.

As word spread outside Boston that 1,000 British troops were occupying the city of about 15,000 people, men and boys from the surrounding countryside began to make their way to the city. They were not an organized opposition, but they were united in their anger.

Meanwhile, the people of Boston were equally upset. There were minor incidents between the soldiers and the citizens. Snowballs with stones in the centers were thrown at the soldiers, but the soldiers were under orders not to fire their guns. In fact, most of the guns were not even loaded. But they used their bayonets to beat whoever attacked them, and sometimes to beat innocent bystanders.

Crispus Attucks was in Boston at that time. A slave named Andrew later said that Attucks had been living in New Providence, in the British colony of the Bahamas, and was in Boston "in order to go [to] North Carolina." The slave Andrew described Attucks as "stout," and since he was over six feet tall he must have been a commanding presence. According to some reports, he was eating supper at a local inn the night of Monday, March 5, 1770, when he heard fire alarms and rushed into the street to see what was happening.

Clashes between soldiers and citizens were occurring in several areas that night. A crowd of young men and boys were battling with soldiers on Brattle Street. Around the same time, on King Street, a British private named Hugh Montgomery hit a barber's apprentice in the face after the boy had insulted a British captain. The boy ran through the streets shouting that he had been "killed."

Someone set fire bells ringing, and Crispus Attucks left his supper to investigate.

He made his way to Dock Square, where a large crowd had gathered. Seeing that the people were milling about aimlessly, he picked up a large stick and shouted to the people to follow him to King Street, where the main guard of the British army was stationed. The crowd followed him to the Customs House, where Private Hugh Montgomery had taken up his post as guard.

Some of the boys in the crowd began to taunt Montgomery, whose musket wasn't loaded. The frightened private called for reinforcements, yelling, "Turn out, main guard!" Captain Preston, who was in charge of the guardhouse that day, ordered seven soldiers to go out and help Montgomery. The soldiers used their bayonets as clubs to cut through the crowd and drive it back. Seeing that the crowd was in no mood to retreat, the soldiers loaded their muskets.

The crowd had swelled, as nearly everyone in Boston heard that something was happening on King Street.

Standing at the front of the crowd was Crispus Attucks. According to the slave named Andrew, who was at the scene, the crowd was crying, "Damn them, they dare not fire, we are not afraid of them." Attucks threw himself into the group of soldiers, said Andrew, and struck at Captain Preston. A group of men followed him, yelling, "Kill the dogs, knock them over."

The soldiers fired. Crispus Attucks was the first to fall, hit by two musket balls. Four other men died: Samuel Gray, rope maker; James Caldwell, a ship's mate; Samuel Maverick, an apprentice joiner (furniture maker); and Patrick Carr, identified only as an Irishman. Six others in the crowd were wounded, but later recovered.

The next day, the bodies of Attucks and Caldwell were taken to Faneuil Hall, because neither man had a home in Boston. Two days after that, all the shops in the city were closed for the public funeral for the five victims. Thousands of people flocked in from the countryside, and the *Boston Gazette* reported that the funeral was attended by the largest crowd ever assembled in North America.

The coffins of Attucks and Caldwell were carried to meet the hearses with the other coffins on King Street. All the bells in the city tolled in the dead men's honor. There was a long procession to the cemetery, where they were all buried together in one grave.

While some called Attucks and the others heroes, others called them villains. But everyone agreed that Crispus Attucks was the main actor in the event, a stranger who had stepped forward to lead the attack on the soldiers.

The soldiers were placed on trial for the murders of the five citizens. In the bill of indictment that the court brought against the soldiers, the main section was devoted to Attucks, presenting his name first and separately from those of the other victims and charging that he had been assaulted "with force and arms, feloniously, willfully, and of malice aforethought."

John Adams was one of the lawyers for the defense. He would become the second president of the United States, but at the time he was loyal to the king of England. He, too, focused on Attucks, saying that it was to his "mad behavior [that], in all probability, the dreadful carnage of that night is chiefly ascribed." Adams claimed that the soldiers had every right to fear the "stout mulatto fellow, whose very looks was enough to terrify any person."

Captain Preston was found not guilty, since the court ruled that he had acted to protect his troops. Two soldiers were found guilty. As punishment, they were branded in the hand with a hot iron. Those who were against the British did not believe that justice had been done.

Clashes between British soldiers and colonists continued. King George III kept levying taxes upon the colonies without giving them a voice in their own government. Within three years, John Adams had changed his mind and no longer supported the king. He had also changed his mind about Crispus Attucks and the event he called the Boston Massacre.

On a Monday in July 1773, Adams wrote in his diary a letter to Governor Thomas Hutchinson of Massachusetts. He may have intended to publish it. He wrote it as if it had come from Crispus Attucks:

You will hear from Us with Astonishment. You ought to hear from Us with Horror. You are chargeable before God and Man, with our Blood. The Soldiers were but passive Instruments, were Machines, neither moral nor voluntary Agents in our Destruction more than the leaden Pelletts, with which we were wounded.—You was a free Agent. You acted, coolly, deliberately, with all that premeditated Malice, not against Us in Particular but against the People in general, which in the sight of the law is an ingredient in the Composition of Murder. You will hear from Us hereafter.

Adams signed the letter "Crispus Attucks."

Five years after Attucks's death, the battle of Lexington, with its "shot heard 'round the world," began the War of Independence. But even earlier Attucks's willingness to take a stand for liberty spurred the slaves of Massachusetts to petition for their freedom. Five separate petitions were presented to the governor, the House of Representatives, and the general court in 1773 and 1774. Unfortunately, none of these petitions were acted upon.

When colonial patriots gathered at Lexington and Concord, Massachusetts, to confront the redcoats from Boston in April 1775, black minutemen were among them. A slave from Lexington named Prince Easterbrooks was one of the first to be wounded at Lexington. Perhaps even more than the white patriots, these black patriots knew what the word *liberty* meant.

Crispus Attucks knew what liberty meant. In 1750 he had seized his own freedom by running away. Twenty years later, he had died fighting for a larger freedom—for himself and for others.

Blacks have honored Crispus Attucks ever since. After the Revolutionary War, black military companies took the name of Attucks Guards. From 1858 to 1870 blacks in Boston held annual Crispus Attucks Days. In 1888 they managed to get the city and state authorities to erect a Crispus Attucks monument on Boston Common. It was the earliest American public monument to a black man.

A WALK IN THE RIVER
AS TOLD BY RACHEL CRUZE

Enslaved blacks did not always passively accept the cruel treatment meted out by slave traders and masters. This haunting story, narrated by a former slave from Tennessee, told of the immense bravery of fifteen captives who would rather die than live as slaves.

Once I heard my colored grandmother and grandfather tell a story of something that happened some years before the War, probably before I was born. A nigger trader had been around the neighborhood buying up tall husky men for the cotton fields down South, and as he bought each one he put handcuffs on him and shackled him to the others. They accompanied him on foot day after day, as he traveled on horseback through that section. He had with him several wagons in which they could lie at night, but during the day they had to walk.

As they walked together, they talked about their future, and they all agreed that death would be preferable to the living death of the cotton fields. And they decided that the first time they had to ferry across a river with the nigger trader, they would walk onto the ferryboat and keep right on walking till they had walked off the other end. At the end of Dr. Sneed's farm was a ferry to carry people over to the Macabee farm on the other side, and when the nigger trader drove those slaves onto the ferry, that is exactly what they did: they all walked off into the deep of the river at the other end. If there was any among them who was lukewarm he was shoved in by the ones behind him.

That nigger trader was nearly crazy because of the money loss. He had not bought all the men outright, but had paid some down on every one of them, with a signed contract to complete payment when he received his money from the cotton raisers. Now he had to make good those notes.

Some years after the War had ended, some boys in the neighborhood were fording the river about a mile downstream from Dr. Sneed's place, and they found fifteen handcuffs, bright and shining and all fastened together. When the father of one of the boys saw them, he recalled the drowning up at Dr. Sneed's place.

THE FLYING AFRICANS

ORAL TESTIMONY

Due in part to their isolation from the mainland, many black folks in the coastal regions of Georgia and South Carolina, particularly the off-shore islands, were able to hold onto African customs and traditions. In the Sea Islands, blacks spoke Gullah, a language said to contain elements of West African dialects. Two islanders recall the story of courageous Africans who literally took flight from slavery. (The text is adapted from interviews recorded in an oral history project.)

I remember one boatload of seven or eight what come down from Savannah. That was just a little before the war. Robbie McQueen was African and Katie and old man Jacob King, they's all African. I remember them all. Old man King, he live till he old, live till I help bury him. But you can't understand much what these people say. They can't understand your talk and you can't understand their talk. They go, "Quack, quack, quack," just as fast as a horse can run, and my pa say, "Ain't no good to listen to 'em."

Ain't you hear about 'em? Well, at that time Mr. Blue, he was the overseer and Mr. Blue put 'em in the field, but he couldn't do nothing with 'em. They gabble, gabble, gabble, and nobody couldn't understand 'em and they didn't know how to work right. Mr. Blue, he go down one morning with a long whip for to whip 'em good. They's foolish acting. He got to whip 'em, Mr. Blue, he ain't have no choice. Anyways, he whip 'em good and they gets together and stick the hoe in the field and then say, "Quack, quack, quack," and they rise up in the sky and turn themselves into buzzards and fly right back to Africa. They sure left the hoe standing in the field and they rise right up and fly right back to Africa.

I ain't seen 'em. I been to Skidaway, but I knowed plenty what did see 'em, plenty what was there in the field with 'em and seen the hoe they left sticking up after they done fly away.

—Wallace Quarterman, Darien

The slaves was out in the field working. All of a sudden they get together and start to move in a ring. Round they go faster and faster. Then one by one they rise up and take wing and fly like a bird. The overseer hear the noise and he come out and he see the slaves rise up in the air and fly back to Africa. He run and he catch the last one by the foot just as he was about to fly off. I don't know if he was near enough to pull him back down and keep him from going off.

—Priscilla McCullough, Darien

IF YOU CAN'T FIGHT, KICK!
CORNELIA

Perhaps the best and most vivid accounts of life under slavery appear in the oral testimonies of former slaves, not in historical tracts and plantation records. Slave narratives provide fascinating glimpses of life in bondage, revealing the interactions of men, women, and children caught in a complex web of emotions, including fear, respect, and contempt. Many accounts tell of unswerving courage and militancy in the face of hopeless prospects for improvement. The following narrative describes life on a small farm in Tennessee and the advice a black mother offers her daughter.

My mother was the smartest black woman in Eden. She was as quick as a flash of lightning, and whatever she did could not be done better. She could do anything. She cooked, washed, ironed, spun, nursed and labored in the field. She made as good a field hand as she did a cook. I have heard Master Jennings say to his wife, "Fannie has her faults, but she can outwork any nigger in the country. I'd bet my life on that."

My mother certainly had her faults as a slave. She was very different in nature from Aunt Caroline. Ma fussed, fought, and kicked all the time. I tell you, she was a demon. She said that she wouldn't be whipped, and when she fussed, all Eden must have known it. She was loud and boisterous, and it seemed to me that you could hear her a mile away. Father was often the prey of her high temper. With all her ability for work, she did not make a good slave. She was too high-spirited and independent. I tell you, she was a captain.

The one doctrine of my mother's teaching which was branded upon my senses was that I should never let anyone abuse me. "I'll kill you, gal, if you don't stand up for yourself," she would say. "Fight, and if you can't fight, kick; if you can't kick, then bite." Ma was generally willing to work, but if she didn't feel like doing something, none could make her do it. At least, the Jennings [sic] couldn't make, or didn't make her.

"Bob, I don't want no sorry nigger around me. I can't tolerate you if you ain't got no backbone." Such constant warning to my father had its effect. My mother's unrest and fear of abuse spread gradually to my father. He seemed to have been made after the timid kind. He would never fuss back at my mother, or if he did, he couldn't be heard above her shouting. Pa was also a sower of all seeds. He was a yardman, houseman, plowman, gardner, blacksmith, carpenter, keysmith, and anything else they chose him to be.

I was the oldest child. My mother had three other children by the time I was about six years old. It was at this age that I remember the almost daily talks of my mother on the cruelty of slavery. I would say nothing to her, but I was thinking all the time that slavery did not seem so cruel. Master and Mistress Jennings were not mean to my mother. It was she who was mean to them.

Master Jennings allowed his slaves to earn any money they could for their own use. My father had a garden of his own around his little cabin, and he also had some chickens. Mr. Dodge, who was my master's uncle, and who owned the hotel in Eden, was pa's regular customer. He would buy anything my pa brought to him; and many times he was buying his own stuff, or his nephew's stuff. I have seen pa go out at night with a big sack and come back with it full. He'd bring sweet potatoes, watermelons, chickens and turkeys. We were fond of pig roast and sweet potatoes, and the only way to have pig roast was for pa to go out on one of his hunting trips. Where he went, I cannot say, but he brought the booty home. The floor of our cabin was covered with planks. Pa had raised up two planks, and dug a hole. This was our storehouse. Every Sunday, Master Jennings would let pa take the wagon to carry watermelons, cider and ginger cookies to Spring Hill, where the Baptist church was located. The Jennings were Baptists. The white folks would buy from him as well as the free Negroes of Trenton, Tennessee. Sometimes these free Negroes would steal to our cabin at a specified time to buy a chicken or barbecue dinner. Mr. Dodge's slaves always had money and came to buy from us. Pa was allowed to keep the money he made at Spring Hill, and of course Master Jennings didn't know about the little restaurant we had in our cabin.

One day my mother's temper ran wild. For some reason Mistress Jennings struck her with a stick. Ma struck back and a fight followed. Mr. Jennings was not at home and the children became frightened and ran upstairs. For half hour they wrestled in the kitchen. Mistress, seeing that she could not get the better of ma, ran out in the road, with ma right on her heels. In the road, my mother flew into her again. The thought seemed to race across my mother's mind to tear mistress' clothing off her body. She suddenly began to tear Mistress Jennings' clothes off. She caught hold, pulled, ripped and tore. Poor mistress was nearly naked when the storekeeper got to them and pulled ma off.

"Why, Fannie, what do you mean by that?" he asked.

"Why, I'll kill her, I'll kill her dead if she ever strikes me again."

I have never been able to find out the why of the whole thing. . . .

Pa heard Mr. Jennings say that Fannie would have to be whipped by law. He told ma. Two mornings afterward, two men came in at the big gate, one with a long lash in his hand. I was in the yard and I hoped they couldn't find ma. To my surprise, I saw her running around the house, straight in the direction of the men. She must have seen them coming. I should have known that she wouldn't hide. She knew what they were coming for, and she intended to meet them halfway. She swooped upon them like a hawk on chickens. I believe they were afraid of her or thought she was crazy. One man had a long beard which she grabbed with one hand, and the lash with the other. Her body was made strong with madness. She was a good match for them. Mr. Jennings came and pulled her away. I don't know what would have happened if he hadn't come at that moment, for one man had already pulled his gun out. Ma did not see the gun until Mr. Jennings came up. On catching sight of it, she said, "Use your gun, use it and blow my brains out if you will." . . .

That evening Mistress Jennings came down to the cabin.

"Well, Fannie," she said, "I'll have to send you away. You won't be whipped, and I'm afraid you'll get killed." . . .

"I'll go to hell or anywhere else, but I won't be whipped," ma answered.

"You can't take the baby, Fannie, Aunt Mary can keep it with the other children."

Mother said nothing at this. That night, ma and pa sat up late, talking over things, I guess. Pa loved ma, and I heard him say, "I'm going too, Fannie." About a week later, she called me and told me that she and pa were going to leave me the next day, that they were going to Memphis. She didn't know for how long.

"But don't be abused, Puss." She always called me Puss. My right name was Cornelia. I cannot tell in words the feelings I had at that time. My sorrow knew no bound. My very soul seemed to cry out, "Gone, gone, gone forever." I cried until my eyes looked like balls of fire. I felt for the first time in my life that I had been abused. How cruel it was to take my mother and father from me, I thought. My mother had been right. Slavery was cruel, so very cruel.

Thus my mother and father were hired to Tennessee. The next morning they were to leave. I saw ma working around with the baby under her arms as if it had been a bundle of some kind. Pa came up to the cabin with an old mare for ma to ride, and an old mule for himself. Mr. Jennings was with him.

"Fannie, leave the baby with Aunt Mary," said Mr. Jennings very quietly.

At this, ma took the baby by its feet, a foot in each hand, and with the baby's head swinging downward, she vowed to smash its brains out before she'd leave it. Tears were streaming down her face. It was seldom that ma cried, and everyone knew that she meant every word. Ma took her baby with her. . . .

An uneventful year passed. I was destined to be happily surprised by the return of my mother and father. They came one day, and found me sitting by the roadside in a sort of trance. . . .

"Puss, we've come back, me and pa, and we've come to stay." . . .

She and pa embraced and caressed me for a long time. We went to the cabin, and Master Jennings was there nearly as soon as we were.

"Hello, Fannie. How did you get along?" he asked.

"Why, Mr. Jennings, you know that I know how to get along," she answered.

"Well, I'm glad to hear that, Fannie."

Ma had on new clothes, and a pair of beautiful earrings. She told Aunt Mary that she stayed in Memphis one year without a whipping or a cross word.

Pa had learned to drink more liquor than ever, it seemed. At least, he was able to get more of it, for there were many disagreements between pa and ma about his drinking. Drinkers will drink together, and Mr. Jennings was no exception. Pa would have the excuse that Master Jennings offered him liquor, and of course he wouldn't take it from anybody else. It was common to see them together, half drunk, with arms locked, walking around and around the old barn. Then pa would put his hands behind him and let out a big whoop which could be heard all over Eden. . . .

Our family was increased by the arrival of a baby girl. Ma was very sick, and she never did get well after that. She was cooking for Mistress Jennings one day when she came home and went to bed. She never got up. I guess ma was sick about six months. During that time she never hit a tap of work. She said she had brought five children in the world for the Jennings, and that was enough; that she didn't intend to work when she felt bad.

On the day my mother died, she called pa and said . . . "Go tell Master Jennings to come in, and get all the slaves too."

Pa went and returned in five minutes with old master.

"Fannie, are you any worse?" said old master.

"No, no, Master Jennings, no worse. But I'm going to leave you at eight o'clock."

"Where are you going, Fannie?" Master Jennings asked as if he didn't know that ma was talking about dying.

Ma shook her head slowly and answered, "I'm going where there ain't no fighting and cussing and damning."

"Is there anything that you want me to do for you, Fannie?"

Ma told him that she reckoned there wasn't much of anything that anybody could do for her now. "But I would like for you to take Puss and hire her out among ladies, so she can be raised right. She will never be any good here, Master Jennings."

A funny look came over Master Jennings' face, and he bowed his head up and down. All the hands had come in and were standing around with him.

My mother died at just about eight o'clock.

❧

Brethren, arise, arise! Strike for your lives and liberties. Now is the day and the hour. Let every slave throughout the land do this, and the days of slavery are numbered. You cannot be more oppressed than you have been—you cannot suffer greater cruelties than you have already. *Rather die freemen than live to be slaves.*

—Henry Highland Garnet,
From An Address to the Slaves
of the United States of America,
August 21, 1843

❧

THE ANTI-SLAVERY ALPHABET
ANONYMOUS

Published as a small book in 1847, this poem was distributed at an anti-slavery fair in Philadelphia.

A is an Abolitionist—
  A man who wants to be free
The wretched slave—and give to all
  An equal liberty.

B is a Brother with a skin
  Of somewhat darker hue,
But in our Heavenly Father's sight,
  He is as dear as you.

C is the Cotton-field, to which
  This injured brother's driven,
When, as the white man's *slave*, he toils
  From early morn till even.

D is the Driver, cold and stern,
  Who follows, whip in hand,
To punish those who dare to rest,
  Or disobey command.

E is the Eagle, soaring high;
  An emblem of the free;
But while we chain our brother man,
  Our type he cannot be.

F is the heart-sick Fugitive,
  The slave who runs away,
And travels through the dreary night,
  But hides himself by day.

G is the Gong, whose rolling sound,
　　　Before the morning light,
Calls up the little sleeping slave,
　　　To labor until the night.

H is the Hound his master trained,
　　　And called to scent the track,
Of the unhappy fugitive,
　　　And bring him trembling back.

I is the Infant, from the arms
　　　Of its fond mother torn,
And, at a public auction, sold
　　　With horses, cows, and corn.

J is the Jail, upon whose floor
　　　That wretched mother lay,
Until her cruel master came,
　　　And carried her away.

K is the Kidnapper, who stole
　　　That little child and mother—
Shrieking, it clung around her, but
　　　He tore them from each other.

L is the Lash, that brutally
　　　He swung around its head,
Threatening that "if it cried again,
　　　He'd whip it till 'twas dead."

M is the Merchant of the north,
　　　Who buys what slaves produce—
So they are stolen, whipped and worked,
　　　For his, and for our use.

N is the Negro, rambling free
　　　In his far distant home,

Delighting 'neath the palm trees' shade
　　And cocoa-nut to roam.

O is the Orange tree, that bloomed
　　Beside his cabin door,
When white men stole him from
　　his home
　　　To see it never more.

P is the Parent, sorrowing,
　　　And weeping all alone—
The child he loved to lean upon,
　　His only son, is gone!

Q is the Quarter, where the slave
　　On coarsest food is fed,
And where, with toil and sorrow worn,
　　He seeks his wretched bed.

R is the "Rice-swamp, dank and lone,"
　　Where, weary, day by day,
He labors till the fever wastes
　　His strength and life away.

S is the Sugar, that the slave
　　Is toiling hard to make,
To put into your pie and tea,
　　Your candy, and your cake.

T is the rank Tobacco plant,
　　Raised by slave labor too:
A poisonous and nasty thing,
　　For gentlemen to chew.

U is for Upper Canada,
　　Where the poor slave has found

Rest after all his wanderings,
　　For it is British ground!

V is the Vessel, in whose dark,
　　Noisome, and stifling hold,
Hundreds of Africans are packed,
　　Brought o'er the seas, and sold.

W is the Whipping post,
　　To which the slave is bound,
While on his naked back, the lash
　　Makes many a bleeding wound.

X is for Xerxes, famed of yore;
　　A warrior stern was he
He fought with swords; let truth
　　and love
　　　Our only weapons be.

Y is for Youth—the time for all
　　Bravely to war with sin;
And think not it can ever be
　　Too early to begin.

Z is a Zealous man, sincere,
　　Faithful, and just, and true;
An earnest pleader for the slave—
　　Will you not be so too?

THE BALLAD OF THE UNDERGROUND RAILROAD

CHARLES L. BLOCKSON

Tonight we ride the underground train.
It runs on tracks that are covered with pain.
The whole of Humanity makes up the crew
And Liberty's the engineer to carry us through.
The North Star will lead us,
And Freedom will greet us
When we reach the end of the line.

The Underground Train,
Strange as it seems,
Carried many passengers
And never was seen.

It wasn't made of wood,
It wasn't made of steel;
A man-made train that
Ran without wheels.

The train was known
By many a name.
But the greatest of all
Was "The Freedom Train."

The Quakers, the Indians,
Gentiles and Jews,
Were some of the people
Who made up the crews.

Free Blacks and Christians
And Atheists, too,
Were the rest of the people
Who made up the crews.

Conductors and agents
Led the way at night,
Guiding the train
By the North Star Light.

The passengers were
The fugitive slaves
Running from slavery
And its evil ways.

Running from the whip
And the overseer,
From the slave block
And the Auctioneer.

They didn't want their masters
To catch them again,
So the men dressed as women
And the women as men.

They hid in churches,
Cellars and barns,
Waiting to hear the
Train's alarm.

Sleeping by day,
And traveling by night,
Was the best way they knew
To keep out of sight.

They waded in the waters
To hide their scent,
And fool those bloodhounds
The slave masters sent.

They spoke in riddles
And sang in codes,

To understand the message,
You had to be told.

Those who knew the secret
Never did tell
The sacred message
Of the "Freedom Train's" bell.

Riding this train
Broke the laws of the land,
But the laws of God
Are higher than man's.

SIGN, SEALED, AND DELIVERED

A few ingenious slaves literally sent themselves to freedom. Special delivery.

In 1856 in Richmond, Virginia, a slave named Henry Brown bought a box that was three feet by two feet by two feet eight inches deep. In it he put a jug of water and biscuits, and then he himself climbed in. A white friend nailed the lid on the box and mailed it, with Henry Brown inside, to Philadelphia. The box arrived twenty-six hours later, having traveled much of the way upside down, despite the markings on its exterior: HANDLE WITH CARE and THIS SIDE UP.

Philadelphia abolitionists, informed that human cargo would arrive, had the box brought directly from the delivery station to Anti-Slavery Society headquarters, where they pried off the lid. Brown stood up and said, "How do you do, gentlemen?"

Three years later, another slave, William Peel Jones, stepped into a box in Baltimore and had a white friend mail him to Philadelphia. Only, Jones's box was smaller than Brown's, so Jones had to keep his legs folded throughout the journey—a seventeen-hour ocean voyage.

The same friend who mailed Jones traveled by land to Philadelphia, found the box on the steamship, and transported it to a safe place, where he opened it. Jones and his devoted friend then celebrated.

WILLIAM STILL,
THE STATIONMASTER
GENE SMITH

William Still (1821–1902), who conducted the Philadelphia station of the Underground Railroad, helped hundreds flee slavery, including his most famous "passenger," Harriet Tubman. One of his strangest encounters involved a member of his own family.

At his death in 1902, at eighty, William Still was very well off, a successful Philadelphia businessman, leaving an estate said to exceed three-quarters of a million dollars, a great sum. But what was it compared in different coin with that owed him by those he had served back then and whose memories and doings he had recorded in the days of the Underground Railroad?

His parents were born in Maryland. His father, Levin, believed that one man could not own another. He would die before he accepted such a concept, he said. His master saw that he meant it and offered "overwork," labor performed on Sundays and holidays, normally times of rest. He would be paid for it. Let him accumulate enough money, the owner said, and Levin might purchase himself. After years he did so. Free, he went to New Jersey. His wife, Charity, followed with their four children, but as an illegal fugitive stealing property—herself and the children. Slave hunters came when Levin was away from home and took his family into custody and back to Maryland, to slavery. The mother did not fight. As a child she had seen her father killed by a drunken master. Although carefully watched and locked up at night, she ran off again, spiriting away her two little girls, whose likely destiny under the slave power she knew too well. She had to leave behind two boys, eight and six. She never ceased to weep for them.

Levin and Charity Still lived in remote Burlington County, New Jersey, farming. Children were born, William in 1821. As a young man he went to Philadelphia, taught himself to read and write, got a three-dollar-a-week clerk-handyman job at the Pennsylvania Society for Promoting the Abolition of Slavery. Family tradition, as described in a book by the Still descendant Lurey Khan, holds that it was his mother's tears for her two lost boys, his brothers in the South, that made him an ardent abolitionist.

From the anti-slavery organization he learned how the Underground Railroad worked. "Passengers," as they were called, were seen along through the South by "conductors" advancing them to a safe house "depot." Money was given by "stockholders" wishing to help. Still became a "stationmaster," receiving self-indicted and self-convicted criminals whose crime under the U.S. Fugitive Slave Law was that they wished to be free. For such, penitentiary, fine, flogging awaited. Those who helped the refugees were also punished. It was the law.

Still wanted to know about these men and women coming to what was called the Vigilance Committee of Philadelphia to be sheltered, fed, clothed, and sent on farther north, as far from Dixie as possible. He asked what it had been like to run from slave catcher and tracking dog through swamp and field, over mountain and water, on top of trains in the night, on stolen horses. He asked about the dens and caves in which people hid and about master, work, punishment, family. For a decade and a half he cached away an accumulating pile of notes that constituted irrefutable proof that he had consciously violated the Fugitive Slave Law. After the Civil War he gathered everything and wrote *The Underground Railroad.*

It seemed to him that those who fled the South were brave, heroic, gallant. They chanced all, leaving behind all they had known, loved ones and security of a kind, in order to ride the Underground Railroad to an unknown future. They were liable to be grabbed in their flight by anyone seeking a reward, tossed into jail, and then sent back to the whipping post and, with likely dispatch in a chain gang, to the most brutal working conditions imaginable. Yet they came.

Once a middle-aged man came. As he answered Still's questions, his identity became clear. He was one of the two little boys left behind when Still's mother ran north, a brother known of since earliest childhood. Their father was dead, but their mother lived to have a reunion with a son not seen in forty years.

After John Brown made his doomed Harpers Ferry raid, his wife and daughter stayed with Still and his wife, Letitia, as they awaited his execution. By then the Stills had four children who had never known a time when there was not a black stranger sitting at the dinner table, fresh from the South and heading on. Nineteen out of twenty fugitives coming through Philadelphia, it is said, stayed with the Stills.

After the Civil War Still grew rich in the coal business, opened a store dealing in stoves, got involved in real estate and finance, and was prominent in charitable work. He helped his Presbyterian church, black veterans of the Union Army, and black orphans.

In the days of slavery it was common for blacks to be assured that sections of the Bible countenanced and endorsed their servitude. But there was that in the Bible that said otherwise, in Deuteronomy 23:15, and it constituted the essence of what the Underground Railroad meant to Still. He put it on the first page of his book: "Thou shalt not deliver unto his master the servant that has escaped from his master unto thee."

FRAGILE FREIGHT
WILLIAM STILL

Here is the story of a daring escape made by a pregnant woman. William Still, a conductor and historian of the Underground Railroad, recorded her story in his book The Underground Railroad, *published in 1872.*

In the winter of 1857 a young woman, who had just turned her majority, was boxed up in Baltimore by . . . a young man, who had the box conveyed as freight to the depot . . . consigned to Philadelphia.

Nearly all one night it remained at the depot with the living agony in it, and after being turned upside down more than once, the next day about ten o'clock it reached Philadelphia. Her companion coming on in advance of the box, arranged with a hackman . . . having it brought from the depot to a designated house, Mrs. Myers . . . where the resurrection was to take place. . . .

The secret had been intrusted to Mrs. M by the young companion of the woman. A feeling of horror came over the aged woman. . . . A few doors from her lived an old friend . . . well known as a brave woman and a friend of the slave, Mrs. Ash, the undertaker or shrouder, whom everybody knew among the colored people. Mrs. Myers felt that it would not be wise to move in the matter of this resurrection without the presence of the undertaker. . . . They mustered courage and pried off the lid. A woman was discovered in the straw. . . . She could not speak, but being assisted, arose. She then went to bed. . . . The third day she began to come to herself and talk quite freely. . . . She had a pair of scissors with her, and in order to procure fresh air she had made a hole in the box, but it was very slight. How she ever managed to breathe and maintain her existence, being in the condition of becoming a mother, it was hard to comprehend. . . .

After spending some three or four days in Mrs. Myers' family she remained in the writer's family about the same length of time, and was then forwarded to Canada.

HARRIET "MOSES" TUBMAN
ANN PETRY

Harriet Tubman (c. 1821–1913) became known as the "Moses of her people." The most famous conductor on the Underground Railroad, she made fifteen trips south to guide an estimated three hundred slaves— including her family—to freedom, and she never lost a "passenger." During the Civil War, she served as a scout, spy, cook, and nurse for the Union army. Her name is synonymous with courage and strength.

When she crossed the line into the free state of Pennsylvania, the sun was coming up. She said, "I looked at my hands to see if I was the same person now I was free. There was such a glory over everything, the sun came like gold through the trees, and over the fields, and I felt like I was in heaven."

When she thought of her family, left behind in Maryland, all of them slaves, her joy in having escaped rapidly left her. She decided that as soon as she could, she would go back to Dorcester County and lead her family North, too. She knew the way now. She knew what a fugitive would do on the nights when it rained, and the North Star was obscured. She had groped her way along, fingering the bark of trees, finding out on which side the moss grew the thickest, moving slowly from tree to tree. Her hands had been cold, and the moss was spongy and wet, the bark of the trees was rough.

But she had done it once, alone, and with the help of the Lord, she would do it again, and again, until she got all of her family out of Maryland.

Though she was not aware of it, she had become a legend in the slave cabins along the eastern shore. She had always had the makings of a legend in her: the prodigious strength, the fearlessness, the religious ardor, the visions she had in which she experienced moments of pre-science. The slaves said she could see in the dark like a mule, that she could smell danger down the wind like a fox, that she could move through thick underbrush without making a sound, like a field mouse. They said she was so strong she could pick up a grown man, sling him over her shoulder and walk with him for miles.

They said, voices muted, awed, that she talked with God every day, just like Moses. They said there was some strange power in her so that no one could die when she was with them. She enveloped the sick and the dying with her strength, sending it from her body to theirs, sustaining them.

They changed her name again. At first she had been called Minta or Minty. After her defiance of an overseer, they called her Harriet, because the pet names, the diminutives, were no longer fitting for a girl who had displayed such courage. Now they called her Moses.

Along the eastern shore of Maryland, in Dorcester County, in Caroline County, the masters kept hearing whispers about the man named

Moses, who was running off slaves. At first they did not believe in his existence. The stories about him were fantastic, unbelievable. Yet they watched for him. They offered rewards for his capture.

They never saw him. Now and then they heard whispered rumors to the effect that he was in the neighborhood. The woods were searched. The roads were watched. There was never anything to indicate his whereabouts. But a few days afterward, a goodly number of slaves would be gone from the plantation. Neither the master nor the overseer had heard or seen anything unusual in the quarter. Sometimes one or the other would vaguely remember having heard a whippoorwill call somewhere in the woods, close by, late at night, though it was the wrong season for whippoorwills.

Harriet Tubman could have told them that there was far more involved in this matter of running off slaves than signaling the would-be runaways by imitating the call of a whippoorwill, or a hoot owl, far more involved than a matter of waiting for a clear night when the North Star was visible.

In December 1851, when she started out with the band of fugitives that she planned to take to Canada, she had been in the vicinity of the plantation for days, planning the trip, carefully selecting the slaves that she would take with her.

She had announced her arrival in the quarter by singing the forbidden spiritual—"Go down, Moses, 'way down to Egypt Land"—singing it softly outside the door of a slave cabin, late at night. The husky voice was beautiful even when it was barely more than a murmur borne on the wind.

Once she had made her presence known, word of her coming spread from cabin to cabin. The slaves whispered to each other, ear to mouth, mouth to ear, "Moses is here." "Moses has come." "Get ready. Moses is back again." The ones who had agreed to go North with her put ashcake and salt herring in an old bandanna, hastily tied it into a bundle, and then waited patiently for the signal that meant it was time to start.

There were eleven in this party, including one of her brothers and his wife. It was the largest group that she had ever conducted, but she was determined that more and more slaves should know what freedom was like.

She had to take them all the way to Canada. The Fugitive Slave Law was no longer a great many incomprehensible words written down on the country's lawbooks. The new law had become a reality.

She had never been to Canada. The route beyond Philadelphia was strange to her. But she could not let the runaways who accompanied her know this. As they walked along she told them stories of her own first flight, she kept painting vivid word pictures of what it would be like to be free.

But there were so many of them this time. She knew moments of doubt when she was half afraid, and kept looking back over her shoulder, imagining that she heard the sound of pursuit. They would certainly be pursued. Eleven of them. Eleven thousand dollars' worth of flesh and bone and muscle that belonged to Maryland planters. If they were caught, the eleven runaways would be whipped and sold South, but she—she would probably be hanged.

They tried to sleep during the day but they never could wholly relax into sleep. She could tell by the positions they assumed, by their restless movements. And they walked at night. Their progress was slow. It took them three nights of walking to reach the first stop. She had told them about the place where they would stay, promising warmth and good food, holding these things out to them as an incentive to keep going.

When she knocked on the door of a farmhouse, a place where she and her parties of runaways had always been welcome, always been given shelter and plenty to eat, there was no answer. She knocked again, softly. A voice from within said, "Who is it?" There was fear in the voice.

She knew instantly from the sound of the voice that there was something wrong. She said, "A friend with friends," the password on the Underground Railroad.

The door opened, slowly. The man who stood in the doorway looked at her coldly, looked with unconcealed astonishment and fear at the eleven disheveled runaways who were standing near her. Then he shouted, "Too many, too many. It's not safe. My place was searched last week. It's not safe!" and slammed the door in her face.

She turned away from the house, frowning. She had promised her passengers food and rest and warmth, and instead of that, there would be hunger and cold and more walking over the frozen ground. Somehow she would have to instill courage into these eleven people, most of them

strangers, would have to feed them on hope and bright dreams of freedom instead of the fried pork and corn bread and milk she had promised
them . . .

That night they reached the next stop—a farm that belonged to a
German. She made the runaways take shelter behind trees at the edge of
the fields before she knocked at the door. She hesitated before she
approached the door, thinking, *Suppose that he, too, should refuse shelter,
suppose*—Then she thought, *Lord, I'm going to hold steady on to You and
You've got to see me through*—and knocked softly.

She heard the familiar guttural voice say, "Who's there?"

She answered quickly, "A friend with friends."

He opened the door and greeted her warmly. "How many this time?"
he asked.

"Eleven," she said and waited, doubting, wondering.

He said, "Good. Bring them in."

He and his wife fed them in the lamplit kitchen, their faces glowing,
as they offered food and more food, urging them to eat, saying there
was plenty for everybody, have more milk, have more bread, have more
meat.

They spent the night in the warm kitchen. They really slept, all that
night and until dusk the next day. When they left, it was with reticence.
They had all been warm and safe and well fed. It was hard to exchange
the security offered by that clean warm kitchen for the darkness and the
cold of a December night. But she urged them on.

Two nights later she was aware that the feet behind her were moving
slower and slower. She heard irritability in their voices, knew that soon
someone would refuse to go on.

She carried a gun with her on these trips. She had never used it—
except as a threat. One of the runaways said, "Let me go back. Let me
go back," and stood still, and then turned around and said, over his
shoulder, "I am going back."

She lifted the gun, aimed it at the despairing slave. She said, "Go on
with us or die." The husky low-pitched voice was grim.

He hesitated for a moment and then he joined the others. They
started walking again. She tried to explain to them why none of them
could go back to the plantation. If a runaway returned, he would turn
traitor, the master and the overseer would force him to turn traitor. The

returned slave would disclose the stopping places, the hiding places, the cornstacks they had used with the full knowledge of the owner of the farm, the name of the German farmer who had fed them and sheltered them. These people who had risked their own security to help runaways would be ruined, fined, imprisoned.

She said, "We got to go free or die. And freedom's not bought with dust."

Finally, they reached Thomas Garrett's house in Wilmington, Delaware. Just as Harriet had promised, Garrett gave them all new shoes, and provided carriages to take them on to the next stop.

By slow stages they reached Philadelphia, where [Underground Railroad stationmaster] William Still hastily recorded their names, and the plantations whence they had come, and something of the life they had led in slavery.

William Still, who was familiar with all the station stops on the Underground Railroad, supplied Harriet with money and sent her and her eleven fugitives on to Burlington, New Jersey.

Harriet felt safer now, though there were danger spots ahead. But the biggest part of her job was over. As they went farther and farther north, it grew colder; she was aware of the wind on the Jersey ferry and aware of the cold damp in New York. From New York they went on to Syracuse, where the temperature was even lower.

From Syracuse they went north again, into a colder, snowier city— Rochester. Here they almost certainly stayed with Frederick Douglass.

Late in December 1851, Harriet arrived in St. Catharines, Canada West (now Ontario), with the eleven fugitives. It had taken almost a month to compete this journey; most of the time had been spent getting out of Maryland.

IN THE FALL of 1854, Harriet Tubman began to feel uneasy about three of her brothers. Benjamin, John, and William Henry were still in Maryland, working on plantations where they had been hired out. She kept having dreams about them sold and sent away in a chain gang. She decided to tell them that she was coming to Maryland that fall, so that they would be ready to go North with her.

It would not be safe to communicate with them directly. She could not read or write. So she had a friend write a cryptic letter to a free

Negro, Jacob Jackson, who lived near the plantation where two of her brothers worked.

Jacob had an adopted son who had gone North to live. Harriet thought that it would be perfectly natural and understandable if this son should write to his foster father, reporting about his health and inquiring about the family. She either did not know or had forgotten that the son, William Henry, had no brothers and no "old folks." But Jacob would know what she meant, for he had often provided shelter for her when she was in Dorcester County.

When the letter arrived in Bucktown, the postmaster opened it and read it. There was always the possibility that mail with a Northern postmark might contain abolitionist propaganda, and when it was addressed to a free Negro, it was almost certain to contain objectionable material.

This is what he found: "Read my letter to the old folks, and give my love to them, and tell my brothers to be always watching unto prayer, and when the good old ship of Zion comes along, to be ready to step on board. Signed—William Henry Jackson."

The postmaster showed the letter to two other men. They agreed that it must mean something—but the meaning eluded them. They knew that William Henry Jackson had no brothers or sisters. He was an orphan. As for "old folks" well, he didn't have any.

They sent for Jacob, showed him the letter, and asked him for an explanation.

Jacob read the letter quickly, though he pretended to read it slowly, stumbling over the words, repeating some of them, using his finger as a guide, back and forth across the sheet of paper. He wondered how Moses had known that her brothers were in trouble. It was common talk in the cabins that they had been sold and were to go South with the chain gang the day after Christmas. She would get here just in time to rescue them.

He handed the paper with its seemingly meaningless words back to the postmaster. "That letter can't be meant for me nohow," he said, shaking his head. "I can't make head or tail of it."

That same night, Jacob told all three of [her] brothers that Moses would be coming for them soon, and to be ready to leave.

Harriet made her way South, slowly, without incident. She reached

Bucktown on the twenty-third of December. The next night she started North again, with a larger party than she had planned for.

When they were ready to start, John Ross, the third brother, had not arrived. Harriet started without him. She never waited for anyone. Delays were dangerous. She left word with Jacob for him, so that if he did come, he could overtake them along the way. The first stop would be in Caroline County, near Ben's cabin. Old Rit and Ben [Harriet's parents] were now living forty miles to the north of Bucktown, in another county, but on a farm that belonged to Dr. Thompson.

John Ross did overtake them, finally. It was daybreak of Christmas morning when he found them. They were concealed in the fodder house, not far away from the cabin where Old Rit and Ben now lived.

John told them why he was late. His wife had just had another baby. He had to go get the midwife. Then after the baby was born, he couldn't bear to leave her. Yet he knew if he didn't run away, go then, he would be separated from her anyway. Because he was to be sold on the day after Christmas. Though she did not know that. He couldn't bring himself to tell her. At least not then.

So he had lingered in the cabin, looking down at his wife and the newborn baby. Then he had edged toward the door, and each time he moved, his wife had said, "Where you goin', John?"

He had told her he was going to see about being hired out on a new job. They all knew that changes in jobs were arranged during Christmas season. He thought she believed him. He couldn't bear to tell her he was taking off, couldn't bear to tell her that he had been sold. When he left the cabin, he stood outside the door, listening. He heard her crying and so went back inside.

She said, "Oh, John, you're going to leave me. I know it. But wherever you go, John, don't forget me and the children."

Then he had told her that he was leaving. He said that he would send Moses back for her, on her next trip. He had promised. It wouldn't be long—and in the dim light in the fodder house he looked at Moses for approval, for agreement. She nodded her head. So he felt better.

There were wide chinks in the walls [of the fodder house]. Through them Harriet could see the sway-backed cabin where Daddy Ben and Old Rit lived . . . Smoke kept pouring out of the clay-daubed chimney, hanging heavy in the air. Old Rit had probably killed her pig, and was cooking it for the Christmas dinner. The master gave her a baby pig every year, and she fattened it, saving food from her own plate to feed the pig, so that she could feed her family with a lavish hand on this one day. She'd have pork and sausage and bacon. Plenty of food. The boys said that Old Rit was expecting them for dinner. They always spent Christmas Day with her.

She had to figure out some way of letting Ben know that she was here, that the boys were with her and that they needed food. It would never do to let Old Rit know this. She would laugh and shout. Then when she learned, as she certainly would, that the boys were running away, going North, she would try to detain them, would create such an uproar that the entire quarter would know their secret.

Harriet remembered two men, John Chase and Peter Jackson. They were strangers. She asked them to go to the cabin, to tell Ben that his children were in the fodder house, badly in need of food. She warned them not to let Old Rit overhear what they said.

John and Peter did exactly as she told them. She watched them knock on the ramshackle door of the cabin, saw the door open, saw Old Ben standing in the doorway. The men motioned to him to come outside. They talked to him. Ben nodded his head. His expression did not change at all. She thought, how wonderful he is. Then he went back inside the cabin.

Late in the afternoon, he tapped on the side of the fodder house, then opened the door, and put part of the Christmas dinner—cooked bacon, hoecake, fried pork, and roasted yams—inside on the floor. He did not look at them. He said, "I know what'll come of this and I ain't goin' to see my children, nohow."

Harriet remembered his reputation for truthfulness. His word had always been accepted on the plantation because he was never known to tell a lie. She felt a kind of wondering admiration for him. He had become an old man in the five years since she had seen him—an old man. Yet the integrity and the strength of his character had not changed. How badly he must have wanted to see them, four of his children, there in the fodder house, on Christmas Day; but he would not lie, and so he would not look at them. Thus, if he was questioned as to the whereabouts of his boys, he could say that he had not seen them.

He made three trips from the cabin to the fodder house. Each time he put a small bundle of food inside the door until he must have given them most of the food intended for the Christmas dinner. Harriet noticed how slow his movements were. He was stooped over. He had aged fast. She would have to come back soon for him and Old Rit. Some time very soon. She remembered his great strength, and his love for his broadax, and the stories he used to tell her about the wonderful things to be seen in the woods. She wanted to put her arms around him and look deep into his eyes and didn't because she respected his right to make this self-sacrificing contribution to their safety. How he must have wanted to look at them, especially at the daughter whom he had not seen for five long years.

They stayed in the fodder house all that day, lying on top of the corn, listening to the drip of the rain, waiting for dark, when they would set out. They spoke in whispers.

Harriet kept reassuring them. They would not be missed for at least two days. At Christmas everyone was busy, dancing, laughing. The masters were entertaining their friends and relatives in their big, comfortable houses. The slaves were not required to work—as long as the Yule logs burned in the fireplaces. She had never lost a passenger, never run her train off the track, they were safe with her, the Lord would see them through.

Late in the afternoon, Ben made one more trip. He pushed another bundle of food inside the door. He kept his eyes closed, tight shut. He said he would be back when it got dark and would walk them just a little way, to visit with them.

At dusk Harriet left the fodder house. She moved quietly toward the cabin. She wanted to get a good look at her mother. The door was ajar. Old Rit was sitting in front of the fireplace, her head on her hand. The flickering light from the fire played over her. Harriet saw a little old woman, rocking her body back and forth, sitting on her heels, in front of the fire, sucking on a clay pipe as she grieved about her boys.

Harriet wanted to say something to her, to offer some word of comfort, of greeting, and dared not for fear Old Rit's uncontrolled joy or her loudly expressed fears would attract attention.

When night came, Ben tapped at the door. He had tied a bandanna tight around his eyes. Harriet took one of his arms and one of the boys took him by the other arm. They started out, walking slowly.

Harriet answered Ben's questions as fast as she could. She told him a little about the other trips she had made, said that she would be back again to get him and Old Rit, told him where some of the people were that she had piloted North, what the North was like, cold in winter, yes, but there were worse things in the world than cold. She told him about St. Catharines, in Canada, and said that she would be back—soon.

They parted from him reluctantly. Ben stood in the middle of the road, listening to the sound of their footsteps. They kept looking back at him. He did not remove the blindfold until he was certain they were out of sight. When he could hear no sound of movement, he untied the bandanna and went back to the cabin.

The next day, Monday, the brothers should have been back on the plantations where they worked. By afternoon, their temporary masters, disturbed by their absence, sent messengers to Dr. Thompson, in Caroline County, asking about them. Dr. Thompson said, "Why, they generally come to see the house servants when they come home for Christmas, but this time they haven't been round at all. Better go down to Old Ben's and ask him."

They questioned Old Rit first. She said, "Not one of 'em came this Christmas. I was looking for 'em all day, and my heart's most broke about 'em not coming."

Ben said, "I haven't seen one of 'em this Christmas."

Meanwhile Harriet led her group through the woods. Sometimes she ventured on the road and they stumbled along behind her over the frozen ruts. Sometimes she took them through the fields, sodden, gray. As they moved slowly North, through Camden, Dover, Smyrna, Blackbird, she became aware of the heavy brooding silence that hung over them. She told them about Thomas Garrett, and the food and warmth of the welcome that awaited them in Wilmington, and thought of the many different times she had invoked the image of the tall, powerfully built Quaker with the kind eyes, to reassure herself, as well as a group of runaways who stumbled along behind her.

They stopped at a house in Middletown and spent the night and part of the day. Then they continued their journey, on through New Castle, down the New Castle Road, until they reached the bank of the Christiana River. Across the river, cold and gray in the dusk of a winter's night, lay Wilmington.

Harriet waited until it was dark and then she herded her party along, over the bridge, and then straight toward Thomas Garrett's house. Garrett fed them and hastily sent them on their way to Philadelphia that same night. The next day Garrett wrote a letter to J. Miller McKim, to let him know that this party of fugitives was on its way.

They arrived safely at the office of the Philadelphia Vigilance Committee on the twenty-ninth of December, late at night. William Still wrote their names down in his record book under the heading "Moses Arrives With Six Passengers."

Harriet Tubman eventually rescued her parents. She led them away from slavery in a horse-drawn wagon.

1,000-MILE SLIPAWAY
WILLIAM AND ELLEN CRAFT

In 1848, William and Ellen Craft, husband and wife, escaped slavery by masquerading as master and slave, and traveling a thousand miles across slave-holding states. Ellen, who was light-skinned and could pass for white, cut her hair and disguised herself as a frail, sickly Southern gentleman. To hide her smooth, beardless skin, she tied a poultice around her head, feigning a toothache; and since she could not read or write, she put her arm in a sling so she would not have to sign hotel registers. Their courage gave them passage to a new life. Their story begins at the door of their cabin in Georgia.

We opened the door, and stepped as softly out as "moonlight upon the water." I locked the door with my own key, which I now have before me, and tiptoed across the yard into the street.

We shook hands, said farewell, and started in different directions for the railway station. I took the nearest possible way to the train, for fear I should be recognized by someone, and got into the Negro car in which I knew I should have to ride; but my *master* (as I will now call my wife) took a longer way round, and only arrived there with the bulk of the passengers. He obtained a ticket for himself and one for his slave to Savannah, the first port, which was about two hundred miles off. My master then had the luggage stowed away, and stepped into one of the best carriages.

But just before the train moved off I peeped through the window, and, to my great astonishment, I saw the cabinetmaker with whom I had worked so long, on the platform. He stepped up to the ticketseller, and asked some question, and then commenced looking rapidly through the passengers, and into the carriages. Fully believing that we were caught, I shrank into a corner, turned my face from the door, and expected in a moment to be dragged out. The cabinetmaker looked into my master's carriage, but did not know him in his new attire, and, as God would have it, before he reached mine the bell rang, and the train moved off.

As soon as the train had left the platform, my master looked round in the carriage, and was terror-stricken to find a Mr. Cray—an old friend of my wife's master, who dined with the family the day before, and knew my wife from childhood—sitting on the same seat.

The doors of the American railway carriages are at the ends. The passengers walk up the aisle, and take seats on either side; and as my master was engaged in looking out of the window, he did not see who came in.

My master's first impression, after seeing Mr. Cray, was, that he was there for the purpose of securing him. However, my master thought it was not wise to give any information respecting himself, and for fear that Mr. Cray might draw him into conversation and recognize his voice, my master resolved to feign deafness as the only means of self-defense.

After a little while, Mr. Cray said to my master, "It is a very fine morning, sir." The latter took no notice, but kept looking out of the window. Mr. Cray soon repeated this remark, in a little louder tone, but my master remained as before. This indifference attracted the attention of the passengers near, one of whom laughed out. This, I suppose, annoyed the old gentleman; so he said, "I will make him hear"; and in a loud tone of voice repeated, "It is a very fine morning, sir."

My master turned his head, and with a polite bow said, "Yes," and commenced looking out of the window again.

One of the gentlemen remarked that it was a very great deprivation to be deaf. "Yes," replied Mr. Cray, "and I shall not trouble that fellow any more." This enabled my master to breathe a little easier, and to feel that Mr. Cray was not his pursuer after all.

The gentlemen then turned the conversation upon the three great topics of discussion in first-class circles in Georgia, namely, Niggers, Cotton, and the Abolitionists.

We arrived at Savannah early in the evening, and got into an omnibus, which stopped at the hotel for the passengers to take tea. I stepped into the house and brought my master something on a tray to the omnibus, which took us in due time to the steamer, which was bound for Charleston, South Carolina.

Soon after going on board, my master turned in; and as the captain and some of the passengers seemed to think this strange, and also questioned me respecting him, my master thought I had better get out the flannels and opodeldoc which we had prepared for the rheumatism, warm them quickly by the stove in the gentleman's saloon, and bring them to his berth. We did this as an excuse for my master's retiring to bed so early.

So I paced the deck till a late hour, then mounted some cotton bags, in a warm place near the funnel, sat there till morning, and then went and assisted my master to get ready for breakfast.

He was seated at the right hand of the captain, who, together with all the passengers, inquired very kindly after his health. As my master had one hand in a sling, it was my duty to carve his food. But when I went out the captain said, "You have a very attentive boy, sir; but you had better watch him like a hawk when you get on to the North. He seems all very well here, but he may act quite differently there. I know several gentlemen who have lost their valuable niggers among them d——d cut-throat abolitionists."

Before my master could speak, a rough slave dealer, who was sitting opposite, with both elbows on the table, and with a large piece of broiled fowl in his fingers, shook his head with emphasis, and in a deep Yankee tone, forced through his crowded mouth the words, "Sound doctrine, captain, very sound." He then dropped the chicken into the plate, leant back, placed his thumbs in the armholes of his fancy waistcoat, and continued, "I would not take a nigger to the North under no consideration. I have had a deal to do with niggers in my time, but I never saw

one who ever had his heel upon free soil that was worth a d———n."
"Now stranger," addressing my master, "if you have made up your
mind to sell that ere nigger, I am your man; just mention your price, and
if it isn't out of the way, I will pay for him on this board with hard silver
dollars." This hard-featured, bristly-bearded, wire-headed, red-eyed
monster, staring at my master as the serpent did at Eve, said, "What do
you say, stranger?" He replied, "I don't wish to sell, sir; I cannot get on
well without him."

"You will have to get on without him if you take him to the North,"
continued this man; "for I can tell ye, stranger, he is a keen nigger, and I
can see from the cut of his eye that he is certain to run away." My
master said, "I think not, sir; I have great confidence in his fidelity."
"Fi*devil,*" indignantly said the dealer, as his fist came down upon the
edge of the saucer and upset a cup of hot coffee in a gentleman's lap. "It
always makes me mad to hear a man talking about fidelity in niggers."

By this time we were near Charleston; my master thanked the captain
for his advice, and they all withdrew and went on deck.

[Later, my master] said to the captain that the air on deck was too
keen for him, and he would therefore return to the cabin. On my master
entering the cabin he found at the breakfast table a young southern
military officer, with whom he had travelled some distance the previous
day.

After passing the usual compliments the conversation turned upon the
old subject—niggers.

The officer, who was also travelling with a manservant, said to my
master, "You will excuse me, Sir, for saying I think you are very likely
to spoil your boy by saying 'thank you' to him. I assure you, Sir,
nothing spoils a slave so soon as saying 'thank you' and 'if you please' to
him. The only way to make a nigger toe the mark, and to keep him in
his place, is to storm at him like thunder. If every nigger was drilled in
this manner, they would be as humble as dogs, and never dare to run
away."

The gentleman urged my master not to go to the North for the
restoration of his health, but to visit the Warm Springs in Arkansas.

My master said, he thought the air of Philadelphia would suit his
complaint best; and, not only so, he thought he could get better advice
there.

The boat had now reached the wharf. The officer wished my master a safe and pleasant journey, and left the saloon.

[In Macon] I ordered a fly to the door, had the luggage placed on; we got in, and drove down to the Custom House Office, which was near the wharf where we had to obtain tickets, to take a steamer for Wilmington, North Carolina. When we reached the building, I helped my master into the office, which was crowded with passengers. He asked for a ticket for himself and one for his slave to Philadelphia. The tickets were handed out, and as my master was paying for them the chief man said to him, "I wish you to register your name here, sir, and also the name of your nigger, and pay a dollar duty on him."

My master paid the dollar, and pointing to the hand that was in the poultice, requested the officer to register his name for him. This seemed to offend the "high-bred" South Carolinian. He jumped up, shaking his head, and, cramming his hands almost through the bottom of his trousers pockets, with a slave-bullying air, said, "I shan't do it."

This attracted the attention of all the passengers. Just then the young military officer with whom my master travelled and conversed on the steamer from Savannah stepped in, somewhat the worse for brandy; he shook hands with my master, and pretended to know all about him. He said, "I know his kin (friends) like a book"; and as the officer was known in Charleston, and was going to stop there with friends, the recognition was very much in my master's favor.

The captain of the steamer, a good-looking jovial fellow, seeing that the gentleman appeared to know my master, and perhaps not wishing to lose us as passengers, said in an off-hand sailorlike manner, "I will register the gentleman's name, and take the responsibility upon myself." He asked my master's name. He said, "William Johnson." The names were put down, I think, "Mr. Johnson and slave." The captain said, "It's all right now, Mr. Johnson." He thanked him kindly, and the young officer begged my master to go with him, and have something to drink and a cigar; but as he had not acquired these accomplishments, he excused himself, and we went on board and came off to Wilmington, North Carolina.

We reached Wilmington the next morning, and took the train for Richmond, Virginia. After changing trains we went on a little beyond Fredericksburg, and took a steamer to Washington.

At Richmond, a stout elderly lady, whose whole demeanor indicated that she belonged to one of the "firstest families," stepped into the carriage, and took a seat near my master. Seeing me passing quickly along the platform, she sprang up as if taken by a fit, and exclaimed, "Bless my soul! there goes my nigger, Ned!"

My master said, "No; that is my boy."

The lady paid no attention to this; she poked her head out of the window, and bawled to me, "You Ned, come to me, sir, you runaway rascal!"

On my looking round she drew her head in, and said to my master, "I beg your pardon, sir, I was sure it was my nigger; I never in my life saw two black pigs more alike than your boy and my Ned."

After the disappointed lady had resumed her seat, and the train had moved off, she closed her eyes, slightly raising her hands, and in a sanctified tone said to my master, "Oh! I hope, sir, your boy will not turn out to be so worthless as my Ned has. Oh! I was as kind to him as if he had been my own son. Oh! sir, it grieves me very much to think that after all I did for him he should go off without having any cause whatever. My dear husband just before he died willed all his niggers free. But I and all our friends knew very well that he was too good a man to have ever thought of doing such an unkind and foolish thing, had he been in his right mind, and, therefore we had the will altered as it should have been in the first place. I sometimes wish that there was not one of them in the world, for the ungrateful wretches are always running away. I have lost no less than ten since my poor husband died. It's ruinous, sir!"

"If freedom will not do for your slaves," replied [another] passenger, "I have no doubt your Ned and the other nine Negroes will find out their mistake, and return to their old home."

"Blast them!" exclaimed the old lady, with great emphasis, "if I ever get them, I will cook their infernal hash, and tan their accursed black hides well for them! God forgive me," added the old soul, "the niggers will make me lose all my religion!"

By this time the lady had reached her destination. The gentleman got out at the next station beyond. As soon as she was gone, the young Southerner said to my master, "What a d——d shame it is for that old whining hypocritical humbug to cheat the poor Negroes out of their liberty! If she has religion, may the devil prevent me from ever being converted!"

Baltimore was the last slave port of any note at which we stopped. [There, an] eagle-eyed officer [said], "It is against our rules, sir, to allow any person to take a slave out of Baltimore into Philadelphia, unless he can satisfy us that he has a right to take him along." "Why is that?" asked my master, with more firmness than could be expected. "Because, sir," continued he, in a voice and manner that almost chilled our blood, "if we should suffer any gentleman to take a slave past here into Philadelphia; and should the gentleman with whom the slave might be travelling turn out not to be his rightful owner, and should the proper master come and prove that his slave escaped on our road, we shall have him to pay for; and, therefore, we cannot let any slave pass here without receiving security to show, and to satisfy us, that it is all right."

This conversation attracted the attention of the large number of bustling passengers. After the officer had finished, a few of them said, "Chit, chit, chit"; not because they thought we were slaves endeavoring to escape, but merely because they thought my master was a slaveholder and invalid gentleman, and therefore it was wrong to detain him. The officer, observing that the passengers sympathized with my master, asked him if he was not acquainted with some gentleman in Baltimore that he could get to endorse for him, to show that I was his property, and that he had a right to take me off. He said, "No," and added, "I bought tickets in Charleston to pass us through to Philadelphia, and therefore you have no right to detain us here." "Well, sir," said the man, indignantly, "right or no right, we shan't let you go." These sharp words fell upon our anxious hearts like the crack of doom, and made us feel that hope only smiles to deceive.

The conductor of the train that we had just left stepped in. The officer asked if we came by the train with him from Washington; he said we did, and left the room. Just then the bell rang for the train to leave, and had it been the sudden shock of an earthquake it could not have given us a greater thrill. The sound of the bell caused every eye to flash with apparent interest, and to be more steadily fixed upon us than before. But, as God would have it, the officer all at once thrust his fingers through his hair, and in a state of great agitation said, "I really don't know what to do; I calculate it is all right." He then told the clerk to run and tell the conductor to "let this gentleman and slave pass," adding, "As he is not well, it is a pity to stop him here. We will let him go." My master thanked him, and stepped out and hobbled across the platform as quickly as possible. I tumbled him unceremoniously into one of the best carriages, and leaped into mine just as the train was gliding off towards our happy destination.

As soon as the train had reached the [Philadelphia] platform, before it had fairly stopped, I hurried out of my carriage to my master, whom I got at once into a cab, placed the luggage on, jumped in myself, and we drove off to the boarding house which was so kindly recommended to me. On leaving the station, my master—or rather my wife, as I may now say—who had from the commencement of the journey borne up in a manner that much surprised us both, grasped me by the hand, and said, "Thank God, William, we are safe!" then burst into tears, leant upon me, and wept like a child.

William and Ellen Craft settled in Boston for two years. After the Fugitive Slave Act of 1850 was passed, and slave catchers threatened their freedom, they fled to London. After the Civil War, the Crafts returned to Georgia and purchased a plantation near Savannah, not far from their old home.

THE SLAVE WHO STOLE A CONFEDERATE SHIP
EDWARD A. MILLER JR.

Wearing a captain's hat and commanding a crew of slaves, Robert Smalls (1839–1915), a slave from Beaufort, South Carolina, delivered a Confederate vessel with a cargo of guns to a Union blockade ship. "I thought the Planter *might be of some use to Uncle Abe," the twenty-three-year-old said, referring to President Lincoln and explaining one of the bravest maritime operations of the Civil War.*

In the early morning hours of May 13, 1862, a lookout on the Union warship *Onward,* part of the blockading squadron off Charleston, South Carolina, raised the alarm. His vessel was the inside ship assigned to monitor traffic in the channel from Charleston and over the bar to the open sea. His impression was that *Onward* was under attack by a Confederate ram, a type of ship feared by the crews of wooden sailing vessels in the Union blockading force. Immediately, the crew of the anchored *Onward* took action to warp the ship into a position where its guns could be brought to bear on the black shape materializing through the haze and mist off the port quarter. At the moment the number three port gun was being elevated to fire, a sailor cried out, "I see something that looks like a white flag."

Onward's captain, Acting Volunteer Lieutenant J. F. Nickels, ordered the vessel be allowed to come alongside. As it came nearer, no white faces could be seen. Indeed, the crew appeared to consist entirely of black men, women, and children who, when it was seen that the Union ship would not fire, ran out on deck—some dancing, some singing, whistling, jumping; and others stood looking towards Fort Sumter, and muttering all sorts of maledictions against it. One of the black men, elegantly dressed, removed his hat and said, "Good morning, sir! I've brought you some of the old United States guns, sir!" Captain Nickels had in his charge the Confederate armed steamer *Planter,* a cargo of unmounted guns, eight men, five women, and three children "representing themselves to be slaves." The organizer of this successful abduction of the Charleston port commander's dispatch and transportation steamer was the ship's pilot, Robert Smalls, a twenty-three-year-old slave.

Smalls's feat was especially remarkable because of the risk he and his associates took in stealing the *Planter* from Southern dock, directly in front of the office and home of Brigadier General Roswell S. Ripley who was commanding the Second Military District of South Carolina. Smalls's operation was planned some days in advance, and he received agreement from most of the other slaves in the crew to join him. Since the *Planter* was commanded by a white officer, Captain C. J. Relyea, and had a white mate, Samuel H. Smith, and a white engineer, Zerich Pitcher, Smalls had to wait for his opportunity to escape from Charleston. The chance came when all three officers decided to spend the night ashore, contrary to standing orders in the military district.

Smalls's success depended on whether the crew members remaining behind did not inform on him, on his own ability to operate the ship on which he ordinarily served as wheelman, on his ability to get his confederates and families aboard without being noticed by armed guards, and on his understanding of the harbor's security and operational procedures. He felt confident that his knowledge and experience would see him through. He said later he was more apprehensive that the Union ships would fire on the *Planter* than would the forts. Smalls got up steam at about 3 A.M., hoisted the Palmetto and Confederate flags, and proceeded to the North Atlantic wharf where he took on board his wife, two children, and others concealed on the ship *Etowah*. He piloted the ship down the South Channel and gave the correct steam whistle signal at Fort Johnson and again at Fort Sumter. The tide was against the vessel, and it was daylight when Sumter was passed. At the fort, his signal was acknowledged, and the *Planter*, perhaps mistaken for the guard boat coincidentally out of service that morning, was given authority to pass. Smalls took the precaution of standing in the pilothouse window with his arms folded as did Captain Relyea, and he wore the captain's large straw hat. He struck his state and Confederate colors and hoisted a dingy towel or handkerchief. Because Smalls made the proper signal, his feat was less dangerous in rebel controlled waters than it was approaching the perhaps jumpy Union blockading force. Had he been challenged and stopped, however, he "would have paid the penalty with his life."

The *Planter* had been a cotton steamer, owned by John Ferguson, which sailed the Pee Dee River. In March, 1861, it was chartered by the Confederate government along with its crew, including Smalls, and put into service running supplies (primarily munitions and ordnance) between the widespread Charleston fortifications. Built of red cedar and oak, the vessel displaced 300 tons, was 147 feet in length, and drew less than 4 feet of water—making it well-suited for service in the creeks and rivers of South Carolina's coastal areas. A wood-burning sidewheeler, the *Planter* was armed with a 32-pounder cannon and 22-pounder howitzer. Its cargo, when abducted by Smalls, was made up of four guns and a guncarriage. These guns were to be delivered to Charleston's Middle Ground battery (Fort Ripley) and the carriage to Fort Sumter the following morning. Of more importance to the Union was the information possibly provided by papers found aboard and, more certainly, the subsequent information offered by Smalls. The vessel with Smalls sailed on all the waters around Charleston, even as far south as Port Royal/Beaufort, before the area was captured by Union forces. Smalls was also said to have been useful to the federal force "as he knew where the Confederate torpedoes [as mines were then called] were sunk in the harbor, having helped to place many of them." Notwithstanding the military and propaganda values of the *Planter,* Smalls's memory of local waters and rebel dispositions were his most valuable contributions to the Union.

Robert Smalls later became captain of the Planter, *and after the war, rose to brigadier general of South Carolina's state militia. In 1875, Smalls was elected to the U.S. House of Representatives. He served five terms.*

LIKE A THIEF IN THE NIGHT
JOHN P. PARKER

A relatively unknown hero of the Underground Railroad was stationmaster John P. Parker (1827–1900), whose autobiography was recently rediscovered. Parker ferried slaves across the Ohio River to freedom, often at the risk of his own life. He not only exhibited acts of gallantry and bravery, he witnessed them as well. During one mission, with hounds on his trail and a boat too small to fit all the escaping slaves, Parker was forced to leave two men on the riverbank, who were sure to be captured. "Then I witnessed an example of heroism and self-sacrifice . . . For one of the single men safely in the boat, hearing the cry of the woman for her husband, arose without a word [and] walked quietly to the bank. The husband sprang into the boat as I pushed off." Here is the story of how Parker rescued another family.

There was a glow of candles through the windows of the big house, which surprised me at such an hour of the night. I came up opposite the cabins and stood looking at them, wondering how I was going to be able to find which one my man lived in. While I was hesitating, the door of one of the shacks opened, and my man came out. He walked up and down in front of his cabin nervously several times, then started for the cornfield.

As the man was by himself I felt sure there was something wrong, since the understanding between us was that he was to bring his wife and child to the rendezvous. Halfway between his cabin and the field, he stopped and listened for a moment, and then hurried to conceal himself in the growing corn. He entered in touching distance of where I was standing, so I had no trouble in stopping him.

Things had gone wrong, just as I supposed. The man was so scared he could hardly talk to me. The folks in the big house had a suspicion he and his wife were planning to run away, and as a precaution compelled him to bring the baby to them every night. The little one was placed at the foot of the bed in which the owner and his wife slept. The old man had placed a chair at his side, on which was a lighted candle and a pistol, and threatened to shoot the first person he found in the room after dark. Besides, a close watch had been kept on all of the cabins to see that none of their occupants were abroad at night. While he was talking he was looking around constantly, as if he expected someone to swoop down on us.

After hearing his story I told him to go back to his home [and] blow the lights out, leaving his door open so I could enter without attracting attention. Asking no questions as to my purpose, he returned and soon had his cabin in darkness. Getting as near his house as I could under cover of the corn, I hurried across the open space and pushed my way into the room, where the man and his wife were awaiting me.

Without wasting time, I proposed that the two of them go with me, leaving the baby behind. This the woman would not listen to; her mother love prompted her to select bondage with her little one rather than freedom without it. When I endeavored to open the subject again she became hysterical for fear I was going to compel her to go against her will. Seeing my efforts were unavailing, I dropped the discussion.

I then proposed to the man that he enter the sleeping room of the big house and rescue the baby from the foot of the bed. This he refused to do, as he was afraid of the big pistol at his owner's head. I attempted to bolster up his courage by holding up to him the hopes of freedom, but he was not to be moved.

As I did not feel it was my duty to endanger my life as well as my liberty on their behalf, I pressed the woman to go to the rescue of the baby. I think she would have made the effort, but for her husband, who was thoroughly cowed by the fear of the man of the house. . . .

Having gone this far I decided to go all the way, enter the forbidden room, and rescue the child from the bed. Coming to this decision, I made them get their possessions in readiness to move. The woman, who was a servant in the house, described its interior, which was very simple indeed. From the small porch at the rear of the house, she said a door opened into a large living room. From this a door led into the sleeping apartment where the child was to be found. There were no locks on any of the doors, [they] being held by wooden latches.

With these facts known, I began to make my plans. I informed both of them I was going to take the child if I could. In the meantime they were to take their position in the road below the house. If they heard any shooting, they were to go back to their cabin at once and I would take care of myself. At all events they were not to take chances of discovery, for fear it might spoil future plans. With these final instructions, I took off my shoes, handing them to the man, impressing him with the fact that in case of trouble, he was to take them back to his hut and destroy them.

Together we left the cabin. The man and the woman went through the field to take their station on the road. I started for the house, going directly to it from the quarters. As I approached the place I could see the candle glow through one window and I knew that was the sleeping room. Getting into the shadow of the house, I endeavored to peep in, but the curtains were pulled down, shutting off my view. There was nothing for me to do but make my way into the place and trust to my good fortune to pull me through.

Crossing the porch, I came to the kitchen door, which I found unlocked as the woman told me. Raising the latch, I pushed it open and entered the room. I was careful to leave the door wide open so that my retreat in that direction was assured. Standing on the threshold of this strange house, I am frank to say I felt the graveness of my position. For a moment my nerve left me, and I am positive I would have run at the least noise.

As my eyes became used to the darkness of the place, my courage came back to me. The floor of the kitchen was of rough boards, so that my footing was uncertain. As I picked my way across the room it seemed to me I struck every loose board in the place. The large crack at the bottom of the door of the sleeping room, through which the rays of the candle showed, guided me surely to my destination.

At the door I hesitated, for I felt I was taking my life in my hand in opening it. If I only knew whether the man was a sound or a light sleeper, it would have eased my mind just then. The wife too was an unknown quantity. These and a multitude [of] other things came to my mind as I stood with my hand on the latch of the sleeping room, ready to open it, to an unknown fate. Twice I put pressure on the latch and twice my heart failed me. The third time my thumb pushed down on the fastening, and it gave way. It was the last point at which I hesitated, for as the latch noiselessly left its place, I felt I was given over to the execution of the task, whatever might be the results; to retreat now was impossible.

Silently I started to open the door. It swung well for a short distance, then the hinges began to squeak. Everything was quiet and my nerves were so wrought up, it seemed to me that the hinges were making noise enough to waken the household. I stopped pushing the door, and putting my ear to the opening, I could distinguish the regular breathing of the couple.

With this assurance, I persevered in opening the door in spite of the noisy hinges until I got a view of the interior of the room. Then I saw that the bed was one of the old style, with a high footboard, and was standing immediately in front of the door. The heads of the man and woman were in plain view. At the man's side was an old wooden chair on which stood the lighted candle. There also close to the candlestick lay a pair of formidable horse pistols. I could see everything but the baby, which was hidden somewhere on the other side of the high footboard.

While I was standing there, the man turned over restlessly, with his face away from the chair and the pistols. I reasoned it out that the child would be on the woman's side, because she was the one who would take care of it during the night. With this in mind, I stooped down, and under the shadow of the bedstead made my way on my hands and knees across the floor to the woman's side of the bed. As I was about to peer around the corner of the footboard, I heard the door close behind me. I certainly felt I was in a predicament shut in the room with a desperate man [and] a noisy woman, in search of someone else's baby. Being concealed by the high bed, I stopped long enough to look around and locate the door and its latch in case of trouble. There was nothing for me to do but to secure the baby and get away as quietly as I could.

Peeping around the foot of the bed, I saw a bundle lying close to the edge. Without waiting to see what it was, I dragged it toward me, and getting a firm hold pulled it off the bed. As I did there was a creak of the [bed]springs and the next moment the room was in darkness. There was no cause for secrecy now, so I jumped to my feet and rushed to the door. I heard the stool upset and the pistols fall. I heard the quick breathing of the man as he sprung out of bed and began feeling around on the floor in the dark for his weapons. Opening the door with a jerk, I ran across the kitchen out into the yard, with the bundle still in my arms. From their position in the room the man and woman saw me hurry out of the house, toward the road.

Confident of my success, they [my two adult fugitives] started toward the river. When I was within a few rods of them, I heard the crack of a pistol and a bullet went singing over my head. Instantly the two ahead of me swerved to one side of the road and started toward the cornfield. By this time I was opposite them and seeing their purpose, I called to them that I had the baby. The man said something about going back to the cabin and started in that direction with the woman after him.

There was no time to argue, seeing the two were about to desert me. I yelled as I went by them I had the baby, and if they wanted it, they would have to follow me. In a few minutes I heard the patter of their feet on the hard road as they came running after me. We soon reached the top of the riverbank.

There was a skiff at the landing, which I made the man turn loose, so that we could not be pursued. My own little craft was soon made ready, and I made the man lie down in the bottom of the boat, so that only two persons could be seen from the shore. Instead of going directly across, which would land me in front of my own house, I rowed up the river. I could see the other boat float down with the current, so that I felt there was no danger from that quarter.

We were about a third of the way across the river when we saw lights down at the landing which we had just left. We were still in plain sight, and I heard the voice of my [white] employee shouting the name of the man in the bottom of the boat, warning him to come back. His threats fell on deaf ears, as I only increased my efforts to get across the river.

Arriving on the opposite side, I asked the man for my shoes, but much to my astonishment, he said that he had dropped them in his flight. They were a new pair of heavy shoes, coarse and different from what I was accustomed to wear. Still the shoes were a clue, and I was nervous as to how close the matter would come home to me. While I was provoked I could not stop to find fault, as the party had to be in hiding or out of town before morning.

Securing my skiff, we hurried up the bank to the home of my friend the attorney. I only took time to tell him he must look after the fugitives, and then hastened home to prepare for the visit I expected would follow. Without striking a light I undressed and got into bed. It was not time to sleep, so I lay awake arranging my plans.

Soon I heard voices outside, then a loud knocking at the door. I was out of bed at the first sound, and throwing up the window I demanded who was making such a row. There were three men below, and the man who worked for me was spokesman. He was evidently surprised to find me, as he suspicioned me the first one, and expected I was away with the fugitives. In spite of finding me at home he began accusing me of running away his father's people. I protested.

"But you run them away," he cried. "No one but you would steal that baby."

"What baby?" was my response.

"You know all about that baby, and it is in your house."

Ordinarily I never permitted anyone to search my premises. This time I did not care, so I told them to wait while I put on my clothes, and I would come down and take the party through the house myself. This seemed to take them back completely, but I knew the longer I kept them busy with me the less likely they were to find their people. After consuming considerable time in dressing I went down.

The old man had his horse pistols in his hand, and he was mad clear through. I am sure if the old man had found his people in the house, he would have shot me down in cold blood. We went through the place room by room. They were completely crestfallen when the last corner was searched, and they failed to find their runaways. As the young fellow went out he turned and said, "I believe you were over the river just the same, and know where my people are."

THE NIGHT'S SEARCH was nothing compared to the scene I had when [my employee] Srofe came into the shop the next morning dangling across his arm my new shoes, which had been dropped the night before by his runaway slave. He shoved the shoes in my face, again declaring I had dropped them in getting his people away. I just as stoutly denied the accusation. He had me scared when he said he was going from store to store in the town until he had the shoes identified.

While I put up a good bluff I . . . [did] try to beat him uptown to tip off the merchant from whom I had purchased the shoes on the previous day. All I could do was to hope and pray that the merchant would not give me away. Srofe, true to his word, did go from shoe shop to shoe shop, and not a soul had ever seen the shoes before.

IF WE MUST DIE
CLAUDE MCKAY

Racial violence during what became known as the "Red Summer" of 1919 prompted Claude McKay (1889–1948) to write this sonnet. More than twenty-five race riots erupted across the nation that season. Newspapers reported the lynching of African Americans in gruesome detail (eighty-three were recorded that year). This poem, McKay's most famous, exhorted "kinsmen" to a brave, noble defense, inspiring Winston Churchill years later to cite the poem in an anti-Nazi speech. The poem served as a rallying cry for Allied Forces in World War II.

If we must die, let it not be like hogs
Hunted and penned in an inglorious spot,
While round us bark the mad and hungry dogs,
Making their mock at our accursèd lot.
If we must die, O let us nobly die,
So that our precious blood may not be shed
In vain; then even the monsters we defy
Shall be constrained to honor us though dead!
O kinsmen! we must meet the common foe!
Though far outnumbered let us show us brave,
And for their thousand blows deal one deathblow!
What though before us lies the open grave?
Like men we'll face the murderous, cowardly pack,
Pressed to the wall, dying, but fighting back!

CONQUEST
GEORGIA DOUGLAS JOHNSON

Courage cuts across routes seldom trod.

My pathway lies through worse than death;
I meet the hours with bated breath.
My red blood boils, my pulses thrill,
I live life running up a hill.

Ah, no, I need no paltry play
Of make-shift tilts for holiday:
For I was born against the tide
And I must conquer that denied.

I shun no hardship, fear no foe;
The future calls and I must go:

I charge the line and dare the spheres
As I go fighting down the years.

WANTED: BLACK WARRIORS

A newspaper advertisement in 1863 called for African American soldiers for the famed Massachusetts Volunteer Infantry, the black unit that courageously stormed South Carolina's Fort Wagner that same year and was eventually portrayed in the movie Glory. *President Lincoln had refused to enlist black troops earlier in the Civil War. But eventually, he realized he could not win without them. In June of 1861, Tennessee passed the first law for enlisting free blacks. In 1862, South Carolina and Rhode Island formed black regiments. In all, African Americans fought in 166 all-black units.*

TO COLORED MEN.

Wanted. Good men for the Fifty-fourth Regiment of Massachusetts Volunteers of African descent, Col. Robert G. Shaw. $100 bounty at expiration of term of service. Pay $13 per month, and State aid for families. All necessary information can be obtained at the office, corner Cambridge and North Russell Streets.

Lieut. J. W. M. Appleton,
Recruiting Officer.

THE UNSUNG HEROES
PAUL LAURENCE DUNBAR

By the end of the Civil War, more than 200,000 black soldiers and sailors had fought for the Union in more than 449 battles, suffering more than 38,000 casualties. For their "gallantry in action," sixteen black soldiers and four black seamen received the nation's highest award for valor, the Medal of Honor. Yet black troops did not march in the two-day victory parade that marked the end of the war because, historians say, the general in charge of the parade specifically excluded them. Paul Laurence Dunbar later honored their bravery with a poem.

A song for the unsung heroes who rose in the
    country's need,
When the life of the land was threatened by the slaver's
    cruel greed,
For the men who came from the cornfield, who came
    from the plough and the flail,
Who rallied round when they heard the sound of the
    mighty man of the rail.

They laid them down in the valleys, they laid them down
    in the wood,
And the world looked on at the work they did, and
    whispered, "It is good."
They fought their way on the hillside, they fought their
    way in the glen,
And God looked down on their sinews brown, and said,
    "I have made them men."

They went to the blue lines gladly, and the blue lines
    took them in,
And the men who saw their muskets' fire thought not
    of their dusky skin.
The gray lines rose and melted beneath their scathing
    showers,

And they said, " 'T is true, they have force to do, these
 old slave boys of ours."

Ah, Wagner saw their glory, and Pillow knew their blood,
That poured on a nation's altar, a sacrificial flood.
Port Hudson heard their war-cry that smote its smoke-
  filled air,
And the old free fires of their savage sires again were
  kindled there.

They laid them down where the rivers, the greening
  valleys gem.
And the song of the thund'rous cannon was their sole
  requiem,
And the great smoke wreath that mingled its hue with
  the dusky cloud,
Was the flag that furled o'er a saddened world, and the
  sheet that made their shroud.

Oh, Mighty God of the Battles Who held them in
  Thy hand,
Who gave them strength through the whole day's length,
  to fight for their native land,
They are lying dead on the hillsides, they are lying dead
  on the plain,
And we have not fire to smite the lyre and sing them
  one brief strain.

Give, Thou, some seer the power to sing them in
  their might,
The men who feared the master's whip, but did not fear
  the fight;
That he may tell of their virtues as minstrels did of old,
Till the pride of face and the hate of race grow obsolete
  and cold.

A song for the unsung heroes who stood the awful test,
When the humblest host that the land could boast went
    forth to meet the best;
A song for the unsung heroes who fell on the bloody
    sod,
Who fought their way from night to day and struggled
    up to God.

CLEANING UP THE WILD WEST

Like gods in the mythology of the Old West, white marshals and villains have loomed larger-than-life for more than a century. Lawman Wyatt Earp always got his man, and killer Billy the Kid never failed to terrorize a foe. But African American lawmen and criminals were equally heroic—or ruthless: Deputy Sheriff Ben Boyer of Coaldale, Colorado, struck fear into the meanest outlaws, and Cherokee Bill began a murderous career at age fourteen by killing his own brother-in-law. The adventures of black lawmen are particularly fascinating, though largely ignored by historians. They faced hostility on two fronts: from white gunslingers and from whites who would rather protect the gunslinger than see an "uppity nigger" bring them to justice. Here are two African American lawmen who helped tame the Wild West.

WILLIE KENNARD

Spirits were high in Cleveland in 1874, the year that the Women's Christian Temperance Union was founded. And in Philadelphia that same year, the city proudly celebrated the opening of the nation's first zoo. But far to the west, the gold-mining hamlet of Yankee Hill, Colorado, was in the grip of more pressing concerns. The citizens of this boom town were living under a reign of terror imposed by renegades and drifters. Desperate to bring an end to the rampant violence and lawlessness, the town fathers advertised for a marshal in Denver's *Rocky Mountain News.*

One man who responded was 42-year-old Willie Kennard, a former trooper in the all-black 9th Cavalry Regiment. Kennard rode into town packing a pistol on each hip and looked up the Yankee Hill mayor, Matt Borden. "I'm puttin' in for your marshalin' job," Kennard announced.

Borden, lingering over his morning coffee with the four men who sat with him on the town council, could hardly believe his ears. For a black man to ride into a place as wild as Yankee Hill and apply to be the lawman made no sense at all. Surely he would provoke hostility simply by being in town; as marshal, he would be lucky to live long enough to draw his first pay.

But Kennard would not be put off. Faced with his persistence, the mayor devised a way to get rid of the unwelcome applicant while having some cruel fun at his expense. Kennard would first have to pass a test, Borden told him, by bringing in Barney Casewit, a cold-blooded criminal no one wanted to tangle with. Casewit had raped a 15-year-old girl and then shot her father dead when he tried to avenge her.

The mayor and councilmembers, eager to see the uppity black man taken down a peg, scurried after Kennard as he strode to Gaylor's Saloon, a rowdy establishment where Casewit and other ruffians hung out. After sizing up the desperado, Kennard walked up to his table and announced that he was under arrest. The outlaw sprang from his chair, reaching for his Colt .44s. But Kennard outdrew him, firing directly at the gunman's holsters. As the story goes, the bullets shattered the cylinders of Casewit's six-shooters, leaving him so dumbstruck that he quietly shuffled off to jail.

Mayor Borden, apparently more pleased to have Casewit put away than to see the black stranger humbled, gave Kennard a tin star. Barney Casewit was tried, convicted, and ultimately hanged. For the next three years the black marshal enforced the law in Yankee Hill, quelling the violence and putting many more desperadoes behind bars. Then, in typical western fashion, Kennard pulled up stakes in 1877 and moved on; little is known of his life after that.

—*From* African Americans: Voices of Triumph: Perseverance,
by the Editors of Time-Life Books © 1993 Time-Life Books, Inc.

BASS REEVES

An ex-slave, Bass Reeves was the first black deputy U.S. Marshal west of the Mississippi.

Bass Reeves was born around 1838 in Paris, Texas. As a young man, he was the personal "body servant" of former Confederate Colonel and Grayson County Sheriff George Reeves. Young Bass was unusually bright, strong, skilled with guns, and highly regarded by the colonel and everyone else who knew him. Then a shadowy event changed his life. The most likely version was that during a card game with the colonel, Bass was somehow provoked into knocking him unconscious. He then fled north across Red River into Indian Territory where he remained a fugitive until Emancipation.

While in Indian Territory, the ruggedly handsome six-foot-two, two-hundred-pound Reeves married; settled in tiny Van Buren above Fort Smith; ran a prosperous farm; raised ten children; was so fast and accurate with his Colt pistols and Winchester rifles that he was barred from turkey shoots at local picnics and fairs (it was said "he could shoot the left hind leg off of a contented fly sitting on a mule's ear at a hundred yards and never ruffle a hair"); and, though illiterate, during his extensive travel across Indian Territory he taught himself to speak not only fluent Creek but every language of the Five Civilized Tribes.

In 1875, when Reeves signed on with Judge Isaac Parker [as deputy U.S. marshal], Indian Territory was swarming with outlaws who specialized in ducking the law. No matter how proficient you were with a gun, you first had to get close to your man. Since Reeves was devoted to doing the job right, he was more original and relentless than his fellow deputies. It was not unusual for him to depart from Fort Smith on his regular circuit, hunting killers, rapists, bootleggers, and thieves, and return months later with a wagonful of prisoners. He did not just ride up, pull out his guns, and take the bad guys in. He often had to use subterfuge—something few lawmen did in those days; for example, the use of disguises. No one in law enforcement was more daring or masterly at this ruse. He stated many times to Judge Parker and fellow deputies that he used disguises to *avoid* shootouts and, therefore, need-less violence. This philosophy alone cast him as singular among Wild West lawmen whose common creed—fee or no fee—was something like: *Shoot first and ask no questions.*

Reeves was so adept at operating undercover as a cowboy, tramp, gunslinger, or bandit, stories about his courage and ingenuity spread across the West to friends and foes alike. For instance: The tale of the legendary twenty-eight-mile hike. Sometime in the 1880s, Reeves de-cided to track two wanted brothers in order to earn a five-thousand-dollar reward. Using his sources, he learned they were holed up in their mother's cabin in southern Indian Territory, near the Texas border. So he formed a small posse, including a cook and wagoner, and they headed south. Eventually, they set up camp twenty-eight miles from the hideout. Reeves later explained he chose this distance so he could study the surrounding land for approach and escape routes, and plan carefully without spooking his prey. He did not want campfires, which could give them away, or chance encounters with the outlaws' allies, who could quickly tip them off. So the twenty-eight miles was not arbitrary; it was key to the element of surprise.

Reeves decided to impersonate a saddle tramp on the lam. So he cut the heels off some old boots and shot three bullet holes in a floppy hat as a disguise. Stuffing his handcuffs, badge, and Colt revolvers under his coat, he started walking to the hideout alone. [H]e knew that Territory outlaws posted lookouts for teams of lawmen on strategic hills. So they would rarely expect anyone to track in alone, especially in disguise.

After hiking the twenty-eight miles and arriving at the mother's cabin, Reeves knocked on the door. When the mother answered, Reeves told her he was a robber running from a posse that had shot the bullet holes in his hat. She believed him and invited him in. While cooking him a meal, she mentioned that her two boys were also on the run and suggested it might be smart if they all protected one another. At dark, someone whistled from across the creek. When the mother went outside, up rode her fugitive sons.

Once inside, they met Reeves, bought his detailed story, and agreed to team up with him for mutual gain. That night, Reeves talked them into sleeping in the same room with him, in case they were rushed by the law. While the unsuspecting brothers slept on the floor, Reeves handcuffed them so expertly they did not awaken. In the morning, the game was up; Reeves ordered them outside. The mother was irate, following them for miles, cursing and screaming at Reeves's back, until she could go no farther. Meantime, he led the outlaws back to his camp where the brothers were shackled to the wagon for the night. Next morning, Reeves led his prisoners, cook, and posse back to Fort Smith. He did not have to wait for the brothers' inevitable conviction to collect his five-thousand-dollar reward—and add another notch to his legend.

Another of his storied undercover jobs happened in the 1890s when he decided to investigate a robbery in the crude saloon town of Keokuk Falls, one of the most dangerous outposts on the Seminole border of Indian Territory. But he was intrepid; he was widely known as one of the few deputy marshals courageous enough to come through the border towns where disputes were settled on the porches of saloons or by shootouts in the streets. He met with the robbery victim, John F. Brown, Jr., chief of the Seminole Nation, who provided directions to the desperadoes' hideout, an abandoned cabin inside the Creek Nation. When Reeves arrived at the cabin and saw chimney smoke, he concocted a plan: He would return the next day as a tenant farmer and try to draw them outside on a ruse. The following morning, he put on dirty, patched overalls, rented a yolk of old oxen and a rickety wagon and intentionally drove the wagon onto a tree stump in front of the cabin. When the four outlaws came out to run him off, Reeves persuaded them to help. They grudgingly obliged by lifting the wagon free of the stump. But when they finished, they were staring down the barrels of his shiny Colts. Reeves disarmed them without incident—a Bass Reeves trademark because he detested unnecessary violence. Afterward, he chained the four to the wagon; recovered the stolen money from the cabin; then marched them to the county seat at Tecumseh, thirty miles away. They were later convicted and imprisoned.

In 1884, Reeves came the closest to losing his life—and yet still added to his legend. Riding the Seminole whiskey trail with warrants for four badmen, he was intercepted by the three Brunter brothers. They were wanted for robbery and murder and must have known that Reeves would eventually hunt them down.

The Brunters ordered him off his horse at gunpoint, so he had to think fast. He did—by talking about the warrant he had for their arrest and showing it to them and asking what day of the week it was so he could list it on the warrant for the government. This baffled the Brunters; why would Reeves so stupidly seal his fate by confirming he was, in fact, hunting them? Of course, that was the point; Reeves knew this would divert them. It did; because in the split second when they called him crazy and started to laugh, Reeves pulled his revolver and dropped two of them while grabbing the barrel of the third one's gun. The doomed Brunter got off three deflected shots before Reeves killed him with blows to the head from his Colt. Reeves collected no fees for the Brunter brothers, but it was widely known that he was more concerned with serving justice than accumulating cash. Besides, Reeves was so relentless in pursuing fugitives and so devoted to bringing them in alive that by the end of his thirty-two-year career he had arrested over three thousand (killing fourteen—seven more than Wild Bill Hickok—without ever being wounded) and earned more money than any dozen deputies put together.

[T]he event in Bass Reeves's life that took the true measure of the man was when he arrested his own son. Late in Reeves's career, one of his three sons, Benjamin, was having marital problems because his wife was unhappy that his work kept him from home so much. One night, Benjamin came home to find his wife with another man. He kept his control, forgave her, and took a less demanding job. But she betrayed him again. This time, he flew into a rage, beat the man severely, and murdered his wife. Panicking, Benjamin then fled to Indian Territory.

It was a touchy issue for the Muskogee marshal; he felt another deputy should go after Reeves's son. But despite being shaken, Bass Reeves insisted that it was his responsibility to bring in his son. Sure enough, two weeks later Bass rode in with Benjamin and completed the hardest assignment of his career by turning his son over to the marshal. At trial, Benjamin manfully owned up to his crime and was convicted and sent to the federal prison at Leavenworth, Kansas. Bass stood by him, all the way to the prison doors. For years, Benjamin served as a model prisoner. And though Bass Reeves was too proud to plead for mercy, Muskogee citizens learned from others the details of the circumstances that led Benjamin to commit the uncharacteristic crime. Finally, out of respect for Bass Reeves and based on Benjamin's exemplary behavior in prison, they circulated a petition and pressed for a pardon. It was eventually granted and Benjamin was released—and he later became one of the most popular barbers in Muskogee.

GREAT BLACK HOPE
RICHARD BAK

If Jack Johnson were to fight today, he might well be packaged as a head-shaven, mean-and-lean media darling capable of drawing tens of millions of dollars for pay-per-view bouts. But in his own time, he was hated by whites. After capturing the world heavyweight championship in 1908, public pressure mounted for a "great white hope" to reclaim the crown and white honor. But Papa Jack, as he was affectionately known by some, defeated all opponents. He held the title until April 5, 1915, when he met Jess Willard for twenty-six rounds under the broiling sun in Havana, Cuba.

John Arthur Johnson, the son of a religious school janitor, was born into a poor family of nine in the port city of Galveston, Texas, in 1878. He worked as a stevedore on the docks and also as a part-time gym attendant. Both occupations provided him with a rudimentary education in handling his fists. His first experiences included participating in the infamous "battle royals," back-alley spectacles where eight or more blacks were thrown into a ring and fought amongst themselves until only one was left standing.

Johnson saw the world as so many adventuresome young men did in those days, hopping freight trains and living in hobo jungles. His travels took him to cities like San Francisco, Chicago, Boston, and New York, where he filled in the time between his sporadic appearances on fight cards by working at odd jobs and finding occasional work as a sparring partner. Contrary to his later reputation as some kind of superman, Johnson could be beaten during his early years. In 1901, he fought the aging but still dangerous Joe Choynski, a storied performer who had once broken the great Jim Jeffries' nose. Choynski knocked out Johnson, at which point Texas Rangers raided the place and tossed both fighters in jail. This turned out to be a stroke of good fortune for Johnson, because he used his jail time sparring with Choynski and soaking up all that the old master could teach him. [Jack Johnson] was a marvelous defensive boxer, possibly the best that ever was. According to Ed "Gunboat" Smith, a leading heavyweight and one-time sparring partner, "Johnson was a fellow that used to stand flat-footed and wait for you to come in. And when you came in, he'd rip the head off of you with uppercuts, cut you all to pieces." When people remarked that [heavyweight champion Tommy] Burns had cleared the heavyweight field of all worthy contenders, they meant of course *white* contenders. Talented Negro pugilists like Johnson and Sam Langford were treated as if they were invisible. This was in keeping with the unspoken but implicit color bar that was an integral part of American sports. There were no blacks in organized baseball, nor were there any in tennis or golf. Just a handful of blacks played collegiate football or competed in track and field. Even horse racing, once dominated by Negro jockeys, had become practically an all-alabaster affair.

Still, it was hard to ignore the claims of Johnson, whose lopsided victories . . . logically made him the number-one challenger. To drive home his case, Johnson literally chased Burns around the globe, showing up in every country—England, Ireland, France, Australia—during Burns's world tour. Burns denied that he was avoiding Johnson, saying that it was all a matter of money, not race. Veteran observers knew this not to be the case. John L. Sullivan had publicly proclaimed that he would not fight Negroes as a matter of principle, and subsequent heavyweight champions had followed his lead. Shortly before Burns died in 1955, he admitted that at the time the "idea of a Negro challenging me was beyond enduring." However, money proved thicker than blood. When promoters approached Burns with an offer of $30,000 to meet Johnson (who would receive $5,000), he readily accepted. It was the first time a black man had been allowed a crack at the heavyweight title.

The fight was held December 26, 1908, inside a wooden amphitheatre on the outskirts of Sydney, Australia. Bettors installed the incumbent as a 3-to-1 favorite. Burns was not afraid of the much bigger Johnson, who stood a shade over six feet tall and weighed 205 pounds. In fact, he displayed the customary arrogance in such matters, assuming the superiority of the Caucasian race would prevail. He told the press that Johnson had "a yellow streak."

"Who told you I was yellow?" Johnson yelled at the start of the fight, just before he leveled Burns with a left uppercut. It turned into a slaughter, Johnson toying with his overmatched opponent. The sun glinted off Johnson's gold-capped teeth as he smiled and kept up a constant obscene banter. Burns, sputtering expletives through bloodied lips, never quit, but finally police jumped into the ring and stopped the debacle in the fourteenth round. Novelist Jack London, then covering the fight for the *New York Herald,* characterized it as a battle between "a pygmy and a colossus . . . a playful Ethiopian at loggerheads with a small white man." His ringside report ended: "But one thing now remains. Jim Jeffries must emerge from his alfalfa farm and remove the golden smile from Jack Johnson's face. Jeff, it's up to you. The White Man must be rescued."

And thus began the quest for the great white hope to unseat the swaggering, grinning Johnson.

JACK JOHNSON

In the following excerpt from his autobiography, In the Ring and Out, *Jack Johnson recalled his historic bout with Jim Jeffries.*

The day of the fight finally arrived. It was a beautiful one—the weather, excepting for the intense heat, was superb. The atmosphere was clear as crystal, and one could see for miles. More than 25,000 people had gathered to watch the fight, and as I looked about me, and scanned the sea of white faces I felt the auspiciousness of the occasion. There were few men of my own race among the spectators. I realized that my victory in this event meant more than on any previous occasion. It wasn't just the championship that was at stake—it was my own honor, and in a degree the honor of my race. I was well aware of all these things, and I sensed that most of that great audience was hostile to me. These things, while they impressed me with the responsibilities that lay upon me, did not disturb or worry me. I was cool and perfectly at ease. I never had any doubt of the outcome.

I was the first to enter the ring. There was one shady corner and in this I seated myself. Jeff followed a little later with his seconds, and proposed that we toss a coin for the shady corner. I declined to toss, but offered to relinquish the shade to him, an offer which he accepted, and I moved over into the sun. The crowd gave me a very hearty reception, but that given Jeff was twenty times greater than mine. When the fight started Jeff was a 10 to 4 favorite, but in the fourth round I was the favorite by the same odds.

Hardly had a blow been struck when I knew that I was Jeff's master. From the start the fight was mine, and, as I have just observed, the fourth round brought the crowd to a realization that Jeff had little chance to win. He fought in his usual style and I think with as much of his vigor, speed and endurance as ever. If he had not been fit, and if there had been the smallest particle of dope in him, as some have contended, he never could have stood under that hot sun for fifteen rounds withstanding the punishment I gave him. He fought his best. He brought into play some of the old swings and blows for which he had been noted. His brain was working keenly, but he found it almost impossible to get through my defense and at no time did he hurt me. He landed on me frequently but with no effect. He devoted his attention to fighting and did not take much part in the run of conversation which was going on. About all he said, was, once, when I struck him on the head:

"Say, but that's a tough old head," he remarked.

As for me, I took part in the palaver that went on, addressing myself particularly to Jim Corbett, a member of Jeff's training staff, who took occasion to send a few jeering remarks in my direction. I told Corbett to come on in the ring, that I would take him on too. At the same time I was demonstrating, that, contrary to Jim's disparaging remarks, I was putting over a good, fast fight. I hit Jeff at will. There was no place that was beyond my reach, and I landed some stiff jolts on him, but not as stiff as I might have, for I really did not have any desire to punish him unnecessarily. The cheering for Jeff never ceased. The spectators urged him on and gave him every possible encouragement, but their cheering turned to moans and groans when they saw that he was suffering as he was. There came up to me from the ringside gasps of astonishment that turned to cries of pity, and more than once I heard them shout:

"Stop it! Stop it!"

The great crowd cheered Jeffries for his grit and supreme effort and they pitied him in his suffering, but they did not for a moment lose their admiration for him. As for me, they learned that I was not a quitter; they realized that I had not entered into any crookedness, and that . . . Langford and others who had swung much of the betting against me had let them in for a good trimming. However, it was not enough that the fight should be a meritorious one and that the best man had won on his worth or that the entire mill had been clean and square; the crowd was by no means pleased. The "white hope" had failed, and as far as the championship was concerned it was just where it was before the beginning of the fight, except that I had established my rightful claim to it beyond all possible dispute. But from that minute on the hunt for the "white hope" was redoubled, and when it proceeded with so little success other methods were taken to dispose of me.

ARCTIC EXPLORER
MATTHEW HENSON

African American adventurer Matthew Henson (1866–1958) is known as the man who codiscovered the North Pole in the spring of 1909. However, Henson is said to have actually reached what Robert Peary, expedition leader, had first projected as the North Pole forty-five minutes ahead of Peary himself. Here are entries from Henson's own diary about the dash to the Pole.

JULY 6, 1908

We're off! For a year and a half I have waited for this order, and now we have cast off. The shouting and the tumult ceases, the din of whistles, bells, and throats dies out, and once again the long, slow surge of the ocean hits the good ship that we have embarked in. . . .

Naturally there were frequent storms and intense cold, and in regard to the storms of the Arctic regions of North Greenland and Grant Land, the only word I can use to describe them is "terrible," in the fullest meaning it conveys. The effect of such storms of wind and snow, or rain, is abject physical terror, due to the realization of perfect helplessness. I have seen rocks a hundred and a hundred and fifty pounds in weight picked up by the storm and blown for distances of ninety or a hundred feet to the edge of a precipice, and there of their own momentum go hurtling through space to fall in crashing fragments at the base. Imagine the effect of such a rainfall of death-dealing bowlders on the feelings of a little group of three or four, who have sought the base of the cliff for shelter. I have been there and I have seen one of my Esquimo companions felled by a blow from a rock eighty-four pounds in weight, which struck him fairly between the shoulder-blades, literally knocking the life out of him. I have been there, and believe me, I have been afraid.

FEBRUARY 18, 1909

There is an irresistible fascination about the regions of northernmost Grant Land that is impossible for me to describe. Having no poetry in my soul, and being somewhat hardened by years of experience in that inhospitable country, words proper to give you an idea of its unique beauty do not come to mind. Imagine gorgeous bleakness, beautiful blankness. It never seems broad, bright day, even in the middle of June, and the sky has the different effects of the varying hours of morning and evening twilight from the first to the last peep of day. Early in February, at noon, a thin band of light appears far to the southward, heralding the approach of the sun, and daily the twilight lengthens, until early in March, the sun, a flaming disk of fiery crimson, shows his distorted image above the horizon. This distorted shape is due to the mirage caused by the cold, just as heat-waves above the rails on a railroad-track distort the shape of objects beyond.

The south sides of the lofty peaks have for days reflected the glory of the coming sun, and it does not require an artist to enjoy the unexampled splendor of the view. The snows covering the peaks show all of the colors, variations, and tones of the artist's palette, and more. Artists have gone with us into the Arctic and I have heard them rave over the wonderful beauties of the scene, and I have seen them at work trying to reproduce some of it, with good results but with nothing like the effect of the original. As Mr. Stokes said, "it is color run riot."

FEBRUARY 26

This from my log: "Clear, no wind, temperature 57° below zero."
Listen! I will tell you about it. At seven A.M. we quit trying to sleep and
started the pot a-boiling. A pint of hot tea gave us a different point of
view, and Professor Marvin handed me the thermometer, which I took
outside and got the reading; 57° below; that is cold enough. I have seen
it lower, but after forty below the difference is not appreciable.

MARCH 19

We left camp in a haze of bitter cold; the ice conditions about the same
as the previous day; high rafters, huge and jagged; and we pickaxed the
way continuously. By noontime, we found ourselves alongside of a lead
covered by a film of young ice. We forced the dogs and they took it on
the run, the ice undulating beneath them, the same as it does when little
wanton boys play at *tickley benders,* often with serious results, on the
newly formed ice on ponds and brooks down in civilization. Our *tickley
benders* were not done in the spirit of play, but on account of urgent
necessity, and as it was I nearly suffered a serious loss of precious
possessions.

   One of the sledges, driven by Ahwatingwah [an Eskimo companion],
broke through the ice and its load, which consisted of my extra equipment, such as kamiks, mittens, etc., was thoroughly soaked Luckily for
the boy, he was at the side of the sledge and escaped a ducking. Fool-
ishly I rushed over, but, quickly realizing my danger, I slowed down,
and with the utmost care he fished out the sledge, and the dogs, shaking
as with palsy, were gently urged on. Walking wide, like the polar bear,
we crept after, and without further incident reached the opposite side of
the lead. My team had reached there before me and, with human intelligence, the dogs had dragged the sledge to a place of safety and were
sitting on their haunches, with ears cocked forward, watching us in our
precarious predicament. They seemed to rejoice at our deliverance, and
as I went among them and untangled their traces I could not forbear
giving each one an affectionate pat on the head.

MARCH 28

Exactly 40° below zero when we pushed the sledges up to the curled-up
dogs and started them off over rough ice covered with deep soft snow. It

was like walking in loose granulated sugar. Indeed I might compare the
snow of the Arctic to the granules of sugar, without their saccharine
sweetness, but with freezing cold instead; you can not make snowballs of
it, for it is too thoroughly congealed, and when it is packed by the wind
it is almost as solid as ice. It is from the packed snow that the blocks
used to form the igloo-walls are cut.

MARCH 29

You have undoubtedly taken into consideration the pangs of hunger and
of cold that you know assailed us, going Poleward; but have you ever
considered that we were thirsty for water to drink or hungry for fat? To
eat snow to quench our thirsts would have been the height of folly, and
as well as being thirsty, we were continuously assailed by the pangs of a
hunger that called for the fat, good, rich, oily, juicy fat that our systems
craved and demanded.

Had we succumbed to the temptations of thirst and eaten the snow,
we would not be able to tell the tale of the conquest of the Pole; for the
result of eating snow is death. True, the dogs licked up enough moisture
to quench their thirsts, but we were not made of such stern stuff as they.
Snow would have reduced our temperatures and we would quickly have
fallen by the way. We had to wait until camp was made and the fire of
alcohol started before we had a chance, and it was with hot tea that we
quenched our thirsts. The hunger for fat was not appeased.

From the land to 87° 48′ north, Commander [Robert] Peary had had
the best of the going, for he had brought up the rear and had utilized the
trail made by the preceding parties, and thus he had kept himself in the
best of condition for the time when he made the spurt that brought him
to the end of the race. From 87° 48′ north, he kept in the lead and did
his work in such a way as to convince me that he was still as good a man
as he had ever been. We marched and marched, falling down in our
tracks repeatedly, until it was impossible to go on. We were forced to
camp, in spite of the impatience of the Commander, who found himself
unable to rest, and who only waited long enough for us to relax into
sound sleep, when he would wake us up and start us off again. I do not
believe that he slept for one hour from April 2 until after he had loaded
us up and ordered us to go back over our old trail, and I often think that

from the instant when the order to return was given until the land was again sighted, he was in a continual daze.

Onward we forced our weary way. Commander Peary took his sights from the time our chronometer-watches gave, and I, knowing that we had kept on going in practically a straight line, was sure that we had more than covered the necessary distance to insure our arrival at the top of the earth.

We were crossing a lane of moving ice. Commander Peary was in the lead setting the pace, and a half hour later the four boys and myself followed in single file. They had all gone before, and I was standing and pushing at the upstanders of my sledge, when the block of ice I was using as a support slipped from underneath my feet, and before I knew it the sledge was out of my grasp, and I was floundering in the water of the lead. I did the best I could. I tore my hood from off my head and struggled frantically. My hands were gloved and I could not take hold of the ice, but before I could give the "Grand Hailing Sigh of Distress," faithful old Ootah had grabbed me by the nape of the neck, the same as he would have grabbed a dog, and with one hand he pulled me out of the water, and with the other hurried the team across.

He had saved my life, but I did not tell him so, for such occurrences are taken as part of the day's work, and the sledge he safeguarded was of much more importance, for it held, as part of its load, the Commander's sextant, the mercury, and the coils of piano-wire that were the essential portion of the scientific part of the expedition. My kamiks (boots of sealskin) were stripped off, and the congealed water was beaten out of my bearskin trousers, and with a dry pair of kamiks, we hurried on to overtake the column.

APRIL 6

When we halted and started to build the igloos, the dogs and sledges having been secured, I noticed Commander Peary at work unloading his sledge and unpacking several bundles of equipment. He pulled out from under his *kooletah* (thick, fur outer-garment) a small folded package and unfolded it. I recognized his old silk flag, and realized that this was to be a camp of importance.

APRIL 7

It was about ten or ten-thirty A.M., on the 7th of April, 1909, that the Commander gave the order to build a snow-shield to protect him from the flying drift of the surface-snow. I knew that he was about to take an observation, and while we worked I was nervously apprehensive, for I felt that the end of our journey had come. When we handed him the pan of mercury the hour was within a very few minutes of noon. Laying flat on his stomach, he took the elevation and made the notes on a piece of tissue-paper at his head. With sun-blinded eyes, he snapped shut the *vernier* (a graduated scale that subdivides the smallest divisions on the sector of the circular scale of the sextant) and with the resolute squaring of his jaws, I was sure that he was satisfied, and I was confident that the journey had ended. Feeling that the time had come, I ungloved my right hand and went forward to congratulate him on the success of our eighteen years of effort, but a gust of wind blew something into his eye, or else the burning pain caused by his prolonged look at the reflection of the limb of the sun forced him to turn aside; and with both hands covering his eyes, he gave us orders to not let him sleep for more than four hours, for six hours later he purposed to take another sight about four miles beyond, and that he wanted at least two hours to make the trip and get everything in readiness.

I unloaded a sledge, and reloaded it with a couple of skins, the instruments, and a cooker with enough alcohol and food for one meal for three, and then I turned in to the igloo where my boys were already sound asleep. The thermometer registered 29° below zero. I fell into a dreamless sleep and slept for about a minute, so I thought, when I was awakened by the clatter and noise made by the return of Peary and his boys.

The Commander gave the word, "We will plant the stars and stripes—*at the North Pole!*" and it was done; on the peak of a huge paleocrystic floeberg the glorious banner was unfurled to the breeze, and as it snapped and crackled with the wind, I felt a savage joy and exultation. Another world's accomplishment was done and finished, and . . . I felt all that it was possible for me to feel, that it was I, a lowly member of my race, who had been chosen by fate to represent it. . . .

When I reached the ship again and gazed into my little mirror, it was the pinched and wrinkled visage of an old man that peered out at me, but the eyes still twinkled and life was still entrancing. This wizening of our features was due to the strain of travel and lack of sleep; we had enough to eat, and I have only mentioned it to help impress the fact that the journey to the Pole and back is not to be regarded as a pleasure outing, and our so-called jaunt was by no means a cake-walk.

A BUS TO FREEDOM
ROSA PARKS

On December 1, 1955, Rosa Parks of Montgomery, Alabama, refused to give up her seat for a white man on a segregated bus. It was a simple gesture of fed-up defiance, but a defining moment in the history of race relations in the United States as well. Her bus ride set in motion a movement that made Martin Luther King Jr. a national leader and culminated in historic civil rights legislation in the 1960s. As one black congressman, John Conyers, later explained it, "Rosa Parks moved civil rights issues from the back of the bus to the front of America's conscience." Here is how she described that fateful time.

When I got off from work that evening of December 1, I went to Court Square as usual to catch the Cleveland Avenue bus home. I didn't look to see who was driving when I got on, and by the time I recognized him, I had already paid my fare. It was the same driver who had put me off the bus back in 1943, twelve years earlier. He was still tall and heavy, with red, rough-looking skin. And he was still mean-looking. I didn't know if he had been on that route before—they switched the drivers around sometimes. I do know that most of the time if I saw him on a bus, I wouldn't get on it.

I saw a vacant seat in the middle section of the bus and took it. I didn't even question why there was a vacant seat even though there were quite a few people standing in the back. If I had thought about it at all, I would probably have figured maybe someone saw me get on and did not take the seat but left it vacant for me. There was a man sitting next to the window and two women across the aisle.

The next stop was the Empire Theater, and some whites got on. They filled up the white seats, and one man was left standing. The driver looked back and noticed the man standing. Then he looked back at us. He said, "Let me have those front seats," because they were the front seats of the black section. Didn't anybody move. We just sat right where we were, the four of us. Then he spoke a second time: "Y'all better make it light on yourselves and let me have those seats."

The man in the window seat next to me stood up, and I moved to let him pass by me, and then I looked across the aisle and saw that the two women were also standing. I moved over to the window seat. I could not see how standing up was going to "make it light" for me. The more we gave in and complied, the worse they treated us.

I thought back to the time when I used to sit up all night and didn't sleep, and my grandfather would have his gun right by the fireplace, or if he had his one-horse wagon going anywhere, he always had his gun in the back of the wagon. People always say that I didn't give up my seat because I was tired, but that isn't true. I was not tired physically, or no more tired than I usually was at the end of a working day. I was not old, although some people have an image of me as being old then. I was forty-two. No, the only tired I was, was tired of giving in.

The driver of the bus saw me still sitting there, and he asked was I going to stand up. I said, "No." He said, "Well, I'm going to have you arrested." Then I said, "You may do that." These were the only words we said to each other. I didn't even know his name, which was James Blake, until we were in court together. He got out of the bus and stayed outside for a few minutes, waiting for the police.

As I sat there, I tried not to think about what might happen. I knew that anything was possible. I could be manhandled or beaten. I could be arrested. People have asked me if it occurred to me then that I could be the test case the NAACP had been looking for. I did not think about that at all. In fact if I had let myself think too deeply about what might happen to me, I might have gotten off the bus. But I chose to remain.

Meanwhile there were people getting off the bus and asking for transfers, so that began to loosen up the crowd, especially in the back of the bus. Not everyone got off, but everybody was very quiet. What conversation there was, was in low tones; no one was talking out loud. It would have been quite interesting to have seen the whole bus empty out. Or if the other three had stayed where they were, because if they'd had to arrest four of us instead of one, then that would have given me a little support. But it didn't matter. I never thought hard of them at all and never even bothered to criticize them.

Eventually two policemen came. They got on the bus, and one of them asked me why I didn't stand up. I asked him, "Why do you all push us around?" He said to me, and I quote him exactly, "I don't know, but the law is the law and you're under arrest." One policeman picked up my purse, and the second one picked up my shopping bag and escorted me to the squad car.

She was jailed, then released on bail. But her arrest sparked a yearlong bus boycott.

THE SKY WAS dark on Monday morning, but that didn't make any difference. Most black people had finally had enough of segregation on the buses. They stayed off those buses. They waited at the bus stops for the black-owned cabs to come along. Or they walked or got a ride. As a result, the Montgomery city buses were practically empty. Oh, a few black people took the buses, but they were mostly people who had not heard about the protest. Some of them were scared away from the buses. The city police had vowed to protect anyone who wanted to ride, and each bus had two motorcycle escorts. But some of the people who didn't know what was going on thought the police were there to arrest them for riding the buses, not to protect them. And then there were those few who didn't want to be inconvenienced. When the bus they were on passed a bus stop full of black people waiting for cabs, they ducked down low so nobody would see them.

That day I had no idea what the result was going to be, but I think everybody was quite amazed at that demonstration of people staying off the buses. It was a surprise to everybody, I think. As Mr. [E. D.] Nixon [former head of the Montgomery NAACP] said, "We surprised ourselves." Never before had black people demonstrated so clearly how much those city buses depended on their business. More important, never before had the black community of Montgomery united in protest against segregation on the buses.

The boycott lasted through that week, and then through the next. No one had any idea how long it would last. Some people said it couldn't last, but it seemed like those who said that were the white people and not us. The whites did everything they could do to stop it.

The police started getting after the groups of blacks who were waiting at the bus stops for the black-owned cabs to pick them up. Then they threatened to arrest the cab drivers if they did not charge their regular fare, which I think was forty-five cents, to go downtown instead of ten cents like the buses charged. White private citizens resisted the boycott too.

When the police started arresting cab drivers for not charging full fare, the [Montgomery Improvement Association] asked for volunteer drivers. Jo Ann Robinson was one. The churches collected money and bought several station wagons. Ordinary black people contributed, and so did some important white people in Montgomery. As a dispatcher, I was responsible for taking calls from people who needed rides and then making calls to the drivers of private cars and the church station wagons to see that the people were picked up wherever they were.

After a while quite a sophisticated system was developed. There were twenty private cars and fourteen station wagons. There were thirty-two pickup and transfer sites, and scheduled service from five-thirty in the morning until twelve-thirty at night. About 30,000 people were transported to and from work every day.

The white people were getting angrier and angrier. I remember somebody said that the memberships of the Montgomery chapters of the Ku Klux Klan and the White Citizens' Council went way up during that time. Even Mayor W. A. Gayle went out and joined the White Citizens' Council and was proud to announce it in public. He called the leaders of the boycott a bunch of Negro radicals. There was real violence against the people by this time. Dr. King's home was bombed at the end of January. Two days later Mr. Nixon's home was bombed. Nobody tried to bomb my home, but I did get a lot of threatening telephone calls. They'd say things like, "You're the cause of all this. You should be killed."

Summer came and [we] still stayed off the buses. The white people tried to break the boycott by not giving the church cars any insurance. All the churches operated the station wagons, and had their names on the sides. Without insurance, the cars could not operate legally. Every time they got insurance from a new company, the policy would suddenly be canceled. But Dr. King got in touch with a black insurance agent in Atlanta named T. M. Alexander, and T. M. Alexander got Lloyd's of London, the big insurance company in England, to write a policy for the church-operated cars.

Next, Mayor Gayle went to court to try to get an order preventing black people from gathering on street corners while waiting for the church cars. Mayor Gayle said they were a "public nuisance" because they sang loudly and bothered other people. He got a court to issue such an order, but that order came on the very same day that the U.S. Supreme Court ruled in our favor, that segregation on the Montgomery buses was unconstitutional.

Integrating the Montgomery buses did not go smoothly. Snipers fired at buses, and the city imposed curfews on the buses, not letting them run after five P.M., which meant that people who worked from nine to five couldn't ride the buses home. A group of whites tried to form a whites-only bus line, but that didn't work. The homes and churches of some ministers were bombed, as I mentioned. But eventually most of the violence died down. Black people were not going to be scared off the buses any more than they were going to be scared onto them when they refused to ride.

African Americans in other cities, like Birmingham, Alabama, and Tallahassee, Florida, started their own boycotts of the segregated buses. The direct-action civil-rights movement had begun.

LUNCH AT THE 5 & 10
MILES WOLFF

On February 1, 1960, four black college students sat down at a whites-only lunch counter in Greensboro, North Carolina. Their simple but brave gesture—ordering coffee—launched the sit-in movement. A nonviolent protest movement consisting mostly of black youth, sit-ins spread through-out the South, eventually causing establishments to end their segregationist practices or suffer dire economic consequences. Like the Montgomery bus boycott, sit-ins galvanized people and proved that nonviolent action could bring on momentous change.

At four-thirty the four boys sat down at the lunch counter. They were Negroes, students at North Carolina Agricultural and Technical College (A&T), a state Negro college located in Greensboro. It was not the first time that Negroes had sat at a Woolworth's lunch counter, nor the first time A&T students had asked for service, and the reaction would be the same as in any white eating establishment in the South in 1960: "We don't serve colored here." The boys were not newcomers ignorant of local customs, and they knew Woolworth's served Negroes only at the stand-up snack bar, but they took seats on the stools at the counter and waited for their orders to be taken.

The four had entered the store a little earlier. Two of them had bought toothpaste, combs, and other small articles in the toiletries area, and they brought these items and their receipts with them to the lunch counter. On the counter, a small stand advertised a turkey club sandwich at sixty-five cents. As the waitress approached, Ezell Blair Jr., the small-est of the group, spoke: "I'd like a cup of coffee, please." The waitress answered as expected: "I'm sorry. We don't serve Negroes here." But the four did not leave, and the boy said: "I beg to disagree with you. You just finished serving me at a counter only two feet away from here." The waitress pointed to the stand-up counter and said, "Negroes eat at the other end."

The boy went on. "What do you mean? This is a public place, isn't it? If it isn't, then why don't you sell membership cards? If you do that, then I'll understand that this is a private concern." The waitress re-sponded a little more heatedly, "Well, you won't get any service here!"

and walked away. The boys remained in their seats, and a Negro girl, a helper on the steam table, approached them and told the four that Negroes were not served at the lunch counter. When they did not move, she became angry. "You're acting stupid, ignorant! That's why we can't get anywhere today. You know you're supposed to eat at the other end." The boys stayed seated.

The date was February 1, 1960, and the four boys were starting a sit-in. There had been earlier demonstrations at variety stores and earlier sit-ins. One of the early movements of the Congress of Racial Equality (CORE) had been against segregated eating facilities of Woolworth's in Baltimore. And in Wichita, Kansas, and in Oklahoma City, Oklahoma, in 1958, there had been a partially successful lunch-counter protest, with more than thirty restaurants opening their doors as a result. In Greensboro there had been a sit-in when Jackie Robinson, catching a plane out of the city, refused to go to the Negro waiting room and continued sitting in the white section of the terminal. But these protests had stopped where they started, and throughout the South the pattern of segregated facilities remained.

The aim of the students was purely local: to obtain service in a store which welcomed Negroes at all but one counter. But these particular four Negro students, sitting at a Woolworth's lunch counter dressed in coats and ties, were starting something that was not to stop with one lunch counter.

The four [Blair, Franklin McCain, Joseph McNeil, and David Richmond] were freshmen at A&T, eighteen years old, and like many freshmen, they had dreams and plans. They were idealistic and perhaps a little naïve. The four boys had been discussing the idea of asking for service at Woolworth's for almost a month. Joe McNeil had brought it up, and as McCain put it, "McNeil had an idea we should do something different from most people and I decided I could be as big a fool as he could." Then on the night of January 31, McNeil came into his room where the other three were talking and asked if they were ready to go. At first the others thought he was kidding, but then Franklin McCain, the largest of the four, spoke up: "Are you guys chicken or not?" The answer, of course, was No.

As the four sat at the counter, they were scared ("Sure we were scared. I suppose if anyone had come up behind me and yelled 'Boo' I think I would have fallen off my seat"), but as they continued sitting and no one else came up to tell them to go and no policeman came in to arrest them, an idea hit McCain. "We didn't know what they could do to us, we didn't know how long we could sit. Now it came to me all of a sudden: Maybe they can't do anything to us. Maybe we can keep it up."

They did keep it up, others joined them, and the idea for lunch counter sit-ins spread throughout the South.

Outside of Greensboro, the list of cities that were experiencing sit-ins was growing. Charleston, Columbia, Miami, Houston, San Antonio, and even Xenia, Ohio, were added to the list, and by the end of the month sixty-eight cities in thirteen states had had some form of sit-in. There were interesting variations. At Petersburg, Virginia, and Memphis, Tennessee, students started sit-ins or read-ins at the local public libraries for whites, and at Elizabeth City, North Carolina, students who had been refused service at the local lunch counter staged a picnic. Memphis had a sit-in at a local art gallery; some Southern churches had kneel-ins; and at Biloxi, Mississippi, in April, Negroes staged a wade-in at the white public beach in that city.

At Columbia, South Carolina, a light-skinned Negro was served, but when he passed his hamburger over to a darker friend, the counter was immediately closed. The Governor of Tennessee charged that demonstrations in Nashville had been "instigated, planned by, and staged for the convenience of CBS," after television crews were on hand when students resumed sit-ins. Southern legislatures and city governments began working on laws that would prohibit the sit-ins, and arrests became more frequent. On March 15 alone, some five hundred protesters were jailed across the South.

Different Southern communities were finding different patterns of behavior, and these were not always just or honorable. In Montgomery, Alabama, a white man clubbed a demonstrating Negro woman with a baseball bat. In Tallahassee, tear gas was used to break up a march, and at Bessemer, Alabama, a white man beat Negroes with iron pipes. At Orangeburg, South Carolina, in 40-degree weather, firemen and police turned high-powered hoses on marching students, sending several who had been hit squarely to the hospital. The 350 students, still wet, were then herded into an open stockade.

On April 11, the activities of the [Greensboro] students widened as they expanded their protest to local shopping centers and other establishments that served Negroes at merchandise counters but not at lunch counters. At a number of places they were served standing up, but most counters closed when the Negroes took seats. It was during the first weeks in April that the strategy of the Negroes and their demands for equal service took a significant turn with a boycott. A boycott had been going on for some weeks in Nashville, where a merchant was quoted as saying, "This thing has frightening ramifications. It is more serious than most people realize. It has now become an economic situation affecting the entire community." The Negroes realized they had a powerful weapon, and the CORE boycott coordinator reported that Woolworth's national business had dropped 8.9 percent in the month of March. . . .

The movement was that of youth, and across the South some fifty thousand Negro students, both college and high school, were sitting in, demonstrating, and picketing. In some cases adult Negroes advised, but there were few participating in the sit-ins, and the younger ones really didn't care whether adults were present. It was their movement. In Alabama, one student expressed Negro students' feelings about adult participation when she talked about the college administrators: "We never were seriously interested in the approval or disapproval of our school administration. We decided that they should stay out of the movement for their own good, that we would not pull them into our activities." These young Negroes saw that their parents living under the Southern system of segregation had done little to change things outwardly, and they did not want to rear their children in the same atmosphere.

Most of the students realized that in the society in which their parents had been brought up, dissent would not have been tolerated.

But now the students were impatient with attacking the "foothills of segregation," as one head of the Southern Regional Council had expressed the goal of his organization, and it was time for direct action. The parents had helped pave the way, but they had not achieved the final goal.

The demonstrations also had important effects on Negro leadership and organizations in the community, for they became a form of protest against the Negro establishment. Bayard Rustin wrote, "What the student movement has done is to have broken the back of professional Uncle Tomism. For years the Negro middle class has profited from segregation. . . ."

ON JULY 25, it was all over. At 2 P.M. three well-dressed Negroes sat down at the Woolworth's lunch counter and were served. There had been no advance publicity, and there was no trouble. The three were employees of Woolworth's. The afternoon paper headlined, "Lunch Counters Integrated Here," and reported that the action by both Woolworth's and Kress's had been purely voluntary. In the first week, approximately three hundred Negroes were served at Woolworth's.

In discussing the sit-ins, the people involved have expressed many different opinions. But to the question of what drove the variety stores to serve Negroes at their counters, the answer has always been the same. [I]t was the tremendous economic pressure put on the stores by the Negroes' boycott, along with the reticence of whites to trade there because of fear of trouble.

The loss of people who simply stopped trading at Woolworth's nearly wiped out the profits for 1960. That year alone cost the store $200,000 in sales, and it dropped from fourth to eighth in food sales and from eighth to tenth in merchandise in its district.

Moral considerations and the rights of the Negro, then, had little to do with Woolworth's decision to desegregate. They were mentioned often enough, but when it came to a solution money was the deciding factor.

BLACK VALOR

BEYOND THE CALL OF DUTY

On January 13, 1997, President Bill Clinton awarded seven black veterans the Medals of Honor they had earned more than fifty years earlier, during World War II, but had never received because of racial discrimination. In 1995, a U.S. Army–contracted study of military archives and veteran interviews, recommended ten black soldiers for the nation's highest honor for bravery. An Army board selected seven winners. Citations for the black Medal of Honor winners are profiles in courage, telling of bravery above and beyond the call of duty. The citations are excerpted below.

PVT. GEORGE WATSON, BIRMINGHAM, ALABAMA

Private Watson was on board a troop ship [near Porlock Harbor, New Guinea] when it was attacked and hit by enemy bombers [March 8, 1943]. Before it sank, the ship was abandoned. Private Watson remained in deep waters long enough to assist several soldiers who could not swim to reach the safety of a life raft. Weakened by continuous physical exertion Private Watson drowned when the suction of the sinking ship dragged him beneath the surface of the swirling waters.

STAFF SGT. RUBEN RIVERS, OKLAHOMA CITY

On 16 November 1944, while advancing toward the town of Guebling, France, Staff Sergeant Rivers's tank hit a mine at a railroad crossing. Although severely wounded, his leg slashed to the bone, Staff Sergeant Rivers declined an injection of morphine, took command of another tank and advanced with his company into Guebling the next day. [On Nov. 19], Company A's tanks advanced toward Bourgaltroff, their next objective, but were stopped by enemy tanks. Staff Sergeant Rivers, however, radioed that he had spotted the German antitank positions: "I see 'em. We'll fight 'em!" While doing so, Staff Sergeant Rivers's tank was hit, killing him and wounding the rest of the crew.

MAJ. CHARLES L. THOMAS, DETROIT

One platoon of Company C, 614th Tank Destroyer Battalion, was designated as the leading element in a task force formed to storm and capture the village of Climbach, France [on Dec. 14, 1944]. Lieutenant Thomas, the Commanding Officer of Company C, volunteered to command the selected platoon of his company and ride in the column's leading vehicle. As his scout car advanced to an exposed position on the heights, he received intense direct fire from enemy artillery, self-propelled guns, and small arms. Lieutenant Thomas received multiple gunshot wounds in his chest, legs and left arm. [He] ordered and directed the dispersion and emplacement of his first two antitank guns. In a few minutes these guns were effectively returning the enemy fire. Lieutenant Thomas refused evacuation until he felt certain that his junior officer was in full control of the situation. [He was promoted later.]

FIRST LIEUT. JOHN R. FOX, CINCINNATI

An organized attack by uniformed German formations was launched [near Sommocolonia, Italy] around 0400 hours, 26 December 1944. Although most of the U.S. infantry forces withdrew from the town, Lieutenant Fox reported at 0800 hours that the Germans were in the streets and attacking in strength. He called for artillery fire increasingly close to his own position. His commander protested that the bombardment would be too close. The Germans continued to press forward in large numbers, surrounding the position. Lieutenant Fox again called for artillery fire with the commander protesting again, "Fox, that will be on you!" The last communication from Lieutenant Fox was: "Fire it! There's more of them than there are of us. Give them hell!" The bodies of Lieutenant Fox and his party were found in the vicinity of his position when his position was taken. [His action] inflicted heavy casualties, causing the deaths of approximately 100 German soldiers, thereby delaying the advance of the enemy.

STAFF SGT. EDWARD CARTER JR., LOS ANGELES

At approximately 0830 hours, 23 March 1945, near Speyer, Germany, the tank upon which Staff Sergeant Carter was riding received bazooka and small arms fire from the vicinity of a large warehouse to its left front. Staff Sergeant Carter and his squad took cover behind an intervening road bank. Staff Sergeant Carter volunteered to lead a three-man patrol to the warehouse where other unit members noticed the original bazooka fire. As the patrol left this covered position, they received intense enemy small arms fire killing one member of the patrol instantly. This caused Staff Sergeant Carter to order the other two members of the patrol to return to the covered position and cover him with rifle fire while he proceeded alone. The enemy fire killed one of the two soldiers while they were returning and seriously wounded [the other].

An enemy machine gun burst wounded Staff Sergeant Carter three times in the left arm as he continued the advance. He continued and received another wound in his left leg that knocked him from his feet. As Staff Sergeant Carter took wound tablets and drank from his canteen, the enemy shot it from his left hand, with the bullet going through his hand. [He] continued the advance by crawling until he was within 30 yards of his objective. The enemy fire became so heavy that Staff Sergeant Carter took cover behind a bank. Eight enemy riflemen approached apparently to take him prisoner. Staff Sergeant Carter killed six of the enemy soldiers and captured the remaining two. The two enemy soldiers later gave valuable information concerning the number and disposition of enemy troops.

FIRST LIEUT. VERNON BAKER, ST. MARIES, IDAHO

At 0500 hours on 5 April 1945, Lieutenant Baker advanced at the head of his weapons platoon, along with Company C's three rifle platoons, toward their objective: Castle Aghinolfi—a German mountain strongpoint. Moving more rapidly than the rest of the company, Lieutenant Baker and about 25 men reached the south side of a draw [ravine] some 250 yards from the castle within two hours. Lieutenant Baker observed two cylindrical objects pointing out of a slit in a mount at the edge of a hill. Crawling up and under the opening, he stuck his M-1 into the slit and emptied the clip, killing the observation post's two occupants. Moving to another position in the same area, Lieutenant Baker stumbled upon a well-camouflaged machine gun nest, the crew of which was eating breakfast. He shot and killed both enemy soldiers. After Captain John F. Runyon, Company C's Commander, joined the group, a German soldier appeared from the draw and hurled a grenade, which failed to explode. Lieutenant Baker shot the enemy soldier twice as he tried to flee. Lieutenant Baker then went down into the draw alone. There he blasted open the concealed entrance of another dugout with a hand grenade, shot one German soldier who emerged after the explosion, tossed another grenade into the dugout and entered firing his sub-machine gun, killing two more. Enemy machine gun and mortar fire began to inflict heavy casualties among the group of 25 soldiers. Captain Runyon ordered a withdrawal [during which] Lieutenant Baker, supported by covering fire from one of his platoon members, destroyed two machine gun positions. The following night, Lieutenant Baker voluntarily led a battalion advance through enemy mine fields and heavy fire toward the division objective.

PFC. WILLY F. JAMES JR., KANSAS CITY, MISSOURI

On 7 April 1945, Company G, 413th Infantry, fought its way across the Weser River in order to establish a crucial bridgehead. The company then launched a fierce attack against the town of Lippoldsberg, possession of which was vital to security and expanding the important bridgehead. Private First Class James was first scout of the lead squad. The mission of the unit was to seize and secure a group of houses on the edge of town. Far out in front, Private First Class James was the first to draw enemy fire. But poor visibility made it difficult for [him] to point out enemy positions. [He] volunteered to go forward. Furious crossfire from enemy snipers and machine guns finally pinned down Private First

Class James after making his way forward approximately 200 yards across open terrain. Lying in an exposed position for more than an hour, Private First Class James intrepidly observed the enemy's positions, which were given away by the fire. Then, with utter indifference to his personal safety, in a storm of enemy small arms fire, Private First Class James made his way back more than 300 yards and gave a full, detailed report on the enemy disposition. [He then] volunteered to lead a squad in an assault on the key house.

SHOOTOUT AT THE BEAUTY SALON

A HAIR-RAISING STORY

On February 5, 1994, Brooklyn beauty salon customers thought they were going to be killed by three armed men who attempted to rob the salon. But a hero was under the hair dryer.

Arlene Beckles walked into a crowded beauty salon in downtown Brooklyn Saturday to get her hair done and emerged a hero.

A police officer who was off duty at the time, Officer Beckles emerged from under a hair dryer to shoot and wound three robbers and to face death.

Ms. Beckles, a thirty-year-old Police Academy instructor, was sitting under a hair dryer when three armed men came in about 5:45 P.M. and announced a robbery. She stood up, she recalled, announced she was a police officer and opened fire. After she emptied her five-shot, off-duty revolver, a gunman who had been shot in the hand rushed her, knocked her down, and put his gun to her head.

He pulled the trigger.

Click.

He tried to unjam the weapon and pulled the trigger again.

Click.

"I really didn't think I had a chance," she said. "There were three of them and there was just me." She added quickly, "I should say, me and God. And we won."

The gunman ran away, followed by a companion whom Officer Beckles had shot in the elbow and buttocks. They were arrested later when they showed up at hospitals.

But then the third gunman, who had been shot in the nose and was lying on the floor, jumped up and began to scuffle with her.

A transit police sergeant, William O'Brien, who was walking by on a meal break and heard the commotion, ran into the salon and helped Ms. Beckles make the arrest.

Ms. Beckles, five feet seven inches tall and weighing 110 pounds, has been an officer for six years, with the housing police and then with the city Police Department. She had never before fired her gun in the line of duty.

Officer Beckles's mother, Ethel, praised her as "nervy." Her father, Cuthbert, said that "even the perpetrators would commend her for what she has done."

Officer Beckles said she had been frightened at first, but then "I thought to myself, 'Arlene, remember your Academy training, take your time, take a deep breath, think about what you're going to do.'"

"I was just glad, glad she was alive," her fiance said. "She only had five shots, and if you're not a cop, you don't really understand. Three guys. Two or three guns. She thought she was going to die."

She had said she was not a Dirty Harriet. But with police officers, she said, "there's a hero inside all of us."

—Adapted from The New York Times

TO ACT OR NOT TO ACT
SIDNEY POITIER

Sidney Poitier, the son of a poor Bahamian farmer, overcame the stereotyping and racism of Hollywood to become a box-office sensation and Academy Award winner. But not before suffering through the agony of giving less-than-stellar performances. He eventually won over audiences, but his initial slow progress gives us some indication of the courage he finally mustered in order to master his craft.

I arrived at the [American Negro Theatre] on the afternoon of [auditions for a new class of actors] to find about seventy-five other people gathered for the same purpose. I sat down in the audience and waited, ready with my material. The clatter in the auditorium came from clusters of auditioners having a last-minute run-through of *their* material. Some like me will be auditioning alone. Some will play scenes with other people. All—unlike me—will be reading from plays. I wonder where the hell they got those plays, because what I've got is a *True Confessions* magazine that I've bought and memorized two paragraphs from, and I'm growing fearful that I may be disqualified for not having a scene from a play for my audition. At that point the lights start down and someone in authority calls the applicants to order and makes a brief welcoming speech in which he explains the aims and aspirations of the American Negro Theatre and officially opens the auditions by calling the first applicant up onto the stage to show his stuff. I think to myself: Hell, it's too late for me to worry about my material now. It's sink or swim with *True Confessions* magazine. I sit there watching intently as other applicants go up on the stage and play out dramatic scenes, comedy scenes, monologues, pantomime . . . and then my turn comes. I hear them say, "Sidney Poitier"—panic! I think: Oh, Lord—here I go now. Do I know how to speak without my accent? I run a few lines in my mind to see if I'm accent-free, and in my mind I say: That's not too bad. Then I go.

The theater holds two hundred or so people. Besides those taking auditions, there are also friends, parents, and others who've come along to lend encouragement and support. Then there are members of the

American Negro Theatre's staff, including the president and the drama coaches. The president's name is Abram Hill.

I walk up on the stage from the little steps on the side, and immediately I feel self-conscious standing under those two bright lights that seem to accentuate everything and will no doubt accentuate the fact that I'm carrying a *True Confessions* magazine instead of a play. And I'm further disquieted by the fact that, though I'm under the spotlight where everybody can see me, I can't see anybody out in the auditorium. A voice coming from the direction of the faculty table asks, "Sidney Poitier?" "Yes," I reply. "Mr. Poitier, what are you going to do for us?" I say, "I am going to read something from *True Confessions* magazine." I hear a snicker in the audience and I say to myself: I must have made a mistake, because why would they be laughing? The teacher says, *"True Confessions* magazine?" I say, "Yes, ma'am." She says, "All right. You can begin whenever you're ready." Out of the breast pocket of my suit I pull my magazine. The best suit I've owned to that point in my life is a brown suit, and needless to say, I'm dressed in my brown suit with my brown tie and my brown socks and my brown shoes and my brown shirt. I am dap! Most of the other kids are not as sartorially stunning as I am because, apparently, they are intelligent enough to know that you don't dress up to come to an audition. So I begin to read this *True Confessions* magazine that I've whipped out of my breast pocket. I turn to a page of some innocuous story about "Frank and Melinda." All of these stories are told from a woman's point of view, and in this one Melinda is telling how she first met Frank, and I'm reading: "I met Frank as I walked down the street going towards so-and-so and there coming towards me is this handsome man and I said to myself 'just look at—' " Well, I can feel the people in the audience—I can feel their jaws drop. I can feel them thinking: What is he doing up there? Such thoughts are reverberating everywhere. Mercifully, Osceola Archer, the drama coach, interrupts. "All right, that's enough," she says. I stop. After a few seconds she says, "Mr. Poitier." I say, "Yes, ma'am." She says, "I would like you to do an improvisation for us. Would you do that?" I say, "Yes, ma'am." Now I don't know what an improvisation is. I just hope that they'll explain it to me so that I won't have to expose my ignorance. She says, "All right, let us presuppose that you are in the jungle . . ." I'm thinking, what has the jungle got to do with that big word "improvisation." She says, ". . . and you are in the Army and you are in the middle of combat." I'm hearing what she's saying, but I'm trying to put it together to see how the word "improvisation" fits, because I still don't know what the word means. Well, finally it dawns on me what it means. It means that I'm supposed to act out the part of a guy in the Army who's caught in the jungle behind enemy lines and there's no way to escape and the enemy is shooting at me from everywhere and I have to make my last-ditch stand—how do I do it? I say, "All right." She says, "Take a few minutes and think it over and let us know when you're ready." So I turn my back to the audience, because I've seen other people do that to prepare themselves, but I'm not preparing anything, I'm thinking: Now, what am I going to do here? This place ain't no jungle. I don't see no jungle, but now I've got to create all that stuff in my imagination. Well, I think, I'm going to give it a shot because I've seen some movies like this. I turn back around and I say, "I'm ready." She says, "All right, begin." I hold my arms out in the shape of a machine gun and I start looking around—I spin around suddenly as if I'm being surrounded by enemies and I'm saying like James Cagney— that's the only thing that comes into my mind—I'm saying, "Oh, you dirty rats, you can come and get me. I'll kill you." And I go brrr— rrrr—rrrr, bang, bang, bang. I'm carrying on like this and suddenly I get shot in the belly by one of the enemy's bullets and start sinking slowly and agonizingly to the floor—when I suddenly realize that this is a dirty floor and I'm wearing my best suit! My very best suit in all my life! What's going to happen if I fall down on this floor and dirty up my suit! So on the way down to the floor, in the most dramatic moment of my improvisation, I reach out my arm and hold myself half on the floor and half off the floor, and I go on holding that position in the hope that all concerned will realize that I'm supposed to be *on* the floor but am just not going to [mess] up my suit doing this improvisation. At which point the drama coach says, "All right, thank you—thank you." I get up and walk off. Now, I don't know whether I've done good or bad. I have a feeling I've done terribly, but I figure I'll brave it out, so I go back and sit in the audience and watch some of the other kids audition, and some of them are really brilliant, but mostly the girls. I finally leave with the understanding that they'll be sending me a card within a week to let me know if I'm accepted or rejected.

A week goes by, and a card arrives that says, "Would you come down and visit with us. We would like to have a talk with you." I dash down there and talk with someone representing the school who says, "We're going to take you on a trial basis for three months. We don't feel that you'll make it, but we want to give you every opportunity. If we feel, at the end of three months, that there hasn't been sufficient improvement we ask you not to continue. Is that understandable, and if so, is it agreeable to you?" I said, "That's understandable and it's agreeable." Little did I realize what the real bottom-line reason for my being accepted on a trial basis was. As it turned out, they had forty students who got passing marks and all forty of them were girls. No men. As rotten as the men were, they had to take ten or twelve of us to fill up the new class, and I was the least likely to succeed among the twelve. . . .

After three months, the faculty of the Theatre School said my first twelve weeks suggested I really wasn't improving and they would rather I didn't come back. I said, "Please! I'm just beginning to get a feel for what it's all about. I realize that there's a hell of a lot more to it than I had thought, but that only strengthens my determination. So please, please reconsider." They said, "No." Devastated at being cut from the class roster, I drifted about in confusion for a week or so before I struck on an idea. I said to myself: Maybe I can barter. I went back to the school, searched out Abram Hill, the president, and said, "Mr. Hill, I want to continue to be a student here. What I would like to do is this: You don't have a regular janitor to clean the theater, to sweep down the hallway and take care of the steps and the stage. You leave that haphazardly to students and they don't do a very good job. I will take over the cleaning of the auditorium and I will take over the cleaning of the stage if you will let me continue on for another semester." He said, "Well, I'll think about it. It's unusual, but I'll think about it. You really want to study that badly?" I said, "Yes, sir." He said, "I'll think about it." I came back a few days later and asked if he *had* thought about it and he said, "Yes. We've discussed it and you've got a deal." So back into the class I go, delighted to be back on track again, happily closing out each evening with a little floor scrubbing, stairway mopping, and whatever other janitorial tidbit I laid on the institution under our agreement.

• • •

FINALLY, [A BROADWAY director] called me in to sign a contract, offering me $65 to $75 per week for [*Lysistrata*]. My Lord! Can you beat that? I thought to myself. . . .

From day one of rehearsal I was well prepared, on my toes, paying attention to everything. I was fascinated by the other people in the cast—watching them move around, listening to the way they read their lines. It was from watching these gifted black American artists that I began to understand the real magic of theater. The rehearsal month for *Lysistrata* was the best four weeks of my life.

Opening night of *Lysistrata*. After all the rehearsals and run-throughs, I am opening in New York on Broadway, and I'm feeling pretty good with myself. In fact, I've decided not only can I become an actor, I *am* an actor. I've proved that—I have an Equity card. "Half hour" comes and goes. I'm all dressed and ready. Somebody says, "Everybody get ready, curtain in five minutes." The actors take their places on the stage. I don't enter for a little while, but I'm ready.

Babe Wallace, on his way to the stage, stops and looks through a little hole about the size of a dime in the proscenium curtain. I wonder why he's peeking through that little hole. Soon he turns to another actor, whispers something, then peeks through the hole again before turning once more to the actor who is waiting for *his* peek. Smiling to himself, Babe wanders off to take his place on the stage. The other actor looks through the hole, shakes his head, and also drifts off to his first-act position.

So I say, "What in the world are they peeking at through there?" An overwhelming urge instantly develops in me: I walk up to the curtain, I look through the hole, and I discover that it looks directly out on the audience—about 1,200 people! As the lights begin to dim, I suddenly realize that I'm going out in front of those 1,200 people (most of whom are white). Lord have mercy—what have I gotten myself into? I quickly dash away from the curtain, but the damage is done. I am now petrified. I've got stage fright.

At that moment, the stage manager says, "Curtain going up." Sure as hell that curtain goes up, boy. I hear this thunderous applause and it sounds as though there are 12 million people out there. The play is supposed to be a Greek *comedy,* the audience is supposed to be laughing, but they ain't laughing. I don't know why. From the wings, I just hear the lines going and the audience quiet. My time grows nearer and nearer. Finally my cue is there and I have got to go out on the stage.

I can't move. The stage manager gives me a shove and I go stumbling out. The first thing I do, instead of looking at the actor I'm supposed to give my first line to, I look dead into the audience, where I see nothing but faces (most of them white). I say to myself: Mama, what am I doing here? It's time for my line. I don't remember it. The first line has gone completely out of my mind. I hear the silence, however, and I say to myself: Come on, Sidney, you've got to say something. You've got to start it. The first line that comes to my mind is line number three, so I give that line to the actor. His eyes open wide, indicating: That's not the right line. He tries to get me back to the head of the scene by giving me the line that was supposed to come after my *first* line. I'm stuck now, and can't pick it up, so I give him line number seven—at which point the juxtaposition of lines is coming out hilariously to the audience. We finally have to wait for them to calm down from laughing.

I know they are laughing at me. They can't be laughing at the humor in the play, because my scene isn't supposed to be funny. The other actor gives me line number three. I give him line number twelve. Now, the audience is not only laughing—they're beginning to applaud. Oh, no, I realize, they want me to get off the stage. I'm finished. I've taken all the humiliation I can stand. The other actor, in desperation, throws yet another line at me. Instead of answering him, I gear myself up, turn around, and walk away. I walk off the stage and the audience is applauding. I'm saying, "You're just applauding because I've left."

Backstage nobody says anything to me about having messed up the lines—they're ecstatic because, they say, the audience thinks I'm so terrific. But I don't believe they think I'm terrific, nor do I listen to anybody who tries to tell me so. I rush upstairs to my dressing room, whip out of my costume, put on my street clothes, and get out of that theater. Everyone is supposed to wait for the curtain calls; I'm not there. They have a party after the show; I'm not there either.

Next morning, after what felt like the most agonizing night of my life, I reluctantly went out to buy some of the thirteen newspapers that were expected to carry reviews on the disaster of the previous evening. I just knew I was about to read about a certain young boy named Sidney Poitier who called himself an actor but was in fact a dishwasher and who messed up a good play. All thirteen reviewers panned the play—more correctly they "destroyed" the play. But according to a few reviews, the only saving grace of the evening was an unknown young actor who came out in the first act and absolutely devastated the audience with his acute comedic approach to the part of Polydorus. I said, "Uh-oh. Wait a minute now. Back up here a second."

I read and reread each paper. The words never changed. According to them, I was a hit. Overnight I was a hit! In a play that lasted only four days, of course, but I was a hit.

Sidney Poitier went on to win an Academy Award for best actor for his role in the 1963 movie Lilies of the Field. *It was the first time an African American male was awarded an Oscar. In 1997, he was officially appointed Ambassador of the Bahamas to Japan. The appointment reflects the high esteem that Bahamians have for Poitier, whose parents were born on the islands.*

YOUR WORLD
GEORGIA DOUGLAS JOHNSON

The most daring—and rewarding—exploits involve stepping outside the bounds and safety of one's own world. That is the only way to soar on a breeze of endless possibilities.

Your world is as big as you make it.
I know, for I used to abide
In the narrowest nest in a corner,
My wings pressing close to my side.

But I sighted the distant horizon
Where the sky line encircled the sea
And I throbbed with a burning desire
To travel this immensity.

I battered the cordons around me
And cradled my wings on the breeze
Then soared to the uttermost reaches
With rapture, with power, with ease!

STRENGTH AND WEAKNESS
ANDY RAZAF

Andy Razaf (1895–1973) was forced to quit school at age sixteen to support his mother. He ended up writing many hit songs, blazing a song-writing career with Thomas "Fats" Waller, and he dabbled in poetry as well. Here is Razaf's advice for pressing forward into parts unknown or untraveled.

I scorn the chicken-hearted kind
Of man, who can't make up his mind;
Who, when it's time for action, yaps:
"I guess so," "Maybe," or "Perhaps."
He never cares to follow through,
Or dare to try out something new.
He'll never risk life or limb
On unknown paths—they're not for him.

He never leaves his yesterdays,
And much prefers the safest ways.
"Let good enough alone," says he,
"New problems were not meant for me."
And so thru life he doubts and sneers
At people we call pioneers.
If we depended on his will,
The world would soon be standing still.

Give me the cool, stout-hearted man
Who says, "I will," "I must," "I can";
Who, in the toughest kind of spot,
Will snap: "Come on," "Let's go," "Why not?"
While weaklings wait and never try,
Just hesitate and alibi,
The strong press forward, seldom fail.
It takes real men to blaze a trail.

LIFTOFF!

A BROTHER ORBITS EARTH

J. ALFRED PHELPS

Few people get to leave the planet—and return. Those who get launched into the "final frontier" are more than just a little brave. They're extraordinary. Colonel Guion S. Bluford Jr. (b. 1942) became the first African American to fly in space. Here is the story of his two-million-mile flight aboard the space shuttle Challenger *in August 1983.*

The rains came, beating and swirling about the orbiter on the launchpad as it pointed majestically toward the sky. For eighteen hours the rain slashed and sluiced in the wind. Thunder rumbled grotesquely. Lightning crackled and scorched. A hold was ordered. Weather parameters across the board were "No Go!"

Seventeen minutes after scheduled liftoff, the rain stopped and the wind died. It seemed almost miraculous. Visibility was tolerable. Countdown resumed. T-minus-ten minutes and counting. Invited guests and members of the media peered from under dripping umbrellas and sodden, makeshift coverings, their hair matted.

Guy Bluford was honored to be the first black American chosen to venture into space, but that fact was not uppermost in his mind. Instead, he thought of the enormity of leaving planet Earth. Of flying higher into the firmament than most men had ever been. Fear was not an issue; there was no time for that. "It was," Bluford recalled, "like preparing for an exam. You study as much as you can, the better prepared you are, the less frightened you are about taking the exam."

The exam grew closer as the countdown dwindled to T-minus-thirty seconds. Second hands swept across watch dials; digital prompts pulsated on the faces of electronic clocks. Launchpad 39-A glistened under powerful searchlights. The 154-foot-high external tank seemed somehow larger, its 28.6-foot diameter fatter. The two 150-foot solid-rocket boosters flanking the [external tank] seemed to glow, providing their assent to the coming test. The orbiter, its nose pointed toward the heavens, shone with an unearthly whiteness.

Computers had taken over the countdown. The propellant tank vents were long closed. Couch-bound, Captain Richard Truly and Daniel Brandenstein stared fixedly at the instrument panels. Bluford and the other mission specialists lay cinched into their seats. Every indicator was green as the countdown moved to T-minus-fifteen seconds. Out in the darkness, cameras set to record the launch began their maniacal, electronic song.

"Liftoff!"

The roar shook houses miles away. Flames flashed and blazed into huge, wedge-shaped deflectors, sending searing exhaust from the solid-rocket boosters into a forty-two-foot trench underneath the launchpad, roaring out the sides, white smoke and brilliant orange flames billowing into the air. The temperature around the launchpad soared to 6,000°F, as the "rain birds" strategically placed around it disgorged three hundred thousand gallons of water onto the pad in thirty seconds, cushioning the shuttle from acoustic energy damage generated by the powerful boosters. Night turned into momentary day as someone observed that, even though it was 2:32 A.M., they could read their newspapers in the monumental glow. Birds, thinking themselves ensconced for the night, took momentary flight, silhouetted against the bright fire. Some died, killed by the sheer level of noise.

"Ooohs" and "aaaaahs" soughed through the crowds on the ground. Some wept. Others cheered as the orbiter leapt into space, grudgingly at first, then headed out over the Atlantic, a fitting denouement to a brilliant spectacle.

They call it "rocket dawn" when the space shuttle takes to the air in the middle of the night. People from as far away as North Carolina saw it light their skies.

Inside *Challenger,* Guy Bluford and the crew thought it was like being in the middle of a great bonfire, riding in some strange elevator through roaring flames. It was a major surprise. They'd purposely turned down the cockpit lights so they could look out the window—just in case they had to land. But it was a night launch, and when they lit the rocket boosters, they "lit up the cockpit so much that whatever night vision we were trying to maintain was lost," Bluford said later.

The solid-fuel rockets exerted 5.3 million pounds of thrust in four-hundredths of a second, lighting the entire circle of the sky. "Rocket dawn" dappled the clouds orange, as the orbiter zoomed through and the color suffused. Within two minutes of liftoff, the shuttle was twenty-seven miles above the earth, where the two booster rockets fell away, tiny explosive devices separating them from the great fuel tank. Parachutes soon deployed and the boosters fell into the sea where recovery ships would bring them back. For the next six minutes, the main engines burned, hurling *Challenger* to the very edge of space. As the main engines shut down, the huge external tank jettisoned, tumbling along a ten-thousand-mile arc into the sea. One hundred eighty miles above the earth, *Challenger* slipped into orbit.

About an hour into the flight, Guy Bluford unstrapped from his seat and, although having been trained for the weightless state aboard an aircraft test bed, he had only experienced it at one degree of gravity. It hadn't really dawned on him that, 180 miles into space, he would be dealing with a zero-gravity state. "The next thing I knew," he recalled, "I was floating off the top of the cockpit!" It wasn't panic that took over, but the searching for a viable answer to the simple question: How do I get down from here? He began wiggling around for a while, trying to figure out how to move about the cabin. It was a new experience, and he quickly found that the rules were somehow different in a weightless state. You learn to push off walls and ceilings because you realize you can't walk around like you used to. It was like floating around in water, but without any water. The bulky space suit and helmet made him feel clumsy as he made unintentional mistakes as he went about flipping switches. But, after two hours, he began to get the hang of it. To his surprise, it was loads of fun: "I mean, it doesn't take much to get things floating across the room. . . . I like to walk on walls and ceilings and all that sort of stuff!"

The launch had been timed to coordinate with one of the mission's prime objectives—launch of the $45-million Indian national satellite, designed to provide communications and weather information to that country. Twenty-five hours and sixteen minutes into the flight on mission day two, Bluford and Dale Garner popped the satellite, INSAT-1B, from the payload bay during sunset over the Pacific.

"Roger, Houston, we're happy to let you know that INSAT was deployed on time with no anomalies and the satellite looked good!" Bluford reported to Mission Control.

"You guys have maintained the shuttle's perfect record!" the ground controllers responded.

They knew President Reagan would probably call, so the communications link was established and, also on their second day in orbit, the presidential call came through.

"Guy," said the president, "you are paving the way for many others and making it plain that we are in an era of brotherhood here in our land. You will serve as a role model for so many others and be so inspirational."

Bluford thanked the president. His response was low key because he is a low-key kind of person. Later, he remembered telling the president simply "that I was part of a team. We were doing a great job, and I was pleased to be there. [And] I *was* pleased."

On the sixth day, the crew concentrated on cabin stowage preparing for reentry and landing. As engineer, Bluford helped Truly and Brandenstein initiate the 160-second deorbit burn early on the morning of 5 September—at the end of their ninety-seventh orbit and after covering 2.22 million miles in space. Truly flew *Challenger* through the prescribed flight profiles and the blast furnace of the earth's heavy atmosphere, taking manual control below Mach 1. Landing at night, they were guided in by twin, powerful light beacons—one white, the other red—punching up from the vast emptiness of the Mojave Desert. Positioning *Challenger* between the two beams, Truly held the orbiter steady

on a steep, nineteen-degree angle of approach to the landing site—
carved from the desert darkness by six Xenon arc lamps shining with the
power of 4.8 billion candles.

Jump at the sun. You may not land on the sun, but at least you'll be off
the ground.

—Traditional

HONESTY

Honesty is more than simply the absence of lies. It deals also in truthfulness, candor, forthrightness, and righteousness—and it has always been among our most cherished values. Those who are honest with others, and with themselves, are held in the greatest esteem, even if the truths they speak sometimes hurt.

Why is dishonesty so common? Lies often provide convenient ducking places and hidden corners. Some people masquerade lies as fact in order to reap rewards for erecting facades of falsehood. Dishonesty thrives where selfishness and lack of caring rule. In short, wherever profits, motives, or truths are concealed, lies and deception usually lurk. Honest people, and pure truth, prefer the broad light of day.

For African Americans, as for others, the truth has served as a shield against lies. To destroy myths about their supposed inferiority, blacks armed themselves with historical facts about black accomplishments and the truth about blacks' capabilities and capacity for greatness. Speaking plain truths is not always an easy thing to do, though, when society continues to foist mythology about black inferiority and white superiority. It takes courage, wisdom, and survival skills to know when to speak up and when to hold one's tongue.

Over time, there have been some exceptions to truth-telling and openness. Fleeing slaves could escape only by using deception. Such an extraordinary condition as slavery called for extraordinary measures, including deceit, guile and duplicity, particularly because getting caught often meant being maimed or killed. Slaves hid during the day and traveled through the wilderness by the light of the moon and the stars. Survival, then, took precedence over frankness and naivete. That was— and still is—understandable and acceptable.

Slaves' disposition to lie in order to survive is discussed by Frederick Douglass, Julius Lester, and others in the following pages. Their opinions on the consequences of honesty when confronting brutal racists are complex and controversial.

More straightforward are short stories by Lerone Bennett Jr. and Chester Himes. Bennett's story deals with the tough choice a man must make in court in the segregated South; Himes's young character discovers the pain that stealing can bring.

These opinions and stories underscore different aspects of honesty and make valuable reading for both children and adults. When highly valued and consistently practiced, honesty becomes so ingrained, it is a given in one's affairs.

◔◐◔

Truth could move multitudes with untutored language.

—*Carter G. Woodson*

◔◐◔

SPEAK THE TRUTH TO THE PEOPLE
MARI EVANS

Hearing the truth can "free the mind" so people can concentrate on constructive work. This poem admonishes blacks to be truthful in speech so audiences can "identify the enemy," distance themselves from conventions that enslave African Americans, and build a strong black nation with its own ideals.

Speak the truth to the people
Talk sense to the people
Free them with reason
Free them with honesty
Free the people with Love and Courage and Care for their Being
Spare them the fantasy
Fantasy enslaves
A slave is enslaved
Can be enslaved by unwisdom
Can be enslaved by black unwisdom
Can be re-enslaved while in flight from the enemy
Can be enslaved by his brother whom he loves
His brother whom he trusts
His brother with the loud voice
And the unwisdom
Speak the truth to the people
It is not necessary to green the heart
Only to identify the enemy
It is not necessary to blow the mind
Only to free the mind
To identify the enemy is to free the mind

A free mind has no need to scream
A free mind is ready for other things
To BUILD black schools
To BUILD black children
To BUILD black minds
To BUILD black love
To BUILD black impregnability
To BUILD a strong black nation
To BUILD.

Speak the truth to the people.
Spare them the opium of devil-hate.
They need no trips on honky-chants.
Move them instead to a BLACK ONENESS.
A black strength which will defend its own
Needing no cacophony of screams for activation
A black strength which attacks the laws
exposes the lies disassembles the structure
and ravages the very foundation of evil.

Speak the truth to the people
To identify the enemy is to free the mind
Free the mind of the people
Speak to the mind of the people
Speak Truth.

You never find yourself until you face the truth.

—*Pearl Bailey*

THE CONVERT
LERONE BENNETT JR.

A black preacher is beaten to death, and folks in town wonder how a witness will testify in a Mississippi courthouse reeking with contempt for blacks. Will Booker Taliaferro Brown lie to save his own skin? Has the preacher died in vain, trying to integrate a train? Lerone Bennett Jr. (b. 1928), author of the classic book, Before the Mayflower, *wrote this story of courage and honesty in 1963, the same year four black girls were killed when segregationists bombed a church in Birmingham, Alabama.*

A man don't know what he'll do, a man don't know what he is till he gets his back pressed up against a wall. Now you take Aaron Lott: there ain't no other way to explain the crazy thing he did. He was going along fine, preaching the gospel, saving souls, and getting along with the white folks; and then, all of a sudden, he felt wood pressing against his back. The funny thing was that nobody knew he was hurting till he preached that Red Sea sermon where he got mixed up and seemed to think Mississippi was Egypt. As chairman of the deacons board, I felt it was my duty to reason with him. I appreciated his position and told him so, but I didn't think it was right for him to push us all in a hole. The old fool—he just laughed.

"Brother Booker," he said, "the Lord—He'll take care of me."

I knew then that that man was heading for trouble. And the very next thing he did confirmed it. The white folks called the old fool downtown to bear witness that the colored folks were happy. And you know what he did: he got down there amongst all them big white folks and he said: "Things ain't gonna change here overnight, but they gonna change. It's inevitable. The Lord wants it."

Well sir, you could have bought them white folks for a penny. Aaron Lott, pastor of the Rock of Zion Baptist Church, a man white folks had said was wise and sound and sensible, had come close—too close—to saying that the Supreme Court was coming to Melina, Mississippi. The surprising thing was that the white folks didn't do nothing. There was a lot of mumbling and whispering but nothing bad happened till the terrible morning when Aaron came a-knocking at the door of my funeral home. Now things had been tightening up—you could feel it in the air—and I didn't want no part of no crazy scheme and I told him so right off. He walked on past me and sat down on the couch. He had on his preaching clothes, a shiny blue suit, a fresh starched white shirt, a black tie, and his Sunday black shoes. I remember thinking at the time that Aaron was too black to be wearing all them dark clothes. The thought tickled me and I started to smile but then I noticed something about him that didn't seem quite right. I ran my eyes over him closely. He was kinda middle-sized and he had a big clean-shaven head, a big nose, and thin lips. I stood there looking at him for a long time but I couldn't figure out what it was till I looked at his eyes: they were burning bright, like light bulbs do just before they go out. And yet he looked contented, like his mind was resting some-wheres else.

"I wanna talk with you, Booker," he said, glancing sideways at my wife. "If you don't mind, Sister Brown—"

Sarah got up and went into the living quarters. Aaron didn't say nothing for a long time; he just sat there looking out the window. Then he spoke so soft I had to strain my ears to hear.

"I'm leaving for the Baptist convention," he said. He pulled out his gold watch and looked at it. "Train leaves in 'bout two hours."

"I know *that*, Aaron."

"Yeah, but what I wanted to tell you was that I ain't going Jim Crow. I'm going first class, Booker, right through the white waiting room. That's the law."

A cold shiver ran through me.

"Aaron," I said, "don't you go talking crazy now."

The old fool laughed, a great big body-shaking laugh. He started talking 'bout God and Jesus and all that stuff. Now, I'm a God-fearing man myself, but I holds that God helps those who help themselves. I told him so.

"You can't mix God up with these white folks," I said. "When you start to messing around with segregation, they'll burn you up and the Bible, too."

He looked at me like I was Satan.

"I sweated over this thing," he said. "I prayed. I got down on my knees and I asked God not to give me this cup. But He said I was the one. I heard Him, Booker, right here"—he tapped his chest—"in my heart."

The old fool's been having visions, I thought. I sat down and tried to figure out a way to hold him, but he got up, without saying a word, and started for the door.

"Wait!" I shouted. "I'll get my coat."

"I don't need you," he said. "I just came by to tell you so you could tell the board in case something happened."

"You wait," I shouted, and ran out of the room to get my coat.

We got in his beat-up old Ford and went by the parsonage to get his suitcase. Rachel—that was his wife—and Jonah were sitting in the living room, wringing their hands. Aaron got his bag, shook Jonah's hand, and said, "Take care of your Mamma, boy." Jonah nodded. Aaron hugged Rachel and pecked at her cheek. Rachel broke down. She throwed her arms around his neck and carried on something awful. Aaron shoved her away.

"Don't go making no fuss over it, woman. I ain't gonna be gone forever. Can't a man go to a church meeting 'thout women screaming and crying."

He tried to make light of it, but you could see he was touched by the way his lips trembled. He held his hand out to me, but I wouldn't take it. I told him off good, told him it was a sin and a shame for a man of God to be carrying on like he was, worrying his wife and everything.

"I'm coming with you," I said. "Somebody's gotta see that you don't make a fool of yourself."

He shrugged, picked up his suitcase, and started for the door. Then he stopped and turned around and looked at his wife and his boy and from the way he looked I knew that there was still a chance. He looked at the one and then at the other. For a moment there, I thought he was going to cry, but he turned, quick-like, and walked out of the door.

I ran after him and tried to talk some sense in his head. But he shook me off, turned the corner, and went on up Adams Street. I caught up with him and we walked in silence, crossing the street in front of the First Baptist Church for whites, going on around the Confederate monument where, once, they hung a boy for fooling around with white women.

"Put it off, Aaron," I begged. "Sleep on it."

He didn't say nothing.

"What you need is a vacation. I'll get the board to approve, full pay and everything."

He smiled and shifted the suitcase over to his left hand. Big drops of sweat were running down his face and spotting up his shirt. His eyes were awful, all lit up and burning.

"Aaron, Aaron, can't you hear me?"

We passed the feed store, Bill Williams' grocery store, and the movie house.

"A man's gotta think about his family, Aaron. A man ain't free. Didn't you say that once, didn't you?"

He shaded his eyes with his hand and looked into the sun. He put the suitcase on the ground and checked his watch.

"Why don't you think about Jonah?" I asked. "Answer that. Why don't you think about your own son?"

"I am," he said. "That's exactly what I'm doing, thinking about Jonah. Matter of fact, he started *me* to thinking. I ain't never mentioned it before, but the boy's been worrying me. One day we was downtown here and he asked me something that hurt. 'Daddy,' he said, 'how come you ain't a man?' I got mad, I did, and told him: 'I am a man.' He said that wasn't what he meant. 'I mean,' he said, 'how come you ain't a man where white folks concerned.' I couldn't answer him, Booker. I'll never forget it till the day I die. I couldn't answer my own son, and I been preaching forty years."

"He don't know nothing 'bout it," I said. "He's hot-headed, like my boy. He'll find out when he grows up."

"I hopes not," Aaron said, shaking his head. "I hopes not."

Some white folks passed and we shut up till they were out of hearing. Aaron, who was acting real strange, looked up in the sky and moved his lips. He came back to himself, after a little bit, and he said: "This thing of being a man, Booker, is a big thing. The Supreme Court can't make you a man. The NAACP can't do it. God Almighty can do a lot, but even He can't do it. Ain't nobody can do it but you."

He said that like he was preaching and when he got through he was all filled up with emotion and he seemed kind of ashamed—he was a man who didn't like emotion outside the church. He looked at his watch, picked up his bag, and said, "Well, let's git it over with."

We turned into Elm and the first thing I saw at the end of the Street was the train station. It was an old red building, flat like a slab. A group of white men were fooling around in front of the door. I couldn't make them out from that distance, but I could tell they weren't the kind of white folks to be fooling around with.

We walked on, passing the dry goods store, the barber shop, and the new building that was going up. Across the street from that was the sheriff's office. I looked in the window and saw Bull Sampson sitting at his desk, his feet propped up on a chair, a fat brown cigar sticking out of his mouth. A ball about the size of a sweet potato started burning in my stomach.

"Please Aaron," I said. "Please. You can't get away with it. I know how you feel. Sometimes I feel the same way myself, but I wouldn't risk my neck to do nothing for these niggers. They won't appreciate it; they'll laugh at you."

We were almost to the station and I could make out the faces of the men sitting on the benches. One of them must have been telling a joke. He finished and the group broke out laughing.

I whispered to Aaron: "I'm through with it. I wash my hands of the whole mess."

I don't know whether he heard me or not. He turned to the right without saying a word and went on in the front door. The string-beany man who told the joke was so shocked that his cigarette fell out of his mouth.

"Y'all see that," he said. "Why, I'll—"

"Shut up," another man said. "Go git Bull."

I kept walking, fast, turned at the corner, and ran around to the colored waiting room. When I got in there, I looked through the ticket window and saw Aaron standing in front of the clerk. Aaron stood there for a minute or more, but the clerk didn't see him. And that took some not seeing. In that room, Aaron Lott stood out like a pig in a chicken coop.

There were, I'd say, about ten or fifteen people in there, but didn't none of them move. They just sat there, with their eyes glued on Aaron's back. Aaron cleared his throat. The clerk didn't look up; he got real busy with some papers. Aaron cleared his throat again and opened his mouth to speak. The screen door of the waiting room opened and clattered shut.

It got real quiet in that room, hospital quiet. It got so quiet I could hear my own heart beating. Now Aaron knew who opened that door, but he didn't bat an eyelid. He turned around real slow and faced High Sheriff Sampson, the baddest man in South Mississippi.

Mr. Sampson stood there with his legs wide open, like the men you see on television. His beefy face was blood-red and his gray eyes were rattlesnake hard. He was mad; no doubt about it. I had never seen him so mad.

"Preacher," he said, "you done gone crazy?" He was talking low-like and mean.

"Nosir," Aaron said. "Nosir, Mr. Sampson."

"What you think you doing?"

"Going to St. Louis, Mr. Sampson."

"You must done lost yo' mind, boy."

Mr. Sampson started walking towards Aaron with his hand on his gun. Twenty or thirty men pushed through the front door and fanned out over the room. Mr. Sampson stopped about two paces from Aaron and looked him up and down. That look had paralyzed hundreds of niggers; but it didn't faze Aaron none—he stood his ground.

"I'm gonna give you a chance, preacher. Git on over to the nigger side and git quick."

"I ain't bothering nobody, Mr. Sampson."

Somebody in the crowd yelled: "Don't reason wit' the nigger, Bull. Hit 'em."

Mr. Sampson walked up to Aaron and grabbed him in the collar and throwed him up against the ticket counter. He pulled out his gun.

"Did you hear me, deacon. I said, 'Git.' "

"I'm going to St. Louis, Mr. Sampson. That's cross state lines. The court done said—"

Aaron didn't have a chance. The blow came from nowhere. Laying there on the floor with blood spurting from his mouth, Aaron looked up at Mr. Sampson and he did another crazy thing: he grinned. Bull Sampson jumped up in the air and came down on Aaron with all his two hundred pounds. It made a crunchy sound. He jumped again and the mob, maddened by the blood and heat, moved in to help him. They fell on Aaron like mad dogs. They beat him with chairs; they beat him with sticks; they beat him with guns.

Till this day, I don't know what come over me. The first thing I know I was running and then I was standing in the middle of the white waiting room. Mr. Sampson was the first to see me. He backed off, cocked his pistol, and said: "Booker, boy, you come one mo' step and I'll kill you. What's a matter with you niggers today? All y'all gone crazy?"

"Please don't kill him," I begged. "You ain't got no call to treat him like that."

"So you saw it all, did you? Well, then, Booker you musta saw the nigger preacher reach for my gun?"

"He didn't do that, Mr. Sampson," I said. "He didn't—"

Mr. Sampson put a big hairy hand on my tie and pulled me to him.

"Booker," he said sweetly. "You saw the nigger preacher reach for my gun, didn't you?"

I didn't open my mouth—I couldn't I was so scared—but I guess my eyes answered for me. Whatever Mr. Sampson saw there musta convinced him 'cause he throwed me on the floor besides Aaron.

"Git this nigger out of here," he said, "and be quick about it."

Dropping to my knees, I put my hand on Aaron's chest; I didn't feel nothing. I felt his wrist; I didn't feel nothing. I got up and looked at them white folks with tears in my eyes. I looked at the women, sitting crying on the benches. I looked at the men. I looked at Mr. Sampson. I said, "He was a good man."

Mr. Sampson said, "Move the nigger."

A big sigh came out of me and I wrung my hands.

Mr. Sampson said, "Move the nigger."

He grabbed my tie and twisted it, but I didn't feel nothing. My eyes were glued to his hands; there was blood under the fingernails, and the fingers—they looked like fat little red sausages. I screamed and Mr. Sampson flung me down on the floor.

He said, *"Move the nigger."*

I picked Aaron up and fixed his body over my shoulder and carried him outside. I sent for one of my boys and we dressed him up and put him away real nice-like and Rachel and the boy came and they cried and carried on and yet, somehow, they seemed prouder of Aaron than ever before. And the colored folks—they seemed proud, too. Crazy niggers. Didn't they know? Couldn't they see? It hadn't done no good. In fact, things got worse. The Northern newspapers started kicking up a stink and Mr. Rivers, the solicitor, announced they were going to hold a hearing. All of a sudden, Booker Taliaferro Brown became the biggest man in that town. My phone rang day and night: I got threats, I got promises, and I was offered bribes. Everywhere I turned somebody was waiting to ask me: "Whatcha gonna do? Whatcha gonna say?" To tell the truth, I didn't know myself. One day I would decide one thing and the next day I would decide another.

It was Mr. Rivers and Mr. Sampson who called my attention to that. They came to my office one day and called me a shifty, no-good nigger. They said they expected me to stand by "my statement" in the train station that I saw Aaron reach for the gun. I hadn't said no such thing, but Mr. Sampson said I said it and he said he had witnesses who heard me say it. "And if you say anything else," he said, "I can't be responsible for your health. Now you know"—he put that bloody hand on my shoulder and he smiled his sweet death smile—"you *know* I wouldn't threaten you, but the boys"—he shook his head—"the boys are real worked up over this one."

It was long about then that I began to hate Aaron Lott. I'm ashamed to admit it now, but it's true: I hated him. He had lived his life; he had made his choice. Why should he live my life, too, and make me choose? It wasn't fair; it wasn't right; it wasn't Christian. What made me so mad was the fact that nothing I said would help Aaron. He was dead and it wouldn't help one whit for me to say that he didn't reach for that gun. I tried to explain that to Rachel when she came to my office, moaning and crying, the night before the hearing.

"Listen to me, woman," I said. "Listen. Aaron was a good man. He lived a good life. He did a lot of good things, but he's *dead, dead, dead!* Nothing I say will bring him back. Bull Sampson's got ten niggers who are going to swear on a stack of Bibles that they saw Aaron reach for that gun. It won't do me or you or Aaron no good for me to swear otherwise."

What did I say that for? That woman liked to had a fit. She got down on her knees and she begged me to go with Aaron.

"Go wit' him," she cried. "Booker. *Booker!* If you's a man, if you's a father, if you's a friend, go wit' Aaron."

That woman tore my heart up. I ain't never heard nobody beg like that.

"Tell the truth, Booker," she said. "That's all I'm asking. Tell the truth."

"Truth!" I said. "Hah! That's all you niggers talk about: truth. What do you know about truth? Truth is eating good and sleeping good. Truth is living, Rachel. Be loyal to the living."

Rachel backed off from me. You would have thought that I had cursed her or something. She didn't say nothing; she just stood there pressed against the door. She stood there saying nothing for so long that my nerves snapped.

"Say something," I shouted. "Say something—anything!"

She shook her head, slowly at first, and then her head started moving like it wasn't attached to her body. It went back and forth, back and forth, back and forth. I started towards her, but she jerked open the door and ran out into the night, screaming.

That did it. I ran across the room to the filing cabinet, opened the bottom drawer, and took out a dusty bottle of Scotch. I started drinking, but the more I drank the soberer I got. I guess I fell asleep 'cause I dreamed I buried Rachel and that everything went along fine until she jumped out of the casket and started screaming. I came awake with a start and knocked over the bottle. I reached for a rag and my hand stopped in midair.

"Of course," I said out loud and slammed my fist down on the Scotch-soaked papers.

I didn't see nothing.

Why didn't I think of it before?

I didn't see nothing.

Jumping up, I walked to and fro in the office. Would it work? I rehearsed it in my mind. All I could see was Aaron's back. I don't know whether he reached for the gun or not. All I know is that *for some reason* the men beat him to death.

Rehearsing the thing in my mind, I felt a great weight slip off my shoulders. I did a little jig in the middle of the floor and went upstairs to my bed, whistling. Sarah turned over and looked me up and down.

"What you happy about?"

"Can't a man be happy?" I asked.

She sniffed the air, said, "Oh," turned over, and mumbled something in her pillow. It came to me then for the first time that she was 'bout the only person in town who hadn't asked me what I was going to do. I thought about it for a little while, shrugged, and fell into bed with all my clothes on.

When I woke up the next morning, I had a terrible headache and my tongue was a piece of sandpaper. For a long while, I couldn't figure out what I was doing laying there with all my clothes on. Then it came to me: this was the big day. I put on my black silk suit, the one I wore for big funerals, and went downstairs to breakfast. I walked into the dining room without looking and bumped into Russell, the last person in the world I wanted to see. He was my only child, but he didn't act like it. He was always finding fault. He didn't like the way I talked to Negroes; he didn't like the way I talked to white folks. He didn't like this; he didn't like that. And to top it off, the young whippersnapper wanted to be an artist. Undertaking wasn't good enough for him. He wanted to paint pictures.

I sat down and grunted.

"Good morning, Papa." He said it like he meant it. He wants something, I thought, looking him over closely, noticing that his right eye was swollen.

"You been fighting again, boy?"

"Yes, Papa."

"You younguns. Education—that's what it is. Education! It's ruining you."

He didn't say nothing. He just sat there, looking down when I looked up and looking up when I looked down. This went on through the grits and the eggs and the second cup of coffee.

"Whatcha looking at?" I asked.

"Nothing, Papa."

"Whatcha thinking?"

"Nothing, Papa."

"You lying, boy. It's written all over your face."

He didn't say nothing.

I dismissed him with a wave of my hand, picked up the paper, and turned to the sports page.

"What are you going to do, Papa?"

The question caught me unawares. I know now that I was expecting it, that I wanted him to ask it; but he put it so bluntly that I was flabbergasted. I pretended I didn't understand.

"Do 'bout what, boy? Speak up!"

"About the trial, Papa."

I didn't say nothing for a long time. There wasn't much, in fact, I could say; so I got mad.

"Questions, questions, questions," I shouted. "That's all I get in this house—questions. You never have a civil word for your pa. I go out of here and work my tail off and you keep yourself shut up in that room of yours looking at them fool books and now soon as your old man gets his back against the wall you join the pack. I expected better than that of you, boy. A son ought to back his pa."

That hurt him. He picked up the coffee pot and poured himself another cup of coffee and his hand trembled. He took a sip and watched me over the rim.

"They say you are going to chicken out, Papa."

"Chicken out? What that mean?"

"They're betting you'll 'Tom.' "

I leaned back in the chair and took a sip of coffee.

"So they're betting, huh?" The idea appealed to me. "Crazy niggers—they'd bet on a funeral."

I saw pain on his face. He sighed and said: "I bet, too, Papa."

The cup fell out of my hand and broke, spilling black water over the tablecloth.

"You did what?"

"I bet you wouldn't 'Tom.' "

"You little fool." I fell out laughing and then I stopped suddenly and looked at him closely. "How much you bet?"

"One hundred dollars."

I stood up.

"You're lying," I said. "Where'd you get that kind of money?"

"From Mamma."

"Sarah!" I shouted. "Sarah! You get in here. What kind of house you running, sneaking behind my back, giving this boy money to gamble with?"

Sarah leaned against the door jamb. She was in her hot iron mood. There was no expression on her face. And her eyes were hard.

"I gave it to him, Booker," she said. "They called you an Uncle Tom. He got in a fight about it. He wanted to bet on you, Booker. *He* believes in you."

Suddenly I felt old and used up. I pulled a chair to me and sat down.

"Please," I said, waving my hand. "Please. Go away. Leave me alone. Please."

I sat there for maybe ten or fifteen minutes, thinking, praying. The phone rang. It was Mr. Withers, the president of the bank. I had put in for a loan and it had been turned down, but Mr. Withers said there'd been a mistake. "New fellow, you know," he said, clucking his tongue. He said he knew that it was my lifelong dream to build a modern funeral home and to buy a Cadillac hearse. He said he sympathized with that dream, supported it, thought the town needed it, and thought I deserved it. "The loan will go through," he said. "Drop by and see me this morning after the hearing."

When I put that phone down, it was wet with sweat. I couldn't turn that new funeral home down and Mr. Withers knew it. My father had raised me on that dream and before he died he made me swear on a Bible that I would make it good. And here it was on a platter, just for a word, a word that wouldn't hurt nobody.

I put on my hat and hurried to the courthouse. When they called my name, I walked in with my head held high. The courtroom was packed. The white folks had all the seats and the colored folks were standing in the rear. Whoever arranged the seating had set aside the first two rows for white men. They were sitting almost on top of each other, looking mean and uncomfortable in their best white shirts.

I walked up to the bench and swore on the Bible and took a seat. Mr. Rivers gave me a little smile and waited for me to get myself set.

"State your name," he said.

"Booker Taliaferro Brown." I took a quick look at the first two rows and recognized at least ten of the men who killed Aaron.

"And your age?"

"Fifty-seven."

"You're an undertaker?"

"Yessir."

"You been living in this town all your life?"

"Yessir."

"You like it here, don't you, Booker?"

Was this a threat? I looked Mr. Rivers in the face for the first time. He smiled.

I told the truth. I said, "Yessir."

"Now, calling your attention to the day of May 17th, did anything unusual happen on that day?"

The question threw me. I shook my head. Then it dawned on me. He was talking about—

"Yessir," I said. "That's the day Aaron got—" Something in Mr. Rivers' face warned me and I pulled up—"that's the day of the trouble at the train station."

Mr. Rivers smiled. He looked like a trainer who'd just put a monkey through a new trick. You could feel the confidence and the contempt oozing out of him. I looked at his prissy little mustache and his smiling lips and I got mad. Lifting my head a little bit, I looked him full in the eyes; I held the eyes for a moment and I tried to tell the man behind the eyes that I was a man like him and that he didn't have no right to be using me and laughing about it. But he didn't get the message. The bastard—he chuckled softly, turned his back to me, and faced the audience.

"I believe you were with the preacher that day."

The water was getting deep. I scrooched down in my seat, closed the lids of my eyes, and looked dense.

"Yessir, Mr. Rivers," I drawled. "Ah was, Ah was."

"Now, Booker—" he turned around—"I believe you tried to keep the nigger preacher from getting out of line."

I hesitated. It wasn't a fair question. Finally, I said: "Yessir."

"You begged him not to go in the white side?"

"Yessir."

"And when that failed, you went over to *your* side—the *colored* side—and looked through the window?"

"Yessir."

He put his hand in his coat pocket and studied my face.

"You saw *everything*, didn't you?"

"Just about." A muscle on the inside of my thigh started tingling.

Mr. Rivers shuffled some papers he had in his hand. He seemed to be thinking real hard. I pushed myself against the back of the chair. Mr. Rivers moved close, quick, and stabbed his finger into my chest.

"Booker, did you see the nigger preacher reach for Mr. Sampson's gun?"

He backed away, smiling. I looked away from him and I felt my heart trying to tear out of my skin. I looked out over the courtroom. It was still; wasn't even a fly moving. I looked at the white folks in front and the colored folks in back and I turned the question over in my mind. While I was doing that, waiting, taking my time, I noticed, out of the corner of my eye, that the smile on Mr. Rivers' face was dying away. Suddenly, I had a terrible itch to know what that smile would turn into.

I said, "Nosir."

Mr. Rivers stumbled backwards like he had been shot. Old Judge Sloan took off his glasses and pushed his head out over the bench. The whole courtroom seemed to be leaning in to me and I saw Aaron's widow leaning back with her eyes closed and it seemed to me at that distance that her lips were moving in prayer.

Mr. Rivers was the first to recover. He put his smile back on and he acted like my answer was in the script.

"You mean," he said, "that you didn't see it. It happened so quickly that you missed it?"

I looked at the bait and I ain't gonna lie: I was tempted. He knew as well as I did what I meant, but he was gambling on my weakness. I had thrown away my funeral home, my hearse, everything I owned, and he was standing there like a magician, pulling them out of a hat, one at a time, dangling them, saying: "Looka here, looka here, don't they look pretty?" I was on top of a house and he was betting that if he gave me a ladder I would come down. He was wrong, but you can't fault him for trying. He hadn't never met no nigger who would go all the way. I looked him in the eye and went the last mile.

"Aaron didn't reach for that gun," I said. "Them people, they just fell on—"

"Hold it," he shouted. "I want to remind you that there are laws in this state against perjury. You can go to jail for five years for what you just said. Now I know you've been conferring with those NAACP fellows, but I want to remind you of the statements you made to Sheriff Sampson and me. Judge—" he dismissed me with a wave of his hand— "Judge, this *man*—" he caught himself and it was my turn to smile— "this *boy* is lying. Ten niggers have testified that they saw the preacher reach for the gun. Twenty white people saw it. You've heard their testimony. I want to withdraw this witness and I want to reserve the right to file perjury charges against him."

Judge Sloan nodded. He pushed his bottom lip over his top one.

"You can step down," he said. "I want to warn you that perjury is a very grave offense. You—"

"Judge, I didn't—"

"Nigger!" He banged his gavel. "Don't you interrupt me. Now git out of here."

Two guards pushed me outside and waved away the reporters. Billy Giles, Mr. Sampson's assistant, came out and told me Mr. Sampson wanted me out of town before sundown. "And he says you'd better get out before the Northern reporters leave. He won't be responsible for your safety after that."

I nodded and went on down the stairs and started out the door.

"Booker!"

Rachel and a whole line of Negroes were running down the stairs. I stepped outside and waited for them. Rachel ran up and throwed her arms around me. "It don't take but one, Booker," she said. "It don't take but one." Somebody else said: "They whitewashed it, they whitewashed it, but you spoiled it for 'em."

Russell came out then and stood over to the side while the others crowded around to shake my hands. Then the others sensed that he was waiting and they made a little aisle. He walked up to me kind of slow-like and he said, "Thank you, sir." That was the first time in his whole seventeen years that that boy had said "sir" to me. I cleared my throat and when I opened my eyes Sarah was standing beside me. She didn't say nothing; she just put her hand in mine and stood there. It was long about then, I guess, when I realized that I wasn't seeing so good. They say I cried, but I don't believe a word of it. It was such a hot day and the sun was shining so bright that the sweat rolling down my face blinded me. I wiped the sweat out of my eyes and some more people came up and said a lot of foolish things about me showing the white folks and following in Aaron's footsteps. I wasn't doing no such fool thing. Ol' Man Rivers just put the thing to me in a way it hadn't been put before— man to man. It was simple, really. Any man would have done it.

❧

One falsehood spoils a thousands truths.

—*Ashanti proverb*

❧

BUILDING ON TRUTH
JOSEPH LANGSTAFF

A Virginia-born man dispenses some wisdom about truth and honesty.

If you teach your children to be fair and honest only some of the time and only to some people, you are really telling them that the truth is unimportant. If you live so that your children see that you think it is all right to lie and cheat, then who can correct them? If I had seen my mother giving food to people which was not fit for dogs and lying about the quality of that food, then I could not have believed her about anything else. Children don't just listen to you, they watch you, too, and if your life is not a good example, you are certain to fail to make them the kind of adult you want them to be.

It is more complicated to live a lie than the truth. If God gives me thirty more years to live and you are so favored and we should meet, I will not have to think, "Well, what did I tell that man?" You see, if you build a country on lies, then all of the successful men in that country will have to be liars before they are anything else. Keeping the lie going is almost all they can do. The truth about anything is the truth of its making. The rightness of anything is in the first step you take in building it. If you make a poor cake you will have poor cake to eat. And you know—because your mother told you—that good bread is better than poor cake. It is just like white men to build a bad building higher than they used to build good buildings. Nothing anyone can ever say or do can make a bad job good. Every time I turn on my television set or look at a wall or listen to a radio, I hear somebody trying to convince me that that thing or this thing just can't be done without, or that thing or this thing will make me a young man that young ladies just cannot resist. All that is vain and foolish because I buy what I need or want and I don't want anything to be anything but what it is. I hear much talk about truth in the packaging of things. Well, to me that means not lying about what you are selling. There is just too much lying, there always has been, but there has never been as much as there is now. Try to find one thing that is true as you go through the day. That's much worse than being unable to get through the day without having to tell a lie or finding that you have been lied to at least once. That's how it used to be. My mother would say, for instance, that there was at least one lie in every hour, but now there are whole weeks in which there is no real truth at all.

You know that people can tell you the truth and make it have the same effect as a lie. People can tell you a lie and have it affect you like the truth. It depends on what you mean to do with the truth whether it comes out to be a bad thing or a good thing. There is much spite in some people's frankness and much sympathy in some people's untruthfulness. You must have found this out very early in life. It depends on how you are in your heart. If you mean well, the right you do will not be against your own nature, and it is death to live against your own nature.

It is easier for some people to do right when they know what it is than it is for other people. Some people like peace and others despise it. Some people are happiest when it is quiet and some people are never happy unless there is some kind of fighting. If you know what kind of person you are, you can watch yourself. If you like quiet and you know it, you will watch yourself to make sure that you do not do something dishonorable just so things will be quiet. If you are the kind of person who must have a circus going on all the time to be happy, you can watch yourself to see that your love of noise and jumping up and down is not making a fool out of you. But you can do nothing for yourself if you don't know what kind of person you are. You should make sure that you are controlling your feelings and that you are doing what you think is right, not just what you want to do. You must not do anything to death.

HUMAN WEAKNESS
COLLECTED BY HAROLD COURLANDER

Nobody is perfect, and some people may be "less perfect" than others.
But one "imperfection" really gets a town talking.

There was a big camp meeting going on over at Selma, one of the biggest they'd had for a long time. The preachers had come from all over, and they were spelling each other in the pulpit. First one would get up and give those people a sermon on Noah, then another would get up and preach on Jonah, and after him another one would preach on the Revelations of John the Revelator. The ones who weren't preaching at the moment sat behind and urged the preacher on. There was a lot of moaning, groaning, and jumping in the tent that day, and lots of folks being saved. After a while it got pretty hot, and the preachers gave a one-hour intermission so people could go get some lemonade and refresh themselves.

There were seven or eight preachers in the bunch, and they went next door, where they had pitched a small tent, and took off their coats and fanned themselves and had some lemonade. After they'd sat around a while, one of them said, "Brothers, we done a lot of talking this morning about the Good Book and human weakness. I got to say something on that. There ain't none of us is perfect in the sight of the Lord, and that includes us. I believe it would do us a powerful lot of good to humble ourselves and speak out on our own human weaknesses. Ain't that a fact?"

"Yes, Brother, it's the truth," the other preachers said, "ain't no one without a human weakness."

"Well, then," the first preacher said, "who want to begin?" Since no one else seemed ready to speak out on the subject of human weakness, he said, "Looks like I am the one got to get the ball rolling. Brothers, my human weakness is laziness. I can't tell you how lazy I get sometimes in doing the Lord's work. I don't mind putting in a *day*, mind you, but I get downright sluggish on the *overtime*. I surely got to reform myself."

"That," said another preacher, "ain't nothing at all compared to *my* human weakness, which is liquid corn. I just can't resist it. That's what my human weakness is all about, Brothers, and I'm a sorry man for it."

"Yes, that's bad, brother," another preacher said, "and I got something to match it. My weakness is gambling. That old Jack of Diamonds and Ace of Spades got me going. There ain't nothing makes me feel so good as playing cards at one dime a point. It sure give me shame to say it, but all Satan got to do is flash a deck at me and I'm lost."

"Brothers," the next preacher said, "we're all in need of reform, but of all the human weaknesses I heard of in here today, mine is the weakest. My problem is women. I just can't keep my mind off any good-looking gal, or any ugly gal neither. Seem like the Devil has got his hold on me for sure."

Every one of those preachers testified what was on his mind, all except one who never said a word. And at last the one who started the testifying in the first place said to him, "Well, Brother John, we heard from everybody except you. Ain't you going to join in?"

Brother John said, "Yes, I been thinking on it, but my weakness is a bad one."

"Ain't nothing too bad for the Lord to hear," the first one said. "Get on with it, Brother John."

Brother John said, "Brothers, my weakness ain't just *bad*, it's *terrible*."

"Tell it out," one of the preachers said, "it'll wash your soul clean."

"I sure hate to tell you," Brother John said, "but my human weakness is *gossip*, and I can't hardly wait to get out of here."

THE MOSES MOUSE
ANDY RAZAF

Here is the story, in verse, of a mouse who roared selfishly and dishonestly, misleading his followers. Before placing trust in people, we should be certain that they are upright, honest, and trustworthy.

A certain Mr. M. T. Squeak,
     A mouse who longed for cheese,
Conceived a plan to win himself
     Much luxury and ease.
Said he, "Since mice are stupid folk
     I'll use them and grow fat;
By organizing them into
     A movement anti-cat."

Straightway he sought his people
     And, within a single week,
He made himself their idol
     With the loudness of his squeak.
Cried he, "I'll save you from our foe
     And fix it so you'll live
Free from his claws—but first of all
     Much cheese you'll have to give!"

Continued he, "Our enemy,
     The cat, we'll quickly check.
If you'll contribute t'ward a bell
     To tie around his neck.
Of course, we first must organize—
     Right here, let me comment;
That I'd prefer some other mouse
     To be the President!"

And instantly the meeting 'rose
     And shouted out as one:
"No! No! you shall be President!"
     Said he, "Well done! Well done!

Now since you've given me the pow'r,
     The first thing I will do
Is name our great protective league
     The squeakers' I.O.U.!"

And then our hero made a speech
  That mice will ne'er forget;
So sad and eloquent was he
  All eyes, with tears, were wet.
"Thru me, our race shall be redeemed"
  He squeaked, defiantly—
"Now step up, comrades, with your
   cheese
  And you will soon be free!"

And in an endless line they came
  Each with a gift of cheese;
"This," said their leader, "will buy ships
  To cross the seven seas!"
This statement brought forth much
   applause,
  Said they, "won't that be nice?"
And seeing them elated;
  He took up collection—twice.

Next meeting-night our hero was
  As timely as before.
Said he, "My comrades, you've done well
  But you must still do more;
I've found and priced a handsome bell
  Which we can never buy;
Without a mighty sacrifice
  For bells are very high!"

Once more they came up eagerly
  And freely gave their cheese,
While, to himself, their leader said:
  "What liberal mice are these—
Such wealth! and oh! so much of it!
  Limburger, swiss and snappy,
American and Liederkranz!"
  Our hero sure was happy.

The squeaky months that followed
    Never once annoyed the cat—
In fact their plans amused him
    And his stomach, round and fat,
Seemed larger than it ever was—
    "What fools mice are!" laughed he,
"What mouse would risk his precious
    self
      To tie a bell on me?"

Of all the mice there was but one
    Who had no cause to kick
And that was Mr. M. T. Squeak;
    He never worked a lick;
Yet had a town and country house
    And many pounds of cheese;
While every day some homeless mouse
    Would starve to death or freeze.

One day an old, but thoughtful, mouse
    Sat down and scratched his head;
Said he, "My people puzzle me—
    I believe their brains are dead;
Week in, week out, for three long years
    They've purchased bells and ships
And vanquished every cat on earth—
    But only with their lips!"

"What's more," said he, "I wonder what
    This M. T. Squeak will do
With all the cheese he's taken
    From his loyal I.O.U.?
If they would only stop and think
    And ask each other why;
Their 'Moses' caters to the ear
    But never to the eye!"

"If they would only hear me out
    I'd tell them what I fear
But in their present state of mind;
    T'would mean my funeral bier."
"I 'spose," went on this wise old mouse,
    "That they'll wake up some day;
But it's a shame to see them throw
    Their hard-earned cheese away!"

Ten years have passed; but up to date
    The mice have seen no bell
Nor have they crossed a single sea—
    And here, I might as well
Acquaint you with the dreadful news:
    They've gone thru every house
Each day, in quest of M. T. Squeak,
    The missing Moses Mouse.

❦❧

De only way tuh keep a lie frum gittin' foun' out is tuh stop tellin' it.
                        —Bert Williams

❦❧

MAMA'S MISSIONARY MONEY
CHESTER HIMES

In this story by Chester Himes (1909–84), a young boy's plunge into theft and deceitfulness is revealed—and corrected—before it is too late. Himes himself was arrested in 1928 for armed robbery and sentenced to twenty years in prison. He was able to reform himself, however, publishing his first short story in Esquire *magazine from behind bars and going on to write eighteen books in his career. Three were produced as films:* Cotton Comes to Harlem, A Rage in Harlem *(from the book originally entitled* For Love of Imabelle), *and* The Heat's On, *renamed* Come Back, Charleston Blue. *He wrote this short story in 1949.*

"You Lem-u-wellllll! You-u-uuuu Lem-u-welllllllLLLLLLLLL!"

Lemuel heard his ma call him. Always wanting him to go to the store. He squirmed back into the corner of the chicken house, out of sight of the yard. He felt damp where he had sat in some fresh chicken manure, and he cursed.

Through a chink in the wall he saw his ma come out of the house, shading the sun from her eyes with her hand, looking for him. Let her find Ella, his little sister, or get somebody else. Tired of going to the store all the time. If it wasn't for his ma it was for Miss Mittybelle next door. Most every morning soon's he started out the house here she come to her door. "Lem-u-well, would you lak t' go to t' the sto' for me lak a darlin' li'l boy?" Just as soon's he got his glove and started out to play. Why din she just say, "Here, go to the sto'." Why'd she have to come on with that old "would you lak t' go" stuff? She knew his ma 'ud beat the stuffin's outen him if he refused.

He watched his ma looking around for him. She didn't call anymore, trying to slip up on him. Old chicken came in the door and looked at him. "Goway, you old tattle tale," he thought, but he was scared to move, scared to breathe. His ma went on off, 'round the house; he saw her going down the picket fence by Miss Mittybelle's sun flowers, going on to the store herself.

He got up and peeped out the door, looked around. He felt like old Daniel Boone. Wasn't nobody in sight. He went out in the yard. The dust was deep where the hens had burrowed hollows. It oozed up twixt the toes of his bare feet and felt hot and soft as flour. His long dark feet were dust-powdered to a tan color. The dust was thick on his ankles, thinning up his legs. There were numerous small scars on the black skin. He was always getting bruised or scratched or cut. There were scars on his hands too and on his long black arms.

He wondered where everybody was. Sonny done gone fishing with his pa. More like Bubber's ma kept him in 'cause he was feeling a little sick. From over toward Mulberry Street came sounds of yelling and screaming. He cocked his long egg-shaped head to listen; his narrow black face was stolid, black skin dusty dry in the noonday sun. Burrhead was getting a licking. Everybody knew everybody's else's cry. He was trying to tell whether it was Burrhead's ma or pa beating him.

Old rooster walked by and looked at him. "Goan, old buzzard!" he whispered, kicking dust at it. The rooster scrambled back, ruffling up, ready to fight.

Lemuel went on to the house, opened and shut the screen door softly, and stood for a moment in the kitchen. His ma'd be gone about fifteen minutes. He wiped the dust off his feet with his hands and started going through the house, searching each room systematically, just looking to see what he could find. He went upstairs to his ma's and pa's room, sniffed around in the closet, feeling in the pockets of his pa's Sunday suit, then knelt down and looked underneath the bed. He stopped and peeped out the front window, cautiously pulling back the curtains. Old Mr. Diggers was out in his yard 'cross the street, fooling 'round his fence. His ma wasn't nowhere in sight.

He turned back into the room and pulled open the top dresser drawer. There was a big rusty black pocketbook with a snap fastener back in the corner. He poked it with a finger. It felt hard. He lifted it up. It was heavy. He opened it. There was money inside, all kinds of money, nickels and dimes and quarters and paper dollars and even ten dollar bills. He closed it up, shoved it back into the corner, slammed shut the drawer, and ran and looked out the front window. Then he ran and looked out the back window. He ran downstairs and went from room to room, looking out all the windows in the house. No one was in sight. Everybody stayed inside during the hot part of the day.

He ran back upstairs, opened the drawer, and got to the pocketbook. He opened it, took out a quarter, closed it, put it away, closed the drawer, ran downstairs and out the back door and across the vacant lot to Mulberry Street. He started downtown, walking fast as he could without running. When he came to the paved sidewalks, they were hot on his feet and he walked half dancing, lifting his feet quickly from the pavement. At the Bijou he handed up his quarter, got a dime in change, and went into the small, hot theatre to watch a gangster film. Pow! Pow! Pow! That was him shooting down the cops. Pow! Pow! Pow!

"Where you been all day, Lem-u-well?" his ma asked as she bustled 'round the kitchen fixing supper.

"Over tuh the bayou. Fishin'. Me 'n Bluebelly went."

His ma backhanded at him but he ducked out of range. "Told you t' call Francis by his name."

"Yas'm. Francis. Me 'n Francis."

His pa looked up from the hydrant, where he was washing his hands
and face. "Ummmmp?" he said. His pa seldom said more than
"Ummmmp." It meant most everything. Now it meant did he catch any
fish. "Nawsuh," Lemuel said.

His little sister, Ella, was setting the table. Lemuel washed his hands
and sat down and his pa sat down and said the blessing while his ma
stood bowed at the stove. It was very hot in the kitchen and the sun
hadn't set. The reddish glow of the late sun came in through the windows, and they sat in the hot kitchen and ate greens and side meat and
rice and baked sweet potatoes and drank the potliquor with the corn
bread and had molasses and corn bread for dessert. Afterwards Lemuel
helped with the dishes, and they went and sat on the porch in the late
evening while the people passed and said hello.

Nothing was said about the quarter. Next day Lemuel took four
dimes, three nickels, and two half dollars. He went and found Burrhead.
"What you got beat 'bout yesdiddy?"

"Nutton. Ma said I sassed her."

"I got some money." Lemuel took the coins from his pocket and
showed them.

"Where you git it?" Burrhead's eyes were big as saucers.

"Ne you mind. I got it. Les go tuh the show."

" 'Gangster Guns' at the Bijou."

"I been there. Les go downtown tuh the Grand."

On the way they stopped in front of Zeke's Grill. It was too early for
the show. Zeke was in his window turning flapjacks on the grill. They
were big, round flapjacks, golden brown on both sides, and he'd serve
'em up with butter gobbed between. Lemuel never had no flapjacks like
that at home. Burrhead neither. They looked like the best tasting flapjacks in the world.

They went inside and had an order, then they stopped at Missus
Harris's and each got double ice-cream cones and a bag of peanut brittle.
Now they were ready for the show. It was boiling hot way up in the
balcony next to the projection room, but what'd they care. They
crunched happily away at their brittle and laughed and carried on. . . .
"Watch out, man, he slippin' up 'hind yuh."

Time to go home. Lemuel had a quarter, two nickels, and a dime left. He gave Burrhead the nickels and dime and kept the quarter. That night after supper his ma let him go over to the lot and play catch with Sonny, Bluebelly, and Burrhead. They kept on playing until it was so dark they couldn't see and they lost the ball over in the weeds by the bayou.

Next day Lemuel slipped up to his ma's dresser and went into the magic black pocketbook again. He took enough to buy a real big-league ball and enough for him and Burrhead to get some more flapjacks and ice cream too. His ma hadn't said nothing yet.

As the hot summer days went by and didn't nobody say nothing at all, he kept taking a little more each day. He and Burrhead ate flapjacks every day. He set up all the boys in the neighborhood to peanut brittle and ice cream and rock candy and took them to the show. Sundays, after he'd put his nickel in the pan, he had coins left to jingle in his pocket, although he didn't let his ma or pa hear him jingling them. All his gang knew he was stealing the money from somewhere. But nobody tattled on him and they made up lies at home so their parents wouldn't get suspicious. Lemuel bought gloves and balls and bats for the team and now they could play regular ball out on the lot all day.

His ma noticed the new mitt he brought home and asked him where he got it. He said they'd all been saving their money all summer and had bought the mitt and some balls. She looked at him suspiciously. "Doan you dast let me catch you stealin' nothin', boy."

About this time he noticed the magic black bag was getting flat and empty. The money was going. He began getting scared. He wondered how long it was going to be before his ma found out. But he had gone this far, so he wouldn't stop. He wouldn't think about what was going to happen when it was all gone. He was the king of the neighborhood. He had to keep on being king.

One night after supper he and his pa were sitting on the porch. Ella was playing with the cat 'round the side. He was sitting on the bottom step, wiggling his toes in the dust. He heard his ma come downstairs. He could tell something was wrong by the way she walked. She came out on the porch.

"Isaiah, somebody's tuk all my missionary money," she said. "Who you reckin it was?"

Lemuel held his breath. "Ummmmp!" his pa said.

"You reckin it were James?" He was her younger brother who came around sometimes.

"Ummmmp! Now doan you worry, Lu'belle. We find it."

Lemuel was too scared to look around. His pa didn't move. Nobody didn't say anything to him. After a while he got up. "I'm goin' tuh bed, ma," he said.

"Ummmmp!" his pa noticed.

Lemuel crawled into bed in the little room he had off the kitchen downstairs. But he couldn't sleep. Later he heard Doris Mae crying from way down the street. He just could barely hear her but he knew it was Doris Mae. Her ma was beating her. He thought Doris Mae's ma was always beating her. Later on he heard his ma and pa go up to bed. All that night he lay half awake, waiting for his pa to come down. He was so scared he just lay there and trembled.

Old rooster crowed. The sun was just rising. Clump-clump-clump. He heard his pa's footsteps on the stairs. Clump-clump-clump. It was like the sound of doom. He wriggled down in the bed and pulled the sheet up over his head. He made like he was sleeping. Clump-clump-clump. He heard his pa come into the room. He held his breath. He felt his pa reach down and pull the sheet off him. He didn't wear no bottoms in the summer. His rear was like a bare tight knot. He screwed his eyes 'round and saw his pa standing tall in mudstained overalls beside the bed, with the cord to his razor strop doubled over his wrist and the strop hanging poised at his side. His pa had on his reformer's look, like he got on when he passed the dance hall over on Elm Street.

"Lem-u-well, I give you uh chance tuh tell the truth. What you do with yo' ma's missionary money?"

"I didn't take it, pa. I swear I didn', pa."

"Ummmmp!" his pa said.

Whack! The strap came down. Lemuel jumped off the bed and tried to crawl underneath it. His pa caught him by the arm. Whack! Whack! Whack! went the strap. The sound hurt Lemuel as much as the licks. "Owwwwwww-owwwwwwWWWW!" he began to bawl. All over the neighborhood folks knew that Lemuel was getting a beating. His buddies knew what for. The old folks didn't know yet but they'd know before the day was over.

"God doan lak thieves," his pa said, beating him across the back and legs.

Lemuel darted toward the door. His pa headed him off. He crawled between his pa's legs, getting whacked as he went through. He ran out into the kitchen. His ma was waiting for him with a switch. He tried to crawl underneath the table. His head got caught in the legs of a chair. His ma started working on his rear with the switch.

"MURDER!" he yelled at the top of his voice. "HELP! POLICE! Please, ma, I ain't never gonna steal nothin' else, ma. If you jes let me off this time, ma. I swear, ma."

"I'm gonna beat the truth into you," his ma said. "Gonna beat out the devil."

He pulled out from underneath the table and danced up and down on the floor, trying to dodge the licks aimed at his leg.

"He gone, ma! Oh, he gone!" he yelled, dancing up and down. "Dat ol' devil gone, ma! I done tuk Christ Jesus to my heart!"

Well, being as he done seen the light, she sighed and let him off. Her missionary money wasn't gone clean to waste nohow if it'd make him mend his stealin' ways. She guessed them heathens would just have to wait another year; as Isaiah always say, they done wanted this long 'n it ain't kilt 'em.

The way Lemuel's backsides stung and burned he figured them ol' heathens was better off than they knew 'bout.

JIM'S EXAMINATION

Resisting the temptation to cheat is always a wise course of action.
Students who cheat do not benefit from their studies, and they run the risk
of getting caught and suffering the consequences.

Jim was taking the engineering course in a large university, and the time
for final examination was approaching. He was anxious about it; in fact,
he seemed to be much more concerned about the examination than many
of his fellow students. He remarked to a friend that he was studying hard
that he might be ready when the test came.

"Aren't you wise to the fact, Jim," his friend asked, "that you can
buy a copy of the questions for five dollars—the very questions which
will be asked in the examination?"

"You don't mean that!" said Jim.

"Surely I mean it. Most of the students have bought the questions.
They don't have to worry now. Just study up the answers to the questions and you will be ready. Would you like to get a set, Jim?"

"How do they get the questions, and from whom?" inquired Jim.

"I can get you a set. It is a secret, and we don't want to let the news
out. But the janitor has been taking carbon paper from the waste baskets,
holding them up to a lookingglass and getting the examination questions. He is making some easy money, and the students have been
getting good grades without studying."

It was a shock to Jim, and he couldn't get the consent of his conscience to do such a thing. It was a temptation to him. But he fought a
battle in his heart, and won. Either he would pass the examination
honestly or he would fail in the attempt. He would not deceive.

So he told the lady where he roomed that he wanted to have two or
three days alone to study for examination, that he was going away and
would leave no address. He didn't want to be bothered. He would return
the morning of the examination.

Finding a place where he could study unmolested, he spent two days
in reviewing the work that would be covered on examination day. It was
a real struggle, for he knew many of the young men and women were
having a good time while he worked. They knew the questions which

would be asked, and had the answers ready. But he was happy in the struggle. He was being fair.

On examination morning he climbed the steps of the university building with a clear conscience and a light heart. He felt prepared. A number of the students, however, cast glances his way, which he knew very well did not come from any love in their hearts for him. And some of them said, "You're a fool, Jim, for being so particular. Why go to so much effort when you can get along without it? Why wear out your brain studying for examination? You are easy, Jim."

At just one minute before the examination was to begin, the door to the room was unlocked, and the teacher entered, papers in hand. He seemed to have an unusually serious look on his face. When all was quiet he said, "Students, we have made a rather startling discovery. The examination papers have been tampered with, and it has been made possible for any one who wished to do so to buy the examination questions for a small sum of money. This news came as a real shock to us. So it became necessary for a number of the faculty to sit up all night last night writing out new questions. But they are ready for you, and you may begin to write."

Faces paled, some reddened, others showed signs of real disappointment. There was tenseness in the air. The examination papers were passed out. Some made an attempt to write, but others got up and walked out. They knew there was no use trying, for they had not studied.

In Jim's heart there was a sense of real joy, a feeling of victory, a happiness that he had been man enough to be honest. He with a number of others wrote their examinations. And Jim passed with honors.

He resolved then and there that he would always be fair and honest.

—*From* Little Journeys into
Storyland—Stories That Will Live and Lift,
by Luis B. Reynolds and Charles L. Passock

THE YEARLING
AS TOLD BY WILLIAM BROWN LEE

Thousands of slaves went hungry. Today many people are convinced that the inhumane conditions of slavery created extraordinary circumstances, often pitting one's ability to survive against the virtues of being completely honest. In this lighthearted story, honesty was put on hold—until Judgment Day.

In the old days the only things the slaves got good to eat is what they stole. Old Marster lost a yea'ling, and some of the preacher's members knowed its whereabouts. So Old Marster told him to preach the hell out of the congregation that Sunday, so that whosomever stole the yea'ling would confess having it.

The preacher got up and pernounced to the crowd: "Some of you have stole Old Marster's yea'ling. So the best thing to do is to go to Old Marster and confess that you stole the yea'ling. And get it off right now. Because if you don't, Judgment Day, the man that stole the Marster's yea'ling will be there. Old Marster will be there too, the yea'ling will be there too—the yea'ling will be *staring* you in the face."

John gets up and says to the preacher, "Mr. Preacher, I understand you to say, Judgment Day, the man that stole Old Marster's yea'ling will be there, Old Marster will be there, the yea'ling will be there, yea'ling will be *staring* you in the face."

Preacher says, "That's right."

John replied then, "Let Old Marster git his yea'ling on Judgment Day—that'll be time enough."

OF TWO MINDS

In his book Lovesong, *Julius Lester wrote:*

"When I describe life in the South before The Movement, globules of pain like phlegm come to my throat and tears flare in my eyes, and I am aware of a massive trauma of anger and terror within me. This is not the melodrama of rhetoric; it is the consequence of surviving in a land where terror was as omnipresent as sunlight and starshine.

"You do not make friends with terror. You can defy it, challenge it. There was a black photographer in The Movement who rode all over Mississippi on his motorcycle the summer of 1964, his blond girlfriend behind him, her arms tightly around his waist. One day some white men beat him almost to death, and he left Mississippi. You can laugh and joke with terror, a time-honored technique that Southern blacks refined into an art form. Or you can try to reach an agreement with it, as in the famous blues line: 'Got one mind for the captain to see, got another mind for what I know is me.' That is most dangerous of all, because it is a statement of functional schizophrenia, of the psyche divided against itself. Ultimately, you become your own victim and never know it."

One may argue the point today. However, so-called "schizophrenia" enabled many a slave to survive the everyday terror and danger of slavery. Frederick Douglass tells why slaves kept their true thoughts to themselves.

FREDERICK DOUGLASS

To describe the wealth of Colonel Lloyd would be almost equal to describing the riches of Job. He kept from ten to fifteen house-servants. He was said to own a thousand slaves, and I think this estimate quite within the truth. Colonel Lloyd owned so many that he did not know them when he saw them; nor did all the slaves of the out-farms know him. It is reported of him, that, while riding along the road one day, he met a colored man, and addressed him in the usual manner of speaking to colored people on the public highways of the south: "Well, boy, whom do you belong to?" "To Colonel Lloyd," replied the slave. "Well, does the colonel treat you well?" "No, sir," was the ready reply. "What, does he work you too hard?" "Yes, sir." "Well, don't he give you enough to eat?" "Yes, sir, he gives me enough, such as it is."

The colonel, after ascertaining where the slave belonged, rode on; the man also went on about his business, not dreaming that he had been conversing with his master. He thought, said, and heard nothing more of the matter, until two or three weeks afterwards. The poor man was then informed by his overseer that, for having found fault with his master, he was now to be sold to a Georgia trader. He was immediately chained and handcuffed; and thus, without a moment's warning, he was snatched away, and forever sundered, from his family and friends, by a hand more unrelenting than death. This is the penalty of telling the truth, of telling the simple truth, in answer to a series of plain questions.

It is partly in consequence of such facts, that slaves, when inquired of as to their condition and the character of their masters, almost universally say they are contented, and that their masters are kind. The slaveholders have been known to send in spies among their slaves, to ascertain their views and feelings in regard to their condition. The frequency of this has had the effect to establish among the slaves the maxim, that a still tongue makes a wise head. They suppress the truth rather than take the consequences of telling it, and in so doing prove themselves a part of the human family. If they have any thing to say of their masters, it is generally in their masters' favor, especially when speaking to an untried man. I have been frequently asked, when a slave, if I had a kind master, and do not remember ever to have given a negative answer; nor did I, in pursuing this course, consider myself as uttering what was absolutely false; for I always measured the kindness of my master by the standard of kindness set up among slaveholders around us.

WILLIAM LOREN KATZ

Further survival lessons are offered in the following passage from another text on slavery.

Masters liked to think of themselves as kindly ladies and gentlemen converting childlike, ignorant heathens into civilized, Christian workers. "We never thought of them as slaves; they were 'ours,' our own dear black folks," said a Florida woman.

"They joyed with us and sorrowed with us; they wept when we wept, and laughed when we laughed. Often our best friends, they were rarely our worst enemies," recalled a Richmond woman.

Slaves had little choice but to follow their owners' demands and to live with their insulting attitudes. Once out of master's reach, however, slaves showed they had not been fooled. Jarmain Loguen fled bondage, wrote a book, became a noted New York minister and leading abolitionist voice. One day his old mistress wrote and angrily asked him for $1,000 for running away. She argued, "We raised you as we did our own children." The Reverend Mr. Loguen replied, "Woman, did you raise your own children for the market? Did you raise them for the whipping post? . . . Shame on you."

Despite planters' efforts at mind control, African Americans were guided by their own sense of dignity, morality, and community. William Craft's old master had a reputation of being a devout Christian, "but he thought nothing of selling my poor old father, and dear aged mother, at separate times, to different persons, to be dragged off never to behold each other again," wrote Craft. He "also sold a dear brother and sister, in the same manner as he did my father and mother. The reason . . . 'they were getting old, and would soon become valueless in the market.' "

For the African-American community the breakup of families through sale or auction was one of the worst threats of slave life. Josiah Henson was about six when an auction divided his family. His mother, older brothers, and sisters were sold first. "Then I was offered to the assembled purchasers. My mother, half distracted with the thought of parting forever from all her children, pushed through the crowd, while the bidding for me was going on, to the spot where Riley [her owner] was standing. She fell at his feet and clung to his knees, entreating him in tones that a mother can only command, to buy her baby as well as herself, and spare to her one, at least, of her little ones." Riley kicked and struck at her until she had to crawl away.

Once he escaped, Henson wrote a book of his experiences, helped other slaves escape, and became the model that novelist Harriet Beecher Stowe used for her lead character in *Uncle Tom's Cabin*.

"Slaves are taught ignorance as we teach our children knowledge," recalled Leonard Black. They were not told their ages, and those near water were not allowed to learn to swim. They were told free states were ten thousand miles away, and that whites who called themselves abolitionists would eat them.

James W. C. Pennington received a doctorate degree from Heidelberg University in Germany, and in 1841 he wrote the first textbook history of African Americans. But as a slave until he was twenty-one, "I was as profoundly ignorant as a child of five years old."

Finding that intelligence, knowledge, and talents might arouse suspicion or jealousy, slaves often played dumb. Lunsford Lane ran a profitable tobacco business, owned property, saved money, and "I never appeared to be so intelligent as I was." Blacks pretended to be meek, happy, and dumb. They learned to answer a master's questions with the words he wanted to hear. To fool whites, recalled Betty Jones of Virginia, people said, "Going to see Jenny tonight," which meant there was going to be a dance.

Henry Bibb concluded that "the only weapon of self-defense I could use successfully was that of deception." African Americans developed deception to a high art. "Got one mind for the boss to see, got another for what I know is me," went a slave song. A worker who laughed with his master in the afternoon might plan to escape that evening.

Laborers became too ignorant to do a decent day's work and too dense to understand or remember orders. "Under the cloak of great stupidity," said a Virginia planter, slaves made "dupes" of whites. Masters and overseers did not know when their hands were ill or just shamming, really physically disabled or just putting on a limp, a bent back, blindness, pregnancy.

In the evening among loved ones, souls were soothed with humor and faith to try to restore hope. People dreamed of, sang songs about, and prayed to God for deliverance. Solomon Northup, captured as a free man living in the North and held in bondage for twelve years, played his violin softly at midnight. "Had it not been for my beloved violin, I scarcely can conceive how I could have endured the long years of bondage." His autobiography tells the story of his kidnapping and his final escape.

Around quiet campfires or in the privacy of their huts, the slave community gathered to swap tales of turtles that outdistanced hares, of little Davids who slew huge Goliaths, and of tiny animals that tricked lions and bears who wanted to eat them. People nourished morale with jokes about refusing to be buried near their masters because the devil might take the wrong body.

❧

Soul is honesty.

—*Aretha Franklin*

❧

SELF-ESTEEM

Since the first black person set foot in America, African Americans have been waging a fierce battle not only for human rights or civil rights, but for thinking rights, too—for control over self-perception. To be truly free, blacks have had to plant the flag of dignity in their own minds. The task was often difficult.

Over the years, the collective psyche of African Americans has been battered and debased. Blacks have been told their skin color was "wrong," their hair texture was "bad," and that the "correct" image of God was certainly not "black like us," but white. It came as no great surprise, then, when studies in the 1940s found that little black girls chose to play with white dolls instead of black ones.

It's all a matter of self-esteem, which can be defined as an easy assurance that stems from an inner source of pride, self-respect, and self-satisfaction. Self-esteem blossoms or wilts with confidence in your ability to carry out your own plans, or fulfill an intention. Even though self-esteem radiates from within, it does not develop out of thin air. Society can play a critical role in affirming or threatening our self-value and self-esteem. In America—where slavery once drove an entire economic sector and racial discrimination was upheld with legal sanctions—society's effects on self-esteem have been devastating for many blacks: diminished confidence, low-sighted goals that sometimes seem hardly worth pursuing, and a distorted sense of self that is handed down from generation to generation.

Still, despite past setbacks or tragedies, black self-esteem often shines through triumphantly.

In this chapter, Langston Hughes remembers ancient dusky rivers where his "soul has grown deep"; America's first black Rhodes Scholar, Alain Locke, introduces the assertive and racially proud "New Negro"; Zora Neale Hurston revels in being—and acting—"colored"; and Dick Gregory questions the belief that blacks are of "inferior stock."

"The American mind must reckon with a fundamentally changed

Negro," Locke insisted. That, of course, involves smashing idols of the past and developing a healthy regard for oneself. These pieces, and others included here, help do exactly that—by challenging racist assumptions, celebrating self-definition and personal integrity, and offering lessons for heightening self-esteem.

∾

Who can be born black and not exult!

—*Mari Evans*

∾

THE PERFECT DOLL

Dolls are rarely meaningless playthings. Children imbue them with personalities. As such, black dolls can reflect pride or shame in one's race, depending on how dolls are presented and how children feel about black features.

In 1987, Darlene Powell Hopson, a clinical psychologist, conducted a study of children's perceptions of dolls. She replicated the landmark study conducted in the 1940s by black therapists that was used to argue the Brown v. Board of Education *desegregation case. As in the 1940s, Dr. Powell Hopson found that children overwhelmingly favored white dolls over black ones when asked to choose which was "good" or "right."*

However, children responded differently with intervention. When black dolls were cast in a positive light as beautiful and heroic beforehand, the children, both black and white, selected them over white dolls.

In the past, American doll manufacturers went to little trouble to make sales in the black community. One collector pointed out that "Many American doll manufacturers would not take the extra effort to make black dolls with Negroid features but were content to paint white dolls brown or black."

There were exceptions to this rule. The Crisis *magazine carried advertisements for dolls that were race-specific.*

NEGRO DOLLS FOR SALE

GIVE THE CHILD A DOLL
THE MOST BEAUTIFUL OF ALL THE TOYS
ON THE MARKET ARE THE
NEGRO DOLLS

Your child would be happy if it had a Negro doll such as are sent out by the National Negro Doll Company, Nashville, Tennessee. Every race is trying to teach their children an object lesson by giving them toys that will lead to higher intellectual heights. The Negro doll is calculated to help in the Christian development of our race. All dolls are sent by express, charges paid.

DOLLS FOR THE SEASON 1911–1912 NOW READY

Prices from 50¢. Up to $8.50

National Negro Doll Company

519 Second Avenue N., Nashville, Tenn.

—*Advertisement in* The Crisis, *July 1911*

COLORED DOLLS FOR YOUR CHILDREN

Teach your children pride of race and appreciation of race. Early impressions are lasting. These beautifully dressed, unbreakable, brown skin dolls designed and made by colored girls in a factory owned and controlled entirely by colored people. These are not the old time, black face, red lip aunt Jemima colored dolls but dolls well made and truly representative of the race in hair and features.

16 inches with long flowing curls, beautifully dressed $3.50
16 inches with carcel wave, nicely dressed 3.00

16 inches Buster Brown style hair,
very neat 2.50
Soldier boy in full uniform 1.50

So far as we know this is the only
Negro doll factory in the world.

BERRY & ROSS, Inc.
Factory: 36-38 W. 135th St.
NEW YORK CITY

—*Advertisement in* The Crisis, *February 1919*

Say it loud: I'm black and I'm proud!

—*James Brown*

THE NEW NEGRO
ALAIN LOCKE

As mentor of much of Harlem's burgeoning creativity during the 1920s, Alain Locke (1886–1954) encouraged a generation of black writers, poets, and artists. In 1925, he published an anthology in which he announced the death of the apologetic "Old Negro" and the arrival of the "New Negro," who is assertive, racially proud, culturally aware, and open to interracial relations. The New Negro, *which contained poetry, short fiction, articles, essays, commentary, and artwork, became a manifesto of the movement popularly known today as the Harlem Renaissance. Here is an excerpt from Locke's title essay.*

In the last decade something beyond the watch and guard of statistics has happened in the life of the American Negro and the three norns* who

* The three Fates in Norse mythology.

have traditionally presided over the Negro problem have a changeling in their laps. The Sociologist, the Philanthropist, the Race-leader are not unaware of the New Negro, but they are at a loss to account for him. He simply cannot be swathed in their formulae. For the younger generation is vibrant with a new psychology; the new spirit is awake in the masses, and under the very eyes of the professional observers is transforming what has been a perennial problem into the progressive phases of contemporary Negro life.

Could such a metamorphosis have taken place as suddenly as it has appeared to? The answer is no; not because the New Negro is not here, but because the Old Negro had long become more of a myth than a man. The Old Negro, we must remember, was a creature of moral debate and historical controversy. His has been a stock figure perpetuated as an historical fiction partly in innocent sentimentalism, partly in deliberate reactionism. The Negro himself has contributed his share to this through a sort of protective social mimicry forced upon him by the adverse circumstances of dependence. So for generations in the mind of America, the Negro has been more of a formula than a human being—a something to be argued about, condemned or defended, to be "kept down," or "in his place," or "helped up," to be worried with or worried over, harassed or patronized, a social bogey or a social burden. The thinking Negro even has been induced to share this same general attitude, to focus his attention on controversial issues, to see himself in the distorted perspective of a social problem. His shadow, so to speak, has been more real to him than his personality. through having had to appeal from the unjust stereotypes of his oppressors and traducers to those of his liberators, friends and benefactors he has had to subscribe to the traditional positions from which his case has been viewed. Little true social or self-understanding has or could come from such a situation.

But while the minds of most of us, black and white, have thus burrowed in the trenches of the Civil War and Reconstruction, the actual march of development has simply flanked these positions, necessitating a sudden reorientation of view. We have not been watching in the right direction; set North and South on a sectional axis, we have not noticed the East till the sun has us blinking. . . .

The mind of the Negro seems suddenly to have slipped from under the tyranny of social intimidation and to be shaking off the psychology of imitation and implied inferiority. By shedding the old chrysalis of the Negro problem we are achieving something like a spiritual emancipation. Until recently, lacking self-understanding, we have been almost as much of a problem to ourselves as we still are to others. But the decade that found us with a problem has left us with only a task. The multitude perhaps feels as yet only a strange relief and a new vague urge, but the thinking few know that in the reaction the vital inner grip of prejudice has been broken.

With this renewed self-respect and self-dependence, the life of the Negro community is bound to enter a new dynamic phase, the buoyancy from within compensating for whatever pressure there may be of conditions from without. The migrant masses, shifting from countryside to city, hurdle several generations of experience at a leap, but more important, the same thing happens spiritually in the life-attitudes and self-expression of the Young Negro, in his poetry, his art, his education and his new outlook, with the additional advantage, of course, of the poise and greater certainty of knowing what it is all about. From this comes the promise and warrant of a new leadership. As one of them has discerningly put it:

We have tomorrow
Bright before us
Like a flame.

Yesterday, a night-gone thing
A sun-down name.

And Dawn today
Broad arch above the road we came.
We march!

This is what, even more than any "most creditable record of fifty years of freedom," requires that the Negro of to-day be seen through other than the dusty spectacles of past controversy. The day of "aunties," "uncles" and "mammies" is equally gone. Uncle Tom and Sambo have passed on, and even the "Colonel" and "George" play barnstorm roles from which they escape with relief when the public spotlight is off.

The popular melodrama has about played itself out, and it is time to scrap the fictions, garret the bogeys and settle down to a realistic facing of facts. . . .

The American mind must reckon with a fundamentally changed Negro. . . .

The Negro too, for his part, has idols of the tribe to smash. If on the one hand the white man has erred in making the Negro appear to be that which would excuse or extenuate his treatment of him, the Negro, in turn, has too often unnecessarily excused himself because of the way he has been treated. The intelligent Negro of to-day is resolved not to make discrimination an extenuation for his shortcomings in performance, individual or collective; he is trying to hold himself at par, neither inflated by sentimental allowances nor depreciated by current social discounts. For this he must know himself and be known for precisely what he is, and for that reason he welcomes the new scientific rather than the old sentimental interest. Sentimental interest in the Negro has ebbed. We used to lament this as the falling off of our friends; now we rejoice and pray to be delivered both from self-pity and condescension. The mind of each racial group has had a bitter weaning, apathy or hatred on one side matching disillusionment or resentment on the other; but they face each other to-day with the possibility at least of entirely new mutual attitudes. . . .

The Negro to-day is inevitably moving forward under the control largely of his own objectives. What are these objectives? Those of his outer life are happily already well and finally formulated, for they are none other than the ideals of American institutions and democracy. Those of his inner life are yet in process of formation, for the new psychology at present is more of a consensus of feeling than of opinion, of attitude rather than of program. Still some points seem to have crystallized.

Up to the present one may adequately describe the Negro's "inner objectives" as an attempt to repair a damaged group psychology and reshape a warped social perspective. Their realization has required a new mentality for the American Negro. And as it matures we begin to see its effects; at first, negative, iconoclastic, and then positive and constructive. In this new group psychology we note the lapse of sentimental appeal, then the development of a more positive self-respect and self-reliance;

the repudiation of social dependence, and then the gradual recovery from hyper-sensitiveness and "touchy" nerves, the repudiation of the double standard of judgment with its special philanthropic allowances and then the sturdier desire for objective and scientific appraisal; and finally the rise from social disillusionment to race pride, from the sense of social debt to the responsibilities of social contribution, and offsetting the necessary working and commonsense acceptance of restricted conditions, the belief in ultimate esteem and recognition. Therefore the Negro to-day wishes to be known for what he is, even in his faults and short-comings, and scorns a craven and precarious survival at the price of seeming to be what he is not. He resents being spoken of as a social ward or minor, even by his own, and to being regarded a chronic patient for the sociological clinic, the sick man of American Democracy. For the same reasons, he himself is through with those social nostrums and panaceas, the so-called "solutions" of his "problem," with which he and the country have been so liberally dosed in the past. Religion, freedom, education, money—in turn, he has ardently hoped for and peculiarly trusted these things; he still believes in them, but not in blind trust that they alone will solve his life-problem.

Each generation, however, will have its creed, and that of the present is the belief in the efficacy of collective effort, in race co-operation. This deep feeling of race is at present the mainspring of Negro life. It seems to be the outcome of the reaction to proscription and prejudice; an attempt, fairly successful on the whole, to convert a defensive into an offensive position, a handicap into an incentive. It is radical in tone, but not in purpose and only the most stupid forms of opposition, misunderstanding or persecution could make it otherwise. Of course, the thinking Negro has shifted a little toward the left with the world-trend, and there is an increasing group who affiliate with radical and liberal movements. But fundamentally for the present the Negro is radical on race matters, conservative on others, in other words, a "forced radical," a social protestant rather than a genuine radical. Yet under further pressure and injustice iconoclastic thought and motives will inevitably increase. Harlem's quixotic radicalisms call for the ounce of democracy to-day lest to-morrow they be beyond cure.

The Negro mind reaches out as yet to nothing but American wants, American ideas. But this forced attempt to build his Americanism on race values is a unique social experiment, and its ultimate success is impossible except through the fullest sharing of American culture and institutions. There should be no delusion about this. American nerves in sections unstrung with race hysteria are often fed the opiate that the trend of Negro advance is wholly separatist, and that the effect of its operation will be to encyst the Negro as a benign foreign body in the body politic. This cannot be—even if it were desirable. The racialism of the Negro is no limitation or reservation with respect to American life; it is only a constructive effort to build the obstructions in the stream of his progress into an efficient dam of social energy and power. Democracy itself is obstructed and stagnated to the extent that any of its channels are closed. Indeed they cannot be selectively closed. So the choice is not between one way for the Negro and another way for the rest, but between American institutions frustrated on the one hand and American ideals progressively fulfilled and realized on the other.

There is, of course, a warrantably comfortable feeling in being on the right side of the country's professed ideals. We realize that we cannot be undone without America's undoing. It is within the gamut of this attitude that the thinking Negro faces America, but with variations of mood that are if anything more significant than the attitude itself. Sometimes we have it taken with the defiant ironic challenge of [Claude] McKay:

> Mine is the future grinding down to-day
> Like a great landslip moving to the sea.
> Bearing its freight of debris far away
> Where the green hungry waters restlessly
> Heave mammoth pyramids, and break and roar
> Their eerie challenge to the crumbling shore.

Sometimes, perhaps more frequently as yet, it is taken in the fervent and almost filial appeal and counsel of [James] Weldon Johnson's:

> O Southland, dear Southland!
> Then why do you still cling
> To an idle age and a musty page,
> To a dead and useless thing?

But between defiance and appeal, midway almost between cynicism and hope, the prevailing mind stands in the mood of the same author's *To America*, an attitude of sober query and stoical challenge:

How would you have us, as we are?
    Or sinking 'neath the load we bear,
Our eyes fixed forward on a star,
    Or gazing empty at despair?

Rising or falling? Men or things?
    With dragging pace or footsteps fleet?
Strong, willing sinews in your wings,
    Or tightening chains about your feet?

More and more, however, an intelligent realization of the great discrepancy between the American social creed and the American social practice forces upon the Negro the taking of the moral advantage that is his. Only the steadying and sobering effect of a truly characteristic gentleness of spirit prevents the rapid rise of a definite cynicism and counter-hate and a defiant superiority feeling. Human as this reaction would be, the majority still deprecate its advent, and would gladly see it forestalled by the speedy amelioration of its causes. We wish our race pride to be a healthier, more positive achievement than a feeling based upon a realization of the shortcomings of others. But all paths toward the attainment of a sound social attitude have been difficult; only a relatively few enlightened minds have been able as the phrase puts it "to rise above" prejudice. The ordinary man has had until recently only a hard choice between the alternatives of supine and humiliating submission and stimulating but hurtful counter-prejudice. Fortunately from some inner, desperate resourcefulness has recently sprung up the simple expedient of fighting prejudice by mental passive resistance, in other words by trying to ignore it. For the few, this manna may perhaps be effective, but the masses cannot thrive upon it.

Fortunately there are constructive channels opening out into which the balked social feelings of the American Negro can flow freely.

Without them there would be much more pressure and danger than there is. These compensating interests are racial but in a new and enlarged way. One is the consciousness of acting as the advance-guard of the African peoples in their contact with Twentieth Century civilization; the other, the sense of a mission of rehabilitating the race in world esteem from that loss of prestige for which the fate and conditions of slavery have so largely been responsible. Harlem, as we shall see, is the center of both these movements; she is the home of the Negro's "Zionism." The pulse of the Negro world has begun to beat in Harlem. A Negro newspaper carrying news material in English, French and Spanish, gathered from all quarters of America, the West Indies and Africa has maintained itself in Harlem for over five years. Two important magazines, both edited from New York, maintain their news and circulation consistently on a cosmopolitan scale. Under American auspices and backing, three pan-African congresses have been held abroad for the discussion of common interests, colonial questions and the future cooperative development of Africa. In terms of the race question as a world problem, the Negro mind has leapt, so to speak, upon the parapets of prejudice and extended its cramped horizons. In so doing it has linked up with the growing group consciousness of the dark-peoples and is gradually learning their common interests. As one of our writers has recently put it: "It is imperative that we understand the white world in its relations to the non-white world." As with the Jew, persecution is making the Negro international.

As a world phenomenon this wider race consciousness is a different thing from the much asserted rising tide of color. Its inevitable causes are not of our making. The consequences are not necessarily damaging to the best interests of civilization. Whether it actually brings into being new Armadas of conflict or argosies of cultural exchange and enlightenment can only be decided by the attitude of the dominant races in an era of critical change. With the American Negro, his new internationalism is primarily an effort to recapture contact with the scattered peoples of African derivation. Garveyism may be a transient, if spectacular, phenomenon, but the possible role of the American Negro in the future development of Africa is one of the most constructive and universally helpful missions that any modern people can lay claim to.

Constructive participation in such causes cannot help giving the Negro valuable group incentives, as well as increased prestige at home and abroad. Our greatest rehabilitation may possibly come through such channels, but for the present, more immediate hope rests in the revaluation by white and black alike of the Negro in terms of his artistic endowments and cultural contributions, past and prospective. It must be increasingly recognized that the Negro has already made very substantial contributions, not only in his folk-art, music especially, which has always found appreciation, but in larger, though humbler and less acknowledged ways. For generations the Negro has been the peasant matrix of that section of America which has most undervalued him, and here he has contributed not only materially in labor and in social patience, but spiritually as well. The South has unconsciously absorbed the gift of his folk-temperament. In less than half a generation it will be easier to recognize this, but the fact remains that a leaven of humor, sentiment, imagination and tropic nonchalance has gone into the making of the South from a humble, unacknowledged source. A second crop of the Negro's gifts promises still more largely. He now becomes a conscious contributor and lays aside the status of a beneficiary and ward for that of a collaborator and participant in American civilization. The great social gain in this is the releasing of our talented group from the arid fields of controversy and debate to the productive fields of creative expression. The especially cultural recognition they win should in turn prove the key to that revaluation of the Negro which must precede or accompany any considerable further betterment of race relationships. But whatever the general effect, the present generation will have added the motives of self-expression and spiritual development to the old and still unfinished task of making material headway and progress. No one who understandingly faces the situation with its substantial accomplishment or views the new scene with its still more abundant promise can be entirely without hope. And certainly, if in our lifetime the Negro should not be able to celebrate his full initiation into American democracy, he can at least, on the warrant of these things, celebrate the attainment of a significant and satisfying new phase of group development, and with it a spiritual Coming of Age.

NOCTURNE VARIAL
LEWIS ALEXANDER

The stars shine most brightly in a velvety black sky. Likewise, some highly esteemed souls reveal their warmth and brilliance only amid darkness.

I came as a shadow,
I stand now a light;
The depth of my darkness
Transfigures your night.

My soul is a nocturne
Each note is a star;
The light will not blind you
So look where you are.

The radiance is soothing.
There's warmth in the light.
I came as a shadow,
To dazzle your night!

A PRAYER ON SELF-WORTH
JESSE L. JACKSON

The indefatigable Jesse L. Jackson (b. 1941) was active in the civil rights movement, founded a social justice organization (the National Rainbow Coalition), ran for the U.S. presidency in 1984 and 1988, and won election as Washington, D.C.'s "shadow senator" (with no voting rights) in 1990. Here is his best-known prayer.

I am somebody.
I may be poor,

                    but I am somebody.

I may be uneducated,
I may be unskilled

                    but I am somebody.

I may be on welfare,
I may be prematurely pregnant,
I may be on drugs,
I may be victimized by racism,

                    but I am somebody.
Respect me. Protect me. Never neglect me.
I am God's child.

Definitions belong to the definer—not the defined.

—*Toni Morrison*

GAINING SELF CONTROL THROUGH SELF-DEFINITION
HAKI R. MADHUBUTI

We are not a tribe,
we are a nation.
We are not wandering groups,
we are people.
We are not without land,
there is Africa.
If we let others define us,
our existence,
our definition will be dependent upon
the eyes, ears and minds of others.

Other people's definitions of us cannot be accurate for us
because their hurt is not our hurt,
their laughter is not our laughter,
their view of the world is not our view of the world.
Others' definition of the world
is necessary for their survival and control of the world
and for us to adopt their view of the world is a necessary
step toward their continued control over us.
Therefore, to let others define us is to assure
we will be a tribe,
we will be wandering groups,
we will be landless.
Self-definition is the first step toward self-control.

THAT WORD *BLACK*
LANGSTON HUGHES

Langston Hughes (1902–67) created Simple, *or* Jesse B. Semple, *in 1943, when the comic character first appeared in the* Chicago Defender, *a black-owned newspaper. Based on one of Hughes's acquaintances,* Simple *was a barstool philosopher who lived in Harlem. Readers followed his exploits in syndicated columns in black newspapers and, eventually, in the white-owned* New York Post. *In this story, Simple makes himself feel better by revising the definition of the word* black.

"This evening," said Simple, "I feel like talking about the word *black*."

"Nobody's stopping you, so go ahead. But what you really ought to have is a soap-box out on the corner of 126th and Lenox where the rest of the orators hang out."

"They expresses some good ideas on that corner," said Simple, "but for my ideas I do not need a crowd. Now, as I were saying, the word *black*, white folks have done used that word to mean something bad so often until now when the N.A.A.C.P. asks for civil rights for the black man, they think they must be bad. Looking back into history, I reckon it all started with a *black* cat meaning bad luck. Don't let one cross your path!

"Next, somebody got up a *blacklist* on which you get if you don't vote right. Then when lodges come into being, the folks they didn't want in them got *blackballed*. If you kept a skeleton in your closet, you might get *blackmailed*. And everything bad was *black*. When it came down to the unlucky ball on the pool table, the eight-rock, they made it the *black* ball. So no wonder there ain't no equal rights for the *black* man."

"All you say is true about the odium attached to the word *black*," I said. "You've even forgotten a few. For example, during the war if you bought something under the table, illegally, they said you were trading on the *black* market. In Chicago, if you're a gangster, the *Black Hand Society* may take you for a ride. And certainly if you don't behave yourself, your family will say you're a *black* sheep. Then, if your mama burns a *black* candle to change the family luck, they call it *black magic*."

"My mama never did believe in voodoo, so she did not burn no black candles," said Simple.

"If she had, that would have been a *black* mark against her."

"Stop talking about my mama. What I want to know is, where do white folks get off calling everything bad *black?* If it is a dark night, they say it's *black* as hell. If you are mean and evil, they say you got a *black* heart. I would like to change all that around and say that the people who Jim Crow me have got a *white* heart. People who sell dope to children have got a *white* mark against them. And all the white gamblers who were behind the basketball fix are the *white* sheep of the sports world. God knows there was few, if any, Negroes selling stuff on the black market during the war, so why didn't they call it the *white* market? No, they got to take me and my color and turn it into everything *bad*. According to white folks, black is bad.

"Wait till my day comes! In my language, bad will be *white*. Black-mail will be *white*mail. Black cats will be good luck, and *white* cats will be bad. If a white cat crosses your path, look out! I will take the black ball for the cue ball and let the *white* ball be the unlucky eight-rock. And on my blacklist—which will be a *white*list then—I will put everybody who ever Jim Crowed me from Rankin to Hitler, Talmadge to Malan, South Carolina to South Africa.

"I am black. When I look in the mirror, I see myself, daddy-o, but I am not ashamed. God made me. He also made F.D., dark as he is. He did not make us no badder than the rest of the folks. The earth is black and all kinds of good things comes out of the earth. Everything that grows comes up out of the earth. Trees and flowers and fruit and sweet potatoes and corn and all that keeps mens alive comes right up out of the earth—good old black earth. Coal is black and it warms your house and cooks your food. The night is black, which has a moon, and a million stars, and is beautiful. Sleep is black, which gives you rest, so you wake up feeling good. I am black. I feel very good this evening.

"What is wrong with black?"

The blacker the berry, the sweeter the juice.

—*Folk saying*

THE NEGRO SPEAKS OF RIVERS
LANGSTON HUGHES

The summer after he graduated from high school, Langston Hughes traveled by train from Cleveland to Mexico. At sunset, while the muddy Mississippi River rolled by outside the Pullman car window, Hughes thought about blacks' historical links to rivers. Within "10 or 15 minutes" he scribbled this poem on the back of an envelope. The poem was published in 1921, when Hughes was nineteen. Eventually, he was called "the poet laureate of the Negro race."

I've known rivers:
I've known rivers ancient as the world and older than the
      flow of human blood in human veins.

My soul has grown deep like the rivers.

I bathed in the Euphrates when dawns were young.
I built my hut near the Congo and it lulled me to sleep.

I looked upon the Nile and raised the pyramids above it.
I heard the singing of the Mississippi when Abe Lincoln
      went down to New Orleans, and I've seen its muddy
      bosom turn all golden in the sunset.

I've known rivers:
Ancient, dusky rivers.

My soul has grown deep like the rivers.

NEGRITUDE
JAMES A. EMANUEL

In this poem, James A. Emanuel (b. 1921) gives new meaning to the word black.

    Black is the first nail I ever stepped on;
    Black the hand that dried my tears.
    Black is the first old man I ever noticed;
    Black the burden of his years.

    Black is waiting in the darkness;
    Black the ground where hoods have lain.
    Black is the sorrow misted story;
    Black the brotherhood of pain.

    Black is a quiet iron door;
    Black the path that leads behind.
    Black is a detour through the years;
    Black the diary of the mind.

Black is Gabriel Prosser's knuckles;
Black Sojourner's naked breast.
Black is a schoolgirl's breathless mother;
Black her child who led the rest.

Black is the purring of a motor;
Black the foot when the light turns green.
Black is last year's dusty paper;
Black the headlines yet unseen.

Black is a burden bravely chanted;
Black cross of sweat for a nation's rise.
Black is a boy who knows his heroes;
Black the way a hero dies.

∾

Nobody will think you're somebody if you don't think so yourself.
—*Traditional*

NURTURING THE BELIEVING SELF
SHELBY STEELE

Shelby Steele outlines a strategy for conquering self-doubt and strug-
gling against assumptions of one's own inferiority.

As children we are all wounded in some way and to some degree by the
wild world we encounter. From these wounds a disbelieving *anti-self* is
born, an internal antagonist and saboteur that embraces the world's
negative view of us, that believes our wounds are justified by our own
unworthiness, and that entrenches itself as a lifelong voice of doubt. This
anti-self is a hidden aggressive force that scours the world for fresh
evidence of our unworthiness. When the believing self announces its
aspirations, the anti-self always argues against them, but never on their
merits (this is a healthy function of the believing self). It argues instead

against our worthiness to pursue these aspirations and, by its lights, we are never worthy of even our smallest dreams. The mission of the anti-self is to deflate the believing self and, thus, draw it down into inertia, passivity, and faithlessness.

The anti-self is the unseen agent of low self-esteem; it is a catalytic energy that tries to induce low self-esteem in the believing self as though it were the complete truth of the personality. The anti-self can only be contained by the strength of the believing self, and this is where one's early environment becomes crucial. If the childhood environment is stable and positive, the family whole and loving, the schools good, the community safe, then the believing self will be reinforced and made strong. If the family is shattered, the schools indifferent, the neighborhood a mine field of dangers, the anti-self will find evidence everywhere with which to deflate the believing self.

This does not mean that a bad childhood cannot be overcome. But it does mean—as I have experienced and observed—that one's *capacity* for self-doubt and self-belief are roughly the same from childhood on, so that years later when the believing self may have strengthened enough to control the anti-self, one will still have the same capacity for doubt whether or not one has the *actual* doubt. I think it is this struggle between our capacities for doubt and belief that gives our personalities one of their peculiar tensions and, in this way, marks our character. . . .

I think black Americans are today more oppressed by doubt than by racism and that the second phase of our struggle for freedom must be a confrontation with that doubt. Unexamined, this doubt leads us back into the tunnel of our oppression where we reenact our victimization just as society struggles to end its victimization of us. We are not a people formed in freedom. Freedom is always a call to possibility that demands an overcoming of doubt. We are still new to freedom, new to its challenges, new even to the notion that self-doubt can be the slyest enemy of freedom. For us freedom has so long meant the absence of oppression that we have not yet realized it also means the conquering of doubt.

Of course, this does not mean that doubt should become a lake we swim in, but it does mean that we should begin our campaign against doubt by acknowledging it, by outlining the contours of the black anti-self so that we can know and accept exactly what it is that we are afraid of. This is knowledge that can be worked with, knowledge that can point with great precision to the actions through which we can best mitigate doubt and advance ourselves. This is the sort of knowledge that gives the believing self a degree of immunity against the anti-self and that enables it to pile up little victories that, in sum, grant even more immunity.

Certainly inferiority has long been the main theme of the black anti-self, its most lethal weapon against our capacity for self-belief. And so, in a general way, the acceptance of this piece of knowledge implies a mission: to show *ourselves* and (only indirectly) the larger society that we are not inferior in any dimension. That this should already be assumed goes without saying. But what "should be" falls within the province of the believing self, where it has no solidity until the doubt of the anti-self is called out and shown false by demonstrable action in the real world. This is the proof that grants the "should" its rightful solidity, that transforms it from a well-intentioned claim into a certainty.

The temptation is to avoid so severe a challenge, to maintain a black identity, painted in the colors of pride and culture, that provides us with a way of seeing ourselves apart from this challenge. It is easier to be "African-American" than to organize oneself on one's own terms and around one's own aspirations and then, through sustained effort and difficult achievement, put one's insidious anti-self quietly to rest. No black identity, however beautifully conjured, will spare blacks this challenge that, despite its fairness or unfairness, is simply in the nature of things. But then I have faith that in time we will meet this challenge since this, too, is in the nature of things.

HOW IT FEELS TO BE COLORED ME
ZORA NEALE HURSTON

Novelist, folklorist, and anthropologist Zora Neale Hurston (1891–1960), whose mother encouraged her early on to "jump at de sun," is now recognized as one of the most important black writers of the twentieth century. Imbued with what writer Alice Walker later called "racial health," Hurston wrote the following autobiographical essay in 1928. In it, she celebrates her cultural and instinctual differences.

I am colored but I offer nothing in the way of extenuating circumstances except the fact that I am the only Negro in the United States whose grandfather on the mother's side was *not* an Indian chief.

I remember the very day that I became colored. Up to my thirteenth year I lived in the little Negro town of Eatonville, Florida. It is exclusively a colored town. The only white people I knew passed through the town going to or coming from Orlando. The native whites rode dusty horses, the Northern tourists chugged down the sandy village road in automobiles. The town knew the Southerners and never stopped cane chewing when they passed. But the Northerners were something else again. They were peered at cautiously from behind curtains by the timid. The more venturesome would come out on the porch to watch them go past and got just as much pleasure out of the tourists as the tourists got out of the village.

The front porch might seem a daring place for the rest of the town, but it was a gallery seat to me. My favorite place was atop the gate-post. Proscenium box for a born first-nighter. Not only did I enjoy the show, but I didn't mind the actors knowing that I liked it. I actually spoke to them in passing. I'd wave at them and when they returned my salute, I would say something like this: "Howdy-do-well-I-thank-you-where-you-goin'?" Usually automobile or the horse paused at this, and after a queer exchange of compliments, I would probably "go a piece of the way" with them, as we say in farthest Florida. If one of my family happened to come to the front in time to see me, of course negotiations would be rudely broken off. But even so, it is clear that I was the first "welcome-to-our-state" Floridian, and I hope the Miami Chamber of Commerce will please take notice.

During this period, white people differed from colored to me only in that they rode through town and never lived there. They liked to hear me "speak pieces" and sing and wanted to see me dance the parse-me-la, and gave me generously of their small silver for doing these things, which seemed strange to me for I wanted to do them so much that I needed bribing to stop. Only they didn't know it. The colored people gave no dimes. They deplored any joyful tendencies in me, but I was their Zora nevertheless. I belonged to them, to the nearby hotels, to the county—everybody's Zora.

But changes came in the family when I was thirteen, and I was sent to school in Jacksonville. I left Eatonville, the town of the oleanders, as Zora. When I disembarked from the riverboat at Jacksonville, she was no more. It seemed that I had suffered a sea change. I was not Zora of Orange County any more, I was now a little colored girl. I found it out in certain ways. In my heart as well as in the mirror, I became a fast brown—warranted not to rub nor run.

But I am not tragically colored. There is no great sorrow dammed up in my soul, nor lurking behind my eyes. I do not mind at all. I do not belong to the sobbing school of Negrohood who hold that nature somehow has given them a low-down dirty deal and whose feelings are all hurt about it. Even in the helter-skelter skirmish that is my life, I have seen that the world is to the strong regardless of a little pigmentation more or less. No, I do not weep at the world—I am too busy sharpening my oyster knife.

Someone is always at my elbow reminding me that I am the granddaughter of slaves. It fails to register depression with me. Slavery is sixty years in the past. The operation was successful and the patient is doing well, thank you. The terrible struggle that made me an American out of a potential slave said "On the line!" The Reconstruction said "Get set!"; and the generation before said "Go!" I am off to a flying start and I must not halt in the stretch to look behind and weep. Slavery is the price I paid for civilization, and the choice was not with me. It is a bully adventure and worth all that I have paid through my ancestors for it. No one on earth ever had a greater chance for glory. The world to be won and nothing to be lost. It is thrilling to think—to know that for any act of mine, I shall get twice as much praise or twice as much blame. It is quite exciting to hold the center of the national stage, with the spectators not knowing whether to laugh or to weep.

The position of my white neighbor is much more difficult. No brown specter pulls up a chair beside me when I sit down to eat. No dark ghost thrusts its leg against mine in bed. The game of keeping what one has is never so exciting as the game of getting.

I do not always feel colored. Even now I often achieve the unconscious Zora of Eatonville before the Hegira.* I feel most colored when I am thrown against a sharp white background.

For instance at Barnard. "Beside the waters of the Hudson" I feel my race. Among the thousand white persons, I am a dark rock surged upon, overswept by a creamy sea. I am surged upon and overswept, but through it all, I remain myself. When covered by the waters, I am; and the ebb but reveals me again.

Sometimes it is the other way around. A white person is set down in our midst, but the contrast is just as sharp for me. For instance, when I sit in the drafty basement that is The New World Cabaret† with a white person, my color comes. We enter chatting about any little nothing that we have in common and are seated by the jazz waiters. In the abrupt way that jazz orchestras have, this one plunges into a number. It loses no time in circumlocutions, but gets right down to business. It constricts the thorax and splits the heart with its tempo and narcotic harmonies. This orchestra grows rambunctious, rears on its hind legs and attacks the tonal veil with primitive fury, rending it, clawing it until it breaks through to the jungle beyond. I follow those heathen—follow them exultingly. I dance wildly inside myself; I yell within, I whoop; I shake my assegai‡ above my head, I hurl it true to the mark *yeeeeoowww!* I am in the jungle and living in the jungle way. My face is painted red and yellow, and my body is painted blue. My pulse is throbbing like a war drum. I want to slaughter something—give pain, give death to what, I do not know. But the piece ends. The men of the orchestra wipe their lips and rest their fingers. I creep back slowly to the veneer we call civilization with the last tone and find the white friend sitting motionless in his seat, smoking calmly.

"Good music they have here," he remarks, drumming the table with his fingertips.

Music! The great blobs of purple and red emotion have not touched him. He has only heard what I felt. He is far away and I see him but dimly across the ocean and the continent that have fallen between us. He is so pale with his whiteness then and I am *so* colored.

---

* Forced flight of Muhammad from Mecca to Medina in A.D. 622; hence a journey undertaken especially to escape danger.

† A Harlem nightclub of the 1920s.

‡ A slender wooden spear used by some South African tribes; it is usually tipped with iron.

At certain times I have no race, I am *me*. When I set my hat at a certain angle and saunter down Seventh Avenue, Harlem City, feeling as snooty as the lions in front of the Forty-Second Street Library, for instance. So far as my feelings are concerned, Peggy Hopkins Joyce* on on the Boule Mich† with her gorgeous raiment, stately carriage, knees knocking together in a most aristocratic manner, has nothing on me. The cosmic Zora emerges. I belong to no race nor time, I am the eternal feminine with its string of beads.

I have no separate feeling about being an American citizen and colored. I am merely a fragment of the Great Soul that surges within the boundaries. My country, right or wrong.

Sometimes, I feel discriminated against, but it does not make me angry. It merely astonishes me. How *can* any deny themselves the pleasure of my company! It's beyond me.

But in the main, I feel like a brown bag of miscellany propped against a wall. Against a wall in company with other bags, white, red and yellow. Pour out the contents, and there is discovered a jumble of small things priceless and worthless. A first-water diamond, an empty spool, bits of broken glass, lengths of string, a key to a door long since crumbled away, a rusty knife-blade, old shoes saved for a road that never was and never will be, a nail bent under the weight of things too heavy for any nail, a dried flower or two, still a little fragrant. In your hand is the brown bag. On the ground before you is the jumble it held—so much like the jumble in the bags, could they be emptied, that all might be dumped in a single heap and the bags refilled without altering the content of any greatly. A bit of colored glass more or less would not matter. Perhaps that is how the Great Stuffer of Bags filled them in the first place—who knows?

May 1928

---

* A much-photographed socialite and heiress.
† Boulevard St. Michel, a street on the Left Bank of Paris.

◐◑

They laugh to themselves when they hear white folks refer to them as ugly and black. Thanks to the whites who are always talking about racial purity, the Negroes possess within their group the most handsome people in the United States, with the greatest variety of color, hair and features. Here is the real melting-pot, and a glorious sight it is to see. Ugly people there are, certainly, but the percentage of beautiful folk is unquestionably larger than among the ofay brethren. One has but to venture abroad in a crowd of whites and then go immediately to a fashionable Negro thoroughfare to be impressed with this fact. Black? Well, yes, but how beautiful! How well it blends with almost every color! How smooth the skin; how soft and rounded the features! But there are browns, chocolates, yellows and pinks as well. Here in Aframerica one finds such an array of beauty that it even attracts Anglo-Saxons, despite their alleged color aversion. . . .

—*George S. Schuyler*

◐◑

THIS LITTLE LIGHT OF MINE

This little light of mine,
I'm goin' to let it shine.
This light of mine,
I'm goin' to let it shine.
This little light of mine,
I'm goin' to let it shine.
Let it shine,
Let it shine,
Let it shine.

Everywhere I go,
I'm goin' to let it shine.
Everywhere I go,
I'm goin' to let it shine.
Everywhere I go,
I'm goin' to let it shine.
Let it shine,

Let it shine,
Let it shine.

All through the night,
I'm goin' to let it shine.
All through the night,
I'm goin' to let it shine.
All through the night,
I'm goin' to let it shine.
Let it shine,
Let it shine,
Let it shine.

ON GETTING A NATURAL
DUDLEY RANDALL

A poem for a woolly-crowned queen who inspires black pride.

FOR GWENDOLYN BROOKS

She didn't know she was beautiful
though her smiles were dawn,
her voice was bells,
and her skin deep velvet Night.
She didn't know she was beautiful,
although her deeds,
kind, generous, unobtrusive,
gave hope to some,
and help to others,
and inspiration to us all. And
beauty is as beauty does,
they say.

Then one day there blossomed
a crown upon her head,
bushy, bouffant, real Afro-down,
Queen Nefertiti again.
And now her regal woolly crown
declares,
I know
I'm black
AND
beautiful.

❧

God made us in His perfect creation. He made no mistake when He made us black with kinky hair.

—*Marcus Garvey*

❧

INFERIOR STOCK?
DICK GREGORY

With his piercing wit, Dick Gregory, entertainer—and 1968 candidate for U.S. President—helped change the face of stage comedy in the 1960s. He let his audiences know how black folks really felt about racism and racists. Here, he sets the record straight on the myth of black inferiority.

White America has curiously become the victim of the very myths it has created. It is one thing to tell a lie and quite another thing to believe it. Since the days of slavery, white mythology has insisted that black people were of inferior stock. But a quick glance at social reality in America will show that white folks do not believe the inferior stock myth.

If I marry a woman of any ethnic background—Italian, Chinese, Puerto Rican, Irish, or whatever—a child produced through that union will be considered black in the eyes of white America. The child will be said to have "Negro blood," will be considered "a Negro" and frequently called "a nigger." The same pattern holds true for any black woman who marries a man of any other ethnic background. Black genes are considered so socially (if not biologically) dominant that a child is designated black regardless of the mixture. Does that sound like inferior stock to you?

Black is beautiful!

—*Anonymous*

AFRICAN AMERICAN HISTORY RAP
SHARON JORDAN HOLLEY

An elementary education—from A to Z.

I say A B C D E F G
African-American History
H I J K L M N O P
African-American History
Q R S, T U V
African-American History
W X Y and Z.
This is a story all about me:
A for African-American,
My true identity.
B for Benjamin Banneker,
Surveyor of Washington, D.C.
C for my community,
A place that I call home.
D for all the discoveries
I made just on my own.
E for education
We use from day to day.
F for all the families
And the love that they portray.

G for all the talents and gifts
Of those who entertain.
H for the writers—Hughes and Hurston—
Who wrote about the people plain.
I for rhythm, blues, and jazz
And all our instruments.
J for Jesse Jackson
Who ran for president.
K for Martin Luther King
We honor with a holiday.
L for the cowboy, Nat Love,
"Deadwood Dick" they say.
M for Madam C. J. Walker
A black woman millionaire.
N for the prophet Nat Turner,
A freedom fighter who dared
O for oppression that we must fight
To keep our struggle alive.
P for the principles some have held
that fill our hearts with pride.
Q for the questions that I ask
about my history.
R for religion
Islam to Christianity.
S for the seven days
Of the Kwanzaa celebration.
T for Harriet Tubman,
Conductor on Freedom's station.
U for the Underground Railroad,
A secret passageway.
V for the values that make me strong
From unity to faith, I pray.
W for Woodson, Carter G.,
A vision he did see
When he proclaimed February
For Black History.
X for the name that Malcolm took

Because it means unknown.
Y for You—to be all you can
From the first day you are born.
Z for zenith, the highest point
In this universe.
You're reaching up
When you learn
An African-American history verse.
I say A B C D E F G
African-American History
H I J K L M N O P
African-American History
Q R S, T U V
African-American History
W X Y and Z.
This is a story all about me.
This is a story all about me.
This is a story all about me.

There's a lot of talk about self-esteem these days. It seems pretty basic to me. If you want to feel proud of yourself, you've got to do things you can be proud of.

—*Oseola McCarty*

WORK

These days, some people call their jobs "slavery," and regard work as pure drudgery, an unimaginative way to squander precious energy.

But for anyone who takes pride in what they do, hard work is not merely profitable; it's an enjoyable, satisfying, and ennobling experience—whether building an airplane, hanging a shelf, designing a skyscraper, or teaching a class. Our attitude about work speaks volumes about who we are, what we like doing, and where we're headed in life. After all, what we produce through work may well end up being our greatest contribution to society.

Yes, certain jobs can be menial, task-oriented, or downright burdensome. But the individual who does them well can still find dignity in them.

African Americans have always had a strong work ethic. Hard work, in fact, is one of our most enduring legacies, in spite of its wretched origins in slavery.

Slaves survived beatings, torture, and back-breaking labor under the hot sun. They worked from "can to can't" (from "can" see at sunrise to "can't" see at night), reaching deep within for strength and stamina. Even if they were planting cotton or digging a ditch, their work became an expression of their own great nobility. And when slaves did not reap rewards for their toil and trouble, many considered that they might get it "by and by," in heaven.

In this atmosphere of extraordinary cruelty, African Americans managed to create a new culture of work, reflected in their work songs and field hollers, the oral testimonies of former slaves, and even the skills of artists such as George Moses Horton, who sold composed-to-order love poems in an effort to buy his freedom [see page 623].

The strong work ethic continued after emancipation. Some blacks stayed on the plantations they had farmed all their lives. Others spread out across the land—to lay train tracks from coast to coast, settle outposts, erect bridges and buildings, and fight the nation's battles. Meanwhile, an increasing number of blacks learned to *do for self*. Some picked up new agricultural techniques and trade skills. Others earned degrees, gained professional skills, or established their own businesses. Whole new classes of black workers emerged whose success stories still provide inspiration.

Our appreciation for work is one of the most valuable gifts we can give our children. When we work hard, we show them that work is worth our time and effort. When we *really* enjoy what we're doing, we prove that work has intrinsic value. The trick is to be imaginative and to find the fun in what we do.

The lessons in this chapter can be applied in almost any occupation, whether you're a high school student or a university instructor, a secretary or a surgeon. Here you will discover how former slave Booker T. Washington built a world-class educational institution from the ground up. Also included is the story of an internationally renowned surgeon, Ben Carson, who recalls a summer job he once held—picking up litter. From these stories, it's easy to see that a job well done—no matter how high or low the work—can be a source of great pride.

~

Hard work gives life meaning. Everyone needs to work hard at something to feel good about themselves. Every job can be done well and every day has its satisfactions.

—*Oseola McCarty*

~

HOME ON THE RANGE
PHILIP DURHAM and EVERETT L. JONES

Traditionally, historians, novelists, and Hollywood producers have dismissed the contributions of African Americans in exploring and settling the Old West. Blacks were among the first settlers of Los Angeles. One fifth of the United States Cavalry were African American troopers, the Buffalo Soldiers. Hundreds of thousands of black pioneers marched West in search of better lives, and dozens of all-black towns sprang up on the Plains. Even the origin of a well-used term deserves a closer look: Some folks say the word "cowboy" contemptuously referred to a black cowhand, regardless of his age, whereas white cowhands were called "cattlemen." The following story brings relatively obscure facts to light about blacks' work in the West.

There had always been Negroes in the West. They had, indeed, been scattered throughout the Western Hemisphere since their first importation as slaves at the beginning of the sixteenth century. Estevánico, a Spanish slave from the west coast of Morocco, was a member of an unfortunate party of four hundred explorers who landed near Tampa Bay in 1528. After a series of disasters, all of the party were lost except Estevánico, his master and two companions, who were marooned on the Texas coast. They were enslaved by Indians and spent seven years freeing themselves and making their way across Texas and Mexico to the frontiers of New Spain. Once there, they told stories they had heard of the Seven Cities of Cíbola, and their reports were directly responsible for the Coronado expedition. Estevánico continued his explorations, discovered the pueblos of New Mexico, and was killed by the Zuñis in 1539.

More than two hundred years later, Negroes and Negro-Indian families helped to found what is now the largest city in the West. Their settlement was established to grow food for the military, and it was called El Pueblo de Nuestra Señora La Reina de Los Angeles. Negroes and descendants of Negroes were literally among the first families of Los Angeles just as they were among the first settlers in the Spanish colonies of New Mexico.

Negroes also took part in American exploration of the West. When Lewis and Clark commanded the first official attempt to extend the "geographical knowledge of our continent," a Negro went with them. Clark's slave, a man named York, accompanied the expedition from the time it hoisted sail near the mouth of the Missouri River in 1804 until it returned in 1806 after having crossed the Rocky and Bitterroot Mountains and pushed to the mouth of the Columbia River. Nearly forty years later a free Negro, Jacob Dodson, accompanied John C. Frémont on his 1843 expedition to search for a new pass through the High Sierra. Another free Negro, Saunders Jackson, joined Frémont's fourth expedition in 1848.

Several Negroes ranged through the Rocky Mountains searching for beaver. One was James P. Beckwith (sometimes Beckwourth), the son of a white father and a Negro slave, who in 1823 was the blacksmith for General William Ashley's fur brigade. In time, he became one of the most famous of the mountain men (as well as a famous storyteller), his exploits rivaling those of Kit Carson and Jim Bridger, with both of whom he associated. During the last years of his life he was a chief among the Crows, earning new fame as a warrior and horse thief. Even his early death before the middle of the century was a subject of legend: it was said that his own tribe poisoned him, using a poison so deadly that not even his own powerful medicine (a bag containing a hollow bullet and two oblong beads) could save his life. Edward Rose was another such mountain man, "a morose, moody misfit of mixed blood and lawless disposition," who "eventually joined the Crow tribe and abandoned civilization entirely."

The explorations of Lewis and Clark, Frémont and the mountain men helped open the way to Oregon. Ironically, although Negroes participated in these expeditions, they were early barred from the Oregon frontier settlements. Many of the first settlers of the Willamette Valley were Southerners, and while they could not change the ruling of the

1843 provisional constitution that prohibited slavery, they added a provision in 1844 which expelled all the Negroes and mulattoes. So in that same year, when George W. Bush, a free Negro, joined an expedition to Oregon, he was refused settlement there. He moved north to Puget Sound and took up a homestead, where he lived the rest of his life. One of the earliest settlers, he helped later arrivals with interest-free loans of grain and other foodstuffs, assisting hundreds of white newcomers to survive their first months on the new frontier.

Another free Negro worked at the start of the Oregon Trail in Independence, Missouri. There Hiram Young operated wagon factories and engaged in a general blacksmithing business, at one time employing more than fifty men on twenty-five forges. He also owned and employed slaves.

After 1848 many travelers of the Oregon Trail turned south to California, where gold had been discovered. Among them were Negroes, both slave and free, who staked claims and formed mining companies. Negro prospectors and miners also joined in later developments in Nevada, Idaho and Montana, and they were among those who headed for Colorado to become part of the Pikes Peak gold rush of 1858. Other Negroes appeared in the West as muleskinners, hostlers, hotelkeepers and unskilled laborers. Some worked for Russell, Majors and Waddell and their Pony Express. Negro women cooked for hungry trappers in isolated mountain forts and for travelers on the Butterfield stages that rolled through Texas and Arizona. . . .

No story of the seizure and settlement of the West would be complete without including an account of the Negro soldiers in the 24th and 25th Infantry Regiments and the Negro troopers in the 9th and 10th Cavalry Regiments. Organization of Negro regiments in the Regular Army was first authorized in 1866. During the Civil War, 178,975 Negro soldiers wore the blue uniforms of the Union Armies, and Negroes took part in 449 engagements. More than 38,000 were listed as killed, wounded or missing in action. With such a record, Negroes proved their effectiveness as soldiers, and the federal government prepared to use them.

The Congressional Act of July 28, 1866 (later modified by supplementary legislation in 1869), established two Negro infantry regiments and two Negro cavalry regiments. All four saw continuous service in the West during the three decades following the Civil War. Negro infantry served in both Texas and the Dakota Territory, and Negro cavalry fought in almost every part of the West from Mexico to Montana. Both General Miles and General Merritt, as well as other officers who commanded Negro troops during the Indian campaigns, praised their courage and skill: "I have always," wrote General Merritt, "found the colored race represented in the army obedient, intelligent and zealous in the discharge of duty, brave in battle, easily disciplined, and most efficient in the care of their horses, arms and equipment."

The story of either cavalry regiment alone would be an exciting history. The men were carefully picked, held to high standards of physical fitness and mental alertness, and were commanded by some of the Army's best white officers. (Three Negroes graduated from West Point in the years before 1900, and a few Negroes were commissioned as chaplains, but all other officers were white.)

The men took quickly to the routine of fort and camp, maintained excellent morale and proved to be excellent soldiers. Because few of them had received more than a smattering of education, a company commander's biggest problem was training men for the inevitable War Department paper work. The men believed that wearing the Army uniform was a privilege and an honor, and they equaled and sometimes surpassed white troops in the field. "Their desertion rate was lower, court-martial record better, and general physical fitness superior."

During the years before the Spanish-American War, troops of the 9th Cavalry served in Texas, New Mexico, Kansas, Oklahoma, Nebraska, Utah and Montana. The 10th Cavalry served in Kansas, Oklahoma, Texas, New Mexico and Arizona. Negro troopers fought against Comanches, Apaches and Sioux. They fought against Crazy Horse and his warriors, and they captured Geronimo.

The Indians called the Negro troopers Buffalo Soldiers because of the similarity between their tightly curled hair, generally short, and that of the buffalo. The white soldiers called them the Brunettes. The War Department knew they were efficient.

Frederic Remington posed a rhetorical question: "Will they fight?" And he answered it himself: "They have fought many, many times. The old sergeant sitting near me, as calm of feature as a bronze statue, once deliberately walked over a Cheyenne rifle pit and killed his man. One little fellow near him once took charge of a lot of stampeded cavalry horses when Apache bullets were flying loose and no one knew from what point to expect them next. These little episodes prove the sometimes doubted self-reliance of the Negro."

Negro soldiers and troopers were also called to keep the peace among white cattlemen and settlers. When Billy the Kid was trapped in a burning building in Lincoln, New Mexico, Negro troops surrounded him. When settlers tried to preempt lands in the Indian Nations, and when Sooners tried to sneak into Oklahoma Indian lands before they were officially opened for settlement, Negro cavalry stopped them. When Wyoming cattlemen started the Johnson County War, only to find themselves outnumbered and pinned down by angry settlers, Negro cavalry rescued them.

The soldiers helped to make the expansion of the cattle empire possible. Sometimes with their help and sometimes without it, cattlemen drove through Kansas and Nebraska to the Dakota Territory or through New Mexico and Colorado to Wyoming and Montana. And with the Texas cattlemen came the Negro cowboys.

These cowboys crossed the Red River and the Cimarron to ride the streets of all the early cowtowns. They stood in the saloons and slept in the jails. They fought Indians and other cowboys, and some of them were buried on Boot Hill or in unmarked graves along the trail. At the end of the long drives, a few remained on northern ranges to become horsebreakers, ranch hands or even outlaws, but most of them drew their pay and rode back to Texas.

While the trail drives lasted, Negroes had a conspicuous place in the life of the cattleman's West. They fought with guns and bullwhips on the streets of Dodge City, and they roamed the streets of Cheyenne. They carried gold through outlaw country, and they took part in bloody range wars. If one got drunk, he could crash through a plate glass window, shoot up a saloon or land in jail. If he turned outlaw, he usually died young.

Negro cowboys hunched in their saddles during blizzards and thunderstorms, fought grass fires and turned stampedes, hunted wild mustangs and rode wild horses. Wolves threatened their cattle, and rattlesnakes crawled into their camps. Their lives were like those of all other cowboys—hard and dangerous.

❧

Rails split 'fo' breakfast'll season de dinner.

—*Plantation proverb*

❧

PICK A BALE OF COTTON

During slavery and afterward, workers used the rhythm of songs to pace themselves in backbreaking work in plantation fields or on chain gangs. Often, they matched the movements of a monotonous task to the beat of a song. Singing also helped pass time.

Jump down, turn around to pick a bale of cotton.
Jump down, turn around, pick a bale a day.
Jump down, turn around to pick a bale of cotton.
Jump down, turn around, pick a bale a day.

Oh, Lordy, pick a bale of cotton!
Oh, Lordy, pick a bale a day!

Me and my gal can pick a bale of cotton,
Me and my gal can pick a bale a day. . . .
Me and my wife can pick a bale of cotton,
Me and my wife can pick a bale a day. . . .

Me and my friend can pick a bale of cotton,
Me and my friend can pick a bale a day. . . .

Me and my poppa can pick a bale of cotton,
Me and my poppa can pick a bale a day.
Oh, Lordy, pick a bale of cotton!
Oh, Lordy, pick a bale a day!

THE BALLAD OF JOHN HENRY

This ballad is one of the best-known songs in African American folk tradition. It tells the epic story of man versus machine—a courageous and stubborn "natural man" in a heroic struggle against technology, the steam drill. John Henry was a track worker on the Chesapeake and Ohio Railroad, and the ballad is based on the digging of the Big Bend Tunnel in the Allegheny Mountains of West Virginia, folklorists say. But the legend has grown to such mythological proportions that his true identity no longer matters.

When John Henry was a little fellow,
  You could hold him in the palm of your hand,
He said to his pa, "When I grow up
  I'm gonna be a steel-driving man.
    Gonna be a steel-driving man "

When John Henry was a little baby,
  Setting on his mammy's knee,
He said "The Big Bend Tunnel on the C. & O. Road
  Is gonna be the death of me,
    Gonna be the death of me."

One day his captain told him,
  How he had bet a man
That John Henry would beat his steam-drill down,
  Cause John Henry was the best in the land,
    John Henry was the best in the land.

John Henry kissed his hammer,
  White man turned on steam,
Shaker* held John Henry's trusty steel,
  Was the biggest race the world had ever seen,
    Lord, biggest race the world ever seen.

* The railroad worker who holds the drill upright for the hammerer, rotating it between blows.

John Henry on the right side
    The steam drill on the left,
"Before I'll let your steam drill beat me down,
    I'll hammer my fool self to death,
        Hammer my fool self to death."

John Henry walked in the tunnel,
    His captain by his side,
The mountain so tall, John Henry so small,
    He laid down his hammer and he cried,
        Laid down his hammer and he cried.

Captain heard a mighty rumbling,
    Said "The mountain must be caving in,"
John Henry said to the captain,
    "It's my hammer swinging in de wind,
        "My hammer swinging in de wind."

John Henry said to his shaker,
    "Shaker, you'd better pray;
For if ever I miss this piece of steel,
    Tomorrow'll be your burial day,
        Tomorrow'll be your burial day."

John Henry said to his shaker,
    "Lordy, shake it while I sing,
I'm pulling my hammer from my shoulders down,
    Great Gawdamighty, how she ring,
        Great Gawdamighty, how she ring!"

John Henry said to his captain,
    "Before I ever leave town,
Gimme one mo' drink of dat tom-cat gin,
    And I'll hammer dat steam driver down,
        I'll hammer dat steam driver down."

John Henry said to his captain,
    "Before I ever leave town,
Gimme a twelve-pound hammer wid a whale-bone handle,
    And I'll hammer dat steam driver down,
        I'll hammer dat steam drill on down."

John Henry said to his captain,
    "A man ain't nothin' but a man,
But before I'll let dat steam drill beat me down,
    I'll die wid my hammer in my hand,
        Die wid my hammer in my hand."

The man that invented the steam drill
    He thought he was mighty fine,
John Henry drove down fourteen feet,
    While the steam drill only made nine,
        Steam drill only made nine.

"Oh, lookaway over yonder, captain,
    You can't see like me,"
He gave a long and loud and lonesome cry,
    "Lawd, a hammer be the death of me,
        A hammer be the death of me!"

John Henry had a little woman,
    Her name was Polly Ann,
John Henry took sick, she took his hammer,
    She hammered like a natural man,
        Lawd, she hammered like a natural man.

John Henry hammering on the mountain
    As the whistle blew for half-past two,
The last words his captain heard him say,
    "I've done hammered my insides in two,
        Lawd, I've hammered my insides in two."

The hammer that John Henry swung
    It weighed over twelve pound,
He broke a rib in his left hand side
    And his intrels fell on the ground,
       And his intrels fell on the ground.

John Henry, O, John Henry,
    His blood is running red,
Fell right down with his hammer to the ground,
    Said, "I beat him to the bottom but I'm dead,
       Lawd, beat him to the bottom but I'm dead."

When John Henry was laying there dying,
    The people all by his side,
The very last words they heard him say,
    "Give me a cool drink of water 'fore I die,
       Cool drink of water 'fore I die."

John Henry had a little woman,
    The dress she wore was red,
She went down the track, and she never looked back,
    Going where her man fell dead,
       Going where her man fell dead.

John Henry had a little woman,
    The dress she wore was blue,
De very last words she said to him,
    "John Henry, I'll be true to you,
       John Henry, I'll be true to you."

"Who's gonna shoes yo' little feet,
    Who's gonna glove yo' hand,
Who's gonna kiss yo' pretty, pretty cheek,
    Now you done lost yo' man?
       Now you done lost yo' man?"

"My mammy's gonna shoes my little feet,
    Pappy gonna glove my hand,
My sister's gonna kiss my pretty, pretty cheek,
    Now I done lost my man,
        Now I done lost my man."

They carried him down by the river,
    And buried him in the sand,
And everybody that passed that way,
    Said, "There lies that steel-driving man,
        There lies a steel-driving man."

They took John Henry to the river,
    And buried him in the sand,
And every locomotive come a-roaring by,
    Says "There lies that steel-drivin' man,
        Lawd, there lies a *steel*-drivin' man."

Some say he came from Georgia,
    And some from Alabam,
But its wrote on the rock at the Big Bend Tunnel,
    That he was an East Virginia man,
        Lord, Lord, an East Virginia man.

∽

If a man is called to be a streetsweeper, he should sweep streets even as Michelangelo painted, or Beethoven composed music, or Shakespeare wrote poetry. He should sweep streets so well that all the hosts of heaven and earth will pause to say, here lived a great streetsweeper who did his job well.

                                       —*Martin Luther King Jr.*

∽

CHANGE THE RULES
BEN CARSON

*Motivated workers often accomplish more than others. And what moti-
vates some people comes as no surprise: time off. World-renowned neurosurgeon Ben Carson—who led a seventy-person surgical team in a twenty-
two-hour operation to separate Siamese twins in 1987—reveals the simple
strategy he has used to complete almost every job he has ever done, from
picking up highway litter to practicing medicine.*

During my college years I worked at several different summer jobs, a
practice I had started in high school where I worked in the school
laboratory. The summer between my junior and senior year of high
school, I worked at Wayne State University in one of the biology laboratories.

Between high school graduation and entering Yale I needed a job
badly. I had to have clothes for college, books, transportation money,
and the dozens of other expenses I knew I'd face.

One of the counselors at our high school, Alma Whittley, knew my
predicament and was very understanding. One day I poured out my
story, and she listened with obvious concern. "I've got a few connections with the Ford Motor Company," she said. While I sat next to her
desk, she phoned their world headquarters. I particularly remember her
saying, "Look, we have this young fellow here named Ben Carson. He's
very bright and already has a scholarship to go to Yale in September.
Right now the boy needs a job to save money for this fall." She paused
to listen, and I heard her add, "You have to give him a job."

The person on the other end agreed.

The day after my last high school class my name went on the list of
employees at the Ford Motor Company in the main administration building in Dearborn. I worked in the payroll office, a job I considered
prestigious, or as my mother called it, big time, because they required
me to wear a white shirt and tie every day.

That job taught me an important lesson about employment in the
world beyond high school. Influence could get me inside the door, but
my productivity and the quality of my work were the real tests. Just

knowing a lot of information, while helpful, wasn't enough either. The principle goes like this: It's not what you know but the kind of job you do that makes the difference.

That summer I worked hard, as I did at every job, even the temporary ones. I determined that I would be the best person they had ever hired.

After completing my first year at Yale, I received a wonderful summer job as a supervisor with a highway crew—the people who clean up the trash along the highways. The federal government had set up a jobs program, mostly for inner-city students. The crew walked along the Interstate near Detroit and the western suburbs, picking up and bagging trash in an effort to keep the highways beautiful.

Most of the supervisors had a horrible time with discipline problems, and the inner-city kids had hundreds of reasons for not putting any effort into their work. "It's too hot to work today," one would say. "I'm just too tired out from yesterday," another said. "Why we gotta do all this? Tomorrow people will just litter it all up again. Who'll know if we cleaned it up or not?" "Why should we kill ourselves at this? The job just doesn't pay enough to do that."

The other supervisors, I learned, figured that if each of the five to six young men in the crew filled two plastic bags a day, they were doing well.

These guys could do that much in one hour, and I knew it. I may be an overachiever, but it seemed a waste of my time to let my crew laze around picking up 12 bags of litter a day. From the first my crew consistently filled between 100 and 200 bags a day, and we covered enormous stretches of highway.

The amount of work my crew did flabbergasted my supervisors in the Department of Public Works. "How come your guys can get so much work done?" they asked. "None of the other crews do that much."

"Oh, I have my little secrets," I'd say, and make a joke out of what I was doing. If I said too much, someone might interfere and make me change my rules.

I used a simple method, but I didn't go by the standard procedures— and I share this story because I think it illustrates another principle in my life. It's like the popular song of a few years ago that says "I did it my way." Not because I oppose rules—it would be crazy to do surgery without obeying certain rules—but sometimes regulations hinder and need to be broken or ignored.

For example, the fourth day on the job I said to my guys, "It's going to be real hot today—"

"You can say that again!" one of them said, and immediately they all eagerly agreed.

"So," I said, "I'm going to make you a deal. First, beginning tomorrow, we start at six in the morning while it's still cool—"

"Man, nobody in the whole world gets up that early—"

"Just listen to my whole plan," I said to the interrupter. Our crews were supposed to work from 7:30 a.m. until 4:30 p.m. with an hour off for lunch. "If you guys—and it has to be all six of you—will be ready to start work so that we can get out on the road at six, and you work fast to fill up 150 bags, then after that you're through for the day." Before anyone could start questioning me I clarified what I meant.

"You see, if you can collect all that trash in two hours, I'll take you back, and you're off the rest of the day. You still earn a full day's pay. But you have to bring in 150 bags no matter how long it takes."

We bashed the idea back and forth, but they saw what I wanted. It had only taken a couple of days to get them to pick up 100 bags a day, and it was hot, hard work in the afternoon. But they loved taunting the other crews and telling how much they had done, and they were ready for the new challenge. These kids were learning to take pride in their work, as lowly as many of them considered their jobs.

They agreed with my arrangement. The next morning all six of them were ready to go at 6:00 a.m. And how they worked—hard and fast. They learned to clean a whole stretch of highway in two to three hours—the same amount of work that they had previously stretched out for the whole day.

"OK, guys," I'd say as soon as I counted the last bag. "We take the rest of the day off."

They loved it and worked with a joyful playfulness. Their best moments came when we'd be hauling ourselves into the Department of Transportation by 9:00, just as the other crews were getting started.

"You guys going to work today?" one of my guys would yell.

"Man, not much trash out there today," another one would say. "Superman and his hot shots have cleaned up most of it."

"Hope you don't get sunburned out there!" they yelled as a truck pulled out.

Obviously the supervisors knew what I was doing, because they saw us coming back in, and they certainly had reports of our going out early. They never said anything. If they had, all I would have had to do was produce evidence of our work.

We weren't supposed to work that way, because the rules set the specific work hours. Yet not one supervisor ever commented on what I was doing with my crew. More than anything else, I believe they kept silent because we were getting the job done and doing it faster and better than any of the other crews.

Some people are born to work, and others are pushed into it by their moms. But doing what must be done as quickly and as well as possible has been my strategy for everything, including medicine. We don't necessarily have to play by the strict rules if we can find a way that works better, as long as it's reasonable and doesn't hurt anybody. Someone told me that creativity is just learning to do something with a different perspective. So maybe that's what it is—being creative.

DANCING SPIRIT
JUDITH JAMISON

Dance emanates from the very core of one's being and extends beyond the body's physical limitations—beyond the tips of one's fingers. Great performance artists dig deep and then set their spirits free on stage. Here, Judith Jamison, a legendary figure in the dance world, describes the gut-wrenching preparation and energy put into one of her most memorable performances. Extraordinary art often depends on this sort of exhausting, behind-the-scenes work.

When people ask me what *Cry* is about I always say that it's about dancing for sixteen minutes, nonstop, as if you're running around the block full speed. It starts out with the weight of the world. The shawl you're holding is representative of a woman scrubbing a floor, of a mantle around your head, of a stole around your shoulder, a burden lovingly carried. Of a protective blanket spread beneath the floor. The cloth carries the weight of many experiences.

Exactly where the woman is going through the ballet's three sections was never explained to me by Alvin Ailey [the choreographer]. In my interpretation, she represented those women before her who came from the hardships of slavery, through the pain of losing loved ones, through overcoming extraordinary depressions and tribulations. Coming out of a world of pain and trouble, she has found her way—and triumphed.

In the first section she celebrates her beauty, but in the meantime she's out there scrubbing floors. She celebrates life by acting as if she's smoothing a blanket for a baby she's been cradling. She walks across the stage defiantly as if to say, "Look at me. I'm a gorgeous being. I have something to say. I'm *here.*" Her tone of voice is of one who presents herself and displays the burdens she carries as well as the blessings.

In the second section she's really wracked with the devastations of what's going on in this world. Here Alvin used Laura Nyro's song "Been on a Train," which speaks of the catastrophe of drugs—how, instead of eating life, you let life eat away at you.

The third and last section is very celebratory, matching the music— the Voices of East Harlem's "Right On, Be Free." In the end, she acknowledges what's going on in the world, but decides to press on. She is going to keep her "eyes on the prize" despite the odds. She is full of pride and elegance, and represents the strength of women who have endured since the beginning of time—the head is held high. It's steeped in tradition and love. If you look at grandmothers, mothers, and daughters, you'll see that. You can see the strength in their faces, the pain that they've been through, and the wisdom that they have. I think Alvin was trying to convey that through movement. . . .

Until the night of the premiere, we hadn't done the ballet from beginning to end. We ran out of time in the tech rehearsal. If you run out of time and the crew goes to dinner, that's it. My first experience of going from start to finish was at the premiere, May 4, 1971. It was quite an experience. Sixteen minutes later, my lungs were on one side of the stage and my heart on the other. The audience went wild, as they still do, no matter who dances. That's what I love about *Cry.* The dance has passed from dancer to dancer to dancer, from generation to generation. *Cry* is about the dance *and* the dancer, but the dance holds up by itself. . . .

Clive Barnes's review from the New York *Times* was like one big bouquet. My name was in headlines. Here's an excerpt:

> For years it has been obvious that Judith Jamison is no ordinary dancer. She looks like an African goddess and her long body has an unexpected gracefulness to it, but it moves in a manner almost more elemental than human. Her face is fantastic.
>
> It is a long Modigliani face, like a black sculpture. It is a tragic face, a mask of sorrow. It is a face born to cry the blues, but when she smiles it is with an innocent radiance, a joyfulness that is simple and lovely. And she dances with an articulated beauty, serene, together and womanly. She holds herself a little aloof from the audience, but she is reserved rather than shy. She never tries consciously to please an audience. She is wonderfully proud, from the poise of her head set perfectly on a long, strong neck, to the lightly sculptured muscles of her long legs.
>
> So for years it has been obvious that Judith Jamison was no ordinary dancer. Now Alvin Ailey has given his African queen a solo that wonderfully demonstrates what she is and where she is. It was given the world premiere at the New York City Center last night, and it was a sensation. Rarely have a choreographer and dancer been in such accord.
>
> The solo, which lasts some 15 minutes and must be one of the longest solos ever choreographed, is called "Cry." Ailey has dedicated it: "For all black women everywhere—especially our mothers." You can see why, for here crystallized is the story of the black woman in America told with an elliptic and cryptic poetry and a passionate economy of feeling.

I hadn't thought after the first performance that anything spectacular had happened, other than that I made it through the dance. I hadn't even known about Alvin's dedication. If I had been told that I was to represent every Black woman in the world, I would have dropped the cloth and left the stage *immediately*. My focus was on getting through the dance, in one piece. Dudley Williams saw me from the front of the house. He told me that during the end of the last section he didn't know if I was going to be able to get from one side of the stage to the other. 'Round about the second section, I couldn't feel my legs. By the third section, I was so far inside of the movement that nothing else was going on. I couldn't hear anything but the music, and what was going on in my mind. You could see but you couldn't see. You could feel but you couldn't feel. There were many contradictions. . . .

There *is* such a thing as pacing in *Cry*. But after you see someone do *Cry*, if you're backstage when she finishes, she's flat-out on the floor gasping for breath. But when the curtain goes up for the bow, you pull your nerves together quickly as if you haven't been in a collapsed state—winded, sweating, tired—two seconds before.

I would collapse after *Cry*, then pick myself up off the floor because the audience was screaming. I'd get up and take that bow and forget about being tired. When the curtain went down, the exhaustion hit me again. There were times when I'd bow, the curtain would come down and I'd be halfway down the hallway toward the dressing room, and I'd have to come back. By that time, if I didn't have *Revelations* to do, I'd have my makeup half off. I used to wear false lashes and I'd have danced the lashes off. The glue wouldn't hold because I'd sweat so much. There are pictures of me doing the headrolls, with water coming straight off of me. When I danced, I sweat so much the costume would stick to me. Sometimes my feet and knees would split open and there'd be blood on my costume and the stage.

Even though the first part is gentle, your energy is so keyed and pointed to convey that kind of stillness, it takes as much energy to do that as it takes to do the last section. There, you're allowed to vent the energy that you've internalized in the first two sections. You've got to go all over the place. It's emotionally draining and physically exhausting. . . .

EVERYTHING IS LINKED. Movement comes from the center of your body. Spiritually, it comes from the light that is inside. It's supposed to emanate from the very core of your being. If your core is in your kneecap, then have it radiate out from there. You have to think of your body as one instrument from the top of the head to the bottom of your feet. I find that when I'm teaching, I'm constantly telling the dancer that the arm comes from a much deeper point than is anatomically defined on the body. It starts way back there. You want the feeling that it's coming from your "light."

When you get onstage it is an arena, and that arena is a reflection of what is going on in life. Whether you're performing a ballet that is abstract or a dance that has a story to tell, the audience should have a mirror held up before them. I think it is important for a dancer to understand that he or she is that reflection. How can you be that reflection if you know nothing about yourself, if you've explored nothing about yourself, if you haven't tapped into your innermost feelings?

I remember always the need to know myself because if I avoid knowing who I am deep inside then I can't express what I have to say through the talent that I have. I can't say what I need to say as a human being. Dance has its own vocabulary. When you put your foot down in a certain way, everyone knows what it means. You put your foot down in another way and the audience receives the message. You jump and the meaning is clear. You must be clear to me who you are, be generous in the process and try to share what you know about yourself so that you become a recognizable reflection.

You don't have to be five feet ten to be a dancer. Don't let what your body does define what you can do. Think of movement as much bigger than what your body says you're limited to. Your hand can go into the depths of your heart to pull out what you need to communicate with another person. I made a career not on how high my legs were but on how high you *thought* they went. Dance is bigger than the physical body. Think bigger than that. When you extend your arm, it doesn't stop at the end of your fingers, because you're dancing bigger than that; you're dancing spirit. Take a chance. Reach out. Go further than you've ever gone before.

Dance from the top of the head to the bottom of your feet. There is no step that is not justified. Even when you're stationary, you must be moving and alive. Even static sculpture has movement. You may be standing still but you're moving. Energy is coming out. And for that you have to be alert. Every single step has value, has justification. Be clear—it's the only way to bring forth the honesty in the movement.

If you lose the step, turn inside. When you get lost, focus. Believe that the gift is in you. Accept it. If there are mistakes, so be it. God is in you. Let your light shine . . .

STUTTERING TOWARD THE ST-ST-STAGE
JAMES EARL JONES

James Earl Jones's rich, booming voice is among the most recognizable in theater, film, and television. He made movie history as the voice of Darth Vader in Star Wars *and his familiar voice is frequently heard in TV commercials. Yet Jones's early years were made difficult by his childhood stuttering. He fine-tuned his voice with exercises to correct certain speech patterns and harness his vocal power. His story reminds us that through work we can strengthen ourselves and open up a world of new possibilities.*

During the Depression and on into the war, the government shipped surplus food around the country, staples and perishables, any overabundance of fruits. We knew when the food train was coming to town, and we could go get our welfare allotment of whatever the train was handing out on that trip. One winter, we got grapefruit, shipped all the way from Florida to Michigan on the food train. We hardly ever had grapefruit in our house.

The taste of it knocked me out, the pure, juicy luxury of grapefruit in winter. I decided to write a poem about it, patterned after the poem I knew best—Longfellow's "Song of Hiawatha." I forced my grapefruit rhapsody into Longfellow's cadence and rhyme scheme. Fortunately, no copy of that poem survives.

I was proud of my effort, however. Somehow Professor Crouch, to his surprise and pleasure, discovered that I wrote poetry. The boy who had written the poems was the same mute boy who had fought with uncontrolled fury. Both fury and poetry poured out of my silence.

"I'm impressed with your poem, James Earl," Professor Crouch told me after he read my ode to grapefruit. "I know how hard it is for you to talk, and I don't require you to do that. Unfortunately, it is hard for me to know whether these are your words. This is a fine poem. Did you copy it from somebody?"

My honor was at stake. Plagiarism was bad business. I had written every word of this poem myself. I would never copy someone else's poem and claim it for my own.

"I think the best way for you to demonstrate that you wrote this poem yourself is for you to say it aloud to the class," he told me.

It would be a trauma to open my mouth in front of my classmates, who would probably laugh at my poem and my stuttering. But it would be a greater trauma to be disgraced, unfairly charged with plagiarism. Now I would just have to open my mouth in public in self-defense.

I was shaking as I stood up, cursing myself. I strained to get the words out, pushing from the bottom of my soul. I opened my mouth— and to my astonishment, the words flowed out smoothly, every one of them. There was no stutter. All of us were amazed, not so much by the poem as by the performance.

Professor Crouch and I had stumbled on a principle which speech therapists and psychologists understand. The written word is safe for the stutterer. The script is a sanctuary. I could read from the paper the words I had composed there, and speak as fluently as anybody in the class.

"Aha!" my professor exclaimed as I sat down, vindicated. "We will now use this as a way to recapture your ability to speak."

And so, gradually, my powers of speech were resurrected. Throughout the rest of high school, I read Shakespeare aloud in the fields to myself. I remember hearing Uncle Bob Walker, Ozella's husband, reciting Mark Antony's speech from *Julius Caesar*. He was a fine man, not endowed by society or economy with the chance to be highly educated. He had worked in a foundry since his discharge from the Army. He was unpretentious in his speech, but he read Shakespeare with a full appreciation of the English language. I witnessed the joy he took in the words, and found it contagious.

I would have glorious experiences reading Edgar Allan Poe aloud. I could throw back the curtains in the high school gymnasium, step out on the stage with a lighted candle, and read Edgar Allan Poe—and everybody would *listen*. Those were special nights for me.

I played some basketball and ran track, but the time I might have given to honing my athletic skills I gave instead to forensics—public speaking, orations, interpretive readings. That was my extracurricular passion, and it was another of those crucial choices we make in life.

I could not get enough of speaking, debating, orating—acting. I became the school's champion public speaker. During those mute years, of course, my voice had changed, almost without my awareness, so in addition to the novelty of being able to speak, I could now speak in a deep, strong voice. People seemed to like to hear it, and I was overwhelmed to be able to speak aloud, in any voice at all. . . .

ACTING IS NOT something you can learn like calculus or history. It is a nonintellectual process, and that first reading of a play is nonintellectual. The challenge is not intellectual, but emotional: how deeply in tune you are with the emotional, imaginative planes of being. The key lies, I think, in the "heart, the feeling soul."

For years I had been nonverbal. I was coming at drama having been devoid of language. A nonverbal person beginning to speak is not unlike an illiterate person beginning to read: what captures the imagination is not the twisting and turning of ideas, but the flooding of feeling. I discovered that graceful language was fluid with sounds. Passion graces itself.

One of the forces which has shaped my life as an actor has been the weak muscle of speech, the *lost* muscle. The dancer Gwen Verdon had leg problems as a child, and in the process of exercising, found a strength that led to dancing. The orator Demosthenes filled his mouth with pebbles and practiced his speeches to overcome his stuttering, so becoming a great orator. The weak muscle can become the dominant muscle, either out of obsession with the weakness or a genuine endeavor to correct it. Consequently, the weak muscle can define a life and a profession.

I had often frozen or stammered or turned mute when problems confronted me in real life, and sometimes it seemed that the harder I worked, the murkier my speech would become in class. As I probed the emotions of a character in a scene, my voice would betray me, bogging

down as if swamped in the sounds. Sometimes my speech would acceler-
ate with emotion, and my words would race with each other, rapid as
heartbeats in a footrace. Will Lee [who went on to be recognized by
millions of children who watched *Sesame Street*] taught me to confront
the reality of that emotional overload and to begin to harness the emotions to the voice.

He also urged me to tone down my natural instincts toward power in
a scene and to control that energy. "Never use your total power," he
told me. "Use three-quarters of your power only, and let the rest of it
bear you up."

He was giving me a sense of proportion, and some valuable experience in working *with* rather than *against* the emotion and passion I
brought to a characterization.

Because of my muteness, I approached language in a different way
from most actors. I came at language standing on my head, turning
words inside out in search of meaning, making a mess of it sometimes,
but seeing truth from a very different viewpoint. In those years I spent
in virtual silence, I developed a passion for expression. I do not believe
that speech is a natural function for the human species. Therefore, any
barrier to speech—stuttering, for instance—only intensifies the difficulty
of an essentially unnatural process, the futility of words. But as I
regained my powers of speech and began to use them as an actor, I came
to believe that what is valid about a character is not his intellect, but the
sounds he makes.

I had come to the American Theatre Wing wanting to act, but without any real knowledge of the different schools of acting. One strategy
which made sense to me, and which has stayed with me, is the attempt to
discover the motivation of the character. Chekhov called it seeing the
inner life of the character as well as the outer appearance. And I wanted
to discover the character's voice.

When you communicate honestly, whether in your real life or your
stage life, you have to actually inhabit the words, touch the core of their
meanings. You have to enter the character, penetrate his spirit before
you can honestly utter his words. Hard labor stretches muscles, no
matter what kind of work you do. Sometimes, just before you break
through to new possibilities in your work, the muscles resist. They hurt.
They balk. That would happen to me with my speech. I would stretch so

far—and speech would crash. But I learned to wait, and try again, and again. The muscles began to grow.

In October 1957, I had a stroke of good fortune and got my first chance to be in a Broadway production. I understudied for Lloyd Richards, who played the role of Perry Hall in *The Egghead,* starring Karl Malden and directed by Hume Cronyn at the Ethel Barrymore Theatre. This began a long association with Lloyd, whose advice I often sought. No understudy's dream came true this time, but in January 1958, I got a speaking part on Broadway, playing the valet in Dore Schary's *Sunrise at Campobello,* a drama about Eleanor and Franklin D. Roosevelt, starring Ralph Bellamy. Vincent Donahue directed me in the small part as Edward the valet.

One night on stage, my worst fear sabotaged me. Here I was, acting in my first play on Broadway. I only had three lines, but one of them gave me trouble: "Mrs. Roosevelt, supper is served."

"M"—the Mama-letter—the overload Mama-word.

"M-m-m-m-m-Mrs. ———" I said during a performance.

Mary Fickett, the actress playing Mrs. Roosevelt, just stood there and let me get through it. That was the only way. I recovered, and we went on. Miraculously it never happened again.

TEACH WORKERS TO WORK
W. E. B. DU BOIS

Essayist, poet, educator, historian, sociologist, novelist, journalist, critic, W. E. B. Du Bois (1868–1963) was the preeminent African American intellectual of the first half of the twentieth century. His pioneering work—he is considered the founder of African American studies—has inspired generations of black scholars in many fields. But he did not limit his mission to academia. He founded and edited the most widely read black magazine of his day, The Crisis, *and wrote five novels and many poems. His most famous work, however, is* The Souls of Black Folk, *a landmark collection of fourteen essays on African American life. The book had a major impact in 1903, when it was first published. Among its most memorable passages is a prophetic statement in the book's forethought: "The problem of the Twentieth Century is the problem of the color-line." The following excerpt from the book calls for training both carpenters and philosophers, workers and thinkers. All are needed to build a nation.*

Teach workers to work—a wise saying; wise when applied to German boys and American girls; wiser when said of Negro boys, for they have less knowledge of working and none to teach them. Teach thinkers to think—a needed knowledge in a day of loose and careless logic; and they whose lot is gravest must have the carefulest training to think aright. If these things are so, how foolish to ask what is the best education for one or seven or sixty million souls! Shall we teach them trades, or train them in liberal arts? Neither and both: teach the workers to work and the thinkers to think; make carpenters of carpenters, and philosophers of philosophers, and fops of fools. Nor can we pause here. We are training not isolated men but a living group of men—nay, a group within a group. And the final product of our training must be neither a psychologist nor a brickmason, but a man. And to make men, we must have ideals, broad, pure, and inspiring ends of living—not sordid money-getting, not apples of gold. The worker must work for the glory of his handiwork, not simply for pay; the thinker must think for truth, not for fame. And all this is gained only by human strife and longing; by ceaseless training and education; by founding right on righteousness and truth on the unhampered search for truth; by founding the common school on the university, and the industrial school on the common school; and weaving thus a system, not a distortion, and bringing a birth, not an abortion.

HINDRANCES THAT HELP
WILLIAM PICKENS

Obstacles can become ladders to success.

In a Northern school there was just one black boy on the athletic teams. When they were practicing the high jump and the colored lad was among the jumpers, two of the white boys of course had to hold the ends of the pole or bar over which they jumped. There was an involuntary and almost instinctive effort, on the part of the white boys who held the bar, to keep the black boy from seeming to jump as well as the white boys: Therefore, when a white boy came to jump they would lower the pole a little and when the black boy came to jump they would raise the pole a little. And if the black lad jumped over the raise, they would raise it a little more next time he jumped. When the field day and the final test came, this black boy could jump nearly a foot higher than any white boy in the school. They had compelled him to out-jump them.

UP FROM SLAVERY
BOOKER T. WASHINGTON

Part autobiography, part rags-to-riches story, part how-to book, Up from Slavery *is the compelling story of Booker T. Washington (1856– 1915), one of America's most influential black leaders at the dawn of the twentieth century. Born a slave on a Virginia plantation, he rose to build the Tuskegee Normal and Industrial Institute, a major educational center for blacks. Washington was hailed—especially by whites—for his accommodationist stance. He urged blacks to "cast down your buckets where you are" and earn a decent living by practical means, with industrial and agricultural skills. These skills, and not political agitation for civil rights, Washington said, offered the best means for rising "up from slavery," which he described as a "school" from which blacks had graduated with honors. Though criticized for assuaging whites' fears, he was a product of his times and a leader who is often misunderstood today. In the first excerpt, Washington tells of his arrival at school, his "application," and his "tuition." In the second excerpt, he shows how hard he and others worked to build Tuskegee. His story provides valuable insight for anyone struggling to earn an education or teach others.*

HAMPTON

Without any unusual occurrence I reached Hampton, with a surplus of exactly fifty cents with which to begin my education. To me it had been a long, eventful journey; but the first sight of the large, three-story, brick school building seemed to have rewarded me for all that I had undergone in order to reach the place. If the people who gave the money to provide that building could appreciate the influence the sight of it had upon me, as well as upon thousands of other youths, they would feel all the more encouraged to make such gifts. It seemed to me to be the largest and most beautiful building I had ever seen. The sight of it seemed to give me new life. I felt that a new kind of existence had now begun—that life would now have a new meaning. I felt that I had reached the promised land, and I resolved to let no obstacle prevent me from putting forth the highest effort to fit myself to accomplish the most good in the world.

As soon as possible after reaching the grounds of the Hampton Institute, I presented myself before the head teacher for assignment to a class. Having been so long without proper food, a bath, and change of clothing, I did not, of course, make a very favourable impression upon her, and I could see at once that there were doubts in her mind about the wisdom of admitting me as a student. I felt that I could hardly blame her if she got the idea that I was a worthless loafer or tramp. For some time she did not refuse to admit me, neither did she decide in my favour, and I continued to linger about her, and to impress her in all the ways I could with my worthiness. In the meantime I saw her admitting other students, and that added greatly to my discomfort, for I felt, deep down in my heart, that I could do as well as they, if I could only get a chance to show what was in me.

After some hours had passed, the head teacher said to me: "The adjoining recitation-room needs sweeping. Take the broom and sweep it."

It occurred to me at once that here was my chance. Never did I receive an order with more delight. I knew that I could sweep, for Mrs. Ruffner had thoroughly taught me how to do that when I lived with her.

I swept the recitation-room three times. Then I got a dusting-cloth and I dusted it four times. All the woodwork around the walls, every bench, table, and desk, I went over four times with my dusting-cloth. Besides, every piece of furniture had been moved and every closet and corner in the room had been thoroughly cleaned. I had the feeling that in a large measure my future depended upon the impression I made upon the teacher in the cleaning of that room. When I was through, I reported to the head teacher. She was a "Yankee" woman who knew just where to look for dirt. She went into the room and inspected the floor and closets; then she took her handkerchief and rubbed it on the woodwork about the walls, and over the table and benches. When she was unable to find one bit of dirt on the floor, or a particle of dust on any of the furniture, she quietly remarked, "I guess you will do to enter this institution."

I was one of the happiest souls on earth. The sweeping of that room was my college examination, and never did any youth pass an examination for entrance into Harvard or Yale that gave him more genuine satisfaction. I have passed several examinations since then, but I have always felt that this was the best one I ever passed.

I have spoken of my own experience in entering the Hampton Institute. Perhaps few, if any, had anything like the same experience that I had, but about that same period there were hundreds who found their way to Hampton and other institutions after experiencing something of the same difficulties that I went through. The young men and women were determined to secure an education at any cost.

The sweeping of the recitation-room in the manner that I did it seems to have paved the way for me to get through Hampton. Miss Mary F. Mackie, the head teacher, offered me a position as janitor. This, of course, I gladly accepted, because it was a place where I could work out nearly all the cost of my board. The work was hard and taxing, but I stuck to it. I had a large number of rooms to care for, and had to work late into the night, while at the same time I had to rise by four o'clock in the morning, in order to build the fires and have a little time in which to prepare my lessons.

After having been for a while at Hampton, I found myself in difficulty because I did not have books and clothing. Usually, however, I got around the trouble about books by borrowing from those who were more fortunate than myself. As to clothes, when I reached Hampton I had practically nothing. Everything that I possessed was in a small hand satchel. My anxiety about clothing was increased because of the fact that General Armstrong* made a personal inspection of the young men in ranks, to see that their clothes were clean. Shoes had to be polished, there must be no buttons off the clothing, and no grease-spots. To wear one suit of clothes continually, while at work and in the schoolroom, and at the same time keep it clean, was rather a hard problem for me to solve. In some way I managed to get on till the teachers learned that I was in earnest and meant to succeed, and then some of them were kind enough to see that I was partly supplied with second-hand clothing that had been sent in barrels from the North. These barrels proved a blessing to hundreds of poor but deserving students. Without them I question whether I should ever have gotten through Hampton.

When I first went to Hampton I do not recall that I had ever slept in a bed that had two sheets on it. In those days there were not many buildings there, and room was very precious. There were seven other boys in the same room with me; most of them, however, students who had been there for some time. The sheets were quite a puzzle to me. The first night I slept under both of them, and the second night I slept on top of both of them; but by watching the other boys I learned my lesson in this, and have been trying to follow it ever since and to teach it to others.

I was among the youngest of the students who were in Hampton at that time. Most of the students were men and women—some as old as forty years of age. As I now recall the scene of my first year, I do not believe that one often has the opportunity of coming into contact with three or four hundred men and women who were so tremendously in earnest as these men and women were. Every hour was occupied in study or work. Nearly all had had enough actual contact with the world

* General Samuel Chapman Armstrong, a Union Army veteran, was head of the school.

to teach them the need of education. Many of the older ones were, of course, too old to master the text-books very thoroughly, and it was often sad to watch their struggles; but they made up in earnestness much of what they lacked in books. Many of them were as poor as I was, and, besides having to wrestle with their books, they had to struggle with a poverty which prevented their having the necessities of life. Many of them had aged parents who were dependent upon them, and some of them were men who had wives whose support in some way they had to provide for. . . .

TUSKEGEE

After consultation with the citizens of Tuskegee, I set July 4, 1881, as the day for the opening of the school in the little shanty and church which had been secured for its accommodation. The white people, as well as the coloured, were greatly interested in the starting of the new school, and the opening day was looked forward to with much earnest discussion. There were not a few white people in the vicinity of Tuskegee who looked with some disfavour upon the project. They questioned its value to the coloured people, and had a fear that it might result in bringing about trouble between the races. Some had the feeling that in proportion as the Negro received education, in the same proportion would his value decrease as an economic factor in the state. These people feared the result of education would be that the Negroes would leave the farms, and that it would be difficult to secure them for domestic service.

The white people who questioned the wisdom of starting this new school had in their minds pictures of what was called an educated Negro, with a high hat, imitation gold eye-glasses, a showy walking-stick, kid gloves, fancy boots, and what not—in a word, a man who was determined to live by his wits. It was difficult for these people to see how education would produce any other kind of a coloured man.

On the morning that the school opened, thirty students reported for admission. I was the only teacher. The students were about equally divided between the sexes. Most of them lived in Macon County, the county in which Tuskegee is situated, and of which it is the county-seat. A great many more students wanted to enter the school, but it had been decided to receive only those who were above fifteen years of age, and who had previously received some education. The greater part of the thirty were public-school teachers, and some of them were nearly forty years of age. With the teachers came some of their former pupils, and when they were examined it was amusing to note that in several cases the pupil entered a higher class than did his former teacher. It was also interesting to note how many big books some of them had studied, and how many high-sounding subjects some of them claimed to have mastered. The bigger the book and the longer the name of the subject, the prouder they felt of their accomplishment. Some had studied Latin, and one or two Greek. This they thought entitled them to special distinction.

In fact, one of the saddest things I saw during the month of travel which I have described was a young man, who had attended some high school, sitting down in a one-room cabin, with grease on his clothing, filth all around him, and weeds in the yard and garden, engaged in studying a French grammar.

The students who came first seemed to be fond of memorizing long and complicated "rules" in grammar and mathematics, but had little thought or knowledge of applying these rules to the everyday affairs of their life. One subject which they liked to talk about, and tell me that they had mastered, in arithmetic, was "banking and discount," but I soon found out that neither they nor almost any one in the neighbourhood in which they lived had ever had a bank account. In registering the names of the students, I found that almost every one of them had one or more middle initials. When I asked what the "J" stood for, in the name of John J. Jones, it was explained to me that this was a part of his "entitles." Most of the students wanted to get an education because they thought it would enable them to earn more money as school-teachers.

Notwithstanding what I have said about them in these respects, I have never seen a more earnest and willing company of young men and women than these students were. They were all willing to learn the right thing as soon as it was shown them what was right. I was determined to start them off on a solid and thorough foundation, so far as their books were concerned. I soon learned that most of them had the merest smattering of the high-sounding things that they had studied. While they could locate the Desert of Sahara or the capital of China on an artificial globe, I found out that the girls could not locate the proper places for the knives and forks on an actual dinner-table, or the places on which the bread and meat should be set.

I had to summon a good deal of courage to take a student who had been studying cube root and "banking and discount," and explain to him that the wisest thing for him to do first was thoroughly to master the multiplication table.

The number of pupils increased each week, until by the end of the first month there were nearly fifty. Many of them, however, said that, as they could remain only for two or three months, they wanted to enter a high class and get a diploma the first year if possible.

ABOUT THREE MONTHS after the opening of the school, and at the time when we were in the greatest anxiety about our work, there came into the market for sale an old and abandoned plantation which was situated about a mile from the town of Tuskegee. The mansion house—or "big house," as it would have been called—which had been occupied by the owners during slavery, had been burned. After making a careful examination of this place, it seemed to be just the location that we wanted in order to make our work effective and permanent.

But how were we to get it? The price asked for it was very little— only five hundred dollars—but we had no money, and we were strangers in the town and had no credit. The owner of the land agreed to let us occupy the place if we could make a payment of two hundred and fifty dollars down, with the understanding that the remaining two hundred and fifty dollars must be paid within a year. Although five hundred dollars was cheap for the land, it was a large sum when one did not have any part of it.

In the midst of the difficulty I summoned a great deal of courage and wrote to my friend General J. F. B. Marshall, the Treasurer of the Hampton Institute, putting the situation before him and beseeching him to lend me the two hundred and fifty dollars on my own personal responsibility. Within a few days a reply came to the effect that he had no authority to lend me money belonging to the Hampton Institute, but that he would gladly lend me the amount needed from his own personal funds.

I confess that the securing of this money in this way was a great surprise to me, as well as a source of gratification. Up to that time I never had had in my possession so much money as one hundred dollars at a time, and the loan which I had asked General Marshall for seemed a tremendously large sum to me. The fact of my being responsible for the repaying of such a large amount of money weighed very heavily upon me.

I lost no time in getting ready to move the school on to the new farm. At the time we occupied the place there were standing upon it a cabin, formerly used as the dining room, an old kitchen, a stable, and an old hen-house. Within a few weeks we had all of these structures in use. The stable was repaired and used as a recitation-room, and very presently the hen-house was utilized for the same purpose.

I recall that one morning, when I told an old coloured man who lived near, and who sometimes helped me, that our school had grown so large that it would be necessary for us to use the hen-house for school purposes, and that I wanted him to help me give it a thorough cleaning out the next day, he replied, in the most earnest manner: "What you mean, boss? You sholy ain't gwine clean out de hen-house in de *day*-time?"

Nearly all the work of getting the new location ready for school purposes was done by the students after school was over in the afternoon. As soon as we got the cabins in condition to be used, I determined to clear up some land so that we could plant a crop. When I explained my plan to the young men, I noticed that they did not seem to take to it very kindly. It was hard for them to see the connection between clearing land and an education. Besides, many of them had been school-teachers, and they questioned whether or not clearing land would be in keeping with their dignity. In order to relieve them from any embarrassment, each afternoon after school I took my axe and led the way to the woods. When they saw that I was not afraid or ashamed to work, they began to assist with more enthusiasm. We kept at the work each afternoon, until we had cleared about twenty acres and had planted a crop.

In the meantime Miss [Olivia A.] Davidson* was devising plans to repay the loan. Her first effort was made by holding festivals, or "suppers." She made a personal canvass among the white and coloured families in the town of Tuskegee, and got them to agree to give something, like a cake, a chicken, bread, or pies, that could be sold at the

---

* Booker T. Washington later married Miss Davidson, his "co-teacher."

festival. Of course the coloured people were glad to give anything that they could spare, but I want to add that Miss Davidson did not apply to a single white family, so far as I now remember, that failed to donate something; and in many ways the white families showed their interest in the school.

Several of these festivals were held, and quite a little sum of money was raised. A canvass was also made among the people of both races for direct gifts of money, and most of those applied to gave small sums. It was often pathetic to note the gifts of the older coloured people, most of whom had spent their best days in slavery. Sometimes they would give five cents, sometimes twenty-five cents. Sometimes the contribution was a quilt, or a quantity of sugarcane. I recall one old coloured woman, who was about seventy years of age, who came to see me when we were raising money to pay for the farm. She hobbled into the room where I was, leaning on a cane. She was clad in rags; but they were clean. She said: "Mr. Washin'ton, God knows I spent de bes' days of my life in slavery. God knows I's ignorant an' poor; but," she added, "I knows what you an' Miss Davidson is tryin' to do. I knows you is tryin' to make better men an' better women for de coloured race. I ain't got no money, but I wants you to take dese six eggs, what I's been savin' up, an' I wants you to put dese six eggs into de eddication of dese boys an' gals."

Since the work at Tuskegee started, it has been my privilege to receive many gifts for the benefit of the institution, but never any, I think, that touched me so deeply as this one.

CAST DOWN YOUR BUCKETS
BOOKER T. WASHINGTON

With this speech—called "the Atlanta Compromise" or the "Atlanta Exposition"—Booker T. Washington (1856–1915) became a national black spokesman. He delivered it at the Cotton States and International Exposition in Atlanta on September 18, 1895, when he was head of the Tuskegee Institute in Alabama. Initially supported by many, the speech called on blacks to work hard and humbly for their economic upliftment and asked whites for aid and encouragement. Black intellectuals later criticized Washington's accommodationist doctrine. W. E. B. Du Bois said it shifted "the burden of the Negro problem to the Negro's shoulders . . . when in fact the burden belongs to the nation." Here is Washington's most famous speech. His ideas of self-help and mutual aid were echoed in the doctrines of several subsequent black leaders, including the economic empowerment philosophies of Marcus Garvey and Elijah Muhammad.

One-third of the population of the south is of the Negro race. No enterprise seeking the material, civil, or moral welfare of this section can disregard this element of our population and reach the highest success. I but convey to you, Mr. President and Directors, the sentiment of the masses of my race when I say that in no way have the value and manhood of the American Negro been more fittingly and generously recognized than by the managers of this magnificent Exposition at every stage of its progress. It is a recognition that will do more to cement the friendship of the two races than any occurrence since the dawn of our freedom.

Not only this, but the opportunity here afforded will awaken among us a new era of industrial progress. Ignorant and inexperienced, it is not strange that in the first years of our new life we began at the top instead of at the bottom; that a seat in Congress or the State Legislature was more sought than real estate or industrial skill; that the political convention or stump speaking had more attractions than starting a dairy farm or truck garden.

A ship lost at sea for many days suddenly sighted a friendly vessel. From the mast of the unfortunate vessel was seen a signal: "Water, water, we die of thirst." The answer from the friendly vessel at once came back, "Cast down your bucket where you are." A second time the signal, "Water, water; send us water!" ran up from the distressed vessel, and was answered, "Cast down your bucket where you are." And a third and fourth signal for water was answered, "Cast down your bucket where you are." The captain of the distressed vessel, at last heeding the injunction, cast down his bucket, and it came up full of fresh, sparkling water from the mouth of the Amazon River. To those of my race who depend on bettering their condition in a foreign land or who underestimate the importance of cultivating friendly relations with the Southern white man, who is their next-door neighbour, I would say: "Cast down your bucket where you are"—cast it down in making friends, in every manly way of the people of all races by whom we are surrounded.

Cast it down in agriculture, mechanics, in commerce, in domestic service, and in the professions. And in this connection it is well to bear in mind that whatever other sins the South may be called upon to bear, when it comes to business pure and simple, it is in the South that the Negro is given a man's chance in the commercial world, and in nothing is this Exposition more eloquent than in emphasizing this chance. Our greatest danger is that, in the great leap from slavery to freedom we may overlook the fact that the masses of us are to live by the productions of our hands, and fail to keep in mind that we shall prosper in the proportion as we learn to dignify and glorify common labor and put brains and skill into the common occupations of life; shall prosper in proportion as we learn to draw the line between the superficial and the substantial, the ornamental gewgaws of life and the useful. No race can prosper till it learns that there is as much dignity in tilling a field as in writing a poem. It is at the bottom of life we must begin, and not at the top. Nor should we permit our grievances to overshadow our opportunities.

To those of the white race who look to the incoming of those of foreign birth and strange tongue and habits for the prosperity of the South, were I permitted I would repeat what I say to my own race, "Cast down your bucket where you are." Cast it down among the eight millions of Negroes whose habits you know, whose fidelity and love you have tested in days when to have proved treacherous meant the ruin of your firesides. Cast down your bucket among these people who have, without strikes and labour wars, tilled your fields, cleared your forests, builded your railroads and cities, and brought forth treasures from the bowels of the earth, and helped make possible this magnificent representation of the progress of the South. Casting down your bucket among my people, helping and encouraging them as you are doing on these grounds, and to education of head, hand, and heart, you will find that they will buy your surplus land, make blossom the waste places in your fields, and run your factories. While doing this, you can be sure in the future, as in the past, that you and your families will be surrounded by the most patient, faithful, law-abiding, and unresentful people that the world has seen. As we have proved our loyalty to you in the past, in nursing your children, watching by the sick-bed of your mothers and fathers, and often following them with tear-dimmed eyes to their graves, so in the future, in our humble way, we shall stand by you with a devotion that no foreigner can approach, ready to lay down our lives, if need be, in defence of yours; interlacing our industrial, commercial, civil, and religious life with yours in a way that shall make the interests of both races one. In all things that are purely social we can be as separate as the fingers, yet one as the hand in all things essential to mutual progress.

There is no defence or security for any of us except in the highest intelligence and development of all. If anywhere there are efforts tending to curtail the fullest growth of the Negro, let these efforts be turned into stimulating, encouraging, and making him the most useful and intelligent citizen. Effort or means so invested will pay a thousand per cent interest. These efforts will be twice blessed—"blessing him that gives and him that takes."

There is no escape through law of man or God from the inevitable—

The laws of changeless justice bind
Oppressor with oppressed,
And close as sin and suffering joined
We march to fate abreast.

Nearly sixteen millions of hands will aid you in pulling the load upward, or they will pull against you the load downward. We shall constitute one-third and more of the ignorance and crime of the South, or one-third its intelligence and progress; we shall contribute one-third to the business and industrial prosperity of the South, or we shall prove a veritable body of death, stagnating, depressing, retarding every effort to advance the body politic.

Gentlemen of the Exposition, as we present to you our humble effort at an exhibition of our progress, you must not expect overmuch. Starting thirty years ago with ownership here and there in a few quilts and pumpkins and chickens (gathered from miscellaneous sources), remember the path that has led from these to the invention and production of agricultural implements, buggies, steam-engines, newspapers, books, statuary, carving, paintings, the management of drug-stores and banks, has not been trodden without contact with thorns and thistles. While we take pride in what we exhibit as a result of our independent efforts, we do not for a moment forget that our part in this exhibition would fall far short of your expectations but for the constant help that has come to our educational life, not only from the Southern states, but especially from Northern philanthropists, who have made their gifts a constant stream of blessing and encouragement.

The wisest among my race understand that the agitation of questions of social equality is the extremest folly, and that progress in the enjoyment of all the privileges that will come to us must be the result of severe and constant struggle rather than of artificial forcing. No race that has anything to contribute to the markets of the world is long in any degree ostracized. It is important and right that all privileges of the law be ours, but it is vastly more important that we be prepared for the exercise of these privileges. The opportunity to earn a dollar in a factory just now is worth infinitely more than the opportunity to spend a dollar in an opera-house.

In conclusion, may I repeat that nothing in thirty years has given us more hope and encouragement and drawn us so near to you of the white race as this opportunity offered by the Exposition; and here bending, as it were, over the altar that represents the results of the struggles of your race and mine, both starting practically empty-handed three decades ago, I pledge that in your effort to work out the great and intricate problem which God has laid at the doors of the South, you shall have at all times the patient, sympathetic help of my race; only let this be constantly in mind, that, while from representations in these buildings of the product of field, of forest, of mine, of factory, letters, and art, much good will come, yet by far above and beyond material benefits will be that higher good, that, let us pray God, will come, in a blotting out of sectional differences and racial animosities and suspicions, in a determination to administer absolute justice, in a willing obedience among all classes to the mandates of law. This, this, coupled with our material prosperity, will bring into our belovèd South a new heaven and a new earth.

HOW TO MAKE TIMELY DECISIONS
COLIN POWELL

Colin Powell, born in Harlem on April 5, 1937, to immigrant parents from Jamaica, rose to four-star general in the U.S. Army and was the first African American to be appointed Chairman of the Joint Chiefs of Staff and National Security Advisor to the President. Powell developed his own managerial philosophy, using it in matters of enormous importance to national security. The following decision-making formula helped him to survive—and thrive—as a military commander and consummate Washington insider.

My daily life in the West Wing amounted to constant decision-making and then passing along my recommendations, issues ranging from where best to hold a summit in New York to helping craft nuclear disarmament treaties at the summit. By now, I had developed a decision-making philosophy. Put simply, it is to dig up all the information you can, then go with your instincts. We all have a certain intuition, and the older we get, the more we trust it. When I am faced with a decision—picking somebody for a post, or choosing a course of action—I dredge up every scrap of knowledge I can. I call in people. I phone them. I read whatever I can get my hands on. I use my intellect to inform my instinct. I then use my instinct to test all this data. "Hey, instinct, does this sound right? Does it smell right, feel right, fit right?"

However, we do not have the luxury of collecting information indefinitely. At some point, before we can have every possible fact in hand, we have to decide. The key is not to make quick decisions, but to make timely decisions. I have a timing formula, $P = 40$ to 70, in which P stands for probability of success and the numbers indicate the percentage of information acquired. I don't act if I have only enough information to give me less than a 40 percent chance of being right. And I don't wait until I have enough facts to be 100 percent sure of being right, because by then it is almost always too late. I go with my gut feeling when I have acquired information somewhere in the range of 40 to 70 percent.

❧

Do for self!

—*Elijah Muhammad*

❧

AMERICA'S FIRST SELF-MADE MILLIONAIRESS: MADAME C. J. WALKER
JAMES MICHAEL BRODIE

Madame C. J. Walker (1867–1919), the daughter of slaves, rose from poverty to great wealth. She invented and sold hair care products door-to-door, then founded her own cosmetics corporation at a time when the majority of urban black women worked as maids. Madame Walker's company employed women across the nation, and her rags-to-riches story inspired many.

Sarah Breedlove McWilliams, known as Madame C. J. Walker, is credited with the development of the modern hot comb. She also is regarded as the first self-made woman millionaire in the United States. Not bad for a woman who started with less than two dollars in her pocket in 1904.

Despite her financial accomplishments, Madame Walker was not the first Black woman to found a Black hair care company. That honor goes to Annie Turnbo Pope Malone, who apparently counted Walker among her employees at one time. However, Walker did revolutionize the Black hair care industry and challenged accepted marketing strategies with her door-to-door approach.

Walker did not invent the first hot comb—reports dating back to the early 1700s credit French Jews with such a device—but there is a debate about who actually first developed the *modern* hot comb. While many say it was Madame C. J. Walker, it was Malone who received the first patent in 1900. Malone's invention was a steel comb—with teeth spaced far enough apart to work on the thick hair of Black women—that could be heated on a stove top.

Sarah Breedlove was born in poverty in 1867 to Minerva and Owen Breedlove on the shores of the Mississippi River. Sarah's parents, both ex-slaves, were sharecroppers who lived on the Burney plantation in Delta, Louisiana.

Sarah grew up in Louisiana cotton fields during the Reconstruction era. And though slavery had ended, the lives of former slaves had changed little. Often they worked long hours under an unforgiving delta sun, hands calloused and bleeding from the spiny cotton plant. They lived in one-room shacks, with no windows, blankets covering the door-ways, no indoor toilets, and dirt floors. Sarah's parents both died on the plantation when she was a child.

Life got no better for Sarah after she was taken in at age seven by her older sister, Louvinia. Louvinia's husband physically abused the child and may have influenced Sarah to marry Moses McWilliams in 1881 when she was fourteen. The marriage produced Lelia, who became her mother's constant companion. In 1887, two years after his daughter's birth, Moses was murdered by a White lynch mob.

Vicksburg, Mississippi, before the turn of the century was no place for a Black single mother. Sarah didn't stay long there. Rather, she went north to live with her family in St. Louis. She took on a number of odd jobs, from cook to laundress.

In Walker's day, there was little in the way of hair care for Black women. Many relied on a process of straightening their hair by wrap-ping and twisting it. It not only was painful but tended to damage hair and make it fall out.

Walker began experimenting with various chemicals—some say she used sulfur—looking for a way to keep her own hair from falling out. She not only halted her hair loss but noted that some had grown back in. She soon began patenting her discoveries and selling them locally.

Walker later recounted in her promotional material the "unusual" dream that led to her hair care invention: "One night I had a dream. . . . A big Black man appeared to me and told me what to mix up for my hair. Some of the remedy was grown in Africa, but I sent for it, put it on my scalp, and in a few weeks my hair was coming in faster than it had ever fallen out." Walker accompanied her "Wonderful Hair Grower" with her development of the metal hot comb.

Following her brother's death in 1905, Walker moved to Denver, Colorado, to live with his widow and four daughters. Soon after, she founded her hair care company. As it grew, she found that she no longer needed to perform domestic work.

Sarah the businesswoman met and married Denver newspaperman C. J. Walker. He was a marketing expert and apparently came up with the door-to-door sales concept that became Sarah's trademark. For a time their union seemed a good one, but C.J. was not comfortable with his wife's growing success, and they soon divorced. Sarah decided to retain his name.

Walker was unable to read or write until well into adulthood. She routinely scribbled her name in such a way that no one could tell she couldn't spell. The act was so successful that when she finally learned to write her own name on a check, the bank would call her up to verify the strange signature.

Perhaps her lack of a good education spurred Madame Walker to push Lelia into college. Lelia attended historically Black Knoxville College in Tennessee. When she graduated, she joined her mother's company. Lelia helped not only with manufacturing the products but also with sales, training, and other aspects of the business. By 1906 she had taken control of the mail-order operation.

In 1908 Madame Walker and her daughter left the "Mile High City" for Pittsburgh, where they founded a beauty school. Lelia College, run by Lelia herself, taught what became known as the Walker Method. Five years later Lelia moved to New York to establish a second Lelia College.

Meanwhile, Madame Walker toured the country, selling her product. She also sold the concept of self-help, particularly among Black women, encouraging them to get into businesses for themselves. By the time she moved her operation to Indianapolis in 1910, she claimed to have more than five thousand sales agents, nearly all of them Black women, earning as much as seven thousand dollars a week. The number of agents grew to more than twenty-five thousand by 1920, Walker claimed.

Madame Walker continued to build her company by hiring key people to mind the business. Freeman B. Hanson, hired to run the Indianapolis operation, met Walker on a train on which he was a porter. He joined Walker's company after finishing law school.

Walker spent the next few years opening beauty parlors in the United States, the Caribbean, and South America.

Her success rested in her ability to exploit a market that had been overlooked by the mainstream. Her methods, however, often drew the wrath of Black leaders who accused her of trying to make Black women look White with her hair straighteners and cosmetics. Many ministers refused to let her address the women in their congregations.

As a Black woman Madame Walker faced the two-headed monster of racism and sexism. In 1912 Walker was snubbed by the educator Booker T. Washington and the National Negro Business League, which refused to let her speak at its convention. But Madame Walker stood up in the middle of the conference and made her voice heard. The following year she was invited back as a guest speaker.

Black women ignored the protestations of the men and rallied around Madame Walker and her business. Soon her success grew to such an extent that she was worth more than one million dollars by 1914. And Madame Walker knew how to flaunt her wealth.

She had a thirty-four-room mansion built on the Hudson River in Irvington, New York, and called it Lewaro, after her daughter (who had married a man named Robinson). The stylish estate became the scene of some of the most opulent gatherings the Black community had seen in this country. Lelia, too, got in on the image-is-everything act, changing her name to A'Lelia.

Walker always remembered where she'd come from, giving away large sums of money to a number of Black organizations. Gifts ranged from five thousand dollars to the Daytona (Florida) Normal and Industrial Institute for Girls, run by educator Mary McLeod Bethune, to five hundred dollars for the restoration of abolitionist Frederick Douglass's home in Washington, D.C.

Then came 1917, the year of the infamous "Red Summer," in which scores of Black men were lynched and otherwise murdered in the cities and on farms by mobs of Whites. That summer was one of the worst on record for lynchings, which were officially overlooked by the government.

Madame Walker joined a group of Black leaders who went to Washington that year to urge President Woodrow Wilson to enact legislation outlawing the lynchings. Wilson would not see them, saying only that he was too busy.

Undaunted, Madame Walker spoke out on the matter as she toured the country, and she encouraged her sales agents to speak out as well. The women sent telegrams to Wilson and other politicos. Eventually antilynching policies were enacted.

Madame Walker's death on May 25, 1919, was mourned throughout the Black community. After a funeral at the mansion, she was buried at Woodlawn Cemetery in the Bronx. For many among the throng of well-wishers who attended the services, she was a vision of what could be and a rejection of all that was negative about African people in this country.

She willed her house to daughter A'Lelia, with the understanding that when she died, she would in turn will it to the NAACP. A'Lelia died during the Depression, and with money hard to come by, the house was sold and the money given to the civil rights organization.

JOHN H. JOHNSON
ROLAND E. WOLSELEY

Success doesn't only require hard work of the elbow grease variety; skill and brainpower and a healthy dose of good fortune also count. With just five hundred dollars, John H. Johnson worked to build one of America's great publishing empires, the Johnson Publishing Company. He founded a host of magazines, including Ebony *and* Jet, *basing each on a successful formula in publishing. Working wisely, he fashioned* Ebony *into one of the most popular magazines in black America. Here is how he succeeded.*

The Johnson saga begins when he and his mother went from rural Arkansas to visit the Chicago World's Fair of 1933. Like many other visitors, they decided to stay, the elder Johnson having died when the future publisher was six. They lived on relief for a time. But, as *Fortune* reported it, in 1936 John Johnson, the student, gave a talk on "America's

Challenge to Youth" at the annual honors convocation at DuSable High School, and was heard by Harry H. Pace, president of the Supreme Life Insurance Company. Pace encouraged Johnson to go on to college. He liked to help ambitious and talented black youths; another he befriended was Paul Robeson. [Pace] gave young Johnson a part-time job. The future owner of *Ebony* attended the University of Chicago at the same time. At the insurance company offices he met various young black businessmen.

One day he was asked to work on the firm's house magazine. After becoming its editor he conceived the idea of a magazine containing articles of interest to the black population and about black citizens.

The new publisher mortgaged his mother's furniture for $500, so he could pay for his first direct mail advertising about his magazine, *Negro Digest*. That letter, sent in 1942, offered subscriptions at two dollars each and brought 3,000 subscribers. A first issue of 5,000 copies did not sell out. For one matter, distributors did not believe that the newsstands could dispose of a magazine of solely black appeal, a not unreasonable view in those days and still shared by many a newsstand operator. So Johnson persuaded thirty friends to ask for the magazines at the stands and thus create a demand. He then bought from the dealers copies not sold. But the second issue did not require such artificial sales stimulation.

Circulation climbed steadily, helped partly by publication of a series called "If I were a Negro," containing pieces by Mrs. Eleanor Roosevelt, Norman Thomas, Marshall Field, Edward G. Robinson, and other whites. Some issues hit as much as 150,000 circulation, a remarkable figure for any black periodical of serious type and unusual even for a white periodical of the kind.

His first venture a success, Johnson now was ready to consider another, a black version of *Life*. In 1945 *Ebony* was born with the intention of emphasizing the bright side of black life and reporting success by black people in almost any endeavor.

The value of imagination and of luck was proved by what happened in the magazine's early years, as A. James Reichley tells it in *Fortune*. Johnson wrote letters to presidents of various large corporations, seeking entrée so he could sell *Ebony* as an idea and as an advertising medium. Presidents of black firms of any sort were not, at that time, accepted by white corporation counterparts, so Johnson received no encouragement.

And black businessmen prepared to spend money on advertising were few and reluctant. Johnson's letter, however, did at last bring one appointment, this with Commander Eugene McDonald, president of Zenith, the radio set manufacturing firm. The commander, an Arctic explorer as well as a leading business executive, once had known Matthew Henson, the black explorer who worked closely with Admiral Peary in the 1909 journey to the North Pole. The publisher knew of the McDonald-Henson friendship and brought with him on his call a copy of the biography of Henson that had been autographed for the commander. As a result of this rapport, McDonald saw to it that the Zenith Corporation bought advertising space in *Ebony*. It became the Johnson firm's first big account and still is one of the major advertisers.

Ebony went through a temporary decline to rise to new strength, and the rest of the Johnson empire was built gradually by the launching of *Jet, Tan Confessions, Hue, Ebony International,* and *Copper Romance*. *Negro Digest* was temporarily discontinued, and the last three were not successful ventures, for varying reasons. Johnson's method always has been to put out magazines with formulas and formats that have been used, often successfully, by white publishers with primarily white readers. His *Negro Digest* was suggestive of the *Reader's Digest; Ebony* is like *Life; Jet* much like a long-defunct miniature magazine called *Quick; Tan Confessions* (now just *Tan)* has much in common with *True Confessions*. Even his later *Ebony International* was in concept like *Life International*. Such imitativeness is normal in the publications world. Walter Goodman, writing in 1968, noted that Johnson, in his first years in mass journalism, declined to become "all hot and bothered about the race questions." He quotes the publisher as saying that the monthly picture magazine would "mirror the happier side of Negro life." The big money earned by entertainment figures and the lavish lives of some of them were played up, for example. This philosophy *Ebony* has had until recent years; it was modified in the later 1960's from a somewhat Pollyanna-ish view to one of a more strident demand for the righting of wrongs against the race. The struggle for equality with rights finally has led Johnson to realize, apparently, that doing what whites strive to do in the world of business or entertainment perhaps is not the acme of accomplishment for people of the black race.

Perhaps because he smarted from criticism that he was too much concerned with making money and not enough interested in providing talented black writers with an outlet or with being an influence on the serious black citizens, Johnson revived *Negro Digest* just ten years after he had discontinued it. As the civil rights movement gained strength and the philosophy of black power, with its many interpretations and applications, could not be ignored by either whites or blacks, *Negro Digest* began carrying articles with such titles as "Negro Rights and the American Future." Promoting that magazine, which now began attacking white power as expressed through White Citizens' Councils and the like, the Johnson institutional advertising said:

> For more than 100 years, a native-bred philosophy not very different from Herr Hitler's has been preached in this country. With the upward thrust of the civil rights movement, this racist philosophy gains more strident voices. And these enemies of humanity are aided, perhaps unwittingly, by those whites who admonish Negro citizens to "go slow" and to be "more responsible" in the push for full and equal rights, as if Negroes had not gone slowly for a century and as if it is not precisely white America's disdain of its responsibility which has brought the nation to this terrible moment . . . The enemies of Negro rights are both numerous and powerful, and many of them heard the cadences of Herr Schicklgruber's marching spirit and are hypnotized.

By fall, 1965, *Ebony* was carrying articles by such outstanding liberal-minded blacks as Martin Luther King, Jr., Carl T. Rowan, and Kenneth Clark, in a number significantly devoted to the theme of "the white man's burden." Johnson began to give hard looks, often sympathetically, at the actions of rebellious black people, particularly youth. But the magazine did not lose its determination to tell success stories and it still speaks primarily to the middle-class black family which wants to be socially and financially successful.

HOW TO MAKE A BILLION
REGINALD LEWIS

Reginald Lewis (1942–93) built a billion-dollar business empire. At the time of his death, his personal fortune was estimated to be $400 million, making him the richest black man in U.S. history. Time magazine described him as "the first black businessman to gain full access to the giant pools of capital on Wall Street," and Forbes magazine listed him among the four hundred wealthiest Americans. The following story tells how he worked his way to the top, first by buying, managing, and selling a home sewing pattern company and then by buying a billion dollar international food company.

McCALL

Reginald F. Lewis was . . . the chairman of the board of the McCall Pattern Company. He had managed to acquire the company for $22.5 million without putting up a cent of his own money.

Established in 1870, McCall Pattern is one of the nation's oldest home sewing pattern companies. Its executive offices are located in Manhattan, New York City, while its production facilities are in Manhattan, Kansas. In 1984, the company had 580 employees.

At the time of Lewis's acquisition, McCall was making approximately 740 patterns for home sewing. Many of the patterns were based on drawings by such well-known designers as Willi Smith, Liz Claiborne, and Laura Ashley. McCall was then the second-largest company in the home sewing pattern business with 29.7 percent of the market. Its major competitors were Simplicity Patterns with 39.4 percent of the market, Butterick with 19.1 percent of the market and Vogue with 4.7 percent of the market.

The company had revenues of $51.9 million with income of about $6 million.

This was the company that Reginald Lewis took over and by the time he sold McCall three years later in June 1987, Lewis had piloted the company to the two most profitable years in its history. Under him, McCall's income doubled in 1985 and 1986, years the company earned

$12 and $14 million, respectively. And Lewis made himself a very wealthy man in the process.

Lewis ran McCall with a firm, yet innovative, hand. His style was an amalgam of Wall Street financial savvy, Harvard legal acumen and brassknuckle street toughness from East Baltimore.

"When he realized how people reacted when he turned up the heat a little bit, he used it," Kevin Wright says. "It was fun for me to watch this African-American intimidate these very senior, established Caucasian businessmen.

Ultimately though, Lewis was toughest on himself. Whatever his successes, he would invariably ask himself, "Why didn't I accomplish more?"

At home in his study, Lewis would indulge in a lifelong habit of rating his performance as well as those of his executives. Like a hard-to-please schoolmarm, Lewis would dole out A pluses, A's, B minuses, C pluses, and so on.

Nor was his personal life exempt from constant assessing and quantifying. He loved to talk about his tennis game and where it was at a given point in time, but Lewis couldn't resist the impulse to dispassionately analyze the components of his play, be it his net game, serve or return of service. He'd grade himself on his oft-used A to F scale.

Lewis would even rate novels or magazine pieces he was reading. His mind was constantly gauging, seeking ways to fine tune and perfect. It didn't matter that perfection was usually unattainable—the quest for perfection was its own reward.

Lewis actually spent little time at McCall's plush executive offices on the entire 10th floor of 230 Park Avenue in Manhattan. He had a two-office suite created for him there, but his favorite lair was his law firm at 99 Wall Street. He would go to McCall's offices periodically to make his presence felt, however, and to put the executives on notice that the new owner was watching.

Under Lewis's stewardship, McCall undertook a number of innovations that increased its profitability.

Because of the shrinking market for home sewing patterns, its former owners believed that operating profits and market share were critical to the company's survival.

However, under the Lewis regime, a new yardstick for measuring operations emerged: cash flow. Because of the highly leveraged nature of the acquisition, McCall had a sizable amount of debt to retire and thus Lewis devoted most of the company's efforts to conserving and generating cash. That meant many things would be done differently than in the past. For example, whereas bills had always been paid when they came in the door in the past, Lewis decreed that they would be paid within 30 days, freeing up accounts payable money for an additional month.

Under Lewis, McCall's assets were always operated with an eye toward generating additional cash. He came up with the idea of using idle presses not grinding out sewing patterns to make greeting cards. As a result, greeting cards became an important profit center for the company and eventually McCall began to export these cards to overseas markets.

Lewis also shelved McCall's pension plan and instituted a 401k program, freeing up an additional $648,000 in cash that was used to pay down debt.

Not all of Lewis's McCall innovations were financial in nature. He set out to change the home sewing pattern industry's less-than-glamorous image by having the company sign up celebrity licenses with, among others, Diahann Carroll, Shari Belafonte-Harper, and Brooke Shields. All three appeared in publicity photos wearing McCall designs.

One day Lewis was in his office at 99 Wall Street when Earle Angstadt called up and asked to see Lewis right away. Lewis rushed to Angstadt's office to see what earth-shattering crisis was afoot. An executive with McCall for 14 years and 17 years Lewis's senior, Angstadt tossed two huge bound catalogues on his desk, where they landed with a resounding thud. The catalogues had "Patterns at 89 Cents" stamped on their covers and were from Butterick, one of McCall's main competitors.

"They're running a sale," Angstadt said plaintively. "The last time this happened, we lost a fortune. We've got to meet their price." The logic behind Angstadt's argument hadn't quite registered with Lewis.

"Why?" Lewis asked. "Why do we have to meet their price?" Lewis and Angstadt argued heatedly over pricing, with Lewis adamantly opposed to meeting Butterick's price and Angstadt all for it. Exasperated, Lewis decided to defer to Angstadt's years of experience in the pattern business.

"Okay," he said. "I tried to talk you out of it and I don't think it makes sense. But if you think this is the way to go, this is the first time I've been confronted with the issue. We'll go with your judgment."

The move to match Butterick's prices was a disaster. McCall lost $2 million during the course of the promotion. Lewis was livid. He gave McCall's executives hell and vowed never to compete on price again.

The next time the pattern industry became involved in a price war, Lewis stuck to his guns. "No, we will not go on sale with those discounts," he said without hesitation. "I want to show these people that we're not here to basically cannibalize the industry. I'm not going to meet their sales price—we might lose a little money or not make as much, but I'm not going to lose money every time I sell a pattern. The price of a pattern is such a small price, let's raise prices some more."

Instead of lowering its prices to meet the competition, McCall followed Lewis's suggestion and raised its prices. The move led to a double-digit increase in net sales and a small drop in market share. Lewis was more than willing to accept the tradeoff. . . .

LEWIS WANTED A more permanent capital structure for McCall and had talked to a number of investment bankers about how to achieve that objective. Doing so would allow McCall to pay down some of its debt.

Lewis was told that to access public debt and public equity markets, McCall would have to have more than $5 million in equity on its balance sheet. So, Lewis began to explore various ways to raise equity above $5 million.

Selling the Manhattan, Kansas, facility to a third party, then leasing it would put millions on McCall's balance sheet. The problem was that a sale would lead to a significant capital gains tax, plus McCall would be subject to the whims of another entity. Lewis conceived of the idea of a sale-leaseback with himself as the other party. Why not sell the McCall plant to Reginald Lewis, then lease it back to the company? That's exactly what Lewis did on June 18, 1985. . . . [Lewis recalled:]

Business turned up and by December of 1986, two years after the deal, we had $23 million in cash on our balance sheet. That was about $20 million up from what we had when we acquired the company. And we had increased earnings from $6.5 million of operating to roughly $13 million or $14 million. The rest of fiscal year 1987 looked pretty good, also.

All these factors pushed Lewis in the direction of a sale. He decided that an auction would be the best way to sell McCall and retained First Boston to handle the auction. He then got together with McCall's executives to prepare an offering document. It was completed in January 1987, and sent to about 80 prospective buyers.

Lewis was leaving McCall a revitalized company. He had strengthened its balance sheet and led it to the two most profitable years in its history.

"Reg comes in and extracts the highest profit margins they've ever had," notes Howard Mackey, a client from Lewis's attorney days. "I always wondered how he managed to do that from a law firm at 99 Wall Street. That is some testament to the way he managed things and managed people."

The auction ended in June 1987 when a British textile manufacturer, the John Crowther Group, bought McCall for $65 million, nearly three times what Lewis paid for the firm three years earlier. [Lewis said:]

I signed the contract with Trevor Barker of Crowther to sell McCall for $65 million, right on the heels of our recapitalization for $19 million. I sold to the bidder we thought was best for the Company—a publicly-held British concern—at a price of roughly $63 million, plus $2 million for our expenses.

TLC [The Lewis Company] had also managed to keep the real estate, which was easily worth another $6 million to $10 million and we'd also gotten some other dividends, so all in all that was about $90 million on our original investment of $1 million, and it was all in cash. And not only that, we felt that we were leaving the Company in excellent shape because the new buyer was putting up $30 million and had some plans for what he wanted to do with it. I was feeling pretty good.

When Lewis told one of McCall's directors, Lee Archer, about the price that had been paid for McCall, Archer actually laughed out loud. "What idiot would pay us $65 million for a company when it's in the record that we only paid $22.5 million," Archer asked incredulously. Lewis just smiled broadly.

TLC BEATRICE

On the 24th of June, Salomon Bros. vice president Graham Cunningham picked up the telephone and called the offices of TLC Group at 99 Wall Street. Salomon was handling the sale of Beatrice for KKR [Kohlberg, Kravis, Roberts & Co.]. "We have received from your group an offer to buy Beatrice International for $950 million," Cunningham said. "We have a small problem—nobody knows who the hell you are!"

Cunningham came over half an hour later to meet with Lewis. Cunningham was brought up to speed on the TLC Group and what it had accomplished: specifically, Lewis's acquisition and sale of McCall.

Lewis derived pleasure from the fact no one expected a black man to be going after a two-billion dollar, international food company. He had paid his dues and had played the game by the rules and, miraculously, found they hadn't been changed in mid-game. Nor did he expect them to, because a central tenet of his was that hard work and dedication invariably take a person where he or she wants to go. Lewis had traveled a road bumpier than that traversed by his white compatriots, but despite that, he'd made it to his destination anyway. [Lewis recalled:]

Now, in terms of the bid process itself, I pretty much felt that the price was around $950 million. We bid $950 million to be preemptive. But I was nervous about it. I was nervous because a lot of the operating units had sizable minority stakeholders, meaning you couldn't automatically bring the cash back into the United States. If the market for assets fell, then I would be stuck with a high-cost debt structure in a business that was generating all this cash out of the country.

We explored a number of different alternative financing structures, but none of them could be implemented under the time constraints we had for putting the entire deal together. Essentially, the strategy that evolved was very simple: We would bid $950 million or so and between the time of signing the contract and closing the deal, we would sell off at least three businesses for an aggregate price of $400 million. Then immediately after the closing, we would decide which businesses we wanted to keep and which businesses we wanted to sell. By then we would have a lot more information about them, because I would have had a chance to get out into the field and find out what was going on.

The aim was to retain a core group of businesses that had some synergies and would improve operating results even as we reduced expenses. That was basically the operating strategy, and it was a sound strategy, because we were in effect piggy-backing on the auction work that Morgan Stanley and Salomon had already done. They had effectively heated up the market for sales of pieces of the business. So while the fact that there was an auction was a negative from the standpoint that you knew you were going to pay a high price, it was a positive from the standpoint that the market for the various assets was going to be well heated. And that's the way we looked at it.

Our bid went in. Word came out that KKR was going with somebody else. Ackerman even called and said, "Well, we got close." I said, "Peter, I don't even want to hear that. Call people— let's create a climate where we can get it done." There was about a 48-hour period where we really turned up the juice and placed a number of phone calls to key decision makers at Beatrice and KKR. To this day, I think KKR knew we were going to have the highest bid and was going to go with us all along, but they created doubt in our minds so that we effectively topped our own bid and increased it to $985 million. But that ultimately took it.

We signed a definitive agreement on August 6, 1987.

Reginald Lewis had done it. He'd managed to pull off a deal so large he could hardly believe it himself. Not only that, but the Beatrice acquisition was the largest offshore leveraged buyout that had been accomplished up to that point. Lewis had worked incredibly hard and very diligently for this moment, and it was every bit as sweet as he fantasized it would be.

The smiling faces of his colleagues flashed before his eyes as though in a dream sequence and he saw hands thrusting toward him to pump his. Everything had an air of unreality about. People who thought Lewis never had any fun should get to know the euphoria that accompanies buying a billion-dollar company. And the thrill and the tremendous surge of accomplishment and pride were magnified three-fold for Lewis, because he had overcome obstacles and impediments that white financiers would never encounter and might not surmount if they did.

Lewis had a secret code that he shared with his wife whenever he accomplished something particularly noteworthy: He would sing the tune, "Raindrops Keep Falling on My Head." Lewis picked up the phone on his desk and, praying the line wouldn't be busy, dialed the villa in the South of France where his family was on vacation and waiting for him to join them. When Loida Lewis picked up, Lewis simply said, "Raindrops, Loida, raindrops."

"Darling, you did it!" Loida Lewis exclaimed excitedly.

FOR THOSE WHO thought Lewis had depleted his bag of tricks when he bought TLC Beatrice, Lewis had another one: He showed them he was one hell of an operator, too. Lewis had done it once with McCall, but that was akin to navigating a yacht, whereas Beatrice was more like the Queen Elizabeth II. This time, Lewis was strutting his stuff on an international stage. From his point of view, though, nothing really had changed. A billion-dollar company could be guided by the same princi ples that worked with a $51.9-million firm like McCall. You just had to do your homework, work hard, and have good managers working for you.

Lewis's divestiture sales had transformed TLC Beatrice International Holdings, Inc. into an international food company whose operations are principally in Europe and are divided into two segments: food distribution and grocery products.

TLC Beatrice is the largest wholesale distributor of food and grocery products to supermarkets in the Paris metropolitan area, primarily through 418 stores operating under the Franprix name. TLC Beatrice franchises 383 of the stores and owns 35. The company also distributes food and grocery products in and around Paris through 95 stores operating under the LeaderPrice name. Of these, 49 are owned by TLC Beatrice and 46 are franchises.

TLC Beatrice's grocery products segment is a major marketer and manufacturer of ice cream in Europe. These products are marketed under well-known local brand names: Premier in Denmark; Artic in France and Belgium; Artigel in Germany; Sanson in Italy; Kalise in the Canary Islands; and La Menorquina in Spain and Portugal. TLC Beatrice is the No. 1 maker of potato chips and snacks in Ireland, under the Tayto and King brand names, among others. Finally, TLC Beatrice's grocery products segment operates soft drink bottling plants located in the Netherlands, Belgium, and Thailand.

When Lewis began divesting himself of TLC Beatrice's operating units in Australia, Latin America, and other international locations, many observers viewed him as a shrewd, callous LBO specialist who would break TLC Beatrice into small pieces, sell them, and enrich himself in the process. Sure Lewis had run McCall, the pundits said, but now he was at the helm of a billion-dollar, multinational firm with far-flung operations.

That Lewis knew little about the food distribution and manufacturing business was no handicap from his point of view. Lewis just took a deep breath and immersed himself in the challenge of running his new business. As at McCall, it was important that management share the Chairman's vision. So Lewis took to the air, visiting his far-flung operating units regularly. Local managers were probably surprised by their omnipresent new boss and his boundless curiosity about their phase of his business.

For one thing, TLC Beatrice would be much more decentralized than McCall had been, giving more autonomy to local managers. The flip side of that was Lewis set higher performance standards than most of his managers were accustomed to.

Lewis taught himself the food business just like he taught himself the home sewing pattern business. The really significant difference this time was that he was spending incredible amounts of time on travel.

It started right after he moved his family to Paris in 1988. On Wednesday, October 12, 1988, Lewis left his apartment at 7:15 A.M. and was on a private jet headed out of Le Bourget Airport by 8 A.M. By 9:30 A.M., Lewis was in Esbjerg, Denmark to meet with a manufacturing manager of one of his operating units, and to take a tour of the plant.

He left Denmark at 11:30 A.M. for a 12:15 ETA in Dortmund, West Germany to meet with some local managers there and to tour another of

TLC Beatrice's plants. At 2:15 P.M., Lewis was back on the jet, where he had lunch as he flew to Paris. This was not an unusual itinerary. In seven hours, Lewis had been to three countries before returning to Paris. Granted, European countries are close to one another, but even continual short-distance commuter hops in the United States take their toll after a while.

On December 6, 1988 at 7 A.M. Paris time, Lewis flew to Zurich to pick up two business associates. After a 10-minute stop in Zurich, Lewis jetted back to France, where he touched down at Strasbourg Airport at 8:30 A.M. in order to tour the headquarters and warehouse of the SES supermarket chain, a TLC Beatrice business in northeastern France that Lewis eventually sold.

At 2:30 P.M., Lewis flew back to Zurich to drop off his passengers, then flew into Paris at 4 P.M. After a half hour layover to refuel, there was a flight back to Strasbourg to pick up TLC Beatrice President Bill Mowry and TLC France executive Daniel Jux. The men flew to Heathrow Airport in London where Lewis attended a business meeting before flying back to Paris at 7:45 P.M.

The return flight marked the end of a grueling 13$^1/_2$ hour day that saw Lewis make 15 takeoffs and landings in the course of hopscotching between three countries.

The following day, Lewis's 46th birthday, he departed from Paris at 8:30 A.M. headed toward Brussels Airport, in order to visit a unit of TLC Beatrice's Artic ice cream division. At 1:15 P.M., the Chairman and CEO of TLC Beatrice was leaving Brussels Airport on the flight path that would take him to Dublin Airport, so he could visit the Tayto potato chip company in Ireland.

Lewis was back in Le Bourget Airport in Paris by 5:15 P.M. Taking it relatively easy on his birthday, Lewis had only worked a 10-hour day.

AMBITIOUS
ANDY RAZAF

Jealousy and envy are a waste of energy and may even hold a person back. We must work our hardest to fulfill our own purpose in life.

A cow looked at a bird and said:
"Why can't I be like him?
I'd give up anything to fly,
And perch up on a limb."
The bird gazed at the cow and sighed:
"Life would be smooth as silk
If I could only moo like you,
And make delicious milk."

A horse, in envy, watched a bee,
And whined: "It may sound funny,
But how I wish I were like you,
So I, too, could make honey."

"To be a horse I'd give my all,"
Replied the mournful bee:
"Now how could one so strong and tall
Want to be small like me?"

A busy ant who overheard,
Just smiled and shook his head:
But they kept on with their complaints
Till finally he said:
"Life has a purpose for us all,
But none of us go far
Unless we do our best to be
The best of what we are!"

❦

Luck is a matter of preparation meeting opportunity.

—*Oprah Winfrey*

❦

TENACITY

If a hailstorm of hard times hits Main Street U.S.A., a twister roars through the black neighborhood. When crime soars, unemployment rises, or disease strikes, African Americans are certain to bear the brunt of it all. But no group has proven tougher and more resilient in facing some of society's biggest dilemmas than black folks. That's because a principle component of the black experience is tenacity.

Tenacious people are nearly impossible to defeat, turn down, or turn around—they're as unyielding as the day is long. Which is a good thing. Much of human progress has depended on tenacity, an essential ingredient in any formula for success. Without tenacity, much that we now take for granted would have been left undiscovered or undone.

There are two basic types of tenacious people: bit players on the world stage, who struggle to survive and lead lives of quiet dignity; and movers and shakers—those key players who bring about momentous change whether on the battlefield, in a laboratory, or at a meeting of world leaders.

Black America has produced its share of both types. Each of them is represented in this chapter.

Here you will find the words of strugglers (the oral testimony of former slave Katie Rowe), poems of persistence (Maya Angelou's "Still I Rise"), and the confessions of world-beaters (athletes LeRoy "Satchel" Paige, Michael Jordan, and Wilma Rudolph).

Tenacity is a central theme in an excerpt from a movie journal by Spike Lee in which he recalls striving to make his first big feature film. The tenacity of civil rights demonstrators is recaptured here in the words of Fannie Lou Hamer, Sheyann Webb, and in a freedom song, "Keep Your Eyes on the Prize."

Other pieces include the story of a boy who struggles to build something for himself (Dorothy West's "The Cart"), a poem of endurance and motherlove by Langston Hughes ("Mother to Son"), a Vietnam war prisoner's harrowing story of survival (recorded by Wallace Terry) and Alex Haley's 12-year research project that resulted in "Roots," the saga that enthralled America and generated interest in family heritage among millions.

By teaching children lessons about the tenacity of black folks, by standing behind them as they remain steadfast, and by helping their efforts to improve themselves as they persist, we will encourage in them survival techniques. This lesson is among the most useful they can learn.

I have learned to take "no" as a vitamin.

—*Suzanne De Passe*

THE FORTY-TWO-YEAR-OLD ROOKIE
LEROY (SATCHEL) PAIGE

The legendary Satchel Paige was forty-two years old when he became a rookie in the American League—a testament to racial discrimination in sports. A star in the Negro Baseball Leagues, he had already been pitching twenty-four years by the time he became the first black pitcher—and the oldest rookie—in the major leagues. He pitched until he was fifty-nine years old. Inducted into the Baseball Hall of Fame in 1971, Satchel was a study in determination. This story appears in his autobiography, Maybe I'll Pitch Forever.

In the 1924 season, I won about thirty games. I lost once. That was the start of a long string of winning streaks for me. I don't know which one was the longest. They were all long. I went by the years without losing a game.

By the next year, every team around town wanted me. And the best team was the team I was on.

But I still was a poor man. I still lived in that shotgun house on South Franklin and we still had to struggle to get money for all the food we needed. That don't sit well when you've found out there is dancing and hunting and fishing, with the fine rods and reels and all the equipment.

That was the fishing I wanted.

So you just keep scratching and trying to get a dollar. Sometimes you do and sometimes you don't. Sometimes you forget you got to go hungry. Sometimes you forget how you can't buy clothes. Sometimes you forget, but usually you don't.

I didn't forget and the more times I remembered how poor I was, the more I wanted to have something better. And the only way I knew how to get something better was with pitching.

That meant I had to get a professional ball club interested in me.

I pitched harder. About halfway through the 1926 season I had me a twenty-five game winning streak going. I was going for number twenty-six when suddenly it looked like that winning streak was going to go up in smoke.

I was pitching for the Down the Bay Boys and we were playing some other Mobile semi-pro club. I slid through the first eight innings of the game without any trouble. The first two guys up in the ninth also were easy outs. Then the troubles began. My infield fell apart.

There were three straight errors and the other team had the bases loaded. Since I only had a one to nothing lead, a hit would tie the game or lose it for me.

I was burning. I walked off the mound and kicked the dirt. I was so mad my stomach felt it. Then I heard the crowd. They sounded like someone was twisting their tail. They were booing to beat all getout, not really booing me but just booing.

Hearing that booing made me even madder.

Somebody was going to have to be showed up for that.

I looked around and then I waved in my outfielders. When they got in around me, I said, "Sit down there on the grass right behind me. I'm pitching this last guy without an outfield."

"What?" one of them said.

The other two started screaming, too. You'd have thought I'd declared war on the government.

But finally I talked them into sitting down.

The crowd went crazy. They weren't booing now. They were watching me and only me.

I heard the roar all around. Everybody was yelling. I took my time, then pumped back and forth and threw.

It was strike one, but you couldn't hear the umpire for all the yelling. He just waved his arm.

He waved strike two and you couldn't even hear yourself.

Back I leaned and then I threw. The batter swung but my quickie hopped right over the wood into the catcher's glove.

The crowd really went crazy. You wouldn't think a few hundred could make that much noise. But they did.

My outfielders danced around like they'd sat on hot coals.

My infielders just walked off the field, but not before I wagged my nose at them.

I GOT TO Cleveland on July 7, 1948. That was my forty-second birthday and I was about to get me the best birthday present I'd ever had. Cleveland Indians owner Bill Veeck told me to go in the locker room and get on a uniform while he was getting Lou Boudreau, the Indians' manager.

I didn't feel anything. I was just numb, I guess.

When I got out on the field, Lou Boudreau was there in his uniform. Mr. Veeck and Abe Saperstein were there, too.

"Can you still throw like you used to?" Mr. Lou asked me.

"I got as fast a ball as anybody pitchin' now, but I got to admit it's not half as fast as it used to be. But I can still pitch it where I want to."

"Can you do that against major leaguers?" Mr. Lou asked.

"Don't you worry about that. The plate's the same size up here."

Mr. Lou just grinned.

"Why don't you catch Satch for about ten minutes and then bat against him," Mr. Veeck told Mr. Lou.

Mr. Lou nodded.

"Maybe you want to warm up first, Satch?" Mr. Lou asked me.

"Yeah, I'd like that."

"Why don't you take a lap around the gravel track, maybe run about fifty paces and then walk fifty like my boys do?"

I looked around that big ball park. But if that was what Mr. Lou wanted me to do, I'd try it. I ran about seventy-five yards and that ball park looked bigger than ever. I stopped and went back.

"You know, Mr. Lou, this is an awful big ball park," I said. "I guess I just won't run after all."

"You think you're warmed up enough?" he asked me.

"I sure am."

Mr. Lou got him a catcher's mitt and went behind the plate. I just tossed a couple real easy and then I started firing. I wasn't thinking. I wasn't trying to get in the majors. I wasn't doing anything except just pitching, like I'd always done.

That was the one thing I really knew how to do.

Finally, Mr. Lou told me I'd thrown enough and I walked up to home plate.

"That's some control, Satch," he told me. "You didn't miss the strike zone more'n four times out of fifty. Those that missed were only an inch or two off the plate, too. Let's see if you can do that good when I try hitting against you now."

"You want me to shag the balls, Lou?" Mr. Veeck said.

"If you want to," Mr. Lou answered. "Get over in right field. After seeing Satch's stuff, I don't think I'm going to pull many balls to left."

He didn't either. After we were done, he told me to go on in the clubhouse. When I walked away, Mr. Lou and Mr. Veeck were up close, real close, jawing away like everything.

A few minutes later Mr. Veeck came in the locker room.

"Lou thinks you can help the club," he told me. "Let's go down to the office and sign a contract."

It was just like that. Just that easy. As easy as it'd been for me to pitch all those years.

I was in the major leagues. The old man'd made it.

I signed that contract real quick. I was going to get a year's salary for only a half-year of ball.

After I'd signed up, Mr. Veeck grinned.

"Satch," he told me, "I'm just sorry you didn't come up in your prime. You'd have been one of the greatest right-handers baseball has ever known if you had."

BEFORE WE LIKED MIKE

MICHAEL JORDAN GETS CUT FROM THE HIGH SCHOOL TEAM

BOB GREENE

Natural talent does not always suffice. To excel, one must work extra hard. And transcending the pack takes unwavering commitment.

Once upon a time, Michael Jordan was merely a "good" basketball player. But he was not good enough to play on the high school varsity team. Coach Clifton "Pop" Herring cut the skinny, five foot ten inch sophomore from the team. Humiliated, Jordan once was reduced to handing out towels to the Laney High team. He got to travel with them only because the student manager was sick. Jordan finally went on to make basketball history in college, international tournaments, the Olympics, and the National Basketball Association. But only because he worked harder than ever on his skills and was supremely dedicated to winning. Here Jordan lets down his guard with author Bob Greene.

"I went to my room and I closed the door and I cried," Michael Jordan said. "For a while I couldn't stop. Even though there was no one else home at the time, I kept the door shut. It was important to me that no one hear me or see me."

We were sitting alone together in the Stadium one late-November night in those hours before the doors to the outside world opened up. I had been thinking a lot about the story of him being cut. Now his likeness and his electronic image were everywhere; sometimes it seemed as if he was as much logo as he was human. I kept wondering how it must have affected him at the time it happened.

We talked about it that night, and it turned out to be the first of many long conversations. Soon I would come to value these conversations every bit as much as I valued the games; the conversations, I know now, will last in my memory well beyond the final scores of the basketball contests. This night was the first, though, and initially I was surprised that Jordan remembered every detail of something that had happened to him long ago. But then I understood: Of course he remembered. How could he not? Back then he didn't know that someday he was going to be Michael Jordan. Back then, all he wanted was the chance to play with the others.

"For about two weeks, every boy who had tried out for the basketball team knew what day the cut list was going to go up," he said. "We knew that it was going to be posted in the gym. In the morning.

"So that morning we all went in there, and the list was up. I had a friend—his name was Leroy Smith—and we went in to look at the list together.

"We stood there and looked for our names. If your name was on the list, you were still on the team. If your name wasn't on the list, you were cut. Leroy's name was on the list. He made it. Mine wasn't on the list."

As we talked, other members of the Chicago Bulls walked past us, arriving at the Stadium. Scottie Pippen came by, and then Horace Grant, and then John Paxson and Bill Cartwright. Jordan's voice was soft, and he nodded hello to each of them and continued with his recollections. The juxtaposition of his words and this setting—an NBA arena on game night—was something you could never invent.

"I looked and looked for my name," he said. "It was almost as if I thought that if I didn't stop looking, it would be there."

I asked him if the list had been in descending order of talent. Were the best players at the top of the list, with the marginal players at the bottom?

"No," he said, as if envisioning the list anew. "It was alphabetical. I looked at the H's, and the I's, and the J's, and the K's, and I wasn't there, and I went back up and started over again. But I wasn't there.

"I went through the day numb. I sat through my classes. I had to wait until after school to go home. That's when I hurried to my house and I closed the door of my room and I cried so hard. It was all I wanted—to play on that team.

"My mother was at work, so I waited until she got home, and then I told her. She knew before I said anything that something was wrong, and I told her that I had been cut from the team. When you tell your mom something like that the tears start again, and the two of you have an aftercry together."

I asked him if he had stayed away from the varsity team that whole

year. He said no; as the regular season was wrapping up, he said, he
went back, but not to request a tryout.

"At the end of the season, I worked up the nerve to ask the coach if I
could ride along on the bus with the team to the district tournament," he
said. "I just wanted to watch the others.

"The coach told me no. But I asked again, and he said I could come.
But when we got to the tournament gym, he said he didn't know if I
could go in. He told me that the only way I could go in was to carry the
players' uniforms.

"So that's what I did. I walked into the building carrying the uniforms for the players who had made the team. What made me feel the
worst about that was that my parents had come to watch the tournament, and when they saw me walking in carrying the uniforms, they
thought I was being given a chance to play.

"That's what hurt me. They thought I was being given a chance. But
I was just carrying the clothes for the others."

There can't be many professional athletes in any sport who were cut
from their high school teams. The men who make it to the pros have
always been the best on every playground, the best in every class, the
best in every school. The men who make it to the pros don't go through
things like that.

"It's okay, though," Jordan said. "It's probably good that it happened."

"Good?" I said.

"I think so," he said. Soon it would be game time in the Stadium, to
that constant soundtrack of shattering, overwhelming, adoring noise.

"It was good because it made me know what disappointment felt like.
And I knew that I didn't want to have that feeling ever again."

THE WORLD'S FASTEST WOMAN
WILMA RUDOLPH

Wilma Rudolph was born almost two months too early, weighing only four and a half pounds. She eventually overcame the crippling effects of a childhood racked by disease to become the first American woman to win three gold medals in track and field at a single Oympiad: the 100-meter dash, the 200-meter dash, and the 400-meter relay at the 1960 Summer Olympic Games in Rome.* Her story—made into a television movie—is testimony that Olympian dreams are not too big for anyone. Tenacity and determination can make a vital difference.

I was safe by the time I was twelve, but it was hard for me to remember all of those terrible days before then. I had a series of childhood illnesses. It started off as scarlet fever and from there it was polio.

My father was the one who sort of babied me and was sympathetic. He was a determined person. He had to be. There were twenty-two children. I am the twentieth. My mother was the one who made me work, made me believe that one day it would be possible for me to walk without braces.

They would take me to a doctor at Meharry Medical College in Nashville, Tennessee, and when we got back home, they would show everybody the massages and exercises that I did when I was in the hospital. It got to the point where everybody could basically share in the exercises, so we used to make a game out of it. When my parents were gone, I would take the braces off and walk around. I think by doing that I probably walked a lot sooner than I would have.

I didn't like any of my friends. Your peers are always the worst. They tease you or if you are playing a game, nobody wants to hold your hand because you have a brace on. I used to hate that. I think my way of getting back at them was through a sport. That was also a form of motivation and determination.

Around nine the braces came off and now I can't remember which leg I wore my braces on. The next thing I knew I was normal. I was doing

---

* Alice Coachman was the first black American woman to win an Olympic gold medal. She won the high jump in 1948 at the Summer Games in London.

everything that everyone else could do. Once I discovered I could run, I spent all of my extra time running.

I was six feet, eighty-nine pounds, and I wanted to be the greatest basketball player that ever came through my tiny high school. My coach said the way I buzzed around so irritated him that he called me "Mosquito." As I grew older, they dropped the first portion and everybody I know calls me "Skeeter."

When the basketball season is over kids are always looking for another sport. You don't want to go home in the afternoon to do chores. So there was my motivation for track and field.

[In college] our coach always protected us. Places he knew we could not use the bathroom, he didn't take us. It made it easier to accomplish something, to be proud and not have to mix any world affairs that we couldn't solve with the accomplishment.

Coming from this small Southern town, I was always determined that I was never going to stay there and not see the rest of the world. When I went to my first Olympics in Melbourne, Australia [1956], I was a green sixteen-year-old, innocent and naive.

After winning the bronze medal in the 4 × 100 relay, the most difficult thing was going back and getting very angry inside about how people perceived black people where I lived. That's when you rebel.

I worked very hard for the next four years. In Rome, I was self-motivated, motivated by my family. It took sheer determination to be able to run a hundred yards and remember all of the mechanics that go along with it. It takes steady nerves and being a fighter to stay out there.

From the moment you walk into the stadium, you block out everything and everybody, until you get the command to start. I could only hear the cheers after the race was over.

After 1960, of course, everything changed. When I got back from the Olympics, my hometown, which had never been integrated, decided to have a parade for me. I told them that I could not come to a parade that would be segregated. So, I sort of broke that barrier in my hometown. I probably did everything that I wasn't supposed to do, but it was to pave the way for other blacks in the town.

Sometimes it takes years to really grasp what has happened to your life. What do you do after you are world-famous and nineteen or twenty and you have sat with prime ministers, kings and queens, the Pope?

What do you do after that? Do you go back home and take a job? What do you do to keep your sanity? You come back to the real world.

I wanted to make more money than I knew other women made. But there was no place for a black woman to make money in the world of advertising and marketing. We know why.

If you listen to everybody else you will feel sorry for yourself, because they will say, "If you had been white, you would have been a millionaire." What kind of answer do you expect me to give you? I am not white. I am a black woman and that is the bottom line.

When I was going through my transition of being famous, I used to ask God, why was I here? what was my purpose? Surely, it wasn't just to win three gold medals. There has to be more to this life than that.

I would be very disappointed if I were only remembered as a runner because I feel that my contribution to the youth of America has far exceeded the woman who was the Olympic champion. The challenge is still there.

In 1981, Wilma Rudolph started her own nonprofit foundation for training young athletes. She died of brain cancer on November 12, 1994. She was fifty-four.

A BULL BY THE HORNS

BILL PICKETT AND LITTLE BEANS

CECIL JOHNSON

Legendary cowboy Bill Pickett invented the rodeo sport of bulldogging, which involves grabbing a steer by its horns and stunning it into submission by biting the steer's upper lip. In 1908, Pickett rode into a Mexico City bullring to battle a killer bull known as Little Beans. The meeting, set to verse, showed Pickett's steely resolve. That day, the fierce bull met his match.

He chose to wear his crimson shirt
Though bulls they say see red,
And blood is also of that hue
When on the sand it's shed.
Bill Pickett's blood they hoped would flow,
That crowd that wished him dead.

He rode into that angry place
His hat cocked to the right,
Mounted on a chestnut steed
Swift Spradley his delight,
And out to greet them charged the bull
Bill Pickett came to fight.

Not fight him like a matador
With blood red cape and sword,
But dog him like a longhorned steer
Or at least stay aboard
The beast for five minutes
Without his getting gored.

It was a contest made in Hell,
Blood thirst would drink its fill,
They knew no cowboy from the north
Possessed the guts or skill
To dominate a fighting bull
That had been bred to kill.

Into that ring of looming death
Came bull and man and horse,
The bet was set, the clock was wound
No time left for discourse,
Just man and beasts and bloody fate,
Too late to show remorse.

The crowd was screaming for his death,
They raised their voices high,

For he had mocked the thing they loved,
And so he had to die.

For all people have a thing they love,
A thing with which their pride
Their sense of being who they are
Is much identified;
Bullfighting was that thing for them
Who in that bullring cried:

"No man can hold a brave bull's horns,
No fool for gold and glory
Could jump onto a brave bull's hump
And live to tell the story."

The bull rushed forth with lowered head
Took aim at Spradley's rear
But the little horse stepped to the side
Just as the horns came near,
So close and yet not close enough
For Pickett to adhere.

Three times the raging Little Beans
(That was the name they cried)
Lunged at horse and rider;
Each time he was denied,
But Pickett could not climb aboard
The spotted killer's hide.

The cowboy had to make a choice,
And yet no choice had he,
To get upon the Little Beans
He had to let Spradley
Be savaged by the cruel horns;
Another way he couldn't see.

He had to watch a thing he loved
Endure that awful fate,
To grace that altar with his blood,
A sacrifice to hate.

With fierce resolve the killer bull
Gathered speed and vaulted;
Spradley tried to move away,
But Pickett held him halted
In the path of the bull's wrath,
Then Pickett somersaulted.

Upon the hump with his strong hands
Those gore-smeared horns he squeezed,
Those needle-sharp and slippery horns
His Spradley's blood had greased;
He held on as the big bull ran
And took him where it pleased.

It took him left, it took him right,
It slammed him on the walls;
It took him east, it took him west,
As if it heard the bawls
Of the crowd in the arena
With its "Death to Pickett" calls.

For he had mocked the thing they loved,
Or so they'd heard it said;
He'd thumbed his nose at their great sport
And so they wished him dead.

"No man can grab a brave, brave bull
For gold and for his glory;
No fool can ride a fighting bull
And live to tell the story."

Around and around ran bull and man,
The cowboy held on fast,
And when the bull came to a stop
The arena was aghast;
Pickett jumped between the horns
And squeezed that neck so vast.

The cowboy squeezed with all his strength
To take the breath away.
He pressed his knees against the nose,
The bull began to sway,
He rocked him left, he rocked him right,
He thought he'd won the day.

That Little Beans so brave and mean
Stood statue still and muzzled,
While in the stands the Mexicans
Looked at each other puzzled;
No man could hold a killer bull . . .
They were totally bumfuzzled.

No man could choke a brave bull down
For money or for glory,
No man could mock their bullfighting
And live to tell the story.

It wasn't Pickett who had bet or scoffed at bullfighting.
His boss, of course, had done all that,
But it was Pickett in the ring,
And it was for Bill Pickett's death the crowd did sing.

The Dusky Demon held his pose
Waiting for the clock;
Then someone in that angry mob
Threw and hit him with a rock.
Other things came flying

Pelting, pounding man and bull,
Then came that awful shock.

The beer bottle that broke his ribs
Made Pickett lose his grip,
And that was all the bull needed
To start another trip
Around the sundrenched bullring
At a much faster clip.

The crowd was yelling for him
To shake Bill off and gore him
To lift him up and toss him high
And let his blood and entrails fly,
For he had mocked the thing they love,
And so he had to die.

Although Bill Pickett lost his hold,
He did not die that day;
Cowboys came and matadors
And helped him get away;
His little horse named Spradley
Survived his goring in the fray.

One man did hold a brave bull's horns
And earned a share of glory.
Bill Pickett rode a killer bull
And lived to tell the story.

ᐇᕽ

It must be borne in mind . . . that the tragedy in life does not lie in not reaching your goal. The tragedy lies in having no goal to reach. It isn't a calamity not to die with dreams unfulfilled, but it is a calamity not to dream . . . It is not a disgrace not to reach the stars, but it is a disgrace to have no stars to reach for. Not failure, but low aim is the sin.

—*Benjamin Mays*

ᐇᕽ

SPIKE'S GOTTA DO IT
SPIKE LEE

Spike Lee wrote, directed, and co-starred in his first feature film, She's Gotta Have It, *which was shot on location in Brooklyn on a shoestring budget of $175,000. Released in 1986, the film grossed $8 million at the box office, launching Lee's career. The success of this independent black-and-white film stems from Lee's tenacity. The following excerpts from his film journal reveal how Lee persevered to get his ideas onto the big screen.*

FEBRUARY 1, 1985

I have to have at least $75,000 in the bank when we start. . . . There are no guarantees in the film industry. People should hope to regain their investments, that's the first step. Hope you don't lose your shirt.

I will not give up casting or final cut for the investors. That's bottom line. If they can't live with that, FORGET IT.

This development with AFI has really sobered me up quick. *She's Gotta Have It* is far from being a lock. I don't have the money so I don't have a picture. Another thing, the actors do not need to know about the financial situation. It's hard enough just trying to act.

FEBRUARY 18, 1985

IDEA. The scene where Jamie and Nola meet should be a semi-chase scene. Jamie is following her, then he loses her. He walks then she ends up following him. He stops and says, "Are you following me?" Nola: "You were following me." "Oh, I was. I was struck by your appearance. I know it sounds corny but if I didn't follow you I know I might not ever see you again." Nola: "Was it worth it?" Jamie: "Don't know yet. What's your name?" Nola: "Nola." Jamie: "Nola, I like you. Would you care to spend some time with me? Maybe a movie or something?" A smile covers his face. Jamie: "You will? Solid."

APRIL 1, 1985

It's becoming apparent that these people I've sent the scripts to won't give me the money. I'm gonna have to raise the money my self with a limited partnership. I have to do it myself, with anybody who will help. It will be a miracle if I can raise the money to shoot in July. One thing, though, I will not become discouraged, I will keep on pushing. I might have to find a job that pays something in the meantime.

APRIL 12, 1985

IDEA. The first time the character of Mars Blackmon is introduced we want to have close-ups of

1. Nike sneakers with fat laces
2. earring
3. gold medallion
4. name belt buckle
5. part in hair
6. Cazals glasses

All of this stuff will be the OFFICIAL B-BOY ATTIRE.

APRIL 25, 1985

In a couple of days the month of May will be here and after that June. Time is moving fast and summer is fast approaching. Either people are gonna get behind me or they won't. It's as simple as that. It's put-up-or-shut-up time. I've just got to get that $53,180 minus my $12,100 which is $41,080, to get it in the can. That's the most important thing, to get it in the can, so I can edit and at least have something to show to people.

MAY 20, 1985

Went to see Tracy Camilla Johns in *Ceremonies in Dark Old Men*. It was good, I could tell it wasn't one of their best performances though, it was a little flat. Tracy was good in her role and she definitely has presence. I also saw another brother, Ruben Hudson, who could definitely read for Greer Childs. The guy is good plus he can act. Tracy says they have grown very close so he'll definitely be down. Then on top of that I ran into another one of Tracy's friends, a costume designer, his name is John Reefer. It was a good, good day yesterday.

JULY 6, 1985

Yesterday was the first official day of shooting. We shot the dog scene. It went well. Earl Smith, Brian Copeland and Erwin Wilson didn't show but we had backup. We shot it in the Bijou at NYU. We have been hit by unexpected expenses—right now I can't worry about that. I pray to God that the $100s come in that we so desperately need.

I'm confident and I will be ready.

Today at the school we finalized the clothes people will wear. It really wasn't the time to work on scenes—we have done that. Monday we start to shoot and I'm getting ready, I can't even think about the money part. We have had seventeen or eighteen people pledge $100, but we are still waiting by the mailbox. I feel good.

Tomorrow we will look at the dance scene in its entirety. Then Monday morning we shoot. I do not foresee any big problems. It's a light day. Maybe transporting people will be a problem but it shouldn't be if we are coordinated.

Right now I'm gonna read the script again.

JULY 20, 1985

All praises due, at 7:40 P.M. the 20th of July in the year of our Lord 1985 we completed principal photography on *She's Gotta Have It*. That's it, done. The whole day was festive. Mr. Strawder, the owner of the Ferry Bank Restaurant, sent us three bottles of champagne. Monty had everybody fired up.

AUGUST 12, 1985

Wednesday morning I start to cut. I will cut six days a week. I'll take Sundays off to go watch football at Uncle Cliff's house. Working six days a week I should have a cut (rough) out by the beginning of

October, from there it's on to a fine cut. Plus the pickup, reshoots, titles, opticals, cut in.

I should be jumping for joy, Cheryl Hill was my last chance. The reason I haven't jumped is because I haven't seen any money yet. There are about $20,000 in back salaries, loans to be paid. People are giving me to September then my phone is really gonna be ringing off the hook. I'm putting the answering machine on.

OCTOBER 16, 1985

Things are getting critical money-wise. My rent was due on October 1st. Cheryl Burr needs her $500. I owe the Black Filmmaker Foundation $500. I can't ask Mama for another cent. Everybody has been real understanding but patience is wearing thin. I have some other possible sources of money. Plus I have more money coming from First Run Features. Things look bleak right now but I can see the light at the end of the tunnel.

OCTOBER 22, 1985

I can't even cut the film in peace. Howard Funsch called today and said I had to come up with $1,000 by today or the negative was definitely being auctioned. I even had a three-way conference call with Kendall, but Funsch wouldn't budge. That was it. I made a desperation call to Nelson George who was just about to leave his house. THANK GOD FOR NELSON GEORGE. He came through like a champ. He and I went into the city to his American Express bank. He gave me $500 in cash and $500 in American Express traveler's checks. I'm at Du Art now waiting for Funsch. He went out to lunch. Nelson also gave me a list of high-powered people who might have the money. So he has really come through. THANK THE LORD. All praises due.

MARCH 20, 1986

Today is my 29th birthday. It was a furious day. Last night I screened *She's Gotta Have It* for Jean-Pierre Deleau and Olivier Jahon of the Cannes Film Festival. I didn't go to the screening—it's bad luck—so I left it up to Pamm Jackson. She took care of everything. After the screening they told her that we had been accepted. I talked to them in person and it's official, plus at the time we were the only film accepted.

When I came back home I had a lot of birthday wishes on the answering machine. Olivier asked me to write a paragraph about the film for tomorrow before he leaves.

It might go something like this:

Today was my twenty-ninth birthday and I received a great present: My first feature film, *She's Gotta Have It,* was invited to Cannes for Director's Fortnight. I now (more than ever) believe that to make a film is one of the hardest tasks in life, and when you're an independent, it takes a miracle. I thank God and all who have been behind me from the start. Now for business: In the history of American cinema, too, too often black people have had to rely on Hollywood to tell our stories. I'm determined to change that even if it's in only a small way. We shouldn't have to rely on the Spielbergs to define our existence. Blacks have to produce their own films, period.

Spike Lee March 20th, 1986. Brooklyn, New York, U.S.A.

APRIL 7, 1986

Last Thursday George Lucas had his secretary call. He wants to see the film. I almost fell out of my chair. We tried to hook it up but it was to no avail. He'll have to wait till we come back from Cannes. It's official, *She's Gotta Have It* as of today is the only American independent film invited to Director's Fortnight. So that's a coup.

Determination and perseverance move the world; thinking that others will do it for you is a sure way to fail.

—*Marva Collins*

THE CART
DOROTHY WEST

Dorothy West has enjoyed one of the longest literary careers in the twentieth century. Born in 1907, she sold stories to a Boston newspaper at fifteen, shared second prize with Zora Neale Hurston in a Harlem Renaissance literary contest, and became friend and colleague to many of the century's brightest literary luminaries—including Hurston, Langston Hughes, and Countee Cullen. In the 1930s, she founded two magazines, hiring Richard Wright as an editor and publishing Ralph Ellison's very first piece. Her first novel, The Living Is Easy, *now a classic, was published in 1938. West's influence continues. Her second novel,* The Wedding, *appeared in 1995, the same year she published a collection of short stories and reminiscences called* The Richer, The Poorer. *One of the stories, "The Cart," tells of a boy who finds a box and turns it into something he will always treasure. The story, and its author's career, bring home the meaning of perseverance.*

One morning in the summer that my nephew Bud was seven and here on school holiday, he went walking in the nearby woods and came across a wooden box. A wooden box has many possibilities, though at that moment Bud could not think of one. Nevertheless he brought it home as being too important a find to leave behind. He felt confident that my mother, who, in his unsophisticated judgment knew everything, would tell him what to do with his discovery.

It was her voice, rising from the region of the side yard, that waked me. My mother often engaged in overstatement. She was doing so now.

"You want to know what to do with a wooden box? I'm sure you're the only boy in the world who's ever asked that question. Every boy in the world knows the answer."

His voice was humble. "Do I have to guess or will you tell me?"

"You'd probably give me a dozen wrong guesses. It will save my time to tell you straight out. Every other boy in the world would make a cart."

Every boy but himself could make such a miracle come to pass. He said in self-defense, "A cart has to have wheels and stuff. I haven't got any wheels and stuff."

"I can see that as well as you can."

His voice was inquiring, not brash. "So?"

"So we take the next step."

"What next step?"

"We go find some."

"Where?"

"I know where. Come on."

In the side yard there was silence now. My mother and Bud had gone to whatever hideaway place where the wheels would materialize. After a while I heard them returning and the sound of something being rolled across the lawn. Curiosity compelled me out of bed, into my robe, and down the stairs. Then, walking quietly into a room that overlooked the side yard, I could see the enterprise in progress. My mother and that boy and an assortment of tools were wrestling with the wheels of my aunt's wheelchair.

The year before, my mother's sister Carrie had suffered a stroke and taken to a wheelchair. When my mother got tired of seeing her let a wheelchair control her existence, she took it out from under her, handed her a cane and told her to get going. And indeed the cane would fit her into places that her wheelchair could not, and give her more freedom of movement.

When the splendid wheels had been wrenched away, both of them stood back for a moment, my mother to take stock, the boy to glow.

"All right," said my mother, "let's start."

"Where do I start?"

"With your common sense."

For the time it took them to turn a wooden box into a moving vehicle, my mother never stopped admonishing the boy for picking up the wrong tool, for asking what she called "fool questions," for taking ten minutes to do what should have taken ten seconds. She rarely lifted a finger to help him. She made him do it all himself, do and undo until he got it right.

My mother's face was deep pink with impatience, a clear indication that her pressure was rising. The boy's face was a deeper pink as he fought to hold back his tears over what my mother was constantly telling him was a "fool mistake."

A half-dozen times I started to rap on the window to attract my mother's attention and make a fiery speech about all that great to-do about a wooden box. As soon as I could dress, I would take the boy downtown and buy him a red cart. Every little boy in the world was entitled to a store-bought cart.

But time and again something stayed my hand, some feeling that I had no right to take part, that I must be a silent witness, and no more. Finally it was over. My mother said, "Well, boy, it's done, and you did it yourself. Always remember you made it yourself. Go try it out, and don't kill yourself."

A look passed between them that I could not fathom. I turned away and went upstairs.

For the rest of that summer, Bud was the golden boy of the neighborhood. No other boy had a moving vehicle made by his own hands. Everybody wanted a ride. Going to the beach took second place.

Then the summer was over. It was time for the round of good-byes. Bud's best friend, Eddie, said that he was going to get a bicycle for Christmas. Bud said joyfully that he was, too.

But when I met Bud at the boat he got off without a bicycle. I didn't go into the why of it. His parents had married young. They could not always keep their promises. I did not want him running behind Eddie's bike like an orphan. We stopped at the bicycle store and bought what I could afford. As far as Bud was concerned there was nothing more he could want.

For the most part, the little cart stayed snug in its nesting place, on occasion surfacing when some younger child asked to play with it, and my mother giving firm instructions about its return before sundown.

She would grumble to me, "That's Bud's cart." I would reply, "He'll never play with it again. Why don't you give it to the next nice child who asks for it."

She would say grimly, "Over my dead body."

Bud entered his teens, then his mid-teens, no longer coming to stay all summer, but working for an uncle in the city, and coming weekends when he could. He and my mother would sit together on the back porch and talk, that communication between an older generation and one much younger.

A young mother, a charming new friend, whose summer cottage was some distance away from mine, asked if her children could play with the cart for the few remaining weeks that they were here. Her children had seen my neighbor's children playing with it and had been entranced. I said of course, without adding the burdensome imposition that they bring it back every sundown.

Fall came, the young mother left, and the cart went with her. She wrote me an endearing little note and sent me a handsome present, explaining that her children were in tears when she told them they must take the cart back. They wouldn't stop crying until she put it in her station wagon. She would bring it back next summer, and she wished me a good winter.

That was the winter my mother died. I wrote Bud's mother that I didn't want him to come. I wanted him to remember her strong and well and full of talk and laughter.

But I was haunted by that cart. I do not really know why. Through the rest of that winter, the feeling of guilt recurred. Bud had not mentioned the cart to me in years. But I could not forget the morning he made it and their remembered faces.

He came that summer. He came on a late boat, and there was a party to go to. He was in and then out of the house. He did not mention my mother, and I sensed it was because he could not.

The next morning he left the house before I waked. He loved to take an early swim, to have the beach to himself, with his thoughts turning inward. He came back. I was on the back porch. I think now he must have looked for his cart, and had not found it. He said to me very quietly, "Where is my cart?"

I had read it in books, but had never believed it, and had certainly never experienced it. My heart lurched. There really is such a feeling. I wanted to make a full confession. "I lent it to somebody who didn't bring it back." Now I wanted absolution.

"That's okay," he said, the way he used to say it when he was a little boy, and he didn't want you to know how much he was hurting.

"Do you remember the morning you made that cart? She never forgot it. We talked about it often and always in a loving way."

"Nobody else had ever helped me make anything. It was one of the happiest days in my life."

He had remembered the good part and forgotten the rest, which is the dictate of wisdom.

MOTHER TO SON
LANGSTON HUGHES

Classic advice to keep on climbing.

Well, son, I'll tell you:
Life for me ain't been no crystal stair.
It's had tacks in it,
And splinters,
And boards torn up,
And places with no carpet on the floor—
Bare.
But all the time
I'se been a-climbin' on,
And reachin' landin's,
And turnin' corners,
And sometimes goin' in the dark
Where there ain't been no light.
So boy, don't you turn back.
Don't you set down on the steps
'Cause you finds it's kinder hard.
Don't you fall now—
For I'se still goin', honey,
I'se still climbin',
And life for me ain't been no crystal stair.

I REMEMBER SLAVERY
AS TOLD BY KATIE ROWE

Former slaves told the harsh truth about bondage when oral histories were collected by federal relief program workers in the 1930s, the last decade when many slaves who had been set free were still alive. Some had felt the lash of slave masters. Others had met Lincoln and Harriet Tubman. From the lips of eyewitnesses to slavery, we can draw lessons in patience and fortitude. Eighty-eight-year-old Katie Rowe, once a slave in Arkansas, told this story about her own emancipation.

I can set on the gallery, where the sunlight shine bright, and sew a powerful fine seam when my grandchildren wants a special pretty dress for the school doings, but I ain't worth much for nothing else, I reckon.

These same old eyes seen powerful lot of tribulations in my time, and when I shuts 'em now I can see lots of little children just like my grandchildren, toting hoes bigger than they is, and they poor little black hands and legs bleeding where they scratched by the brambledy weeds, and where they got whippings 'cause they didn't git out all the work the overseer set out for 'em.

I was one of them little slave gals my own self, and I never seen nothing but work and tribulations till I was a grownup woman, just about.

THE NIGGERS HAD hard traveling on the plantation where I was born and raised, 'cause Old Master live in town and just had the overseer on the place, but iffen he had lived out there hisself I 'speck it been as bad, 'cause he was a hard driver his own self.

He git biling mad when the Yankees have that big battle at Pea Ridge and scatter the 'Federates all down through our country all bleeding and tied up and hungry, and he just mount on his hoss and ride out to the plantation where we all hoeing corn.

He ride up and tell old man Saunders—that the overseer—to bunch us all up round the lead row man—that my own uncle Sandy—and then he tell us the law!

"You niggers been seeing the 'Federate soldiers coming by here look-

ing pretty raggedy and hurt and wore out," he say, "but that no sign
they licked!

"Them Yankees ain't gwine git this far, but iffen they do, you all ain't
gwine git free by 'em, 'cause I gwine free you before that. When they git
here they gwine find you already free, 'cause I gwine line you up on the
bank of Bois d'Arc Creek and free you with my shotgun! Anybody miss
just one lick with the hoe, or one step in the line, or one clap of that bell,
or one toot of the horn, and he gwine be free and talking to the devil
long before he ever see a pair of blue britches!"

That the way he talk to us, and that the way he act with us all the
time.

Before Old Master died he sold off a whole lot of hosses and cattle,
and some niggers too. He had the sales on the plantation, and white men
from around there come to bid, and some traders come. He had a big
stump where he made the niggers stand while they was being sold, and
the men and boys had to strip off to the waist to show they muscle and
iffen they had any scars or hurt places, but the women and gals didn't
have to strip to the waist.

The white men come up and look in the slave's mouth just like he was
a mule or a hoss.

After Old Master go, the overseer hold one sale, but mostly he just
trade with the traders what come by. He make the niggers git on the
stump, though. The traders all had big bunches of slaves, and they have
'em all strung out in a line going down the road. Some had wagons and
the children could ride, but not many. They didn't chain or tie 'em
'cause they didn't have no place they could run to anyway.

I seen children sold off and the mammy not sold, and sometimes the
mammy sold and a little baby kept on the place and give to another
woman to raise. Them white folks didn't care nothing 'bout how the
slaves grieved when they tore up a family.

Old Man Saunders was the hardest overseer of anybody. He would
git mad and give a whipping sometime, and the slave wouldn't even
know what it was about.

I NEVER FORGET the day we was set free!

That morning we all go to the cotton field early, and then a house
nigger come out from Old Mistress on a hoss and say she want the

overseer to come into town, and he leave and go in. After while the old horn blow up at the overseer's house, and we all stop and listen, 'cause it the wrong time of day for the horn.

We start chopping again, and there go the horn again.

The lead row nigger holler, "Hold up!" And we all stop again. "We better go on in. That our horn," he holler at the head nigger, and the head nigger think so too, but he say he afraid we catch the devil from the overseer iffen we quit without him there, and the lead row man say maybe he back from town and blowing the horn hisself, so we line up and go in.

When we git to the quarters, we see all the old ones and the children up in the overseer's yard, so we go on up there. The overseer setting on the end of the gallery with a paper in his hand, and when we all come up he say come and stand close to the gallery. Then he call off everybody's name and see we all there.

Setting on the gallery in a hide-bottom chair was a man we never see before. He had on a big broad black hat like the Yankees wore, but it didn't have no yellow string on it like most the Yankees had, and he was in store clothes that wasn't homespun or jeans, and they was black. His hair was plumb gray and so was his beard, and it come 'way down here on his chest, but he didn't look like he was very old, 'cause his face was kind of fleshy and healthy-looking. I think we all been sold off in a bunch, and I notice some kind of smiling, and I think they sure glad of it.

The man say, "You darkies know what day this is?" He talk kind, and smile.

We all don't know, of course, and we just stand there and grin. Pretty soon he ask again and the head man say, "No, we don't know."

"Well, this the fourth day of June, and this is 1865, and I want you all to 'member the date, 'cause you always gwine 'member the day. Today you is free, just like I is, and Mr. Saunders and your mistress and all us white people," the man say.

"I come to tell you," he say, "and I wants to be sure you all understand, 'cause you don't have to git up and go by the horn no more. You is your own bosses now, and you don't have to have no passes to go and come."

We never did have no passes, nohow, but we knowed lots of other niggers on other plantations got 'em.

"I wants to bless you and hope you always is happy and tell you you got all the right . . . that any white people got," the man say, and then he git on his hoss and ride off.

We all just watch him go on down the road, and then we go up to Mr. Saunders and ask him what he want us to do. He just grunt and say do like we damn please, he reckon, but git off that place to do it, lessen any of us wants to stay and make the crop for half of what we make.

None of us know where to go, so we all stay, and he split up the fields and show us which part we got to work in, and we go on like we was, and make the crop and git it in, but they ain't no more horn after that day.

Old Mistress never git well after she lose all her niggers, and one day the white boss tell us she just drap over dead setting in her chair, and we know her heart just broke.

Next year the children sell off most the place and we scatter off, and I and Mammy go into Little Rock and do work in the town. Grandmammy done dead.

Lots of old people like me say that they was happy in slavery and that they had the worst tribulations after freedom, but I knows they didn't have no white master and overseer like we all had on our place. They both dead now, I reckon, and they no use talking 'bout the dead, but I know I been gone long ago iffen that white man Saunders didn't lose his hold on me.

It was the fourth day of June in 1865 I begins to live, and I gwine take the picture of that old man in the big black hat and long whiskers, setting on the gallery and talking kind to us, clean into my grave with me.

STILL I RISE
MAYA ANGELOU

When Bill Clinton chose her to read at his 1993 presidential inaugura-tion, Maya Angelou instantly became one of America's most famous poets—and the first black and first woman to be so recognized. Suddenly, at sixty-four, Angelou was a symbol of hope and reconciliation for a nation about to embark on a new political course. Part of her appeal no doubt stemmed from her rich and varied life, marked by tragedy but distinguished by talent and a knack for overcoming adversity. Born in 1928 to the granddaughter of a slave, Angelou was raped at age eight by her mother's boyfriend. Coincidentally, after she named the rapist, he was killed. She felt that her own words had sentenced a man to death, so she plunged into silence, remaining mute for five years. She absorbed the voices around her. Eventually, she regained her own. Despite these trau-matic experiences, her writings contain a spirit of triumph. In her many books and poetry volumes, she has documented her experiences as a singer, dancer, producer, composer, actress, journalist, playwright, educator, and writer. Few others can speak with such authority when it comes to the power to endure. This poem captures the unbroken spirit of a tenacious people.

You may write me down in history
With your bitter, twisted lies,
You may trod me in the very dirt
But still, like dust, I'll rise.

Does my sassiness upset you?
Why are you beset with gloom?
'Cause I walk like I've got oil wells
Pumping in my living room.

Just like moons and like suns,
With the certainty of tides,
Just like hopes springing high,
Still I'll rise.

Did you want to see me broken?
Bowed head and lowered eyes?
Shoulders falling down like teardrops,
Weakened by my soulful cries.

Does my haughtiness offend you?
Don't you take it awful hard
'Cause I laugh like I've got gold mines
Diggin' in my own back yard.

You may shoot me with your words,
You may cut me with your eyes,
You may kill me with your hatefulness,
But still, like air, I'll rise.

Does my sexiness upset you?
Does it come as a surprise
That I dance like I've got diamonds
At the meeting of my thighs?

Out of the huts of history's shame
I rise
Up from a past that's rooted in pain
I rise
I'm a black ocean, leaping and wide,
Welling and swelling I bear in the tide.
Leaving behind nights of terror and fear
I rise
Into a daybreak that's wondrously clear
I rise
Bringing the gifts that my ancestors gave,
I am the dream and the hope of the slave.
I rise
I rise
I rise.

FROM PICKING COTTON TO
PICKING PRESIDENTS
FANNIE LOU HAMER

The irrepressible Fannie Lou Hamer (1917–77), one of the most effec-
tive civil rights activists of the 1960s, was committed to bringing change to
Mississippi, a state ruled by racists. For registering to vote and attending
civil rights meetings, she lost her job and was beaten. She pressed on,
helping to organize the Mississippi Freedom Democratic Party. In 1964,
Hamer held the nation spellbound with her impassioned televised request to
unseat the all-white Mississippi Democratic Party and replace it with the
MFDP at the Democratic convention. The party of black sharecroppers
and farm workers did not succeed. But the attempt inspired in others efforts
to improve their lives. They went on to organize schools, daycare centers,
food banks, and farm cooperatives. By 1966, Mississippi magazine se-
lected her as one of six "women of influence" in the state. Here, Hamer
tells part of her life story. It reminds us that rights are won by fearlessness
and sheer resolve.

I was born October sixth, nineteen and seventeen in Montgomery
County, Mississippi. My parents moved to Sunflower County when I
was two years old, to a plantation about four and a half miles from here,
Mr. E. W. Brandon's plantation.

. . . My parents were sharecroppers and they had a big family.
Twenty children. Fourteen boys and six girls. I'm the twentieth child.
All of us worked in the fields, of course, but we never did get anything
out of sharecropping.

My life has been almost like my mother's was, because I married
a man who sharecropped. I married in 1944 and stayed on the plantation until 1962 when I went down to the courthouse in Indianola to
register to vote. That happened because I went to a mass meeting one
night.

Until then I'd never heard of no mass meeting and I didn't know that
a Negro could register and vote. Bob Moses, Reggie Robinson, Jim
Bevel and James Forman were some of the SNCC [Student Nonviolent
Coordinating Committee] workers who ran that meeting. When they
asked for those to raise their hands who'd go down to the courthouse the

next day, I raised mine. Had it up as high as I could get it. I guess if I'd had any sense I'd a-been a little scared, but what was the point of being scared? The only thing they could do to me was kill me and it seemed like they'd been trying to do that a little bit at a time ever since I could remember.

Well, there was eighteen of us who went down to the courthouse that day and all of us were arrested. Police said the bus was painted the wrong color—said it was too yellow. After I got bailed out I went back to the plantation where Pap and I had lived for eighteen years. My oldest girl met me and told me that Mr. Marlow, the plantation owner, was mad and raising sand. He had heard that I had tried to register. That night he called on us and said, "We're not going to have this in Mississippi and you will have to withdraw. I am looking for your answer, yea or nay?" I just looked. He said, "I will give you until tomorrow morning. And if you don't withdraw you will have to leave. If you do go withdraw, it's only how I feel, you might still have to leave." So I left that same night. Pap had to stay on till work on the plantation was through. Ten days later they fired into Mrs. Tucker's house where I was staying. They also shot two girls at Mr. Sissel's.

That was a rough winter. I hadn't a chance to do any canning before I got kicked off, so didn't have hardly anything. I always can more than my family can use 'cause there's always people who don't have enough. That winter was bad, though. Pap couldn't get a job nowhere 'cause everybody knew he was my husband. We made it on through, though, and since then I just been trying to work and get our people organized.

I reckon the most horrible experience I've had was in June of 1963. I was arrested along with several others in Winona, Mississippi. That's in Montgomery County, the county where I was born. I was carried to a cell and locked up with Euvester Simpson. I began to hear the sound of licks, and I could hear people screaming. . . .

After then, the State Highway patrolmen came and carried me out of the cell into another cell where there were two Negro prisoners. The patrolman gave the first Negro a long blackjack that was heavy. It was loaded with something and they had me lay down on the bunk with my face down, and I was beat. I was beat by the first Negro till he gave out. Then the patrolman ordered the other man to take the blackjack and he began to beat. . . .

After I got out of jail, half dead, I found out that Medgar Evers had been shot down in his own yard.

I'VE WORKED ON voter registration here ever since I went to that first mass meeting. In 1964 we registered 63,000 black people from Mississippi into the Freedom Democratic Party. We formed our own party because the whites wouldn't even let us register. We decided to challenge the white Mississippi Democratic Party at the National Convention. We followed all the laws that the white people themselves made. We tried to attend the precinct meetings and they locked the doors on us or moved the meetings and that's against the laws they made for their ownselves. So we were the ones that held the real precinct meetings. At all these meetings across the state we elected our representatives to go to the National Democratic Convention in Atlantic City. But we learned the hard way that even though we had all the law and all the righteousness on our side—that white man is not going to give up his power to us.

We have to build our own power. We have to win every single political office we can, where we have a majority of black people.

THE QUESTION FOR black people is not, when is the white man going to give us our rights, or when is he going to give us good education for our children, or when is he going to give us jobs—if the white man gives you anything—just remember when he gets ready he will take it right back. We have to take for ourselves.

KEEP YOUR EYES ON THE PRIZE

Many of the freedom songs sung in the 1960s sprang from spirituals and gospel tunes. The following song, "Keep Your Eyes on the Prize" (which was based on the gospel tune "Keep Your Hands on the Plow") was sung to help fortify the spirit of those carrying on the civil rights struggle.

KEEP YOUR EYES ON THE PRIZE

Paul and Silas bound in jail,
Had no money for to go their bail.
Keep your eyes on the prize,
Hold on, hold on.
       Hold on, hold on.
Keep your eyes on the prize,
       Hold on, hold on.

Paul and Silas begin to shout,
The jail door open and they walked out.
Keep your eyes on the prize,
       Hold on, hold on.

]Freedom's name is mighty sweet,
Soon one day we're gonna meet.
Keep your eyes on the prize,
       Hold on, hold on.

Got my hand on the Gospel plow,
I wouldn't take nothing for my journey now.
Keep your eyes on the prize,
       Hold on, hold on.

The only chain that a man can stand,
Is that chain of hand in hand.

Keep your eyes on the prize,
> Hold on, hold on.

The only thing that we did wrong,
Stayed in the wilderness a day too long.
Keep your eyes on the prize,
> Hold on, hold on.

But the one thing we did right,
Was the day we started to fight.
Keep your eyes on the prize,
> Hold on, hold on.

We're gonna board that big Greyhound,
Carryin' love from town to town.
Keep your eyes on the prize,
> Hold on, hold on.

We're gonna ride for civil rights,
We're gonna ride both black and white.
Keep your eyes on the prize,
> Hold on, hold on.

We've met jail and violence too,
But God's love has seen us through.
Keep your eyes on the prize,
> Hold on, hold on.

Haven't been to Heaven but I've been told,
Streets up there are paved with gold.
Keep your eyes on the prize,
> Hold on, hold on.

BLOODY SUNDAY
AS TOLD BY SHEYANN WEBB

On March 7, 1965, eight-year-old Sheyann Webb's mother brushed her hair, hugged her, and let her join six hundred civil rights activists who were to march fifty-four miles from Selma to Montgomery, Alabama. They planned to present a petition for their voting rights to Governor George Wallace at the state capitol. Six blocks into the march, the activists began to cross the Edmund Pettus Bridge. When they reached the apex, they were attacked by Alabama state troopers, who "rushed forward in a flying wedge," according to one witness. Here is how Sheyann remembered that day—and the strange sense of calm after the terrible storm. Ultimately, the marchers won. Often, victory depends on tactics and constancy, rather than merely might.

All I knew is I heard all this screaming and the people were turning and I saw this first part of the line running and stumbling back toward us. At that point, I was just off the bridge and on the side of the highway. And they came running and some of them were crying out and somebody yelled, "Oh, God, they're killing us!" I think I just froze then. There were people everywhere, jamming against me, pushing against me. Then, all of a sudden, it stopped and everyone got down on their knees, and I did too, and somebody was saying for us to pray. But there was so much excitement it never got started, because everybody was talking and they were scared and we didn't know what was happening or was going to happen. I remember looking toward the troopers and they were backing up, but some of them were standing over some of our people who had been knocked down or had fallen. It seemed like just a few seconds went by and I heard a shout. "Gas! Gas!" And everybody started screaming again. And I looked and I saw the troopers charging us again and some of them were swinging their arms and throwing canisters of tear gas. And beyond them I saw the horsemen starting their charge toward us. I was terrified. What happened then is something I'll never forget as long as I live. Never. In fact, I still dream about it sometimes.

I saw those horsemen coming toward me and they had those awful masks on; they rode right through the cloud of tear gas. Some of them had clubs, others had ropes or whips, which they swung about them like they were driving cattle.

I'll tell you, I forgot about praying, and I just turned and ran. And just as I was turning the tear gas got me; it burned my nose first and then got my eyes. I was blinded by the tears. So I began running and not seeing where I was going. I remember being scared that I might fall over the railing and into the water. I don't know if I was screaming or not, but everyone else was. People were running and falling and ducking and you could hear the horses' hooves on the pavement and you'd hear people scream and hear the whips swishing and you'd hear them striking the people. They'd cry out; some moaned. Women as well as men were getting hit. I never got hit, but one of the horses went right by me and I heard the swish sound as the whip went over my head and cracked some man across the back. It seemed to take forever to get across the bridge. It seemed I was running uphill for an awfully long time. They kept rolling canisters of tear gas on the ground, so it would rise up quickly. It was making me sick. I heard more horses and I turned back and saw two of them and the riders were leaning over to one side. It was like a nightmare seeing it through the tears. I just knew then that I was going to die, that those horses were going to trample me. So I kind of knelt down and held my hands and arms up over my head, and I must have been screaming—I don't really remember.

All of a sudden somebody was grabbing me under the arms and lifting me up and running. The horses went by and I kept waiting to get trampled on or hit, but they went on by and I guess they were hitting at somebody else. And I looked up and saw it was Hosea Williams who had me and he was running but we didn't seem to be moving, and I kept kicking my legs in the air, trying to speed up, and I shouted at him, "Put me down! You can't run fast enough with me!"

But he held on until we were off the bridge and down on Broad Street and he let me go. I didn't stop running until I got home. All along the way there were people running in small groups; I saw people jumping over cars and being chased by the horsemen who kept hitting them. When I got to the apartments there were horsemen in the yards, galloping up and down, and one of them reared his horse up in the air as I went by, and he had his mask off and was shouting something at me.

When I got into the house my momma and daddy were there and

they had this shocked look on their faces and I ran in and tried to tell them what had happened. I was maybe a little hysterical because I kept repeating over and over, "I can't stop shaking, Momma, I can't stop shaking," and finally she grabbed me and sat down with me on her lap. But my daddy was like I'd never seen him before. He had a shotgun and he yelled, "By God, if they want it this way, I'll give it to them!" And he started out the door. Momma jumped up and got in front of him shouting at him. And he said, "I'm ready to die; I mean it! I'm ready to die!" I was crying there on the couch, I was so scared. But finally he put the gun aside and sat down. I remember just laying there on the couch, crying and feeling so disgusted. They had beaten us like we were slaves.

That night, African Americans gathered in church. "It was like we were at our own funeral," Sheyann said.

BUT THEN LATER in the night, maybe nine-thirty or ten, I don't know for sure, all of a sudden somebody there started humming. I think they were moaning and it just went into the humming of a freedom song. It was real low, but some of us children began humming along, slow and soft. At first I didn't even know what it was, what song, I mean. It was like a funeral sound, a dirge. Then I recognized it—*Ain't Gonna Let Nobody Turn Me 'Round*. I'd never heard it or hummed it that way before. But it just started to catch on, and the people began to pick it up. It started to swell, the humming. Then we began singing the words. We sang, "Ain't gonna let George Wallace [the Governor of Alabama] turn me 'round." And, "Ain't gonna let Jim Clark turn me 'round." "Ain't gonna let no state trooper turn me 'round."

Ain't gonna let no horses . . . ain't gonna let no tear gas—ain't gonna let nobody turn me 'round. *Nobody!*

And everybody's singing now, and some of them are clapping their hands, and they're still crying, but it's a different kind of crying. It's the kind of crying that's got spirit, not the weeping they had been doing.

And me and Rachel are crying and singing and it just gets louder and louder. I know the state troopers outside the church heard it. Everybody heard it. Because more people were coming in then, leaving their apartments and coming to the church—because something was happening.

We was singing and telling the world that we hadn't been whipped, that we had won.

Just all of a sudden something happened that night and we knew in that church that—Lord Almighty—we had really won, after all. We had won!

The news media captured the attack. Network television broadcast footage of the beating nationally, and pictures were flashed around the world, showing the cruel face of Southern racism. People from across America then joined in the crusade for civil rights.

P.O.W.

A SOLDIER'S STORY OF SURVIVAL

RECORDED BY WALLACE TERRY

Many black heroes fought in the Vietnam War. Some spent much of the war behind enemy lines, not as spies but as prisoners. U.S. Air Force Captain Norman McDaniel's reconnaissance plane was shot down near Hanoi on July 20, 1966. With bullets "zinging through the air," he was able to parachute to a hillside but was captured. His dramatic story proves that survival sometimes depends on sheer willpower and a persistence to "make it back."

I could smell the hate.

Some of them had pistols. Some guns. Some shook knives at me, shovels, even hoes. They motioned for me to stand up. Then they inched forward. About fifty of them. Communist militia, like popular forces. And just plain folk, too. All pointing guns at me.

They looked to see what I had and took my .38. They made me strip down to shorts and T-shirt. They took off my boots. They tied my hands behind me.

Then they marched me about a hundred yards, right down this hill to this hut. Then around to the backyard. There was a large hole, like a pit.

They motioned for me to get into that. I hesitated. Then they pushed and shoved me into it.

I thought I was going to be executed.

I said to myself, This is it.

I guess I was in a state of shock. I wasn't afraid. I just thought my time had come.

It was July 20, 1966. Just seven days short of my twenty-ninth birthday. I had come a half world away from Fayetteville, North Carolina—the son of sharecroppers—to die in North Vietnam at the hands of peasants. . . .

We took off early on July 20 from Takhli Air Base. Our missions normally lasted an hour and a half, maybe two hours. The bombers were going after railroads, bridges, storage depots. Pretty much the standard items.

The EB-66C is not armed, so in the daytime, we had fighter coverage—F-100s, F-104s—to keep the MiGs off. If we flew at night, it was assumed that the MiGs couldn't see us. So we flew alone. We flew alone. And some nights it was kind of interesting. Moonlight nights, boy, it was just about like day. We didn't feel too comfortable.

Just as we were completing our support, we were hit by a surface-to-air missile. We were at about thirty thousand feet. The missile was not a direct hit. If it had been, the plane would have just exploded right away, and none of us would have survived. But the missile exploded a little distance from the plane, yet it was close enough for some of the fragments to puncture the fuel tanks. The plane caught on fire immediately and started to disintegrate.

We lost all communications with the front section, where the pilot and the navigator were. Smoke and fumes started filling up our section fast. We didn't even have communications within our compartment with each other.

In our section, I was supposed to eject first. The big question was, are we as bad off as I think we are, or am I jumping the gun. But assessing the situation, I chose to eject.

The history of the EB-66C is such that normally in ejection, those who eject upwards—the pilot and the navigator—survive. Those who eject downward—the EWOs—the survival rate for them is very, very low. Later on, the North Vietnamese said one of the crew members died shortly after he was captured because he was injured severely. I tend to believe them because he was the fourth man out of my compartment. The second guy to go received more severe burns than me. The third guy had a head wound that kept him in and out of consciousness for the first couple of weeks. Probably the fourth guy got banged up far worse than that.

As I was coming down in the chute, I thought I saw the plane burning on the ground. And then I could hear bullets zinging through the air. The Vietnamese were shooting at me as I was descending. I looked up and saw a couple of holes in the chute. I didn't look down at them. I was looking more at where I was going to land.

I had to steer my parachute to keep from landing in some water. And I came down on a small hillside. Thirty miles northwest of Hanoi. Unfortunately, there were no trees, nothing to hide in. Just knee to thigh deep grass.

As soon as I touched ground, I tried to hide the chute. It was a big orange and white signal telling the whole world, here's McDaniel. All I could do was get it a little bit out of sight. Then I grabbed my survival radio to try to let our friendlies in the air know that I was down. That took thirty seconds. Then I looked around to find a place to hide. There was just nowhere. And within a minute after I hit the ground, they were on me.

I thought about using my gun, but I said, Well, I'd better just lay low for a moment. All of a sudden, things got kind of quiet, and I thought, Maybe they've gone away. Then I heard some grunts, and as I looked around, they were everywhere, all around me. They had gotten quiet to see if I were going to make a move.

Whatever they were going to do to me in that pit, they stopped when a jeep drove up with four regular army men. The soldiers said something in Vietnamese and motioned for the others to back away. Then they took me out of the pit, blindfolded me, and drove me about a mile away to a little place where they started interrogating.

They asked me if I could speak French. I said, no, no. Then in English they asked me what kind of plane I was flying, who else was in the plane, what targets we were trying to hit, what plans we had next. They wanted any military information that would help them to better defend themselves. I just kept giving them my name, my rank, my service number, and my date of birth.

After they tried that a few times, they tied me up and put me in a little hut. About an hour later, somebody with a white smock on came in to examine my injuries. When I ejected, I had banged up my ankle and got some face and neck burns. He figured I was going to live whether he did anything or not. So he did nothing. Later, they smocked down the burns with something that remind you of iodine. But that was all.

They took me to the prison camp we called the Hilton for the first extensive interrogations. That's where they had the torture room and can put the screws to you. When I mentioned the Geneva Convention, they laughed in my face. They said, "You're not qualified to be treated as a prisoner of war. You're a criminal. Black American criminal."

After two weeks, they took me to a camp we called the Zoo. And they put me in a concrete cell that was about six by nine feet. You either had a board or a concrete pallet for a bed. And, at first, you were told to sit on it all day. If they saw you moving around, trying to exercise, or trying to communicate with somebody, then they would take you out and beat you.

I kept looking for a break to get out that first evening, but I never got the opportunity. I figured if I could get out of the hut into the jungle, I might have a chance. But I never did. Once they got us to Hanoi, there were several things going against a successful escape. Even though they had guards in towers and barbed wire on the walls, we figured it was possible to scale the walls without being seen. There was something like a moat around the camp. But from there it was people, people, people. There were more people there per square hectare than you can shake a stick at. And, unfortunately, they worked more at night than at daytime because of the bombing raids. Another thing was just our size. And the white guys had a problem with the color of their skin and with their hair. And our features were different enough to the point that a black man would be recognized very, very readily. Even so, we were always planning how to escape, the best route, individually and collectively.

We ate twice a day. A little rice and a little soup made from swamp weed that you would see growing out the window. It tasted a little bit like a very bad-tasting turnip green. Not too bitter, just sort of bland.

You would get about a third of a bowl with a few of the greens, but mostly colored water. That was the standard fare.

Sometimes you would get a side dish of a tablespoon of turnips, cauliflower, or carrots that were kind of steamed. Once in a while, they might put a little pork fat in. If they had any chicken, they could chop it up, bones and all. You might get a smathering. But usually it was the pork fat, about the size of your thumbnail. A lot of guys couldn't eat it. It wasn't half clean. It would have hair on it. And it looked bad. So they would throw it away. My philosophy was that no matter what it is, no matter how bad it tastes, if it's going to keep me alive, I'm going to eat it.

I ate it. I ate. I ate. I ate. If it was edible at all, I ate it.

Most of the time I would go to sleep hungry. For the first ten months I never saw a piece of bread.

I think I lost thirty-five pounds, down from 155. But some of the guys who were shot down were just skeleton and bones because they couldn't eat the food and, in some cases, they wouldn't eat the food. There were guys who had weighed 190 pounds and were down to one hundred.

It gets pretty cold in North Vietnam in the winter months. And it's terrible if you don't have much clothing. We had two sets of prison clothes—shorts, pants, and shirt. But they would only let you wear one set at a time. The first winter I had no socks, just sandals made from rubber tires. And one blanket. The second winter they gave us a pair of socks and a second blanket. But it was still not enough to keep warm.

You had to keep track of time on your own. And the first couple of weeks, I just couldn't put it all together. The interrogations and beatings came in cells where you couldn't see out. You would get so beat out until you might sleep a few minutes and think you'd been asleep all night. But afterwards, you could keep the days together. Being some-what accustomed to the Western way, Sunday was not a big workday for them. And then you knew a week had rolled around.

They didn't want us to communicate, because we could pass informa-tion and keep each other's spirits up. Communicating was one of the quickest ways that you could get tortured.

In the first few days we knocked on walls and made signals if we saw each other. Morse code was too slow. So we put the alphabet in a five by five matrix. The first series of taps located the letter vertically, the next series horizontally. We combined J and K, or we would just use six straight taps for a K. Once in a while you would try to talk very low, but that was very hazardous.

By 1969, the word had gotten around the world that we were being treated very badly. So the powers that took over after Ho Chi Minh's death decided they were going to improve our treatment. So around Christmas we started to get more food and our first packages and letters from home.

My wife, Carol, and I had a close-knit family. It was one of my constant concerns.

I did not tell her that I was flying combat missions. So when the Air Force people came to her house saying I was missing in action, she just went out of it. For weeks her face and hands would swell up, and she had to stay on tranquilizers. And she stayed in a state of limbo for three years, because when my plane went down, the fighter cover said they had saw only two chutes.

Carol didn't know for sure that I was alive until 1969. The Air Force showed her pictures taken of me in the camp, and she said, "My goodness, I'd recognize that guy anywhere." The pictures were taken for propaganda purposes at Easter and Christmas. They would let some of us get together to read Scripture and sing a few songs to show how good they treated American prisoners. We gained some benefit, because it was one of the few times we could pass information and keep morale up.

From 1968 on, they would give you bits and pieces about the peace negotiations. When the bombings picked up in 1972 and the presidential campaign was going on, we thought something was going to happen. One of the provisions in the Paris Accords in 1973 was that the prisoners would be notified. So a few days after the peace agreements were signed, we were called out in a formation, and they announced we would be released soon.

The North Vietnamese agreed to let American C-141 airplanes into Gia Long airport to pick us up. When I got on the plane, I still thought the Communists could change their minds or the engine might not go. It wasn't until wheels up that I said, "Whoooo, man. We made it."

It was February 12, 1973. Six years, six months, and twenty-three days after my capture.

I think they had some candy and some sodas on the plane. When we got to Clark Air Force Base in the Philippines, we went through the chow hall and, boy, we just tore up the ice cream.

I landed at Andrews Air Force Base near Washington, D.C. The first thing I said to Carol was, "I made it back." She was so excited she just screamed.

SILENCED KNIGHT
BENJAMIN O. DAVIS JR.

In 1936, Benjamin O. Davis Jr. became the first African American to graduate from West Point in the twentieth century. * *But his time there was spent in virtual isolation. He was "silenced" for four years; his peers spoke to him only in the line of duty. Still, Davis graduated thirty-fifth in a class of 276 and went on to a distinguished military career. In World War II, he commanded the squadrons popularly known as the Tuskegee Airmen—among the most famous black fighting units in U.S. history. Davis—whose father, Benjamin O. Davis Sr., was the U.S. Army's first black brigadier general—retired in 1970 as a three-star general. His West Point years speak volumes about pluck and determination in the face of adversity.*

SPECIAL TREATMENT

I distinctly remember my first day at the Academy—the picturesque highlands above the Hudson, and West Point's mammoth, fortresslike stone buildings. We were met in a civil manner and driven by bus to the central barracks, where all civility promptly disappeared. There we were greeted by the raucous voices of handsome young men who sought, successfully, to convince us that they were God's chosen creatures and that we were the lowest possible dregs. Later I learned they were "year-

* Henry Flipper was the first black to graduate from West Point, on June 15, 1877.

lings" (sophomores), men who less than a month before had been plebes, and only a year before had been in the same position we found ourselves in now. For our first month, the yearlings of the so-called Beast Detail (from BCT, Basic Cadet Training) were to be our masters in every respect, responsible for our development from the low status of "new cadet" to the exalted position of "cadet."

The Beast Detail seemed to be composed mostly of men from the South, perhaps bearing out the popular notion that southerners held a particularly high belief and pride in military tradition. We new cadets were not permitted to walk; unless in military formation, we were required to double-time everywhere. Several times on that first day I felt as if I could not take another step. The roughest part of it all was standing at an exaggerated position of attention for long periods. On my second day, one man gave me all his attention for the entire day. He did not exactly haze me—hazing was against regulations—but the "training" he dispensed was rigorous, to say the least. I thought at the time that he was testing me as he would have tested any other new cadet.

At first, the only indication that I was being singled out for special treatment was the fact that I was rooming alone in a large room designed for at least two cadets. But shortly after I arrived at West Point, the commandant of cadets told me in what he obviously considered to be an act of kindness that, officially, I was to be "treated like a white man." Of course, I was thoroughly disgusted by this condescending attitude. He also explained that, in accordance with Academy tradition, roommates were voluntary, and no white boy could be asked to room with me. It was hard for me to believe that West Point could take such a stand. Even at this early stage in my career as a cadet, it did not seem consistent with the "Duty, Honor, Country" creed I had read about.

I obviously had much to learn about the Academy. Many years later I learned that in 1925, seven years before I went to West Point, the Army War College had determined in a study forwarded to the Army Chief of Staff that blacks were decidedly inferior to whites and should be relegated to a special status within the Army. The commandant of the War College stated that this report, entitled "The Use of Negro Manpower in War," was the product of "several years study by the faculty and the student body of the Army War College." It concluded that the intelligence of black people was lower than that of whites, that blacks lacked courage, that they were superstitious, and that they were dominated by moral and character weaknesses. It also stated that the "social inequality" of blacks made the close association of whites and blacks in military organizations "inimicable to harmony and efficiency." The Army had approved this "study" and used it as the basis for its discrimination against blacks.

My plebe classmates were too busy coping with the Beast Detail to be hostile toward me. A cadet from Tennessee wanted to know all about me, and a couple of cadets who lived across the hall were friendly for the first two days. They seemed to be as overwhelmed by their new environment as I was. A yearling from Wichita, Kansas, Warren S. Everett, "recognized" me, told me he was my friend, and said he was "going to look out for me," which made me feel better at least temporarily. "Recognition," which implied a friendly and personal relationship, could be bestowed by any upperclassman upon any plebe, but it was usually reserved for the en masse recognition ceremony at the end of plebe year. Everett was the first and only cadet to recognize me until graduation week a year later.

We plebes were routinely forced to stand at extreme attention, among the many forms of physical torture that fell short of actual violence: shoulder blades touching, buttocks rolled forward, back flat, gut sucked up, chest up, chin tightly back and in. Standing at attention for 30 minutes or more at a time made my feet go to sleep and my arms ache, and the constriction of blood vessels produced a pronounced dimness of vision. On my fifth day at West Point, the captain of my company pronounced my room and equipment the best in the company. At that moment, one of his assistants put the finger of his white glove on the woodwork and found some dust. Suddenly commands came from everywhere: "Pull your chin in, mister." "Keep your shiny, green eyes straight to the front." "Roll your buttocks under you." "Get the sway out of your back." "Get some blood in those ears." "Break out in a sweat, mister."

In the mess hall, though the food was excellent, the eating was difficult. We had to keep our eyes on the floor while we double-timed into the dining hall, and then we had to sit on the front 3 inches of our chairs and keep our eyes strictly on our plates. We were required to serve the upperclassmen first, with special attention to the senior cadet, the table

commandant, who sat at the head of the table. We spoke only in prescribed phrases when performing our duties, and in addition, we were
required to recite pieces of "poop," that is, information we had memorized. After the upperclassmen were served, the serving dishes were
passed down to the plebes at the other end of the table. Sometimes we
were kept so busy "sitting up" and answering questions that we did not
have time to eat as much as we liked.

These practices, while tough, actually gave me no problem whatsoever. However, just when I thought that I was getting along extremely
well—that life at West Point, even for plebes, was a piece of cake—the
roof fell in. I was in my room shining my shoes and brass when I heard
a knock on the door announcing a meeting in the sinks (the basement) in
10 minutes. As I approached the assembly where the meeting was in
progress, I heard someone ask, "What are we going to do about the
nigger?" I realized then that the meeting was *about* me, and I was not
supposed to attend. I turned on my heel and double-timed back to my
room.

From that meeting on, the cadets who roomed across the hall, who
had been friendly earlier, no longer spoke to me. In fact, no one spoke to
me except in the line of duty. Apparently, certain upperclass cadets had
determined that I was getting along too well at the Academy to suit
them, and they were going to enforce an old West Point tradition—
"silencing"—with the object of making my life so unhappy that I would
resign. Silencing had been applied in the past to certain cadets who were
considered to have violated the honor code and refused to resign. In my
case there was no question of such a violation, which would have been
formally cited by the Honor Committee; I was to be silenced solely
because cadets did not want blacks at West Point. Their only purpose
was to freeze me out. What they did not realize was that I was stubborn
enough to put up with their treatment to reach the goal I had come to
attain.

AN INVISIBLE MAN

Except for the recognition ceremony at the end of plebe year, I was
silenced for the entire four years of my stay at the Academy. Even

though West Point officialdom could maintain that this silence had no official basis, they knew precisely how I was being treated and that I was the only cadet in the corps treated in this manner. When we traveled to football games on buses or trains, I had a seat to myself; even as a first classman (senior), when we traveled to Fort Benning, Georgia, and Fort Monroe, Virginia, I lived alone in whatever quarters were provided, usually large enough for two or more cadets. Except for tutoring some underclassmen after my plebe year, I had no conversations with other cadets. The situation was ridiculous, but in no way was it funny. To this day I cannot understand how the officials at West Point and the individual cadets, with their continually and vociferously stated belief in "Duty, Honor, Country" as a way of life, could rationalize their treatment of me.

It is true that at the end of plebe year, at the recognition ceremony at Company M, large numbers of upperclass cadets from all over the corps came up to me, recognized me, and congratulated me. But after that I reverted to my status as an invisible man.

This cruel treatment was designed to make me buckle, but I refused to buckle in any way. I maintained my self-respect. First, I did not mention my troubles in letters to my mother and father. Second, I made my mind up that I would continue to hold my head high. At no time did I consciously show that I was hurt; even at this early date, I took solace in the fact that I was mature enough to live through anything other people might submit me to, particularly people I considered to be misguided. I kept telling myself that I was *superior* in character to them, even to the point of feeling sorry for them. Certainly I was not missing anything by not associating with them; instead, I bolstered my feelings by thinking that they were missing a great deal by not knowing me.

I received other forms of special treatment. The commandant called me in three times to ask how I was getting along. My answer was that I intended to graduate, regardless of how I was treated. We did not discuss the particulars of that treatment. Similarly, after the cadet captain of my company had told the company tactical officer that I was a good worker, the tactical officer called me in and asked me whether I was getting proper instruction in tactics and whether I was being treated all right generally. Like the commandant, he said that I was to come to him in case any difficult situation arose. I was well aware that neither of them had any intention to correct or even alleviate the silencing. They quite obviously knew what was going on, and they must have had their own personal reasons for not saying anything more about it.

But I was in no mood to trust anyone, and I had enough intelligence to know that complaints about my situation would not help me. I kept my letters to my parents cheerful and took encouragement from theirs. I asked them for a number of things, just to get mail. For some obscure psychological reason, I ate a prodigious amount of candy. I also read many, many books and magazines, and regardless of the weather, I ran lots of solo cross-country in the hills, after which I always felt better when I returned to my empty room. I never felt sorry for myself. I knew I could push aside any obstacle in my path. My father had taught me to be strong; he had endured adversity, and so could I.

PLEBE YEAR CONTINUES

Our lives as plebes were dominated by the routine of the Blue Book, which told us in clipped and precise language all the things we were supposed to do and when we were supposed to do them, and also the things we were forbidden to do. I enjoyed much of the routine—there was something to be said for being told what was expected, so that one could do it. On Sunday mornings we marched to chapel, where battle flags from the Civil War, the Spanish-American War, and the Philippine Insurrection hung from the triforium. The rest of Sunday was free. Having no one to talk to, I kept up correspondence with my mother, father, and sisters.

My initial grades were not as good as I thought they should be, but they improved as time went on. I liked the method of "teaching"— mostly memorization and regurgitation—and the system of daily grading. Weekly grades were posted each Saturday, so each cadet could find out just how he was doing compared to his classmates. The big problem was finding time to study, what with drill, intramural athletics ("Every man an athlete"), and parade. The old statement was basically true: "You've got time for everything at West Point." I frequently got up before reveille to study.

I won a monogram on our championship lacrosse team, qualified in swimming, and received a perfect grade on my boxing test. I fought a cadet who was about equal to me in ability. He hit me twice where I could feel it, once in the eye, then in the center of my body, where my ribs separated, but I paid him back with a fast blow to the chin as the second round ended. My grade probably reflected effort more than skill. We had been warned that we had to fight as hard as we could; otherwise we would be marked down.

In early October my father wrote Maj. Gen. William D. Connor, the Superintendent, stating his intention to visit me at West Point. General Connor replied immediately to make arrangements, adding, "The good work that Cadet Davis is doing must be evident from the academic reports. In his Conduct he has been a model cadet." The visit went better than either of us expected, and I was proud of the hospitality shown my father by the Corps of Cadets and the Academy. He, too, was pleased with the treatment he received; although he was in civilian clothes, many cadets saluted him. He dined with me on the balcony of the mess hall, usually reserved for distinguished visitors, and he visited with me in my room. Among other things we discussed, he gave me some pointers on military tactics. Although he must have noticed that I was rooming alone, the subject of my silencing never came up. I could think of no way in which my father could appreciably improve my situation, so there was no use in saying anything about it. In the last analysis, only time—precisely, the passage of four years—could solve my problems at West Point. . . .

GRADUATION

My feelings as I approached graduation were bittersweet. I was extremely proud that I had withstood the forces that opposed me so actively for my entire four years as a cadet, and that I would be the first black in the 20th century to graduate from West Point. My father had hoped that I would do well enough to join the Engineers, and I had, ranking 35 in a class of 276. Nevertheless, I still had my heart set on being a pilot. My father had also said more than once that he did not want to leave active duty without at least one black Regular Army line officer on the active list. It was somewhat reassuring to know that when

I graduated, there would be two. I had become stronger and healthier, and I had acquired many valuable skills. I had learned to live with myself and by myself. Living as a prisoner in solitary confinement for four years had not destroyed my personality, nor poisoned my attitude toward other people. I had even managed to keep a sense of humor about the situation; when my father told me of my many supporters, the many people who were pulling for me, I said, "It's a pity none of them were at West Point."

All these positive aspects held great meaning for me that would help sustain me for the rest of my life. But there was no denying the very substantial negatives. I had spent many miserable days, weeks, months, and years at West Point. My problems were not in any way related to basic military training. I believed in the Academy and its educational approach; I actually enjoyed the rigid discipline that was designed to produce leaders who could endure the hardships of war. The silencing imposed on me, however, was an entirely different matter. Upon entering West Point, I had looked forward to making lifelong friends who would endure the Academy experience along with me and with whom I would be closely and sympathetically associated throughout our service. It did not turn out that way; I left West Point without any genuine friends and with only the most distant of acquaintances.

Graduation went well. Gen. John J. Pershing spoke, and though I was too preoccupied to notice, many of those present told me later of the prolonged applause that occurred when he presented me with my commission and degree. Newspapers all over the United States, both black and white, carried articles about the graduation of the first black cadet from West Point in this century, and a prominent black magazine, *The Crisis*, pictured me on its cover as the "Number One Graduate of the Nation." I received many telegrams and letters from people who had read these articles.

꒰꒱

Treat failure as practice shots.

—*Deborah McGriff*

꒰꒱

ALEX HALEY
DISCOVERS HIS ROOTS
ALEX HALEY

In the summer of 1767, Kunta Kinte, the great-great-great-great-grandfather of Alex Haley (1921–92), was kidnapped by a slave-raiding party near the Gambia River in West Africa and shipped to slavery in America with some 140 others. Kinte's story, along with a few words of the African language he spoke, were passed down through generations of his descendants, finally reaching Haley, who decided to trace Kinte's origins. In 1976, Haley published Roots: The Saga of an American Family. *The book, and the two television miniseries it spawned, instilled pride in black Americans' African ancestry.* Roots *took more than a decade to research and write. How Haley uncovered the facts of his family history is a compelling story of perseverance.*

The farthest-back person [my oldest relatives] ever talked about was a man they called "the African," whom they always said had been brought to this country on a ship to some place that they pronounced " 'Naplis." They said he was bought off this ship by a "Massa John Waller," who had a plantation in a place called "Spotsylvania County, Virginia." They would tell how the African kept trying to escape, and how on the fourth effort he had the misfortune to be captured by two white professional slave catchers, who apparently decided to make an example of him. This African was given the choice either of being castrated or having a foot cut off, and—"thanks to Jesus, or we wouldn't be here tellin' it"—the African chose his foot. I couldn't figure out why white folks would do anything as mean and low-down as that.

But this African's life, the old ladies said, had been saved by Massa John's brother, a Dr. William Waller, who was so mad about the entirely unnecessary maiming that he bought the African for his own plantation. Though now the African was crippled, he could do limited work, and the doctor assigned him in the vegetable garden.

Grandma and the others said that Africans fresh off slave ships were given some name by their massas. In this particular African's case the name was "Toby." But they said anytime any of the other slaves called him that, he would strenuously rebuff them, declaring that his name was "Kin-tay." . . .

I WENT TO the National Archives in Washington, D.C., and told a reading-room desk attendant that I was interested in Alamance County, North Carolina, census records just after the Civil War. Rolls of microfilm were delivered. I began turning film through the machine, feeling a mounting sense of intrigue while viewing an endless parade of names recorded in that old-fashioned penmanship of different 1800s census takers. After several of the long microfilm rolls, tiring, suddenly in utter astonishment I found myself looking down there on: "Tom Murray, black, blacksmith—," "Irene Murray, black, housewife—" . . . followed by the names of Grandma's older sisters—most of whom I'd listened to countless times on Grandma's front porch. "Elizabeth, age 6"—nobody in the world but my Great Aunt Liz! At the time of that census, Grandma wasn't even born yet!

It wasn't that I hadn't believed the stories of Grandma and the rest of them. You just *didn't* not believe my grandma. It was simply so uncanny sitting staring at those names actually right there in official U.S. Government records.

Now the thing was where, what, how could I pursue those strange phonetic sounds that it was always said our African ancestor had spoken. It seemed obvious that I had to reach as wide a range of actual Africans as I possibly could, simply because so many different tribal tongues are spoken in Africa. There in New York City, I began doing what seemed logical: I began arriving at the United Nations around quitting time; the elevators were spilling out people who were thronging through the lobby on their way home. It wasn't hard to spot the Africans, and every one I was able to stop, I'd tell my sounds to. Within a couple of weeks, I guess I had stopped about two dozen Africans, each of whom had given me a quick look, a quick listen, and then took off. I can't say I blame them—me trying to communicate some African sounds in a Tennessee accent.

Increasingly frustrated, I had a long talk with George Sims, a master researcher. After a few days, George brought me a list of about a dozen people academically renowned for their knowledge of African linguistics. One whose background intrigued me quickly was a Belgian Dr. Jan Vansina. After study at the University of London's School of African and Oriental Studies, he had done his early work living in African villages. I telephoned Dr. Vansina where he now taught at the University of Wisconsin, and he gave me an appointment to see him. It was a Wednesday morning that I flew to Madison, Wisconsin.

That evening in the Vansinas' living room, I told him every syllable I could remember of the family narrative heard since little boyhood—recently buttressed by Cousin Georgia in Kansas City. Dr. Vansina, after listening intently throughout, then began asking me questions. Being an oral historian, he was particularly interested in the physical transmission of the narrative down across generations.

We talked so late that he invited me to spend the night, and the next morning Dr. Vansina, with a very serious expression on his face, said, "I wanted to sleep on it. The ramifications of phonetic sounds preserved down across your family's generations can be immense." He said that he had been on the phone with a colleague Africanist, Dr. Philip Curtin; they both felt certain that the sounds I'd conveyed to him were from the "Mandinka" tongue. I'd never heard that word; he told me that it was the language spoken by the Mandingo people. Then he guess translated certain of the sounds. One of them probably meant cow or cattle; another probably meant the baobab tree, generic in West Africa. The word *ko,* he said, could refer to the *kora,* one of the Mandingo people's oldest stringed instruments, made of a halved large dried gourd covered with goatskin, with a long neck, and twenty-one strings with a bridge. An enslaved Mandingo might relate the *kora* visually to some among the types of stringed instruments that U.S. slaves had.

The most involved sound I had heard and brought was Kamby Bolongo, my ancestor's sound to his daughter Kizzy as he had pointed to the Mattaponi River in Spotsylvania County, Virginia. Dr. Vansina said that without question, *bolongo* meant, in the Mandinka tongue, a moving water, as a river; preceded by "Kamby," it could indicate the Gambia River.

I'd never heard of it. . . .

I was asked to speak at a seminar held at Utica College, Utica, New York. Walking down a hallway with the professor who had invited me, I said I'd just flown in from Washington and why I'd been there. "The

Gambia? If I'm not mistaken, someone mentioned recently that an out-standing student from that country is over at Hamilton."

The old, distinguished Hamilton College was maybe a half hour's drive away, in Clinton, New York. Before I could finish asking, a Professor Charles Todd said, "You're talking about Ebou Manga." Consulting a course roster, he told me where I could find him in an agricultural economics class. Ebou Manga was small of build, with careful eyes, a reserved manner, and black as soot. He tentatively confirmed my sounds, clearly startled to have heard me uttering them. Was Mandinka his home tongue? "No, although I am familiar with it." He was a Wolof, he said. In his dormitory room, I told him about my quest. We left for The Gambia at the end of the following week.

Arriving in Dakar, Senegal, the next morning, we caught a light plane to small Yundum Airport in The Gambia. In a passenger van, we rode into the capital city of Banjul (then Bathurst). Ebou and his father, Alhaji Manga—Gambians are mostly Moslem—assembled a small group of men knowledgeable in their small country's history, who met with me in the lounge of the Atlantic Hotel. As I had told Dr. Vansina in Wisconsin, I told these men the family narrative that had come down across the generations.

When I had finished, they said almost with wry amusement, "Well, of course 'Kamby Bolongo' would mean Gambia River; anyone would know that." I told them hotly that no, a great many people *wouldn't* know it! Then they showed a much greater interest that my 1760s ancestor had insisted his name was "Kin-tay." "Our country's oldest villages tend to be named for the families that settled those villages centuries ago," they said. Sending for a map, pointing, they said, "Look, here is the village of Kinte-Kundah. And not too far from it, the village of Kinte-Kundah Janneh-Ya."

Then they told me something of which I'd never have dreamed: of very old men, called *griots*, still to be found in the older back-country villages, men who were in effect living, walking archives of oral history. A senior *griot* would be a man usually in his late sixties or early seventies; below him would be progressively younger *griots*—and apprenticing boys, so a boy would be exposed to those *griots'* particular line of narrative for forty or fifty years before he could qualify as a senior *griot*, who told on special occasions the centuries-old histories of villages, of clans, of families, of great heroes. Throughout the whole of black Africa such oral chronicles had been handed down since the time of the ancient forefathers, I was informed, and there were certain legendary *griots* who could narrate facets of African history literally for as long as three days without ever repeating themselves.

Seeing how astounded I was, these Gambian men reminded me that every living person ancestrally goes back to some time and some place where no writing existed; and then human memories and mouths and ears were the only ways those human beings could store and relay information. They said that we who live in the Western culture are so conditioned to the "crutch of print" that few among us comprehend what a trained memory is capable of.

Since my forefather had said his name was "Kin-tay"—properly spelled "Kinte," they said—and since the Kinte clan was old and well known in The Gambia, they promised to do what they could to find a *griot* who might be able to assist my search.

Back in the United States, I began devouring books on African history. It grew quickly into some kind of obsession to correct my ignorance concerning the earth's second-largest continent. It embarrasses me to this day that up to then my images about Africa had been largely derived or inferred from Tarzan movies and my very little authentic knowledge had come from only occasional leafings through the *National Geographic.*

After some weeks, a registered letter came from The Gambia; it suggested that when possible, I should come back.

I flew then to Africa.

The same men with whom I had previously talked told me now in a rather matter-of-fact manner that they had caused word to be put out in the back country, and that a *griot* very knowledgeable of the Kinte clan had indeed been found—his name, they said, was "Kebba Kanji Fofana." I was ready to have a fit. "Where *is* he?" They looked at me oddly: "He's in his village."

I discovered that if I intended to see this *griot,* I was going to have to do something I'd never have dreamed I'd ever be doing—organizing what seemed, at least to me then, a kind of minisafari! It took me three days of negotiating through unaccustomed endless African palaver finally to hire a launch to get upriver; to rent a lorry and a Land-Rover to take supplies by a roundabout land route; to hire finally a total of fourteen people, including three interpreters and four musicians, who had told me that the old *griots* in the back country wouldn't talk without music in the background.

In the launch *Baddibu,* vibrating up the wide, swift "Kamby Bolongo," I felt queasily, uncomfortably alien. Did they all have me appraised as merely another pith helmet? Finally ahead was James Island, for two centuries the site of a fort over which England and France waged war back and forth for the ideal vantage point to trade in slaves. Asking if we might land there a while, I trudged amid the crumbling ruins yet guarded by ghostly cannon. Picturing in my mind the kinds of atrocities that would have happened there, I felt as if I would like to go flailing an ax back through that facet of black Africa's history. Without luck I tried to find for myself some symbol remnant of an ancient chain, but I took a chunk of mortar and a brick. In the next minutes before we returned to the *Baddibu,* I just gazed up and down that river that my ancestor had named for his daughter far across the Atlantic Ocean in Spotsylvania County, Virginia. Then we went on, and upon arriving at a little village called Albreda, we put ashore, our destination now on foot the yet smaller village of Juffure, where the men had been told that this *griot* lived.

When we got within sight of Juffure, the children who were playing outside gave the alert, and the people came flocking from their huts. It's a village of only about seventy people. Like most back-country villages, it was still very much as it was two hundred years ago, with its circular mud houses and their conical thatched roofs. Among the people as they gathered was a small man wearing an off-white robe, a pillbox hat over an aquiline-featured black face, and about him was an aura of "somebodiness" until I knew he was the man we had come to see and hear.

As the three interpreters left our party to converge upon him, the seventy-odd other villagers gathered closely around me, in a kind of horseshoe pattern, three or four deep all around; had I stuck out my arms, my fingers would have touched the nearest ones on either side. They were all staring at me. The eyes just raked me. Their foreheads were furrowed with their very intensity of staring. A kind of visceral surging or a churning sensation started up deep inside me; bewildered, I was wondering what on earth was this . . . then in a little while it was rather as if some full-gale force of realization rolled in on me: Many times in my life I had been among crowds of people, but never where *every one was jet black!*

Rocked emotionally, my eyes dropped downward as we tend to do when we're uncertain, insecure, and my glance fell upon my own hands' brown complexion. This time more quickly than before, and even harder, another gale-force emotion hit me: I felt myself some variety of a hybrid . . . I felt somehow impure among the pure; it was a terribly shaming feeling. About then, abruptly the old man left the interpreters. The people immediately also left me now to go crowding about him.

One of my interpreters came up quickly and whispered in my ears, "They stare at you so much because they have never here seen a black American." When I grasped the significance, I believe that hit me harder than what had already happened. They hadn't been looking at me as an individual, but I represented in their eyes a symbol of the twenty-five millions of us black people whom they had never seen, who lived beyond an ocean.

The people were clustered thickly about the old man, all of them intermittently flicking glances toward me as they talked animatedly in their Mandinka tongue. After a while, the old man turned, walked briskly through the people, past my three interpreters, and right up to me. His eyes piercing into mine, seeming to feel I should understand his Mandinka, he expressed what they had all decided they *felt* concerning those unseen millions of us who lived in those places that had been slave ships' destinations—and the translation came: "We have been told by the forefathers that there are many of us from this place who are in exile in that place called America—and in other places."

The old man sat down, facing me, as the people hurriedly gathered behind him. Then he began to recite for me the ancestral history of the Kinte clan, as it had been passed along orally down across centuries from the forefathers' time. It was not merely conversational, but more as if a scroll were being read; for the still, silent villagers, it was clearly a formal occasion. The *griot* would speak, bending forward from the waist, his body rigid, his neck cords standing out, his words seeming almost physical objects. After a sentence or two, seeming to go limp, he would lean back, listening to an interpreter's translation. Spilling from the *griot's* head came an incredibly complex Kinte clan lineage that reached back across many generations: who married whom; who had what children; what children then married whom; then their offspring. It was all just unbelievable. I was struck not only by the profusion of details, but also by the narrative's biblical style, something like: "—and so-and-so took as a wife so-and-so, and begat . . . and begat . . . and begat . . ." He would next name each begat's eventual spouse, or spouses, and their averagely numerous offspring, and so on. To date things the *griot* linked them to events, such as "—in the year of the big water"—a flood—"he slew a water buffalo." To determine the calendar date, you'd have to find out when that particular flood occurred.

Simplifying to its essence the encyclopedic saga that I was told, the *griot* said that the Kinte clan had begun in the country called Old Mali. Then the Kinte men traditionally were blacksmiths, "who had conquered fire," and the women mostly were potters and weavers. In time, one branch of the clan moved into the country called Mauretania; and it was from Mauretania that one son of this clan, whose name was Kairaba Kunta Kinte—a *marabout*, or holy man of the Moslem faith—journeyed down into the country called The Gambia. He went first to a village called Pakali N'Ding, stayed there for a while, then went to a village called Jiffarong, and then to the village of Juffure.

In Juffure, Kairaba Kunta Kinte took his first wife, a Mandinka maiden whose name was Sireng. And by her he begot two sons, whose names were Janneh and Saloum. Then he took a second wife; her name was Yaisa. And by Yaisa, he begot a son named Omoro.

Those three sons grew up in Juffure until they became of age. Then the elder two, Janneh and Saloum, went away and founded a new village called Kinte-Kundah Janneh-Ya. The youngest son, Omoro, stayed on in Juffure village until he had thirty rains—years—of age, then he took as his wife a Mandinka maiden named Binta Kebba. And by Binta Kebba, roughly between the years 1750 and 1760, Omoro Kinte begat four sons, whose names were, in the order of their birth, Kunta, Lamin, Suwadu, and Madi.

The old *griot* had talked for nearly two hours up to then, and perhaps fifty times the narrative had included some detail about someone whom he had named. Now after he had just named those four sons, again he appended a detail, and the interpreter translated—

"About the time the King's soldiers came"—another of the *griot's* time-fixing references—"the eldest of these four sons, Kunta, went away from his village to chop wood . . . and he was never seen again. . . ." And the *griot* went on with his narrative.

I sat as if I were carved of stone. My blood seemed to have congealed. This man whose lifetime had been in this back-country African village had no way in the world to know that he had just echoed what I had heard all through my boyhood years on my grandma's front porch in Henning, Tennessee . . . of an African who always had insisted that his name was "Kin-tay"; who had called a guitar a *"ko,"* and a river within the state of Virginia, "Kamby Bolongo"; and who had been kidnaped into slavery while not far from his village, chopping wood, to make himself a drum.

I managed to fumble from my dufflebag my basic notebook, whose first pages containing grandma's story I showed to an interpreter. After briefly reading, clearly astounded, he spoke rapidly while showing it to the old *griot,* who became agitated; he got up, exclaiming to the people, gesturing at my notebook in the interpreter's hands, and *they* all got agitated.

I don't remember hearing anyone giving an order, I only recall becoming aware that those seventy-odd people had formed a wide human ring around me, moving counterclockwise, chanting softly, loudly, softly; their bodies close together, they were lifting their knees high, stamping up reddish puffs of the dust. . . .

The woman who broke from the moving circle was one of about a dozen whose infant children were within cloth slings across their backs. Her jet-black face deeply contorting, the woman came charging toward me, her bare feet slapping the earth, and snatching her baby free, she thrust it at me almost roughly, the gesture saying "Take it!" . . . and I did, clasping the baby to me. Then she snatched away her baby; and another woman was thrusting her baby, then another, and another . . . until I had embraced probably a dozen babies. I wouldn't learn until maybe a year later, from a Harvard University professor, Dr. Jerome Bruner, a scholar of such matters, "You didn't know you were participating in one of the oldest ceremonies of humankind, called 'The laying on of hands'! In their way, they were telling you 'Through this flesh, which is us, we are you, and you are us!' "

Later the men of Juffure took me into their mosque built of bamboo and thatch, and they prayed around me in Arabic. I remember thinking, down on my knees, "After I've found out where I came from, I can't understand a word they're saying." Later the crux of their prayer was translated for me: "Praise be to Allah for one long lost from us whom Allah has returned."

Flying homeward from Dakar, I decided to write a book. My own ancestors' would automatically also be a symbolic saga of all African-descent people—who are without exception the seeds of someone like Kunta who was born and grew up in some black African village, some-one who was captured and chained down in one of those slave ships that sailed them across the same ocean, into some succession of plantations, and since then a struggle for freedom. . . .

[T]he *griot* had timed Kunta Kinte's capture with "about the time the King's soldiers came." [In] London, midway during a second week of scurching in records of movement assignments for British military units during the 1760s, I finally found that "King's soldiers" *had* to refer to a unit called "Colonel O'Hare's forces." The unit was sent from London in 1767 to guard the then British-operated Fort James Slave Fort in the Gambia River. The *griot* had been so correct that I felt embarrassed that, in effect, I had been checking behind him.

I went to Lloyds of London. In the office of an executive named Mr. R. C. E. Landers, it just poured out of me what I was trying to do. He got up from behind his desk and he said, "Young man, Lloyds of London will give you all of the help that we can." It was a blessing, for through Lloyds, doors began to be opened for me to search among myriad old English maritime records. Many records seemed never to have been opened after their original storage; apparently no one had felt occasion to go through them.

I hadn't found a single ship bound from The Gambia to Annapolis, when in the seventh week, one afternoon about two-thirty, I was study-ing the 1,023rd sheet of slave-ship records. A wide rectangular sheet, it recorded the Gambia River entrances and exits of some thirty ships during the years 1766 and 1767. Moving down the list, my eyes reached ship No. 18, and automatically scanned across its various data heading entries.

On July 5, 1767—the year "the King's soldiers came"—a ship named

Lord Ligonier, her captain, a Thomas E. Davies, had sailed from the Gambia River, her destination Annapolis. . . .

I don't know why, but oddly my internal emotional reaction was delayed. I recall passively writing down the information, I turned in the records, and walked outside. Around the corner was a little tea shop. I went in and ordered a tea and cruller. Sitting, sipping my tea, it suddenly hit me that quite possibly that ship brought Kunta Kinte!

I still owe the lady for the tea and cruller. By telephone, Pan American confirmed their last seat available that day to New York. There simply wasn't time to go by the hotel where I was staying; I told a taxi driver, "Heathrow Airport!" Sleepless through that night's crossing of the Atlantic, I was seeing in my mind's eye the book in the Library of Congress, Washington D.C., that I had to get my hands on again. It had a light brown cover, with darker brown letters—*Shipping in the Port of Annapolis,* by Vaughan W. Brown.

From New York, the Eastern Airlines shuttle took to Washington; I taxied to the Library of Congress, ordered the book, almost yanked it from the young man who brought it, and went riffling through it . . . and there it was, confirmation! The *Lord Ligonier* had cleared Annapolis' customs officials on September 29, 1767.

Renting a car, speeding to Annapolis, I went to the Maryland Hall of Records and asked archivist Mrs. Phebe Jacobsen for copies of any local newspaper published around the first week of October 1767. She soon produced a microfilm roll of the Maryland *Gazette.* At the projection machine, I was halfway through the October 1 issue when I saw the advertisement in the antique typeface: "JUST IMPORTED, In the ship *Lord Ligonier,* Capt. Davies, from the River Gambia, in Africa, and to be sold by the subscribers, in Annapolis, for cash, or good bills of exchange on Wednesday the 7th of October next, A Cargo of CHOICE HEALTHY SLAVES. The said ship will take tobacco to London on liberty at 6s. Sterling per ton." The advertisement was signed by John Ridout and Daniel of St. Thos. Jenifer.

On September 29, 1967, I felt I should be nowhere else in the world except standing on a pier at Annapolis—and I was; it was two hundred years to the day after the *Lord Ligonier* had landed. Staring out to seaward across those waters over which my great-great-great-great-grandfather had been brought, again I found myself weeping.

The 1766–67 document compiled at James Fort in the Gambia River had included that the *Lord Ligonier* had sailed with 140 slaves in her hold. How many of them had lived through the voyage? Now on a second mission in the Maryland Hall of Records, I searched to find a record of the ship's cargo listed upon her arrival in Annapolis—and found it, the following inventory, in old-fashioned script: 3,265 "elephants' teeth," as ivory tusks were called; 3,700 pounds of beeswax; 800 pounds of raw cotton; 32 ounces of Gambian gold; and 98 "Negroes." Her loss of 42 Africans en route, or around one third, was average for slaving voyages.

I realized by this time that Grandma, Aunt Liz, Aunt Plus, and Cousin Georgia also had been *griots* in their own ways. My notebooks contained their centuries-old story that our African had been sold to "Massa John Waller," who had given him the name "Toby." During his fourth escape effort, when cornered he had wounded with a rock one of the pair of professional slave-catchers who caught him, and they had cut his foot off. "Massa John's brother, Dr. William Waller," had saved the slave's life, then indignant at the maiming, had bought him from his brother. I dared to hope there might actually exist some kind of an actual documenting record.

I went to Richmond, Virginia. I pored through microfilmed legal deeds filed within Spotsylvania County, Virginia, after September 1767, when the *Lord Ligonier* had landed. In time, I found a lengthy deed dated September 5, 1768, in which John Waller and his wife Ann transferred to William Waller land and goods, including 240 acres of farmland . . . and then on the second page, "and also one Negro man slave named Toby."

My God!

❦

You can cut off the concert halls, which you have done already, and I will still speak out . . . and if you silence my voice by making me a nonperson there will be another voice and another voice . . .

　　　　　　　　　　　　　　　　　　　　　　　—Paul Robeson

❦

CREATIVITY

Creativity isn't necessarily magic (as in *abracadabra!*), but it can indeed be magical. Like the compositions of Duke Ellington. Or the slam dunk of a ballplayer who seemingly defies gravity at will. Or the most imaginative story you ever dreamt up.

Technically, creativity is the act of bringing something into existence, of producing an original where there was nothing, or something different. Black folks are old hands at fashioning new uses for old stuff; at "making new" or "making do." We have been doing this for centuries.

Ever since our ancestors arrived in the West, creativity has played a prominent role in black survival, from the first nostalgic songs about Africa to carvings of newfangled farm implements; and from slave-invented gadgets that earned millions for Massa to the infusion of tribal words into the American lexicon.

Black art, literature, and music continue to function as storehouses for creative genius. Blacks, in fact, developed the only musical genre ever created in America—jazz.

But creativity has never been the exclusive province of artists, writers, and musicians. It is a man/woman-on-the-street activity, too—which is clearly evident in our everyday life: in black fashion, hairdos, dance, speech, and humor. Stroll down the street or turn on the radio or television, and you will witness African American creativity. As poet Gwendolyn Brooks noted, "Every Negro has something to say. Simply because he is a Negro. . . . His mere body . . . is an eloquence."

African American creativity has influenced people around the world. Black music, for instance, is a craze on every continent. But the work of black scientists and inventors has had an even greater impact on people worldwide than black music. In this chapter, you will read about black folks who helped to change the way we live or who opened our eyes and ears with their genius—finger-flying banjoists; individuals whose inventions revolutionized entire industries: Norbert Rillieux (sugar refining), Lewis Temple (whaling), Jan Earnst Matzeliger (shoemaking), and George Washington Carver (agriculture).

How can we inspire creativity in young people? By facilitating it. By teaching them the rudiments of a discipline and then encouraging them to test traditional techniques or invent new ones. They might learn to master jazz dance techniques, for example, and apply them to a choreographed movement. In the end, they might develop their very own interpretation of the dance.

Creativity is an important factor in moral development because it is a channel of direct expression, a vent for frustrations, a power that allows the spirit to fly. It can help us mature by teaching us lessons about ourselves and those around us, and it can bring joy and happiness to others.

Here is a small part of the story of black creativity in America.

᠊ᠥᠥᠥ᠊

There are no wrong notes.

—*Thelonius Monk*

᠊ᠥᠥᠥ᠊

ON IMAGINATION
PHILLIS WHEATLEY

Named Phillis for the slaveship that brought her to America, Phillis Wheatley (c. 1753–84) was the first black American to publish a book. The accomplishment astonished whites in her day, an era when whites assumed blacks to be uncivilized, suitable only for slavery and incapable of expressing themselves in high art forms such as literature. But only four years after being sold on a Boston slave block, African-born Wheatley began composing verse—all the more remarkable because she wrote in her newly adopted language. With her writings, she revolutionized American literature, establishing the black literary tradition. She used poetry to gain her freedom and became the first American woman, black or white, to attempt to earn a living by writing. Here, she demonstrates her poetic skill. Though her style is difficult to penetrate today, in her own time Wheatley's poems were considered works of genius.

Thy various works, imperial queen, we see,
How bright their forms! how deck'd with pomp by thee!
Thy wond'rous acts in beauteous order stand,
And all attest how potent is thine hand.

From *Helicon's* refulgent heights attend,
Ye sacred choir,* and my attempts befriend:
To tell her glories with a faithful tongue,
Ye blooming graces, triumph in my song.

Now here, now there, the roving *Fancy* flies,
Till some lov'd object strikes her wand'ring eyes,

---

* This refers to the nine Muses, goddesses of literature and art.

Whose silken fetters all the senses bind,
And soft captivity involves the mind.

Imagination! who can sing thy force?
Or who describe the swiftness of thy course?
Soaring through air to find the bright abode,
Th' empyreal* palace of the thund'ring God,
We on thy pinions can surpass the wind,
And leave the rolling universe behind:
From star to star the mental optics rove,
Measure the skies, and range the realms above.
There in one view we grasp the mighty whole,
Or with new worlds amaze th' unbounded soul.

Though *Winter* frowns to *Fancy's* raptur'd eyes
The fields may flourish, and gay scenes arise;
The frozen deeps may break their iron bands,
And bid their waters murmur o'er the sands.
Fair *Flora*† may resume her fragrant reign,
And with her flow'ry riches deck the plain;
Sylvanus‡ may diffuse his honours round,
And all the forest may with leaves be crown'd:
Show'rs may descend, and dews their gems disclose,
And nectar sparkle on the blooming rose.

Such is thy pow'r, nor are thine orders vain,
O thou the leader of the mental train:
In full perfection all thy works are wrought,
And thine the sceptre o'er the realms of thought.
Before thy throne the subject-passions bow,
Of subject-passions sov'reign ruler Thou,
At thy command joy rushes on the heart,
And through the glowing veins the spirits dart.

---

* Celestial.
† Roman goddess of flowers.
‡ Roman god of the forest.

Fancy might now her silken pinions try
To rise from earth, and sweep th' expanse on high;
From *Tithon's* bed now might *Aurora** rise,
Her cheeks all glowing with celestial dies,†
While a pure stream of light o'erflows the skies.
The monarch of the day I might behold,
And all the mountains tipt with radiant gold,
But I reluctant leave the pleasing views,
Which *Fancy* dresses to delight the *Muse;*
Winter austere forbids me to aspire,
And northern tempests damp the rising fire;
They chill the tides of *Fancy's* flowing sea,
Cease then, my song, cease the unequal lay.‡

1773

HARLEM LITERATI
LANGSTON HUGHES

Few creative ventures were as appropriately named as the magazine
Fire! *It burned up a lot of people—and then was ignited itself. Here is an*
excerpt from Langston Hughes's autobiography, The Big Sea.

During the summer of 1926, Wallace Thurman, Zora Neale Hurston,
Aaron Douglas, John P. Davis, Bruce Nugent, Gwendolyn Bennett, and
I decided to publish "a Negro quarterly of the arts" to be called *Fire*—
the idea being that it would burn up a lot of the old, dead conventional
Negro-white ideas of the past, *épater le bourgeois* into a realization of the
existence of the younger Negro writers and artists, and provide us with
an outlet for publication not available in the limited pages of the small

---

* Roman goddess of dawn, who loved the Trojan Tithonus.
† Colors.
‡ Ballad.

Negro magazines then existing, the *Crisis, Opportunity,* and the *Messenger*—the first two being house organs of inter-racial organizations, and the latter being God knows what.

Sweltering summer evenings we met to plan *Fire.* Each of the seven of us agreed to give fifty dollars to finance the first issue. Thurman was to edit it, John P. Davis to handle the business end, and Bruce Nugent to take charge of distribution. The rest of us were to serve as an editorial board to collect material, contribute our own work, and act in any useful way that we could. For artists and writers, we got along fine and there were no quarrels. But October came before we were ready to go to press. I had to return to Lincoln, John Davis to Law School at Harvard, Zora Hurston to her studies at Barnard, from whence she went about Harlem with an anthropologist's ruler, measuring heads for Franz Boas.

Only three of the seven had contributed their fifty dollars, but the others faithfully promised to send theirs out of tuition checks, wages, or begging. Thurman went on with the work of preparing the magazine. He got a printer. He planned the layout. It had to be on good paper, he said, worthy of the drawings of Aaron Douglas. It had to have beautiful type, worthy of the first Negro art quarterly. It had to be what we seven young Negroes dreamed our magazine would be—so in the end it cost almost a thousand dollars, and nobody could pay the bills.

I don't know how Thurman persuaded the printer to let us have all the copies to distribute, but he did. I think Alain Locke, among others, signed notes guaranteeing payments. But since Thurman was the only one of the seven of us with a regular job, for the next three or four years his checks were constantly being attached and his income seized to pay for *Fire.* And whenever I sold a poem, mine went there, too—to *Fire.*

None of the older Negro intellectuals would have anything to do with *Fire.* Dr. DuBois in the *Crisis* roasted it. The Negro press called it all sorts of bad names, largely because of a green and purple story by Bruce Nugent, in the Oscar Wilde tradition, which we had included. Rean Graves, the critic for the *Baltimore Afro-American,* began his review by saying: "I have just tossed the first issue of *Fire* into the fire." Commenting upon various of our contributors, he said: "Aaron Douglas who, in spite of himself and the meaningless grotesqueness of his creations, has gained a reputation as an artist, is permitted to spoil three perfectly good pages and a cover with his pen and ink hudge pudge. Countee Cullen has written a beautiful poem in his 'From a Dark Tower,' but tries his best to obscure the thought in superfluous sentences. Langston Hughes displays his usual ability to say nothing in many words."

So *Fire* had plenty of cold water thrown on it by the colored critics. The white critics (except for an excellent editorial in the *Bookman* for November, 1926) scarcely noticed it at all. We had no way of getting it distributed to bookstands or news stands. Bruce Nugent took it around New York on foot and some of the Greenwich Village bookshops put it on display, and sold it for us. But then Bruce, who had no job, would collect the money and, on account of salary, eat it up before he got back to Harlem.

Finally, irony of ironies, several hundred copies of *Fire* were stored in the basement of an apartment where an actual fire occurred and the bulk of the whole issue was burned up. Even after that Thurman had to go on paying the printer.

Now *Fire* is a collector's item, and very difficult to get, being mostly ashes.

FIRST LADY OF FASHION:
ANN LOWE

Ann Lowe (c. 1899–1981), among the first African American fashion designers to break through the racial barricade, designed dresses for the rich, the fabulous, and the famous. Her gowns became the pride of top New York boutiques. She eventually opened her own shop on Madison Avenue and paved the way for a generation of new black designers. Creative talent can sometime make its own runway.

Ann Lowe, the great-granddaughter of a slave, became one of high society's most sought-after fashion designers. Her exquisitely hand-sewn, fairy-princess gowns were adored by women across the land.

Her gowns—including those for Jacqueline Bouvier's wedding to John F. Kennedy—were described in great detail in the society pages. But Lowe herself remained relatively unknown for most of her career. One magazine even called her "society's best-kept secret."

The daughter and granddaughter of dressmakers, Lowe was born in Grayton, Alabama, and educated in Mobile. There, as a young child, she learned dressmaking techniques. At age six, she sewed scraps of cloth into miniatures of flowers she saw in the garden.

When Ann was sixteen, her mother died, leaving four gowns commissioned for a New Year's ball unfinished. Ann was so talented by then that she completed them.

Soon afterward, Lowe married a man who was ten years older than she. He insisted that she give up sewing. But one day a wealthy Florida woman spotted Lowe, wearing a dress she had made, in a department store. Impressed with Lowe's talent, the woman invited her to Tampa, commissioning her to make a wedding dress and trousseau. "I could hardly believe it," Lowe recalled. "It was a chance to make all the lovely gowns I'd always dreamed of." Lowe moved to Tampa with her infant son, Arthur, ending her marriage.

In Tampa, Lowe finished the wedding gowns, then knocked on doors in a wealthy residential neighborhood, winning orders for more dresses and becoming a local success.

After spotting an advertisement for New York City's S. T. Taylor Design School, Lowe applied to the school and was accepted. But when she showed up in New York, in April 1917, the school's director nearly turned her away upon learning that she was black. Other students refused to work near Lowe, so she asked to be seated in a separate room. Six months later, when she graduated, the director told her: "There is no more we can teach you. You are *very* good."

Lowe returned to Tampa to open her own shop. By age twenty-one, she headed the city's best dress shop, employing eighteen dressmakers.

But New York, a world fashion center, beckoned. Lowe moved there in 1928, renting a West 46th Street workroom until her savings ran out. She pleaded for jobs. "Just give me a place to work and some fabric, and I'll make dresses for nothing," she told shop owners. "You pay me only if they sell."

Eventually shop owners did—and every dress that Lowe made sold immediately.

Over the next twenty years Lowe built a steady clientele for her original hand-sewn dresses. Divas and wealthy women adored them. Olivia de Havilland wore a Lowe creation to accept the 1947 Academy Award for best actress in *To Each His Own*. The shop owner got public credit for Lowe's dress, however.

Each Lowe dress had its own built-in undergarment. "When [women] wear one of my dresses, they just step in, zip up and they're gone," Lowe once told a reporter.

In 1950 Lowe became a partner in her own shop. Three years later, Jacqueline Bouvier asked her to design her bridal party's gowns. "I want a tremendous dress," Jacqueline told Lowe. "A typical Ann Lowe dress."

Lowe went to work.

But disaster struck just ten days before the wedding. A pipe in the tin ceiling of her workroom burst, and water showered the tables, ruining nine of fifteen wedding party gowns. Jacqueline's French silk chiffon taffeta wedding gown, which had taken two months to make, was also completely destroyed.

In tears, Lowe called her fabric merchant. Fortunately he had more material. Lowe put her seamstresses on an emergency schedule and remade all the gowns in time. The dresses were a fashion success. But Lowe lost a small fortune on them.

Five years later, Lowe's son, who served as her financial adviser, died in a car accident, and she plunged into debt. In 1960, Saks Fifth Avenue opened a boutique for Lowe dresses. The arrangement didn't work out, however, because Lowe was putting more money into her dresses than she was collecting.

She then tried opening her own shop, but the Internal Revenue Service closed it in 1962 for tax delinquency.

Shortly afterward, her glaucoma condition deteriorated, and she had to have her right eye removed. Upon leaving the hospital, she received a call from the IRS. But instead of asking for back taxes, the caller reported that an anonymous friend of Lowe's had paid off her entire debt.

Lowe went to work, this time for Madeleine Couture, a dress shop whose owner sponsored Ann Lowe's first fashion show in New York. But a cataract in her remaining eye threatened to completely cut off her vision. She underwent a delicate operation, risking blindness. "Dresses are my life," she said. "If I can't design dresses I'd rather just fly off the top of the Empire State Building."

The operation was a success, and Lowe eventually went back to work in her own shop, Ann Lowe Originals on Madison Avenue. She retired in the 1970s. Arthur Sages, an importer of fine fabrics who knew Lowe, said her career probably would have flourished in Europe. "If she had lived in France, she'd have been as well known as Chanel or Dior."

Source: The Saturday Evening Post

MY BENT-UP HORN
DIZZY GILLESPIE WITH WILMOT ALFRED FRASER

John "Dizzy" Gillespie (1917–93), a lightning-fast jazz trumpeter, was one of the founding fathers of bebop. He pioneered not only a new musical style but also became known for the distinctive shape for his trumpet. Here he explains how his signature bent-up horn was developed.

The truth is that the shape of my horn was an accident. I could pretend that I went into the basement and thought it up, but it wasn't that way. It was an accident. Actually, I left my horn on a trumpet stand and someone kicked it over, and instead of just falling, the horn bent. I was playing at Snookie's on Forty-fifth Street, on a Monday night, January 6, 1953. I had Monday nights off, but it was my wife's birthday so we had a party and invited all the guys—Illinois Jacquet, Sarah Vaughan, Stump 'n Stumpy, and several other artists, all the people who were in show business who knew Lorraine from dancing. They were down there having a good time and the whiskey was flowing. They had a cake and drinks and everything. This guy, Henry Morgan, who had his own show in New York, invited me to come on his show and be interviewed. This was really another put-on because he wasn't really interested in music.

Anyway, I went out to be interviewed; he was doing the show from a hotel around the corner. My horn was still straight when I left it on one of those little trumpet stands that sticks straight up.

When I got back to the club after making this interview, Stump 'n Stumpy had been fooling around on the bandstand, and one had pushed the other, and he'd fallen back onto my horn. Instead of the horn just falling, the bell bent. Nine hundred and ninety-nine times out of a thousand if someone fell on a horn, it would bend the valves or maybe hit and bend the valve case. The horn would be dented, and the valves would stick, but this horn bent. When I got back, the bell was sticking up in the air. Illinois Jacquet had left. He said, "I'm not going to be here when that man comes back and sees his horn sticking up at that angle. I ain't gonna be here when that crazy [guy] gets back."

When I came back, it was my wife's birthday and I didn't wanna be a drag. I put the horn to my mouth and started playing it. Well, when the bell bent back, it made a smaller hole because of the dent. I couldn't get the right sound, but it was a strange sound that I got from that instrument that night. I played it, and I liked the sound. The sound had been changed and it could be played softly, very softly, not blarey. I played it like that the rest of the night, and the next day I had it straightened out again. Then I started thinking about it and said, "Wait a minute, man, that was something else." I remembered the way the sound had come from it, quicker to the ear—to my ear, the player. A forty-five-degree angle is much closer than ninety degrees. I contacted the Martin Company, and I had Lorraine, who's also an artist, draw me a trumpet at a forty-five-degree angle and sent it to the Martin Company. I told them, "I want a horn like this."

"You're crazy!" they said.

"O.K.," I said, "I'm crazy, but I want a horn like this." They made me a trumpet and I've been playing one like that ever since.

FIDDLIN' FOOL

I fooled Old Marster seven years
Fooled the overseer three;
Hand me down my banjo
And I'll tickle your bel-lee.

THE STORY OF THE BANJO
GERALD HAUSMAN AND KELVIN RODRIQUES

African Americans have shaped and greatly influenced musical expression in the United States and abroad. During slavery, black Americans developed field hollers and spirituals and became virtuoso fiddlers and banjoists. They were forbidden to play the drum, since slave owners feared that this instrument, which was used in Africa to convey messages and orders across forests, might be used in America to excite slaves and stir rebellion.* Here is the story of the banjo, one of black America's first major instruments.

On American plantations, African exiles did not beat drums and chant songs that harked back to Africa, nor were they encouraged to do so by the plantation owners. One might imagine that, given time and acclimatization, they would gravitate toward a plucked instrument like the guitar, an instrument much less forbidding than the ominous-toned skin drum, but in fact, this did not happen until much later during the post-slavery era.

However, West African blacks, brought to America in slave ships, did have an instrument common to their culture: the banjo. Made of skin and string, groundhog and cat, it was similar to instruments made by the

---

* In Africa, drums either are spirits or they contain spirits. So when a drum is played at a feast or celebration or ritual, and dancers dance to the beat, the spirit of the drum is believed to inhabit the dancers. Hence, "the spirit moves them" should be taken literally.

Moors, north of the Sahara. An early French visitor to this country described it as the African *rabouquin:* "a triangular piece of board with three strings made of intestines, supported by a bridge, which may be stretched at pleasure by means of pegs like those of our instruments in Europe; it is indeed nothing else than a guitar with three strings." In 1785, Thomas Jefferson aptly remarked in a footnote of his *Notes on the State of Virginia* that the slave instrument of choice "is the Bonjar, which they brought hither from Africa . . ." A skin-covered gourd with strings, this earliest form of what we now call the banjo might also have been made from a hollowed-out turtleshell or a wooden bowl; its obvious allure was its similarity to the drum.

In the minstrelsy era of the late 1700s and early 1800s, the banjo found a beloved place. Banjoists were close in popularity to bones and tambo players, who in England were called corner men. Visualize, if you will, sixty performers on a stage, line upon line, rising in tiers. On the wings were the end-men with their tambourines and bones. Following their lead, in the second section of a typical minstrel show, came a rousing number of banjo-playing and clog-dancing performers whose antics fitted their musical skills.

The banjo took on a soul of its own, a ringing of rhythm that, behind a thin disguise, was none other than the forbidden Congo drum. With their high-minded antics went the banjo and the bones, the fiddle, and the tambourine. For a long while, the role of the stately interlocutor, who sat in the center of the line of minstrel men, was the banjoist's. Over and over, he hammered out the rhythm beaten down and played up by his musical end-men brothers, Brother Bones and Brother Tambo.

The banjo strikes a pure, three-to-five-stringed note of African intensity: "Cindy got religion, she's had it once before, but when she hears my old banjo, she's the first one on the floor." It may not have been noticed by Southern gentry as an "instrument of origin," a kind of rinky-dink, rappety-tap drum with strings. [But] the West African *bania*, the banjo proper, would become indispensable in American mainstream folk music. As musicologist Frederic V. Grunfeld has pointed out: "In America, where musical integration is a continuous process going back to Colonial times, the banjo player from Africa meets the guitar player from Europe, and the result is that instruments as well as styles are exchanged."

Prior to the appearance of the blues, the banjo filled in for the guitar as a kind of talkative dummy perched upon the ventriloquist's lap. It cried, it sighed, it sang like a river and rang like a stream, a volley of bells on the blue-black Southern plantation night. "From time to time," wrote the European composer Henri Iterz in the 1840s, "while listening to negro banjo players, I have pondered the mysterious law of rhythm which seems to be a universal law, since rhythm is a coordinated movement, and movement is life, and life fills the universe." So it was that four-string cheese-box banjos came into being, to float in sweet accord with the pulsations of the cosmos.

—*From* African-American Alphabet

〰

Every Negro has something to say. Simply because he is a Negro. . . . His mere body . . . is an eloquence.

—*Gwendolyn Brooks*

〰

A POEM FOR "MAGIC"
QUINCY TROUPE

In the 1996–97 basketball season, sportswriters and former National Basketball Association coaches and players voted Earvin "Magic" Johnson one of the fifty greatest players of all time. Johnson, who was born in 1959, joined the Los Angeles Lakers in 1979 and led the team to five NBA titles. The NBA named him its Most Valuable Player three times. The following poem, an ode to Johnson's legendary skills, just might change how you view basketball.

FOR EARVIN "MAGIC" JOHNSON, DONNELL REID, AND RICHARD FRANKLIN

take it to the hoop, "magic" johnson
take the ball dazzling down the open lane
herk & jerk & raise your six feet nine inch

frame into air sweating screams of your neon name
"magic" johnson, nicknamed "windex" way back in high school
cause you wiped glass backboards so clean
where you first juked & shook
wiled your way to glory
a new style fusion of shake & bake energy
using everything possible, you created your own space
to fly through—any moment now, we expect your wings
to spread feathers for that spooky take off of yours—
then shake & glide, till you hammer home
a clotheslining deuce off glass
now, come back down with a reverse hoodoo gem
off the spin, & stick it in sweet, popping nets, clean
from twenty feet, right-side

put the ball on the floor, "magic"
slide the dribble behind your back, ease it deftly
between your bony, stork legs, head bobbing everwhichaway
up & down, you see everything on the court
off the high, yoyo patter, stop & go dribble, you shoot
a threading needle rope pass, sweet home to kareem
cutting through the lane, his skyhook pops cords
now lead the fastbreak, hit worthy on the fly
now, blindside a behind the back pinpointpass for two more
off the fake, looking the other way
you raise off balance into space
sweating chants of your name, turn, 180 degrees

off the move, your legs scissoring space, like a swimmer's
yoyoing motion, in deep water, stretching out now toward free
flight, you double pump through human trees, hang in place
slip the ball into your left hand
then deal it like a las vegas card dealer
off squared glass, into nets, living up to your singular nickname
so "bad," you cartwheel the crowd towards frenzy
wearing now your electric smile, neon as your name

in victory, we suddenly sense your glorious uplift
your urgent need to be champion
& so we cheer, rejoicing with you, for this quicksilver, quicksilver
                                   quicksilver
moment of fame, so put the ball on the floor again, "magic"
juke & dazzle, shake & bake down the lane
take the sucker to the hoop, "magic" johnson,
recreate reverse hoodoo gems off the spin,
deal alley-oop-dunk-a-thon-magician passes
now, double-pump, scissor, vamp through space
hang in place & put it all up in the sucker's face, "magic"
johnson, & deal the roundball, like the juju man that you am
like the sho-nuff shaman man that you am
"magic," like the sho-nuff spaceman, you am

In 1991, Magic Johnson announced he had contracted HIV, the virus that causes AIDS. He then established the Magic Johnson Foundation, which provides funding to nonprofit HIV/AIDS organizations. By 1998, the foundation had given more than $6 million in grants to organizations nationwide.

HEAT
RETOLD BY HAROLD COURLANDER

Boasting to keep up with natural-born storytellers requires a vivid and potent imagination.

One boy says, "It's sure hot around here."

Another one says, "Hot? How come you call this hot? It's pure cool to me. Down where I come from it's so hot you dassent leave your hammer in the sun, cause the heat takes the temper right out of it."

"Hot? You call that hot?" another man say. "Why, down in the bottoms where my daddy lives all the fence posts bend over in the middle when the sun comes up, and the logs and stumps in the fields crawl away to find some shade."

"Well, that sounds kind of *warm* all right," someone say, "but it sure ain't hot. Down in my country when the dogs is chasin' cats down the main street they is all walkin'."

"I forgot to tell you one more thing about my place," says one. "Was so hot down there that when we pumped water nothin' but steam come out. So we had to catch that steam and put it in the ice house at night to turn it back to water."

"Speakin' of the ice house," says another, "we had to keep the popcorn there, else it popped right off the ears and covered the ground like snow."

"Well, that ain't much to mention," says one old boy, "where I come from the railroad tracks set out there in the sun long as they can stand it, then they burrow under the ground and don't come out till dark. That's how come the train don't go through till midnight."

"What you-all are talkin' about is plain cool to me," another man says. "We got a creek down in my country that runs like the devil at night. But when the sun comes up in the morning this creek begins to get sluggish in the heat, and by ten o'clock it just stops in its tracks and don't move at all till the sun goes down."

"We got a creek too down on my daddy's farm," says one, "and if you go out there in the middle of the day you hear all the stones hollerin' something pitiful for somebody to come quick and throw them in the water."

"My mamma had a great big iron kettle," another man say, "and she left it outside one time for just about ten minutes in the sun. And when she took it in it had great big water blisters on it."

"That does it," says another. "When *my* mamma left her iron kettle in the sun it melted down flat and she had to use it for a stove lid."

"Ain't you forget to hear about the big old swamp on my granddaddy's forty acres?" says this man who ain't said nothin' yet up to this point. "When it gets hot there that swamp rises up like a cake till it's thirty feet high, and it don't go down till the frost hits."

Well, about that time the first man to complain, he say, "The way it seem to me is where we're sittin' is just too cold, so somebody go and fetch my coat."

I had to constantly overcome the disadvantages of having no academic training by inventing my own way of doing things.

—*Gordon Parks*

FIRST IN SCIENCE:
BENJAMIN BANNEKER

With practically no formal schooling, Benjamin Banneker (1731– 1806) became America's first black scientist. He carved a clock from wood (though he had never seen one), helped to survey the land that became the District of Columbia, and produced the first scientific text by an African American, an almanac. His endeavors, and his correspondence with Thomas Jefferson, make him an especially important figure in both science and letters.

Benjamin Banneker was born on November 9, 1731, near the Patapsco River in Baltimore County, Maryland. The child of free blacks, he grew up on the family's farm, learned to read and write from his grandmother, and attended a one-room school, developing an early interest in mathematics.

When he was twenty-one, he drew plans for his first scientific achievement, a clock. Sketching wheels, gears, a balancing mechanism, and a spring barrel, and then using his blueprints and a pocket knife, he painstakingly carved the teeth of the wheels and pinions and fit them all together. When he was done, he set the mechanisms, and on the hour, it struck. He had built, almost entirely from wood, a striking clock—a rarity in eighteenth century America, since most clocks were imported from Europe. The clock became a curiosity, and people from across the region visited the farm to marvel at it. It ticked until his death more than fifty years later.

When Banneker was forty, a white neighbor named George Ellicot visited the farm, saw the clock, scanned Banneker's small library, and sensed the two had similar interests. In the fall of 1788, George visited Banneker again and lent him two astronomy books, a pedestal telescope, and drafting instruments. Soon afterward, on starry nights, Banneker explored the heavens, pointing the telescope at stars and planets he identified from his readings. He then studied logarithms and computed a projection for an eclipse of the sun, a difficult calculation in his time.

He set down his projection in a letter to George Ellicot, stating his ambition to compute an entire ephemeris, a chart of complex mathematical calculations based on astronomical observations. Ephemerides included charts of the rising and setting of the sun, the moon, and stars. Seamen used them to calculate their positions and for tidal information so they could navigate inland and coastal waters. Farmers used them for weather forecasts and to schedule planting dates. At the time, ephemerides were published in almanacs, the only secular publications then available in America.

George Ellicot was astonished by Banneker's letter. Banneker went ahead preparing his ephemeris for the year 1791 and sent out letters to publishers. But by the time a prospective publisher had checked the calculations, it was too late for publication, so Banneker was forced to put aside his ephemeris.

But his scientific pursuits had only begun. His next major project would be the greatest adventure of his life: surveying the boundaries of land that would become the nation's capital. President George Washington commissioned the survey on January 24, 1791.

In early February, Banneker, fifty-nine, and George Ellicot's cousin, Major Andrew Ellicot IV, thirty-eight, set up a base camp near Georgetown, on the Potomac River. From there, they carried out Washington's detailed instructions to establish the perimeter of the federal district—a ten-mile-square area of mostly wilderness.

Banneker, too old for fieldwork, remained in the base camp. In the observatory tent, he manned what was probably the most sophisticated clock in the nation, an astronomical clock designed for marking the precise passage of time, so survey calculations would be accurate. Banneker wound the instrument and ensured that the clock operated at a constant rate by cross-checking it with altitudes taken of the sun at periodic intervals. He also made sure the clock's mechanisms were not hampered by cold. Subtle variations could affect its precision, so he kept thermometers nearby and made several readings each day.

The boundary survey for the area, called the District of Columbia, was completed on January 1, 1793. The federal government moved into the district seven years later.

Through his involvement in the survey, Banneker's appreciation grew for mathematical skills and for the value of astronomy, though his health suffered due to his grueling schedule and exposure to cold. He returned to his farm, where, by candlelight, at the oval table strewn with astronomical instruments and books, he prepared an ephemeris for 1792. To do it, he performed seventy separate calculations for each projection of an eclipse. He checked his mathematics and entered his calculations into a 300-page journal. By June 1791 he was done.

Two months later, he composed a letter to Thomas Jefferson, Secretary of State:

> Sir, I am fully sensible of the greatness of that freedom which I take with you on the present occasion; a liberty which Seemed to me Scarcely allowable, when I reflected on that distinguished, and dignifyed station in which you Stand; and the almost general prejudice and prepossession which is so prevalent in the world against those of my complexion.

He reminded Jefferson of the "time in which the Arms and tyranny of the British Crown were exerted with every powerful effort, in order to reduce you to a State of Servitude" and wrote that such a tyranny had inspired Jefferson to "create a document that contained these words: 'We hold these truths to be Self evident, that all men are created equal, and are endowed by their creator with certain inalienable rights, that among these are life, liberty, and the pursuit of happiness.' "

Banneker's letter, then, equated the British tyranny against Americans with America's treachery against blacks. It was a powerful argument, using Jefferson's own words from the Declaration of Independence to mirror the plight of fellow human beings whose "inalienable rights" had been suppressed.

Banneker mailed the letter along with his ephemeris to Jefferson, no doubt impressing him. Jefferson, who is alleged to have fathered children with his slave, had waffled on the slave issue. In his *Notes on Virginia,* he wrote of his hatred for the institution but in fact depended as a planter on the work of his own slaves. He said he hoped to change the status of slaves to that of tenants. But his own financial status relied heavily on the institution.

Four days later, Jefferson wrote a reply to Banneker:

Nobody wishes more than I do to see such proofs as you exhibit, that Nature has given our black brethren talents equal to those of the other colors of men, and that the appearance of a want of them is owing only to the degraded condition of their existence.

He went on to say that he forwarded Banneker's ephemeris to the Secretary of the Royal Academy of Sciences in Paris, as evidence of the intellectual achievement of a black in America. But soon after Jefferson wrote the Marquis de Condorcet, the French Revolution took place, and the Marquis was embroiled in political turmoil and killed. No record has yet been found of Banneker's ephemeris among French archives.

That December, Banneker's first almanac was published, a twenty-four-page volume advertised as *Benjamin Banneker's highly approved Al-Manack, for 1792.* In its introduction, Maryland Senator James McHenry sketched Banneker's life story and added that he considered "this Negro as fresh proof that the powers of the mind are disconnected with the colour of the skin." The almanac was a bestseller, and a second edition was printed.

Banneker's next almanac, published the following year, contained his correspondence with Jefferson. Banneker published almanacs until 1797—twenty-eight known editions over six years, including one featuring a woodcut portrait of the scientist in Quaker dress, the outfit of many abolitionists, but clothes Banneker probably didn't own.

Meanwhile, he let his farming tasks slip and occupied himself with science, calculating ephemerides for eight more years. On October 9, 1806, he took a walk, felt sick, hurried home, and collapsed on his couch. He died that same day, one month before his seventy-fifth birthday. Two days later, as his body was lowered into a grave, his cabin burst into flames. His remarkable clock, which had ticked until that day, was lost.

As a black man, Banneker's fame was unusual in the late eighteenth century, when there were 60,000 free blacks and 750,000 slaves in America. But other blacks almost certainly contributed to scientific, medical, and technological progress. Their names, however, were seldom recorded.

SLAVE INVENTORS: NED AND SAM

Blacks rarely got credit for their ingenuity.

In 1790, the U.S. Patent Act was enacted to encourage innovation, provide detailed information about inventions, and protect the rights of the inventor. Before the Civil War, free blacks had legal rights to patents, but few actually got them. In 1821, Thomas L. Jennings (1791–1859) received a patent for a dry cleaning process, becoming the first black known to have obtained a patent. He used his earnings to promote anti-slavery activities in New York.

While free blacks were subjected to a number of legal restrictions—such as those limiting freedom of travel, disallowing court testimony, or enslaving blacks for minor offenses—slaves had it worse, and rights to their inventions were not recognized by slave owners or the government. In fact, many slave owners undoubtedly claimed slaves' inventions as their own property.

The invention of a slave mechanic named Ned, from Pike County, Mississippi, tested the patent system by provoking the federal government to articulate its position on the legality of his invention and the rights to it. Ned invented a cotton scrapper that enabled one man and two horses to complete the work of two men, four horses, two single scrappers, and two plows. When Ned's owner wrote the U.S. Secretary of the Interior to secure a patent for the invention in his own name, as Ned's master, the matter was referred to U.S. Attorney General Jeremiah Black, who on June 10, 1858, rendered an opinion that an invention by a slave "cannot, in the present state of law, be patented." Essentially, he reasoned that a slave was not recognized as a citizen, and thus could not enter into a legal contract. Thus, any invention of a slave could not be formally recognized by the patent office. The opinion stood until the end of the Civil War and the passage of the Thirteenth and Fourteenth Amendments.

Ned's owner went ahead with his scheme, manufacturing and selling the double cotton scrapper. Ned probably died as a slave, never reaping rewards for his invention.

And Ned was not alone; many other slaves invented labor-saving tools claimed by whites, perhaps even the cotton gin, an invention that revolutionized agriculture. It is said that Eli Whitney may have gotten his idea for the cotton gin from a slave named Sam, who used a comb-like device to clean cotton, culling seeds and debris from it. It was said that Sam had learned to make the device from his father. Whitney's device worked on precisely the same principle. With it, annual U.S. cotton exports soared from 138,000 pounds to six million pounds.

SUGAR DADDY: NORBERT RILLIEUX

Norbert Rillieux (1806–94) was the first major black inventor. His invention, considered by some to be among the greatest in American chemical engineering, revolutionized an entire industry, making sugar plentiful and inexpensive.

Born in 1806 in New Orleans, Louisiana, Norbert Rillieux was the son of a wealthy French planter and a black woman whom he probably set free. Norbert attended Catholic schools in New Orleans, then studied engineering in Paris at L'Ecole Centrale. He graduated at twenty-four and was asked to stay on to teach applied mechanics, becoming the school's youngest instructor.

In Paris, Rillieux recalled how slaves back home produced sugar— they tended steaming vats in a laborious, backbreakingly slow process called the "Jamaica Train." Using long-handled ladles, the slaves stirred thick, boiling sugar cane juice then scooped it into a series of successively smaller kettles. The water boiled away, leaving a thicker mixture of molasses and sugar in each vat. Residue in the last vat was heated until it crystallized, producing crude, caramelized sugar.

In 1840, Rillieux returned to New Orleans. As chief engineer of a new sugar factory, he built a large refining system. It had design flaws. But Rillieux modified his plans and convinced a sugar manufacturer to install the redesigned system. The apparatus, which resembled a stationary locomotive spouting steam clouds, was a complete success.

He called his machine the multiple-effect vacuum evaporator. It harnessed steam, using latent heat from one pan to heat the next in a series of vacuum pans. The method, which is still in use, lowered evaporating temperatures—thus saving fuel—and cut the risk of discoloring sugar with excessive heat. It also turned out fine, granulated sugar.

Rillieux patented his evaporator in 1846. It revolutionized the sugar industry. Thousands of evaporators were installed at refineries in Louisiana, Mexico, and Cuba. Rillieux became famous, and sugar, a luxury through most of the 1800s, became plentiful.

Rillieux had succeeded in stopping the inefficient "Jamaica Train" with its row of slaves with ladles. A single person could work the new system by simply turning valves. Ironically, however, when the production and supply of sugar increased, the demand for slaves did also. More were needed to work in the sugarcane fields.

In 1854, when a law was passed requiring blacks in New Orleans to carry identification cards, Rillieux returned to Paris, where he became headmaster of L'Ecole Centrale. He developed an interest in Egyptology and made valuable contributions in deciphering hieroglyphics. In the final stages of his career, he patented a process of heating juices with multiple-effect vapors. The process is still used in cane and sugar beet factories.

Rillieux died forty years after returning to Paris. His name is missing from most science books today. But he is one of a handful of inventors who could rightly claim to have revolutionized an industry.

WHALE CATCHER: LEWIS TEMPLE

Lewis Temple (1800–54) invented the single most important invention in whaling history.

One day in 1848, Lewis Temple sat in a barbershop chair in New Bedford, Massachusetts, the center of the whaling industry. He listened to seamen complain of how whales broke free from arrowhead-shaped harpoons. The barber's scissors gave him a novel idea for a harpoon.

Lewis, who operated a blacksmith shop in town, went to work, hammering out his newfangled harpoon. With its movable head, or barb, it would have far-ranging implications.

Upon piercing the whale's blubber, the barb was held parallel to the shaft by a thin wooden pin. The pin snapped when the whale pulled away, and the barb toggled at a right angle, anchoring in the whale. The harpoon could not be withdrawn when the whale struggled to get free.

Whaling experts have called Temple's Toggle Iron "the most important single invention in the whole history of whaling" because it helped whalers capture "a far greater proportion of whales" than ever. One whaleship, the *Ohio,* returned home from the Arctic with 2,300 barrels of whale oil. Its whalers had used only eight Toggle Irons to kill twenty-one whales.

Temple, born in Richmond, Virginia, in 1800, may well have been one of the more than 100,000 slaves who fled to northern cities via the Underground Railroad. In New Bedford, he managed to make a living off his invention. But as important to whaling as it was, he never obtained a patent, so other blacksmiths copied it. One blacksmith shop made 30,000 toggle harpoons over twenty years—and there were some eight shops in New Bedford at the time.

In the early 1850s, Temple contracted a construction company to build a bigger shop near Steamboat Wharf. But an accident prevented him from moving in. In 1853, while walking one night near his half-finished shop, he stumbled over a plank left by a sewer worker. The fall injured and weakened him badly, and he never recovered. Temple sued the city for $2,000. But the fifty-four-year-old Temple died before the money was awarded. Though the whaling industry would peak in New Bedford in just three years, partly due to his invention, his entire estate was valued at less than $1,500 when he died. The money went toward his debts.

THE REAL MCCOY: ELIJAH MCCOY

The son of escaped slaves, Elijah McCoy (1843–1929), whose name became synonymous for a genuine, high-quality item ("the real McCoy"), patented more than fifty inventions used by railroad engineers.

In the 1880s, more than 70,000 miles of railroad track were laid, bringing markets closer together and just as often putting great distances between people. The expanding rail network and the mighty steam engines that chugged along them provided jobs for many African Americans. For one man, the hazards of railroad life sparked an idea for a mechanical wonder that ended up saving railroads time and enormous sums of money.

Elijah McCoy was born in 1843 in a community of escaped slaves in Colchester, Ontario. Fascinated by engines, he traveled to Scotland to study mechanical engineering. In Edinburgh, he completed an apprenticeship, then moved to Ypsilanti, Michigan, to work for the Michigan Central Railroad. Although he was a master mechanic and engineer, the best job he could get was the lowly position of locomotive fireman. But he treated the job as a learning experience.

Train engines generated immense heat and friction. To prevent overheating, trains were stopped—often. McCoy's job was to climb off and lubricate the hot, steaming engine by hand then climb back on board. Miles down the track, the process had to be repeated.

McCoy set out to improve upon this lubrication method, and in 1872 he invented a lubricating cup that did the job automatically. His cup dripped oil, continuously, onto gears and other moving engine parts while the train was still in motion. He patented the cup and designed many other automatic lubricating devices. Shipping lines, railroad companies, and factories bought and used them.

Though some white workers referred to them as "nigger oil cups," they installed the device, often under McCoy's direction; and to learn to use the cups, people hung on McCoy's every word of instruction.

No one made better lubricators. McCoy's graphite lubricator, patented in 1915, enabled one engine to travel 300,000 miles without relubricating cylinders. His manufacturing techniques were rigorous, and his lubricating devices were unequaled in quality. They became the industry standard, hence the term "the real McCoy."

But inventions could be expensive to develop and market. So, like many other black inventors, McCoy sold his patent rights to others for cash. His most lucrative inventions made millions for investors in the Elijah McCoy Manufacturing Firm. But McCoy himself owned little stock in the company. He suffered a series of financial setbacks and in 1929 died relatively poor in Eloise, Michigan.

THE BLACK EDISON: GRANVILLE T. WOODS

With his telegraph and telephone systems, Granville T. Woods (1856–1910) was an early competitor with Alexander Graham Bell and Thomas Edison. He also invented the trolley car system. Largely self-taught, Woods was one of America's most versatile inventors.

In 1884, Granville T. Woods opened an electrical engineering shop in Cincinnati—Woods Electric Company—to manufacture his own inventions. As a black engineer, he had been passed over for promotions many times and had lost many jobs. The move to establish his own firm, and the work it produced, caused him to be called the "Black Edison."

In fact, he had modeled his shop after Thomas Edison's Menlo Park, New Jersey, industrial research laboratory.

Woods's first patent was for a steam boiler furnace, and his first electrical invention was a distinct improvement on telephone transmitters then in use. He assigned the transmitter rights to the American Bell Telephone Company of Boston.

Some of America's largest electric engineering companies—among them General Electric and Westinghouse—came knocking as his reputation grew. He invented an apparatus that combined the telephone and telegraph, coining the word "telegraphony." With telegraphony, people could speak over the same wires used to send Morse code, with no additional equipment.

In 1887, he patented his "induction telegraphy" system, which kept trains from colliding. Moving trains could use the system to send and receive messages on the location of other moving trains. The system prevented major accidents, which often occurred when engineers aboard trains relied solely on signalmen in stations.

The following year, Woods invented the overhead conducting system for trains and streetcars. Poles extended from a train or streetcar drew current from electrified power lines strung along the route. Woods also invented the grooved wheel, or "troller," that rolled on the power lines. This "trolley" system practically eliminated friction.

Woods produced many other inventions, including an incubator, an automatic circuit-breaker, and the "third rail," still used by subway systems worldwide. For the latter, he set up a series of electrical conductors parallel to the path of the train. "Collectors" of the electricity, installed on each train car, made contact with the conductors along the route. Woods sold this invention to General Electric in 1901.

In all, Woods patented more than sixty inventions, most of them electrical. His direct competitors were Thomas Edison and Lucius Phelps, each of whom invented a similar telegraph system. Woods won his court battles for patent protection. But he couldn't afford to pay all his legal bills. He died in 1910 in poverty.

LAMP TO THE WORLD: LEWIS LATIMER

Lewis Latimer (1848–1928) produced the patent drawings for the tele-phone, invented an incandescent lamp, and wrote the world's first book on electric lighting. *

Lewis Howard Latimer was born in 1848 in Chelsea, Massachusetts, a free state, but his parents were former slaves. Both had fled Virginia via the Underground Railroad, settling in Boston. Lewis's father, George, became involved in a celebrated case when his former owner visited Boston and demanded his "property." Frederick Douglass, William Lloyd Garrison, and other abolitionists then purchased George's free-dom for $400.

Lewis's childhood was brief. His father abandoned the family when Lewis was only ten. Five years later, Lewis joined the Union navy and saw action as a landsman aboard the U.S.S. *Massasoitt*. After being honorably discharged in 1865, he became an office boy at Crosby & Gould, a Boston patent law firm, where he earned three dollars per week. There, he saw men making detailed drawings, and he set out to become a draftsman. He practiced and mustered the courage to ask his employer to let him draw. The boss laughed, handed him a sheet of drawing paper, and walked off. When he returned, he was startled by Latimer's talent and promoted him to junior draftsman. Latimer later became head draftsman, staying at the firm eleven years.

While there, he drew out Alexander Graham Bell's specifications for the telephone, illustrating each part of the invention to show how it worked. Using Latimer's drawings, Bell applied for and was granted a patent in 1876.

Latimer dreamed of becoming an inventor himself. He moved to Bridgeport, Connecticut, where he worked for Hiram S. Maxim (who later invented the machine gun) at the U.S. Electric Lighting Company. The firm was one of Thomas Edison's biggest competitors.

Latimer's experiments improved electric lighting, invented by Edison

---

* Lewis Latimer was also a poet. See "The Endless Chain," page 690.

in 1879. Specifically, Latimer invented carbon filaments for the electric incandescent lamp, which he patented in 1881. A year later, he devised a process for manufacturing carbon filaments that would last longer and be cheaper to produce than Edison's.

Maxim opened factories to produce Latimer's filaments, which were used across the United States, Canada, and Europe. Latimer himself supervised the installation of electric light plants in New York, Philadelphia, and other cities.

Latimer's tremendous value as an inventive genius became widely known, even to Edison. In 1884, Edison hired Latimer, who worked for thirty years as Edison's draftsman and technical witness in patent lawsuits. Millions of dollars hinged on his court testimony.

In 1890, Latimer wrote *the* book on electric lighting, *Incandescent Electric Lighting: A Practical Description of the Edison System.* The first book on the subject, it became a standard reference in the industry, unveiling the mysteries of incandescence.

LASTING SHOES:
JAN EARNST MATZELIGER

Born in South America, Jan Earnst Matzeliger (1852–89) ranks among the elite group of geniuses who revolutionized industries. He invented the extraordinarily complex "lasting machine," which stitched the top of a shoe to its bottom—a delicate leather-tailoring job formerly done by skilled craftsmen.

At age ten, Jan Earnst Matzeliger worked in machine shops that his father ran in Paramaribo, the capital of Suriname (then known as Dutch Guiana). But he yearned to explore the world. At nineteen, he got his chance, aboard an East Indian vessel. Several years later, he landed in

Philadelphia, where he worked odd jobs before moving to Lynn, Massachusetts, the center of the shoe industry.

In 1877, highly paid, unionized craftsmen stitched a shoe's upper to its sole. "Hand lasting" created a production bottleneck, since shoe parts were pumped out quickly by machines. Manufacturers wanted to mechanize hand lasting, the final stage in the shoe-making process. But no machine invented yet could do the work. Prototypes, costing $250,000, had failed.

The young, frail Matzeliger tried to build one that would work. After operating sole-sewing, heel-burnishing, and buttonhole machines all day, he worked through the night building—from scratch—a machine that could pull, pleat, tuck, tack, and stitch leather around a foot-shaped mold.

Matzeliger's prototype, constructed over six months, was crude, consisting of scrap metal, blocks of wood, cigar boxes, and junk. He was offered fifty dollars for the model, but refused to sell it and went on redesigning it.

Over several years, he constructed a model capable of pleating leather around the toe and heel of a shoe. This time, when he showed his creation, he was offered $1,500. Again, he refused and started from scratch on another machine, this time in a corner of a shoe plant, using a discarded forge.

He lived on a nickel a day for food, but after securing financial support—in return for two thirds interest in his invention—he was able to build another prototype in three years.

Test day arrived. Matzeliger started up his contraption. It held the last in position and moved it forward while other parts punched the leather and drew it over the last, fitting the leather at the toe and heel. Then the machine fed nails into position and drove them over the last. Time from start to finish: one minute. At the end of the day, the factory test had completed seventy-five pairs of women's shoes. With modifications, Matzeliger's machine produced up to seven hundred pairs. A hand laster could finish only fifty pairs in a day.

Matzelinger patented the machine in 1883.

Disgruntled hand lasters called Matzeliger's invention the "niggerhead" machine. But such remarks did not forestall progress. His machine increased shoe production and cut costs in half.

By 1889 the entire shoe industry—worldwide—ordered the machine. Matzeliger and his investors established a company, but it was too small to meet the demand. Eventually, the United Shoe Machinery Corporation was formed. During the next twelve years it earned more than $50 million and had captured 98 percent of the shoe machinery market. By 1955, the company was valued at more than $1 billion.

Matzeliger himself, however, made very little money. Inventing his machine had pushed his fragile health over the limit. He contracted tuberculosis and died in 1889, willing all of his company stock to the only church in Lynn that had welcomed him. The church was able to pay off its entire debt of $10,860.

GIANT OF SCIENCE:
GEORGE WASHINGTON CARVER

George Washington Carver (c. 1864–1943) is perhaps the nation's most celebrated African American scientist. Many remember the slave-born educator and scientist only for his ingenuity with peanuts. But his experiments were wide ranging, and he helped change the course of agriculture in the United States.

George Washington Carver is remembered for having the biggest "green thumbs" in American history. He spent his childhood reportedly talking to flowers and had been known in his adulthood to stay up all night to watch a plant bloom.

Yet his life was anything but pastoral. It started in 1864 or 1865 in Missouri with birth in slavery and with incredible violence. Often bushwhackers would raid farms to demand money. While George was still an infant, a band kidnapped both him and his mother. A Union scout tracked the band to Confederate Arkansas and, as one story goes, swapped the baby for a $300 racehorse. The scout returned with George, who was sickly by then. George's mother was never heard from again.*

When slavery ended, Carver attended a school for black children, then wandered the Midwest, completing high school in Kansas. He went on to study botany and agriculture at Iowa State College, becoming the school's first black graduate in 1894.

Carver studied for his master's degree, concentrating on mycology, a branch of botany dealing with fungi. He often took walks in the woods to gather specimens, eventually contributing some 15,000 specimens to the college herbarium.

While still a postgraduate student—he received his master's degree in 1896—Carver received a teaching offer from Booker T. Washington, founder of Tuskegee Institute. Washington's letter read: "I cannot offer you money, position, or fame. The first two you have; the last, from the place you now occupy, you will no doubt achieve. These things I now ask you to give up. I offer you in their place work—hard, hard work—the task of bringing a people from degradation, poverty, and waste to full manhood."

Carver thought and finally replied, saying it had "always been the one great ideal of my life to be of the greatest good to the greatest number of 'my people' possible" and that education "is the key to unlock the golden door of freedom to our people."

Once Carver arrived at Tuskegee, Washington was frank. He said, "Your department exists only on paper, Carver, and your laboratory will have to be in your head."

Undismayed, Carver improvised, building a makeshift lab from discarded items and scraps found around campus. From a heavy teacup, he made a mortar. A kerosene lamp became his Bunsen burner. He wasted nothing. And in the end, through both his laboratory and his farming activities, he was able to transform agricultural practices across the South, reaching both black and white farmers.

In 1897, Carver was named the first director of the Tuskegee Agricultural Experimental Station, funded by the government. There, he taught farming techniques and printed bulletins on crops suitable for the overworked soil of the region.

* According to another version, George's owner thanked the scout by giving him a $300 racehorse. Whichever version is true, George's life was still bartered for the horse.

He also started the first movable school in the South, a mule-drawn wagon packed with farm-education material. Moving from farm to farm, Carver and his assistant demonstrated farming methods. By the summer of 1906, the wagon reached two thousand farmers a month. Eventually it became part of a federal program employing more than eight hundred black farmers.

Carver taught pragmatic farming methods. On a twenty-acre parcel of poor land, he had his students plant cowpeas, which served as fertilizer and resupplied the overused soil with nitrates. Next Carver planted sweet potatoes and then cotton. The formerly poor land yielded five hundred pounds of crop per acre—more than any farmer in the area had ever harvested. Local farmers took notice, acting on Carver's recommendation for "crop rotation," which could rejuvenate soil that had been depleted for so long by one-crop cotton or tobacco farming.

Carver encouraged farmers to make wise use of natural resources, even waste such as leaves, garbage, paper, grass, and rags. And while other agricultural stations focused on pure science, Carver focused on applied science. His farming bulletins served as "how-to" publications, complete with recipes. Bulletin No. 31 was *How to Grow the Peanut and 105 Ways of Preparing It for Human Consumption*. Over forty-four years he published bulletins touching on subjects of interest to local farmers, from rebuilding depleted soil to pickling and curing meat.

He pushed peanut farming so well that it ended up replacing cotton as the number one crop in the farming belt from Alabama to Florida. The oversupply of peanuts prompted Carver to lock himself in his lab to concoct new uses for them. Days later he reemerged, having devised more than two dozen new products. Over time, he developed three hundred peanut-based products—including milk, cheese, face powder, butter, shampoo, printer's ink, vinegar, coffee, salads, soaps, and wood stains. These efforts alone brought farmers tens of millions of dollars in additional revenue.

He also developed new uses for other crops—including synthetic marble made from sawdust and sweet-potato "rubber." Inventing new industrial uses for agricultural products—or chemurgy—was unknown at the time; and his lab was, in a sense, a forerunner of the research and design departments of many of today's large corporations. Thomas Edison and Henry Ford took note.

Carver's fame spread not just to Washington, D.C., but abroad. Asked to help food efforts in African regions where the disease-ridden tsetse fly infested dairy herds, he invented a nourishing milk made from peanuts, which were widely grown there.

He pointed out that man was a more effective milk producer than cows. "It takes the cow twenty-four hours to make milk. I can make from peanuts better, cleaner, and more healthful milk in five minutes. The cow simply takes out of the food she eats what is soluble. Which is the cleaner process, that of grinding, moistening, heating, and filtering in a machine or pan, or passing cereals, vegetables, or the vegetable matter a cow eats through her stomach?"

Carver's teaching philosophy centered on "understanding relationships." Instead of studying various sciences in isolation, his students studied one particular object in depth, the cowpea, for instance. He showed how each of the sciences—meteorology, chemistry, entomology—produced a combined effect on the cowpea.

He also taught that nature does not produce waste; waste results from man's failure to efficiently use natural resources. In class, he illustrated this concept, holding a tangled knot of string that apparently was no longer useful. Next to it, he held a neatly tied and wound piece of string, which his students could easily see was still useful. Ignorance was like a tangled mass of string, he said. Intelligence brought order and usefulness, he added, holding up the neatly wound string. Natural resources can be used again and again in much the same way.

But Carver gradually shifted his focus from teaching to "creative chemistry," helping industry profit yet not reaping rewards from his own work. He acquired only three patents in his entire career, which earned him little. And he rejected the job Thomas Edison reportedly offered him.

Carver died in 1943. Honors did not end with his death, however. In addition to a museum bearing his name, many public schools were named for him. In 1949, a U.S. postage stamp memorialized his achievements. A naval vessel has been named for him. And the first national monument to commemorate an African American was built at his birth site, near Diamond, Missouri.

FROM STRAIGHTENING HAIR TO SAVING LIVES: GARRETT MORGAN

Garrett Morgan (1877–1963) launched a career of invention by acci-dentally discovering hair straightener. He developed an early version of the gas mask and invented the traffic signal, saving perhaps millions of lives.

Garrett Morgan, whose mother was a former slave, practically stumbled upon a career of invention. The seventh of eleven children, he was raised on a Paris, Kentucky, farm, eventually moving to Cleveland, Ohio, where he opened a sewing machine repair shop in 1907. By 1909 he employed thirty-two people in a prosperous tailoring business.

One night, Morgan, an expert tinkerer, tried to solve a sewing prob-lem. The friction of sewing machine needles left woolen thread scorched. Hoping to reduce the friction, he polished a needle, but was called to dinner by his wife. He hastily wiped polish from his hands onto a swatch of wiry-fibered cloth on his workbench.

After supper, he returned to work and discovered that the polish had straightened the fuzz of the cloth. He decided to see what the polishing fluid would do to hair. His neighbor had an Airedale, a large breed of terrier. With the dog owner's permission, Morgan spread the fluid on the dog's fur. The dog returned home unrecognized by its owner.

Next, Morgan spread the fluid on his own head. It straightened his hair. He packaged his "magic formula" as a cream, sold it through the G. A. Morgan Hair Refining Company and helped change hairdos across America.

But changing hair fashion was just the start of Morgan's new career. In 1912, he invented a precursor to the gas mask—a "breathing device" consisting of a hood with a tube attached. The hood fit over the user's head; the tube extended to the ground. Because dense smoke and fumes rise, the tube enabled the user to draw breaths from the layer of compar-atively clear air at ground level.

Morgan the inventor then became Morgan the traveling salesman. Knowing whites would not buy his gas mask if they knew a black man had invented it, he masqueraded as "Big Chief Mason," a full-blooded

Indian. Big Chief gave a crowd a thrill at a New Orleans exhibition: Wearing his gas mask, Morgan strode into a tent filled with the smoke of burning tar, sulfur, formaldehyde, and manure; he lingered inside and reemerged twenty minutes later miraculously still breathing. The crowd gasped.

He sold many gas masks after putting it to a dramatic, lifesaving test in Cleveland. On July 24, 1916, a violent explosion ripped through a waterworks tunnel. Eleven workers were trapped five miles out into Lake Erie, 250 feet below the surface. Ten rescuers tried to save them, but all ten suffocated in a poisonous atmosphere of fumes, smoke, and dust.

Morgan, his brother, and two volunteers put on gas masks, descended into the tunnel and carried out two survivors and four bodies. The heroic rescue, widely reported, prompted fire departments across the country to order dozens of gas masks. Many departments canceled their orders, however, when they discovered Morgan was black.

Unfazed, he continued inventing, and in 1923, he developed the automated traffic signal. The idea for a device that could manage traffic came to him when he witnessed a collision involving an automobile and a horse and carriage. With the growing number of automobiles, street-corner accidents were increasing. To prevent them, Morgan knew he had to change driving patterns. So he invented an automatic stop-and-go traffic signal system to be placed at intersections. The system was an early version of the traffic light now used worldwide.

Morgan sold the patent rights for the traffic signal to General Electric for $40,000, and began focusing on civic affairs. He died at eighty-six in 1963, having saved perhaps millions of lives.

MAN OF VISION:
JACOB LAWRENCE
SHARON FITZGERALD

The paintings of Jacob Lawrence (b. 1917), one of the greatest American artists of the twentieth century, "read" like an epic narrative of African American history. He has always found inspiration in patterns, shapes, textures, ordinary people, historic figures, and landscapes. His work is the result of an age-old artistic quest—to bring clarity to the clutter of life, explore identities, and search for meaning.

In 1940 and '41, the years during which Jacob Lawrence painted his "Migration of the Negro" series, little attention was being paid to the narrative power of art, and even less consideration was given to the epic relocation of America's black citizens. Lawrence's creation changed all of that. His sequence of 60 paintings guided viewers along the journey—fraught with disappointment, hope and courage—that African Americans took from the rural South into the North's urban quagmire.

The stories Lawrence had been told of black people's struggles united masterfully with his vision of their strength and determination. He considered the series to be in fact one painting beheld at separate stages; in his hands, this exodus of his people became a tour de force.

"During the World War, there was a great migration north by Southern Negroes," reads the artist's caption to the first panel. Beneath three signs, marked "Chicago," "New York" and "St. Louis," a seamless throng of chocolate brown people presses forward, separating only at the passageways that indicate their destinations. Their faces are without discernible features; individuality is conveyed by the shape, tilt or carriage of a head, the curve of a bosom. Most are dressed in earth tones, and, of course, there are hats: black bowlers, a red baseball cap, a black top hat, a red turban. Only behind the railway station's latticed fence does one glimpse the pale blue promise of sky.

"I don't think in terms of history in that series: I think in terms of contemporary life," Lawrence has said. "If it was a portrait of something, it was a portrait of myself, a portrait of my family, a portrait of my peers. In that way, it was like a still life with bread, a still life with flowers; it was like a landscape."

It has been [many] years since the impassioned griot Jacob Armstead Lawrence Jr. sallied forth into the spotlight of modern artists. From the start, he astonished critics with his virtuosity. He inspired audiences, who immediately recognized the purity of his artistic talent and purpose. He took a life slated for anonymity and created a world in which not only he, but all African Americans, would have a powerful identity.

Lawrence was born in Atlantic City, New Jersey, on September 7, 1917. His mother, Rose Lee, had departed from her Virginia birthplace to live in New Jersey, where she met and married Jacob Lawrence, a railroad worker from South Carolina. Shortly after their first child, Jacob, was born, the couple moved to Easton, Pennsylvania, where their daughter, Geraldine, and second son, William, were born.

Hard times followed the family. The marriage ended, and Rose Lawrence set out with the children for Philadelphia. Unable to make ends meet, she placed Jacob and his brother and sister in temporary foster homes and went to New York to find work. She brought them to live with her in Harlem in 1930. "We were a part of that migration," Jacob Lawrence recalls.

Folks expected the world of Harlem. The name alone suggested a fusion of hustle, style, achievement and survival. This crowded, fast-paced community provided Rose Lawrence with neither economic security nor a safe haven in which to raise her children. Especially concerned that Jacob, a quiet teenager, would be susceptible to the dangers of street life, she enrolled the children in the Utopia Children's House, a local settlement that provided an after-school program of meals and activities. It was here—under the tutelage of the artist Charles Alston, then a graduate student at Columbia University—that Jacob Lawrence began to create.

"I took carving, leatherwork, woodwork—things of that sort," Lawrence says. "Charles Alston had a great influence. I liked to make papier-mâché masks, and he introduced me to names like W. T. Benda, the famous mask maker. I liked color. I liked paint. I liked design. I wasn't thinking of becoming a professional artist; I really didn't know what that was."

Alston realized that Lawrence's intense curiosity, independence and intuition were propelled by a tremendous gift. Recalling the play of color and design exhibited on his mother's area rugs, Lawrence boldly juxtaposed shapes, colors and tones. Fascinated by the human and architectural patterns of everyday Harlem, he took large cardboard boxes, removed the tops, opened the sides, and painted street scenes on the stagelike walls. The same muse that inspired Lawrence's papier-mâché masks—months before he first viewed African sculpture—was transporting him into the unknown worlds of social realism, theater design and abstractionism.

"I decided it would be a mistake to try to teach him," Alston later explained. "He was teaching himself, finding his own way." Instead, as Lawrence's first mentor, Alston provided the necessary materials and answered the younger artist's questions about techniques and methods. Having discovered his medium in water-based colors, Lawrence continued to pursue his craft at the Harlem Art Workshop.

The Great Depression also influenced Lawrence's development. He dropped out of New York's Commercial High School after two years and in 1936 joined the Civilian Conservation Corps, where he spent six months in upstate New York, helping to build a dam. He then returned to Harlem, determined to make a living. During the day, he busied himself with assorted odd jobs; at night, he painted. By this time, the Works Progress Administration (WPA) and its Federal Art Project were having a visible impact on the nation's cultural growth. Within Harlem alone there were four separate workshops devoted to art instruction.

"With every negative, there is a positive," says Lawrence. "It's ironic, but we were going through the Depression, and many of us benefited. There have always been those who objected to any federal support of the arts and artisans, but the few years that the Federal Art Project was in existence was one of the most creative periods in the history of the United States."

At the suggestion of Alston, Lawrence began taking free classes at the Harlem Community Art Center, run by sculptor Augusta Savage. During this period, his affinity to uptown syncopation found clear expression in his art. His take on Harlem was riveting. The geometric forms which had long intrigued him became brownstones and front stoops, ladders and streetlights and people. Lawrence filled, but did not clutter, his compositions. He established drama and movement with his spontaneous, albeit precise, placement of line and maintained simplicity with his use of flat, complementary colors.

"The people of the Harlem community led and encouraged me—people who were not necessarily involved in the visual arts," says Lawrence. "I would go to the Apollo Theatre, and I would see the big bands and the chorus girls, all the colors taking place. I would see the comedians, who would tell wonderful stories of great pathos about what was happening in Harlem."

At 306 West 141st Street, Lawrence discovered still more sources of inspiration. "Three-o-six," as it came to be known, had been a deserted barn until Alston, with the help of painter and sculptor Henry "Mike" Bannarn, converted it into the new home of the Harlem Art Workshop.

Artists and art students came in to work or take classes, but 306 was also a hothouse for cultural dialogue among writers, musicians, actors, dancers and other artists. On a given evening one might encounter Langston Hughes, Alain Locke, Rose McClendon, Aaron Douglas, Ernest Crichlow, Ralph Ellison, Richard Wright, Canada Lee, Frank Fields or Countee Cullen. It was here that Lawrence met fellow artist and future wife Gwendolyn Knight, who had studied with Savage and was then a part of the WPA's Harlem Hospital murals project.

"It was like an open house, like a university without the walls," Lawrence recalls. "You know, these things are sort of overromanticized in retrospect, yet there was a wonderful spirit, a flow. There was an interest in what was going on in the arts, outside and within the black community.

"People would talk about the challenges of the theater; someone else would talk about the visual arts; musicians would talk about their challenges. Those like myself who might have been too young to participate in this kind of exchange would overhear these stories. It was only in retrospect that I realized how I benefited from this experience."

In spite of his youth and comparative inexperience, Lawrence was encouraged by those artists at 306, who, like Alston, approached his unique talent with enthusiasm, but without intrusion. "The older artists were content to leave me alone to develop," Lawrence says. "If I put six fingers on a hand, they didn't tell me, 'That's wrong.' They told me, 'Make sure that the sixth finger works in place.' I don't prescribe this for all student-teacher relationships, but for me it worked."

Jacob Lawrence often describes Augusta Savage—a leader both among artists and within the community—as the person who stepped in and made his later success possible. The occasional sales of his paintings to friends, local teachers and librarians were not sustaining him, and his mother had started urging him to take a job in the post office, one of the few secure positions available to blacks. When Savage learned of these difficulties, she took him to the WPA Federal Art Project and had him signed on for the easel project. With the standard weekly salary of $23.80, he was at last a professional artist.

"If Augusta Savage hadn't insisted on getting me onto the project, I don't think I ever would have become an artist," Lawrence has stated. "I'd be doing a menial job somewhere. It was a real turning point for me."

Lawrence turned on a dime. His first narrative series, "Toussaint L'Ouverture," received widespread exposure in 1939, when—at the urging of Howard University professor Alain Locke, artist Elton Fax, and Harmon Foundation Director Mary Beattie Brady—the Baltimore Museum of Art reserved a separate room for all 41 panels at its landmark exhibition of African-American art.

From 1938 to 1940, Lawrence followed his epic account of the Haitian revolutionary with two more historical series—the first, a 32-panel exploration of the life of Frederick Douglass, and the second, a 31-panel chronicle of the courageous Harriet Tubman.

But it was his next project, the "Migration of the Negro" series, that established his position in the art world. Response to the series was stunning by all accounts and unprecedented for the work of an African-American artist. *Fortune* magazine devoted six pages in its November 1941 issue to a display of 26 panels and to an essay describing the movement of blacks as an American saga. Edith Gregor Halpert first displayed the complete series at her prestigious Downtown Gallery. A few months later, the exhibition began a national tour at the Museum of Modern Art.

Over the past five decades, there have been several retrospectives and countless solo exhibitions devoted to Lawrence's early and subsequent work; he is represented in all of the nation's leading collections. He holds chair 41 in the American Academy of Arts and Letters, one of 50 highly prized lifetime appointments given to masters of this nation's art and literature. In 1970, he became the first artist to receive the Spingarn Medal from the NAACP.

In 1974, when Pope Paul VI was invited to select an American artwork for the Vatican Museum's collection, he asked for a creation by Jacob Lawrence. President Jimmy Carter requested that he paint the picture of his 1977 inauguration. Lawrence has taught in several of the country's leading art schools, including the Pratt Institute and the Art Students League, and he retired as a full professor from the University of Washington in Seattle.

"I would not say that I am surprised by the reception I have received," Lawrence says of his life's accomplishments, "but I have been very happy. Gwen and I would be content just to work. I think that those of us who are in the arts are fortunate in that we tend to need to search. That is a part of our philosophy. Therefore, you continue to grow and to realize your full capacity as a human being. It is a quality of life. That is what I think is feeding us."

⚬⚬⚬

Dialect or the speech of the people is capable of expressing whatever the people are.

—*Sterling Brown*

⚬⚬⚬

SAY WHAT?

For many decades, black English has been the subject of controversy, fomenting debate among those who dismiss it as merely broken English and advocates who hold it to be a legitimate language with African roots.

The great debate continues, intensifying every now and then in school districts, in newspaper columns, at podiums. Agreement appears elusive and may even be unwanted. People cannot even seem to agree on a proper term. Is the language that black folks speak "black English" or "ebonics" (from the words ebony and phonics)?

Two things do seem certain: first, insofar as speech plays a pivotal role in self-identity or self-perception, black English will remain central to defining what it means simply to be black in America; and second, black English will continue to serve as the vast and lively respository of a people's creativity. People of other races and ethnicities will continue to imitate its grammar, syntax, and inflections, as many white American artists have done for ages.

Whatever it is called—African dialect, slang, a hybrid, a vernacular of American English—the language of black America holds the imagination of people around the globe. Much of this book appears in what some people classify as black English. The following section only begins to describe the richness, vitality, and range of the language.

O.K.

Africans and African Americans have enriched the American English lexicon. Here's a word that probably originated in Africa.

okay; O.K. n. (1620s–1990s) yes; all right; probably from West African sources: *o-ke* (Djabo); *waw-kayk, waw ke* (Wolof); *o-kay* (Dogno); *o-key* (Mandingo); *eeyi-kay* (Fula West). Also these possibly converged with American "okay," as used by Martin Van Buren in his abbreviation of "old Kinderhook." "OK" ("orally korrect") was, according to Vere, an abbreviation Gen. Andrew Jackson used to initial paperwork as a symbol of his approval; an early American abbreviation of the (incorrect) spelling of orally correct ("orally korrect"). But it seems much more likely that the original African form influenced all such later variations. "Oh ki" was being used by blacks in the South by the late 1770s and in Jamaica at least twenty years before evidence of "okay" in the speech of New England.

—*Juba to Jive: A Dictionary of African American Slang,*
compiled and edited by Clarence Major

IF BLACK ENGLISH ISN'T A LANGUAGE, THEN TELL ME, WHAT IS?

JAMES BALDWIN

Born and raised in Harlem, James Baldwin (1924–87) is ranked among the most influential black authors in U.S. history. His novels, plays, and essays—now part of the canon of American literature—are impassioned works that seek to unveil the brutal forces behind racism in the United States and abroad. The following excerpt, from an article Baldwin published in 1979, explains the genesis and role of black English.

It goes without saying . . . that language is . . . a political instrument, means, and proof of power. It is the most vivid and crucial key to identity: It reveals the private identity, and connects one with, or divorces one from, the larger public, or communal identity. There have been, and are, times, and places, when to speak a certain language could be dangerous, even fatal. Or, one may speak the same language, but in such a way that one's antecedents are revealed, or (one hopes) hidden. This is true in France, and is absolutely true in England. The range (and reign) of accents on that damp little island make England coherent for the English and totally incomprehensible for everyone else. To open your mouth in England is (if I may use black English) to "put your business in the street": You have confessed your parents, your youth, your school, your salary, your self-esteem, and, alas, your future.

Now, I do not know what white Americans would sound like if there had never been any black people in the United States, but they would not sound the way they sound. *Jazz*, for example, is a very specific sexual term, as in *jazz me, baby*, but white people purified it into the Jazz Age. *Sock it to me*, which means, roughly, the same thing, has been adopted by Nathaniel Hawthorne's descendants with no qualms or hesitations at all, along with *let it all hang out* and *right on! Beat to his socks*, which was once the black's most total and despairing image of poverty, was transformed into a thing called the Beat Generation, which phenomenon was, largely, composed of *uptight*, middle-class white people, imitating poverty, trying to *get down*, to get *with it*, doing their *thing*, doing their despairing best to be *funky,* which we, the blacks, never dreamed of doing—we *were* funky, baby, like *funk* was going out of style.

Now, no one can eat his cake, and have it, too, and it is late in the day to attempt to penalize black people for having created a language that permits the nation its only glimpse of reality, a language without which the nation would be even more *whipped* than it is.

I say that this present skirmish is rooted in American history, and it is. Black English is the creation of the black diaspora. Blacks came to the United States chained to each other, but from different tribes: Neither could speak the other's language. If two black people, at that bitter hour of the world's history, had been able to speak to each other, the institution of chattel slavery could never have lasted as long as it did. Subsequently, the slave was given, under the eye, and the gun, of his master, Congo Square, and the Bible—or, in other words, and under these conditions, the slave began the formation of the black church, and it is within this unprecedented tabernacle that black English began to be formed. This was not, merely, as in the European example, the adoption of a foreign tongue, but an alchemy that transformed ancient elements into new language: *A language comes into existence by means of brutal necessity, and the rules of the language are dictated by what the language must convey.*

There was a moment, in time, and in this place, when my brother, or my mother, or my father, or my sister, had to convey to me, for example, the danger in which I was standing from the white man standing just behind me, and to convey this with a speed, and in a language, that the white man could not possibly understand, and that, indeed, he cannot understand, until today. He cannot afford to understand it. This understanding would reveal to him too much about himself, and smash that mirror before which he has been frozen for so long.

Now, if this passion, this skill, this (to quote Toni Morrison) "sheer intelligence," this incredible music, the mighty achievement of having brought a people utterly unknown to, or despised by "history"—to have brought this people to their present, troubled, troubling, and unassailable and unanswerable place—if this absolutely unprecedented journey does not indicate that black English is a language, I am curious to know what definition of language is to be trusted.

A people at the center of the Western world, and in the midst of so hostile a population, has not endured and transcended by means of what is patronizingly called a "dialect." We, the blacks, are in trouble, certainly, but we are not doomed, and we are not inarticulate because we are not compelled to defend a morality that we know to be a lie.

The brutal truth is that the bulk of the white people in America never had any interest in educating black people, except as this could serve white purposes. It is not the black child's language that is in question, it is not his language that is despised: It is his experience. A child cannot be taught by anyone who despises him, and a child cannot afford to be fooled. A child cannot be taught by anyone whose demand, essentially, is that the child repudiate his experience, and all that gives him sustenance, and enter a limbo in which he will no longer be black, and in which he knows that he can never become white. Black people have lost too many black children that way.

And, after all, finally, in a country with standards so untrustworthy, a country that makes heroes of so many criminal mediocrities, a country unable to face why so many of the nonwhite are in prison, or on the needle, or standing, futureless, in the streets—it may very well be that both the child, and his elder, have concluded that they have nothing whatever to learn from the people of a country that has managed to learn so little.

THE TWO FACES OF EBONICS: DISGUISE AND GIVEAWAY
MARGO JEFFERSON

Language says volumes about the speaker, even when he or she utters few words. Many view black English as either an affectation for chic expressions or a crutch, as an asset or a liability. Social mobility and class are key. Here Margo Jefferson, a Pulitzer Prize–winning journalist, dis-

cusses the double edge of ebonics—how one might be respected or patron-
ized for speaking it.

Do let's remember, as the debate over ebonics lurches and struggles along generating polemical fervor and resentment at every turn, that black English plays a complicated, quite fascinating role in the culture, one that Americans of all races are much affected by, possibly even obsessed by. It is easy to dismiss the subject with glib gibes or to enshrine it in sentimental bombast. It's hard work to start making sense of all the contradictions.

For starters, let's call it black English instead of ebonics. Americans can never resist inventing pretentious names for new schools of thought, new religions or aspiring new disciplines: euthenics, Dianetics, ebonics (coined from ebony and phonics). All are meant to convey scientific respectability and a certain grandeur. But the science sounds officious and the grandeur sounds fake.

Americans have never been able to resist making up new histories for themselves either: not those 17th- and 18th-century colonists who devised family trees and coats of arms to live out new world fantasies of old and noble European ancestry; not those 19th- and 20th-century immigrants who changed (and are still changing) their names to sound as much like 17th- and 18th-century colonists as possible. Afrocentric rites and claims are the latest manifestation of this national need. Whenever they think about those Old World ancestors, Americans grow desperately nostalgic; they start mythologizing every more and folkway in sight and competing wildly with one another in the name of equity but with the hope of superiority.

That being said, why, at this moment, are we treating a cultural controversy that has everything to do with class and social status as if it had only to do with race? When black English is an adopted mode of speech, a vernacular chosen for certain expressive purposes or a chic form of slang, when it is clear to all concerned that the speaker has a more standardized language at his or her command, then everyone is content and everything is copacetic.

Many black (and white) American writers draw on the syntax and inflections of black English, as do blues, rock, pop and rap performers of European, Asian, African and Latin American origin, along with upper-

and middle-class teen-agers of every conceivable race, religion and ethnicity. So long as it's a fad, a pose or a clearly calculated style, black English can earn its practitioners money, power and respect as artistic innovators or popularizers.

But the stakes change when the speakers are working class, lower class or just poor black students who need to acquire standardized English skills and conventions to achieve what everybody in America wants: social mobility and respect.

How you talk is either a dead giveaway or a flawless disguise. Grammar, syntax and accent allow or forbid people to patronize and penalize you on the ground of where you came from. If you are middle class or above and not starring in a movie, on television or on a talk-radio show, it is still best not to speak an English that hints at certain areas of Brooklyn, Long Island or the South. If you are an immigrant or visitor, it is certainly best not to speak with the kind of foreign accent and pidgin grammar that imply peasant rather than merchant or aristocratic forebears.

Schools have always been critical to this process of adaptation and transformation: public schools (especially those with tracking systems), private schools, charm schools, boarding schools and colleges. The question no one has answered yet is: How are all those ill-equipped, poorly financed public schools that are supposed to represent educational opportunity for so many in this country going to manage it?

Speaking practically, the middle and upper classes of all races will always look down on those whose speech reads as strictly lower or working class. If you are black and speak only black English, you are likely to be patronized or stigmatized. On the other hand, if you have money, power and style—if you are an athlete or entertainer, say—and speak some form of black English, you will be idolized and imitated (which will not preclude some mockery behind your well-paid back). Race prejudice is obviously part of the package; so is race fascination. Call it attraction-repulsion, call it love-hate: of all the vernaculars that have contributed to American English, it is black vernacular that still has the strongest hold on the collective imagination.

Black English is a hybrid that, like the standardized American English it both mirrors and alters, can be spoken with beauty and power or with utter banality. Here is an example of black English from Zora Neale

Hurston, based on the King James version of the Bible and taken from her folklore and hoodoo narrative, "Mules and Men":

"The way we tell it, hoodoo started way back there before everything. Six days of magic spells and mighty words and the world with its elements above and below was made. And now, God is leaning back taking a seventh day rest. When the eighth day comes around, He'll start to making new again."

And later:

"Moses was the first man who ever learned God's power-compelling words and it took him 40 years to learn 10 words. So he made 10 plagues and Ten Commandments. But God gave him His rod for a present and showed him the back part of His glory. Then too, Moses could walk out of the sight of man. But Moses never would have stood before the Burning Bush if he had not married Jethro's daughter. Jethro was a great hoodoo man. Jethro could tell Moses could carry power as soon as he saw him. In fact he felt him coming. Therefore, he took Moses and crowned him and taught him.

"So Moses passed on beyond Jethro with his rod. He lifted it up and tore a nation out of Pharaoh's side, and Pharaoh couldn't help himself. Moses talked with the snake that lives in a hole right under God's footrest. Moses had fire in his head and a cloud in his mouth. The snake had told him God's making words. The words of doing and the words of obedience. Many a man thinks he is making something when he's only changing things around. But God let Moses make. And then Moses had so much power he made the eight winged angels split open a mountain to bury him in, and shut up the hole behind them."

Hurston was a writer wise enough to have mastered both sides of the language.

A SHORT BOOK OF JIVE
(NOT FOR SQUARES)

*In the late 1930s and early 1940s, a new language evolved in Harlem:
Jive. "Squares" had to consult a Jive dictionary to understand it. Here is
a sampling of Jive talk along with an unofficial dictionary.*

FIRST STEPS IN JIVE

Names of Things

Since Jive talk came into being because of the paucity of words and
inadequacy of the vocabularies of its users, it is of primary interest that
we get a good working knowledge of the Jive names for things. It is also
essential to understand here that really good Jive talk is also accompa
nied by appropriate gestures, inflections of the voice, and other aids
toward making one's meaning clear.

The simplest words in Jive are those relating to things—inanimate
objects, the furniture in a room, objects which can be moved, sold,
bought, exchanged, all concrete and tangible objects.

Alarm clock: Chimer
Body: Frame
Corner: Three pointer
Door: Slammer
Elderly man: Poppa Stoppa
Feet: Groundpads
Gun: Bow-wow
Hands: Grabbers
Moon: Pumpkin
Nose: Sniffer
Overcoat: Benny or Bear

Verbal Nouns

These are the words that move and "jump," the Jive Verbs that give the language its appeal and spontaneity, that make Jive flexible.

Here we are dealing with the words which describe bodily motion, the movement of arms, legs, hands and feet. They also denote intangible action having to do with thought, comprehension, a very important phase of Jive.

We start off by naming simple acts. In the preceding portion of this chapter we discussed the name of things, we had you going home: and, instead of saying, "I am going home," you said, "I'm going to my pile of stone." "Am going" is a perfectly legitimate expression in English denoting an intention and describing an act already taking place. In Jive you would substitute the words "cop" and "trill" in place of "am going," and your statement would be: "I'm copping my trill for my pile of stone." Simple, isn't it? Even your great-aunt Hannah could understand that, couldn't she?

There are relatively few Jive verbs, since Jive is primarily a language consisting of descriptive adjectives, rather than being replete with verbs denoting action. However, the few Jive verbs to balance the enormous number of nouns, or names of things, are thrillingly competent, graphic and commanding. Two in particular are worthy of our attention. The verbs "knock" and "lay" are the basis of Jive. "Knock" in particular is found all through the process of a Jive conversation. It is one of the key words.

"Knock a nod," says the Jiver. He means going to sleep. "Knock a scoff," he says. He means, eat a meal. "Knock a broom" is found to mean a quick walk or brisk trot away from something. "Knock me down to her" means to introduce me to a young lady; "knock off a riff," in musical parlance means for a musician to play a musical break in a certain manner. "Knock a jug" means to buy a drink.

The verb, "Lay," is another vitally important verb in the Jiver's vocabulary. It also denotes action. For example: "Lay some of that cash on me," says a Jiver. His statement means literally what it says. But if he says, "he was really laying it," he means someone was doing something out of the ordinary, as in a stage performance or musical program, or a well-dressed entering a room and suddenly becoming the object of all eyes.

Here are some other important verbs:

Blow: To leave, move, run away
Cop: To take, receive, understand, do
Dig: To understand, take, see, conceive, perceive, think, hand over
Drag: Humiliate, upset, disillusion
Stash: To lay away, hide, put down, stand, a place
Take a powder: Leave, disappear

Jive Adjectives, or Words Signifying Quality

Before the names of things, or objects, as in standard English we need to know a special state or condition regarding them in order to get a clear mental picture in our minds. For example, a *blue* sky, a *soft* chair, the *hot* sun, etc. The language of Jive has plenty of such adjectives, more of which are constantly being added every day. The following list may prove helpful:

Anxious: Wonderful, excellent
Fine· All right, okay, excellent
Frantic: Great, wonderful
Groovy: To one's liking, sensational, outstanding, splendid
Mad: Fine, capable, able, talented
Mellow: State of delight, beautiful, great, wonderful
Righteous: Pleasing to the senses, glorious, pretty, beautiful, mighty
Solid: Very fine, okay, great, terrific

Jive Phrases, Simile and Hyperbole

As in standard English, Jive is flexible and infinitely capable of expressing phrases or rare harmonic beauty and rhythmical force. The language of the hepsters is constantly acquiring new descriptive phrases, narrative and explanatory in content, which constitute an integral and necessary part of one's equipment for gaining proficiency in talking and writing Jive. Here are a few, some of which are self-explanatory.

Mellow as a cello

Like the bear, nowhere

Playing the dozens with my uncle's cousins—doing things wrong

"I'm like the chicken, I ain't stickin' "—broke

"Dig what I'm laying down?"—understand what I'm saying?

"I'm chipper as the China Clipper and in the mood to play"—flying high and personally feeling fine

"Swimps and wice"—Shrimps and rice

"Snap a snapper"—light a match

"Like the farmer and the 'tater, plant you now and dig you later"—means, "I must go, but I'll remember you."

Jive Rhyming and Meter

The language of Jive presents an unusual opportunity for experimentation in rhymes, in fact, a lot of it is built on rhymes, which at first hearing might be considered trite and beneath the notice. However, Jive rhymes and couplets are fascinating and comparatively easy to fashion. As to meter, it is desirable that the syllables form a correct measure, but this is not essential. All that is necessary is that the end words rhyme; they do not necessarily need to make sense. Here are some examples:

"Collars a broom with a solid zoom"—left in a hurry

"No lie, frog eye"

"What's your duty, Tutti-Frutti?"

"Joe the Jiver, the Stranded Pearl-Diver"

"Swing and sweat with Charley Barnet"—means dance to Barnet's music

"Are you going to the function at Tuxedo Junction?"—Tuxedo Junctions are places, dancehalls, candy-stores, etc., where hepsters gather.

"My name is Billie, have you seen Willie?"—used as a greeting or salutation among accomplished hepcats

"Ain't it a pity, you're from Atlantic City?"—salutation

JIVE DICTIONARY

Cop a squat and dig this Jive dictionary. It's a real gasser!

Ace: Bosom friend. *He's my ace boy.*

Alligator: A jitterbug.

Baby kisser: A politician.

Ball: To have riotous fun. *On Saturday we ball!*

Beat: Bad looking, depressed, tired. *I'm beat to my sox.* (Very beat).

Beat up your chops: Talking a lot. *Stop beating up your chops, gal.*

Benders: Knees

Blow: To leave. *I'm gonna blow this town.*

Blow your fuse: To get angry. *That landlady made me blow my fuse.*

Blow your top: Same. *She went to the welfare and blew her top.*

Boon-coon: Same as ace. *Stacy's my boon-coon.*

Boot: To explain, to describe, inform authoritatively. *That chick booted me about love.*

Bread: Money; wages. *He makes good bread.* (Earns good money)

Bring down: Depressing, unseemly, wrong, no good. *Monday is a bring down.*

Brownie: Cent, a penny.

Bug: To irritate. *Get away, you're bugging me.*

Bust your vest: To swell with pride. *That preacher's busting his vest.*

Cat: A male. *That little cat's sure fat.*

Chips: Money. *He's in the chips today.*

Cholly: A dollar bill. *When you beg for a cholly, you're really down.*

Chops: Lips, mouth, jaws. *Don't you put my glass to your chops.*

Clinker: A sour note in music. *The trumpet hit a clinker.*

Collar all jive: To understand everything. *Hipsters collar all jive.*

Cool: Calm, unruffled. *Be cool, man.*

Cop: To take, receive, understand.

Cop a nod: Take a quick nap. *Between acts he cops a nod.*

Cop a deuceways: To buy two dollars worth of something. *Let's cop a deuceways of barbecue.*

Cop a slave: To go to work. *It's time to cop a slave.*

Cop a squat: To take a seat. *Cop a squat and stay awhile.*

Creaker: An aged person. *I hate to see a creaker act so chippyfied.*

Crib: House, home, where you can hang your hat.

Cut out: To depart. *I'm gonna cut out from Harlem.*

Cut some rug: To dance. *Let's dig the Savoy and cut some rug.*

Den: Apartment, room, house, home. *All couples need their own den.*

Deuce: Two. *A deuce of chippies kept my company.*

Dicty: High hat, snooty. *The dicties live on Riverside.*

Dig: To understand, to enjoy, to go to. *I don't dig Dixieland.*

Do a Houdini: To disappear, to leave suddenly. *If [he comes], I'll do a Houdini.*

Doodley-squat: Not caring. *I don't give a doodley-squat.*

Down with it: To get acquainted with, to understand. *I'm down with your jive.*

Dozens: Humorous but vulgar references to someone else's mother. *If you put me in the dozens, I'll hit you sure.*

Drag: To humiliate, upset, disillusion. *You drag when you bring me down.*

Drape: A suit of clothes. *Man, dig my righteous drape!*

Dust: To leave.

Dust your broom: To go away, to leave town. *She dusted her broom on a Greyhound bus.*

Early black: Early evening. *Dig the neons in the early black.*

Early blue: Same as above.

Eighty-eight: (88) A piano. *With Duke at the 88, the music's great.*

Eyeball: To look at someone. *That chick's eyeballing me.*

Fault: To blame. *If I can't make it, don't fault me.*

Flic, flicker: A motion picture. *Sinatra's in a frantic flic.*

Fly: Fresh, impudent, sassy, flirtacious. *She's a real fly chick.*

Fly right: To behave. *Straighten up and fly right.*

Fracture your wig: Same as blow your top. *Love can make you fracture your wig.*

Frantic: Great, wonderful. *Dizzy's a frantic musician.*

Freebye: Free, without charge; a free dance, a free meal.

Gasser: An exciting thing. *Eartha Kitt is a gasser.*

Gate: A big mouth. Used as a salutation. *What you say, gate?*

Get off: To show off, strut your stuff, go over big. *When she rose to sing, she really got off.*

Get straight: To clarify, speak plainly. *My husband really got me straight.*

Gig: A single engagement for a musician. *House parties ain't nothing but gigs.*

Gimme some skin: To slap hands in greeting.

Git-box: A juke box, also piccolo. *Put a dime in the git-box and play a side.*

Go down: The happenings. *Let's see what's going down at the dance.*

Gone: Great, fine, very good. *Rock and Roll is real gone music.*

Grey: A white person. *Nothing but greys go to the Stork Club.*

Grease your chops: To dine. *For a dime you can grease your chops at Father's.*

Groovey: Soothingly pleasant, also In The Groove. *King Cole sings groovey. He's in the groove.*

Gumbeat: To talk a lot, gossip. *Women are always gumbeating.*

Gutbucket: Loud and low-down. *Rock and Roll is real gutbucket sometimes.*

Half-past a colored man: 12:30 A.M.

Hamfat: A phoney, a worthless character, a poser. *I hate hamfats myself.*

Hawkins: The wind, wintertime, cold weather, ice, snow. *In February, Hawkins talks.*

Head knock: The deity. *When the head knock calls, you got to go.*

Hincty: Same as dicty. *Muriel is hincty.*

Hip: Wise, in the know, understanding. *I'm hip to what's going down.*

Hipster: A sophisticate, an all-around wise guy. *Hipsters dig the jive.*

Hustler: One who makes a living at others' expense. *Hustler's use crooked dice.*

Hype: A pretense, a deceitful act. *Don't try to lay a hype on me.*

If push comes to shove: When the final necessity arises. *I'll pay that bill when push comes to shove.*

Igg: To ignore, to high hat. *Miss Dicty tried to igg me.*

In there: All right, fine, very good. *That dress is really in there, girl!*

Jam: To make spontaneous group music, to jazz without music.

Jam-session: Musicians playing spontaneously for fun.

Jive: Kidding, double-talk, pleasant pretending. *He puts down such corny jive.*

Jump: To be very lively. *Let's play the juke box and make the joint jump.*

Kicks: Thrills, satisfaction. *He gets his kicks from gospel singing.*

Killer: A great thing, something or somebody wonderful. *Harlem is a killer, man!*

Kitchen mechanic: A domestic servant. *Kitchen mechanic's night is Thursday.*

Lane: A simpleton, an unhip person. *Country boys are all lanes.*

Latch on: To become aware, to understand, to learn. *I latch on quick to anybody's jive.*

Lay, lay it: To strut, to preen, to show off. *Aw, lay it, girl, in your necklace of pearls!*

Mad: Fine, excellent. *That's real mad meal.*

Map: Face. *What an ugly map!*

Mellow: Agreeable, softly pleasant, nice. *My girl is fine and mellow.*

Moss: Hair. *She's got some mellow moss.*

Most: The greatest. *Smithfield ham is the most.*

Nix out: To freeze out, to eliminate. *Two in love nix out all others.*

Nowhere: Of no value, uninteresting. *That old time jazz is nowhere.*

Onliest: Unique. *Belafonte's the onliest.*

Pad: Same as crib, home, house. *I'm heading for the pad to cop a nod.*

Pecks: Food. *My girl lays some pecks!*

Peepers: Eyes. *Dig them bedroom peepers.*

Pitch a boogie-woogie: Raise sand; fuss, quarrel violently. *His wife pitched a boogie-woogie when he wasn't home for dinner.*

Plant you now and dig you later: I'll leave you now to see you by and by.

Righteous: Excellent, great, very nice indeed. *She's got a righteous smile.*

Roost: Same as crib, pad.

Rug-cutter: A dancer, a jitterbug.

Rubber: An automobile. *Folks like Sugar Ray always ride on rubber.*

Rumble: A fight, a street fight. *I cut out when the rumble started.*

Run in: A quarrel, a minor fight. *Kin folks shouldn't have run ins.*

Salty: Disagreeable, angry, pouting, an evil mood. *When I said let's go, she jumped salty.*

Scat: Singing in nonsense syllables. *Cab and Louis can really scat.*

School: To teach. *That chick can really school a square.*

Scarf: To eat, also scoff. *We scarf good at grandma's.*

Scuffle: To work for a living. *After I scuffled all week, I was tired.*

Send: To thrill, stir enthusiasm, gratify, please greatly. (Noun, *Sender*)

Sharp: Well dressed. *Harlem cats are sharp.*

Signify: To cast aspersions, hint at something wrong. *Tell me plain, baby, and DON'T signify.*

Sky-piece: A hat. *Tip the sky-piece, man.*

Sky-pilot: A preacher. *Get me a sky-pilot when I come to die.*

Slammer: A door. *Knock on the slammer before you enter.*

Snap your cap: To become very angry. *The dozens made him snap his cap.*

So help me: That's the truth, no kidding. *So help me, I went to work.*

Solid: Very fine, okay, great, terrific. *She's a solid sender.*

Spade: A Negro. *Crackers don't like spades.*

Spaginzy: Same as above. Also *Spaginzy-spagade.*

Square: An unsophisticated person. *Teenagers are all squares.*

Square from Delaware: A very square square, completely unhipped.

Stash: To stand arrogantly, also *Stash back* with one's legs benched. *Dressed to kill, he stashed on the corner.*

Stomps: Footwear. *I need some new stomps.*

Stone: Very, really and sure enough whatever the word precedes. *Stone sick, stone crazy, stone ugly. Alaska is stone cold.*

Struggle-buggy: An automobile.

Stud: A man. *He's a hip stud from St. Louis.*

Take it slow: To be careful, cool. *If your old lady blows her top, take it slow.*

Take low: To be humiliated. *Women love to see a man take low.*

The law: The police.

The man: The policeman.

The shorts: Hunger, empty pockets. *I'm troubled with the shorts.*

Twister: Key. *My wife changed the lock so my twister's nowhere.*

Two's and fews: Same as *The shorts.*

Unbooted: Square, state of being a lane, a dull person. *Rev. is unbooted.*

Uncle's: Any pawn shop.

Unhip: Same as unbooted, a square. *She's so unhipped it's a shame.*

Uppity: Same as dicty, hincty, snobbish.

What's your story: How are things? What do you want? Why? Explain yourself. *What's your story, morning glory?*

Wig: Head, hair. *Mary's got a righteous wig.*

Wooden kimona: Coffin. *Most gangsters end in a wooden kimona before their time.*

Yarddog: A low, loud and boisterous person. *He ain't nothing but a yarddog.*

◎◎◎

My people! My people!—Sad and satiric expression in the Negro language: sad when a Negro comments on the backwardness of some members of his race; other times, used for satiric or comic effect.

—*Zora Neale Hurston,* Glossary of Harlem Slang

◎◎◎

WILLIAM COOL SURVEYS THE SITUATION

Here's a brief story on William Cool, who is having a difficult time making ends meet. Short on cash, he is considering a dramatic change in his life.

MY FRIEND:—I am really sick about the way things have gotten so difficult and money so scarce a fellow can hardly hustle any easy money any more. It is so bad that many of the fellows on the street can't even make enough to cover their meals regularly. The once fertile avenues of kowtowing to the whites have been dried up by the virile campaign for equal rights. Single action on the numbers is still a possibility because the writers carry their plays in their heads instead of in writing. But the straight numbers men are either on the lams or inactive because of raids and other difficulties with the law. But things will change when the proper contacts are made with the higher ups. Confidence games are out now, too, because there are no unwary people to use as victims. In fact, you try such tricks and you may wind up falling for the other fellow's story yourself, only to be humiliated when you see the person enjoying himself with your money at a bar. Things are so difficult, Jim, that in desperation it's best to make the most drastic of all moves and go and get yourself a regular job. I'll see you later, pal.

WILLIE COOL DIGS THE SCENE

Now test your Harlem Jive skills with this translation of "William Cool Surveys the Situation."

MY MAN:—The freeze has really set in on the turf, champ, and a kiddie has the toughest kind of time trying to get hold to some long bread so that he can have a ball and come on with frantic plays all up and down the line. Home, it's so bad that a lot of the cats on the stroll can't even get to their grits half the time. There used to be a few hustles that you could always fall back on for your twos and fews but nothing is happening at all. Even the soft shoe or gumshoe plays are cold. It used to be that a man could lay down a real hype by tomming to some grey but most of them plays got nixed by the hard beef laid down by some of the equal rights kids. You can still get some fast action on the single action kick because most of the pickups carry the stuff in their head and pass the scribe. This tricks the bluecoats and bulls trying to pickup on the action for a break job. It's a little tough copping any bread on the straight digit action because the boys from the ace law and order pad have been whaling like mad at the turnin' points. The heavy iron boys who didn't get snagged in the crummy play are blowing the burg if they're straight waiting for the chill to set in or they're just cooling it until somebody gets the contacts straight so that the brass will hold still for an arrangement. Con plays are out, too, cause everybody is so hip, there ain't no fools to drop a shuck on. You move in one a lane or square with the smooth tongue action and half the time he's got a riffle of his own that he drops on you behind a sob story so you wind up giving up some iron to him or her and then blow your stack when you see the action that plays behind it for the next time you eyeball the turkey, he running them around at a giggle juice joint. It is the craziest action, Jim, so it's best to go on the desperate tip and cop a slave for your ends. Later, daddy.

Hi-De-Hi-De-Hi-De-Ho!

—*Cab Calloway*

WORD!

THE ABRIDGED AND UNOFFICIAL RAP DICTIONARY ("BAMMAS": BEWARE)

The freshness and creativity that African Americans once put into Jive today gets put into rap, black America's latest manifestation of hipness in language, music, and clothing. As a language, rap is still evolving. Many terms are introduced and gain currency in the songs of popular rappers. Here is a selection of words heard on the street and in music. So peep this and get the 4-1-1 on rap.

A: Going to. *I'm a do it now.*

All that: In possession of all good qualities. *His music ain't all that.*

Bamma: Person who cannot dress; a loser. *You and the rest of the bammas out there.*

Bank: Money. *She whipped out bank.*

B-boy: From "break boy"; one who breakdances.

Beef: An argument or discrepancy; a complaint or disagreement. *He got a beef with you.*

Boo: Term of endearment, like "baby." *I'll be back later, boo.*

Boyee: Exclamation, often directed to a friend.

Bug: To act strange, crazy, weird. *Don't take him seriously. She's just buggin'.*

Bust this: Pay attention. *Bust this! I'm a tell you somethin'.*

Chill: Relax; mellow. *You better just chill.*

Cronkite: News, after the television news broadcaster, Walter Cronkite. *The brother is droppin' Cronkite.*

Def: Okay; standard of excellence. *You think that music is def?*

Digits: Telephone number. *Gimme her digits.*

Duckets: Money, from "ducats": coins. *I earn my duckets the old-fashioned way.*

Flava: Flavor; style. *She has mad flava.*

Four-one-one: Information. *Let me give you the four-one-one.*

Front: Pretend to be that which you are not; act tough. *He's always frontin'.*

Ghetto bird: Police helicopters. *Here comes the ghetto bird.*

Homeboy: Close friend. *He's my homeboy.*

Honey: Female; generally attractive. *Look at the honey.*

Ill: To be obnoxious, or to act weird. *You illin', man.*

In the house: Present, here. *Brooklyn's in the house.*

Jet: To leave in a hurry. *She had to jet.*

Kickin' it: Relaxing. *I'll be at home kickin' it.*

Kill dat noise: Shut up. *You better kill dat noise.*

Little sumthin-sumthin: A little bit. *Give me a little sumthin-sumthin.*

Live: Great. *Is it live?*

Mad: Extremely, very; a large quantity. *His stereo was pumping mad music.*

Marinate: To chill; hang out. *We was marinatin'.*

No diggety: No doubt, no question. *No diggety, homeboy.*

Oreo: Black person who wants to be white, or people of mixed race. *Give that oreo a message for me.*

Peep: Check this out. *Peep this.*

Phat: Great, addictive; attractive. *She is phat.*

Props: An abbreviation of proper or proper respect. *The deejay gave him mad props.*

Recognize: Take notice of. *You better recognize (my skills).*

Represent: To do something well. *Spike Lee represents on film.*

Scope: Look at something. *Scope that picture.*

Shorty: Girlfriend; youth. *He called his shorty.*

Stupid: Creative; very. *The song has a stupid dope beat.*

Vexed: Very angry. *Don't vex me.*

Wack: Weak. *You know that was wack.*

Word: That's the truth; I agree. *"Maxwell's album's phat." "Word!"*

Yo: You; your.

—*Adapted from the* Totally Unofficial Rap Dictionary

❧

Do a common thing in an uncommon way.

—*Booker T. Washington*

❧

FAITH

Faith has moved mountains, built empires, defeated invincible armies, stirred billions of people through the ages, and generated indescribable love. Aside from love itself, what more powerful virtue could there be in this world—or any other?

We call on our faith to get us through thick and thin, and we have been doing this for centuries. But what exactly is faith?

To some, faith is an unquestioning belief in something that can never be proven—a confidence that stems from an inner certainty. This sort of knowingness is bound not only by evidence made manifest by the senses, but by a complete trust in the presence of things unseen and in powers beyond mortal comprehension.

Others say our faith is our religion. Both definitions are correct. But it's what you do with your faith that really matters.

Ultimately, faith allows us to soar spiritually. Yet since we also live in this world, faith should plant our feet on solid ground, too. It should anchor us socially and provide a framework for moral reasoning.

Black faith in America has done just that for centuries.

Enslaved Africans brought their own religions to America. In time, blacks adopted the slave masters' Christianity, but reinterpreted it to suit their own particular needs. The black church might have retained Christianity's core orthodoxies, but black worshipers chose to express them in new, unreserved ways. Possessed by the Holy Spirit, black churchgoers across the South shouted, or fell into trance-like states. Others waved their hands and signaled their approval of the preacher's sermon with shouts of "Amen!" and "Well?" And then there was the music itself: deeply moving spirituals.

Many people credit religion for helping African Americans get through the hard times of slavery, the first years of freedom and beyond. After emancipation, the church became the center of life for many African Americans, serving as schoolhouse, theater, political forum, social club, courthouse. Today, churches, mosques, and temples provide structure for most black religious life.

Faith is as vital today as it has ever been for African Americans. In a society rife with turmoil, consumerism, and misery, faith still brings joy, peace, fulfillment, love, and kindness to millions, and it is exhibited in every level of black society—the rich, poor, old, young, and middle-aged.

Among the stories in this chapter, Mary McLeod Bethune tells how faith guided her in building a college on a former garbage dump. Thomas A. Dorsey develops a new musical form, gospel (for a time, gospel songs are called "Dorseys"). Martin Luther King Jr. envisions a new America. Malcolm X writes from Mecca to reveal his startling religious transformation from race-based Islam to an orthodoxy that includes whites in the universal brotherhood of man. The principles of Kwanzaa, one of the fastest-growing holidays in America, are explained. And magazine editor Susan L. Taylor discusses her views on the "highest power." These pieces and others offer valuable insight into how faith thrives in black America.

Faith is the flip side of fear.

—Susan L. Taylor

⏒

FAITH TO MOVE MOUNTAINS

A COLLEGE BUILT ON A GARBAGE DUMP

MARY MCLEOD BETHUNE

In the 1930s and 1940s, Mary McLeod Bethune (1875–1955) was the most influential black woman in America—a spellbinding speaker, founder and head of national organizations, a presidential advisor, and Washington power broker. Through it all, Bethune was motivated by her powerful faith.

The daughter of ex-slaves, she founded Bethune–Cookman College and served as president for thirty-eight years. Early on she taught her students spirituals and had them sing while she passed the hat for donations. She founded and led the 800,000-member National Council of Negro Women, then moved on to become a leader in New Deal politics. She served in President Franklin D. Roosevelt's "Black Cabinet," which she herself organized with thirty colleagues. She also directed the National Youth Administration's Negro Affairs Division and in 1945 was a consultant at the charter conference to establish the United Nations.

Bethune selflessly used her great organizational skills and considerable influence to benefit black folks. In this article, written in 1941, she tells of her childhood years and her work to establish Bethune–Cookman. Through her, we can see that prayer and faith can open doors of opportunity.

I was born in Maysville, South Carolina, a country town in the midst of rice and cotton fields. My mother, father, and older brothers and sisters had been slaves until the Emancipation Proclamation. . . . After Mother was freed she continued in the McIntosh employ until she had earned enough to buy five acres of her own from her former master. Then my parents built our cabin, cutting and burning the logs with their own hands. I was the last of seventeen children, ten girls and seven boys.

When I was born, the first free child in their own home, my mother exulted, "Thank God, Mary came under our own vine and fig tree."

Mother was of royal African blood, of a tribe ruled by matriarchs. . . . Throughout all her bitter years of slavery she had managed to preserve a queenlike dignity. She supervised all the business of the family. Over the course of years, by the combined work and thrift of the family, and Mother's foresight, Father was able to enlarge our home site to thirty-five acres.

Most of my brothers and sisters had married and left home when I was growing up—there were only seven or eight children still around. Mother worked in the fields at Father's side, cutting rice and cotton, and chopping fodder. Each of us children had tasks to perform, according to our aptitudes. Some milked the cows, others helped with the washing, ironing, cooking, and house-cleaning. I was my father's champion cotton picker. When I was only nine, I could pick 250 pounds of cotton a day. . . .

[In those days] it was almost impossible for a Negro child, especially in the South, to get education. There were hundreds of square miles, sometimes entire states, without a single Negro school, and colored children were not allowed in public schools with white children. Mr. Lincoln had told our race we were free, but mentally we were still enslaved.

A knock on our door changed my life over-night. There stood a young woman, a colored missionary sent by the Northern Presbyterian Church to start a school near by. She asked my parents to send me. Every morning I picked up a little pail of milk and bread, and walked five miles to school; every afternoon, five miles home. But I walked always on winged feet.

The whole world opened to me when I learned to read. As soon as I understood something, I rushed back and taught it to the others at home. My teacher had a box of Bibles and texts, and she gave me one of each for my very own. That same day the teacher opened the Bible to John 3:16, and read: "For God so loved the world, that He gave His only begotten Son, that whosoever believeth in Him should not perish, but have everlasting life."

With these words the scales fell from my eyes and the light came flooding in. My sense of inferiority, my fear of handicaps, dropped away. "Whosoever," it said. No Jew nor Gentile, no Catholic nor Protestant, no black nor white; just "whosoever." It meant that I, a humble Negro girl, had just as much chance as anybody in the sight and love of God. These words stored up a battery of faith and confidence and determination in my heart, which has not failed me to this day. . . .

By the time I was fifteen I had taken every subject taught at our little school and could go no farther. Dissatisfied, because this taste of learning had aroused my appetite, I was forced to stay at home. Father's mule died—a major calamity—and he had to mortgage the farm to buy another. In those days, when a Negro mortgaged his property they never let him get out of debt.

I used to kneel in the cotton fields and pray that the door of opportunity should be opened to me once more, so that I might give to others whatever I might attain.

My prayers were answered. A white dressmaker, way off in Denver, Colorado, had become interested in the work of our little neighborhood school and had offered to pay for the higher education of some worthy girl. My teacher selected me, and I was sent to Scotia Seminary in Concord, North Carolina. There I studied English, Latin, higher mathematics, and science, and after classes I worked in the Scotia laundry and kitchen to earn as much extra money as I could. . . .

When I was graduated, I offered myself eagerly for missionary service in Africa, but the church authorities felt I was not sufficiently mature. Instead, they gave me another scholarship, and I spent two years at the Moody Bible School, in Chicago. Again I offered myself for missionary service, and again I was refused. Cruelly disappointed, I got a position at Haines Institute, in Augusta, Georgia, presided over by dynamic Lucy C. Laney, a pioneer Negro educator. From her I got a new vision: my life work lay not in Africa but in my own country. And with the first money I earned I began to save in order to pay off Father's mortgage, which had hung over his head for ten years!

During my early teaching days I met my future husband. He too was then a teacher, but to him teaching was only a job. Following our marriage, he entered upon a business career. When our baby son was born, I gave up my work temporarily, so that I could be all mother for one precious year. After that I got restless again to be back at my beloved work, for having a child made me more than ever determined to build better lives for my people. . . .

In 1904 I heard . . . [that] Henry Flagler was building the Florida East Coast Railroad, and hundreds of Negroes had gathered in Florida for construction work. . . .

I [went to] Daytona Beach, a beautiful little village, shaded by great oaks and giant pines. . . . I found a shabby four-room cottage, for which the owner wanted a rental of eleven dollars a month. My total capital was a dollar and a half, but I talked him into trusting me until the end of the month for the rest. This was in September. A friend let me stay at her home, and I plunged into the job of creating something from nothing. I spoke at churches, and the ministers let me take up collections. I buttonholed every woman who would listen to me. . . .

On October 3, 1904, I opened the doors of my school, with an enrollment of five little girls, aged from eight to twelve, whose parents paid me fifty cents' weekly tuition. My own child was the only boy in the school. Though I hadn't a penny left, I considered cash money as the smallest part of my resources. I had faith in a living God, faith in myself, and a desire to serve. . . .

We burned logs and used the charred splinters as pencils, and mashed elderberries for ink. I begged strangers for a broom, a lamp, a bit of cretonne to put around the packing case which served as my desk. I haunted the city dump and the trash piles behind hotels, retrieving discarded linen and kitchenware, cracked dishes, broken chairs, pieces of old lumber. Everything was scoured and mended. This was part of the training to salvage, to reconstruct, to make bricks without straw. As parents began gradually to leave their children overnight, I had to provide sleeping accommodations. I took corn sacks for mattresses. Then I picked Spanish moss from trees, dried and cured it, and used it as a substitute for mattress hair.

The school expanded fast. In less than two years I had 250 pupils. In desperation I hired a large hall next to my original little cottage, and used it as a combined dormitory and classroom. I concentrated more and more on girls, as I felt that they especially were hampered by lack of educational opportunities. . . .

I had many volunteer workers and a few regular teachers, who were paid from fifteen to twenty-five dollars a month and board. I was supposed to keep the balance of the funds for my own pocket, but there was never any balance—only a yawning hole. I wore old clothes sent me by mission boards, recut and redesigned for me in our dress-making classes. At last I saw that our only solution was to stop renting space, and to buy and build our own college.

Near by was a field, popularly called Hell's Hole, which was used as a dumping ground. I approached the owner, determined to buy it. The price was $250. In a daze, he finally agreed to take five dollars down, and the balance in two years. I promised to be back in a few days with the initial payment. He never knew it, but I didn't have five dollars. I raised this sum selling ice cream and sweet-potato pies to the workmen on construction jobs, and I took the owner his money in small change wrapped in my handkerchief.

That's how the Bethune-Cookman college campus started.

We at once discovered the need of an artesian well. The estimate was two hundred dollars. Here again we started with an insignificant payment, the balance remaining on trust. But what use was a plot without a building? I hung onto contractors' coat-tails, begging for loads of sand and secondhand bricks. I went to all the carpenters, mechanics, and plasterers in town, pleading with them to contribute a few hours' work in the evening in exchange for sandwiches and tuition for their children and themselves.

Slowly the building rose from its foundations. The name over the entrance still reads Faith Hall.

I had learned already that one of my most important jobs was to be a good beggar! I rang doorbells and tackled cold prospects without a lead. I wrote articles for whoever would print them, distributed leaflets, rode interminable miles of dusty roads on my old bicycle; invaded churches, clubs, lodges, chambers of commerce. . . .

Strongly interracial in my ideas, I looked forward to an advisory board of trustees composed of both white and colored people. I did my best missionary work among the prominent winter visitors to Florida. I would pick out names of "newly arrived guests," from the newspapers, and write letters asking whether I could call.

One of these letters went to James N. Gamble, of Procter & Gamble. He invited me to call at noon the next day. . . .

Mr. Gamble himself opened the door, and when I gave my name he looked at me in astonishment. "Are you the woman trying to build a school here? Why, I thought you were a white woman."

I laughed. "Well, you see how white I am." Then I told my story. "I'd like you to visit my school and, if it pleases you, to stand behind what I have in my mind," I finished.

He consented. . . . The next day . . . he made a careful tour of inspection, agreed to be a trustee, and gave me a check for $150— although I hadn't mentioned money. For many years he was one of our most generous friends.

Another experience with an unexpected ending was my first meeting with J. S. Peabody, of Columbia City, Indiana. After I had made an eloquent appeal for funds he gave me exactly twenty-five cents. I swallowed hard, thanked him smilingly, and later entered the contribution in my account book.

Two years later he reappeared. "Do you remember me?" he asked. "I'm one of your contributors." I greeted him cordially. He went on: "I wonder if you recall how much I gave you when I was here last?"

Not wishing to embarrass him, I told a white lie: "I'll have to look it up in my account book." Then after finding the entry, I said, "Oh, yes, Mr. Peabody, you gave us twenty-five cents."

Instead of being insulted, he was delighted that we kept account of such minute gifts. He immediately handed me a check for a hundred dollars and made arrangements to furnish the building. When he died, a few years later, he left the school $10,000. . . .

One evening I arranged a meeting at an exclusive hotel, expecting to talk to a large audience of wealthy people. But so many social functions were taking place that same night that I was greeted by an audience of exactly six. I was sick at heart—but I threw all my enthusiasm into my talk. At the end a gentleman dropped a twenty-dollar bill in the hat.

The next day he unexpectedly appeared at the school. He said his name was Thomas H. White, but it meant nothing to me. He looked around, asked where the shabby but immaculate straw matting on the floor came from. I said, "The city dump." He saw a large box of corn meal, and inquired what else there was to eat. I replied, "That's all we have at the moment." Then he walked about the grounds and saw an unfinished building, on which construction work had been temporarily abandoned for lack of funds. That was nothing new—there were always unfinished buildings cluttering up the landscape of our school. But I think the crowning touch was when he saw our dressmaking class working with a broken-down Singer sewing machine.

He turned to me, saying, "I believe you are on the right track. This is the most promising thing I've seen in Florida." He pressed a check in my hand, and left. The check was for $250. The following day he returned again, with a new sewing machine. Only then did I learn that Mr. White was the Singer people's principal competitor.

Mr. White brought plasterers, carpenters, and materials to finish our new building. Week after week he appeared with blankets for the children, shoes and a coat for me, everything we had dreamed of getting. When I thanked him, with tears in my eyes, for his generosity, he waved me aside.

"I've never invested a dollar that has brought greater returns than the dollars I have given you," he told me. And when this great soul died, he left a trust of $67,000, the interest to be paid us "as long as there is a school."

Do you wonder I have faith?

I never stop to plan. I take things step by step. For thirty-five years we have never had to close our doors for lack of food or fuel, although often we had to live from day to day. . . .

As the school expanded, whenever I saw a need for some training or service we did not supply, I schemed to add it to our curriculum. Sometimes that took years. When I came to Florida, there were no hospitals where a Negro could go. A student became critically ill with appendicitis, so I went to a local hospital and begged a white physician to take her in and operate. My pleas were so desperate he finally agreed. A few days after the operation, I visited my pupil.

When I appeared at the front door of the hospital, the nurse ordered me around to the back way. I thrust her aside—and found my little girl segregated in a corner of the porch behind the kitchen. Even my toes clenched with rage.

That decided me. I called on three of my faithful friends, asking them to buy a little cottage behind our school as a hospital. They agreed, and we started with two beds.

From this humble start grew a fully equipped twenty-bed hospital—

our college infirmary and a refuge for the needy throughout the state. It was staffed by white and black physicians and by our own student nurses. We ran this hospital for twenty years as part of our contribution to community life; but a short time ago, to ease our financial burden, the city took it over.

Gradually, as educational facilities expanded and there were other places where small children could go, we put the emphasis on high-school and junior-college training. In 1922, Cookman College, a men's school, the first in the state for the higher education of Negroes, amal-gamated with us. The combined coeducational college, now run under the auspices of the Methodist Episcopal Church, is called Bethune-Cook-man College. We have fourteen modern buildings, a beautiful campus of thirty-two acres, an enrollment in regular and summer sessions of 600 students, a faculty and staff of thirty-two, and 1,800 graduates. The college property, now valued at more than $800,000, is entirely unen-cumbered.

When I walk through the campus, with its stately palms and well-kept lawns, and think back to the dump-heap foundation, I rub my eyes and pinch myself. And I remember my childish visions in the cotton fields.

But values cannot be calculated in ledger figures and property. More than all else the college has fulfilled my ideals of distinctive training and service. Extending far beyond the immediate sphere of its graduates and students, it has already enriched the lives of 100,000 Negroes.

In 1934, President Franklin D. Roosevelt appointed me director of the division of Negro affairs of the National Youth Administration. My main task now is to supervise the training provided for 600,000 Negro children, and I have to run the college by remote control. Every few weeks, however, I snatch a day or so and return to my beloved home.

This is a strenuous program. The doctor shakes his head and says, "Mrs. Bethune, slow down a little. Relax! Take it just a little easier." I promise to reform, but in an hour the promise is forgotten.

For I am my mother's daughter, and the drums of Africa still beat in my heart. They will not let me rest while there is a single Negro boy or girl without a chance to prove his worth.

AMERICA'S FIRST BLACK PREACHING WOMAN: ELIZABETH, DAUGHTER OF THUNDER

BETTYE COLLIER-THOMAS

To white society, the slave woman was a source of cheap labor and a breeder. As such she served as the main "vessel" for passing slavery down through the generations. Added to her terrible burden was the "spiritual sexism" pervasive in America. Whereas African traditions granted females prominent, sacred roles in religious life—as priestesses, queens, diviners, herbalists, or even deities—Christianity in America was preached to the slaves by men, black and white. But it was only a matter of time before black women took up the call.

Early slave women preached clandestinely and held no official church role. Their mid- to late–nineteenth century successors also were not officially recognized or ordained by the black church. Black women's paths to the ministry were principally as exhorters, missionaries, evangelists, writers, teachers, and wives. Still, black female preachers managed to exert a powerful influence on black theology. Here is the story of Elizabeth, America's first black "daughter of thunder."*

The earliest black female preacher was a woman known simply as Elizabeth. Born a slave in Maryland in 1766, she was set free in 1796. Her parents were devout Methodists, and her father read the Bible aloud to his children every Sunday, instilling in them a fervent belief in the Scriptures and the power of prayer.

At the age of eleven, Elizabeth was sent to another farm. Although she was denied permission to visit her family, out of loneliness and despair she risked punishment and possibly death to see them. When she returned to the farm where she resided, the overseer tied her with a rope and lashed her. Recognizing the danger of Elizabeth's actions and her

---

* As a folk idiom, "daughter of thunder" (or "son of thunder") designates a booming voiced, fiery preacher, but according to theologians C. Eric Lincoln and Lawrence H. Mamiya, the term may also be traced to Shango, the West African god of thunder and lightning, whose symbol was the axe.

need for guidance and communion, her mother told her that she had "none in the world to look to but God."

Religion, particularly prayer, became her constant refuge. Every place became an altar. She mourned and moaned "in the corners of the field, and under the fences." For six months she prayed and wept, and gradually she lost her appetite and became extremely weak. It was in this state that she had her first vision and felt "the power of the Holy Ghost."

Elizabeth's description of her conversion experience is remarkably similar to that described by other women preachers. She felt "sustained by some invisible power." Converted to Christ at the age of twelve, she continued to pray and wrestle with the divine invocation that she should live a life of prayer and devotion to Christian principles.

Although Elizabeth had visions of traveling and preaching, it was many years before she actually had these experiences. When she was forty-two, as she later related, it "was revealed to me that the message which had been given to me I had not yet delivered, and the time had come." Lacking sufficient reading skills, Elizabeth questioned whether or not she could deliver the message, because she did not know the Scriptures. She sought guidance from other Christians but was discouraged from pursuing her mission. She was told that the Scriptures did not sanction women's preaching and that women were not suited to the rigors of travel required of an itinerant minister. Thoroughly disheartened, she first resisted the Holy Spirit but then felt the Holy Spirit's urging her to take up her mission.

In 1808, Elizabeth became a preaching woman, holding her first meeting in Baltimore. She was rejected at every turn by the "elders and rulers," and harassed at every meeting she attempted to hold in a church. Some women supported her desire to preach, but they feared expulsion from the Church if they allowed her to hold meetings in their homes. As the persecution against Elizabeth increased, the elders argued more adamantly that because she was a woman, her meetings went against the Methodist Church's discipline.

Elizabeth's perseverance and her firm belief in the holiness doctrine of salvation empowered her to continue preaching. She began to travel in the South and North, preaching and lecturing wherever she could. Despite the risk to her life and the possibility of reenslavement, she held meetings in Virginia and remote places throughout the South. Once in

Virginia, while speaking against slavery, she was challenged and threatened with imprisonment. When asked by what authority she spoke and if she were ordained, she answered, "Not by the commission of men's hands: if the Lord had ordained me, I needed nothing better." Her unprecedented answer, supreme confidence, conviction, and apparent godliness were enough to set aside many a threatening force. Elizabeth preached for almost fifty years before retiring to Philadelphia, where she lived among Quakers and spent her final years.

BORN TO PREACH
LEONTINE TURPEAU CURRENT KELLY

For some people, faith is a calling. It was for Leontine Turpeau Current Kelly (b. 1920), the first African American woman to become bishop of a major religious denomination in the United States. She served as spiritual head of the United Methodist Church in Northern California and Nevada, overseeing 375 churches with more than 100,000 members. Bishop Kelly retired in 1988.

My father was a Methodist minister. I was born in the parsonage of Mount Zion Methodist Episcopal Church in the Georgetown section of Washington, D.C. One of the stories in our family is that the second black bishop elected in the Methodist church baptized me when I was three months old. The story goes that when he handed me back to my mother, he said, "How I wish you were a boy, so that my mantle could fall on you." He'd probably turn over in his grave at the idea of a woman being a bishop in the church.

All four of my father's daughters said that we would never marry a minister. So, certainly, there was no thought of *being* one. I was a schoolteacher and that, I felt, was my ministry. I did not enter the ministry until my husband, a minister, died in 1969. I had been a certified lay speaker in the church for twelve years.

It's difficult for me not to preach. My children would tell you that, even as a mama. When the district superintendent asked my youngest son what he thought about me going in the ministry, he said, "She's been preaching all my life."

There has been an ordination and an acceptance, but women still work toward equality in the church. It isn't there yet, it's like society.

Some people use the Corinthian scripture of Paul saying women should not speak in the church. But we could find our own scriptures to substantiate why women should be allowed to speak.

I believe in a called ministry, a sense of assurance that there is something specific for you to do. For me, it was a year after my husband's death, the people asked me to serve the church that he pastored [in Edwardsville, Virginia]. Paul didn't call me. I believe God called me to the ordained ministry. I was willing to go that journey and it has been sustained.

Many people say you can prove whatever you want to from the Bible. But as a black person, what I look for in the Bible is a sense of my own freedom and acceptance by God and the sense of liberation that is there for me. And that word comes through very clearly.

As a child I asked my father, how could black people be Christian? How could they accept it, when the very persons that enslaved them taught them Christianity? My father said that in God there was the strength and the source for patience to wait for freedom. That was his sense of it. What I have found, of course, is that everybody wasn't waiting. People were working.

As children in Cincinnati, we located a station of the underground railway in the basement of our house. It went from the house to the church. When my father told us about it, he said that the witness of this church was not the wood brought all the way from Italy for the great beams. The real witness of that church was in the cellar. Someone had taken the risk to move against society and the government. It was a sanctuary movement of those days. I was excited about what kind of preaching was going on in a church like that.

My father not only preached, but he also ran a church that was the economic, cultural, and political center of the community. He also became an Ohio legislator.

We were not reared that politics was not a part of a Christian's duty.

If we were going to pray for liberation and equality, then we also had to work for it.

Another question was, Why do we stay in a major denomination that by its own policies does not accept us? Our whole concept was that we were in mission to the church. Where the church saw us as objects of mission, we saw the major church as a mission field for us, knowing that if you ever got the major churches of this country straight, then you were working on the country at the same time.

I was about eight years old and I opened the door one day and there was Mary McLeod Bethune. I remember sitting on the floor playing as my mother and she talked. Mrs. Bethune was saying that colored women need to stop playing bridge and start building bridges.

I've never been accused of not being outspoken. I crusaded for women as well as all ethnics in the church. Our proclamations and resolutions are great. We have yet to live them out.

As a country we have really been lulled into some kind of sense of superiority, as if we deserve some special reward from God. Our American children are about to be the only unilingual children in the world. And we pass legislation as if English were the king's language, I mean, God's language.

We privatize our religion such that it makes it safe for people to be Christian. And Christianity is not safe. If you're going to follow Jesus, then it's risky to do that.

For me, the crux of the gospel message is the way we share power. One of the things women bring to the situation in terms of sharing power is new styles of leadership. I am no less the bishop. I know where the buck stops and who is responsible. But that doesn't mean that I have to exert power in such a way that other people feel they are less than who they are because of who I am.

THE CREATION
JAMES WELDON JOHNSON

"The old-time Negro preacher," wrote James Weldon Johnson (1871–1938), "preached a personal and anthropomorphic God, a sure-enough heaven and a red-hot hell. He had the power to sweep his hearers before him; and so himself was often swept away. At such times his language was not prose but poetry."

"The Creation" is a sermon in verse. Johnson was inspired to write it, and others, by the recollection of sermons he had heard in his youth. This poem is as moving today as it was in 1920, when it was composed.

> And God stepped out on space,
> And he looked around and said:
> I'm lonely—
> I'll make me a world.
>
> And far as the eye of God could see
> Darkness covered everything,
> Blacker than a hundred midnights
> Down in a cypress swamp.
>
> Then God smiled,
> And the light broke,
> And the darkness rolled up on one side,
> And the light stood shining on the other,
> And God said: That's good!
>
> Then God reached out and took the light in his hands,
> And God rolled the light around in his hands
> Until he made the sun;
> And he set that sun a-blazing in the heavens.
> And the light that was left from making the sun
> God gathered it up in a shining ball
> And flung it against the darkness,
> Spangling the night with the moon and stars.
> Then down between

The darkness and the light
He hurled the world;
And God said: That's good!

Then God himself stepped down—
And the sun was on his right hand,
And the moon was on his left;
The stars were clustered about his head,
And the earth was under his feet.
And God walked, and where he trod
His footsteps hollowed the valleys out
And bulged the mountains up.

Then he stopped and looked and saw
That the earth was hot and barren.
So God stepped over to the edge of the world
And he spat out the seven seas—
He batted his eyes, and the lightnings flashed—
He clapped his hands, and the thunders rolled—
And the waters above the earth came down,
The cooling waters came down.

Then the green grass sprouted,
And the little red flowers blossomed,
The pine tree pointed his finger to the sky,
And the oak spread out his arms,
The lakes cuddled down in the hollows of the ground,
And the rivers ran down to the sea;
And God smiled again,
And the rainbow appeared,
And curled itself around his shoulder.

Then God raised his arm and he waved his hand
Over the sea and over the land,
And he said: Bring forth! Bring forth!
And quicker than God could drop his hand,
Fishes and fowls

And beasts and birds
Swam the rivers and the seas,
Roamed the forests and the woods,
And split the air with their wings.
And God said: That's good!

Then God walked around,
And God looked around
On all that he had made.
He looked at his sun,
And he looked at his moon,
And he looked at his little stars;
He looked on his world
With all its living things,
And God said: I'm lonely still.

Then God sat down—
On the side of a hill where he could think;
By a deep, wide river he sat down;
With his head in his hands,
God thought and thought,
Till he thought: I'll make me a man!

Up from the bed of the river
God scooped the clay;
And by the bank of the river
He kneeled him down;
And there the great God Almighty
Who lit the sun and fixed it in the sky,
Who flung the stars to the most far corner of the night,
Who rounded the earth in the middle of his hand;
This Great God,
Like a mammy bending over her baby,
Kneeled down in the dust
Toiling over a lump of clay
Till he shaped it in his own image;

Then into it he blew the breath of life,
And man became a living soul.
Amen. Amen.

THE THREAD IN MY HAND
HOWARD THURMAN

*In this excerpt from a prayer-poem called "The Threads in My Hand"
by Howard Thurman (1900–81), the speaker holds one end of a number
of threads, each extending to him from a different source—the sick, the
old, the troubled. But one thread stands out from all others: a "strange
thread." It is a good idea to hold fast to it.*

One thread is a strange thread—it is my steadying thread;
    When I am lost, I pull it hard and find my way.
When I am saddened, I tighten my grip and gladness glides
            along its quivering path;
When the waste places of my spirit appear in arid confusion,
    the thread becomes a channel of newness in life.
One thread is a strange thread—it is my steadying thread.
        God's hand holds the other end . . .*

---

* This is reminiscent of verse 3:103 in the Qur'an, which is interpreted as: "And hold fast, all
together, by the rope which Allah (stretches out for you) . . ." According to some scholars, the
"rope" represents the Qur'an itself, the holy book of Islam. Holding fast to it will prevent
division among believers. The "rope" metaphor also implies a means of rescue stretched out for
people struggling in deep water.

PRECIOUS LORD, TAKE MY HAND
THOMAS A. DORSEY

In the 1920s, a gifted pianist–composer named Thomas A. Dorsey (1899–1993) worked as an accompanist for the great blues singer Ma Rainey in Chicago. Meanwhile, he was developing a new music that would raise a joyous sound in churches and ultimately form the roots of rock and roll. It was called gospel.

In 1932, Dorsey's wife died during childbirth, and their baby died a few days later. "It was quite a while before I could get myself together," Dorsey said. "And when I got myself together, then I became more prolific in writing than ever before . . . After the baby died, that's where I got 'Precious Lord.' Just sitting talking to myself, and Precious Lord. Great Lord. 'Precious Lord, Take My Hand.' That's my prayer. Every day. Every night."

Dorsey's songs—then called "Dorseys"—struck a nerve. Pop Staples, the great gospel singer who moved to Chicago in the 1930s, said, "When you listened to Mr. Dorsey's music, you could sit back and reminisce about its meaning. You could feast on it." Dorsey sold sheets of his new music door to door, and in 1932 established the first gospel publishing company, Dorsey House. Four years later, he staged the first commercial gospel concert. Great singers traveled to learn gospel directly from Dorsey. His music spread across the world in the 1940s and 1950s. Today, Dorsey is known as "the father of gospel music." Here is perhaps his most famous song.

Precious Lord, take my hand,
Lead me on, let me stand,
I am tired, I am weak, I am worn.
Through the storm, through the night
Lead me on to the light,
Take my hand, precious Lord,
Lead me home.

When my way grows drear,
Precious Lord, linger near.
When my life is almost gone,
Hear my cry, hear my call,

Hold my hand lest I fall.
Take my hand, precious Lord,
Lead me home.

When the darkness appears
And the night draws near,
And the day is past and gone,
At the river I stand,
Guide my feet, hold my hand.
Take my hand, precious Lord,
Lead me home.

UNSPOKEN PRAYERS
ANONYMOUS

We may not get what we ask for, but we often get all we really need.

I asked my God for strength,
that I might achieve . . .

I was made weak,
that I might humbly learn to obey.

I asked for health,
that I might do greater things . . .

I was given infirmity,
that I might do better things.

I asked for riches,
that I might be happy . . .

I was given poverty,
that I might be wise.

I asked for power,
that I might have the praise of men . . .

I was given weakness,
that I might feel the need of God.

I asked for all things,
that I might enjoy life . . .

I was given life,
that I might enjoy all things.

I got nothing that I asked for,
but everything I had hoped for.
Almost despite myself,
my unspoken prayers were answered.

I am among all men, most richly blessed!

Can you feel the spirit? . . . In the dark.
　　　　—Aretha Franklin, "Spirit in the Dark," 1970

THE MOTHER OF GOSPEL MUSIC
WILLIE MAE FORD SMITH

Called the "mother of gospel music," Willie Mae Ford Smith (1906–94) was considered among the greatest gospel singers. She taught and influenced countless others, including Mahalia Jackson (1911–72), who became known as the "queen of the gospel sound." For Smith, singing was both an emotional outlet and a means to rejuvenate her faith. "The gospel

song is the Christian blues," Smith once said. "I'm like the blues singer.
When something's rubbing me wrong, I sing out my soul to settle me
down."

Smith was born in the central Mississippi Delta town of Rolling Fork.*
She became an ordained minister in the 1920s. By "talking it up" between
songs, she originated what is called the "sermonette," now used by almost
all gospel singers. Smith, who helped establish the National Convention of
Gospel Choirs and Choruses, toured the country to preach and sing, and
was featured prominently in the 1983 gospel film, Say Amen, Somebody.
In 1988, she was named a National Heritage Fellow by the National
Endowment for the Arts for her contributions as a master folk artist.
Mother Smith explained how the spirit moved her. Faith put power and
joy in her voice.

My mother would sing "The Lonely Jesus" and it would sound so good
to me. I'd sing "The Long-leg Jesus" 'cause I didn't know. I never got it
different until I got to be a big girl. When I was little I'd get up on the
table and sing, "There's not a friend like the long-leg Jesus, no no not
one." People laughin' at me singin' that, but I thought they was feelin'
good 'cause I was a child.

My mother was a wet-nurse, if you know what I mean. So many
white people had babies that didn't have any milk, breast milk. My
mother was just like a little dairy. She would get babies all the time.
When I was a baby, my milk went to the other white kids and I got the
strippings. . . .

They left Mississippi and came to Memphis and they left Memphis
when [the United States entered] the war in 1917. At that time white
folks were killin' black folks and black folks were killin' white folks. You
get a black man mad, he thinks "You're just goin' to kill me. I'm goin' to
die anyway. So I'm goin' to get you while I'm goin'. We goin' out
together." My daddy didn't want to live in that circumstance so he
thought he better push out with all his children, fourteen children—
seven sisters and seven brothers. I happened to be the seventh of the
fourteen children.

After I received the gift of the holy experience, I began to dig. It was

---

* The birthplace of blues guitarist McKinley Morganfield, better known as Muddy Waters
(1915–83).

a call of God. But I went to a seminary school for training. I knew how to read the Bible. You read the Bible with your eyes, of course, but you don't know how to get the connections.

When the bishop's son was fixing the program up for his father's funeral—who goin' to sing this and what—I told him I didn't want to sing that. He said, "But Dad liked that song." I said okay and I tried all I knew to get up there and sing it. I stood still and breathed a while and then he said, "Use what you got." I got this song in my heart and I sang it. That fitted me, it was a good garment for me. You sing what fits you.

The preachers would say about me, "Don't let her come in your church 'cause she's a bell cow. She'll lead all your people out acting that foolish stuff."

When I would go to their meetings, the preachers would say, "You can sit down there, you don't need to come up here. Don't get in my program. You a woman, didn't you realize?" No respect at all. Well, it don't make no difference to me. So I turn around in my pew and sing to that audience. Next thing I know, "Come on up here, get up and let all of them see you."

I felt like taking my number up the aisle, but you've got to use common sense with whatever you do. You see, when the spirit was taking me away, [one preacher] said, "Control yourself, because the Holy Spirit will use you up in one performance."

See, God don't want no filter on His work. To be a gospel singer, you got to be a gospel person. You know, some people will just woo everybody in church. They'll just dress so fabulous and frilly. People can't get the gospel for looking at you, you know. I don't worry about my fancy clothes. When I get up to carry on, I want to look so they won't wonder, what is that she got on?

I'm the mother of the world. All these children are mine. Anybody let me love 'em, they're mine. Those that don't let me love 'em, then I love 'em anyhow.

Yeah, they love me. I believe they do. If they don't love me, I don't want to find out. . . .

God is not pleased. He's not pleased with all this shackin' business. He's not pleased with all this liquor business and dope. Slippin' and slidin', peepin' and hidin' don't work with God. . . .

Look at the trees now, aren't they bare? But you let a certain day come for spring and they'll come out. They won't be the same leaves that was there last year, but when they come out they're so pretty. I look out at those trees and just think, Oh, you're so beautiful. God sure dressed you up. I say that to a tree. The work I have done, if I have to do it over, I'm willin'. But I don't want to go back. Let me be the leaf just laying at the foot of the tree giving it substance to grow. . . .

When you're walkin' with God you don't worry about what you're gonna get in this life. I told you in my song—you heard it, didn't you? I'm gonna be happy. I'll tell you it makes me happy now when I think about the home over there. I don't need no washing, I don't need no maid. Oh, hallelujah! When I get over there, I believe I'm gonna get that milk and honey. I've read about it, heard about it. I've been taught about it. I want it! I want it! I want to go home with God and rest.

Some said I'm packin' up, gettin' ready to go. But I'm not! Honey, I'm not packing up a handkerchief, you know. But I'm gettin' ready to go. How am I doin' it? I'm layin' aside every weight and a sin that does so easily beset me and I'm gettin' light for the flight.

WE SHALL OVERCOME
MUSIC AND LYRICS BY SILPHIA HORTON, FRANK HAMILTON, GUY CARAWAN, AND PETE SEEGER

This is a modern adaptation of an old Negro spiritual, "I'll Overcome Someday," the lyrics of which were: "I'll be all right . . . I'll be like Him . . . I'll wear the crown . . . I will overcome." The song was adapted for use in a picket line by union workers in a 1945 strike in Charleston, South Carolina. It was adopted as a theme song by High-lander Folk School, introduced to union workers across the South, and eventually passed on to civil rights demonstrators in the 1960s.

We shall overcome,
We shall overcome,
We shall overcome,
Someday.
Oh, deep in my heart,
I do believe, that
We shall overcome
Someday.

We'll walk hand in hand,
We'll walk hand in hand,
We'll walk hand in hand,
Someday.
Oh, deep in my heart,
I do believe, that
We shall overcome
Someday.

We are not afraid,
We are not afraid,
We are not afraid,
Oh, no, no, no,
'Cause deep in my heart,
I do believe, that
We shall overcome
Someday.

I HAVE A DREAM
MARTIN LUTHER KING JR.

Delivered on the steps of the Lincoln Memorial on August 28, 1963,
by Martin Luther King Jr. (1929–68), this moving seventeen-minute
oration is perhaps the most famous by an American in the twentieth
century. More than 200,000 people heard King's speech in person, at the
climax of the March on Washington, the largest rally of the civil rights
era. Millions more heard him on television.

"I Have a Dream" moves from King's nightmarish description of
racial injustice to a vision of peace and equality across the land. It ends on
a hopeful note—a dream of freedom, the joined hands of "all of God's
children," and words of gratefulness taken from an old black spiritual.
Here then is faith in an exalted vision of freedom, spoken in the measured
cadences of one of the greatest preachers and orators of all time.

I am happy to join with you today in what will go down in history as the
greatest demonstration for freedom in the history of our nation.

Fivescore years ago, a great American, in whose symbolic shadow we
stand today, signed the Emancipation Proclamation. This momentous
decree came as a great beacon light of hope to millions of Negro slaves
who had been seared in the flames of withering injustice. It came as a
joyous daybreak to end the long night of their captivity.

But one hundred years later, the Negro still is not free; one hundred
years later, the life of the Negro is still sadly crippled by the manacles of
segregation and the chains of discrimination; one hundred years later,
the Negro lives on a lonely island of poverty in the midst of a vast ocean
of material prosperity; one hundred years later, the Negro is still languished in the corners of American society and finds himself in exile in
his own land.

So we've come here today to dramatize a shameful condition. In a
sense we've come to our nation's capital to cash a check. When the
architects of our republic wrote the magnificent words of the Constitution and the Declaration of Independence, they were signing a promissory note to which every American was to fall heir. This note was the
promise that all men, yes, black men as well as white men, would be

guaranteed the unalienable rights of life, liberty, and the pursuit of happiness.

It is obvious today that America has defaulted on this promissory note in so far as her citizens of color are concerned. Instead of honoring this sacred obligation, America has given the Negro people a bad check; a check which has come back marked "insufficient funds." We refuse to believe that there are insufficient funds in the great vaults of opportunity of this nation. And so we've come to cash this check, a check that will give us upon demand the riches of freedom and the security of justice.

We have also come to this hallowed spot to remind America of the fierce urgency of now. This is no time to engage in the luxury of cooling off or to take the tranquilizing drug of gradualism. Now is the time to make real the promises of democracy; now is the time to rise from the dark and desolate valley of segregation to the sunlit path of racial justice; now is the time to lift our nation from the quicksands of racial injustice to the solid rock of brotherhood; now is the time to make justice a reality for all of God's children. It would be fatal for the nation to overlook the urgency of the moment. This sweltering summer of the Negro's legitimate discontent will not pass until there is an invigorating autumn of freedom and equality.

Nineteen sixty-three is not an end, but a beginning. And those who hope that the Negro needed to blow off steam and will now be content, will have a rude awakening if the nation returns to business as usual.

There will be neither rest nor tranquility in America until the Negro is granted his citizenship rights. The whirlwinds of revolt will continue to shake the foundations of our nation until the bright day of justice emerges.

But there is something that I must say to my people who stand on the warm threshold which leads into the palace of justice. In the process of gaining our rightful place we must not be guilty of wrongful deeds.

Let us not seek to satisfy our thirst for freedom by drinking from the cup of bitterness and hatred. We must forever conduct our struggle on the high plane of dignity and discipline. We must not allow our creative protest to degenerate into physical violence. Again and again we must rise to the majestic heights of meeting physical force with soul force.

The marvelous new militancy which has engulfed the Negro community must not lead us to a distrust of all white people, for many of our white brothers, as evidenced by their presence here today, have come to realize that their destiny is tied up with our destiny and they have come to realize that their freedom is inextricably bound to our freedom. This offense we share mounted to storm the battlements of injustice must be carried forth by a biracial army. We cannot walk alone.

And as we walk, we must make the pledge that we shall always march ahead. We cannot turn back. There are those who are asking the devotees of civil rights, "When will you be satisfied?" We can never be satisfied as long as the Negro is the victim of the unspeakable horrors of police brutality.

We can never be satisfied as long as our bodies, heavy with fatigue of travel, cannot gain lodging in the motels of the highways and the hotels of the cities. We cannot be satisfied as long as the Negro's basic mobility is from a smaller ghetto to a larger one.

We can never be satisfied as long as our children are stripped of their selfhood and robbed of their dignity by signs stating "for whites only." We cannot be satisfied as long as a Negro in Mississippi cannot vote and a Negro in New York believes he has nothing for which to vote. No, we are not satisfied, and we will not be satisfied until justice rolls down like waters and righteousness like a mighty stream.

I am not unmindful that some of you have come here out of excessive trials and tribulation. Some of you have come fresh from narrow jail cells. Some of you have come from areas where your quest for freedom left you battered by the storms of persecution and staggered by the winds of police brutality. You have been the veterans of creative suffering. Continue to work with the faith that unearned suffering is redemptive.

Go back to Mississippi; go back to Alabama; go back to South Carolina; go back to Georgia; go back to Louisiana; go back to the slums and ghettos of the northern cities, knowing that somehow this situation can, and will be changed. Let us not wallow in the valley of despair.

So I say to you, my friends that even though we must face the difficulties of today and tomorrow, I still have a dream. It is a dream deeply rooted in the American dream that one day this nation will rise up and live out the true meaning of its creed—we hold these truths to be self-evident, that all men are created equal.

I have a dream that one day on the red hills of Georgia, sons of former slaves and sons of former slave-owners will be able to sit down together at the table of brotherhood.

I have a dream that one day, even the state of Mississippi, a state sweltering with the heat of injustice, sweltering with the heat of oppression, will be transformed into an oasis of freedom and justice.

I have a dream my four little children will one day live in a nation where they will not be judged by the color of their skin but by content of their character. I have a dream today!

I have a dream that one day, down in Alabama, with its vicious racists, with its governor having his lips dripping with the words of interposition and nullification, that one day, right there in Alabama, little black boys and black girls will be able to join hands with little white boys and white girls as sisters and brothers. I have a dream today!

I have a dream that one day every valley shall be exalted, every hill and mountain shall be made low, the rough places shall be made plain, and the crooked places shall be made straight and the glory of the Lord will be revealed and all flesh shall see it together.*

This is our hope. This is the faith that I go back to the South with.

With this faith we will be able to hear out of the mountain of despair a stone of hope. With this faith we will be able to transform the jangling discords of our nation into a beautiful symphony of brotherhood.

With this faith we will be able to work together, to pray together, to struggle together, to go to jail together, to stand up for freedom together, knowing that we will be free one day. This will be the day when all of God's children will be able to sing with new meaning—"my country 'tis of thee; sweet land of liberty; of thee I sing; land where my fathers died, land of the pilgrim's pride; from every mountain side, let freedom ring"—and if America is to be a great nation, this must become true.

So let freedom ring from the prodigious hilltops of New Hampshire.
Let freedom ring from the mighty mountains of New York.
Let freedom ring from the heightening Alleghenies of Pennsylvania.
Let freedom ring from the snow-capped Rockies of Colorado.
Let freedom ring from the curvaceous slopes of California.

---

* Isaiah 40:4–5: "Every valley shall be exalted, and every mountain and hill shall be made low: and the crooked shall be made straight, and the rough places plain: and the glory of the Lord shall be revealed, and all flesh shall see it together."

But not only that.

Let freedom ring from Stone Mountain of Georgia.

Let freedom ring from Lookout Mountain of Tennessee.

Let freedom ring from every hill and molehill of Mississippi, from every mountainside, let freedom ring.

And when we allow freedom to ring, when we let it ring from every village and hamlet, from every state and city, we will be able to speed up that day when all of God's children—black men and white men, Jews and Gentiles, Catholics and Protestants—will be able to join hands and to sing in the words of the old Negro spiritual, "Free at last, free at last; thank God Almighty, we are free at last."

THE NEGRO'S TEN COMMANDMENTS

JOSEPH S. COTTER SR.

Here are some commandments for living in the United States, written in 1947 by Joseph Seamon Cotter Sr. (1861–1949), a poet, educator, and civic leader from Kentucky.

1. Thy father's God forsake not and thy manhood debase not, and thou shalt cease to say: "I am a Negro, therefore I cannot."

2. Be not ashamed of thy physical self lest thy ideal be lowered and thou proclaim thyself thy brother's servant.

3. Thou must have thine own David to psalm thy praise and thine own Ezekiel to vision thy valley of dry bones.

4. In the fields shalt thou grow brawn and brew ease, but in the city shall come to thee the steel of endurance, the wisdom of conquest.

5. Read not thyself out of toiling with the hands, and toil not thyself out of reading; for reading creates dreams, and toiling makes one akin to the ox. Therefore he who simply dreams is dying, and he who dreams not is already dead.

6. Make thou thy thought inter-racial and thy life artistic, and thy destiny shall be one long path of glory.

7. Learn thou the worth of a dollar and how to keep it from damning thee.

8. So long as thy brother must buy thy daily bread just so long will he lower thy genius, culture and manhood to the price thereof. Secure thou thy own bread, if thou wouldst settle thy standing among men.

9. Socially thou shalt go nearer thy brother than he comes to thee. Aversion in him should slay the thought of advance in thee.

10. If thou hast a mind to live by being honest, industrious, frugal and self-sacrificing, remain . . . where thou shalt surely reap thy character's worth; but if thou hast a mind to die through sloth, ignorance and folly, get thee far from [there], for the burden of burying such is becoming intolerable.

O Lord, help me to understand that you ain't going to let nothing come my way that You and me together can't handle.

—*Anonymous African boy*

WHAT MAN LIVES BY
BENJAMIN E. MAYS

Benjamin E. Mays (1895–1984) was president of Morehouse College in Atlanta for many years. His words influenced many African Americans, including Martin Luther King Jr. Here is one of Dr. Mays's sermons, considered among the most eloquent of the twentieth century.

Some nineteen centuries ago a Palestinian Jew made these words immortal: "Man shall not live by bread alone, but by every word that proceedeth out of the mouth of God" (Matthew 4:4, King James Version). To state it another way: Man shall not live by bread alone but by every good thing that God provides. Man can *exist* on food, air, and water, just as animals can, but man must have more than bread in order to live creatively and constructively.

It is not too much to translate this passage by saying, Man shall not live by material things alone. Money, houses and land, stocks and bonds, silver and gold, iron and ore, silks and diamonds and pearls and furs are all important, but man may have all these and merely exist—not live.

Jesus stated it wisely: Man shall not live by bread alone. He knew that bread—food—is basic to man's life. And the Devil knew that when a man gets hungry, he is vulnerable and may do many abnormal things in order to get food. Facing starvation, most people would steal, if they could, rather than starve. Using bread as a symbol for food, adequate food for all mankind has been a problem since the beginning of time. It is a crucial problem today. It is estimated that half the people of the earth are starving for lack of bread. Bread is so important that if food became too scarce, the strong man would turn on the weak man and cannibalize him in order to survive. The population-explosion threat is no idle dream. If bread becomes too unobtainable, we have the basis for revolution. In man's quest for more bread—more food—and a higher standard of living, labor strikes against management and the common people rise up against the establishment. Those of us who care are appalled by the fact that easily thirty million Americans are living below the poverty line. Bread is important, and man cannot exist without it. But if man had only food, only material things, to live by, he would cease to be a man.

So Jesus says to the Devil that man cannot live by bread alone. If he could, he would be a mere animal. Bread is the means, not the end. Man lives in God, and the circumference of life cannot be rightly drawn until the center is set.

The experience of Jesus in the wilderness is common to all mankind. Simply put, Jesus is trying to decide the basic question that confronts every man: What shall I do with my life? This question faces every man: What shall I do with my life? Although I shall deal with only one of the three temptations, Jesus is getting his priorities straight. Man has to decide what he will put first in his life. This problem faces the young with terrific force. If it is money, material wealth, houses and land, stocks and bonds, silver and gold—as important as these are—if these are central in our lives, human values become secondary. Man may exist, but he will never know the full joy of living. As indispensable as bread is, as vital as material things are, possessions alone have never made a man great. The rich man who achieves a degree of greatness achieves it not because he hoards his wealth but because he gives it away in the interest of good causes—his concern for humanity, his concern for the poor, and his desire to improve the quality of education. The truly great men of history are great not because of the abundance of the things they possessed but because of their dreams and the contributions they made to mankind. It is because they recognized that man cannot live by bread alone.

Bread is vital; it is indispensable; but in appraising a man for greatness, wealth per se is never a criterion. Nobody stops to ask how much wealth persons like Fred Douglass, Harriet Tubman, Thomas Aquinas, Albert Einstein, Booker T. Washington, Mary McLeod Bethune, Shakespeare, and Socrates had when they died. They achieved historical immortality long after bread ceased to sustain their bodies. If man cannot live by bread alone, what else does he need to live by? Jesus answers this by saying: By every word that proceedeth out of the mouth of God.

Any man or woman who has a family knows that man lives by affection and love. There may be material things galore, but if there is no affection, no love in the home, the family falls apart. The baby may have all the food it needs, all the air and sunshine, all the protection from cold and heat; yet if he does not get his mother's kisses, her affectionate hugs, her inviting smiles, and her soothing words when he cries, the baby may exist but he will be an abnormal child. The baby must be made to know that he or she is wanted. The child must have the love of father, mother, sisters, and brothers, and the protection they give—all these the child must receive in order to live and flourish.

No man has ever made his wife really happy merely by giving her an abundance of material things. He may give her gold and silver, diamonds and pearls, houses and land, stocks and bonds—all these she will reject if her husband withholds his love. In truth, love is the thing no man or woman can live without. Affection and love hold the family together; hatred and infidelity tear the family apart. Man cannot live by bread alone. Bread must be accompanied by love and affection.

No man can live without forgiveness. The family cannot hold together without it. The husband and wife must forgive each other for the unkind words they sometimes say to each other, for the unpleasant glances they sometimes give, for being impatient with one another. Even if at times husband and wife are deliberately mean toward one another, they must forgive. Forgiveness is the very essence of happiness in the home. The family cannot survive if the wife seeks opportunities to get revenge for unkind things the husband says and does to her. Nor can the family hold together if the husband seeks retaliation against the wife. Forgiveness is the heart of family life. The father must forgive the son, the son the father; the sister must forgive her brother and the brother the sister; the wife must forgive the husband and the husband the wife. I have even known cases where there was forgiveness where infidelity was involved. It takes a lot of forgiveness to keep a family together.

Man must live by forgiveness, not only family forgiveness but community forgiveness. The prisoner who served his time needs community forgiveness. Man needs forgiveness for the dirty, vicious things that some do to others. How often have we in some little or big way trespassed against a brother? We live by forgiveness of those friends who love us and stick with us though we sin against them.

But most of all, we live by the forgiveness of God. No man is perfect enough, no man is good enough not to need the forgiveness of God. In one sense we are all sinners. If a sinner is one who sins, we all qualify as sinners. All of us sometimes sin. If it is true that when we sin against man, we sin against God; when we lie to man, we lie to God; when we exploit man, we exploit God; when we hate man, we hate God—God must indeed be a forgiving God with man sinning against him all of the time! Man shall not live by bread alone, but man shall live and does live by the forgiveness of a merciful God.

In addition to bread, man lives by the grace of God. One definition of grace is that we get what we do not deserve. Every man who is honest with himself knows of instances when he got what he did not deserve, certainly that which he did nothing to achieve. God sends his rain on the just and the unjust. The moon and the sun shine on us all. The unrighteous live as long as the righteous. The best man does not always get the job. We often get honors and prizes which we have not earned. Someone dies and leaves us a bit of wealth which we never turned a little finger to get. The man we do not like sometimes does us a favor, to our embarrassment. We inherit a good mind by some means we do not understand, a mind which we did nothing to get. We develop into a handsome boy or beautiful girl by nature and nature's God, but we did nothing to get the beauty or the comeliness. Some are born into better circumstances than others, but we are not responsible for where we are born, nor for what we are born with. In some degree, we all get what we do not deserve, and we live by the grace of God.

Man shall not live by bread alone. Man must live by faith—faith in himself and faith in others. However beastly man may be, we must believe in him and rely on him. We trust the doctor to operate on our bodies. We trust the man who drives the automobile. We trust the banks to keep our money. We trust the man who directs us to an unfamiliar place. We trust the pilot who takes us three thousand feet above the ground. We live by faith in others. But most of all we must live by faith in ourselves—faith to believe that we can develop into useful men and women. No man can live without faith in himself—a sense of inner security. A child must learn early to believe that he is somebody worthwhile and that he can do many praiseworthy things. Without this hope, there would be nothing for him to do but commit suicide. Furthermore, man could not live hopefully without believing that he counts for something in this world. The greatest damage that the white man did to the black man through slavery and segregation was to beat him down so much that millions of Negroes believed that they were nobody. The hopelessness and despair of so many black youths today lie in the fact that they have never believed that they have dignity and worth as human beings. If the emphasis on blackness and black awareness today means that black people are beginning to be proud of their heritage and proud of being what they are—black—apologizing to no one, not even to God, for what they are, it is a good thing. Man lives best by a belief that he is somebody, God's creature, and that he has status not given to him by man but given to him by God.

Man must believe that however hard the road, however difficult today, tomorrow things will be better. Tomorrow may not be better, but we must believe that it will be. Wars may never cease, but we must continue to strive to eliminate them. We may not abolish poverty, but we must believe that we can provide bread enough to spare for every living creature and that we can find the means to distribute it. We may not exterminate racism, but we must believe that different racial groups can live together in peace, and we must never cease to try to build a society in which the fatherhood of God and the brotherhood of man become realities.

In other words, many must live by faith in God—faith to believe that God sustains good and not evil, peace and not war, truth and not lies, justice and not injustice, integrity and not dishonesty.

No man is self-sustaining. We are dependent on the labors of many hands for the food we eat, for the clothes we wear, for the cars and planes in which we ride, for the books we read, for the teachers who teach us, for the skill of the surgeon, for the technical training of the pilot. We are dependent on the postman who brings the mail, on the controllers who guide the planes in and out of airports, and on the sanitation workers who take away the garbage. Our lives are interlaced, interwoven, and intertwined with the lives of all classes of men, and whether we like it or not we all need each other and every man is our brother.

Man shall not live by bread alone, but man must live by his dreams, by the goals he strives to reach, and by the ideals which he chooses and chases. What is man anyway? Man is flesh and blood, body and mind, bones and muscle, arms and legs, heart and soul, lungs and liver, nerves and veins—all these and more make a man. But man is really what his dreams are. Man is what he aspires to be. He is the ideals that beckon him on. Man is the integrity that keeps him steadfast, honest, true. If a young man tells me what he aspires to be, I can almost predict his future.

It must be borne in mind, however, that the tragedy in life does not lie in not reaching your goal. The tragedy lies in having no goal to reach. It isn't a calamity to die with dreams unfulfilled, but it is a calamity not to dream. It is not a disaster to be unable to capture your ideal, but it is a disaster to have no ideal to capture. It is not a disgrace not to reach the stars, but it is a disgrace to have no stars to reach for. Not failure, but low aim is the sin.

Man shall not live by bread alone. Man must live by affection and love; by forgiveness—forgiveness of man and the forgiveness of God; by God's grace; by the labors of many hands; by faith—faith in himself, faith in others, and faith in God. And finally man must live by his dreams, his ideals, the unattainable goal, and what he aspires to be. Man shall not live by bread alone.

WHY ME?

ARTHUR ASHE

Tennis great Arthur Ashe (1943–93) was not only a world-class athlete, but a champion of many causes. He fought racism both on and off the tennis court, opposed South Africa's apartheid and protested U.S. immigration policy toward Haitians. Finally, he battled AIDS, which he contracted in 1983. During his last few years, his faith enabled him to face death with great dignity.

Believing that pain has a purpose, I do not question either its place in the universe or my fate in becoming so familiar with pain through disease. Quite often, people who mean well will inquire of me whether I ever ask myself, in the face of my diseases, "Why me?" I never do. If I ask "Why me?" as I am assaulted by heart disease and AIDS, I must ask "Why me?" about my blessings, and question my right to enjoy them. The morning after I won Wimbledon in 1975 I should have asked "Why me?" and doubted that I deserved the victory. If I don't ask "Why me?"

after my victories, I cannot ask "Why me?" after my setbacks and disasters. I also do not waste time pleading with God to make me well. I was brought up to believe that prayer is not to be invoked to ask God for things for oneself, or even for others. Rather, prayer is a medium through which I ask God to show me God's will, and to give me strength to carry out that will. God's will alone matters, not my personal desires or needs. When I played tennis, I never prayed for victory in a match. I will not pray now to be cured of heart disease or AIDS.

I do not brood on the prospect of dying soon. I am not afraid of death. Perhaps fear will come to haunt me when the moment of death is closer. On the other hand, perhaps I will be even less fearful, more calm and at peace. I think of my lack of fear as being, in some ways, different from true courage. My bouts of surgery have made me a veteran in fighting death. Familiarity has not bred contempt of death but has given me practice in learning to face it calmly. In any event, the courage I yearn for is that described by Dr. Howard Thurman: "There is a quiet courage that comes from an inward spring of confidence in the meaning and significance of life. Such courage is an underground river, flowing far beneath the shifting events of one's experience, keeping alive a thousand little springs of action."

I think that we must do our best to face death with dignity. I hope that I can be strong when my time comes. A true hero in facing death was Senator Hubert Humphrey of Minnesota, once vice-president of the United States and, in 1968, candidate for the presidency against Richard Nixon. Ten years later, as he faced the final onslaught of death by cancer at his house on the shore of Lake Waverly, near Minneapolis, Senator Humphrey's glowing optimism, even ebullience, was an example of true heroism I will never forget. I remember how it was said of him that in his splendid career as a liberal he taught us how to live, and that in his magnificent battle with cancer he taught us later how to die. I hope that I learned something from his example and can emulate it when my time comes.

I believe with Dr. Thurman that "death is an event in life. It is something that occurs *in* life rather than something that occurs *to* life." Death is but one of many occurrences in life, "none of which exhausts life or determines it." I believe, too, "that what a man discovers about the meaning of life . . . need not undergo any change as he meets death." So I go calmly on with my life. Keeping as busy as my health allows, I press on with my modest efforts at striving and achieving.

Above all, I have faith in God. Dr. Thurman has looked at the fear of death and reminded us of the infinite power of divine grace. "When I *walk* through the *valley* of the *shadow* of death," he writes, alluding to the Twenty-third Psalm, "I will fear no evil because God is with me." God's presence "makes the difference, because it cancels out the threatening element of the threat, the evil element of evil." God does not promise a pleasant end; far from it. "Of course I may linger, or I may die; I may suffer acutely, or all my days may rest upon an undercurrent of muted agony." Nevertheless, God is sufficient: "I shall not be overcome; God is with me. My awareness of God's presence may sound like magic, it may seem to some to be the merest childlike superstition, but it meets my need and is at once the source of my comfort and the heart of my peace."

AFTERWARDS
ANDY RAZAF

Death is a time of great sadness for family and friends of the deceased. In this poem, Andy Razaf, who died in 1973, tells us not to weep, for the body is just a shell and eternal peace has begun.

When death draws down the veil and is done,
And you gaze on my features, one by one . . .
Say to thyself, "This body laying here
Is but the shell of him I loved so dear.
He, at this moment, dwells amongst the blest,
Free from all cares, all dangers and unrest.
Thus, he has found but fortune in this calm,
So then, why weep at this, Life's sweetest balm?"

And what is sadder than this life of ours,
That buds and blooms and withers like flowers?
To me, it is a heartless, ugly thing,
A month of winter to each day of spring.
So when the last sleep seals my weary eyes,
To put an end to all my woes and sighs,
'Twill mean eternal peace and joys begun,
When death draws down the veil—and all is done.

THE CIRCLE OF FAITH
TIAUDRA RILEY

I
have faith in you
because I trust you. I trust you
because I like you. I like you because I
understand you. I understand you because I
care for you. I care for you because I am a part
of you. I am a part of you because I depend on
you. I depend on you because I am honest with
you. I am honest with you because I can talk to
you. I can talk to you because I am for you. I
am for you because I need you. I need you
because I love you. I love you because I
believe in you. I believe in you
because I have faith in
you. . . .

FROM MALCOLM X TO EL-HAJJ MALIK EL-SHABAZZ
MALCOLM X (EL-HAJJ MALIK EL-SHABAZZ)

Malcolm X is one of the most misunderstood black leaders of the twentieth century. Today he is remembered more for his political ideology—black nationalism—and for his eloquent rejection of racism than for his struggles for salvation. Over the course of his life, Malcolm X was able to transform himself completely, from a hoodlum to a minister who called whites "blue-eyed devils" to a Sunni Muslim who believed in the brotherhood of all mankind. His pilgrimage to Mecca in 1964 was a spiritual turning point. There, Malcolm X tossed out his old race-based religious principles and embraced "color-blind" Islam as practiced throughout the world. In doing so, he became El-Hajj Malik El-Shabazz. This letter, which he sent to colleagues back in New York, reminds us that change is a process of spiritual growth.

Never have I witnessed such sincere hospitality and the overwhelming spirit of true brotherhood as is practiced by people of all colors and races here in this Ancient Holy Land, the home of Abraham, Muhammad, and all the other prophets of the Holy Scriptures. For the past week, I have been utterly speechless and spellbound by the graciousness I see displayed all around me by people *of all colors.*

I have been blessed to visit the Holy City of Mecca. I have made my seven circuits around the Ka'ba,* led by a young *Mutawaf* named Muhammad. I drank water from the well of Zem Zem. I ran seven times back and forth between the hills of Mt. Al-Safa and Al-Marwah. I have prayed in the ancient city of Mina, and I have prayed on Mt. Arafat.

There were tens of thousands of pilgrims, from all over the world. They were of all colors, from blue-eyed blonds to black-skinned Africans. But we were all participating in the same ritual, displaying a spirit of unity and brotherhood that my experiences in America had led me to believe never could exist between the white and the non-white.

America needs to understand Islam, because this is the one religion

---

* The sacred house in Mecca around which pilgrims circumambulate during hajj. The building, toward which Muslims worldwide turn in prayer five times daily, is not worshipped by the faithful, but regarded as a spiritual center.

that erases from its society the race problem. Throughout my travels in the Muslim world, I have met, talked to, and even eaten with people who in America would have been considered "white"—but the "white" attitude was removed from their minds by the religion of Islam. I have never before seen *sincere* and *true* brotherhood practiced by all colors together, irrespective of their color.

You may be shocked by these words coming from me. But on this pilgrimage, what I have seen, and experienced, has forced me to *rearrange* much of my thought-patterns previously held, and to *toss aside* some of my previous conclusions. This was not too difficult for me. Despite my firm convictions, I have been always a man who tries to face facts, and to accept the reality of life as new experience and new knowledge unfolds it. I have always kept an open mind, which is necessary to the flexibility that must go hand in hand with every form of intelligent search for truth.

During the past eleven days here in the Muslim world, I have eaten from the same plate, drunk from the same glass, and slept in the same bed (or on the same rug)—while praying to the *same* God—with fellow Muslims, whose eyes were the bluest of blue, whose hair was the blondest of blond, and whose skin was the whitest of white. And in the *words* and in the *actions* and in the *deeds* of the "white" Muslims, I felt the same sincerity that I felt among the black African Muslims of Nigeria, Sudan, and Ghana.

We were *truly* all the same (brothers)—because their belief in one God had removed the "white" from their *minds*, the "white" from their *behavior*, and the "white" from their *attitude*.

I could see from this, that perhaps if white Americans could accept the Oneness of God, then perhaps, too, they could accept *in reality* the Oneness of Man—and cease to measure, and hinder, and harm others in terms of their "differences" in color.

With racism plaguing America like an incurable cancer, the so-called "Christian" white American heart should be more receptive to a proven solution to such a destructive problem. Perhaps it could be in time to save America from imminent disaster—the same destruction brought upon Germany by racism that eventually destroyed the Germans themselves.

Each hour here in the Holy Land enables me to have greater spiritual insights into what is happening in America between black and white. The American Negro never can be blamed for his racial animosities—he is only reacting to four hundred years of the conscious racism of the American whites. But as racism leads America up the suicide path, I do believe, from the experiences that I have had with them, that the whites of the younger generation, in the colleges and universities, will see the handwriting on the wall and many of them will turn to the *spiritual* path of *truth*—the *only* way left to America to ward off the disaster that racism inevitably must lead to.

Never have I been so highly honored. Never have I been made to feel more humble and unworthy. Who would believe the blessings that have been heaped upon an *American Negro?* A few nights ago, a man who would be called in America a "white" man, a United Nations diplomat, an ambassador, a companion of kings, gave me *his* hotel suite, *his* bed. By this man, His Excellency Prince Faisal, who rules this Holy Land, was made aware of my presence here in Jedda. The very next morning, Prince Faisal's son, in person, informed me that by the will and decree of his esteemed father, I was to be a State Guest.

The Deputy Chief of Protocol himself took me before the Hajj Court. His Holiness Sheikh Muhammad Harkon himself okayed my visit to Mecca. His Holiness gave me two books on Islam, with his personal seal and autograph, and he told me that he prayed that I would be a successful preacher of Islam in America. A car, a driver, and a guide have been placed at my disposal, making it possible for me to travel about this Holy Land almost at will. The government provides air-conditioned quarters and servants in each city that I visit. Never would I have even thought of dreaming that I would ever be a recipient of such honors— honors that in America would be bestowed upon a King—not a Negro.

All praise is due to Allah, the Lord of all the Worlds.

Sincerely,
El-Hajj Malik El-Shabazz
(Malcolm X)

KWANZAA AND ITS PRINCIPLES
ERIC V. COPAGE

Kwanzaa, the seven-day African American holiday celebrated annually between December 26 and January 1, is a synthesis of African harvest festivals. But there is no festival known as Kwanzaa in any African society; it is purely an African American creation, launched at the height of the civil rights and Black Power era.

Kwanzaa, today observed by some eighteen million people in the United States, was invented in 1966 by Maulana Karenga, who is now a professor of black studies at California State University in Long Beach. Kwanzaa means "first fruits of the harvest" in Swahili, the language spoken by forty-nine million people in East Africa and the Congo region.

The holiday is intended to reestablish blacks' connections with their African origins, impart a sense of their ancestors' agrarian past, and provide a culturally viable alternative to the "white Christmas" dreamed of by many. In his writings, Karenga explained that Kwanzaa would "give Blacks an opportunity to celebrate themselves."

In the 1960s, he developed a value system he called Kawaida, meaning "tradition" or "reason" in Swahili. At the core of the system were seven principles that he called the Nguzo Saba. Karenga believed these guidelines for living—which today govern Kwanzaa—formed the underlying values that black people must adopt in order to "rescue and reconstruct our history and lives."

Intended from the beginning as a noncommercial holiday, Kwanzaa is a cultural celebration with a difference—it has its own value system. Here are guidelines for celebrating the holiday, which focuses on principles dealing with self-mastery and empathy.

If you want to adhere strictly to the Kwanzaa program as Karenga conceived it, here is what you need to have and what they mean:

1. *Mazao:* fruits and vegetables, which stand for the product of unified effort.

2. *Mkeka:* a straw place mat, which represents the reverence for tradition.

3. *Vibunzi:* an ear of corn for each child in the family.

4. *Zawadi:* simple gifts, preferably related to education or to things African or African-influenced.

5. *Kikombe cha umoja:* a communal cup for the libation (I like to look at this as a kind of homage to past, present, and future black Americans).

6. *Kinara:* a seven-branched candleholder, which symbolizes the continent and peoples of Africa.

7. *Mishumaa saba:* the seven candles, each one symbolizing one of the Nguzo Saba, or seven principles, that black Americans should live by on a daily basis and which are reinforced during Kwanzaa.

On each day of Kwanzaa, a family member lights a candle, then discusses one of those seven principles. The principles, along with Karenga's elucidation of them in 1965, are:

1. *Umoja (Unity):* To strive for and maintain unity in the family, community, nation, and race.

2. *Kujichagulia (Self-determination):* To define ourselves, name ourselves, create for ourselves, and speak for ourselves instead of being defined, named, created for, and spoken for by others.

3. *Ujima (Collective Work and Responsibility):* To build and maintain our community together, and to make our sisters' and brothers' problems our problems and to solve them together.

4. *Ujamma (Cooperative Economics):* To build and maintain our own stores, shops, and other businesses and to profit from them together.

5. *Nia (Purpose):* To make our collective vocation the building and developing of our community in order to restore our people to their traditional greatness.

6. *Kuumba (Creativity):* To do always as much as we can, in whatever way we can, in order to leave our community more beautiful and beneficial than we inherited it.

7. *Imani (Faith):* To believe with all our heart in our people, our parents, our teachers, our leaders, and in the righteousness and victory of our struggle.

The next-to-last day of the holiday, December 31, is marked by a lavish feast, the *Kwanzaa Karamu*, which, in keeping with the theme of black unity, may draw on the cuisines of the Caribbean, Africa, South

America . . . wherever Africans were taken. In addition to food, the Karamu is an opportunity for a confetti storm of cultural expression: dance and music, readings, remembrances. Here is Karenga's suggested way of conducting a Karamu:

1. *Kukaribisha (Welcoming)*
   Introductory remarks and recognition of distinguished guests and elders.
   Cultural expression through songs, music, dance, unity circles, etc.
2. *Kukumbuka (Remembering)*
   Reflections of a man, a woman, and a child.
   Cultural expression
3. *Kuchunguza tena na kutoa ahadi tena (Reassessment and Recommitment)*
   Introduction of distinguished guest lecturer, and short talk.
4. *Kushungilla (Rejoicing)*
   Tamshi la tambiko (libation statement)
   Kikombe cha umoja (unity cup)
   Kutoa majina (calling names of family ancestors and black heroes)
   Ngoma (drums)
   Karamu (feast)
   Cultural expression
5. *Tamshi la tutaonana* (Farewell Statement)

THE HIGHEST POWER
SUSAN L. TAYLOR

Susan Taylor, editor-in-chief of Essence *magazine since 1981, writes monthly editorials that serve as a source of inspiration and self-affirmation for thousands of readers. Here she focuses on the power within.*

There is a force that supports all existence. It is the energy that governs every aspect of the universe and orders every cell in every living thing.

It is unfailing, always at work. It is our source and our substance, an unlimited power that we call by many names: Jehovah, Yahweh, Allah, Divine Intelligence, Spirit, God.

Most of us agree that there is a Highest Power. We testify to that truth. But to experience the inner peace we are seeking, we must do more than speak and sing its name to the heavens. We must keep the awareness that the Power lives within us. It's difficult to sustain trust in the unseen when we're taught to believe only in what is visible. So we put our faith in the material world, when the greatest power is in the nonvisible, spiritual world.

We all want material things, and we work hard to get them. But we surrender the very freedom we are seeking when we believe possessions will make us happy, secure or content. We will always hunger for more when we look to the material world to sustain us. We can see the result of this misplaced faith all around us. It fuels most of the pain and suffering in the world. Even the wealthiest people don't feel they have enough money. Most want more, and some use any means to get it. They create wars, foul the environment, hook children on drugs, market cancer-causing foods, close factories and ship jobs offshore where even poorer people can be exploited—all to make more money.

When we believe that money gives us our essential power, we let down our moral guard and give up our humanity. We no longer concern ourselves with preserving and enhancing life, so our divinity is stifled and demeaned. When we believe our power is in the material world, we never feel quite strong enough or confident enough or attractive enough to live fully and freely. We always feel that something is lacking, that we should have more. We will violate ourselves trying to boost our self-image so that people will admire us more.

We all want people to like and admire us, but when we *need* their confirmation or adulation, we don't live our lives on our own terms. We are focused outward, intent on surrounding ourselves with the trappings they undoubtedly admire. We were not created to please people. We were created to please God, to recognize the Highest Power in ourselves and make it manifest in our daily lives.

The Highest Power is love and it protects us and all of creation. Love is the very nature of the energy we call God. It is the force that orders this universe and is greater than we can fully comprehend. It choreographs the movements of the more than 200 billion stars, including our sun, hurtling through space—all spinning, spiraling, whirling and revolving in billions of galaxies like the one we live in. Imagine such a power, ordering planets and comets and moons through aeons, in a perfect cosmic dance. Our African ancestors discovered the laws of life thousands of years ago. They understood that the same power that governs the cosmos and protects the lilies of the field sustains us too.

Love yourself as a beautiful and necessary light that was created by God. Remember that the Highest Power is alive within you. It is alive as you. You are human and divine. As is true of the universe, nothing about you is haphazard or accidental. Know that the channels for your existence were put into place in the very beginning. You were created on purpose, with a purpose. You are exactly who and where you need to be, with all the power you need to take your next steps forward. Accept yourself as you are, and make any changes in your life based on your discoveries of what is best for you, what nourishes you and celebrates God through you.

Lift up your faith in yourself and in the miracle that is your being. You never doubt that tomorrow the sun will rise. Have faith that you, too, are an important part of creation. You, too, are protected by love. Don't put your faith in transitory things: They are here today and gone tomorrow. Put your faith in God, the unseen source of all goodness. Make a ritual of spending quiet time, time to focus inward so that you can experience God, the Highest Power, the source of wisdom and strength in you. The Holy Spirit that awaits you at the center of your being.

WE'VE COME THIS FAR BY FAITH
ALBERT A. GOODSON

We've come this far by faith
Leaning on the Lord,
Trusting in His Holy Word,

He's never failed me yet.
Oh, can't turn back,
We've come this far by faith.

Don't be discouraged with trouble in your life
He'll bear your burdens and move all misery and strife.

Thank God, We've come this far by faith
Leaning on the Lord,
Trusting in His Holy Word,
He's never failed me yet.
Oh, can't turn around,
We've come this far by faith.

❧

Keep the faith, baby!

—*Adam Clayton Powell Jr.*

❧

THE BOOK OF
EMPATHY

FAMILY

Nothing embraces us more lovingly, from cradle to grave, than family. It nurtures us, protects us, grounds us, eases us out into the world, and provides us with links to history and to our future. We gather on holidays, and we pay homage to our bonds through reunions that bring together dozens, or hundreds, from across the nation and even from overseas.

The family is our nest in just about every stage of life. During our formative years, family love and support help guide us over the rougher spots of our development. Later in life, we still turn to the family for love and understanding.

We are, in a sense, family emissaries. Most of us even carry our relatives with us, in wallet photographs. Resemblances can be strikingly apparent to those we meet—and to ourselves when, in adulthood, we finally realize that we *are* our parents. Practically, anyway.

Still, few people fully appreciate the miracle that the black family represents, considering what it has endured.* From the outset, slavery not only severed familial ties to Africa and to age-old societies, it fragmented families in America, placing no value on black kinship. For example, to punish a recalcitrant slave or simply to make a profit, a slave owner might tear apart an entire black family, separating husband and wife, or selling off children, parents, siblings, or grandparents.

Yet the black family survived even this. After the Civil War, African Americans searched far and wide to rejoin families or to officially pronounce wedding vows in places where laws had prohibited slave marriages. The more fortunate families regrouped and grew stronger, offering some protection from often violent racial discrimination not just in the South but in many other sections of the country.

Today, the black family, as resilient as ever, continues to thrive. At

* Among the first African American families was that of Antonio and Isabella, who arrived in Jamestown, Virginia, around 1619, and their son, William, the first known black child born in English North America, in 1624. In his book *Before the Mayflower*, Lerone Bennett Jr. reports that Antonio and Isabella were not slaves, but were brought to America as indentured servants. They named their son after a local farmer. Some years later, the colonies made race a determining factor in slavery. Enslaved Africans were then imported by the thousands from villages along the West African coast.

the time of the signing of the Declaration of Independence, there were a half-million blacks in America, most of them slaves. By the end of the twentieth century, the number of black family households in the United States will grow to 8.5 million, averaging more than three persons per family, according to projections of the U.S. Census Bureau. These statistics, though, are merely cold calculations that say nothing, really, of the nature of black families, whose relations often transcend bloodlines.

Black families come in all shapes and sizes—as small as two persons (a parent and child) or as large as 20-and-then-some. Black families are not limited to spouses, siblings, children, uncles, aunts, cousins, grandparents, and in-laws, but are also graced by a host of "virtual relatives"—godparents and their godchildren, "would-be aunts and uncles," "should-be brothers and sisters," "practically cousins," and even "ain't really related" relatives—all members of extended families that sometimes appear to stretch as far as forever, possibly even back to Africa. Indeed, they sometimes do, as you will see in the case of the American woman who discovered her Mende tribal roots by singing a song that had been passed down for centuries. You might say her "family of the heart" extends from Georgia to Sierra Leone and from the 1790s through the 1990s.

In this chapter you will read stories about extended families, poems dedicated to expectant mothers, current mothers, and ancestors. Also included are folk rhymes, stories on fatherhood, and some issues faced by family members. All of the stories focus on the blessings of the African American family.

A stream cannot rise higher than its source. The home is no rarer, purer and sweeter than the mothers in those homes. A race is but a total of families. The nation is the aggregate of its homes.

—*Anna J. Cooper*

AFRICAN AMERICAN MAMA-TO-BE PRAYER
CHRISENA COLEMAN

A prayer for pregnancy.

Now I lay me down to rest,
may baby lay comfy in my nest.

A healthy boy or healthy girl,
another blessing into this world.

If dreams really do come true,
Mama dreams only the best for you.

Ten fingers, ten toes, and a heart of gold,
intelligent and kind with a God-fearing soul.

I had a dream that you were already here,
Mama smothered you with kisses,
tender love, and lots of care.

We played by day and read books at night,
You looked just like GrandMa—such a pretty sight.

You learned about the family and our African kin,
You laughed, and smiled, and gave me a big grin.

The happiest baby in all the land,
A perfect shade of brown, just like a honey tan.

Now it's time to really sleep,
I pray all dreams are ours to keep.

EXTENDED FAMILIES
BARBARA EKLOF

Extended family—aunts, uncles, nephews, nieces, cousins, and other relatives who are not blood relations—are all important members of the black family, stretching back through slavery and beyond: to Africa. Each relative plays a special role in keeping African American culture intact.

The call to make families may very well be God's gift. The generosity of our people often expands our families even more, when we invite others into our folds. Aunt Mabel may not really be kin, but your grandmother's lifelong pal. And maybe Kalil isn't your actual blood brother, but the son of a struggling former neighbor, whom your folks "took in" long ago. Yet, no less love is spilled upon these pseudo-family members than on the generations of grandparents, aunts, uncles, cousins, nieces, nephews, and in-laws you adore because they are all members of your extended family dynasty.

Unfortunately, the proximity of African American extended family members was forever challenged and changed by migration. Aside from the African slave trade's creation of the greatest forced migration in world history and the mammoth migrations of American slaves to wherever southern agricultural development flourished, even after slavery, members of our forefamilies dispersed across the map in an ongoing search for economic opportunities and an escape from racism. And now, in our contemporary world, mobility, urbanization, and differing lifestyles are still challenging the development of extended family dynasties.

Fortunately, African American families have faithfully upheld the tradition of family reunions, or homecomings as a celebratory means of validating and reinforcing our roots. Differing from family gatherings abruptly inspired by funerals, a homecoming is the long-anticipated *planned* gathering of kin that honors its ever-growing and ever-improving circle of love.

When I was a child nicknamed Bobbie, my family's reunions were held in Littleton, North Carolina, when the roads still kicked up dust and outhouses kicked my ego. For a city kid, I remembered reunions at Grandma's home as being held in a "free" place. That's how I thought of that breathe-easy, tree-lined amusement park tickling cool grass between my toes and crowded with merry-go-rounds of startling introductions—"You're who? Grandma Pat's brother-in-law's cousin's child?" And if heaven had a taste, it would have to be like those six-layer pineapple upside-down cakes that didn't last a minute.

But the passing years were marked with tarred roads, indoor plumbing, and reunions too grand for Grandma's advancing years to handle. That's when my father, her eldest of seven, became the family patriarch—since my grandfather had long since passed away—and the reunions were relocated to his huge, tree-lined backyard in Baltimore (my parents had divorced). Days before the celebration, Daddy and the crew would mow grass, trim shrubbery, set out picnic tables, spit-shine the brick grill, and anchor the big yellow tent off to the side. That's where I'd eventually settle; that's where bushels of spicy steamed crabs begged for mercy.

As with the ancestors, feasting remained synonymous with celebration. On the big reunion day, family members moseyed into the yard in groves as excited greetings welcomed: "Go get some food! Bar-be-cue's on platters by the grill; potato salad, baked beans, corn on the cob and stuff's over there; cakes and pies are coming in heaps; and crabs and coolers are under the tent by Bobbie. Go say hello."

Then, the passing years were marked by the family youngsters becoming parents, new in-laws and children expanding the dynasty, and a more elaborate weekend-long family reunions. Oh, they still ended up at Daddy's house, but the first day hosted a banquet and talent show in a facility hung with the "Royster Family" banner. Among the carnival of entertainment, my younger son, Carl, risked joints and limbs showing off break-dance moves, my daughter, Zelinda, performed death-defying leaps and twirls in leotards and tights, and my elder son, Bill, stunned us with a rhythm-and-blues guitar medley. That's one thing about having the family as an audience: Regardless of your talent and level of expertise, you're made to feel like pros.

That was a good thing because years later, I sang. Actually, I was obsessed with reworking the words of the song "You Are So Beautiful to Me" to honor my father as a surprise. At the reunion, I asked him to join me on stage, where he sat by my side. I sang, Daddy began to weep, and soon we embraced earnestly and lovingly on stage. Afterward, my Aunt Erleen, in tears herself, said she'd never seen my father cry.

I'm blessed with the tradition of family reunions, for the feeling of belonging to a loving flock of folks who enjoy belonging to me. But mostly, I'm blessed that that intimate public venue had offered me the opportunity to show my father just how much I loved him. As God would have it, that was to be my father's last family reunion on earth. He died shortly afterward, taking "You Are So Beautiful to Me" with him.

THANKSGIVING IS THE GREATEST HOLIDAY
ROBERT C. MAYNARD

Robert C. Maynard (1937–93), bought the Oakland Tribune *in 1983, becoming the first African American to own a major metropolitan newspaper. Under his leadership, the daily newspaper built a solid national reputation. In addition to other duties, Maynard wrote a twice-weekly syndicated column, drawing much of his material from his own family life. In this piece, published November 21, 1982, he recalls how his family celebrated Thanksgiving and shares some of the lessons he learned from the holiday.*

NOVEMBER 21, 1982—Thanksgiving. To hear the word when we were children was enough to swell the heart with joy. It might be July, and someone would make some vague reference to Thanksgiving, and we would stop and reflect with pleasure.

Thanksgiving was not a holiday to our household. It was a concept. Much planning went into it, the whole family was involved in all the preparatory chores, and we seemed to celebrate it for about a week.

No holiday bore for us the significance of Thanksgiving. We paid very little attention to Christmas because my father's religious doctrine dismissed as fallacy the idea that anyone knew when Christ was born. Easter suffered similar defects, in my father's way of thinking.

July 4 was always a great deal of fun and so was Labor Day, both of them occasions for fine family picnics. We celebrated birthdays with great family fervor, but with six children, it must have seemed to my parents there was always a birthday celebration going on in our home.

Nothing made us feel the richness of oneness as Thanksgiving did. It must have been the combination of fabulous food and fabulous faith.

Forgive me for talking about the food first. My father and his younger brother migrated to New York toward the end of World War I. Their parents had been able to send them off with a few dollars, but it was assumed they would be earning money soon after they arrived in the big city of dreams.

Instead, it took awhile for them to find work. They lived in a furnished flat and neither of them knew enough about how to cook "to boil an egg," as my father put it so often in telling the tales of his youthful adventures.

Their money ran out quickly because they were eating every meal in restaurants. They nearly starved to death. When my father met my mother and discovered she was a masterly cook, he took it as a sure sign their marriage had been arranged in heaven.

My father was a great believer in the philosophy that no life experience is for naught. Each experience, no matter how painful, held a life lesson for him. So he always taught us. The only problem was that sometimes they were his life experiences but his children were the beneficiaries of the lesson.

That's the way it was with cooking. Even though it was he who almost starved to death, it was we who had to learn to cook. He died not knowing much more about cooking than he knew when he came to New York a half-century before. But he laid down an edict that no son of his would pass his 14th birthday without being able to produce all or most of a major meal.

He might have made the same rule for my sisters but he did not. It was assumed they would learn to cook in the natural course of things. But he was taking no chance on any son of his finding himself in a faraway place unable to fend for himself at a stove.

My mother and sisters were our tutors and tormentors in the kitchen. Each of us boys was oriented to the kitchen first by becoming experts in pot and pan washing. When we displayed due diligence in that department, we moved on to vegetable peeling with a paring knife.

Chickens and turkeys came from the butcher shop in those days with their feathers firmly in place and it fell to us boys to master the art of feather removal. (I never mastered that one.) Little by little, you got a chance to cook something under the watchful eye of my mother and my sisters.

The day you presented a dish to the whole family was the day you passed in our house from useless boy to promising young man. That kitchen was its own form of school, and the great annual celebration of the virtues of the institution of the kitchen was Thanksgiving Day.

We scrubbed vegetables, chopped onions and scurried about from early morning in an atmosphere of family euphoria. The aromas told us "the bird" was nearing readiness and that spurred us to bring it all together in a grand finale orchestrated by my mother.

I remember as if it were yesterday the Thanksgiving I was assigned to make the marshmallow sweet potatoes all by myself. I burned the marshmallows the first time and got it almost right the second time. When the dish reached the table, my father tasted it and declared that he was pleased that his last born might actually learn to cook. No medal could have pleased me more.

My father's faith was simple, but it was the center of his being. He lived to worship God and he lived for his family. He cared for little besides church and home. All this came to fit nicely with Thanksgiving.

In this holiday he found the nexus of his love of God and family. He was a man in a constant state of thanksgiving. He felt richly blessed by the simple rewards of health and a home.

So at Thanksgiving, he encouraged us to share with each other those things for which we felt most thankful from the previous year. Usually, we were most grateful for good grades, but he stretched us and pushed us to think deeper and search for the really important reasons to be thankful.

That turned out to be difficult to do without thinking about some of our disappointments, things we had to admit had not turned out as well as we might have hoped. He always wanted to hear about those because he always wanted to know what we planned to do to make our disappointments eventually become triumphs.

Well, we would always say to that question, we will try harder.

Yes, yes, he would always say, but how? How?

At such times, he would often exhort us to have a bold spirit and an inquiring mind. None of us ever asked him exactly what a bold spirit was. We surmised from the tone of his voice when he said those words that he wanted us to think first of what had to be done and think only after that about the obstacles.

I remember one of my sisters at the Thanksgiving table describing some excruciating challenge she faced as a freshman in college. She seemed truly daunted by all she faced. She finished describing the challenge and there was a long silence. Finally, she asked my father what she should do.

"A little more prayer will take care of it," he said.

In truth, although he exhorted us to prayer and faith, he never allowed us to overlook the benefits of preparation and hard work. That to me is what was so fabulous about his faith. He gave God the credit for all his successes and ours, but he was not about to allow any of us to say we would pray instead of study for an exam.

He believed in rigorous study and the applied use of knowledge. Knowledge that was acquired and not shared was no knowledge at all as far as he was concerned. One of his favorite phrases was "educated fool," a term he often used to describe people with impressive degrees and an unimpressive degree of common sense.

I still awaken excited on Thanksgiving morning. I still love to make marshmallow sweet potatoes and dressing with mushrooms and sausage. But I rarely find myself thinking of those objects purely as food. They have become, for me, much as they were intended to be, symbols of

Thanksgiving in its truest sense, a thankfulness for blessings that have no name.

MY MOTHER'S DAY REFLECTION
ANDY RAZAF

We are forever in debt to our mothers.

There's a check that I've cashed on mother
And it's long been over-drawn,
On the bank of love and sacrifice,
From the day that I was born;
A check in terms of endless care,
Of sleeping nights and tears,
Signed by her hand that has toiled for me
From childhood to manhood years.

This check has drawn so much interest
'Till its total leaves me dismayed,
For I know if I live a million years
It can never be fully repaid.
The priceless love of a mother
Can never be bought with gold;
It's God's greatest gift from heaven,
A blessing that cannot be sold.

Now since this is true, darling mother,
It leaves me with just one plan:
I'll make you happy by doing my best,
And always playing the man.
I'll never forget or neglect you;
I'll write (if it's only a line)—

May heaven bless and protect you,
Wonderful mother of mine.

THE WIFE OF HIS YOUTH
CHARLES W. CHESNUTT

Published in 1899, this story first appeared in a collection of color-line stories by Charles W. Chesnutt (1858–1932), the most popular African American fiction writer at the beginning of the twentieth century. The story is about a man who moved from his black Southern roots to Groveland (patterned after Cleveland), Ohio, where he joined an exclusive, light-skinned social set. Along came former slave Liza Jane, on a twenty-five-year search for her lost husband.

Chesnutt's story has tragic overtones. Nevertheless, it tells of the reunion of a husband and wife. Familial loyalty was—and still is—a moral imperative in the black community. After the Civil War, many thousands of newly freed slaves traveled far and wide to reestablish connections and save their fragmented families.

I

Mr. Ryder was going to give a ball. There were several reasons why this was an opportune time for such an event.

Mr. Ryder might aptly be called the dean of the Blue Veins. The original Blue Veins were a little society of colored persons organized in a certain Northern city shortly after the war. Its purpose was to establish and maintain correct social standards among a people whose social condition presented almost unlimited room for improvement. By accident, combined perhaps with some natural affinity, the society consisted of individuals who were, generally speaking, more white than black. Some envious outsider made the suggestion that no one was eligible for membership who was not white enough to show blue veins. The suggestion was readily adopted by those who were not of the favored few, and since that time the society, though possessing a longer and more pretentious name, had been known far and wide as the "Blue Vein Society," and its members as the "Blue Veins."

The Blue Veins did not allow that any such requirement existed for admission to their circle, but, on the contrary, declared that character and culture were the only things considered; and that if most of their members were light-colored, it was because such persons, as a rule, had had better opportunities to qualify themselves for membership. Opinions differed, too, as to the usefulness of the society. There were those who had been known to assail it violently as a glaring example of the very prejudice from which the colored race had suffered most; and later, when such critics had succeeded in getting on the inside, they had been heard to maintain with zeal and earnestness that the society was a lifeboat, an anchor, a bulwark and a shield—a pillar of cloud by day and of fire by night, to guide their people through the social wilderness. Another alleged prerequisite for Blue Vein membership was that of free birth; and while there was really no such requirement, it is doubtless true that very few of the members would have been unable to meet it if there had been. If there were one or two of the older members who had come up from the South and from slavery, their history presented enough romantic circumstances to rob their servile origin of its grosser aspects.

While there were no such tests of eligibility, it is true that the Blue Veins had their notions on these subjects, and that not all of them were equally liberal in regard to the things they collectively disclaimed. Mr. Ryder was one of the most conservative. Though he had not been among the founders of the society, but had come in some years later, his genius for social leadership was such that he had speedily become its recognized adviser and head, the custodian of its standards, and the preserver of its traditions. He shaped its social policy, was active in providing for its entertainment, and when the interest fell off, as it sometimes did, he fanned the embers until they burst again into a cheerful flame.

There were still other reasons for his popularity. While he was not as white as some of the Blue Veins, his appearance was such as to confer distinction upon them. His features were of a refined type, his hair was almost straight; he was always neatly dressed; his manners were irreproachable, and his morals above suspicion. He had come to Groveland a young man, and obtaining employment in the office of a railroad company as messenger had in time worked himself up to the position of stationery clerk, having charge of the distribution of the office supplies for the whole company. Although the lack of early training had hindered the orderly development of a naturally fine mind, it had not prevented him from doing a great deal of reading or from forming decidedly literary tastes. Poetry was his passion. He could repeat whole pages of the great English poets; and if his pronunciation was sometimes faulty, his eye, his voice, his gestures, would respond to the changing sentiment with a precision that revealed a poetic soul and disarmed criticism. He was economical, and had saved money; he owned and occupied a very comfortable house on a respectable street. His residence was handsomely furnished, containing among other things a good library, especially rich in poetry, a piano, and some choice engravings. He generally shared his house with some young couple, who looked after his wants and were company for him; for Mr. Ryder was a single man. In the early days of his connection with the Blue Veins he had been regarded as quite a catch, and young ladies and their mothers had maneuvered with much ingenuity to capture him. Not, however, until Mrs. Molly Dixon visited Groveland had any woman ever made him wish to change his condition to that of a married man.

Mrs. Dixon had come to Groveland from Washington in the spring, and before the summer was over she had won Mr. Ryder's heart. She possessed many attractive qualities. She was much younger than he; in fact, he was old enough to have been her father, though no one knew exactly how old he was. She was whiter than he, and better educated. She had moved in the best colored society of the country, at Washington, and had taught in the schools of that city. Such a superior person had been eagerly welcomed to the Blue Vein Society, and had taken a leading part in its activities. Mr. Ryder had at first been attracted by her charms of person, for she was very good-looking and not over twenty-five; then by her refined manners and the vivacity of her wit. Her husband had been a government clerk, and at his death had left a considerable life insurance. She was visiting friends in Groveland, and, finding the town and the people to her liking, had prolonged her stay indefinitely. She had not seemed displeased at Mr. Ryder's attentions, but on the contrary had given him every proper encouragement; indeed, a younger and less cautious man would long since have spoken. But he had made up his mind, and had only to determine the time when he would ask her to be his wife. He decided to give a ball in her honor, and at some time during the evening of the ball to offer her his heart and hand. He had no special fears about the outcome, but, with a little touch of romance, he wanted the surroundings to be in harmony with his own feelings when he should have received the answer he expected.

Mr. Ryder resolved that this ball should mark an epoch in the social history of Groveland. He knew, of course—no one could know better—the entertainments that had taken place in past years, and what must be done to surpass them. His ball must be worthy of the lady in whose honor it was to be given, and must, by the quality of its guests, set an example for the future. He had observed of late a growing liberality, almost a laxity, in social matters, even among members of his own set, and had several times been forced to meet in a social way persons whose complexions and callings in life were hardly up to the standard which he considered proper for the society to maintain. He had a theory of his own.

"I have no race prejudice," he would say, "but we people of mixed blood are ground between the upper and the nether millstone. Our fate lies between absorption by the white race and extinction in the black. The one doesn't want us yet, but may take us in time. The other would welcome us, but it would be for us a backward step. 'With malice towards none, with charity for all,' we must do the best we can for ourselves and those who are to follow us. Self-preservation is the first law of nature."

His ball would serve by its exclusiveness to counteract leveling tendencies, and his marriage with Mrs. Dixon would help to further the upward process of absorption he had been wishing and waiting for.

II

The ball was to take place on Friday night. The house had been put in order, the carpets covered with canvas, the halls and stairs decorated with palms and potted plants; and in the afternoon Mr. Ryder sat on his front porch, which the shade of a vine running up over a wire netting made a cool and pleasant lounging place. He expected to respond to the toast "The Ladies" at the supper, and from a volume of Tennyson—his favorite poet—was fortifying himself with apt quotations. The volume was open at "A Dream of Fair Women." His eyes fell on these lines, and he read them aloud to judge better of their effect:

> "At length I saw a lady within call,
>   Stiller than chisell'd marble, standing there;
> A daughter of the gods, divinely tall,
>   And most divinely fair."

He marked the verse, and turning the page read the stanza beginning—

> "O sweet pale Margaret,
>   O rare pale Margaret."

He weighed the passage a moment, and decided that it would not do. Mrs. Dixon was the palest lady he expected at the ball, and she was of a rather ruddy complexion, and of lively disposition and buxom build. So he ran over the leaves until his eye rested on the description of Queen Guinevere:

> "She seem'd a part of joyous Spring:
> A gown of grass-green silk she wore,
> Buckled with golden clasps before;
> A light-green tuft of plumes she bore
> Closed in a golden ring.

> "She look'd so lovely, as she sway'd
> The rein with dainty finger-tips,
> A man had given all other bliss,
> And all his worldly worth for this,
> To waste his whole heart in one kiss
> Upon her perfect lips."

As Mr. Ryder murmured these words audibly, with an appreciative thrill, he heard the latch of his gate click, and a light footfall sounding on the steps. He turned his head, and saw a woman standing before his door.

She was a little woman, not five feet tall, and proportioned to her height. Although she stood erect, and looked around her with very bright and restless eyes, she seemed quite old; for her face was crossed and recrossed with a hundred wrinkles, and around the edges of her bonnet could be seen protruding here and there a tuft of short gray wool. She wore a blue calico gown of ancient cut, a little red shawl fastened around her shoulders with an old-fashioned brass brooch, and a large bonnet profusely ornamented with faded red and yellow artificial flowers. And she was very black—so black that her toothless gums, revealed when she opened her mouth to speak, were not red, but blue. She looked like a bit of the old plantation life, summoned up from the past by the wave of a magician's wand, as the poet's fancy had called into being the gracious shapes of which Mr. Ryder had just been reading.

He rose from his chair and came over to where she stood.

"Good afternoon, madam," he said.

"Good evenin', suh," she answered, ducking suddenly with a quaint curtsy. Her voice was shrill and piping, but softened somewhat by age. "Is dis yere whar Mistuh Ryduh lib, suh?" she asked, looking around her doubtfully, and glancing into the open windows, through which some of the preparations for the evening were visible.

"Yes," he replied, with an air of kindly patronage, unconsciously flattered by her manner, "I am Mr. Ryder. Did you want to see me?"

"Yas, suh, ef I ain't 'sturbin' of you too much."

"Not at all. Have a seat over here behind the vine, where it is cool. What can I do for you?"

" 'Scuse me, suh," she continued, when she had sat down on the edge of a chair, " 'scuse me, suh, I's lookin' for my husban'. I heerd you wuz a big man an' had libbed heah a long time, an' I 'lowed you wouldn't min' ef I'd come roun' an' ax you ef you'd ever heerd of a merlatter man by de name er Sam Taylor 'quirin' roun' in de chu'ches ermongs' de people fer his wife 'Liza Jane?"

Mr. Ryder seemed to think for a moment.

"There used to be many such cases right after the war," he said, "but it has been so long that I have forgotten them. There are very few now. But tell me your story, and it may refresh my memory."

She sat back farther in her chair so as to be more comfortable, and folded her withered hands in her lap.

"My name's 'Liza," she began, " 'Liza Jane. W'en I wuz young I us'ter b'long ter Marse Bob Smif, down in ole Missoura. I wuz bawn down dere. W'en I wuz a gal I wuz married ter a man named Jim. But Jim died, an' after dat I married a merlatter man named Sam Taylor. Sam wuz freebawn, but his mammy and daddy died, an' de w'ite folks 'prenticed him ter my marster fer ter work fer 'im 'tel he wuz growed up. Sam worked in de fiel', an' I wuz de cook. One day Ma'y Ann, ole miss's maid, came rushin' out ter de kitchen, an' says she, ' 'Liza Jane, ole marse gwine sell yo' Sam down de ribber.'

" 'Go way f'm yere,' says I; 'my husban' 's free!'

" 'Don' make no diff'ence. I heerd ole marse tell ole miss he wuz gwine take yo' Sam 'way wid 'im ter-morrow, fer he needed money, an' he knowed whar he could git a t'ousan' dollars fer Sam an' no questions axed.'

"W'en Sam come home f'm de fiel' dat night, I tole him 'bout ole marse gwine steal 'im, an' Sam run erway. His time wuz mos' up, an' he swo' dat w'en he wuz twenty-one he would come back an' he'p me run erway, er else save up de money ter buy my freedom. An' I know he'd 'a' done it, fer he thought a heap er me, Sam did. But w'en he come back he didn' fin' me, fer I wuzn' dere. Ole marse had heerd dat I warned Sam, so he had me whip' an' sol' down de ribber.

"Den de wah broke out, an' w'en it wuz ober de cullud folks wuz scattered. I went back ter de ole home; but Sam wuzn' dere, an' I couldn' l'arn nuffin' 'bout 'im. But I knowed he'd be'n dere to look fer me an' hadn' foun' me, an' had gone erway ter hunt fer me.

"I's be'n lookin' fer 'im eber sence," she added simply, as though twenty-five years were but a couple of weeks, "an' I knows he's be'n lookin' fer me. Fer he sot a heap er sto' by me, Sam did, an' I know he's be'n huntin' fer me all dese years—'less'n he's be'n sick er sump'n, so he couldn' work, er out'n his head, so he couldn' 'member his promise. I went back down de ribber, fer I 'lowed he'd gone down dere lookin' fer me. I's be'n ter Noo Orleens, an' Atlanty, an' Charleston, an' Richmon'; an' w'en I'd be'n all ober de Souf I come ter de Norf. Fer I knows I'll fin' 'im some er dese days," she added softly, "er he'll fin' me, an' den we'll bofe be as happy in freedom as we wuz in de ole days befo' de wah." A smile stole over her withered countenance as she paused a moment, and her bright eyes softened into a faraway look.

This was the substance of the old woman's story. She had wandered a little here and there. Mr. Ryder was looking at her curiously when she finished.

"How have you lived all these years?" he asked.

"Cookin', suh. I's a good cook. Does you know anybody w'at needs a good cook, suh? I's stoppin' wid a cullud fam'ly roun' de corner yonder 'tel I kin git a place."

"Do you really expect to find your husband? He may be dead long ago."

She shook her head emphatically. "Oh no, he ain' dead. De signs an' de tokens tells me. I dremp three nights runnin' on'y dis las' week dat I foun' him."

"He may have married another woman. Your slave marriage would not have prevented him, for you never lived with him after the war, and without that your marriage doesn't count."

"Wouldn' make no diff'ence wid Sam. He wouldn' marry no yuther 'ooman 'tel he foun' out 'bout me. I knows it," she added. "Sump'n 's be'n tellin' me all dese years dat I's gwine fin' Sam 'fo' I dies."

"Perhaps he's outgrown you, and climbed up in the world where he wouldn't care to have you find him."

"No, indeed, suh," she replied, "Sam ain' dat kin' er man. He wuz good ter me, Sam wuz, but he wuzn' much good ter nobody e'se, fer he wuz one er de triflin'es' han's on de plantation. I 'spec's ter haf ter suppo't 'im w'en I fin' 'im, fer he nebber would work 'less'n he had ter. But den he wuz free, an' he didn' git no pay fer his work, an' I don' blame 'im much. Mebbe he's done better sence he run erway, but I ain' 'spectin' much."

"You may have passed him on the street a hundred times during the twenty-five years, and not have known him; time works great changes."

She smiled incredulously. "I'd know 'im 'mongs' a hund'ed men. Fer dey wuzn' no yuther merlatter man like my man Sam, an' I couldn' be mistook. I's toted his picture roun' wid me twenty-five years."

"May I see it?" asked Mr. Ryder. "It might help me to remember whether I have seen the original."

As she drew a small parcel from her bosom he saw that it was fastened to a string that went around her neck. Removing several wrappers, she brought to light an old-fashioned daguerreotype in a black case. He looked long and intently at the portrait. It was faded with time, but the features were still distinct, and it was easy to see what manner of man it had represented.

He closed the case, and with a slow movement handed it back to her.

"I don't know of any man in town who goes by that name," he said, "nor have I heard of anyone making such inquiries. But if you will leave me your address, I will give the matter some attention, and if I find out anything I will let you know."

She gave him the number of a house in the neighborhood, and went away, after thanking him warmly.

He wrote the address on the flyleaf of the volume of Tennyson, and, when she had gone, rose to his feet and stood looking after her curiously. As she walked down the street with mincing step, he saw several persons whom she passed turn and look back at her with a smile of kindly amusement. When she had turned the corner, he went upstairs to his bedroom, and stood for a long time before the mirror of his dressing case, gazing thoughtfully at the reflection of his own face.

III

At eight o'clock the ballroom was a blaze of light and the guests had begun to assemble, for there was a literary programme and some routine business of the society to be gone through with before the dancing. A black servant in evening dress waited at the door and directed the guests to the dressing rooms.

The occasion was long memorable among the colored people of the city; not alone for the dress and display, but for the high average of intelligence and culture that distinguished the gathering as a whole. There were a number of schoolteachers, several young doctors, three or four lawyers, some professional singers, an editor, a lieutenant in the

United States army spending his furlough in the city, and others in various polite callings; these were colored, though most of them would not have attracted even a casual glance because of any marked difference from white people. Most of the ladies were in evening costume, and dress coats and dancing pumps were the rule among the men. A band of string music, stationed in an alcove behind a row of palms, played popular airs while the guests were gathering.

The dancing began at half past nine. At eleven o'clock supper was served. Mr. Ryder had left the ballroom some little time before the intermission, but reappeared at the supper table. The spread was worthy of the occasion, and the guests did full justice to it. When the coffee had been served, the toastmaster, Mr. Solomon Sadler, rapped for order. He made a brief introductory speech, complimenting host and guests, and then presented in their order the toasts of the evening. They were responded to with a very fair display of after-dinner wit.

"The last toast," said the toastmaster, when he reached the end of the list, "is one which must appeal to us all. There is no one of us of the sterner sex who is not at some time dependent upon woman—in infancy for protection, in manhood for companionship, in old age for care and comforting. Our good host has been trying to live alone, but the fair faces I see around me tonight prove that he too is largely dependent upon the gentler sex for most that makes life worth living—the society and love of friends—and rumor is at fault if he does not soon yield entire subjection to one of them. Mr. Ryder will now respond to the toast—The Ladies."

There was a pensive look in Mr. Ryder's eyes as he took the floor and adjusted his eyeglasses. He began by speaking of woman as the gift of Heaven to man, and after some general observations on the relations of the sexes he said: "But perhaps the quality which most distinguishes woman is her fidelity and devotion to those she loves. History is full of examples, but has recorded none more striking than one which only today came under my notice."

He then related, simply but effectively, the story told by his visitor of the afternoon. He gave it in the same soft dialect, which came readily to his lips, while the company listened attentively and sympathetically. For the story had awakened a responsive thrill in many hearts. There were some present who had seen, and others who had heard their fathers and grandfathers tell, the wrongs and sufferings of this past generation, and all of them still felt, in their darker moments, the shadow hanging over them. Mr. Ryder went on:

"Such devotion and confidence are rare even among women. There are many who would have searched a year, some who would have waited five years, a few who might have hoped ten years; but for twenty-five years this woman has retained her affection for and her faith in a man she has not seen or heard of in all that time.

"She came to me today in the hope that I might be able to help her find this long-lost husband. And when she was gone I gave my fancy rein, and imagined a case I will put to you.

"Suppose that this husband, soon after his escape, had learned that his wife had been sold away, and that such inquiries as he could make brought no information of her whereabouts. Suppose that he was young, and she much older than he; that he was light, and she was black; that their marriage was a slave marriage, and legally binding only if they chose to make it so after the war. Suppose, too, that he made his way to the North, as some of us have done, and there, where he had larger opportunities, had improved them, and had in the course of all these years grown to be as different from the ignorant boy who ran away from fear of slavery as the day is from the night. Suppose, even, that he had qualified himself, by industry, by thrift, and by study, to win the friendship and be considered worthy the society of such people as these I see around me tonight, gracing my board and filling my heart with gladness; for I am old enough to remember the day when such a gathering would not have been possible in this land. Suppose, too, that, as the years went by, this man's memory of the past grew more and more indistinct, until at last it was rarely, except in his dreams, that any image of this bygone period rose before his mind. And then suppose that accident should bring to his knowledge the fact that the wife of his youth, the wife he had left behind him—not one who had walked by his side and kept pace with him in his upward struggle, but one upon whom advancing years and a laborious life had set their mark—was alive and seeking him, but that he was absolutely safe from recognition or discovery, unless he chose to reveal himself. My friends, what would the man do? I will presume that he was one who loved honor, and tried to deal justly with all men. I will even carry the case further, and suppose that perhaps he had set his heart upon another, whom he had hoped to call his own. What would he do, or rather what ought he to do, in such a crisis of a lifetime?

"It seemed to me that he might hesitate, and I imagined that I was an old friend, a near friend, and that he had come to me for advice; and I argued the case with him. I tried to discuss it impartially. After we had looked upon the matter from every point of view, I said to him, in words that we all know:

> 'This above all: to thine own self be true,
> And it must follow, as the night the day,
> Thou canst not then be false to any man.'

Then, finally, I put the question to him, 'Shall you acknowledge her?'

"And now, ladies and gentlemen, friends and companions, I ask you, what should he have done?"

There was something in Mr. Ryder's voice that stirred the hearts of those who sat around him. It suggested more than mere sympathy with an imaginary situation; it seemed rather in the nature of a personal appeal. It was observed, too, that his look rested more especially upon Mrs. Dixon, with a mingled expression of renunciation and inquiry.

She had listened, with parted lips and streaming eyes. She was the first to speak: "He should have acknowledged her."

"Yes," they all echoed, "he should have acknowledged her."

"My friends and companions," responded Mr. Ryder, "I thank you, one and all. It is the answer I expected, for I knew your hearts."

He turned and walked toward the closed door of an adjoining room, while every eye followed him in wondering curiosity. He came back in a moment, leading by the hand his visitor of the afternoon, who stood startled and trembling at the sudden plunge into this scene of brilliant gaiety. She was neatly dressed in gray, and wore the white cap of an elderly woman.

"Ladies and gentlemen," he said, "this is the woman, and I am the man, whose story I have told you. Permit me to introduce to you the wife of my youth."

CARVER'S KIDS
GEORGE WASHINGTON CARVER

Brilliant scientist-educator George Washington Carver (c. 1864–1943), who taught for forty-seven years at Tuskegee Institute in Alabama, never married, but still had a "family." He considered his Tuskegee students to be his children, often advising them on matters outside of the classroom, and even loaning them money. His students remembered him warmly. He wrote this thank-you note to a representative of the Class of 1922, after receiving a gift from the class.

JANUARY 9, 1922

Mr. L. Robinson

I wish to express through you to each member of the Senior class my deep appreciation for the fountain pen you so kindly and thoughtfully gave me Christmas.

This gift, like all the others, is characterized by simplicity and thoughtfulness, which I hope each member will make the slogan of their lives.

As your father, it is needless for me to keep saying, I hope, except for emphasis, that each one of my children will rise to the full height of your possibilities, which means the possession of these eight cardinal virtues which constitutes a lady or a gentleman.

1st. Be clean both inside and outside.

2nd. Who neither looks up to the rich or down on the poor.

3rd. Who loses, if needs be, without squealing.

4th. Who wins without bragging.

5th. Who is always considerate of women, children and old people.

6th. Who is too brave to lie.

7th. Who is too generous to cheat.

8th. Who takes his share of the world and lets other people have theirs.

May God help you to carry out these eight cardinal virtues and peace and prosperity be yours through life.

Lovingly yours,
G. W. Carver

I am not a role model . . . I am paid to wreak havoc on a basketball court. Parents should be role models. Just because I dunk a basketball doesn't mean I should raise your kids.

—*Charles Barkley*

FATHER'S PLEDGE
HAKI R. MADHUBUTI

Born in 1942 in Little Rock, Arkansas, Haki R. Madhubuti is a poet, critic, educator, editor, and publisher. His name at birth was Don L. Lee, but he changed it to Madhubuti in 1973 to reflect his ideological beliefs. A major voice in the Black Arts movement of the 1960s and 1970s, which labeled black arts the "aesthetic and spiritual sister of the Black Power concept," Madhubuti published many volumes of poetry, addressing his work to black audiences. In 1967, with $400 in earnings from readings, he founded Third World Press in his basement apartment on Chicago's South Side. In his poems of the 1980s and 1990s, Madhubuti points out that many of the political, economic, and cultural issues that confronted blacks in the 1960s still must be addressed. In the following pledge, he stresses the responsibilities of fathers.

1. I will work to be the best father I can be. Fathering is a daily mission, and there are no substitutes for good fathers. Since I have not been taught to be a father, in order to make my "on the job" training easier, I will study, listen, observe and learn from my mistakes.

2. I will openly display love and caring for my wife and children. I will listen to my wife and children. I will hug and kiss my children often. I will be supportive of the mother of my children and spend quality time with my children.

3. I will teach by example. I will try to introduce myself and my family to something new and developmental each week. I will help my children with their homework and encourage them to be involved in extracurricular activities.

4. I will read to or with my children as often as possible. I will

provide opportunities for my children to develop creatively in the arts: music, dance, drama, literature and visual arts. I will challenge my children to do their best.

5. I will encourage and organize frequent family activities for the home and away from home. I will try to make life a positive adventure and make my children aware of their extended family.

6. I will never be intoxicated or "high" in the presence of my children, nor will I use language unbecoming for an intelligent and serious father.

7. I will be nonviolent in my relationships with my wife and children. As a father, my role will be to stimulate and encourage my children rather than carry the "big stick."

8. I will maintain a home that is culturally in tune with the best of African-American history, struggle and future. This will be done, in part, by developing a library, record/disc, video and visual art collections that reflect the developmental aspects of African people worldwide. There will be *order* and *predictability* in our home.

9. I will teach my children to be responsible, disciplined, fair and honest. I will teach them the value of hard work and fruitful production. I will teach them the importance of family, community, politics and economics. I will teach them the importance of the Nguzo Saba (Black value system) and the role that ownership of property and businesses plays in our struggle.

10. As a father, I will attempt to provide my family with an atmosphere of love and security to aid them in their development into sane, loving, productive, spiritual, hard-working, creative African-Americans who realize they have a responsibility to do well and help the less fortunate of this world. I will teach my children to be *activists* and to *think* for themselves.

❦❧

Mamas only do things cause they love you so much. They can't help it. It's flesh to flesh, blood to blood. No matter how old you get, how grown and on your own, your mama always loves you like a newborn.

—*Ntozake Shange, in* Betsy Brown

❦❧

TICKLE TICKLE
DAKARI HRU

Are you ticklish?

me papa tickle me feet
he call it "finger treat"
me scream and run each time he come
me papa tickle me feet

he tickle me tummy, me chest, me arm
his fingers fly so wild
he say, "Come here, little man.
You my ticklin' chile."

me papa say he love me
me papa look so proud
he say, "Sonny, what a joy
to see you laugh out loud."

he tickle me ribs, me neck, me back
his fingers grow longer each day
me twist and swing and laugh and kick
but he hold me anyway

me eyes, they water
me throat be sore
me weak, me dizzy
but me want more

he throw me high up in the air
and catch me from behind
me say, "Go higher!" and he say,
"Don't you know you're mine?"

me papa tickle me feet
he call it "finger treat"
me scream and run (but OH, WHAT FUN!)
when papa tickle me feet

UNDERGROUND DADS
WIL HAYGOOD

Often, bighearted black men stand in for absentee fathers, teaching black boys right from wrong.

For years, while growing up, I shamelessly told my playmates that I didn't have a father. In my neighborhood, where men went to work with lunch pails, my friends thought there was a gaping hole in my household. My father never came to the park with me to toss a softball, never came to see me in any of my school plays. I'd explain to friends, with the simplicity of explaining to someone that there are, in some woods, no deer, that I just had no father. My friends looked at me and squinted. My mother and father had divorced shortly after my birth. As the years rolled by, however, I did not have the chance to turn into the pitiful little black boy who had been abandoned by his father. There was a reason: other men showed up. They were warm, honest (at least as far as my eyes could see) and big-hearted. They were the good black men in the shadows, the men who taught me right from wrong, who taught me how to behave, who told me, by their very actions, that they expected me to do good things in life.

There are heartbreaking statistics tossed about regarding single-parent black households these days, about children growing up fatherless. Those statistics must be considered. But how do you count the other men, the ones who show up—with perfect timing, with a kind of soft-stepping loveliness—to give a hand, to take a boy to watch airplanes lift off, to show a young boy the beauty of planting tomatoes in the ground and to tell a child that all of life is not misery?

In my life, there was Jerry, who hauled junk. He had a lean body and a sweet smile. He walked like a cowboy, all bowlegged, swinging his shoulders. It was almost a strut. The sound of his pickup truck rumbling down our alley in Columbus, Ohio, could raise me from sleep.

When he wasn't hauling junk, Jerry fixed things. More than once, he fixed my red bicycle. The gears were always slipping; the chain could turn into a tangled mess. Hearing pain in my voice, Jerry would instruct me to leave my bike on our front porch. In our neighborhood, in the 60's, no one would steal your bike from your porch. Jerry promised me he'd pick it up, and he always did. He never lied to me, and he cautioned me not to tell lies. He was, off and on, my mother's boyfriend. At raucous family gatherings, he'd pull me aside and explain to me the importance of honesty, of doing what one promised to do.

And there was Jimmy, my grandfather, who all his life paid his bills the day they arrived: that was a mighty lesson in itself—it taught me a work ethic. He held two jobs, and there were times when he allowed me to accompany him on his night job, when he cleaned a Greek restaurant on the north side of Columbus. Often he'd mop the place twice, as if trying to win some award. He frightened me too. It was not because he was mean. It was because he had exacting standards, and there were times when I didn't measure up to those standards. He didn't like shortcutters. His instructions, on anything, were to be carried out to the letter. He believed in independence, doing as much for yourself as you possibly could. It should not have surprised me when, one morning while having stomach pains, he chose not to wait for a taxi and instead walked the mile to the local hospital, where he died a week later of stomach cancer.

My uncles provided plenty of good background music when I was coming of age. Uncle Henry took me fishing. He'd phone the night before. "Be ready. Seven o'clock." I'd trail him through woods—as a son does a father—until we found our fishing hole. We'd sit for hours. He taught me patience and an appreciation of the outdoors, of nature. He talked, incessantly, of family—his family, my family, the family of friends. The man had a reverence for family. I knew to listen.

I think these underground fathers simply appear, decade to decade, flowing through the generations. Hardly everywhere, and hardly, to be sure, in enough places, but there. As mystical, sometimes, as fate when fate is sweet.

Sometimes I think that all these men who have swept in and out of my life still couldn't replace a good, warm father. But inasmuch as I've never known a good, warm father, the men who entered my life, who taught me right from wrong, who did things they were not asked to do, have become unforgettable. I know of the cold statistics out there. And yet, the mountain of father-son literature does not haunt me. I've known good black men.

UNCLE JOHN
NORMA JEAN AND CAROLE DARDEN

Two sisters, the coauthors of Spoonbread and Strawberry Wine, *a bestselling cookbook of family recipes, remember one of their favorite uncles.*

Uncle John was the oldest son of Charles and Dianah Darden. The dreams and hopes of the family centered on him, and he proved worthy of their confidence. From the beginning, John was a carbon copy of his father. Even in his youth, he was disarmingly self-assured and knew how to survive and to protect others. But from the age of ten, when he was unable to find medical assistance for his unconscious sister Annie, John had one driving goal, and that was to become a doctor.

At the age of thirteen, he was sent by Papa Darden to high school in Salisbury, North Carolina. Lean years followed as he worked his way through Livingstone College, medical school, and an internship on Long Island, New York. His was a long, hard struggle, but when he made it, he established a pattern the younger children would follow. Summer jobs, mainly on the railroad and ships, took John all over the country. But he always found his way back to Wilson to share what he had seen and learned of the world, and to encourage his brothers and sisters in their pursuits. By the time he was ready to put out his shingle in 1903, Wilson already had Black medical service, so John went deeper south, settling in Opelika, Alabama, where, as the only Black doctor in a thirty-mile radius, he was greeted with an eighteen-hour workday.

His overloaded practice in that remote little town almost caused him to lose his fiancée, Maude Jean Logan, who questioned his long absences from her. But Uncle John's persuasive letter, which we found in Aunt Maude's Bible, saved the wedding day:

Sat. Noon

My own darling Jean:

Here on the very verge of our approaching happiness comes the saddest news pen could write . . . Sweetheart Jean, the condition of a half dozen patients demands that I keep constant watch over them for at least three days. Had thought to see you at the cost of their lives; but you would care so much less for me then . . . Won't you sympathize with me just a little, the responsibilities on this end and realize that no man under the canopy of heaven could love you more . . .

Soon after, John, making calls with his new wife in his horse and buggy, became a familiar sight on the narrow dirt roads around the Opelika countryside.

Emulating his father's diversified business tactics, John opened a drugstore on Avenue A, the main street of town. His brother J.B. had just earned his degree in pharmacy from Howard University, so he was recruited as a partner. The two brothers dispensed prescriptions, cosmetics, ice cream, and a lot of good cheer, and the store became a meeting place for the community. Local residents tell us that their Sundays were not complete without a stroll to the drugstore for a chat and a scoop of John's homemade ice cream. After the death of their mother, baby brother Bud, our father, joined the group and, at the age of nine, became the ace soda fountain man, specializing in a tutti-frutti sundae. Eventually Opelika proved to be too quiet for J.B., so, with John's blessings, he returned to medical school in livelier Nashville, Tennessee, leaving the oldest and the youngest brothers together. John was like a second father to Bud, who nicknamed him Toad because of his protruding abdomen.

According to Bud, John was a natural leader of men and was considered the guardian of minority rights. People brought him their sorrows, their joys, and news of gross community injustices. Long outraged at the lack of public medical facilities for Black people, he established a private

hospital. It was a simple one-story wooden building, but many complicated operations were performed there and many lives saved. Like most
country doctors, he had his thumb glued to the pulse of the community
and became the town chronicler. He knew who had been born, who had
died, and who had moved in or out. (Because of his two additional jobs
as the Lee County jail doctor and a conscription doctor, he even knew
who was incarcerated or who was inducted into the army.) Thus, he had
firsthand knowledge of the jailing of people for minor infractions of the
law, of assaults on defenseless females, and of the countless other indignities perpetuated on Blacks. During his time, the air was indeed perme-
ated with clouds of sudden and irrational violence.

Once Dr. John's quick presence of mind was able to avert the lynching of a Black stranger. Bud remembers that he and John were in the
drugstore when they heard a commotion coming from the street and
upstairs, where John's brother-in-law, a dentist, had an office. Dr. John
Clark came down to tell them that a stranger seeking refuge from a
lynching mob had run into his office quite out of the blue. With no
questions asked, John left and returned in a flash with a few fearless and
daring Black citizens and the white Republican postmaster (a federal
appointee in those days when Republicans were considered liberals).
The mob had gathered momentum and was threatening to storm the
building. But the postmaster, whom John knew to be sympathetic to the
plight of Blacks, had arrived heavily armed, and he kept the mob distracted while John and his friends spirited the man out of town. The
man's crime? A visitor from Chicago unfamiliar with local customs, he
had almost lost his life for taking a seat in an empty white restaurant
while waiting for directions to another town.

Afterward, some local residents conducted a campaign of harassment
against John and Maude, who remained cautious, cool, and armed until
the fervor died down. We asked Aunt Maude if John had ever considered leaving town. She answered that in the darkest days in the backwoods of Alabama, he had never wavered in his determination to remain
in the community he loved and to aid others.

She also told us that the balance and harmony so sorely missing in
John's hostile environment were supplied by his love of music, of religion, of gardening, and, surprisingly, of fashion. A meticulous dresser,
he had developed an appreciation for good fabric and fit from his

mother, the seamstress. He was a steward in his church, raised livestock and pigeons, and kept a beautiful flower and vegetable garden, as had his father. However, the talent that set him apart was his melodious baritone voice, and it is said that he could be heard singing a mile away.

In a life that had so many parallels to Papa Darden's, it is interesting to note that after John's death the local Black high school was named for him in appreciation for the many things that he had done for the citizens of Opelika.

LIFE IMITATES TV
HENRY LOUIS GATES JR.

In small-town black America, the civil rights era was both real and imagined: real because blacks heroically battled the ways of racist white folks on so many fronts; imagined because so much of the era and its spectacular scenes flickered by on black-and-white televisions in living rooms around the nation. These life-altering, sometimes brutal scenes were occurring hundreds, if not thousands, of miles away. So for millions, the struggle for civil rights became very much a prime-time TV event. The whole family gathered to watch it, as if with one set of eyes, and then went about the day's business. While the civil rights movement lasted, though, TV-watching was truly a family experience. So were the antics of black TV comics.

Seeing somebody colored on TV was an event.

"Colored, colored, on Channel Two," you'd hear someone shout. Somebody else would run to the phone, while yet another hit the front porch, telling all the neighbors where to see it. And *everybody* loved *Amos and Andy*—I don't care what people say today. For the colored people, the day they took *Amos and Andy* off the air was one of the saddest days in Piedmont, about as sad as the day of the last mill pic-a-nic.

What was special to us about *Amos and Andy* was that their world was *all* colored, just like ours. Of course, *they* had their colored judges and lawyers and doctors and nurses, which we could only dream about having, or becoming—and we *did* dream about those things. Kingfish ate his soft-boiled eggs delicately, out of an egg cup. He even owned an acre of land in Westchester County, which he sold to Andy, using the facade of a movie set to fake a mansion. As far as we were concerned, the foibles of Kingfish or Calhoun the lawyer were the foibles of individuals who happened to be funny. Nobody was likely to confuse them with the colored people we knew, no more than we'd confuse ourselves with the entertainers and athletes we saw on TV or in *Ebony* or *Jet,* the magazines we devoured to keep up with what was happening with the race. And people took special relish in Kingfish's malapropisms. "I denies the allegation, Your Honor, and I resents the alligator."

In one of my favorite episodes of *Amos and Andy,* "The Punjab of Java-Pour," Andy Brown is hired to advertise a brand of coffee and is required to dress up as a turbaned Oriental potentate. Kingfish gets the bright idea that if he dresses up as a potentate's servant, the two of them can enjoy a vacation at a luxury hotel for free. So attired, the two promenade around the lobby, running up an enormous tab and generously dispensing "rubies" and "diamonds" as tips. The plan goes awry when people try to redeem the gems and discover them to be colored glass. It was widely suspected that this episode was what prompted two Negroes in Baltimore to dress like African princes and demand service in a segregated four-star restaurant. Once it was clear to the management that these were not American Negroes, the two were treated royally. When the two left the restaurant, they took off their African headdresses and robes and enjoyed a hearty laugh at the restaurant's expense. "They weren't like our Negroes," the maître d' told the press in explaining why he had agreed to seat the two "African princes."

Civil rights took us all by surprise. Every night we'd wait until the news to see what "Dr. King and dem" were doing. It was like watching the Olympics or the World Series when somebody colored was on. The murder of Emmett Till was one of my first memories. He whistled at some white girl, they said; that's all he did. He was beat so bad they didn't even want to open the casket, but his mama made them. She wanted the world to see what they had done to her baby.

In 1957, when I was in second grade, black children integrated Central High School in Little Rock, Arkansas. We watched it on TV. All of us watched it. I don't mean Mama and Daddy and Rocky. I mean *all* the colored people in America watched it, together, with one set of eyes. We'd watch it in the morning, on the *Today* show on NBC, before we'd go to school; we'd watch it in the evening, on the news, with Edward R. Murrow on CBS. We'd watch the Special Bulletins at night, interrupting our TV shows.

The children were all well scrubbed and greased down, as we'd say. Hair short and closely cropped, parted, and oiled (the boys); "done" in a "permanent" and straightened, with turned-up bangs and curls (the girls). Starched shirts, white, and creased pants, shoes shining like a buck private's spit shine. Those Negroes were *clean.* . . .

The children would get off their school bus surrounded by soldiers from the National Guard and by a field of state police. They would stop at the steps of the bus and seem to take a very deep breath. Then the phalanx would start to move slowly along this gulley of sidewalk and rednecks that connected the steps of the school bus with the white wooden double doors of the school. All kinds of crackers would be lining that gulley, separated from the phalanx of children by rows of state police, who formed a barrier arm in arm. Cheerleaders from the all-white high school that was desperately trying to stay that way were dressed in those funny little pleated skirts, with a big red *C* for "Central" on their chests, and they'd wave their pom-poms and start to cheer: "Two, four, six, eight—We don't want to integrate!" And all those crackers and all those rednecks would join in that chant as if their lives depended on it. Deafening, it was: even on our twelve-inch TV, a three-inch speaker buried along the back of its left side.

The TV was the ritual arena for the drama of race. In our family, it was located in the living room, where it functioned like a fireplace in the proverbial New England winter. I'd sit in the water in the galvanized tub in the middle of our kitchen, watching the TV in the next room while Mama did the laundry or some other chore as she waited for Daddy to come home from his second job. We watched people getting hosed and cracked over their heads, people being spat upon and arrested, rednecks siccing fierce dogs on women and children, our people responding by singing and marching and staying strong. Eyes on the prize. Eyes on the prize. George Wallace at the gate of the University of Alabama, blocking Autherine Lucy's way. Charlayne Hunter at the University of Georgia. President Kennedy interrupting our scheduled program with a special address, saying that James Meredith will *definitely* enter the University of Mississippi; and saying it like he believed it (unlike Ike), saying it like the big kids said "It's our turn to play" on the basketball court and walking all through us as if we weren't there.

THE HISTORY OF THINGS TO COME
JOHN EDGAR WIDEMAN

John Edgar Wideman (b. 1941) writes eloquently on how the "cloud of race" hovers over the cradles of newborns. The "paradigm of race," a legacy passed from our parents to us, forms an indelible part of our consciousness and our fate as Americans. And family history is tied to cultural recollections. The following passages are taken from Wideman's Fatheralong, *the book in which he documents an odyssey with his father to Promised Land, South Carolina, a small town that is not on most maps of the state, "just as you won't discover any mention of Africans or slaves or slavery in the closely printed eight-page outline of the* Chronological History of South Carolina (1662–1825)." *In Promised Land, Wideman attempts to remap and recover his history and cultural memory. "In our minds," he writes, "our memories beat the pulse of history."*

Parents viscerally bond with likenesses they discover or invent in tiny, newborn Mary or Tommy all freshly bathed, powdered, and swaddled in hospital linen. This identification, this celebration of self reproduced, self extended yet also miraculously transcended, may be normal and necessary to get us in the proper spirit for the rigors of child rearing. But in America this positive identification with likeness is also the beginning of trouble because we impose a thing called "race" on the face in the cradle. On the basis of observable, external features—lips, nose, color, hair, and paradoxically, even in the absence of these signs if we know the "race" of the parents—a newborn's destiny is assigned. Assumptions about the infant's character, intelligence, ability to launch a jump shot, manage a baseball team or a corporation are swiftly, unalterably ascribed.

If you're a black man gazing through the nursery window at your newborn son, whatever else you're feeling, love, joy, wonder, gratitude, the tipsiness of the universe whirling around you as you step aside, make room for a new star at the dead center, you cannot entirely escape the chill of the cloud passing momentarily between you and your boy. The cloud of *race*.

No, it doesn't pass. It settles in the tiny mirror of the face you're searching, darkens the skin with a threat of bad weather. Sooner or later, whether you're rich or poor, whether your blackness is wrapped in ivory or ebony, you must address this threat: the legacy of being despised, 'buked and scorned, of inequality and powerlessness. You've passed it on to your son. It may become as hateful and corrosive for him as it's been for his fathers. Wealth, position have no bearing on the deep, general levels of resistance he will encounter, except to add a tinge of irony to success, teach the futility of certain compromises, the bitterness of how close to winning losing can be.

Will you be able to protect him from what's dogged you and yours. Are your face, your skin admissions of defeat. Have you failed to redress crimes committed against you. Where is the clean slate upon which he can write his name. Your name.

Sorry is not enough. Sorry won't do. You acknowledge with a sinking feeling—how far, how long you sink is the worst moment, what can't be written—acknowledge how little things have changed. It could drive you wild, the face, the race in the crib is yours and the [cycle's] about to start all over again. He must go out into the world and fight too many of the same battles you did, perhaps bearing the irony of a white name, a pale face that leads to the same compromising, unanswerable questions the darkest orphan in this society of white over black must confront. Who is your father?

You are your son's biological link to past and future. Are you also his burden. To claim you, say yes to you, must he also accept the stigma of race. Does your dark face doom him to be an outsider, force him to address one way or another the lives his fathers, his brothers and sisters have pursued on the margins of society. Damned if he does, damned if he doesn't. If he denies you, he doesn't need to look any farther than the nose on his face, the skin on the back of his hands, to realize he's denying himself. Saying no to himself. No to the power within himself to achieve what no one can give: freedom and equality.

Are you proof he's less than a man because you're not able to give him what white men give to their sons at birth: full, unquestioned, unconditional citizenship. You can attempt to arm him, to prepare him to face the hard facts, but in the innocence of your first glimpses of him, you cannot pretend the facts don't exist. You can't pretend "race" doesn't exist, and "race" defines you both as something other, something less than a white man. All that mess seemed like old news, nasty, sweepable-under-the-rug news, and you could fight it or forget it . . . until the moment you peer into the mirror of those still unfocused dark eyes. Are you guilty of an unforgivable miscalculation. Have you passed on to him what your daddy passed on to you. The broken circle—unbroken.

I'm making up this father-son exchange. I have no evidence the nursery scene I'm sketching ever happened. No actual father or son may recognize themselves in what I've written. It's as much about a father and daughter as a father and son. Many would deny the relevance, its applicability to their experience. The words and thoughts I attribute to fathers and sons are not drawn directly from my experience, either. As I wrote I listened as much as composed. Stillness spread within me as I entered a space where boundaries are breached. Inner quiet merges with a larger stillness and voices not mine begin to speak, not to me, but through me. I listen, neither affirm nor deny the authenticity of what I'm hearing. The voices are not mine, the story they're unfolding just might be.

No one's asking for sympathy. No tears, no hand wringing or prayers or handouts. I'm setting down part of a story, a small piece of what needs to be remembered so when we make up the next part, imagine our lives, our history, this piece will be there, among the fragments lost, found, and remembered.

The paradigm of race works to create distance between sons and fathers. One of the worst aspects of this distance is the unwitting complicity of the victims perpetuating it. Because we don't talk or can't talk father to son, son to father, each generation approaches the task of becoming men as if no work has been accomplished before. Treats an unfinished building as if it's a decaying, useless building and feels compelled to tear it down, start over, instead of utilizing solid foundations bought and paid for with the ancestor's blood. Imagine how different we might be if we really listened to our fathers' stories. If we preserved them, learned to make them part of our lives. Wouldn't the stories, if known and performed over generations, be infused with the power of our music. Transforming power, engendering power, get-happy and stay-strong power. Power to link us as our music links, power to plant seeds, nurture them, celebrate their growth.

Our fathers' stories, like their songs, their bodies, can be stolen, silenced, alienated from them, sold, corrupted. We must learn to resist those who would come between us, those who would destroy the messages we must pass on.

HISTORY IS NOT something given, a fixed, chronological, linear outline with blank spots waiting to be filled with newly unearthed facts. It's the activity over time of all the minds comprising it, the sum of these parts that produces a greater ecological whole. History, the past, is what you're thinking, what you've thought. *You*, the individual, you the enabler and product of the collective enterprise of mind.

History is mind, is driven by mind in the same sense a flock of migratory birds, its configuration, destination, purpose, destiny are propelled, guided by the collective mind of members of the immediate flock and also the species, all kindred birds past and present inhabiting Great Time. Collective experience feeds this "mind" with a sort of accumulated, biological, experiential wisdom, knowledge both within and external to individuals. The minute-by-minute precarious survival of each individual is also work that insures perpetuation of kind. Conscious articulation of common goals, common stakes in a common struggle to survive is one means of acknowledging and also building upon the past, asserting a sense of belongingness to something greater than ourselves.

〰

I have looked into
    my father's eyes and seen an
        african sunset.

                        —*Sonia Sanchez*

〰

ANCESTORS
DUDLEY RANDALL

    Let's remember all of our ancestors—kings and queens and common folk, too.

Why are our ancestors
always kings and princes
and never the common people?

Was the Old Country a democracy
where every man was a king?
Or did the slave catchers
steal only the aristocrats
and leave the fieldhands
laborers
street cleaners
garbage collectors
dish washers
cooks
and maids
behind?

My own ancestor
(research reveals)
was a swineherd
who tended the pigs
in the Royal Pigstye

and slept in the mud
among the hogs.

Yet I'm as proud of him
as of any king or prince
dreamed up in fantasies
of bygone glory.

LYRICAL ROOTS

HOW A SONG LINKED AN AMERICAN WOMAN TO AFRICA

HERB FRAZIER

Here is the story—published in Newsday *on April 7, 1997—of how an American woman discovered her long-lost connection to the Mende people of Africa through a funeral song. The song had been handed down through generations, just as Alex Haley's family legends were. Incidentally, Cinque and the Africans who rebelled on the* Amistad *in 1839 were of Mende ancestry.*

Ah wakah muh monuh kambay yah lay kwambay
Ah wakah muh monuh kambay yah lay kwan
Hah suh wiligo seeyah yuh banga lilly
Hah suh wiligo dwellin duh kwan
Hah suh wiligo seeyah yuh kwendieyah

Everyone come together, let us struggle
The grave is not yet finished
Let his heart be perfectly at peace
Sudden death commands everyone's attention like a firing gun

Sudden death commands everyone's attention, oh elders, oh heads of
the family
Sudden death commands everyone's attention, like a distant drum beat
— *Mary Moran's family song in the Mende language,*
with English translation.

HARRIS NECK, GEORGIA—The song came from Mary Moran's mother,
Amelia Dawley, who got it from her mother, Tawba Shaw, and her
grandmother Catherine, both born in slavery.

Shaw and Catherine probably got it from their ancestors, whose
names are lost in time.

The song had no meaning to them. It's in a language they do not
know. Still, they sang the lyrics, thinking it came from Gullah, an
Africa-based culture and dialect that arose among slaves and their descendants on the Sea Islands of South Carolina and Georgia and on the
mainland nearby. They used it to entertain the children, to make them
dance.

"We took it to be a happy little song," Mary Moran said.

Four thousand miles away on the west coast of Africa in Sierra Leone,
another woman passed a song along in a similar fashion.

Mariama Suba sang to her granddaughter Baindu. Unlike the Moran
family, Suba knew the meaning of her song. In the decades before Suba
died, the advent of Christianity and Islam forced her people to abandon
the song. But Suba passed it on anyway, believing it to be an important
part of her heritage.

For about 200 years, each song stood apart. But in 1989, they began
gradually inching closer, unlocking secrets along the way.

Now, Mary Moran, a 75-year-old mother of 13 who lives in this small
town 80 miles south of Savannah, knows the song she sings is a funeral
song from the Mende people of southern Sierra Leone.

Baindu Jabati knows the Mende funeral song traveled on a slave ship
to America in the 1790s, twisted some by time but not changed much
from the way it has been sung through the generations of Moran's
family.

The song is believed to be the longest text in an African language that has been preserved by a black family in the United States, said Cynthia Schmidt, an ethnomusicologist who teaches at the University of Nebraska at Omaha.

On a steamy March morning, Mary Moran of the coastal Georgia hamlet of Harris Neck met Baindu Jabati in her home of Senehun Ngola, a rural rice-farming village hacked out of a dense tropical forest. They hugged. They cried. They exchanged their cultures and their songs.

The government of Sierra Leone invited Moran to visit as a demonstration of the closeness between the African country and the Sea Islands of South Carolina and Georgia. After her family coaxed her out of a fear of flying to the distant land, she agreed. Twelve of her relatives and the pastor of the family's church arrived in Freetown on February 26 for an 11-day visit. It was a dizzying tour during which Moran sang the five-line song for the country's president and other leaders and was greeted on the streets of Freetown, a capital city of some 500,000 people, like a rock star.

Banners strung up around Freetown welcomed her. People stopped her on the street and in her hotel lobby to shake her hand. One woman, who appeared to be waiting for a taxi, approached the small bus carrying the Morans and waved at Mary Moran. "Welcome," the woman shouted.

"It is amazing that this little song has brought me to Africa," Moran said before arriving in Senehun Ngola. She fanned herself with a Freetown newspaper that carried a story on her visit. "This doesn't seem real. It seems like I'm still in America."

All of what the Morans had seen and done and would do seemed unimportant when compared with Senehun Ngola and Jabati. But first, they had to get there. After a nervous one-hour flight from Freetown on an old Russian-made helicopter, the Morans arrived in the village, about 80 miles from the Liberian border.

When the thick red dust in the village's school yard, kicked up by the whirling rotors, had settled back to earth, the craft was quickly surrounded by a crowd of singing people.

When Moran and her brother, the Rev. Robert Thorpe of Savannah, stepped off the helicopter, the crowd scooped them up and dropped them in hammocks suspended from the heads of men stationed at their four corners.

As she swung in the hammock, Moran laughed wildly as if she were on an amusement-park ride. "This is kinda funny," she said. "I've never in my life gotten a welcome like this."

During the lengthy musical welcoming procession, an honor reserved for local chiefs and visiting VIPs, hundreds swarmed through the village of Senehun Ngola to greet Moran and her family. The procession stopped in the center of the village. Then all eyes were focused on the Morans, seated in the Barri Court where village elders settle disputes.

"We are so happy to find our roots, the Mende," Moran told the approving crowd. "We will come again."

Joseph Opala, an American anthropologist who lives in Freetown, leads a team of two other scholars who've researched and translated the Mende song to English and brought Moran and Jabati together. Opala told the Mende audience their song went to America on a slave ship and today it has come back.

With those words, Jabati was overcome. She fell to her knees and buried her face in Moran's lap. She sobbed. And sobbed. Later, she said the occasion would have been better if her ancestors could have welcomed Mary Moran, too.

Opala, Schmidt and Tazief Koroma, a lecturer in linguistics at Njala University College in Sierra Leone, would not have found the song had it not been for coincidences and good fortune. The song—on each side of the Atlantic—teetered on the edge of being lost forever.

But to understand that, go back to 1932, when a linguist met Amelia Dawley and heard her song.

During the late 1920s and early 1930s, Lorenzo Dow Turner taught summer school at black colleges in South Carolina and his native North Carolina. The peculiar speech of his students from coastal South Carolina and Georgia piqued his interest in Gullah words and culture and its influence by African cultures. Soon, Turner traveled the Sea Islands collecting words and stories.

In 1932, Turner, a Howard University linguist, recorded Dawley singing in a language he later identified as Mende. His translation of the song, along with other Gullah words, were published in his 1949 book *Africanism in the Gullah Dialect*.

In 1989, Opala and Schmidt located Turner's recording of Dawley. In Sierra Leone, they gave it to a Freetown choral group, who sang it for visitors from South Carolina and Georgia who had come on a Gullah homecoming. Mende people were surprised to learn that a song in their language had been recorded in Georgia.

Schmidt and Opala were surprised too in 1991, when Mary Moran sang the same song for them that her mother had sung for Turner.

In Sierra Leone, Koroma, from the Mende tribe, helped Schmidt search for the area where people spoke the Mende dialect of the funeral song. Then Schmidt went from village to village. Finally, she came upon Baindu Jabati. When Schmidt played a tape recording of the song, Jabati sang along.

Now the mission became getting Moran and Jabati together. That would not come quickly.

In April, 1992, Liberian rebels attacked villages in Sierra Leone. Soon the violence spread. Within a few years, Senehun Ngola was burned and razed. Jabati, apparently the last person in the country who knew the Mende funeral song, was captured and held by rebels for eight months. She came close to being killed, and her granddaughter Sattu died from starvation.

Jabati's grandmother, Mariama Suba, and her family owned the song because it was Suba's job in the Mende village to conduct the funerals. No one else had that right. When Suba died, the responsibility fell to Jabati.

Even though Jabati could sing the funeral song, she had no reason to perform it within its original context. The song and the funeral rite, Tenjamei, that went along with it were shunned as pagan rituals by Christians and Muslims, she said.

The song took on a new meaning. It became a social song. But with little to cheer about in a village smashed by war, she had not sung it in years. Jabati said the song came to her lips the night she buried Sattu.

Because Mary Moran did not know the Mende words or the song's context, she did not teach it to her children until 1991, when Opala and Schmidt visited her and told her the song was connected to the Mende people.

Women in the Mende culture preside over funerals and births. The men in the Moran family, however, are learning the song now because of its newfound celebrity.

Mary Moran's son, Wilson Moran, of Harris Neck, said, "If the song hadn't been found and revived, it would have been lost. It will be here for another 200 years.

"This song is going to heal a lot of wounds left by slavery, and it is going to bring two cultures together. My mother is alive. She is real, and she is the other link in the chain."

QUILTING
RECORDED BY ROLAND L. FREEMAN

Quilting is an important link to the past. Slaves sewed and knitted and quilted both for the plantation mistress and for themselves. But quilts served as so much more than blankets. They were things of beauty, made of whatever material was available. And they were also signs. According to quilt lore, quilts in a certain pattern were hung outside houses on the Underground Railroad to signal fleeing slaves that a home was safe harbor. Some quilts were said to serve as maps for travelers.

Beyond such practical uses, quilts were also a "canvas" for preserving and passing on African techniques and motifs. Slaves channeled their expressions through appliqués, cutting and stitching as they saw fit, or as tradition demanded. Quilting also provided a support network and a sense of camaraderie for stitchers. Their creations expressed what life under slavery was like.

But quilting is as much alive today as it was yesterday. Here is what two poets had to say about quilts and quilting.

SONIA SANCHEZ

I am saying physically and initially, something happens when you put a quilt on your bed. And wow, when you sleep under it, it's like you are sheltered, like nothing can happen to you. Maybe what I'm saying is you feel protected, and I mean it's like what some people call "ooga booga" stuff. These quilts can be a form of intellectual nourishment. When I look at some of these quilts, I see the blood, I see the tears, and I see the sweat. I see women who could not say what I say on paper—but they certainly say it loud and clear in their quilts. You can hear the spirits of the sisters moaning, moaning, moaning. They're not crying, they're just moaning. And all I'm saying is, in these quilts, there is life that gives love.

NIKKI GIOVANNI

Now my mommy never did quilt. My grandmother, her name is Emma Louvenia, was born in 1890 or so, and she grew up of course as the quintessential housewife. As for me, I started to quilt when I was expecting a child. I'm very futuristic. So I said to myself, "If I have this child and everything is all right (which I sincerely hope it will be), what are going to be my responsibilities?" I thought, "Okay. You have to be a parent, but there's no school for parenting. But it's easy to figure out how to be a grandparent because grandparents—at least in my opinion—bake bread, make cobblers, and give you a quilt." So I thought I should really make a quilt because the quilt that I have, in fact, was made by my great-grandmother Cornelia Watson, whom we called Mama Dear, and my mother had given it to me.

Now I remember my grandmother doing a number of things, but I don't have a recollection of her sitting and quilting per se. But she would tell me stories of her mother quilting, and I watched her repair things. But when I made my quilt, when I was expecting Thomas, I forgot the one thing that she had always stressed about it. She had laughed about people who messed up making quilts and had to start again, because you start at the center, not at the ends, and I had started this quilt that I made for my son at the ends.

I've always liked quilts and of course, if I had real money, I would have quilts from the 1820s, because all those 1820 quilts are basically African American. The mistress of the house did not sit around and quilt. Some of them are more beautiful than others, and you can see those that were quilted for the slaves and those that were quilted for the big house. But there's no question of who did the work. I mean, there's no question . . .

I have used quilts as a metaphor. That's because I have a line in a poem called "Hands" which is a poem I wrote for Mother's Day. It says, "Quilts are the way our lives are lived. We survive on the scraps, the leftovers from a materially richer society." Quilts are such a—what's the word I'm looking for—banner to black women. Because what they ended up taking was that which nobody wanted, and making something totally beautiful out of it. Making something in fact quite valuable. At least to this day. But that's like the spirituals. We took a bad situation and found a way to make a song. So it's a definite part of the heritage.

When the quilt I have, which you see is worn, when it finally dissolves, there will be a few pieces—and that would be a couple more generations presumably—what you hope is your great-grandchild will then say, "Well, I'll take these pieces from Grandma Nik's quilt, which she got from Mama Dear, and make another quilt and start the pattern all over again." It will be modern, I mean it will probably have materials we don't even know.

I think quilting, in particular, teaches you patience. Because you can't do it in a hurry. There's probably nothing worse than a quilt that's machine-made. I don't even know how to say it; it just goes against the whole nature of a quilt. Why would you do that? I mean, if you're good (which I am not) you're supposed to [use] a single thread. Mine was done with double thread. Mama Dear's was done with single thread, and that's good sewing. But it teaches you just to stop and think about all the little ways. But my house is a quilt. I think if you could take the top off of it and photograph it, anybody who looked at it would say, "Oh, that's Nikki."

⨀

God loves you, child; no matter what, he sees you as his precious idea.
—*India Anette Peyton*
to her granddaughter Melba Pattillo, one of nine teenagers
who integrated Little Rock's Central High School in 1957.

⨀

THE NEGRO MOTHER
LANGSTON HUGHES

Written in 1931 and inspired by Mary McLeod Bethune, this poem praises the black mother and depicts her as nurturing and encouraging her children to look upward and keep on climbing "up the great stairs" of life.

Children, I come back today
To tell you a story of the long dark way
That I had to climb, that I had to know
In order that the race might live and grow.
Look at my face—dark as the night—
Yet shining like the sun with love's true light.
I am the child they stole from the sand
Three hundred years ago in Africa's land.
I am the dark girl who crossed the wide sea
Carrying in my body the seed of the free.
I am the woman who worked in the field
Bringing the cotton and the corn to yield.
I am the one who labored as a slave,
Beaten and mistreated for the work that I gave—
Children sold away from me, husband sold, too.
No safety, no love, no respect was I due.
Three hundred years in the deepest South:
But God put a song and a prayer in my mouth.
God put a dream like steel in my soul.
Now, through my children, I'm reaching the goal.
Now, through my children, young and free,
I realize the blessings denied to me.
I couldn't read then. I couldn't write.
I had nothing, back there in the night.
Sometimes, the valley was filled with tears,
But I kept trudging on through the lonely years.
Sometimes, the road was hot with sun,
But I had to keep on till my work was done:
I *had* to keep on! No stopping for me—

I was the seed of the coming Free.
I nourished the dream that nothing could smother
Deep in my breast—the Negro mother.
I had only hope then, but now through you,
Dark ones of today, my dreams must come true:
All you dark children in the world out there,
Remember my sweat, my pain, my despair.
Remember my years, heavy with sorrow—
And make of those years a torch for tomorrow.
Make of my past a road to the light
Out of the darkness, the ignorance, the night.
Lift high my banner out of the dust.
Stand like free men supporting my trust.
Believe in the right, let none push you back.
Remember the whip and the slaver's track.
Remember how the strong in struggle and strife
Still bar you the way, and deny you life—
But march ever forward, breaking down bars.
Look ever upward at the sun and the stars.
Oh, my dark children, may my dreams and my prayers
Impel you forever up the great stairs—
For I will be with you till no white brother
Dares keep down the children of the Negro mother.

My great-great-grandmother walked as a slave from Virginia to Eatonton, Georgia—which passes for the Walker ancestral home—with two babies on her hips. She lived to be a hundred and twenty-five years old and my own father knew her as a baby. It is in memory of this walk that I chose to keep and to embrace my maiden name, Walker.

—*Alice Walker*

COMMUNITY

We *dwell* in neighborhoods—on our streets, in our homes, in our buildings. But we truly *live* in our communities. The difference can be subtle, but it is real.

Neighborhoods have borders. Geography rules. In neighborhoods, people come and go. And when an unwanted change occurs, somebody never fails to utter that familiar refrain:

"There goes the neighborhood."

Communities, however, cannot be so neatly mapped out. They are not bound by the laws of physics or geography. And we can live in many simultaneously.

Actually, our communities resemble concentric circles. The innermost one tends to be our family and loved ones. Next come close friends. Then, in some order, are our neighbors, colleagues, co-workers, and others. We may be members of artistic circles, cultural communities, social sets, political groups, religious communities—people with similar interests or shared concerns.

The African American community is large and dynamic—a mosaic of tens of millions of people bound by African heritage and, unfortunately, a common history as victims of discrimination in America. This community has been changing and evolving for centuries. It arrived on ships. It survived slavery. It packed up and departed certain "neighborhoods" (at emancipation, and in migrations north). It founded new townships and cities. It settled in the Harlems of America, in the new South. It developed its own politics, sociology, class structure. It did its own thing.

Over the course of the twentieth century, the black community has expressed itself uniquely: Brothers doo-wopping on street corners. Little girls double Dutching. Strolling through Harlem. Dancing to the new music of jazz bands. Making quilts. Watching Satchel Paige pitch. Marching in Selma, Alabama. Touring the "chitlin' circuit." Dancing to the Motown sound. Signifying in barbershops. Preaching and schooling. Celebrating emancipation (late) in Texas. Cheering the "heavyweight champeen" of the world. Identifying with the poetry of Langston Hughes. Listening to Martin Luther King Jr.'s speeches.

The following stories describe much of this, including the legendary community of Harlem ("Black Manhattan" and "The Great Black Way"), where thousands sought a better life; the segregated days of black baseball ("The Negro Leagues"); the founding of Motown ("Hitsville, U.S.A."); how a community fought for its rights to travel on city transportation at the start of the civil rights era ("Organizing the Bus Boycott"); and black holidays ("John Canoe, An Original Slave Holiday" and "Juneteenth").

This chapter shows how the destiny of individuals was—and still is—tied to the fate of the community at large.

֍

Up, you mighty race! You can accomplish what you will!

—*Marcus Garvey*

֍

FOUNDERS

Blacks have founded communities across America, including cities that people of all races and ethnicities now call home. Here are three of the many U.S. cities first settled by blacks.

Los Angeles, California: Population 1990 (metropolitan area): 3,485,557

Los Angeles (Reina de los Angeles, or Queen of the Angels) was founded on September 4, 1781, by forty-four persons from eleven families. Twenty-six of the founders had some degree of African ancestry. Maria Rita Valdez, whose black grandparents were among the founding members of Los Angeles, owned Rancho Rodeo de Las Aguas, today known as Beverly Hills. Francisco Reyes, another black resident, owned San Fernando Valley, selling it in the 1790s. Reyes was mayor of Los Angeles from 1793 to 1795.

Chicago, Illinois: Population 1990 (metropolitan area): 2,783,726

In the world of Daniel Boone and Chief Pontiac, their friend Jean Baptiste Pointe Du Sable was an anomaly. This tall, handsome, urbane black foreigner, Paris-educated and an admirer of European art, was known far and wide on the frontier both for his skills as a fur trapper and his ease in getting along with red and white men. Yet his niche in history is based simply on the trading post he established in 1779 at the mouth of the Chicago River. As the first permanent settlement of Chicago, it made Du Sable the city's founder. (Indians later pointed out to visitors that the first white man to come to Chicago was black.)

Du Sable was born in 1745 in Haiti to a French mariner father and an African slave woman. After his mother's death, his father sent young Du Sable to Paris for an education. Later he worked as a seaman on his father's ships. At twenty he was shipwrecked near New Orleans; fearful that he might be enslaved, he persuaded Jesuits to hide him until he was strong enough to leave the South.

He headed northwest and became a fur trapper. A British report of July 4, 1779, pinpointed both his geographical and political position: "Baptiste Pointe Du Sable, a handsome Negro, well educated and settled at Eschikagou, but was much in the interest of the French." This suspicion led to Du Sable's arrest for "treasonable intercourse with the enemy," for the British and French were at war. The charges were soon dropped, the official report admitting Du Sable "has in every way behaved in a manner becoming to a man of his station, and has many friends who give him a good character."

During the sixteen years Du Sable lived at the mouth of the Chicago River, he devoted himself to building his business and attending to his domestic duties. He brought to his crude log cabin a Potawatomi Indian woman named Catherine, and twenty-three European works of art. Soon the couple had a daughter and a son. Though Du Sable acquired eight hundred acres of land in Peoria, he always considered Chicago his home. His settlement grew to include a 40-by-22-foot log house, a bakehouse, a dairy, a smokehouse, a poultry house, a workshop, a stable, a barn, and a mill. Besides trading in furs, Du Sable was a miller, a cooper, a husbandman and whatever else was needed around the settlement.

In 1788 Du Sable and Catherine were married before a Catholic priest at Cahokia. Two years later their daughter was married and in 1796 they became grandparents. That same year Du Sable, closely aligned with the Indians of the region, decided to run for election as chief of the neighboring tribes. He lost. In 1800, perhaps as a result of this defeat, he sold his Chicago property for twelve hundred dollars and left the area forever. He lived on, fearing only two things—that he would become a public charge and that he would not be buried in a Catholic cemetery. As old age overtook him he did have to ask for public relief. But in 1818, when he died, he was buried in the St. Charles Borromeo Cemetery.

Centralia, Washington: Population 1990: 12,101

In 1817 George Washington was born in Virginia to a slave father and white mother. His mother gave him in adoption to a white family who moved to frontier settlements, first in Ohio and then northern Missouri. By the time he was a teen-ager, he was an expert marksman with rifle or revolver. He had also picked up skills as a miller, distiller, tanner, cook, weaver and spinner, and had learned to read, write and do arithmetic. Six feet tall and weighing almost two hundred pounds, he was known locally for his strength. The Missouri legislature granted him almost all the rights of a citizen.

But in 1850 he and his foster parents left the state in a train of fifteen wagons that took four months to reach the Oregon Territory. As an independent homesteader on a 640-acre plot purchased for him by his foster father, he grew cereal and vegetable crops. He did not marry until after he had repaid his foster parents and after they had died. He was fifty when he wedded an attractive Negro widow, Mary Jane Cooness. Together the two prospered. In 1872 when the Northern Pacific Railroad decided to build across his land, he decided to establish a town he called Centerville, halfway between the Columbia River and Puget Sound. To insure the town's growth, he sold lots at only five dollars if the buyers would agree to build a house worth at least a hundred dollars on the land. Then he donated money to build churches, a cemetery and aid less fortunate townspeople. In 1890, two years after his first wife died, he remarried, and Washington, then in his mid-seventies, shortly had a son.

The Panic of 1893 severely tested Washington's generosity and resources, but he became a one-man relief agency. His wagons brought rice, flour, sugar, meat and lard from as far away as Portland to his starving town. He provided jobs and "he saved the town."

In 1905 and still in good health, he died in an accident, thrown from his horse and buggy. The mayor proclaimed a day of mourning and Centralia had its biggest funeral. It was entirely fitting that it was held in a church he had donated, on ground he had donated, and he was laid to rest in a cemetery he had donated to the town. The city park still bears the name of this sturdy and compassionate black man whose skilled hands and resourceful mind had helped to build the West. Those who knew him, and many who did not, all benefited.

SOS
IMAMU AMIRI BARAKA (LEROI JONES)

Amiri Baraka, a leading poet, playwright, lecturer, and essayist in the late 1950s and 1960s, is considered the father of the Black Arts movement, the so-called "aesthetic and spiritual sister" of Black Power. Born LeRoi Jones in 1934, he changed his name in the 1960s to reflect traditional African practices and beliefs. His work has been dedicated to raising the consciousness of black people—waking them from a sleep that has lasted hundreds of years. Here, Baraka sends out a call to black folks everywhere.

Calling black people
Calling all black people, man woman child
Wherever you are, calling you, urgent, come in
Black People, come in, wherever you are, urgent, calling
you, calling all black people
calling all black people, come in, black people, come on in.

❧

I'd rather be a lamppost in Harlem than the governor of Georgia.
—*Anonymous*

❧

BLACK MANHATTAN
JAMES WELDON JOHNSON

In the 1920s New York City became a powerful magnet, drawing many thousands of blacks from the rural South, from other places across the nation, from the West Indies, and from Africa. Harlem beckoned. Loudly. It became the capital of black America and "the Negro capital of the world," as one of its leading residents, James Weldon Johnson, said. Harlem was the sophisticated nucleus of the New Negro Movement, otherwise known as the Harlem Renaissance, a movement that prompted international interest in black culture.

Harlem wasn't always a black community. At the turn of the century, mostly white upper–middle class New Yorkers resided there, on streets lined with beautiful brownstones. But by 1914, it was a community of 14,000 blacks. The black population swelled to 175,000 by 1925. By the Great Depression, when more than 200,000 blacks lived in Harlem, most white Harlemites had fled the community.

Here Johnson describes his Harlem, a place bursting with activity and great potential,* a neighborhood rich in its diversity of black folk and unique in all the world.

The fact that within New York, the greatest city of the New World, there is found the greatest single community anywhere of people descended from age-old Africa appears at a thoughtless glance to be the climax of the incongruous. Harlem is today the Negro metropolis and as such is everywhere known. In the history of New York the name Harlem has changed from Dutch to Irish to Jewish to Negro; but it is through this last change that it has gained its most widespread fame.

Within the past ten years Harlem has acquired a world-wide reputation. It has gained a place in the list of famous sections of great cities. It is known in Europe and the Orient, and it is talked about by natives in the interior of Africa. It is farthest known as being exotic, colourful, and sensuous; a place of laughing, singing, and dancing; a place where life wakes up at night. This phase of Harlem's fame is most widely known because, in addition to being spread by ordinary agencies, it has been proclaimed in story and song. And certainly this is Harlem's most striking and fascinating aspect. New Yorkers and people visiting New York from the world over go to the night-clubs of Harlem and dance to such jazz music as can be heard nowhere else; and they get an exhilaration impossible to duplicate. Some of these seekers after new sensations go

---

* James Weldon Johnson lived at 187 West 135th Street, next door to the Harlem Young Men's Christian Association and on an historic block. Among the YMCA's guests were George Washington Carver, Matthew Henson, Charles Drew, Langston Hughes, and Ralph Ellison. Booker T. Washington served on the board of the Y.

Ellison lived at the Y when he moved to Harlem from Alabama. (He first met Langston Hughes and Alain Locke on the steps of the Y on June 5, 1936.) The block had other famous residents: entertainer Florence Mills, at 230 West 135th Street, and Claude McKay, at 180 West 135th Street (now a part of the Y). Also, the New York Public Library's 135th Street branch, at 103 West 135th Street, was the unofficial headquarters of black writers during the Harlem Renaissance.

beyond the gay night-clubs; they peep in under the more seamy side of things; they nose down into lower strata of life. A visit to Harlem at night—the principal streets never deserted, gay crowds skipping from one place of amusement to another, lines of taxicabs and limousines standing under the sparkling lights of the entrances to the famous night-clubs, the subway kiosks swallowing and disgorging crowds all night long—gives the impression that Harlem never sleeps and that the inhabitants thereof jazz through existence. But, of course, no one can seriously think that the two hundred thousand and more Negroes in Harlem spend their nights on any such pleasance. Of a necessity the vast majority of them are ordinary, hard-working people, who spend their time in just about the same way that other ordinary, hard-working people do. Most of them have never seen the inside of a night-club. The great bulk of them are confronted with the stern necessity of making a living, of making both ends meet, of finding money to pay the rent and keep the children fed and clothed neatly enough to attend school; their waking hours are almost entirely consumed in this unromantic task. And it is a task in which they cannot escape running up against a barrier erected especially for them, a barrier which pens them off on the morass—no, the quicksands—of economic insecurity. Fewer jobs are open to them than to any other group; and in such jobs as they get, they are subject to the old rule, which still obtains, "the last to be hired and the first to be fired."

Notwithstanding all that, gaiety is peculiarly characteristic of Harlem. The people who live there are by nature a pleasure-loving people; and though most of them must take their pleasures in a less expensive manner than in nightly visits to clubs, they nevertheless, as far as they can afford—and often much farther—do satisfy their hunger for enjoyment. And since they are constituted as they are, enjoyment being almost as essential to them as food, perhaps really a compensation which enables them to persist, it is well that they are able to extract pleasure easily and cheaply. An average group of Negroes can in dancing to a good jazz band achieve a delightful state of intoxication that for others would require nothing short of a certain per capita imbibition of synthetic gin. The masses of Harlem get a good deal of pleasure out of things far too simple for most other folks. In the evenings of summer and on Sundays they get lots of enjoyment out of strolling. Strolling is almost a lost art in New York; at least, in the manner in which it is so generally practised in Harlem. Strolling in Harlem does not mean merely walking along Lenox or upper Seventh Avenue or One Hundred and Thirty-fifth Street; it means that those streets are places for socializing. One puts on one's best clothes and fares forth to pass the time pleasantly with the friends and acquaintances and, most important of all, the strangers he is sure of meeting. One saunters along, he hails this one, exchanges a word or two with that one, stops for a short chat with the other one. He comes up to a laughing, chattering group, in which he may have only one friend or acquaintance, but that gives him the privilege of joining in. He does join in and takes part in the joking, the small talk and gossip, and makes new acquaintances. He passes on and arrives in front of one of the theatres, studies the bill for a while, undecided about going in. He finally moves on a few steps farther and joins another group and is introduced to two or three pretty girls who have just come to Harlem, perhaps only for a visit; and finds a reason to be glad that he postponed going into the theatre. The hours of a summer evening run by rapidly. This is not simply going out for a walk; it is more like going out for adventure.

In almost as simple a fashion the masses of Harlem get enjoyment out of church-going. This enjoyment, however, is not quite so inexpensive as strolling can be made. Some critics of the Negro—especially Negro critics—say that religion costs him too much; that he has too many churches, and that many of them are magnificent beyond his means; that church mortgages and salaries and upkeep consume the greater part of the financial margin of the race and keep its economic nose to the grindstone. All of which is, in the main, true. There are something like one hundred and sixty coloured churches in Harlem. A hundred of these could be closed and there would be left a sufficient number to supply the religious needs of the community. There would be left, in fact, just about the number of churches that are regularly organized and systematically administered and that could be adequately supported. The superfluous one hundred or more are ephemeral and nomadic, belonging to no established denomination and within no classification. They are here today and gone somewhere else or gone entirely tomorrow. They are housed in rented quarters, a store, the floor of a private dwelling, or even the large room of a flat; and remain as long as the rent can be met or until a move is made, perhaps, to other quarters. Doubtless some of the founders of these excess churches are sincere, though ignorant; but it is certain that many of them are parasitical fakers, even downright scoundrels, who count themselves successful when they have under the guise of religion got enough hard-working women together to ensure them an easy living.

In Harlem, as in all American Negro communities, the fraternal bodies also fill an important place. These fraternities, too, are in a very large degree social organizations, but they have also an economic feature. In addition to providing the enjoyment of lodge meetings, lodge balls and picnics, and the interest and excitement of lodge politics, there are provisions for taking care of the sick and burying the dead. Both of these latter provisions are highly commendable and are the means of attracting a good many members; however, the criticism can be made that very often the amount of money spent for burying the dead is out of proportion to that spent in caring for the living. Indeed, this is so general that it makes "the high cost of dying" a live question among Negroes.

Harlem is also a parade ground. During the warmer months of the year no Sunday passes without several parades. There are brass bands, marchers in resplendent regalia, and high dignitaries with gorgeous insignia riding in automobiles. Almost any excuse for parading is sufficient—the funeral of a member of the lodge, the laying of a cornerstone, the annual sermon to the order, or just a general desire to "turn out." Parades are not limited to Sundays; for when the funeral of a lodge member falls on a weekday, it is quite the usual thing to hold the exercises at night, so that members of the order and friends who are at work during the day may attend. Frequently after nightfall a slow procession may be seen wending its way along and a band heard playing a dirge that takes on a deeply sepulchral tone. But generally these parades are lively and add greatly to the movement, colour, and gaiety of Harlem. A brilliant parade with very good bands is participated in not only by the marchers in line, but also by the marchers on the sidewalks. For it is not a universal custom of Harlem to stand idly and watch a parade go by; a good part of the crowd always marches along, keeping step to the music.

Now, it would be entirely misleading to create the impression that all Harlem indulges in none other than these Arcadian-like pleasures. There is a large element of educated, well-to-do metropolitans among the Negroes of Harlem who view with indulgence, often with something less, the responses of the masses to these artless amusements. There is the solid, respectable, bourgeois class, of the average proportion, whose counterpart is to be found in every Southern city. There are strictly social sets that go in for bridge parties, breakfast parties, cocktail parties, for high-powered cars, week-ends, and exclusive dances. Occasionally an exclusive dance is held in one of the ballrooms of a big downtown hotel. Harlem has its sophisticated, fast sets, initiates in all the wisdom of worldliness. And Harlem has, too, its underworld, its world of pimps and prostitutes, of gamblers and thieves, of illicit love and illicit liquor, of red sins and dark crimes. In a word, Harlem possesses in some degree all of the elements of a cosmopolitan centre. And by that same word, striking an average, we find that the overwhelming majority of its people are people whose counterparts may be found in any American community. Yet as a whole community it possesses a sense of humour and a love of gaiety that are distinctly characteristic.

THE GREAT BLACK WAY
JERVIS ANDERSON

Some streets stir the imagination. In the 1920s and 1930s, Harlem's Seventh Avenue wasn't simply a street. It was a boulevard of dreams, a place with dash and style. This account paints a vivid picture of "the Great Black Way" deep in the heart of Harlem.

When the great bandleader Cab Calloway, who grew up in Rochester and Baltimore, first saw Harlem, in 1929, he was, he said, "awestruck by the whole scene." Never had he beheld "so many Negroes in one place," or a street as glamorous as Seventh Avenue. "It was beautiful," he added. "Just beautiful . . . night clubs all over, night clubs whose names were legendary to me." The young Duke Ellington—a native of

Washington, D.C.—is said to have remarked on first seeing Harlem, in the early twenties, "Why, it is just like the Arabian Nights."

Seventh Avenue was the most handsome of the boulevards running through Harlem. It was bisected into an uptown and a downtown drive by a narrow strip of park, planted with trees and flowers. Despite the renown and importance of 125th Street—the district's main commercial artery—it was Seventh Avenue that deserved to be called the main street of Harlem. It reflected almost every form of life uptown—with its stores, churches, beauty parlors, doctors' offices, theatres, night clubs, nice-looking apartment buildings, and private brownstones. The novelist Wallace Thurman referred to it as Harlem's "most representative" avenue, "a grand thoroughfare into which every element of the Harlem population ventures either for reasons of pleasure or of business." From 125th Street to 145th Street, he added, Seventh Avenue was "majestic yet warm," and reflected "both the sordid chaos and the rhythmic splendor of Harlem."

In the twenties, Seventh Avenue was the headquarters of Harry Pace's Black Swan phonograph company, which produced some of the earliest recordings of jazz and the blues. On the avenue, there were the Renaissance ballroom and such fine theatres as the Roosevelt, the Alhambra, and the Lafayette. Among the churches there, Salem Methodist was perhaps the largest, and among the cabarets, the most famous were Connie's Inn and Smalls' Paradise. During the thirties, James Van Der Zee, Harlem's best-known photographer, had his studio on the avenue. Of Van Der Zee, a sympathetic and indefatigable recorder of Harlem life, Cecil Beaton wrote in 1938: "In Harlem he is called upon to capture the tragedy as well as the happiness in life, turning his camera on death and marriage with the same detachment." Several of the left-wing ideologues who harangued crowds at the corner of Lenox Avenue and 135th Street edited their little magazines from offices on Seventh. The Blyden Bookstore and the National Bookstore, virtual academies of black consciousness, were on the avenue. Owned by Dr. Willis Huggins and Lewis Michaux, respectively, their stocks leaned heavily to volumes on African and Afro-American history. "If we couldn't find a book anywhere else," a customer of the National Bookstore later said, "we always knew that Michaux had a copy on hand; but perhaps more important than the availability of books was the kind of books he had—books on

Africa now out of print; books on the history of *us.*" At the corner of
Seventh and 125th Street—across the way from Michaux's bookstore—
was Harlem's best hotel, the Theresa. It was not until around 1940,
however, that the Theresa began admitting blacks, at which point, according to *Ebony*, it became "the social headquarters for Negro America, just as the Waldorf is the home for the white elite." The magazine
added: "To its famous registration desk flock the most famous Negroes
in America. It is the temporary home of practically every outstanding
Negro who comes to New York. . . . Joe Louis stays there, along with
every big-time Negro fighter. So does Rochester and the Hollywood
contingent, all the top bandleaders who haven't the good fortune to have
their own apartments in town, Negro educators, colored writers, and the
Liberian and Haitian diplomatic representatives. Big men in the business
world jostle top labor leaders in the flowered, mirrored lobby."

To many in Harlem, Seventh Avenue, a boulevard of high style, was
"the Great Black Way." One requirement of a grand funeral procession
in Harlem was that it make its way up or down Seventh Avenue at some
point. Father Divine's religious marches and Marcus Garvey's black
nationalist parades—resplendent with colorful banners and uniforms—
achieved a special swagger only when, from other streets and thorough-
fares, they swung into Seventh Avenue. When the great black fraternal
organizations (the Elks, the Odd Fellows, the Monarchs, the Masons, or
the Pythians) came to Harlem for an annual convention, a high point of
their gathering was an extravaganza of march and music that they staged
on Seventh. Perhaps none of these shows was more attractive than the
one in 1927, when some thirty thousand lodge brothers and sisters,
stepping to the accompaniment of twenty-five marching bands,
cakewalked and Charlestoned down the avenue to tunes like "Me and
My Shadow" and "Ain't She Sweet."

But Seventh Avenue presented no finer spectacle than its Easter Parades and its Sunday-afternoon promenades, when the high and low of
Harlem—in their best clothes or wearing the latest in fashion—strolled
leisurely up and down the avenue. Here is what a writer for *The New
Yorker* observed on a Sunday in 1926:

> Now that Fifth Avenue is no longer a promenade, only a fashion-
> able procession of shoppers . . . we have been seeking elsewhere

for a street which still retains the loafing stroll as a tempo. . . .
Seventh Avenue between 127th and 134th Streets . . . is still the
real thing in promenades. . . . Here the elite of colored New
York stroll almost any evening in a true Sunday-afternoon-in-the-
park manner. Here the young men in evening clothes and jaunty
derbies or in more sporting outfits of spats, colored shirts, trick
canes, loiter on the corners or in front of the theatres and laugh.
. . . dusky young school girls go arm in arm, sometimes four or
five abreast. Here old women waddle along, leading their favorite
hound or poodle; and a group of mammies, exchanging gossip as
though in a small-town back yard, mingle with flashy young flap-
pers. . . . Prosperous old men with heavy gold watch chains
slung ponderously over wide bellies stroll. . . . Harlem takes its
ease on one of the widest and more lovely avenues in the city.

On other Sunday afternoons, male strollers were to be seen in silk
toppers, homburgs, cutaways, velvet-collared Chesterfields, bouton-
nieres, monocles, lorgnettes, gaiters, frock coats, and white gloves.
Women carried Yankee sand pocketbooks, and wore high-cuffed peek-a-
toe slippers, wide-brimmed hats (decorated with flower bouquets), and
veils in chartreuse, lime, pink, blue, black, and white. In 1932, a journal
in Harlem reported that many women were wearing "sleek black
carouls" with "silver fox and sable trimmings" and "white satin or
velvet evening frocks, with draped bodies." Waistlines were "anywhere
from the hip top to a high empire line." Dresses were trimmed with fur,
"kolinsky fur, the preference." Popular that year was a Paris-designed
beret, with "a perky feather" shooting skyward. Shoes were generally
suede, in various shades of gray. And almost all the women of fashion
showed signs of having had an "oatmeal facial."

Of course, not all the strollers on Seventh Avenue were *that* smart-
looking. And not all belonged to the better classes. It was not so hard to
spot the prostitutes. Accustomed to their own style of street walking,
they could not quite conceal the habitual rhythms of their gait or suppress the erotic insolence of their derrieres. Prosperous pimps and racke-
teers—at the wheels of expensive automobiles—cruised up and down
the avenue, trolling for the attention of the young, the pretty, and the
innocent. Men dressed as exquisitely as Adolphe Menjou—the "dicty's,"

as such classy types in Harlem were called—shared the stroll with day laborers, elevator operators, and shoeshine boys, whose humbler duds were probably what the cut-rate economies of Delancey Street permitted. Servants of rich Park and Fifth Avenue families wore the hand-me-downs of their employers, striving, with amusing result, to look the part of what they had on. A number of women were out in ensembles that, as any knowing eye could tell, had been put together on their own sewing machines.

The *Age* was surely correct when it said, of a promenade in 1934, that "the creme de la creme" mingled with the "has beens," the "would-be's," the "four flushers," the "shallow fops," and the "humble."

But it was the relaxed and neighborly air of the stroll that mattered the most.

THE NEGRO LEAGUES
WILLIE MAYS

Before 1947, when Jackie Robinson crossed professional baseball's color line, major league baseball was "a white man's place."* Hall of Famer Willie Mays remembers the segregated leagues of yesteryear. Teams like

---

* Jackie Robinson (1919–72), the grandson of slaves and the son of sharecroppers, broke into historically white major league baseball by joining the Brooklyn Dodgers in 1947. His breakthrough changed sports history and eventually made him a prominent spokesman for racial integration and civil rights during the 1950s and 1960s.

But fifty years after his historic season with the Brooklyn Dodgers, team scouts, managers, and major league officials were worried that professional baseball was alienating blacks. One scout reportedly predicted that blacks would soon disappear from the sport without vigorous recruiting. The reason for this alienation, according to a *New York Times* reporter, was that baseball "preserved apartheid far too long, barring African-American talent that was often superior to that of the white majors." Sadly, baseball's "residue of racism" still lingers on, affecting how the game is managed and played. One study found that black pros consistently must outplay whites in order to stay in the league and that blacks customarily get put on the "athletic" track (positions such as outfielder), while whites are directed toward "thinking" posts (pitcher, catcher, infielder). Also, white players can go on to coaching careers more easily than blacks.

*the Kansas City Monarchs, the Homestead Grays, and others drew huge
crowds. As many as 50,000 fans attended Negro League All-Star Games
in Chicago. Blacks took special pride in their favorite teams.*

Jackie Robinson wasn't the first black ballplayer to wear a big-league
uniform. He was just the first who didn't pretend not to be black. For
years, players had "passed" or were described as "Indian" or "Cuban."
Back in 1872, a Negro named Bud Fowler broke into organized ball.
And in 1884, two brothers, Welday and Moses Fleetwood Walker,
played with Toledo of the American Association.

Since blacks and whites weren't allowed to compete on the same field
in most places in America—although a black jockey did win the Kentucky Derby—a group of waiters at a Babylon, Long Island, restaurant
passed themselves off as Cubans and played semipro white teams. They
became the noted Cuban Giants, the first outstanding black team in
America. Their Spanish probably was limited to "no."

But there were always "situations." The most noted ballplayer of the
1880s was Adrian (Cap) Anson of the Chicago White Sox. In an exhibition game with Newark of the Eastern League he simply walked off the
field rather than perform on the same field with Newark's light-skinned
pitcher.

John McGraw, in 1902, tried to sneak a black in when he was manag-
ing the Orioles. The player's name was Charley Grant, but McGraw
called him Chief Tokahoma. The plot failed, and Grant was forced to
leave the team.

Ty Cobb, whose .367 career batting average remains untouched by
any other ballplayer, toured Cuba in 1910, and some of the players on
his team were blacks. He came back disgruntled that three of them had
outhit him.

Meanwhile, New York was developing into the capital of black baseball, as tens of thousands of Southern blacks made the migration north
to settle in the major cities. Harlem quickly became the political, cultural, and residential capital of New York blacks. When World War I
ended, a Negro National League was formed, joined by an Eastern
Colored League. Teams in both leagues played white teams every fall
after the World Series was over.

But this caused some embarrassment to major league baseball when the black teams won. So Commissioner Kenesaw Mountain Landis ruled that if any of his major league teams played a black team, that major league team had better not wear its regular uniform—instead, they had to call themselves all stars. This way, it wasn't the Yankees or Giants or White Sox getting beaten by Negro ballplayers, it was just some collection of white ballplayers.

My team, the Black Barons, joined the Negro National League in 1917, along with their rookie pitcher, Satchel Paige, but it had been formed some years earlier. By the time the Depression rolled around, the players were grateful for a chance to play two and three games a day, even though they traveled in buses.

World War II changed attitudes. Perhaps the first stirrings of blacks concerning big-league baseball actually happened during the war. Bill Veeck, who was to do some unpopular things as an owner—such as make Larry Doby the American League's first black ballplayer, and put a midget up to bat—had been aware of the existence of great black players for decades. It went back to his years with the Chicago Cubs, when his father was president of the club. During the war, Veeck owned the Milwaukee Brewers of the American Association. But as he did with most things in life, he got tired of them after they had some success and he had made some money.

In 1945, the war was about to end and Veeck was searching for a team. Now, Veeck took off on his most outrageous plan of all. The Philadelphia Phillies were for sale. Veeck planned not only to buy those losers—but to stock the team with black baseball stars. After all, there was no law preventing an owner from hiring a black ballplayer. When Landis got wind of Veeck's plans, the old judge quickly found a more conservative buyer for the team.

While I was growing up, a way of life and a cast of characters with a wonderful history evolved in the black leagues that rivaled anything organized ball could muster. Goose Tatum played first base for the Indianapolis Clowns, for example, before becoming the star attraction of the Harlem Globetrotters.

Players used to recall the days of two-dollar meal money. The problem even with the two bucks was that they couldn't always find a place to spend it. They ate out of grocery stores in the South because often they couldn't find a restaurant that would serve them.

What ironies they must have appreciated. They would go to the Polo Grounds and draw thirty thousand fans. The annual East-West game in Chicago between the black teams attracted as many as fifty thousand fans. The blacks played in South America, Puerto Rico, Cuba—they were America's ambassadors. Did fans know the reason the players were traveling men, going so far from home?

They used a Wilson ball, a store-bought item. Their bats came off the shelves, and were not customized in Louisville by Hillerich and Bradsby. The ball wasn't as lively as the major league ball, the bats not as solid, and certainly not tailor made. In 1948, though, Artie Wilson of Birmingham led everyone, black and white, with a .402 batting average.

Teams would travel in baggage cars. If they were playing in Pittsburgh on Saturday night, why they'd play a doubleheader in Washington on Sunday. If they were staying overnight someplace, they might rent three rooms and squeeze in all nine players.

But what if you got hurt?

"We didn't have a paid trainer," Buck Leonard told me. "We rubbed each other."

Night games presented problems. Teams brought along portable lights, and players would string them up over the field before game time. A pitcher on each team was also a scorer, and kept track of runs and hits and errors. But if he had to come in as a relief pitcher, someone else would finish handling the scoring. No wonder Negro League records are hard to come by.

In nonleague exhibition games against a semipro team, the winner would get 60 percent and the loser 40 percent. Since the umpires were local guys, they favored the semipro teams.

This was the game of baseball in America as it was played outside the big-league parks, in the Texas League or in Triple A places or the Sally League. People think that black baseball somehow was like a minor league version of white baseball. No way. It was baseball for the best black ballplayers in America. And what kind of teams do you think were composed of the best black players in America? What kind of team do you think we'd have today if it contained the best black players? I think we'd have a shot at the pennant. But there have been a lot of myths about those times and leagues and players, as if we were just a bunch of characters flitting around in a sagging old yellow school bus, as if it was unorganized and sort of played just for fun, not following the rules.

That is so far from the truth. I'm not talking now about the exhibition games we played in Yankee Stadium or Comiskey Park in Chicago. We did fine right in Birmingham, too. On Sundays there would be anywhere from six thousand to ten thousand fans at Rickwood Field. It might have been black baseball, but the white fans got the best seats. Maybe five hundred white folks would show up on Sundays. They sat in a special section along the third-base line. The Black Barons were owned by Tom Hayes, an undertaker from Memphis, and we shared the field with the white Barons. They had the first choice of the playing dates, and we scheduled our games when they were on the road.

Despite its seemingly unorganized nature, black baseball did have its organization, and each season was crowned by the Negro World Series. And we felt that we were as good as the other world champions.

THE CHITLIN CIRCUIT
BELL HOOKS

In the South during the days of segregation, blacks were not served meals in white establishments unless they were willing to suffer the indignities of eating in the kitchen. But those who were willing to do so sometimes ate better fare at cheaper prices than white patrons out in the dining area. Black cooks and waiters, themselves subject to the same discrimination, often eased the burden of racism with warmth and consideration. And this "kitchen kindness"—the flip side of Jim Crowism—was not limited to the restaurant business. When blacks traveled and could not sleep in white hotels, local blacks opened their doors to travelers.

bell hooks recalls the days of segregation with nostalgia for the "sweet communion" that black people felt, which was rooted in love for one another. Assimilation, she says, has so divided the black community that many young people today do not have a clear concept of what the "black

experience" actually is. Here, hooks outlines an agenda for regaining the
communal feelings of the old "chitlin circuit"—the network of blacks who
knew and helped one another in times of deprivation and despair.

One of the most intense, vivid memories of childhood relives itself in
my mind often, the memory of school desegregation, which meant then
the closing of black schools, our beloved Booker T. Washington and
Crispus Attucks, schools in segregated black neighborhoods. We loved
going to school then, from the moment we rushed out of the door in the
morning to the lingering strolls home. In that world, black children were
allowed innocence. We did not really understand the meaning of segregation, the brutal racism that had created apartheid in this society, and
no one explained it. They wanted us to live childhood life not knowing.
We only knew the world we lived in, and as children we loved that
world in a deep and profound way.

It was the world of Southern, rural, black growing up, of folks sitting
on porches day and night, of folks calling your mama 'cause you walked
by and didn't speak, and of the switch waiting when you got home so
you could be taught some manners. It was a world of single older black
women schoolteachers, dedicated, tough; they had taught your mama,
her sisters, and her friends. They knew your people in ways that you
never would and shared their insight, keeping us in touch with generations. It was a world where we had a history. There grandfathers and
great-grandfathers, whose knees we sat on, gave us everything wonderful they could think about giving. It was a world where that something
wonderful might be a ripe tomato, found as we walked through the rows
of Daddy Jerry's garden, or you thought it was his garden then, 'cause
you did not know that word you would learn later—"sharecropper."
You did not know then that it was not his property. To your child mind
it had to be his land, 'cause he worked it, 'cause he held that dirt in his
hands and taught you to love it—land, that rich Kentucky soil that was
good for growing things. It was a world where we had a history. At tent
meetings and hot Sunday services we cooled ourselves with fans that
waved familiar images back to us. Carried away by pure religious ec-
stasy we found ourselves and God. It was a sacred world, a world where
we had a history.

That black world of my growing up began to fundamentally change when the schools were desegregated. What I remember most about that time is a deep sense of loss. It hurt to leave behind memories, schools that were "ours," places we loved and cherished, places that honored us. It was one of the first great tragedies of growing up. I mourned for that experience. I sat in classes in the integrated white high school where there was mostly contempt for us, a long tradition of hatred, and I wept. I wept throughout my high school years. I wept and longed for what we had lost and wondered why the grown black folks had acted as though they did not know we would be surrendering so much for so little, that we would be leaving behind a history.

Scenes in Paule Marshall's novel *Praisesong for the Widow* remind me of that loss; there the black couple is so intent on "making it" economically in the white world that they lose the sense of who they are, their history. Years later, older, and going through a process of self-recovery, the black woman has the insight that "they had behaved as if there had been nothing about themselves worth honoring." Contemplating the past, she thinks:

> Couldn't we have done differently? Hadn't there perhaps been another way! . . . Would it have been possible to have done both? That is, to have wrested, as they had done all those years, the means to rescue them from Halsey Street and to see the children through, while preserving, safeguarding, treasuring those things that had come down to them over the generations, which had defined them in a particular way. The most vivid, the most valuable part of themselves.

That line "they had behaved as if there had been nothing about themselves worth honoring" echoes in my dreams. She could have been writing about us back then when we let our schools go, when no one talked about what we would be losing, when we did not make ways to hold on.

With no shame, I confess to bearing a deep nostalgia for that time, for that moment when I first stood before an audience of hundreds of my people in the gymnasium of Crispus Attucks and gave my first public presentation. I recited a long poem. We had these talent shows before pep rallies, where we performed, where we discovered our artistry.

Nostalgia for that time often enters my dreams, wets my pillow (for a long time the man lying next to me, whose skin is almost soot black like my granddaddy's skin, woke me to say "stop crying, why you crying?"). I cannot imagine daily life without the brown and black faces of my people.

Nostalgic for a sense of place and belonging and togetherness I want black folks to know again, I learn anew the meaning of struggle. Words hardly suffice to give memory to that time, the sweetness of our solidarity, the heaviness of our pain and sorrow, the thickness of our joy. We could celebrate then; we knew what a good time looked like.

For me, this experience, of growing up in a segregated small town, living in a marginal space where black people (though contained) exercised power, where we were truly caring and supportive of one another, was very different from the nationalism I would learn about in black studies classes or from the Black Muslims selling papers at Stanford University my first year there. That nationalism was linked to black capitalism. I had come from an agrarian world where folks were content to get by on a little, where Baba, mama's mother, made soap, dug fishing worms, set traps for rabbits, made butter and wine, sewed quilts, and wrung the necks of chickens; this was not black capitalism. The sweet communion we felt (that strong sense of solidarity shrouding and protecting my growing-up years was something I thought all black people had known) was rooted in love, relational love, the care we had toward one another. This way of loving is best described by Linell Cady in her essay "A Feminist Christian Vision":

> Love is a mode of relating that seeks to establish bonds between the self and the other, creating a unity out of formerly detached individuals. It is a process of integration where the isolation of individuals is overcome through the forging of connections between persons. These connections constitute the emergence of a wider life including yet transcending the separate individuals. This wider life that emerges through the loving relationship between selves does not swallow up individuals, blurring their identities and concerns. It is not an undifferentiated whole that obliterates individuality. On the contrary, the wider life created by love constitutes a community of persons. In a community, persons retain their identity, and

they also share a commitment to the continued well-being of the relational life uniting them.

It is this experience of relational love, of a beloved black community, I long to know again.

At this historical moment, black people are experiencing a deep collective sense of "loss." Nostalgia for times past is intense, evoked by awareness that feelings of bonding and connection that seemed to hold black people together are swiftly eroding. We are divided. Assimilation rooted in internalized racism further separates us. Neonationalist responses do not provide an answer, as they return us to an unproductive "us against them" dichotomy that no longer realistically addresses how we live as black people in a postmodern world. Many of us do not live in black neighborhoods. Practically all of us work for white people. Most of us are not self-sufficient; we can't grow, build, or fix nothing. Large numbers of us are educated in predominantly white institutions. Interracial relations are more a norm. The "chitlin circuit"—that network of black folks who knew and aided one another—has been long broken. Clearly, as Marshall suggests in her novel, things must be done differently. We cannot return to the past. While it is true that we lost closeness, it was informed by the very structure of racist domination black civil rights struggle sought to change. It is equally true that this change has meant advancement, a lessening of overt racist brutality toward all black people. Looking back, it is easy to see that the nationalism of the sixties and seventies was very different from the racial solidarity born of shared circumstance and not from theories of black power. Not that an articulation of black power was not important; it was. Only it did not deliver the goods; it was too informed by corrosive power relations, too mythic, to take the place of that concrete relational love that bonded black folks together in communities of hope and struggle.

Black women, writing from a feminist perspective, have worked hard to show that narrow nationalism with its concomitant support of patriarchy and male domination actually helped erode an organic unity between black women and men that had been forged in struggles to resist racism begun in slavery time. Reinvoking black nationalism is not an adequate response to the situation of crisis we are facing as a people. In many ways, ours is a crisis of identity, not that "I need to find out who I am" lifestyle brand. The identity crisis we suffer has to do with losing a sense of political perspective, not knowing how we should struggle collectively to fight racism and to create a liberatory space to construct radical black subjectivity. This identity has to do with resistance, with reconstructing a collective front to re-vision and renew black liberation struggle.

In his provocative book *The Death of Rhythm and Blues* Nelson George sees this crisis as informed by a split between assimilationists and those black folks who wish to be, as he calls it, self-sufficient. This simplistic account is problematic. There are many black people who are not positioned to be self-sufficient, who are also not assimilationist. It is not simply a matter of personal choice. Much of the "new racism" bombarding us undermines black solidarity by promoting notions of choice and individual rights in ways that suggest "freedom" for a black person can be measured by the degree to which we can base all decisions in life on individualistic concerns, what feels good or satisfies desire. This way of thinking militates against bonding that is rooted in relational love, nor is it countered by nationalism.

When black people collectively experienced racist oppression in similar ways, there was greater group solidarity. Racial integration has indeed altered in a fundamental way the common ground that once served as a foundation for black liberation struggle. Today black people of different classes are victimized by racism in distinctly different ways. Despite racism, privileged black people have available to them a variety of life choices and possibilities. We cannot respond to the emergence of multiple black experiences by advocating a return to narrow cultural nationalism. Contemporary critiques of essentialism (the assumption that there is a black essence shaping all African-American experience, expressed traditionally by the concept of "soul") challenge the idea that there is only "one" legitimate black experience. Facing the reality of multiple black experiences enables us to develop diverse agendas for unification, taking into account the specificity and diversity of who we are.

Teaching Black Studies, I find that students are quick to label a black person who has grown up in a predominantly white setting and attended similar schools as "not black enough." I am shocked and annoyed by the growing numbers of occasions where a white person explains to me that another black person is really "not black-identified." Our concept of black experience has been too narrow and constricting. Rather than assume that a black person coming from a background that is not predominantly black is assimilationist, I prefer to acknowledge that theirs is a different black experience, one that means that they may not have had access to life experiences more common to those of us raised in racially segregated worlds. It is not productive to see them as enemies or dismiss them by labeling them "not black enough." Most often they have not chosen the context of their upbringing, and they may be suffering from a sense of "loss" of not knowing who they are as black people or where they fit in. Teaching students from these backgrounds (particularly at Yale), I found myself referring often to traditional black folk experience and they would not know what I was talking about. It was not that they did not want to know—they did. In the interest of unity, of strengthening black community, it is important for us to recognize and value all black experiences and to share knowledge with one another. Those of us who have a particularly rich connection to black folk traditions can and should share.

Years ago I would begin my introduction to African-American literature classes by asking students to define blackness. Usually they simply listed stereotypes. Often folks evoke the experience of Southern rural black folks and make it synonymous with "authentic" blackness, or we take particular lifestyle traits of poor blacks and see them as "the real thing." Even though most black folks in the United States have Southern roots (let's not forget that for a long time ninety percent of all black people lived in the agrarian South), today many know only an urban city experience. A very distinctive black culture was created in the agrarian South, by the experience of rural living, poverty, racial segregation, and resistance struggle, a culture we can cherish and learn from. It offers ways of knowing, habits of being, that can help sustain us as a people. We can value and cherish the "meaning" of this experience without essentializing it. And those who have kept the faith, who embody in our life practices aspects of that cultural legacy, can pass it on. Current trends in postmodernist cultural critiques devaluing the importance of this legacy by dismissing notions of authenticity or suggesting that the very concept of "soul" is illusory and not experientially based are disturbing. Already coping with a sense of extreme fragmentation and alienation, black folks cannot afford the luxury of such dismissal.

Philosopher Cornel West, an influential black scholar committed to liberation struggle, calls attention to the crisis we are facing in his discussions of postmodernism. Commenting on the nihilism that is so pervasive in black communities, he explains:

> Aside from the changes in society as a whole, developments like hedonistic consumerism and the constant need of stimulation of the body which make any qualitative human relationships hard to maintain, it is a question of a breakdown in resources, what Raymond Williams calls structures of meaning. Except for the church, there is no longer any potent tradition on which one can fall back in dealing with hopelessness and meaninglessness.

West is speaking about the black underclass, yet the patterns he cites are equally manifest among black people who have material privilege. Poverty alone does not create a situation of nihilism; black people have always been poor. We need to re-examine the factors that gave life meaning in the midst of deprivation, hardship, and despair. I have already cited relational love as one of these forces; that way of being can be consciously practiced.

We can begin to build anew black communal feelings and black community by returning to the practice of acknowledging one another in daily life. That way "downhome" black folks had of speaking to one another, looking one another directly in the eye (many of us had old folks tell us, don't look down, look at me when I'm talking to you), was not some quaint country gesture. It was a practice of resistance undoing years of racist teachings that had denied us the power of recognition, the power of the gaze. These looks were affirmations of our being, a balm to wounded spirits. They opposed the internalized racism or alienated individualism that would have us turn away from one another, aping the dehumanizing practices of the colonizer. There are many habits of being that were a part of traditional black folk experience that we can re-enact, rituals of belonging. To reclaim them would not be a gesture of passive nostalgia; it would reflect awareness that humanizing survival strategies employed then are needed now.

Another important practice we need to reconstruct is the sharing of stories that taught history, family genealogy, and facts about the African-American past. Briefly, during the contemporary black power movement, tremendous attention was given to the importance of learning history. Today young black people often have no knowledge of black history and are unable to identify important black leaders like Malcolm X. The arts remain one of the powerful, if not the most powerful, realms of cultural resistance, a space for awakening folks to critical consciousness and new vision. Crossover trends in black music, film, etc., that require assimilation have a devastating anti-black propagandistic impact. We need to call attention to those black artists who successfully attract diverse audiences without pandering to a white supremacist consumer market while simultaneously creating a value system where acquisition of wealth and fame are not the only measures of success.

The most important agenda for black people concerned with unity and renewed struggle is the construction of a visionary model of black liberation. To complete this task we would need to examine the impact of materialist thinking in black lives. Nowadays many black folks believe that it is fine to do anything that will make money. Many of us have lost a needed sense of ethics, that morality Mama evokes in *A Raisin in the Sun* when she asks Walter Lee, "Since when did money become life?" Black people must critically examine our obsession with material gain and consumer goods. We need to talk about the way living simply may be a necessary aspect of our collective self-recovery. We need to look at the way addiction to drugs, food, alcohol and a host of other substances undermines our individual sense of self and our capacity to relate to one another. Addiction must be seen politically as both sickness and a manifestation of genocidal practices that have a grip on black life and are destroying it.

In *Freedom Charter,* a work which chronicles resistance strategies in South Africa, the phrase "our struggle is also a struggle of memory against forgetting" is continually repeated. Memory need not be a passive reflection, a nostalgic longing for things to be as they once were; it can function as a way of knowing and learning from the past, what Michael M.J. Fischer in his essay "Ethnicity and the Art of Memory" calls "retrospection to gain a vision for the future." It can serve as a catalyst for self-recovery. We are talking about collective black self-recovery. We need to keep alive the memory of our struggles against racism so that we can concretely chart how far we have come and where we want to go, recalling those places, those times, those people that gave a sense of direction. If we fall prey to the contemporary ahistorical mood, we will forget that we have not stayed in one place, that we have journeyed away from home, away from our roots, that we have lived drylongso and learned to make a new history. We have not gone the distance, but we can never turn back. We need to sing again the old songs, those spirituals that renewed spirits and made the journey sweet, hear again the old testimony urging us to keep the faith, to go forward in love.

HITSVILLE, U.S.A.
BERRY GORDY JR.

Berry Gordy Jr., the son of a construction contractor, founded a musical dynasty in a Detroit house in 1959. He signed a cast of stars who dominated the nation's pop-music charts and played a vital role in shaping popular culture. His stars were the Supremes, Smokey Robinson, Marvin Gaye, Diana Ross, Michael Jackson, the Temptations, the Four Tops, and others. The company was Motown.

At the time, the nation was torn by racial violence. But Motown—a black-owned company of black artists—wielded tremendous crossover appeal. That appeal was stage-managed by Gordy. The story of Motown was very much one of family and community. Family got it off the ground, loaning Berry Jr. $800 to start his company. Community provided enough momentum for it to thrive.

I had sent everyone out looking for a larger place, but it was Raynoma Liles who found the one I liked, a two-story house at 2648 West Grand Boulevard with a big picture window in the front and a photography studio in the back. Perfect for my growing operation. I put a down payment on it and we moved in.

A couple of weeks later, George Kelly, the local club owner who had earlier hired Roquel and me to work with his singer, Frances Burnett, came by to check things out. The two of us stood out on the sidewalk, looking back at the building.

"What are you going to call it?" he asked. This was something I'd been thinking hard about, wanting to come up with the perfect name. Standing there looking at that unique picture window, I came up with it.

"Hitsville," I proclaimed.

He laughed. "You're joking."

"No, I'm serious. That's the only name I can think of that expresses what I want it to be—a hip name for a factory where hits are going to be built. That's it, Hitsville."

Thanks to my brief training in electronics school, where I had gone on the GI Bill, I was able to set up a two-track recorder that I bought from Bristol Bryant. Mother was right . . . "Whatever you learn is never wasted." And again, my family was right there with me, pitching in. While I set up the microphones and strung wires to assemble my first mixing board, Pop and my brother George handled the plastering, sealing of cracks and installation of soundproofing material.

The house needed a major top-to-bottom scrubbing and repainting, and many of the artists and creative people I was working with came to help.

In no time at all that house at 2648 West Grand Boulevard took on a whole new life. From a photo studio, the garage was turned into a recording studio, the first floor became the lobby and the control room. Between the basement and first and second floors we had to cram everything in, including living quarters for me, Ray, Kerry, and Cliff.

Down in the studio, finishing up our work, surrounded by all this activity there was Pop, finding an opportunity to give me advice: "Well, just remember, son, a smart man profits from his mistakes."

Now that I was my own boss I could add my own variations to my father's philosophies. "But a *wise* man," I said, "also profits from the mistakes of others." I told him if I had to make all my own mistakes I would not live long enough to do half the things I wanted to do in my lifetime.

Pop chuckled. . . .

The white lady who had sold me the house came around a few times making repairs—fixing little things, painting, trying to keep it up. She had gotten it back twice before in foreclosures. And with no credit rating and no visible means of support, and her seeing young black kids running in and out and making all that noise, she was certain it would soon be hers again.

I don't think she realized that we were there to stay until one day she came by and saw the place looking better than ever. And above the big picture window, stretching from door to door, were big beautiful letters spelling out HITSVILLE USA.

My privacy began to disappear as more people became drawn to what I was doing. Besides aspiring artists, writers and producers who had started hanging around, others who had business skills were also looking for ways to get involved.

Upstairs, in a bedroom-turned-bookkeeping-office, my sister Esther ran a tight ship handling the money matters, helped by her husband, George Edwards, a Michigan state representative and an accountant.

In another upstairs office my sister Loucye, who left her government job with the Army Reserves, set up her area. It wasn't much then, but would soon be what was loosely called the Manufacturing Department. She would handle everything from the pressing plants, shipping, billing and collections, to sales, graphics and liner notes for the album covers. A real dynamo!

Downstairs Ray had her own office area. Because of her knowledge of music and lead sheets, I put her in charge of the publishing operation, where she got tremendous help from her brother, Mike Ossman, and Janie Bradford, our first receptionist.

Janie Bradford was something else. While she was hardworking and capable, she never lost her demented sense of fun. One July day in '59 I was walking through the lobby on my way to the studio, studying a lyric sheet, when I felt someone pinching my butt.

One of her favorite things to do was sneak up behind me and do that. It never mattered to her who I was talking to at the time. As I'd jump and look around, there she'd be, smiling as if nothing happened. Then she'd whisper, "Just couldn't help it. You're sooo special."

I sort of bought that special line until later I found out Brian, Smokey and a few others were "special," too.

When she did it that day, I jumped a little but seeing who it was I kept walking. From my attitude, she could see I was in no mood for talking—or being pinched.

She caught up with me again. "Mr. Gordy," I heard her say cheerfully, "I'm sorry but I couldn't help it, you are just—"

"Unh, unh," I said, cutting her off. "I'm trying to finish a song."

Janie, a songwriter herself, was interested in any song I might be writing. "Oh yeah? That's great! What's it about?"

Magic words. I was always a sucker when someone really wanted to hear my new song ideas. It was a throwback to my youthful days when people saw me coming and would go the other way. "Well," I began, "it's a long story."

"Tell me about it," she said. "I got plenty of time."

"Okay. A couple days ago while walking down the street I decided to write a song. So I asked myself the same question I always do whenever I start a new song. What am I really feeling right now?" I told her I was having a mixed bag of emotions: anticipation, exhilaration, motivation. I was thinking about what most other hit songs were written about—love! "Yeah, love," I said, "the most beautiful thing in the world."

"You sho' ain't lying there, baby. That's great," she shouted.

"Yeah, I know, but I didn't want to write about that. Everybody writes about love. *I* wanted to write about something different. But what? Then it popped into my head, the most obvious thing of all, the thing I needed most—money. And I'm almost finished. Got one more verse to go."

"But won't people think that's all you care about?" Janie said.

"So what? Some will be shocked, some will think it's cute, some will think it's funny. I think I'll make money. What do you think?"

"How's it go?"

By this time we had reached the studio. Standing at the piano, I began to play some of the chords to my song, telling her how as a kid I'd heard people say, *"The best things in life are free,"* but knowing how much easier that was to say when you had money I sarcastically added, *"But you can give them to the birds and bees, I need money . . ."*

She laughed.

I loved the fact that she laughed so I rushed into the next verse singing the song as I played—*"Money don't get everything it's true, but what it don't get I can't use, I need money."*

She laughed again.

Then I really got into it, singing the chorus—*"Money, that's what I want. Yeah, yeah, that's what I want . . ."*

Janie was ecstatic. Still laughing, she offhandedly threw in her own line—*"Your love gives me such a thrill, but your love don't pay my bills, gimme some money, baby."*

"Great! That's great," I said, continuing to jam on the chorus line. "I'm gonna use that."

Barrett Strong, an artist I had started working with, who was writing a song in another room, ran into the studio and started jamming along with us. He slid next to me on the piano bench, playing away and joining me singing the chorus—uninvited. This was uncharacteristic of Barrett, who always seemed quiet, shy and a little in awe of me. But not this day. His voice was soulful and passionate. I didn't have to think twice about who I could get to sing my song. Barrett was it.

Janie didn't realize I was serious about using the line she had just blurted out spontaneously in a moment of fun. She was more convinced when she saw the songwriter's contract. Thinking her verse was the best of all, I gave her fifty percent.

"Money (That's What I Want)" was one of the first records cut at our own little studio. It was less like any record session I can remember. More like an in-house rehearsal—a party. One long party. It lasted a few days. We took take after take. Fun. I no longer had to worry about the cost of the studio. I owned it.

Being one of the earlier sessions, we recorded everything together, the singer, the band and the background voices. That gave it a raw, earthy feel.

At the beginning we did our sound engineering with the existing equipment—the little two-track I had bought from Bristol Bryant. Then I hired a young technical genius named Mike McLean. He slowly rebuilt our equipment, creating as he went along. Very worried about how "his" equipment was going to be used, he made all the producers and engineers take classes from him on how to operate it—including me.

I was never really happy with our studio sound. But as it turned out, its many limitations forced us to be innovative. For example, having no room in the studio for a vocal booth, we made one out of the hallway that led from the control room to the stairs that took you into the studio. Since there were no windows we couldn't see the singer, so we communicated only over the microphones. But the end result was a good, clean vocal.

Our first echo chamber was the downstairs bathroom. We had to post a guard outside the door to make sure no one flushed the toilet while we were recording.

Later we also adapted an attic area as an echo chamber. That worked very well, except for an occasional car horn, rain, thunder or any other outside sounds that came in through the roof. Eventually we started recording the songs dry and adding echo afterward. Echoes gave the recording a bigger sound and made the voice sound fatter with a lingering feel to it. We bought a German electronic echo chamber, called an EMT, which we installed in the basement. That worked the best of all.

We put partitions around the different instruments to keep the horn sounds from bleeding into the bass, or the drums into the piano, and so on.

To get a clean, clear sound on the guitars, without any hum or feedback from the amps, we started feeding the guitars directly into the control room. (Several years later we brought in Armin Steiner from the West Coast to rebuild and modernize our studio.)

Long before there were electronic synthesizers, I was looking for new ways to create different sound effects. We would try anything to get a unique percussion sound: two blocks of wood slapped together, striking little mallets on glass ashtrays, shaking jars of dried peas—anything. I might see a producer dragging in big bike chains or getting a whole group of people stomping on the floor.

Never having forgotten that big orchestral sound from the Jackie Wilson "Lonely Teardrops" session, I tried to re-create it in our own studio, often bringing in string players from the Detroit Symphony. At first they had no idea what to make of me or how their music would fit into ours. But in time they became an integral part of the Motown family and our sound.

Another regular aspect of our early productions was the background voices of the Andantes—Judith Barrow, Louvain Demps, Jacqueline Hicks—another backup group.

Since many producers, myself included, lacked a lot of formal music education, when it came time to merge all these different elements, we sometimes looked for help from some of our arrangers. In the process, the talents of such people as Johnny Allen, Willie Shorter, Paul Riser and Hank Cosby would also leave a distinctive mark on our music.

Mixing was so important to me that it seemed I spent half my life at the mixing board. To get just the right sound, just the right blend, I would mix and mix and then remix. Smokey and I had a running joke over what a mix maniac I was.

Often the differences between the various mixes were subtle; but those subtleties, I felt, could make or break a record.

Whether I was cutting a record, mixing it or listening to someone else's, I was open to just about anything.

I may not have always known what I was looking for exactly, but when I found it I knew it. While open to a broad range of influences— Gospel, Pop, Rhythm & Blues, Jazz, Doo-Wop, Country—I always emphasized simple, clear communication.

As other independent record companies were failing, we were thriving. I am often asked, "How did you do it? How did you make it work at a time when so many barriers existed for black people and black music?" There are many answers to those questions but at the base of them is atmosphere. Hitsville had an atmosphere that allowed people to experiment creatively and gave them the courage not to be afraid to make mistakes. In fact, I sometimes encouraged mistakes. Everything starts as an idea and as far as I was concerned there were no stupid ones. "Stupid" ideas are what created the lightbulb, airplanes and the like. I never wanted people to feel how I felt in school—dumb. It was an atmosphere that made you feel no matter how high your goals, they were reachable, no matter who you were.

I had always figured that less than 1 percent of all the people in the world reach their full potential. Seeing that potential in others, I realized that by helping them reach theirs, maybe I could reach mine.

❧

Sticks in a bundle are unbreakable.

—*Kenyan proverb*

❧

BLACK FRATERNITIES AND SORORITIES STEP LIVELY

Black Greek-letter organizations have a strong tradition of community service. They sponsor fund-raising drives for black organizations, voter registration campaigns, college scholarships, and mentoring programs. Fraternities and sororities also pushed to establish the Martin Luther King Jr. national holiday. A large number of the nation's black achievers are proudly affiliated with these organizations, in which bonds often last a lifetime.

Since the early years of the twentieth century, black fraternities and sororities have played an important role in black society, offering fellowship, a culture of achievement, leadership, and community service.

The first black fraternity emerged from a literary society at Cornell University in Ithaca, New York, on October 23, 1906, when a study group of seven undergraduates, barred from white fraternities, formed their own: Alpha Phi Alpha. A week later, the group rented a Masonic hall, where they toasted with punch, enjoyed a communal smoke, and enrolled the first group of initiates, who were said to be "trembling," into the exclusive brotherhood. In just two years, it became an international organization with a second chapter at Howard University in Washington, D.C., a third at the University of Toronto, and a basic set of ideals, adopted at its first convention, held in 1908: "manly deeds, scholarship, and love for all mankind."

Following Alpha Phi Alpha's lead, other black Greek-letter organizations sprang up quickly. Five of the eight major African American Greek-letter student societies were founded at Howard University over the next several years—Alpha Kappa Alpha Sorority (1908), Omega Psi Phi Fraternity (1911), Delta Sigma Theta Sorority (1913), Phi Beta Sigma Fraternity (1914), and Zeta Phi Beta Sorority (1920). Kappa Alpha Psi Fraternity was founded in 1911 at Indiana University in 1911, and the youngest major Greek-letter society, Sigma Gamma Rho Sorority, was established at Butler University in 1922.

During the days of segregation, these organizations—which now form the National Pan-Hellenic Council—served as "survival networks," particularly at predominately white schools, which excluded blacks from campus activities. Black fraternities and sororities provided housing for black students who were not admitted to campus dormitories, and lessened the sense of social isolation for blacks on campus.

These groups also have a long and distinguished tradition of service off campus. The Alpha Phi Alpa Fraternity began a national higher education campaign in 1916 called "Go to High School, Go to College." Each June, fraternity brothers disseminated educational literature, made speeches on the value of higher education, and sponsored counseling sessions. The Kappa Alpha Psi Fraternity began its Guide Right program for mentoring young black men in 1922. In 1935, Alpha Kappa Alpha Sorority began its Mississippi Health Project, which sent teams of physicians and nurses in the backwoods of Mississippi to provide treatment and educate residents. Two years later, Delta Sigma Theta Sorority launched its National Library Program, sending bookmobiles throughout the South.

Today, African American Greek-letter societies remain among the few black-led and -financed organizations that give millions of dollars annually in scholarships. They provide funding for black colleges, social institutions, and the arts. They also manage low-income housing for the elderly, provide prenatal counseling and legal aid for teenagers in many cities, operate job training centers, run drug-prevention and literacy programs, and offer international aid. Alpha Kappa Alpha, which became an accredited observer at the United Nations in the 1940s, has "adopted" more than two hundred African villages over the years, sending money to build wells and provide supplies for schools and health centers.

What has differentiated black Greek-letter organizations from their white counterparts is black organizations' unabashed commitment to social and political action. Soon after it was founded in 1913, Delta Sigma Theta participated in a mass march on Washington for women's suffrage. Many black organizations have worked for civil rights legislation and litigation, allying themselves with the National Association for the Advancement of Colored People, the National Urban League, and other groups. African American Greek-letter chapters have also assisted the political campaigns of members.

Though the popularity of black Greek-letter organizations dipped in the late 1960s and early 1970s, when black militancy on campus took root, their memberships have increased over the years as the number of black college students and graduates grew. By 1990, some 700,000 blacks were members of one of the eight major black organizations. In 1992, Delta Sigma Theta alone claimed a membership of some 175,000 sorors.

Since their inception, black fraternities and sororities have provided a steady flow of black leadership, including some of the most prominent figures in government and entertainment. U.S. Supreme Court Justice Thurgood Marshall and Martin Luther King Jr. were members of Alpha Phi Alpha. Bill Cosby, Jesse Jackson, and Michael Jordan are members of Omega Psi Phi. Other fraternity and sorority members have included Marian Anderson, Mary McLeod Bethune, Shirley Chisolm, W.E.B. Du Bois, Nikki Giovanni, Dorothy I. Height, Lena Horne, Barbara Jordan, Ernest Just, Jesse Owens, Leontyne Price, Paul Robeson, Mary Church Terrell, and Walter White.

Hundreds of thousands have felt the bonds of brotherhood and sister-hood, which differ in character or style from one organization to an-other. Fraternity and sorority pledges undergo grueling indoctrinations involving boot-camp style discipline and secret initiation rites. In the weeks prior to "crossing over," some carry ducks or bricks or plants, which symbolize an aspect of the organization; others shave their heads and paint their faces. Each group has its own special colors, songs, and "step dances," including call-and-response participation and the creation of music from synchronized, percussive stomping, tapping, and hand clapping. "Step dances," some people say, are rooted in African tradi-tions.

While known by letters of the Greek alphabet, these organizations have not lost sight of their members' heritage. According to author Paula Giddings, a soror of Delta Sigma Theta, "the choice of using Greek names for these organizations was, in part, a response to the beliefs of those like former U.S. Vice President John C. Calhoun, who said that a 'Negro would never learn to parse a Greek verb or solve a problem in Euclid.' " Regardless of whose alphabet is used to identify these groups—or why—many people would agree that these organizations celebrate the values of a rich black past.

Community cannot feed for long on itself, it can only flourish with the coming of others from beyond, their unknown and undiscovered brothers.

—Howard Thurman

I am we.

—African axiom

I, TOO

LANGSTON HUGHES

Written at the dawn of the Harlem Renaissance, this poem illustrates that African Americans are as much a part of the fabric of America as any other group.

I, too, sing America.

I am the darker brother.
They send me to eat in the kitchen
When company comes,
But I laugh,
And eat well,
And grow strong.

Tomorrow,
I'll be at the table
When company comes.
Nobody'll dare
Say to me,

"Eat in the kitchen,"
Then.

Besides,
They'll see how beautiful I am
And be ashamed—

I, too, am America.

❧

Democracy is a collectivity of individuals.

—*Ralph Ellison*

❧

WE, TOO, SING "AMERICA"
DUKE ELLINGTON

Suave and sophisticated Edward Kennedy Ellington (1899–1974), better known as Duke Ellington, was an American musical genius who created more than 1,500 compositions, including some of our best-loved jazz classics. The maestro delivered this speech in Los Angeles in 1941. It was inspired by Langston Hughes's poem "I, Too."

America is reminded of the feats of Crispus Attucks, Peter Salem, black armies in the Revolution, the War of 1812, the Civil War, the Spanish-American War, the World War. Further, forgetful America is reminded that we sing without false notes, as borne out by the fact that there are no records of black traitors in the archives of American history. This is all well and good, but I believe it to be only half the story.

We play more than a minority role, in singing "America." Although numerically but 10 per cent of the mammoth chorus that today, with an eye overseas, sings "America" with fervor and thanksgiving, I say our 10 per cent is the very heart of the chorus: the sopranos, so to speak, carrying the melody, the rhythm section of the band, the violins, pointing the way.

I contend that the Negro is the creative voice of America, is creative America, and it was a happy day in America when the first unhappy slave was landed on its shores.

There, in our tortured induction into this "land of liberty," we built its most graceful civilization. Its wealth, its flowering fields and handsome homes; its pretty traditions; its guarded leisure and its music, were all our creations.

We stirred in our shackles and our unrest awakened Justice in the hearts of a courageous few, and we recreated in America the desire for true democracy, freedom for all, the brotherhood of man, principles on which the country had been founded.

We were freed and as before, we fought America's wars, provided her labor, gave her music, kept alive her flickering conscience, prodded her on toward the yet unachieved goal, democracy—until we became more than a part of America! We—this kicking, yelling, touchy, sensitive, scrupulously-demanding minority—are the personification of the ideal begun by the Pilgrims almost 350 years ago.

It is our voice that sang "America" when America grew too lazy, satisfied and confident to sing . . . before the dark threats and fire-lined clouds of destruction frightened it into a thin, panicky quaver.

We are more than a few isolated instances of courage, valor, achievement. We're the injection, the shot in the arm, that has kept America and its forgotten principles alive in the fat and corrupt years intervening between our divine conception and our near tragic present.

༒

It's nation time!

—Anonymous

༒

ORGANIZING THE BUS BOYCOTT
JO ANN ROBINSON

Community spirit can spread quickly and have a powerful effect. We saw how fast it can spread in 1955, after Rosa Parks refused to give up her seat on a Montgomery, Alabama, bus and was arrested for defying segregation laws. Her arrest sent shock waves through the black community, prompting immediate action. To protest the arrest and support Parks, a local group led a citywide bus boycott. Nearly all area blacks joined in. A local newspaper reported, "Negroes were on almost every street corner in the downtown area, silent, waiting for rides or moving about to keep warm, but few got on buses."

The boycott also showed how effective community spirit can be: thirteen months after it had begun, blacks could sit in any seat on the bus. In the following paragraphs, Jo Ann Robinson, who played a crucial role in the bus boycott, tells how black people were prepared for the boycott.

The Women's Political Council was an organization begun in 1946 after dozens of black people had been arrested on the buses. We witnessed the arrests and humiliations and the court trials and the fines paid by people who just sat down on empty seats. We knew something had to be done.

We organized the Women's Council and within a month's time we had over a hundred members. We organized a second chapter and a third, and soon we had more than 300 members. We had members in every elementary, junior high, and senior high school. We had them organized from federal and state and local jobs; wherever there were more than ten blacks employed, we had a member there. We were organized to the point that we knew that in a matter of hours we could corral the whole city.

The evening that Rosa Parks was arrested, Fred Gray called me and told me that her case would be [heard] on Monday. As president of the main body of the Women's Political Council, I got on the phone and called all the officers of the three chapters. I told them that Rosa Parks had been arrested and she would be tried. They said, "You have the plans, put them into operation."

I didn't go to bed that night. I cut those stencils and took them to

[the] college. The fellow who let me in during the night is dead now . . . he was in the business department. I ran off 35,000 copies.

I talked with every member [of the Women's Council] in the elementary, junior high and senior high schools and told them to have somebody on the campus. I told them that I would be there to deliver them [the handbills]. I taught my classes from 8:00 to 10:00. When my 10:00 class was over, I took two senior students with me. I would drive to the place of dissemination and a kid would be there to grab [the handbills].

After we had circulated those 35,000 circulars, we went by the church. That was about 3:30 in the afternoon. We took them to the minister. The [ministers] agreed to meet that night to decide what should be done about the boycott after the first day. You see, the Women's Council planned it only for Monday, and it was left up to the men to take over after we had forced them really to decide whether or not it had been successful enough to continue, and how long it was to be continued.

They had agreed at the Friday night meeting that they would call this meeting at Holt Street Church and they would let the audience determine whether or not they would continue the bus boycott or end it in one day.

Monday night, the ministers held their meeting. The church itself holds four or five thousand people. But there were thousands of people outside of the church that night. They had to put up loudspeakers so they would know what was happening. When they got through reporting that very few people had ridden the bus, that the boycott was really a success—I don't know if there was one vote that said "No, don't continue that boycott"—they voted unanimously to continue the boycott. And instead of it lasting one day as the Women's Council had planned it, it lasted for thirteen months.

The spirit, the desire, the injustices that had been endured by thousands of people through the years . . . I think people were fed up, they had reached the point that they knew there was no return. That they had to do it or die. And that's what kept it going. It was the sheer spirit for freedom, for the feeling of being a man or a woman.

Now when you ask why the courts had to come in, they had to come in. You get 52,000 people in the streets and nobody's showing any fear, something had to give. So the Supreme Court had to rule that segregation was not the way of life . . . We [met] after the news came through. All of these people who had fought got together to communicate and to rejoice and to share that built-up emotion and all the other feelings they had lived with during the past thirteen months. And we just rejoiced together.

Building community is not that hard. It just takes ordinary friendliness. The woman who took me to the doctor when my arthritis got bad is a checkout person at my grocery store.

When she helped me with my groceries all those years, we spoke. I didn't stand there looking at the floor or the ceiling. We became acquainted.

—*Oseola McCarty*

SIMPLE ARITHMETIC
LANGSTON HUGHES

Pride in historical accomplishments can inspire a sense of community. Langston Hughes's fictional folk philosopher Jesse B. Semple—or Simple—makes note of Negro History Week and reflects on his own genealogy. Negro History Week was initiated in 1926 by historian and educator Carter G. Woodson. Fifty years later, it was expanded into Black History Month.

"Next week is Negro History Week," said Simple. "And how much Negro history do you know?"

"Why should I know *Negro* history?" I replied. "I am an American."

"But you are also a black man," said Simple, "and you did not come over on the *Mayflower*—at least, not the same *Mayflower* as the rest."

"What rest?" I asked.

"The rest who make up the most," said Simple, "then write the history books and leave *us* out, or else put in the books nothing but prize fighters and ballplayers. Some folks think Negro history begins and ends with Jackie Robinson."

"Not quite," I said.

"Not quite is right," said Simple. "Before Jackie there was Du Bois and before him there was Booker T. Washington, and before him was Frederick Douglass and before Douglass the original Freedom Walker, Harriet Tubman, who were a lady. Before her was them great Freedom Fighters who started rebellions in the South long before the Civil War. By name they was Gabriel and Nat Turner and Denmark Vesey."

"When, how, and where did you get all that information at once?" I asked.

"From my wife, Joyce," said Simple. "Joyce is a fiend for history. She belongs to the Association for the Study of Negro Life and History.* Also Joyce went to school down South. There colored teachers teach children about *our* history. It is not like up North where almost no teachers teach children anything about themselves and who they is and where they come from out of our great black past which were Africa in the old days."

"The days of Ashanti and Benin and the great trade routes in the Middle Ages, the great cities and great kings."

"Amen!" said Simple. "It might have been long ago, but we had black kings. It is from one of them kings that I am descended."

"You?" I exclaimed. "How so? After five hundred years it hardly seems possible that you can trace your ancestry back to an African king."

"Oh, but I can," said Simple. "It is only just a matter of simple arithmetic. Suppose great old King Ashanti in his middle ages had one son. And that one son had two sons. And them two sons each had three sons—and so on down the line, each bigger set of sons having bigger sets of children themselves. Why, the way them sons of kings and kings' sons multiplied, after five hundred years, every black man in the U.S.A. must be the son of one of them African king's grandsons' sons—including me. A matter of simple arithmetic—I am descended from a king."

"It is a good thing to think, anyhow," I said.

"Furthermore, I am descended from the people who built the pyramids, created the alphabets, first wrote words on stones, and first added up two and two."

* The ASNLH was founded in 1915 by Carter G. Woodson and other scholars. The association's subsidiary, Associated Publishers, was the leading black-owned press in the U.S. for many years. Woodson founded the *Journal of Negro History* in 1916.

"Who said all those wise men were colored?"

"Joyce, my wife—and I never doubts her word. She has been going to the Schomburg Collection all week reading books which she cannot take out and carry home because they is too valuable to the Negro people, so must be read in the library. In some places in Harlem a rat might chaw one of them books which is so old and so valuable nobody could put it back in the library. My wife says the Schomburg in Harlem is one of the greatest places in the world to find out about Negro history. Joyce tried to drag me there one day, but I said I had rather get my history from her after she has got it from what she calls the archives. Friend, what is an archive?"

"A place of recorded records, books, files, the materials in which history is preserved."

"They got a million archives in the Schomburg library," said Simple.

"By no stretch of the imagination could there be that many."

"Yes there is," said Simple. "Every word in there is an archive to the Negro people, and to me. I want to know about my kings, my past, my Africa, my history years that make me proud. I want to go back to the days when I did not have to knock and bang and beg at doors for the chance to do things like I do now. I want to go back to the days of my blackness and greatness when I were in my own land and were king and I invented arithmetic."

"The way you can multiply kings and produce yourself as a least common denominator, maybe you did invent arithmetic," I said.

"Maybe I did," said Simple.

JOHN CANOE, AN ORIGINAL SLAVE HOLIDAY
BARBARA EKLOF

Each year, millions of American families celebrate holidays that pay homage to black figures and historical events. But before there was Martin

Luther King Jr.'s Birthday (January 15), Black History Month (Febru-
ary), Juneteenth (June 19), and Kwanzaa (December 26–January 1),
there were other African American holidays of joy and upliftment. In the
North, these included the Parade of Governors, Pinkster King, and Cris-
pus Attucks Day.

Begun in 1750 and celebrated for nearly a century, the Parade of
Governors was a mock election day holiday in which blacks in New
England campaigned among themselves for government posts. Imitating
whites, they made campaign promises, practiced mudslinging, then voted
and held an inaugural ball.

Pinkster King, named for Pinkster Hill in Albany, New York, was a
weeklong festival of parades and dances celebrated in the North until
1811. Slaves honored the man they considered royalty, King Charley, who
was supposedly kidnapped from southwestern Africa and sold in slavery.

Crispus Attucks Day was celebrated on March 5 in Boston, beginning
in 1858. Attucks was shot and killed by British soldiers in the Boston
Massacre on March 5, 1770, one of the events that precipitated the
American Revolution.

In the South, slaves celebrated yet another festival, John Canoe. Here
is how they observed it.

A costumed king appeared amid mass joviality. A processional court of
musicians and assistants followed close behind. "John Canoe!" shouted
the slave children and adults, pointing and gasping at his hideous white
mask. The audience was held spellbound by his magnificent costume of,
it seemed, a million colors and textures—grass, animal skins, and assorted fabrics, to name a few, with a glorious house- or boat-shaped
headdress shadowing it all. Suddenly, his musicians broke into intoxicat-
ing beats, and John Canoe began to sing and dance down the road in a
profusion of jerks and gyrations. The crowd cheered, imitated his steps,
and threw coins at his feet. Still, the show didn't end there. Between the
songs, John Canoe bestowed a repertoire of folklore long into the feast-
filled night.

This nineteenth-century, Mardi Gras–style festival emerged as a private celebration of slaves in North Carolina that coincided with the
slaveholders' major holidays. Depending on what part of the state you're
in and who you're talking to, the holiday has a multitude of additional
nicknames with various spellings: John Conny, John Connu, John

Kuner, John Kooner, John Crow, John Crayfish, Joncooner, Jonkanoo, Jonkeroo, Jonkonnu, Koo-Koo, Kunering, and even Who-Who's. However, our Diasporan family in the West Indies remained loyal to the name Kunering and still celebrates the holiday today. Unfortunately, Jonkonnu was put to an end in North Carolina around 1900 by the police, who represented offended Whites, and by upper-class Blacks, who thought the festival a racial blemish.

Blemish? Well, you decide for yourself after you learn who the John Canoe Festival truly honors.

Since this event is an African-born tradition, it's believed that the symbolic name is derived from the king of Axim, John Conny, from Africa's Gold Coast. During his life, from 1660 to 1732, Conny was known as one of the Gold Coast's finest Black African merchants, having initiated trade between the Ashanti and Germans. His fame spread, however, when, as commander of the Prussian Fort Brandenburg, he outfoxed and defeated Dutch merchants who were attempting to take control of the fort. This triumph gained him many honors, including the renaming of the fort to Conny's Castles and the bestowed title of the Last Prussian Negro Prince.

JUNETEENTH
LISA JONES

Abraham Lincoln issued the Emancipation Proclamation—a presidential decree to free slaves and admit blacks into the armed forces—on January 1, 1863. Most slaves in the South did not hear about the Proclamation for years, learning of it from various sources. Free blacks in New Orleans, Louisiana, spread word of Lincoln's directive in their own French–English newspaper, L'Union. But in Texas, news may have come to blacks via mule-back messenger. In 1992, a New York journalist investigated how—and when—Texans celebrate an annual holiday commemorating freedom.

There are three legends told of how enslaved Africans in the Texas territory came to know of their freedom, and why the word didn't get to them until two months after the Civil War ended, which was a good two and half years after Lincoln's Emancipation Proclamation. Or, to make it plain, rather late. One legend says the messenger, a black Union soldier, was murdered. Another says he arrived, but had been delayed by mule travel. (A variation on this is that he had stopped to get married.) The third and favored is that the news was withheld by white landowners so they could bleed one last crop from slave labor. What *is* held as fact is that June nineteenth—the day that federal troops rode into Galveston with orders to release those kept as slaves—has been celebrated for 127 years, in Texas and beyond, as Emancipation Day, as Jubilation Day, as Juneteenth. The day the last ones heard.

Juneteenth, the name, is one of those fab African-Americanisms, functional, rhythmic, at once concise and not too concise. It fuses the month of June with the number nineteen, and eludes to the fact that the holiday was held in adjoining states on different days of the month as folks got the word. Early emancipation rituals were not exclusive to Texas (South Carolina and Mississippi's fall in May)—or to the South. What may have been the first emancipation ceremony was held in New York as early as 1808 to mark the legal cessation of the slave trade.

No state comes close to Juneteenth in Texas, the black folks' Fourth of July, with its parades, feasting, pageants, and preachifying. Emancipation day organizations in Texas date back to the turn of the century. The most powerful image from the early days must have been former slaves themselves, who, according to tradition, marched together at the end of parade lines. By the 1950s Juneteenth Day came to be linked with, not freedom from slavery, but segregation. On Juneteenth, Texas's Jim Crow cities would allow blacks to be citizens for twelve hours a year by granting them entry into whites-only parks and zoos. With the passage of civil rights legislation in the sixties, refined black Texans abandoned Juneteenth to their country cousins and took to celebrating Independence Day in July along with their white brethren.

A Juneteenth renaissance has been gathering steam since the mid eighties, spurred by the Afrocentricity crusade. Beyond being a hootenanny for black Texas (the condescending folksy portrait favored by the local press), it's become a holiday eagerly adopted nationwide by African Americans in search of cultural signposts. Not to mention one that offers, as is required these days, a dramatic tube-and-T-shirt-friendly soundbite of black history.

The J-Day momentum is due in large part to the efforts of a man you might call Daddy Juneteenth, state representative Al Edwards from Houston. Edwards sponsored the bill that made Juneteenth an official Texas holiday thirteen years ago, a feat in a state that still closes banks for Confederate Heroes Day. Juneteenth U.S.A., Edwards's organization, tracks J-Day rites across the country and is fundraising for a national educational headquarters. To Edwards the holiday has tremendous secular and sacred promise. He sees it as an economic vehicle for African Americans, as well as a day that should be observed with almost holy remembrance: "The Jews say if they ever forget their history, may their tongues cleave to the roof of their mouth. . . . Let the same happen to us."

You can find Juneteenth rituals in all regions of the country now. States like California, where Texans migrated en masse, have held Juneteenth festivities for decades. The New York area's largest is in Buffalo, tapping into upstate's rich history of antislavery activity. Wisconsin counts at least five, including Milwaukee's, where Juneteenth has been celebrated since 1971 and is the best attended single-day cultural event in the state. Far from being family picnics, these festivals sometimes last for days, made possible by the legwork of community groups, city cooperation, and private sector donations. Juneteenth in Minneapolis, now in its seventh year, is building a rep as one of the most progressive and trendsetting J-Day celebrations in the Texas diaspora. What began as a poetry reading in a church basement is now two weeks of programming, including a film festival and an Underground Railroad reenactment. At these celebrations old world often knocks against new world, when Miss Juneteenth pageants (inherited from towns like Brenham, Texas, which crowns a "Goddess of Liberty") share the stage with Afro-chic street fairs ablaze in faux kente.

There are those who think Juneteenth is an embarrassment. That the holiday tells more of our ignorance and subjugation than of an inheritance that predates slavery in the Americas. Or that it's "too black" because it promotes a separate but not equal Fourth of July, or "not black enough" as it's often funded by white purses. And of course that it's far too symbolic and doesn't solve anything. What does a Juneteenth celebration mean anyway when the Freeman's Bureau never gave us our forty acres and a mule? (Not thrilled about news of the state holiday, one former Texas legislator had this to say: "Dancing up and down the streets, drinking red soda water, eating watermelons. . . . I grew out of that.") But Juneteenth critics haven't put a dent in the holiday's grass-roots popularity.

Folks are hungrier than ever for rituals that enshrine our identity as hyphen Americans. Kwanzaa's metamorphosis in the last few years speaks to this need. And merchandising opportunities are never far behind: Evolving in two short decades from cultural nationalist position paper to mainstream ethnic festival profiled in the *Times*'s Living section, Kwanzaa has spawned its own designer cookbook and Santa surrogate, Father Kwanzaa. Now Juneteenth spreads like spring fever. Also gaining steam are rites of passage ceremonies for young men and women that are based on ancient African models and seek to address modern urban ills. (The National Rites of Passage Organization held its fifth annual conference this year.) And spotted last year in *Sage: A Scholarly Journal on Black Women:* plans for a Middle Passage memorial holiday that would fall near Thanksgiving.

Buried in their shopping ethos, we tend to forget holidays were once holy days that defined us in more profound ways than what Nintendo jumbo pack we got for Christmas. Michael Chaney, an arts activist in Minneapolis, believes that Juneteenth rituals could be more than acts of racial communion; they could have a role in redefining America: "We have to realize our own role as historians. We need to ascribe our treasures and offer them to the world. Juneteenth should be a day for all Americans to get in touch with the Africanism within."

Juneteenth does have great possibilities as a new American holiday. Along with reuniting blood relatives, the families that emancipated slaves made embraced family beyond kin, family as community. In this tradition, modern Juneteenth doesn't circumscribe any Dick-and-Jane paean to the nuclear family. You can be a single parent, gay, from D.C. or Ann Arbor; it's a history that includes you. You can read the Emancipation Proclamation out loud or drink some red soda water if you damn please. Or just take a moment out of your day to think about all the folks that laid down nothing less than their lives so that you could see the twentieth century.

FOR MY AMERICAN FAMILY

JUNE JORDAN

June Jordan, one of America's most prolific writers, was born in Harlem in 1936 to Jamaican parents who had escaped poverty by immigrating to the United States. Her parents, who became proud American citizens, raised her in the Bedford-Stuyvesant section of Brooklyn. To Jordan, Bed-Stuy certainly was no "breeding ground for despair," as black neighborhoods often were labeled in her youth. In fact, it was an exciting, richly rewarding cultural stew of working-class "American Negroes" and "West Indians," a breeding ground for high achievers and solid citizens. Bed-Stuy also turned out a distinguished American poet—Jordan herself. The author of poetry collections, children's books, plays, essays, and articles, Jordan has won numerous fellowships and awards, and was nominated for a National Book Award in 1972 for her novel "His Own Where." Much of her work has been influenced by her family and her sense of community. In the following essay, she describes an ideal she wants "to uphold."

A BELATED TRIBUTE TO A LEGACY OF GIFTED INTELLIGENCE AND GUTS*

I would love to see pictures of the Statue of Liberty taken by my father. They would tell me so much about him that I wish I knew. He couldn't very well ask that lady to "hold that smile" or "put on a little something

---

* This essay, written April 29, 1986, was originally published in a special section of *New York Newsday*, July 4, 1986.

with red to brighten it up." He'd have to take her "as is," using a choice of angles or focus or distance as the means to his statement. And I imagine that my father would choose a long-shot, soft-focus, wide-angle lens: that would place Miss Liberty in her full formal setting, and yet suggest the tears that easily spilled from his eyes whenever he spoke about "this great country of of ours: America."

A camera buff, not averse to wandering around the city with both a Rolleiflex and a Rolleicord at the ready, my father thought nothing of a two or three hours' "setup" for a couple of shots of anything he found beautiful.

All of this took place in the 1940s. We lived in the Bedford-Stuyvesant neighborhood of Brooklyn, one of the largest urban Black communities in the world. Besides the fruit and the flowers of my father's aesthetic preoccupation, and just beyond those narrow brownstone dining-room windows, there was a burly mix of unpredictable street life that he could not control, despite incessant telephone calls, for example, to the Department of Sanitation: "Hello. This is a man by the name of Granville Ivanhoe Jordan, and I'm calling about garbage collection. What happened? Did you forget?!"

The unlikely elements of my father's name may summarize his history and character rather well. Jordan is a fairly common surname on the island of Jamaica where he was born, one of perhaps twelve or thirteen children who foraged for food, and who never forget, or forgave, the ridicule his ragged clothing provoked in school. Leaving the classroom long before the normal conclusion to an elementary education, my father later taught himself to read and, after that, he never stopped reading and reading everything he could find, from Burpee seed catalogues to Shakespeare to the *National Geographic* magazines to "Negro" poetry to liner notes for the record albums of classical music that he devoured. But he was also "the little bull"—someone who loved a good rough fight and who even volunteered to teach boxing to other young "Negroes" at the Harlem YMCA, where he frequently participated in political and militant "uplifting-the-race" meetings, on West 135th Street.

Except for weekends, my father pursued all of his studies in the long early hours of the night, 3 or 4 A.M., after eight hours' standing up at the post office where he speed-sorted mail quite without the assistance of computers and zip codes which, of course, had yet to be invented.

Exceptionally handsome and exceptionally vain, Mr. G. I. Jordan, immaculate in one of his innumerable, rooster-elegant suits, would readily hack open a coconut with a machete, or slice a grapefuit in half, throw his head back, and squeeze the juice into his mouth—carefully held a tricky foot away—all to my mother's head-shaking dismay: "Why now you have to act up like a monkey chaser, eh?"

It is a sad thing to consider that this country has given its least to those who have loved it the most. I am the daughter of West Indian immigrants. And perhaps there are other Americans as believing and as grateful and as loyal, but I doubt it. In general, the very word *immigrant* connotes somebody white, while *alien* denotes everybody else. But hundreds and hundreds of thousands of Americans are hardworking, naturalized Black citizens whose trust in the democratic promise of the mainland has never been reckoned with, fully, or truly reciprocated. For instance, I know that my parents would have wanted to say, "Thanks, America!" if only there had been some way, some public recognition and welcome of their presence, here, and then some really big shot to whom their gratitude might matter.

When I visited the birthplace of my mother, twelve years ago, I was embarrassed by the shiny rented car that brought me there: even in 1974, there were no paved roads in Clonmel, a delicate dot of a mountian village in Jamaica. And despite the breathtaking altitude, you could not poke or peer yourself into a decent position for "a view": the vegetation was that dense, that lush, and that chaotic. On or close to the site of my mother's childhood home, I found a neat wood cabin, still without windowpanes or screens, a dirt floor, and a barefoot family of seven, quietly bustling about.

I was stunned. There was neither electricity nor running water. How did my parents even hear about America, more than a half century ago? In the middle of the Roaring Twenties, these eager Black immigrants came, by boat. Did they have to borrow shoes for the journey?

I know that my aunt and my mother buckled into domestic work, once they arrived, barely into their teens. I'm not sure how my father managed to feed himself before that fantastic 1933 afternoon when he simply ran all the way from midtown Manhattan up to our Harlem apartment, shouting out the news: A job! He had found a job!

And throughout my childhood I cannot recall even one utterance of disappointment, or bitterness with America. In fact, my parents hid away any newspaper or magazine article that dealt with "jim crow" or "lynchings" or "discrimination." These were terms of taboo status neither to be spoken nor explained to me. Instead I was given a child's biography of Abraham Lincoln and the Bible stories of Daniel and David, and, from my father, I learned about Marcus Garvey and George Washington Carver and Mary McLeod Bethune. The focus was relentlessly upbeat. Or, as Jimmy Cliff used to sing it, "You can make it if you really try."

My mother's emphasis was more religious, and more consistently race-conscious, and she was equally affirmative: God would take care of me. And, besides, there was ("C'mon, Joe! C'mon!") the Brown Bomber, Joe Louis, and then, incredibly, Jackie Robinson who, by himself, elevated the Brooklyn Dodgers into a sacred cult worshipped by apparently dauntless Black baseball fans.

We had a pretty rich life. Towards the end of the 1960s I was often amazed by facile references to Black communities as "breeding grounds of despair" or "culturally deprived" or "ghettos." That was not the truth. There are grounds for despair in the suburbs, evidently, and I more than suspect greater cultural deprivation in economically and racially and socially homogeneous Long Island commuter towns than anything I ever had to overcome!

In Bedford-Stuyvesant, I learned all about white history and white literature, but I lived and learned about my own, as well. My father marched me to the American Museum of Natural History and to the Planetarium, at least twice a month, while my mother picked up "the slack" by riding me, by trolley car, to public libraries progressively farther and farther away from our house. In the meantime, on our own block of Hancock Street, between Reid and Patchen Avenues, we had rice and peas and curried lamb or, upstairs, in my aunt and uncle's apartment, pigs' feet and greens. On the piano in the parlor there was boogie-woogie, blues, and Chopin. Across the street, there were cold-water flats that included the Gumbs family or, more precisely, Donnie Gumbs, whom I saw as the inarguable paragon of masculine cute. There were "American Negroes," and "West Indians. Some rented their housing, and some were buying their homes. There were Baptists, Holy Rollers, and Episcopalians, side by side.

On that same one block, Father Coleman, the minister of our church, lived and worked as the first Black man on New York's Board of Higher Education. There was Mrs. Taylor, whose music studio was actually a torture chamber into which many of us were forced for piano lessons. And a Black policeman. And a mail carrier. And a doctor. And my beloved Uncle Teddy, with a Doctor of Law degree from Fordham University. And the tiny, exquisite arrow of my aunt, who became one of the first Black principals in the entire New York City public school system. And my mother, who had been president of the first Black class to graduate from the Lincoln School of Nursing, and my father, who earned the traditional gold watch as a retiring civil servant, and Nat King Cole and calypso and boyfriends and Sunday School and confirmation and choir and stickball and roller skates and handmade wooden scooters and marbles and make-believe tea parties and I cannot recall feeling underprivileged, or bored, in that "ghetto."

And from such "breeding grounds of despair," Negro men volunteered, in droves, for active duty in an army that did not want or honor them. And from such "limited" communities, Negro women, such as my mother, left their homes in every kind of weather, and at any hour, to tend to the ailing and heal the sick, regardless of their color, or ethnicity. And in such a "culturally deprived" house as that modest home created by my parents, I became an American poet.

And in the name of my mother and my father, I want to say thanks to America. And I want something more:

My aunt has survived the deaths of her husband and my parents in typical, if I may say so, West Indian fashion. Now in her seventies, and no longer principal of a New York City public school, she rises at 5 A.M., every morning, to prepare for another day of complicated duties as the volunteer principal of a small Black private academy. In the front yard of her home in the Crown Heights section of Brooklyn, the tulips and buttercups have begun to bloom already. Soon every passerby will see her azaleas and jonquils and irises blossoming under the Japanese maple tree and around the base of the Colorado blue spruce.

She is in her seventies, and she tells me:

I love the United States and I always will uphold it as a place of opportunity. This is not to say that you won't meet prejudice along the way but it's up to you to overcome it. And it can be overcome!

Well, I think back to Clonmel, Jamaica, and I visualize my aunt skipping along the goat tracks, fast as she can, before the darkness under the banana tree leaves becomes too scary for a nine-year-old. Or I think about her, struggling to fetch water from the river, in a pail. And I jump-cut to Orange High School, New Jersey, U.S.A., where my aunt maintained a 95 average, despite her extracurricular activities as a domestic, and where she was denied the valedictory because, as the English teacher declared, "You have an accent that the parents will not understand." And I stay quiet as my aunt explains, "I could have let that bother me, but I said, 'Naw, I'm not gone let this keep me down!' "

And what I want is to uphold this America, this beckoning and this shelter provided by my parents and my aunt. I want to say thank you to them, my faithful American family.

ᕫᕬᕬ

A tree cannot stand without its roots.

—*African proverb*

ᕫᕬᕬ

LOVE

Love is *the* soul-stirring ingredient of poetry . . . summer songs . . . newborns . . . 50-year unions . . . courtships . . . flowery letters . . . rendezvous . . . heartwarming recipes . . . cherished friendships . . . and extra-long telephone calls.

It is also much more—a desire and devotion that will drive you to do good, a tenderness that arouses delight and elicits deep affection in the heart and soul. With love, minor miracles appear routine (songs sound sweeter), and major ones come to pass with ease (the sun shines brighter). Love, then, is no ordinary moral value. It glows as we do. And yet it continues to mystify much of humanity.

Actually, black love is easy to define. The simplest definition is: the tenderhearted affections and expressions of endearment of African Americans. A more complex definition is: the tenderhearted affections and expressions of endearment of African Americans, along with the blues. (It hurts to sing the blues, but the blues can help one to transcend pain and sorrow.)

Black love arrived in America centuries ago with the first Africans. Since then, it has survived centuries of racial discrimination. More specifically it has survived slavery, the Civil War, emancipation, segregation, two World Wars, mass migration, the civil rights era, desegregation, Black Arts poetry, blaxploitation cinema, several assassinations, the mainstreaming of Motown, and rap music videos—all without skipping a beat.

This chapter celebrates the beauty, endurance, and strength of love by honoring a few golden moments, including the work of slave poet George Moses Horton, various love potions from the South, a love letter from a G.I. in World War II, the secrets of a long-married celebrity couple (Ruby Dee and Ossie Davis), and more.

From these stories, poems, and prescriptions, the glory of love shines brightly. If the past is any indication of what's to come, the future of black love looks very promising . . .

◈

Life is the first gift, love is the second, and understanding is the third.

—*Anonymous*

◈

BLACK LOVE
GWENDOLYN BROOKS

Gwendolyn Brooks has devoted much of her time to popularizing poetry and teaching that it is within everyone's grasp. In this poem, she asks black love to make a call on us.

Black love, provide the adequate electric
for what is lapsed and lenient in us now.

Rouse us from blur. Call us.

Call adequately the postponed corner brother.
And call our man in the pin-stripe suiting and restore
     him to his abler logic; to his people.

Call to the shattered sister and repair her
in her difficult hour, narrow her fever.

Call to the Elders—
our customary grace and further sun
loved in the Long-ago, loathed in the Lately;
a luxury of languish and of rust.

Appraise, assess our Workers in the Wild, lest they
     descend to malformation and to undertow.

Black love, define and escort our romantic young, be means and
     redemption, discipline.

Nourish our children—proud, strong
little men upright-easy:
quick
flexed
little stern-warm historywomen. . . .
I see them in Ghana, Kenya, in the city of Dar-es-
      Salaam, in Kalamazoo, Mound Bayou, in Chicago.

Lovely loving children
with long soft eyes.

Black love, prepare us all for interruptions;
assaults, unwanted pauses; furnish for leavings and
      for losses.

Just come out Blackly glowing!

On the ledges—in the lattices—against the failing
      light of candles that stutter,
and in the chop and challenge of our apprehension—
be
the Alwayswonderful of this world.

ANTEBELLUM COURTSHIP INQUIRY

*Before the Civil War, a courtship might have gotten started with these
words.*

HE: Is you a flyin' lark or a settin' dove?
SHE: I'se a flyin' lark, my honey Love.
HE: Is you a bird o' one fedder, or a bird o' two?

SHE: I'se a bird o' one fedder, w'en it comes to you.

HE: Den, Mam:

> I has desire, an' quick temptation,
> To jine my fence to yō' plantation.

A longer version of a courtship conversation might have sounded like this:

HE: My dear kin' miss, has you any objections to me drawing my cher to yer side, and revolvin' de wheel of my conversation around de axle of your understandin'?

SHE: I has no objection to a gentleman addressin' me in a proper manner, kin' sir.

HE: My dear miss, de worl' is a howlin' wilderness full of devourin' animals, and you has got to walk through hit. Has you made up yer min' to walk through hit by yersef, or wid some bol' wahyer?

SHE: Yer 'terrigation, kin' sir, shall be answered in a ladylike manner, ef you will prove to me dat it is not for er form and er fashion dat you puts de question.

HE: Dear miss, I would not so impose on a lady like you as to as' her a question for a form an' a fashion. B'lieve me, kin' miss, dat I has a pertickler objick in ingagin' yer in conversation dis afternoon.

SHE: Dear kin' sir, I has knowed many a gentleman to talk wid wise words and flatterin' looks, and at de same time he may have a deceivin' heart. May I as' yer, kin' gentleman, ef you has de full right to address a lady in a pertickler manner?

HE: I has, kin' miss. I has seen many sweet ladies, but I has never up to dis day an' time lef' de highway of a single gentleman to foller dese beacon lights. But now, kin' miss, as I looks in yer dark eyes, and sees yer hones' face, and hears yer kind voice, I mus' confess, dear lady, dat I would be joyous to come to yer beck and call in any time of danger.

SHE: Den, kin' sir, I will reply in anser to your 'terrigation in de fus place, sence I think you is a hones' gentleman, dat I feels dat a lady needs de pertection of a bol' wahyer in dis worl' where dere's many wil' animals and plenty of danger.

HE: Den, kin' honored miss, will you condescen' to encourage me to hope dat I might, some glorious day in de future, walk by yer side as a perteckter?

SHE: Kin' sir, ef you thinks you is a bol' warrior I will condescend to let you pass under my observation from dis day on, an' ef you proves wuthy of a confidin' ladies' trus', some lady might be glad to axcept yer pertection—and dat lady might be me.

Here's a marriage proposal with a provisional acceptance.

HE: Oh Miss Lizie, how I loves you!
My life's jes los' if you hain't true.
If you loves me lak I loves you,
No knife cain't cut our love in two.

SHE: Grapevine warp, an' cornstalk fillin';
I'll marry you if mammy an' daddy's willin'.
HE: Rabbit hop an' long dog trot!
Let's git married if dey say "not."

FROG WENT A-COURTING

This call-and-response rhyme (the response is "Uh-huh! Uh-huh!") tells the story of a frog's courtship and the gathering at his and Miss Mousie's wedding. Some scholars say this song has been traced as far back as 1580. Today, children still enjoy it.

De frog went a-co'tin', he did ride. Uh-huh! Uh-huh!
De frog went a-co'tin', he did ride.
Wid a sword an' a pistol by 'is side. Uh-huh! Uh-huh!

He rid up to Miss Mousie's do'. Uh-huh! Uh-huh!
He rid up to Miss Mousie's do',
Whar he'd of'en been befo. Uh-huh! Uh-huh!

Says he: "Miss Mousie, is you in?" Uh-huh! Uh-huh!
Says he: "Miss Mousie, is you in?"
"Oh yes, Sugar Lump! I kyard an' spin." Uh-huh! Uh-huh!

He tuck dat Mousie on his knee. Uh-huh! Uh-huh!
He tuck dat Mousie on his knee,
An' he say: "Dear Honey, marry me!" Uh-huh! Uh-huh!

"Oh Suh!" she say, "I cain't do dat." Uh-huh! Uh-huh!
"Oh Suh!" she say, "I cain't do dat,
Widout de sayso o' uncle Rat." Uh-huh! Uh-huh!

Dat ole gray Rat, he soon come home. Uh-huh! Uh-huh!
Dat ole gray Rat, he soon come home,
Sayin': "Whose been here since I'se been gone?" Uh-huh! Uh-huh!

"A fine young gemmun fer to see." Uh-huh! Uh-huh!
"A fine young gemmun fer to see,
"An' one dat axed fer to marry me." Uh-huh! Uh-huh!

Dat Rat jes laugh to split his side. Uh-huh! Uh-huh!
Dat Rat jes laugh to split his side.
"Jes think o' Mousie's bein' a bride!" Uh-huh! Uh-huh!

Nex' day, dat rat went down to town. Uh-huh! Uh-huh!
Nex' day dat rat went down to town,
To git up de Mousie's Weddin' gown. Uh-huh! Uh-huh!

"What's de bes' thing fer de Weddin' gown?" Uh-huh! Uh-huh!
"What's de bes' thing fer de Weddin' gown?"—
"Dat acorn hull, all gray an' brown!" Uh-huh! Uh-huh!

"Whar shall de Weddin' Infar' be?" Uh-huh! Uh-huh!
"Whar shall de Weddin' Infar' be?"—
"Down in de swamp in a holler tree." Uh-huh! Uh-huh!

"What shall de Weddin' Infar' be?" Uh-huh! Uh-huh!
"What shall de Weddin' Infar' be"—
"Two brown beans an' a blackeyed pea." Uh-huh! Uh-huh!

Fust to come in wus de Bumblebee. Uh-huh! Uh-huh!
Fust to come in wus de Bumblebee.
Wid a fiddle an' bow across his knee. Uh-huh! Uh-huh!

De nex' dat come wus Khyernel Wren. Uh-huh! Uh-huh!
De nex' dat come wus Khyernel Wren,
An' he dance a reel wid de Turkey Hen. Uh-huh! Uh-huh!

De nex' dat come wus Mistah Snake. Uh-huh! Uh-huh!
De nex' dat come wus Mistah Snake,
He swallowed de whole weddin' cake! Uh-huh! Uh-huh!

De nex' come in wus Cap'n Flea. Uh-huh! Uh-huh!
De nex' come in wus Cap'n Flea,
An' he dance a jig fer de Bumblebee. Uh-huh! Uh-huh!

An' now come in ole Giner'l Louse. Uh-huh! Uh-huh!
An' now come in ole Giner'l Louse.
He danced a breakdown 'round de house. Uh-huh! Uh-huh!

De nex' to come wus Major Tick. Uh-huh! Uh-huh!
De nex' to come wus Major Tick,
An' he e't so much it make 'im sick. Uh-huh! Uh-huh!

Dey sent fer Mistah Doctah Fly. Uh-huh! Uh-huh!
Dey sent fer Mistah Doctah Fly.
Says he: "Major Tick, you's boun' to die." Uh-huh! Uh-huh!

Oh, den crep' in ole Mistah Cat. Uh-huh! Uh-huh!
Oh, den crep' in ole Mistah Cat,
An' chilluns, dey all hollered, "Scat!!" Uh-huh!!! Uh-huh!!!

It give dat frog a turble fright. Uh-huh! Uh-huh!
It give dat frog a turble fright,
An' he up an' say to dem, "Good-night!" Uh-huh! Uh-huh!

Dat frog, he swum de lake aroun'. Uh-huh! Uh-huh!
Dat frog, he swum de lake aroun',
An' a big black duck come gobble 'im down. Uh-huh! Uh-huh!

"What d'you say 'us Miss Mousie's lot?" Uh-huh! Uh-huh!
"What d'you say 'us Miss Mousie's lot?"—
"W'y—, she got swallered on de spot!" Uh-huh! Uh-huh!

Now, I don't know no mo' 'an dat. Uh-huh! Uh-huh!
Now, I don't know no mo' 'an dat.
If you gits mo' you can take my hat. Uh-huh! Uh-huh!

An' if you thinks dat hat won't do. Uh-huh! Uh-huh!
An' if you thinks dat hat won't do,
Den you mought take my head 'long too. Uh-huh!!! Uh-huh!!!

THE LOVER'S FAREWELL
GEORGE MOSES HORTON

*George Moses Horton (c. 1797–c. 1883) was the only man to publish
volumes of poetry while still a slave, and the first black Southerner to
publish a book.* He taught himself to read, and based on his ability to
compose verse on demand, he built a reputation at the University of North
Carolina's Chapel Hill campus. A daily presence on campus for more than
thirty years, he sold a dozen made-to-order poems a week either for poetry
books or for twenty-five to seventy-five cents per lyric. His owner refused to*

---

* *The Hope of Liberty, Containing a Number of Poetical Pieces,* published in 1829. Over his
lifetime, he published three collections containing more than 150 poems.

sell Horton his freedom, so he remained in bondage until the end of the
Civil War. Here, he speaks of a lover's despair.

And wilt thou, love, my soul display,
And all my secret thoughts betray?
I strove but could not hold thee fast,
My heart flies off with thee at last.

The favorite daughter of the dawn,
On love's mild breeze will soon be gone
I strove but could not cease to love,
Nor from my heart the weight remove.

And wilt thou, love, my soul beguile,
And gull thy fav'rite with a smile?
Nay, soft affection answers, nay,
And beauty wings my heart away.

I steal on tiptoe from these bowers,
All spangled with a thousand flowers;
I sigh, yet leave them all behind,
To gain the object of my mind.

And wilt thou, love, command my soul,
And waft me with a light controul?—
Adieu to all the blooms of May,
Farewell—I fly with love away!

I leave my parents here behind,
And all my friends—to love resigned—
'Tis grief to go, but death to stay:
Farewell—I'm gone with love away!

Love is a itchin' round the heart you can't get at to scratch.
—*Sally Nealy, former slave*

LOVE 'N SLOP
VIOLET GUNTHARPE

Love expresses itself in the oddest places. An eighty-two-year-old woman tenderly recalls how she was wooed back in the days of slavery.

My mammy stay on wid de same marster 'til I was grown, dat is fifteen, and Thad got to lookin' at me, meek as a sheep and dumb as a calf. I had to ask dat nigger, right out, what his 'tentions was, befo' I get him to bleat out dat he love me. Him name Thad Guntharpe. I glance at him one day at de pigpen when I was sloppin' de hogs, I say: "Mr. Guntharpe, you follow me night and mornin' to dis pigpen; do you happen to be in love wid one of these pigs? If so, I'd like to know which one 'tis; then sometime I come down here by myself and tell dat pig 'bout your 'fections." Thad didn't say nothin; but just grin. Him took de slop bucket out of my hand and look at it, put upside down on de ground, and set me down on it; then he fall down dere on de grass by me and warm my fingers in his hands. I just took pity on him and told him mighty plain dat he must limber up his tongue and say what he mean, wantin' to visit them pigs so often. Us carry on foolishness 'bout de little boar shoat pig and de little sow pig, then I squeal in laughter over how he scrouge so close; de slop bucket tipple over and I lost my seat. Dat ever remain de happiest minute of my eighty-two years.

DEADWOOD DICK CATCHES
A TRAIN
NAT LOVE

The outrageous Nat Love, the only black cowboy to write an autobiog-raphy, was born a slave in Tennessee in 1854. He participated in many cattle drives and arrived in Dodge City in 1869. His exaggerated claims have become the stuff of legend. He said he had been shot fourteen times and that he once rode his horse into a saloon and ordered a drink for himself and the horse. The nickname Deadwood Dick was given to him after he won a shooting contest in Deadwood, South Dakota, he said. Tall tales and all, his autobiography—The Life and Adventures of Nat Love, Better Known in the Cattle Country as "Deadwood Dick"—*is a rare account of black life in the West. The book informs us that even a tough-riding legend could go soft on love and try his hand at an amazingly crazy feat, like catching a train—literally.*

During my wild career on the western plains I had met many handsome women, and they often made much of me, but somehow I had never experienced the feeling called love, until I met my charming sweetheart in Old Mexico. I had perhaps been too much absorbed in the wild life of the plains, in the horses, and cattle which made up my world, to have the time or inclination to seek or enjoy the company of the gentler sex. But now that I had met my fate, I suppose I became as silly about it as any tenderfoot from the east could possibly be, as evidence of how badly I was hit. While on the trail with the herd our route lay along a narrow gauge railroad, and I was feeling up in the air caused no doubt partly from the effects of love and partly from the effects of Mexican whiskey, a generous measure I had under my belt, however I was feeling fine, so when the little engine came puffing along in the distance I said to the boys I have roped nearly everything that could be roped, so now I am going to rope the engine. They tried to persuade me not to make the attempt, but I was in no mood to listen to reason or anything else, so when the engine came along I put my spurs to my horse and when near enough I let fly my lariat. The rope settled gracefully around the smoke stack, and as usual my trained horse set himself back for the shock, but the engine set both myself and my horse in the ditch, and might have continued to set us in places had not something given way, as it was the rope parted, but the boys said afterwards that they thought they would have to send for a wrecking train to clean the track or rather the ditch.

Roping a live engine is by long odds worse than roping wild Buffalo on the plains or Uncle Sam's cannon at the forts. This incident cleared the atmosphere somewhat, but my love was as strong as ever and I thanked my lucky start she did not see me as they dragged me out of the ditch.

I PUT A SPELL ON YOU

To attract love, some people turn to conjuring, or hoodoo—a folk system of magic blended from Christianity and African religions. Here are a few old-time love potions.

From *Zora Neale Hurston's* Mules and Men.

TO MAKE PEOPLE LOVE YOU

Take nine lumps of starch, nine of sugar, nine teaspoons of steel dust. Wet it all with Jockey Club cologne. Take nine pieces of ribbon, blue, red or yellow. Take a dessertspoonful and put it on a piece of ribbon and tie it in a bag. As each fold is gathered together call his name. As you wrap it with yellow thread call his name till you finish. Make nine bags and place them under a rug, behind an armoire, under a step or over a door. They will love you and give you everything they can get. Distance makes no difference. Your mind is talking to his mind and nothing beats that.

From Gumbo Ya-Ya: A Collection of Louisiana Folktales

TO WIN A MAN'S LOVE

- Wrap a thimble in a small piece of silk and carry this in your pocket for three days. Every time you enter or leave the house, make a wish regarding your sweetheart. Your wish will come true in three months.
- Place the man's picture behind a mirror.
- Write the man's name and yours on separate pieces of paper. Pin them together in the form of a cross with yours on top. Put them in a glass of water containing sugar and orange-flower water and burn a red candle before this glass for nine days.

TO WIN A WOMAN'S LOVE

- Take some of the desired one's hair and sleep with it under the pillow.
- Carry a piece of weed called John the Conqueror in your pocket.
- Rub love oil into the palm of your right hand.

NEVER OFFER YOUR HEART TO SOMEONE WHO EATS HEARTS
ALICE WALKER

To some people, a soft and tender heart is merely something delectable. Beware.

Never offer your heart
to someone who eats hearts
who finds heartmeat
delicious
but not rare

who sucks the juices
drop by drop
and bloody-chinned
grins
like a God.

Never offer your heart
to a heart gravy lover.
Your stewed, overseasoned
heart consumed
he will sop up your grief
with bread
and send it shuttling
from side to side
in his mouth
like bubblegum.

If you find yourself
in love
with a person
who eats hearts
these things
you must do:

Freeze your heart
immediately.
Let him—next time
he examines your chest—
find your heart cold
flinty and unappetizing.

Refrain from kissing
lest he in revenge
dampen the spark
in your soul.

Now,
sail away to Africa
where holy women
await you
on the shore—
long having practiced the art
of replacing hearts
with God
and Song.

GOOD MORNING, BLUES
COUNT BASIE, ED DURHAM, AND JIMMY RUSHING

Nothing colors a mood quite like the blues.

The blues is considered one of the finest forms of expression to evolve from the African American experience. It first appeared in the early twentieth century as a new kind of music inspired by the trials and tribulations of love or trouble or both. Many blues songs are melancholic grievances, suspended sometimes by fleeting moments of pleasure; some are simply expressions of woe. Paradoxically, through re-creating sad situations and articulating agonizing pain, the blues can bring a sense of relief, escape, or even transcendent joy. Many versions of the following blues song exist. Jimmy Rushing recorded this one in 1937.

Good mornin', blues,
Blues, how do you do?
Good mornin', blues,
Blues, how do you do?
Good morning, how are you?

I laid down last night,
Turning from side to side;
Yes, I was turning from side to side,

I was not sick,
I was just dissatisfied.

When I got up this mornin',
Blues walking round my bed;
Yes, the blues walkin' round my bed,
I went to eat my breakfast,
The blues was all in my bread.

I sent for you yesterday baby,
Here you come a walking today;
Yes, here you come a walking today,
Got your mouth wide open,
You don't know what to say.

Good mornin', blues,
Blues, how do you do?
Yes, blues, how do you do?
I'm doing all right,
Good morning, how are you?

〰

You never miss the water till the well runs dry.
You'll never miss your baby till she says goodbye.

—Blues lyrics

〰

THE LETTER
BEATRICE M. MURPHY

Please excuse this letter;
I know we said we're through
But there's something very precious

Of mine you took with you
And I must have it back.

I'm sure that you will find it
If you search among your pack
Way down in the innermost part.

Please wrap it carefully
Before you mail—
You see, it is my heart.

WHY WOMEN ALWAYS TAKE
ADVANTAGE OF MEN
ZORA NEALE HURSTON

In 1935, Zora Neale Hurston published Mules and Men, *the first book of black folklore written by an African American. In this collection of folk tales, told by Florida townspeople to the book's narrator, we learn how marriage became a give-and-take proposition.*

You see in de very first days, God made a man and a woman and put 'em in a house together to live. 'Way back in them days de woman was just as strong as de man and both of 'em did de same things. They useter get to fussin' 'bout who gointer do this and that and sometime they'd fight, but they was even balanced and neither one could whip de other one.

One day de man said to hisself, "B'lieve Ah'm gointer go see God and ast Him for a li'l mo' strength so Ah kin whip dis 'oman and make her mind. Ah'm tired of de way things is." So he went on up to God.

"Good mawnin', Ole Father."

"Howdy man. Whut you doin' 'round my throne so soon dis mawnin'?"

"Ah'm troubled in mind, and nobody can't ease mah spirit 'ceptin' you."

God said: "Put yo' plea in de right form and Ah'll hear and answer."

"Ole Maker, wid de mawnin' stars glitterin' in yo' shinin' crown, wid de dust from yo' footsteps makin' worlds upon worlds, wid de blazin' bird we call de sun flyin' out of yo' right hand in de mawnin' and consumin' all day de flesh and blood of stump-black darkness, and comes flyin' home every evenin' to rest on yo' left hand, and never once in all yo' eternal years, mistood de left hand for de right, Ah ast you *please* to give me mo' strength than dat woman you give me, so Ah kin make her mind. Ah know you don't want to be always comin' down way past de moon and stars to be straightenin' her out and it's got to be done. So give me a li'l mo' strength, Ole Maker and Ah'll do it."

"All right, Man, you got mo' strength than woman."

So de man run all de way down de stairs from Heben till he got home. He was so anxious to try his strength on de woman dat he couldn't take his time. Soon's he got in de house he hollered "Woman! Here's yo' boss. God done tole me to handle you in which ever way Ah please. Ah'm yo' boss."

De woman flew to fightin' 'im right off. She fought 'im frightenin' but he beat her. She got her wind and tried 'im agin but he whipped her agin. She got herself together and made de third try on him vigorous but he beat her every time. He was so proud he could whip 'er at last, dat he just crowed over her and made her do a lot of things she didn't like. He told her, "Long as you obey me, Ah'll be good to yuh, but every time yuh rear up Ah'm gointer put plenty wood on yo' back and plenty water in yo' eyes."

De woman was so mad she went straight up to Heben and stood befo' de Lawd. She didn't waste no words. She said, "Lawd, Ah come befo' you mighty mad t'day. Ah want back my strength and power Ah useter have."

"Woman, you got de same power you had since de beginnin'."

"Why is it then, dat de man kin beat me now and he useter couldn't do it?"

"He got mo' strength than he useter have. He come and ast me for it and Ah give it to 'im. Ah gives to them that ast, and you ain't never ast me for no mo' power."

"Please suh, God, Ah'm astin' you for it now. Jus' gimme de same as you give him."

God shook his head. "It's too late now, woman. Whut Ah give, Ah never take back. Ah give him mo' strength than you and no matter how much Ah give you, he'll have mo'.''

De woman was so mad she wheeled around and went on off. She went straight to de devil and told him what had happened.

He said, "Don't be dis-incouraged, woman. You listen to me and you'll come out mo' than conqueror. Take dem frowns out yo' face and turn round and go right on back to Heben and ast God to give you dat bunch of keys hangin' by de mantel-piece. Then you bring 'em to me and Ah'll show you what to do wid 'em."

So de woman climbed back up to Heben agin. She was mighty tired but she was more out-done than she was tired so she climbed all night long and got back up to Heben agin. When she got befo' de throne, butter wouldn't melt in her mouf.

"O Lawd and Master of de rainbow, Ah know yo' power. You never make two mountains without you put a valley in between. Ah know you kin hit a straight lick wid a crooked stick."

"Ast for whut you want, woman."

"God, gimme dat bunch of keys hangin' by yo' mantel-piece."

"Take 'em."

So de woman took de keys and hurried on back to de devil wid 'em. There was three keys on de bunch. Devil say, "See dese three keys? They got mo' power in 'em than all de strength de man kin ever git if you handle 'em right. Now dis first big key is to de do' of de kitchen, and you know a man always favors his stomach. Dis second one is de key to de bedroom and he don't like to be shut out from dat neither and dis last key is de key to de cradle and he don't want to be cut off from his generations at all. So now you take dese keys and go lock up everything and wait till he come to you. Then don't you unlock nothin' until he use his strength for yo' benefit and yo' desires."

De woman thanked 'im and tole 'im, "If it wasn't for you, Lawd knows whut us po' women folks would do."

She started off but de devil halted her. "Jus' one mo' thing: don't go home braggin' 'bout yo' keys. Jus' lock up everything and say nothin' until you git asked. And then don't talk too much."

De woman went on home and did like de devil tole her. When de man come home from work she was settin' on de porch singin' some song 'bout "Peck on de wood make de bed go good."

When de man found de three doors fastened what useter stand wide open he swelled up like pine lumber after a rain. First thing he tried to break in cause he figgered his strength would overcome all obstacles. When he saw he couldn't do it, he ast de woman, "Who locked dis do'?"

She tole 'im, "Me."

"Where did you git de key from?"

"God give it to me."

He run up to God and said, "God, woman got me locked 'way from my vittles, my bed and my generations, and she say you give her the keys."

God said, "I did, Man, Ah give her de keys, but de devil showed her how to use 'em!"

"Well, Ole Maker, please gimme some keys jus' lak 'em so she can't git de full control."

"No, Man, what Ah give Ah give. Woman got de key."

"How kin Ah know 'bout my generations?"

"Ast de woman."

So de man come on back and submitted hisself to de woman and she opened de doors.

He wasn't satisfied but he had to give in. 'Way after while he said to de woman, "Le's us divide up. Ah'll give you half of my strength if you lemme hold de keys in my hands."

De woman thought dat over so de devil popped and tol her, "Tell 'im, naw. Let 'im keep his strength and you keep yo' keys."

So de woman wouldn't trade wid 'im and de man had to mortgage his strength to her to live. And dat's why de man makes and de woman takes. You men is still braggin' 'bout yo' strength and de women is sittin' on de keys and lettin' you blow off till she git ready to put de bridle on you.

SLAVE MARRIAGE CEREMONY SUPPLEMENT

Words that made marriage official.

> Dark an' stormy may come de wedder;
> I jines dis he-male an' dis she-male to-gedder.
> Let none, but Him dat makes de thunder,
> Put dis he-male an' dis she-male asunder.
> I darfore 'nounce you bofe de same.
> Be good, go 'long, an' keep up yō' name.
> De broomstick's jumped, de worl's not wide.
> She's now yō' own. Salute yō' bride!

LOVE & WAR
EDWARD A. CARTER II

Staff Sgt. Edward A. Carter II (1916–63) was awarded the Medal of Honor posthumously in 1997, more than a half century after it was denied him because of racism. He was one of seven black soldiers in World War II to receive the nation's highest military award for bravery. [See "Black Valor," page 149.] Carter wrote this letter to his wife, Mildred, two months before his act of heroism.

Jan. 3rd 1945
France

Dear Lover,

I have always found, that is the way I feel, that the time I spend writing you to be my holy and sacred hour of the day. The time that I spend in writing to you my sweets is the only time that I ever make a confession. And it seems to me that I'll always be guilty of the same sin. Or is it a sin? Well it seems that I am guilty of Loving You.

Please do not condemn me, because I shall only continue to confess my Love and devotion to you alone. There is an old saying that "Absence makes the heart grow fonder for somebody else." I find this saying to be very much untrue. My reactions have been just the opposite. Please don't write saying that it is my imagination working over time. Married life I have found to be one of the sweetest of all experiences. Life was tragic until my lucky star, You, came into this life of mine. For Love's sake alone, I promise you there will never be, let's see, I guess you might call it the state of stagnation, for us. Again I promise, as I have in my other letters, to reimburse you for every lonely second, hour, day, week, month, and year that I have been forced to spend away from your *charms* and that radiant, tender, consuming Love that you alone possess and have given unto me so freely. Is my confession complete sweetheart? I am trying to confess that which is in this heart of mine. My way of expression I admit is crude, but please try and comprehend. What I have written comes from the heart and not from reasoning. If I were to follow the code that I have always tried to live by, I would never admit my Love and feelings to any woman, not even to myself. Because I have always felt, that is until meeting you, that to express one's Love and devotion could only mean that the person or persons were weak. And I the one who has lived by these same codes have broken them. "I was blind and now I see!" Now I am quoting the Bible and that's not at all like myself. If there is anything that I have failed to admit or own up to, please let me know. (Amen.)

Kiss the children by proxy for me. Give my Love and good wishes to the family . . .

As for myself, I am still in the very best of health and will continue to make the best of a bad situation. The harder I work and fight to draw this war to a speedy close, the sooner my return. Keep my chin [up]? I do. Keep your chin up, you must do. Keep smiling and sing whenever you get the blues.

Sweets, I must sound retreat until another day of light. Loads of Love, all of my Love. Thumbs up. Write whenever your time permits.

For Ever and Ever,
Eddie (Amen)

P.S.
I still Love You only.

LANGUAGES OF THE HEART
JAMES WELDON JOHNSON

The firstborn son of a schoolteacher and a hotel headwaiter, James Weldon Johnson (1871–1938) was a man of many talents—lawyer, diplomat, songwriter, journalist, critic, novelist. He was also a versatile poet able to write in many styles. Here are two very different kinds of poems to describe lost love.

Sence You Went Away

Seems lak to me de stars don't shine so bright,
Seems lak to me de sun done loss his light,
Seems lak to me der's nothin' goin' right,
   Sence you went away.

Seems lak to me de sky ain't half so blue,
Seems lak to me dat eve'ything wants you,
Seems lak to me I don't know what to do,
   Sence you went away.

Seems lak to me dat eve'ything is wrong,
Seems lak to me de day's jes twice ez long,
Seems lak to me de bird's forgot his song,
   Sence you went away.

Seems lak to me I jes can't he'p but sigh,
Seems lak to me ma th'oat keeps gittin' dry,
Seems lak to me a tear stays in ma eye,
   Sence you went away.

The Glory of the Day Was in Her Face

The glory of the day was in her face,
The beauty of the night was in her eyes.
And over all her loveliness, the grace
Of Morning blushing in the early skies.

And in her voice, the calling of the dove;
Like music of a sweet, melodious part.
And in her smile, the breaking light of love;
And all the gentle virtues in her heart.

And now the glorious day, the beauteous night,
The birds that signal to their mates at dawn,
To my dull ears, to my tear-blinded sight
Are one with all the dead, since she is gone.

NAMOMMA'S DEEP LOVE
VERTAMAE SMART-GROSVENOR

Romantic tales have been passed down to us from slavery, including stories about African forebears. The Gullah—descendants of former slaves living on the Sea Islands and isolated coastal areas of South Carolina and Georgia—still speak an English creole dialect that retains some of the grammar and vocabulary of West African languages. Vertamae Smart-Grosvenor, author, broadcast journalist, and "culinary anthropologist," wrote of her Gullah ancestor's devotion and what it led a slave master to do.

My great great grandfather was a Jack of all trades. He could make anything. I remember Granddaddy Charlie weaving baskets and making wagons. He told us how his grandfather from Africa had taught him. My great great granddaddy had an African name. I don't know what it really was, but folks say it was something like "Ifana." Anyhow, this is what happened:

H E BOUGHT HIS freedom, but fell in love with a very beautiful slave girl named Namomma. Since he did some work for the master of Namomma, he saw her often. He was free; she was a slave, and slaves couldn't get married like other people—not really. They didn't know what to do. He wanted to have her for his wife, so he asked the master how much it would cost for her freedom. The master said $500. The master thought that was a fair price cause she would make a good breeder.

For seven years my great great grandfather worked to get that $500— and when he got it, he went to the master and offered to buy her freedom. The master said that the price had gone up to $1500. My great great grandfather knew it wouldn't be possible to save that much money, so he took out his free man's pass and burned it, and offered himself to the master as his slave as long as Namomma was his slave. He made one clause in the bargain. If the master ever tried to sell her or any of their children, he said to kill him first. Otherwise he would kill the master and his whole family. And he said if the master tried to sell them after he was dead, he and the ghosts of his ancestors would put a curse on the house of Johnson and all their children thereafter would be cursed with ugliness. Master Johnson was so taken back that he let Namomma go and gave them *both* free issue passes.

LOVING A BLACK SHINING PRINCE
AS TOLD BY BETTY SHABAZZ

Betty Shabazz (1936–97) was married to Malcolm X (El-Hajj Malik El-Shabazz) for seven years before he was gunned down by a ring of assassins in 1965. Shabazz, pregnant with twins, witnessed the killing, shielding her four daughters from the gunfire with her own body. Here, Betty Shabazz remembers her relationship with Malcolm X, who, according to eldest daughter Attallah, lovingly called his wife "My Apple Brown Betty." Shabazz went on to raise her six daughters alone and earn a doctorate in education. She died tragically from burns suffered in a fire in June 1997.

MEETING MALCOLM

. . . It was very interesting how I met Malcolm. I had come to New York City from Tuskegee Institute in Alabama to go to nursing school. My father had graduated from Tuskegee, but after I got there I decided I wanted to change my major from elementary education to nursing. The dean of nursing suggested that I attend a three-year nursing school, and the school I attended in New York was one that Tuskegee student nurses were affiliated with for psychiatric nursing. In my junior year I was invited to dinner by a nurse's aide who worked at the hospital. I wasn't really dating, but I was going out with a young intern who is now a prominent psychiatrist, and I invited him to accompany me to dinner.

The food was delicious. I'd never tasted food like that. It was seasoned with corn oil, margarine, onions, garlic, celery, green pepper and chives—just all sorts of good things. After dinner the woman, who was a little older than me, asked us if we would go with her to a lecture. Now, how are you going to sit and eat all that food and say no? So we went to the lecture, which I hoped would be over any minute. The woman wanted me to meet her minister, but he was not there that night.

After the lecture she asked me why didn't I join the Temple, and I told her that number one, I was not familiar with the philosophy, and number two, my parents would kill me if they knew I joined another religion and gave up being a Methodist. "Just wait until you hear my minister talk," she said. "He's very disciplined, he's good-looking, and all the sisters want him."

Well, if I was going to go back to her house to eat, which I really wanted to do, I would have to go to this place to listen to her minister. It wasn't called a mosque then. It was called the Temple. Temple Seven. The next time the intern and I went to the temple, our hostess was sitting behind me and she whispered in my ear, "The minister is here." I said to myself, *Big deal.* But then I looked over and saw this man on the extreme right aisle sort of galloping to the podium. He was tall, he was thin, and the way he was galloping it looked as though he was going someplace much more important than the podium. Have you ever seen people who are going someplace and you just know they are focused? Well, he got to the podium—and I sat up straight. I was impressed with him—clean-cut, no-nonsense.

I felt that somewhere in life I had met this energy before. Isn't that strange? At that time I was totally unaware of such things as vibrations, spiritual connections—chemistry. But it was like I knew him. So what struck me next after seeing him walk down the aisle and feeling connected to him was the point at which he took off his glasses to clean them as he talked. I looked up at him and thought, *Oh, my God—hurry up, please put your glasses back on!* You know, I wanted to hold something in front of him so no one else could see what I saw: His face, his eyes, his hair were all the same color. I remember thinking, *My God, this man is totally malnourished. He needs some liver, some spinach, some beets and broccoli.* You know what I'm saying? He was rhiny. I could tell just by looking at him that he was overworked.

When he put his glasses back on, those dark-rimmed glasses, he looked a little better. And when he spoke you just knew he was no-nonsense. I remember thinking I'd better not get close to him in case he could read minds too—I would be in terrible trouble! I don't really remember what he talked about during his lecture that night—something about his travels and our people and the need for all of us to refocus. I can't remember his exact words, but he talked about having the strength to do what you know is right. And that you have to take one day at a time.

When I was introduced to him after the lecture, he said, "Will you be back? We'd love to have you."

That was my first meeting, and I was impressed. But I was willing to leave it right there. The nurse's aide who had first invited me would always look for me at the hospital and say, "Are you going to the temple?" And I would say, "No, I'm on duty" or give some other excuse.

But one night I was invited to a dinner at somebody's house in Brooklyn, and Malcolm was there. He said, "Sister, how are you doing?" I told him I was doing fine, but he said, "Are you sure? Because you look worried." I told him I really was not worried, but then we started talking. About school. About life. I told him about living in Alabama and the hostilities I encountered there, and how my parents did not want to deal with it. They thought it was my fault. I'm talking about the irritation between the races in the South. Malcolm started talking to me about the condition of Black people. This was the first time I heard the word *racism* used. He started giving me a history lesson—told me racism was not my fault. I began to see why people did certain things. I began to see myself from a different perspective.

I started going to his lectures, and we started having conversations afterward. He would actively seek me out, ask me questions. He was different. He was refreshing, but I never suspected that he thought of me in any way other than as a sister who was interested in the Movement. Besides, there were too many people in line for his affection, his attention. I was not about to be in line, ever. Plus some of the older women used to always say, "These young sisters need not have any notions about marrying Brother Minister, because he likes good food, and he likes it cooked in a Muslim way—and if you don't know how to do that, forget it."

I think they started saying that because he started paying attention to me, you know? And I was obviously pleased. By this time I had joined the Nation.

DATING MALCOLM

I never "dated" Malcolm as we think of it because at the time single men and women in the Muslims did not "fraternize," as they called it. Men and women always went out in groups. Whenever I went out in a group with Malcolm he would always drive, and I always sat in the backseat directly behind him. I never understood why I was supposed to sit behind him, until one day I was talking and happened to look up into the rearview mirror. I saw him looking at me. When he saw me looking, he smiled and I smiled back. That was as much as we could do.

Malcolm traveled a lot, but whenever he was in town I would try to get time off. I would tell Ella Yates, a young supervisor at the hospital, "I've got to go." She would laugh and say, "You've got to do what?"

"I've got to go."

"Did that man come into town again?"

"Yes, and he's coming to my dorm to pick me up and take me to dinner."

"Well, did you tell him you were working?"

"No. No, I didn't."

Malcolm would always take me to dinner accompanied by another Muslim brother. For me, it was a whole new way of living and learning and eating and being. Malcolm treated me really special, but he treated everybody special. But what most attracted me to him was his nobility. He always made me feel very comfortable. If he said he was going to call, you could bank on it. If he said he was going to do something, you could be assured that it would be done. He did not play games.

MARRYING MALCOLM

I kind of had an idea of Malcolm's intentions. He wanted to know all about me—my plans for the future, what I thought about the Movement. He would say, "So, sister, you'll be graduating next month, and what are you going to do?"

The day he actually asked me he was in Detroit. He called me from a public phone. "Are you ready to make that move?" he asked.

I screamed. I was so happy—I don't remember being that happy in my entire life. I was on a plane headed for Detroit practically the next day. I went home to my parents, and Malcolm came by and met them. They thought he was nice. "The one thing we can say about you is that you've always had nice friends," they told me. "We've never had to worry about you. We're very pleased—he's a nice young man."

They were so sing-songy about liking Malcolm that I said to my mother, "So, how would you like to have him for a son-in-law?" Well, the floodgates opened. My mother almost had a breakdown. She went on and on. He was too old. He would take me from them. He belonged to a different religion. My father was consoling her and saying to me, "See what you're doing to your mother?" Then my father looked at me with tears in his eyes and said, "What have we done to you to make you hate us so?"

Then, of course, I started crying. I felt so bad I went to bed. Now I'm supposed to be leaving the next day, going someplace in Indiana where we could get married in twenty-four hours. So the next morning Malcolm called from a little store around the corner. "Are you ready?" he asked.

"Ready? I'm still in bed."

"Why are you in bed? You know we have a long drive ahead."

"Listen, I'm in my mother's house. I've *got* to appear relaxed. I can't get up rushing. I can't tell them I'm leaving to get married."

"Okay," Malcolm said. "I'll call you back in a few minutes."

He called me back in a few minutes. "Did you tell them yet?"

"No." I had gone back to bed. I was trying to appear calm and cool. Then Malcolm said, "Well, I'm around the corner. I told you that, now. If you're going with me . . . you'd better get up."

Well, I got up rushing. I told my mother I had to get back to New York. And when Malcolm called the third time, I told him to come pick me up, but to please not come in. "Just sit outside. And please don't park directly in front of the house," I said. And I got my bag and said good-bye to my parents, went outside, got in the car and told Malcolm, "Drive quick, quick!" And he did.

I had tears in my eyes because I knew my parents loved me and wanted the best for me. My mother always wanted to give me a big wedding, so I felt bad—but not as bad as I felt when we got to Indiana and found that the law allowing marriages within twenty-four hours had been changed a few days before.

Malcolm called one of his older brothers, who told him to go to Lansing. Then Malcolm called his brother in Lansing to let them know we were coming. As soon as we got there we went to take the blood test and, while the analysis was being done, we went out and got two gold rings. We went back to get the results of the blood test and went to the courthouse—and got married. I still had my wedding dress in the suitcase. The dress and the little headgear had seemed extremely important, but I forgot all about the dress after we found we couldn't get married in Indiana. We knew the sun could not set with us together and not married. This was the first time I had ever been alone with Malcolm, and I sat way on the other side of the car, practically crushed up against the window.

After the marriage ceremony, I got on my tiptoes and kissed my husband on the cheek. He was grinning. He was happy. His older brother had invited us to spend the night with him and his wife, but Malcolm wouldn't hear of it.

We went to a hotel, and I showed him my wedding dress. We both laughed. I had brought along a modest little nightgown. I undressed in the bathroom, then ran to the bed. "Don't hurt yourself," my husband said. He was trying to pretend he wasn't looking, but you know a hotel room is just so large. But yes, I was nervous. Being alone with him. Undressing and getting into bed with him. *Oh, my God*, I thought, *what am I doing?*

LOVING MALCOLM

One of the things my husband said before he got married is that it would be very difficult for him to tell a wife where he was, where he was going, when he was coming back—you know, those simple things. It was basically that fear of a woman having control. So when we got married, I never asked his whereabouts.

But then after we were married, he started telling me. He would be at such-and-such a place from ten until about eleven-thirty, and then he'd be back at the office, he would say. Or if he was going out, he would leave me two or three numbers where I could reach him. "This is where I'll be staying," he would say. "And if nobody is there, you can always call and leave a message."

"What is all of this?" I would ask him. We laughed about his single days and his apprehension about letting a woman know where he was at all times. He didn't know where that fear of a woman having control came from. But after we were married it became very easy for him to volunteer information. He said that any mature man knows that if he is married to a woman and is concerned about her, she would also be concerned about him—about his coming and going. So sharing became very easy. He said it was the only civilized thing to do in a committed relationship. . . .

BLACK MAGIC
DUDLEY RANDALL

As this poem indicates, black girls possess powerful charms.

Black girl black girl
lips as curved as cherries
full as grape bunches
sweet as blackberries

Black girl black girl
when you walk you are
magic as a rising bird
or a falling star

Black girl black girl
what's your spell to make
the heart in my breast
jump   stop   shake

MY BROTHERS
HAKI R. MADHUBUTI

my brothers i will not tell you
who to love or not love
i will only say to you
that
Black women have not been
loved enough.

i will say to you
that
we are at war & that
Black men in america are
being removed from the
earth
like loose sand in a wind storm
and that the women Black are
three to each of us.

no
my brothers i will not tell you
who to love or not love
but
i will make you aware of our
self hating and hurting ways.
make you aware of whose bellies
you dropped from.
i will glue your ears to those images
you reflect which are not being
loved.

TREATING MY LADY RIGHT
DENNIS RAHIIM WATSON

This poet has set a standard of adoration that almost any woman would love.

Every other morning . . .
I wake up early and serve my lady
breakfast in bed
And if she's running late for work,
I iron her blouse or dress

Throughout the week
I do her feet and nails.
On Fridays it's dinner and Broadway
Because she's such a wonderful and
special friend, hang partner, advisor
and supporter, I surprise her with
bouquets of flowers, gifts and
plenty of loving.

I enjoy shopping for her clothes
I help her with the housework, homework
and career
On Saturday I do our laundry
If she's out jogging
I run her bubble bath . . .
and massage her tired body
with my finest oils

Because I don't like to fuss or fight . . .
I make it my business
to treat my lady right . . .
So she won't replace me overnight!

APPRECIATION
DOROTHY E. KING

This poem offers complete instructions for appreciating the one you love.

you ask me what i want from you

well, i'll tell you

i want to be appreciated
i want you to acknowledge my specialness
i want my achievements
to be lined up in your memory
like trophies on a mantel

i want you to be overwhelmed sometimes
by my talents

i want you to feel in awe

i want you to applaud my successes
& celebrate my triumphs

i want you there with champagne for my victories
i want you there with a shoulder for my tears

i want you to realize that the time i have put/do put
into myself
is to make our relationship better

i want you to encourage my efforts
even if it means i surpass you!
i want you to take my seriousness, seriously
& respond accordingly

i want to be appreciated

for all the special, little things
that make me, me
i want to be appreciated

LEARNING TO LOVE
FREDERICK J. GOODALL

For some men, learning to hug a friend means reeducating oneself.

I hugged my friend James today. Even though he thought I had lost my mind, it felt good to show him some love.

"What the hell is wrong with you?" he demanded as he pushed me away.

"Nothing," I replied. "I just wanted to let you know I love you, that's all."

Puzzled, he looked at me for several seconds. Suddenly his eyes widened as if he'd seen a ghost.

"Are you gay?" he whispered.

I laughed. "No, I'm not gay, just content."

After several years of harboring ill feelings toward Black men, I am finally content. There was a time in my life when I would never have considered expressing affection for another Black man, or for any man, for that matter. I was too cold, too hard. It was difficult for me even to love myself.

In retrospect, I understand why. I can't remember ever hearing a Black man say "I love you" when I was growing up. I can only remember Black men talking badly about one another and telling me to watch my back. They didn't teach me love, only fear.

My mother tried her best to put love in my heart, but her efforts weren't enough to save me. Without a strong male figure in the home, I had no one to emulate or show me how to love. I'm not saying women can't be role models for young boys; they can. What I'm saying is that a boy also needs a man to talk to.

As an adolescent, I started hanging with some older neighborhood boys, fighting, drinking and getting into mischief. If someone we didn't know stared at us for too long or (God forbid) touched us in any way, we felt compelled to attack. It sounds silly, but back then it seemed like the right thing to do. I don't know why I felt threatened by these young men. Maybe I saw things in them that I hated about myself, maybe I was venting my frustration about my father's absence, maybe I was insecure. Whatever it was kept me on the defensive.

My soul grew darker as I grew older (notice I didn't say "matured"). I continued to raise hell with my homeboys. But after a while I outgrew them and began to keep my distance. I had been drawn to them in the first place because they were hard: To me they epitomized true manhood. Actually, they were as confused and emotionally void as I. They walked around with gangsta leans and carried guns, but all they really needed was to be loved.

Sometimes I would see men embracing or otherwise displaying emotion toward each other. I would always label these men sissies or punks. In reality, they were neither. Unlike me, they were secure in their manhood and could express themselves without foul language, violence or hardness. They felt safe in the presence of other men. They knew how to love.

When I entered college, I tried to follow their example and give up the hate, but it wasn't easy. Tearing down walls around your heart never is. My old thought patterns kept creeping in. When someone would try to reach out to me, I'd think, *This guy is corny*. When I walked across campus, I threw on my hard persona when another Black man walked by—as I occasionally still do when I'm walking in the 'hood and a brotherman passes me. I see his dark skin and my parasympathetic nervous system yells danger!

A talk with my father turned my life around. We hadn't spoken in years, but something made me call him. The conversation was heavy with silence. We had so much to say but didn't know how to say it. Out of nowhere he said, "I love you." I was stunned. I'd never heard him utter those words to anyone. Hearing him say them to me was almost surreal. I felt confused, happy and relieved at once. I'd been hating my father for not being around when I needed him, and those three words lifted all the tension that had built up. It was as if I had been in the dark for years and someone had finally turned on the light.

It took several years, but today I can finally tell another brother that I love him and mean it. More important, I can mean it when I say it to myself.

YOU WERE NEVER MORE LOVABLE
ALLISON WEST

A father expresses his love.

December 23, 1994

Dear Tracey,

I haven't had an opportunity to talk to you since this lovable despot came into the family. His whimpers are our commands. All I can do is watch you care for him and listen to you lecture your mother and me on baby-sitting for our grandchild. I won't test your love and tell you what we say about you after you are out of ear reach.

The more I see your child, the more I see my daughter, and a kaleidoscope of colorful memories, unique and precious, crystallizes inside me. At his age, you decided my shoulder was more appetizing and soothing than your teething ring. You gummed me, then bit me, and if I would have allowed you, I'm certain you would've nibbled away my shoulder. You taught me how painless your needs were.

The years were greedy with us. They gobbled up my little girl and left a young lady who tried to conceal the child I visioned. On numerous occasions you informed me you were a woman. Even when you became a lawyer, your voicing it was unacceptable evidence. When we marched down the aisle at your wedding, I didn't feel I was giving you away, just adding to our life. And all that has happened since has proven me correct. It was not until I saw you with your child did I see you anew.

The happiness in your face when you looked at him. The way you talked and played with him, burying your face in his stomach, entangling your hair in his grasping hands. Both laughing as if laughter were the song of love.

What I saw I never imagined. All the other phases of your life I peeped into your future and glimpsed them before they arrived. Why was it that I never saw you with child? Did I knowingly blind that vision because of its irrefutability: my child would be gone and replaced by a woman? What do I see now when I look at you holding your child? You were never lovelier. You were never more loving. You were never more lovable. You were never more.

I don't know if it is possible for me to love you more. But I do know there is so much for me to love and to know about my love.

Love,
DAD

THOSE WINTER SUNDAYS
ROBERT HAYDEN

A father's love often is expressed in the thankless tasks he performs, many of which pass unnoticed by those who benefit.

Sundays too my father got up early
and put his clothes on in the blueblack cold,
then with cracked hands that ached
from labor in the weekday weather made
banked fires blaze. No one ever thanked him.

I'd wake and hear the cold splintering, breaking.
When the rooms were warm, he'd call,
and slowly I would rise and dress,
fearing the chronic angers of that house,

Speaking indifferently to him,
who had driven out the cold
and polished my good shoes as well.
What did I know, what did I know
of love's austere and lonely offices?

A LASTING LOVE
RUBY DEE AND OSSIE DAVIS

Long-time veterans of screen and stage, Ruby Dee and Ossie Davis first met in 1946 at a rehearsal for a play called Jeb. *Many decades later, they are very much together and very much in love. Their names are linked in the public mind with love and marriage. When interviewed by* Essence *magazine for an article appropriately entitled "A Love Supreme," they had been married for nearly fifty years. Here is what they said.*

INTERVIEWER: One of the things that really impressed us about your relationship is the admiration and tenderness you have for each other after all these years.

RUBY DEE: Well, I didn't always think that Ossie admired me or respected my talent. I think he came to that.

OSSIE DAVIS: I had to learn to appreciate you in terms of respecting you as an equal, but as a woman and as a wife, in the sense that I had been taught, I always respected you. The one continuing thing about you since I first met you, and I suppose the source of my greatest admiration, is that you always have something that you want to do. And that fascinated me. A lot of the most exciting things that have ever happened to me have come from following you into whatever you wanted to do. The spine of my life, intellectual and otherwise, has essentially been Ruby.

DEE: That's interesting. For a while I thought you were so traditionally male. But then I remember those times when you seemed to turn around and really look at me. I'm always looking for that. I desperately needed sanctioning and approving, you know, lacking confidence, being Black, being a woman . . .

DAVIS: It took me longer to understand that about you than any other thing. I thought you were self-motivated and thoroughly accepting of yourself and knew exactly what you wanted. I didn't know for the longest time that a little encouragement would have gone a long way. So I didn't give it.

INTERVIEWER: Ruby, were you a traditional wife? And even though you had a career as an actress, did you feel Ossie expected you to be a traditional wife?

DEE: When we first got married, neither of us was working. I'm cooking the breakfast and cleaning dishes and doing housework and so on, and he is sitting in the living room reading the paper. And I guess I thought this was the way it was supposed to be. But suddenly something broke loose in me, and we had many wrangles about men, women, equality and employment, and the Black man, and the whole business of having a baby, that it's my responsibility. He bucked, and we had terrible arguments, but one thing about Ossie, always after a week or two I could feel a qualitative change with him. He washed diapers, he got up and gave the early feedings and let me sleep. So we overcame something.

INTERVIEWER: Was either of you ever jealous of the other's career—perhaps when one of you was working a lot and the other wasn't?

DEE: There were times when I would physically beat the walls with my fists because I couldn't see any way out, being a mother and wife. There was a horrible jealousy, and I wanted the same kind of freedom that I felt men had. But wishing each other well is something that you have to practice doing—wishing each other well and believing that your light will shine also.

DAVIS: I'm not a jealous person. And I think it's because I'm a little too selfish to be jealous and a little too preoccupied. And not only did I trust Ruby implicitly but I also trusted myself, no matter what Ruby did, not to throw away a good marriage. I wasn't about to let my manhood or my maleness put me in a position where I would have to say good-bye to Ruby. No way was that ever going to be. If Ruby wanted to leave home, I would say, "Ruby, leave, but take me with you." Somehow I was going to work that thing out.

DEE: Once when I was working and Ossie wasn't, he came with me on location and brought the children and took care of them while I worked. And he has taken us all along when he went on a job.

INTERVIEWER: Would either of you forgive an affair or a lie or unfaithfulness to preserve your marriage?

DEE: Well, I made up my mind that, given infidelity, I would have to do battle. Because I'm not willing to let this man go for any such reason. I want him. So if you want something, you put your weight on it. You just get in there and fight for it. Or you come to other kinds of rationales. And just because you're married to each other, you're not half dead or blind. You're forever going to meet attractive people, especially in this business. And there are certain things you have to tell yourself about that. So you try all sorts of things as the marriage matures, and we came to a conclusion: Love and sex are two different things, and you don't just junk the thing up, but an affair is not the end of the world.

DAVIS: But Ruby, an affair, that's not the correct word. But maybe infatuations and flirtations on location . . .

DEE: You get smitten.

DAVIS: But I think we'd all be amazed at what simple conversation, truly held, can achieve in human relationships. Equally important is a profound sense of humor. Ruby has been the screen wife or love interest of Sidney [Poitier] four times [*Edge of the City, A Raisin in the Sun, Virgin Island* and *Buck and the Preacher*], of Jackie Robinson [*The Jackie Robinson Story*] and of Nat King Cole [*St. Louis Blues*]. And I look up there at the movies and wonder how I'm going to survive except to laugh.

INTERVIEWER: Has your relationship changed over the years?

DAVIS: You start out with love, passion, blind sex, fulfillment and the joy of all the physical aspects of it. And then that tapers off, and you become husband and wife. And it's a steady love, but other things are involved, furniture and unpaid bills and, when you become parents, children and diapers. And then the true objective of marriage finally comes into focus. Marriage was invented so children would have a chance to grow. And the love broadens and deepens in another way. Then you become partners, working together and appreciating each other as creative and productive people. And finally, if you're smart and lucky and wise, you end up friends. It's a never-ending process, because—speaking for myself

now—the one I'm in love with is continually capable of delightful sur-
prises and growth and things I didn't imagine she was capable of, though
we've been married for forty-six years. There's always something to
look forward to with Ruby. It's still interesting, still exciting, and the
best is yet to be. She's the best friend I have.

DEE: Once your kids are grown, if you're lucky, you almost find yourself
back like you were when you first met. I've found that it's very exciting
in a lot of ways that you might not think when you're young in your
twenties and thirties. You may think that people in their sixties and
seventies are not very good lovers, but believe me, you can get better.
Maybe because there are a lot of things out of the way, and you can
relax and pay attention. It's wonderful.

INTERVIEWER: Couples like you, who have been together a long time, are
an inspiration to us and, I'm sure, to others. Is that something you ever
think about—that your relationship might have meaning and be important to people beyond your own family?

DAVIS: A good marriage belongs among the vital statistics of any people.
It is a credit to the people who are married, and to the group the married
people belong to. Being a part of life, being part of the tribe, being part
of the group, part of the community, involves all of you.

DEE: I used to say, "Oh, I don't want to talk about it"—this business of
being married. But we've come to the point now where we do want to
talk about it. We must talk about it. We are older, we have to say things,
we have to hand down messages. We have to *be* elders because the tribe
needs its elders.

INTERVIEWER: Do you think we have failed our children?

DEE: Yes. And I am concerned because it's like an accusation. But we're
confronted with an unprecedented phenomenon. When television first
came into our homes, we didn't take stock of what it was doing to our
children's minds and of the images that were put before them, especially
as they relate to Black people. We were glad to have this thing. I'm not
blaming television for everything, but we let it just come in and claim
our children's minds without demanding credentials, because we were
too busy "doing our own thing."

DAVIS: When we in this house had to face very grave issues with our
children, it usually took place at the dinner table. The dinner table was a

place where much more than food was being exchanged. We learned our history, and we learned the values, attitudes and propositions of the past. Definitions are made and the culture passes from one generation to the other around the dinner table. Now the elimination of the dinner table as a fact in how the family conducts its business means that a marketplace for the transfer of very important ideas, ideas relevant to cultural identity, was lost, creating a kind of vacuum. Into that vacuum came television, which looked upon our children as a market where sales could be made. So our children at the most tender phases of their lives are being manipulated. Now they hear things that relate to consumption, to self-gratification and self-indulgence. And children reflect those values—or that lack of values —they get from having their minds misused. We are guilty in the sense that we were not the elders of the tribe when we needed to be, the way we needed to be.

DEE: To begin to heal our communities, parents have to take charge. There's no substitute for somebody being in charge. Being an elder is more than sitting on a stoop with a pipe. Being an elder today is putting your ass on the line.

INTERVIEWER: Your entire career and marriage have been characterized by political activism—from speaking at forums organized by Paul Robeson's periodical, *Freedom,* to arranging a meeting between Malcolm X and the mainstream Black leadership of the day, to organizing a fundraiser for Angela Davis. Yet during the McCarthy era, taking a political stand on certain issues was risky for people in the entertainment business.

DAVIS: When Ruby and I came into the professional theater in 1946 and 1947, World War II was just over and America was saying, "We're going to do something about racism and get rid of it, because look at that Hitler over there." But Black soldiers were coming back and getting killed in Macon, Georgia, and four more down in Monroe, Georgia. Another Black soldier, Isaac Woodard, was coming through the South on a bus when he was dragged off and his eyes were gouged out. Two more out on Long Island were killed. And the theater was responding. Every night somebody would have a party to raise money for somebody about to be lynched. We raised money for Rosalie Ingram, whose two sons came to her defense after she was attacked by a White man on a farm down in Florida. The state was going to execute all three of them. We in the theater had a sense of purpose. It wasn't about money. It wasn't about your name on the marquee.

DEE: It was how, as artists, we could respond.

INTERVIEWER: So where are we as a people today?

DEE: We're doing well, considering what we're up against—a society that lacks a solid spiritual base and is increasingly characterized by the immorality and stupidity of greed and disruptive economics. The family is the basis of society, the nation and civilization. But this society does not support the family.

DAVIS: If I could add to what Ruby is saying: The Civil Rights Movement was organized around education and the conviction that, whatever was wrong, education could fix it. Well, we won the right to an education, but, like so much that we fought for, it has come to us in a deteriorated state. As a people, I think, we are in transition, and it seems as if we're wandering around in the wilderness, but so is everyone. What we need to do now is to make some definitions, to define equality.

DEE: Yes, and define freedom. Freedom can only exist if it is bound to principles and anchored in economics. We need an interlocking structure of systems and values. Bottom line, we must know—and poet Gwendolyn Brooks said it simply and so beautifully—that "We are each other's harvest. We are each other's business. We are each other's magnitude and bond."

LOVE RHYMES
COLLECTED BY J. MASON BREWER

Le's go across the ocean, le's go across the sea,
Le's lock our hearts together and throw away the key.

•

I'm a cute little girl, with very sweet kisses,
But it won't change my name from Miss to Mrs.

•

Up the hickory, an' down the pine;
Good-looking boys is hard to find.

❧

Love is or it ain't. Thin love ain't love at all.
                    —*Toni Morrison,* Beloved

❧

FRIENDSHIP

A friend will take your secrets to the grave. But even more importantly, a friend will sit through videotapes of your family reunion, accompany you on shopping sprees (to help you spend your money), lend you a listening ear, tolerate your poetry (and advise you tactfully not to expand your limited audience), eat your best soul food dish and smile (regardless of the taste), and send you postcards from Shangri-las you wish you could visit. A good friend will also stand by you in good times or bad. Who could ask for anything more caring than that.

As we grow older, we learn to treasure our best friends, to value their loving concern and counsel. We also begin to realize how similar (or complementary) they are to us. Indeed, in friendships, we learn as much about ourselves as others, for our friends mirror our likes, dislikes, interests, and concerns. A Senegalese proverb states, "When you know who his friend is, you know who he is." This bit of wisdom rings as true in America as it does in Africa or anywhere else.

Choosing the right friends is vitally important to our outlook on life. They can bring out the best or the worst in us; they will either embellish our strengths or enlarge our weaknesses. Not only do friends reflect our own positive or negative traits, they reveal the choices we are likely to make and the roads we are likely to follow. They either help us mature, or hold us back.

We must work to keep our friends. Friendships, like other relationships, are seldom completely smooth. But true friends can tolerate rocky roads. They can also take criticism. What they will *not* tolerate are senseless restrictions imposed by others, or by society. Racism, for example, did not prevent blacks and whites from forming friendships.*

Distance, also, will not sever true friendships. An enduring friendship existed between Langston Hughes and Arna Bontemps, though for many

---

* In 1859, a slave named William Peel Jones enlisted his white friend's support to escape slavery. The white friend participated in a plan to mail Jones from a slave-holding state—Maryland—to a state where slavery was prohibited—Pennsylvania. Jones's white friend mailed Jones in a large box, then traveled from Baltimore to Philadelphia, collected the box, and transported it to a safe destination, where he opened it. The two friends then celebrated the successful plan.

years they lived in separate cities. Several of their letters appear in this chapter.

Friendships can be found almost anywhere, even within our families. In a newspaper editorial reprinted here, Robert C. Maynard explains how he and his wife continued their friendship as husband and wife. From his piece, we can see that friendship is, in fact, an expression of love—an emotional bonding that is as powerful as just about any other kind.

We must teach children to make friends and cherish them and to distinguish rewarding friendships from harmful ones. Their friendships—from preschool through adulthood—will stimulate their moral development and lend to their lives a richness, depth, vitality, and variety that cannot be duplicated by any other means.

WHEN THE LONG RACE IS RUN
JAMES S. WATSON

James S. Watson (1882–1952) was the first black judge in New York State. This poem was included in a speech he delivered before the Biosophy Society in New York City on October 26, 1938.

When the long race is run
And all the tasks are done,
    Men find that peace depends
Not on the goals attained
Or the high fortunes gained,
    But on good friends.

Laughter and song and mirth
And the rich joys of earth
    No mortal here attend,
Unless with him each day
'Neath sunny skies or gray
    Walks a true friend.

Pride, pomp and power of place
Lack that consoling grace
    Which soothes and mends
Heartache and sorrow's pain,
Who weeps shall smile again
    If he has friends.

Though on a golden throne,
He, who must dwell alone,
    Time sadly spends,
All that makes life complete,
All that makes memories sweet,
    Comes from our friends.

THE STORY OF LAZARUS
INTERPRETED BY P. K. MCCARY

What happened to a friend of Jesus' was a miracle to behold.

Jesus' friends, Mary and Martha, had a favorite brother named Lazarus. And Lazarus took sick and was dying. Mary and Martha pleaded with Jesus 'cuz they knew He loved Lazarus, too.

"Please, come see 'bout Lazarus, Jesus. We don't want him to die."

And Jesus told them not to worry. *"This sickness is not the dying kind. Don't worry. Whatever will happen will be to the glory of the Almighty."*

When Jesus got to Lazarus' house, the funeral had already taken place 'cuz Lazarus had died while Jesus was away. Jesus told them He was glad that He hadn't come early 'cuz now they could watch Him work.

Jesus had them take Him to Lazarus' grave even though Martha was upset that her brother had died.

"You know, Jesus, if you had been there, Lazarus would still be here," she said sadly.

But Jesus understood. *"Don't worry, sister. Your brother will rise."*

Martha said, "Yes, I know. Glory, 'cuz he'll rise in the resurrection in the last day."

But Jesus said, *"Nope, that's not what I mean, Martha. I'm the resurrection and the life. I got the power."* And then He set out to show just what He meant. Jesus had Mary and Martha take Him to where Lazarus was buried.

Then Jesus came to the tomb and told them to open it up.

Martha hesitated. "Jesus, I'm sure it stinks in there. Lazarus has been dead for a while."

But Jesus wouldn't hear of them not believing Him. He insisted that they move it immediately. And when they had, Jesus first thanked the Almighty and then He called out, *"Hey, Lazarus, my brother. Come on out of there."*

It was a sight. All bound up with tape and cloth, Lazarus came hopping out of the tomb and everybody was amazed.

"Let him out of those things," Jesus urged. Many brothers who saw this now believed.

SHARING THE STAGE WITH THE KING OF BEBOP

Jazz musicians often develop special bonds, communicating through their music. Dizzy Gillespie (1917–93), one of the chief architects of bebop, struck up a "stage relationship" with tenor saxophonist James Moody. Here is a story of how the two musicians got along.

Dizzy developed funny routines as fast as he developed original music. With them he attracted and held audiences that might not have understood everything he was playing. Thus he kept his band working and was free to play what interested him.

Some of his funny ideas developed into classic clowning routines as good as anything ever seen in vaudeville. One of the best was the mock fight he developed with James Moody. After the opening chorus of a tune with both horns playing in unison, Moody and Dizzy would step to the microphone at the same time. They would bump into each other, stop, look at each other, and pantomime a dispute, while the rhythm section continued to play. The following is a free translation of the mimed gestures.

MOODY: I'm supposed to solo first.
DIZZY: No, I'm going to play first.
MOODY: But I play first on this tune.
DIZZY: It's my band, and I'm going to play first. (Pushes Moody.)

MOODY: Don't push me.

DIZZY: I'll push you again if you don't get out of my way!

MOODY: Put your hand on me again if you dare!

DIZZY: Get out of my way! (Pushes Moody again.)

At this point Moody reaches quickly into his pocket and keeps his hand there, with an obvious sharp point showing through the material of his pants. Dizzy's eyes pop open in alarm, and he reaches into his own pocket. They crouch warily and circle each other as the tension mounts. Then, simultaneously, they whip their hands from their pockets and spring dangerously at each other—and dance an elegant foxtrot together as the rhythm section plays on.

～

The tree of love gives shade to all.

—*Traditional*

～

INTEGRATED PATHS
CHARLAYNE HUNTER-GAULT

Before going on to a career as a newspaper reporter and nationally known television broadcast journalist, Charlayne Hunter-Gault was one of the first black students to attend the University of Georgia, helping to desegregate the institution. Her companion—and competitor—in those historic days was Hamilton Holmes. In the following selection, she recalls their friendship.

The year Hamilton Holmes was our high school football co-captain and I was the homecoming queen, we became a team. It was the spring of 1959, and until then, Hamp, the scholar-jock who wanted to be a doctor, and I, the aspiring journalist, had mostly gone our seperate ways. But we became the team that was Georgia's entry into the civil rights revolution after we were admitted as the first Black students to the 176-year-old University of Georgia—an institution into which the governor had vowed that "no, not one" Black student would ever be allowed.

Hamp, a straight-A student, was more deeply hurt then I was by the university's year and a half of ruses to keep us out. The officials had rejected him as unqualified during the admissions procedure, and after we were admitted, they refused to let him play football. They said it was too risky. He could be killed. Deliberately. But with his old-fashioned sense of loyalty, commitment, and duty, he blocked and tackled for me, even as he ran the gauntlet of insults, including finding the air let out of his tires by some white kid who just didn't get it. When from time to time I had to go to the infirmary with stomach pains of uncertain origin, the first person to appear at my bedside would be Hamp.

"You all right, Char?" he would ask. And whatever was on my mind or in my gut would recede. This must have been the manner he later brought to the bedside of his patients, after he had graduated, Phi Beta Kappa, and then become the first Black graduate of Emory University School of Medicine.

Not long before his enormously good heart failed him and he died, Hamp, a prominent orthopedic surgeon and teacher, had been asked to introduce me at a public event. I was in Atlanta for a reading of my book, *In My Place*, a memoir of our college days. At one point, I heard him say, "Of course, she's a lot nicer now than she was then." As he flashed that big face-filling grin of his, we exchanged knowing glances that took us all the way back to our intense competitions at Turner High, when they eliminated the Best All-Around Student honor because both of us insisted on having it.

Hamp had all but buried the unhappy ghosts of the past; he had even forgiven the university, becoming one of its governing officials and biggest boosters. In fact, at the foot of the blanket of flowers that adorned his coffin lay a red-and-black Georgia Bulldogs cap.

He had told me that *his* book, were he ever to write it, would probably tell our story a bit differently than mine did, and I allowed that he was probably right, especially given the importance he attached to proving to whites that he was as good as any of their best.

When I finished my reading, I assumed that Hamp was gone. As I headed for a table in the lobby, a long line of people were waiting in line for me to sign their books. At one point, I turned to a page and saw that big, round, curving signature that I used to poke fun at in high school—unmistakably that of Hamilton Earl Holmes. I looked up, and there was Hamp working the line from the back, talking with people and signing everyone's copy of my book. Our book. About the best team I ever joined.

WHAT HOLDS A MARRIAGE TOGETHER?
ROBERT C. MAYNARD

Robert C. Maynard (1937–93), founder of the Institute for Journalism Education, which trained hundreds of minority journalists, wrote a syndicated column for the Oakland Tribune, *which he owned and managed. This piece, published on August 27, 1987, tells us that something extra— in addition to love—is a key ingredient in a successful marriage.*

AUGUST 27, 1987—We never heard them argue, and yet they had many spirited discussions. My parents were married a half century and went to their graves adoring each other more, they said, than when they first courted.

As children, the thing I suppose we admired—and feared—most about my parents was the way they thought. That is to say, the degree to which they seemed to us to be both emotionally and intellectually inseparable.

Try as we might, we could never maneuver them onto opposite sides of a parental issue. If my mother said no to a request or proposal, chances were excellent my father would say the same, even if he had no idea what my mother's position had been. We used to call their solidarity "the stone wall" long before Watergate.

What started me thinking about that long, loving and impressive relationship was a recent cover story in *Newsweek* magazine about the improving state of marriage. It seems the divorce rate is dipping slightly after years of unremitting increase.

The statistics surrounding this issue are always open to differing interpretations, but it does appear marriages are lasting longer and the divorce option is losing some of its previous appeal. AIDS, it is thought, might be contributing to some sober reflections about the appeal of sexual freedom.

This trend toward less divorce is entirely too new to contribute to many useful conclusions. Why people divorce, or don't, depends on too many variables. But buried in the *Newsweek* piece was something that struck me as an overlooked constant.

It has to do with why some couples stay together through thick and thin. It's also why I believe my parents remained married and devoted to each other despite all the problems you might expect a couple to face raising six children during the Depression and World War II. Those were tough times to be parents.

The special ingredient, I believe, was friendship. My parents were not head-over-heels romantics. In fact, they were rarely demonstrably affectionate around us. But they were friends. Best friends. That, I believe, was the great secret of their devotion.

For a time when I was in high school, my father did some remodeling that required me temporarily to give up my room for an anteroom to my parents' bedroom. That is when I discovered what good friends they were.

Long into the night, especially on weekends, they would talk about the doings of the previous day, the funny things that happened to one or the other of them.

The thing I noticed was the calm, even tone of their voices. They talked almost in a code of their own. They laughed at each other's silly mistakes and foibles. And when they disagreed about something, there was an odd silence. They listened very carefully to each other until each understood the reason for the argument of the other.

Later, I was to learn that most people who argue have ceased listening to what the other person has to say. My parents were the opposite. My father once explained to me why he listened so carefully to my mother's arguments.

"I always learn something by listening to your mother," he said simply. He was by no means a docile person. He often argued back just as vigorously. But they never raised their voices to each other and they clearly respected each other's views on just about everything.

They ran a business together for most of that half century, and there were myriad tough decisions to be made. They had little trouble working those problems out together. It was impressive to see the way they anticipated each other and finished each other's sentences.

Where their true unity of purpose shone was in the manner in which they raised six children together. As we later came to understand, my parents had spent long hours as newlyweds establishing their mutual goals for the family.

They agreed on the code and spirit by which their children would be raised. Above all, they agreed that love was the thing of which their children would have the most. Discipline turned out to hold a solid second place on their agenda. Material things were a distant third.

And when they disagreed, they did it in a friendly fashion that said to the rest of us that they were sure to still love each other at the end of the argument. As I said, it is difficult to know all the reasons people divorce, but one thing I am sure holds couples together. It's friendship.

UP THE HILL
VIVIAN H. GRASTY

Composed primarily of parents and children between the ages of two and nineteen, Jack and Jill of America was organized June 1, 1938, in Philadelphia with two main objectives: (1) to create a medium of contact for children, and (2) to provide constructive recreational, social, and cultural programs for children and mothers. Here's a 1948 Jack and Jill song that embodied the spirit of the organization.

Sung to the tune of "Jingle Bells."

Friends are far and near
In Jack and Jill today,
Happiness and cheer
Meet us on our way.
Boys and girls soon learn
That friendship is the thing,
Oh what friends we all can have;
Jacks and Jills—Let's Sing.

Jack and Jill—Jack and Jill,
Happy days are here,
Oh what fun it is to come,
You bring us so much cheer.
Jack and Jill—Jack and Jill,
Picnics—Parties—Gym,
Stories—Music—Sewing—Art
Fun filled to the brim.

FRIENDS
ANDY RAZAF

True friends will remain loyal to you whether you are present or not.

Acquaintances are many,
But friends are very few;
If you must call someone your friend,
Think twice before you do.

The face-to-face variety
Of Friends you'll never lack;

But who knows which of these remains
A friend behind your back?

SELECTED CORRESPONDENCE
LANG AND ARNA

*Authors Langston Hughes (1902–67) and Arna Bontemps (1902–73)
were close friends and collaborators. They met in 1924 and together wrote
several books. In 1932, they collaborated on* Pop and Finfina, *a children's
book about Haiti, following it with two invaluable anthologies—*The
Poetry of the Negro *in 1949 and* The Book of Negro Folklore *in 1958.
At one point, the voluminous manuscript for the latter weighed seven and a
half pounds.*

*Between 1925 and 1967, when Hughes died, they exchanged some
2,300 letters. Here are a few of them.*

April 30, 1946

Dear Lang:

Just a quickie to raise two or three small questions in connection with
the article I am writing this week about you for *Ebony*.

1. Which is the exact title and description of the citation and honor
which you are about to receive from the American Academy—also the
full and exact name of the Academy?

2. Can you estimate the number of lectures you have made this year?
The number in your whole career? The number of people to whom you
lecture in a big year and in an average year? The total number to whom
you have given your lecture readings in your life-time as a poet? I would
just like to play with these figures in some sort of way. Any other
estimates involving dramatic numbers would come in handy. I still don't
know what I'll do with them, but I have a vague impression that something interesting might be possible.

3. Will you jot down a quick list of novelties and interesting and
important items which might otherwise be neglected or forgotten by me.

You know I am doing this strictly off the top of my head—no notes, no nothing.

Please rush this data to my house number via airmail special.

More anon.

> Ever,
> Arna
> 923 - 18th Avenue, North

❦

> 634 St. Nicholas Avenue
> New York 30, New York
> May 2, 1946.

Dear Arna,

How was Chicago and did you get my letter there?

Dick Wright and wife and also child have gone to Paris.

Now as to your piece on me. You should have an invite by now. It is an "Arts and Letters Grant" from The American Academy of Arts and Letters—One Thousand Dollars. (Cash.)

2. 15 lectures in fall, and 40 since New Years, not counting freebies— I'd say about 75 all told this season including the schools they drug me by against my will sleepy and just off the train. My first was in Washington in 1924, so in 22 years I'd estimate from Mississippi to Moscow and Chicago to Shanghai well over a thousand public appearances reading my poems. There are seldom less than a hundred people in an audience, average I'd say five hundred, often a thousand, and high school or college assemblies frequently 2 to 3 thousand, so I'd say at least 500,000 or a half million folks have heard me read *Rivers* myself in person. (Although I doubt if the Chinese understood it.)

Six cross country tours, and up and down and back between times, so probably have travelled at least 100,000 miles in this country alone. Recent cross country tour as you know entirely by air.

More Negro audiences and sponsors in America than white, but white sponsors growing all the time. This season from Town Hall, New York, to Parent-Teachers Association (colored) Tupelo, Mississippi, fashionable Oak Park Nineteenth Century Women's Club to Colored Community Center, Anderson, Indiana, the University of Colorado to Lanier High School, Jackson, Mississippi, the sixth grades assembly of Kalamazoo, Michigan to the Brooklyn Academy of Arts and Sciences—all within a year. And reading the *same* poems from kids on up to whoever goes to Town Hall or Brooklyn at 11 A.M., same poems in Mississippi as in Boston, to colored or white or mixed—which proves something or other!

3. Translated into Uzbek among other languages. . . . Singers of my songs range from Lawrence Tibbett to Josh White, Marian Anderson to Marion Oswald. . . . I get two sets of fan letters, some to me, some to Simple. . . . Hobbies: Collecting House Rent Party cards and attending Gospel Song Battles. . . . In only one railroad wreck in all my travels. Got an overcoat out of that, and nary a scratch. . . . Sometimes sleep 15 hours at a time. . . . Lately (more and more) am invited to deliver the Sunday morning message at churches (Paid). Recently Community Church of Boston and Unity Church, Unitarian, of Montclair, N.J. . . . Did Tour USO's and army camps during war. . . . Enormous fan mail from soldiers overseas re Defender column and Bedside Esquire story, "A Good Job Gone" which by the way brought Esquire its largest mail in pre-publication controversy. . . . Have only received one threatening communication—about ten years ago from Ku Klux Klan. . . . As you know, have no mechanical sense. Took me eight years to learn to close vegetable bin in Aunt Toy's kitchen. Never turn on right burner on a gas stove. Still can't close a folding table (much). . . . Have a long head, but just recently learned I should always buy an oval shaped hat. Even then they get out of shape quick. . . . Give away as many books as I sell. All of my books (except *Fine Clothes*) still in print. *Weary Blues* never out of print in twenty years. . . . Try to answer every letter I receive at least once, but in recent years unable to keep up steady correspondences. (Haven't yet read all the mail that accumulated during my recent winter tour—a suitcase full still unread. Have only *part time* secretary—but two portable typewriters—one of which has been around the world with me and is over twenty years old. . . . Like to eat. Gain weight on tour from the good dinners folks fix. . . . Get sick if get mad. . . . Have several hundred unpublished poems as far as book form goes. . . . Read slowly. . . . Read books I like over and over, but don't read many new ones. . . . Never had a thousand dollars all at once until I was forty. Haven't had two thousand dollars all at once yet. . . . Pay bills promptly. . . . Arrested once in Cuba for defying Jim Crow at Havana Beach. Put out

of Japan for visiting Madame Sun Yat Sen in China. . . . Picketed by Gerald L. K. Smith's Mothers of America at Wayne College in Detroit. . . . By Aimee Semple McPherson in Pasadena. Never sued. . . . Never married, but once reported engaged to Elsie Roxborough in public press (niece Joe's manager). . . . Friends include Mrs. Bethune and Bricktop, Diego Rivera and Bootsie's creator, Ollie Harrington, Paul Robeson and Willie Bryant, Still and Duke, Margot and Butterbeans and Susie, Hemingway and Roy Wilkins! . . . Hey, now! . . . Love kids. . . . Love dogs. . . . Hate parsnips, narrative poems, bridge, breakfast invitations, Jim Crow cars, and people who recite poetry in a faraway voice. . . . Also "Trees" sung just before I am introduced. . . . Chain smoker. . . . Height of ambition to live in Arizona. Love that there sun. . . . Also to have plenty time to just stand on the street and loaf like street corner colored do. . . . Also to have enough wall space to hang all the pictures and paintings friends give me. . . . And shelves to pile the records I own. . . . And time to write another novel.

C'est tout.

> Sincerely,
> Langston

ℰ—ⅠⅠ—৯

> 20 East 127th Street
> New York 35, N. Y.
> February NAY March 2, 1955

Dear Arna,

*Lonesome Boy** is a perfectly charming and unusual book. I read it right off it came in the mail today. I LOVE books that short and easy and pretty to read. It ought to make a wonderful gift book. I must tell Frances Reckling's Gift Shop about it.

When I went to the bank up the street today I saw your son, Pablo, in a restaurant ordering a great big (albeit chopped) steak—so I asked him what he was in training for!

Did I tell you I had dinner with Elton Fax, the artist who's been living in Mexico? He's going next week to five South American countries lecturing on his art as a cultural mission for the State Dept. (All expenses and 700 bucks per month!) Why don't you get Charles S. to get

---

* *Lonesome Boy,* a children's book, was published in 1955.

you such a trip—like Redding and several others have had? You look cultural.

When do you leave for California? Train or plane? Why not fly back via New York and relax yourself after all that speaking?

Man, I have almost 50 stories now selected for my African anthology! Been dreaming Nigeria in my sleep. The Nigerians write the most vividly, the South Africans the most poetically. The Liberians *not at all*— inhibited by being part American, I reckon. Griff Davis says there's not a writer in the whole Republic! He's been here on leave and about to return.

We had Chinese food for dinner tonight.

水廾玄廾

Lan Sin Hews

⟨───⟩

10 December '56

Dear Lang,

Yesterday I had the long sleep I've been craving for nearly a month, and it did a world of good. I'm on the pace again today. Meanwhile, I've given the *Pictorial History* the close reading it deserves, and I agree with the fine recommendation it receives in the *Library Journal*. It is certainly a job well done. Despite a few minor slips, like using one of Douglass' early pictures twice (also Gwen Brooks), it is over all something of which we can all be proud. It should be active a long time—saleswise, that is. In our living room on the table it attracts immediate attention, and even the nonbookish say: "That's something I must get."

The prospectus for our prize book, *The Book of Negro Folklore*, arrived Saturday (8) and gave me another spin. This should work into a really big item in every sense. The stuff from our Humor job reads awfully good after this lapse of time, and I think the sections you have indicated are fine. Maybe the wording could be changed in a few cases (would *Recollections* sound more folklorish than *Remembrances*, for example?), but there will be time for such fine points. The others I'm thinking about in this connection are "Past-time Rymes," "Race Relations," and "Humorous Anecdotes," but none *need* be changed unless we think up better wordings.

I'm collecting like a weaver. I have something in just about all the categories, and in some quite a bit. There is good stuff here in the

Source Documents of the Social Science Department (none published), and I'm having myself a time while reading it. The book resources of the library are just about complete, and I'm digging in that too. John Work is expected back from Europe with the Jubilees toward the end of this week, and I expect to get some leads from him. I also expect to start playing recordings made by him and others on folklore sorties into Mississippi and elsewhere. All told, a thrilling operation! It's easy to get folks to help on this because it's so much fun.

The idea of paragraphs or pages by us to introduce each section also appeals to me—for several reasons. A Fisk thesis I've found on the Folk Sermon will help me do a good statement on "Sermons, Prayers, Testimonials." I'm also primed for several others. Maybe we could divide these up and initial the ones we do. This would simplify the matter of possible quotation, etc. Also we might get going and want to do a short article on one or another. You would obviously want to do the little piece on "Blues" and "Rhymed Jive, Etc." While I am rather up for "Ghost Stories" and "Recollections," for example. Your introduction to "Party Cards and Advertisements" could easily touch off an article that you could sell.

By the way, I favor leaving *American* out of the title. People will probably understand or guess that it's American, coming from us, and by opening the book they'll soon find out for sure. But more important, James Weldon Johnson used that adjective so conspicuously in his several "Books" (American Negro Poetry, American Negro Spirituals) ours might get mixed up with his—or at least seem to lean a bit too heavily on his titles. Besides, the title is shorter without it and probably better for promotion.

Alberta* re-arranged and improved my working room while I was away. The only trouble is that it may take me a few months to find everything. But I'm certainly set up better now. I wish I had more hours to spend in it.

The lectures helped out a lot on the budget this month. One more windfall (will it be the *Folklore?*) and I should be up even again.

Best ever,
Arna

* Arna Bontemps's wife.

ᔪᕐᔭ

20 East 127th Street
New York 35, N.Y.
October 28, 1963
4 A. M. after a
long production
conference.

Dear Arna:

Thanks a lot for those schoolboard clippings you sent me. But the bit of excitement down there is as nothing to the current goings on at the Little Theatre*—near knock-down-and-drag-out in the aisle after dress rehearsal between producers and the young and most cocky 27-year-old theatre owner (who, by the way, made his million in buying marsh land in Nigeria then selling it to the government there at 10 times its purchase price, I hear). "Hold him!". . . . No, let him go, I'll knock his teeth out! . . . "Call the police" in this lovely old bandbox of a playhouse. . . . The next night at the first preview *between the acts*, the same thing, only this time on the sidewalk in full view of the public. All parties forcibly restrained by others. Then the theatre owner called for his bouncer-manager who barred two of the three producers from the Little Theatre forever and would not let them re-enter to see the second act. (They haven't been back yet. A million dollar lawsuit threatened, also "We'll move the show to a Schubert house". . . . "You can't because you have a contract with me and I dare you to move." (Owner). . . . "Don't threaten us—or you'll find yourself with all the fire-violations in the book on your theatre before opening night!" Etc., Etc. . . . Anyhow, we're still there and performing—and things on stage look pretty good. Cullud behaving (on the whole) beautifully. But the white folks!!!!!. . . . Incidentally the backer's millions come mainly from housing for Negroes (projects, etc.) in Texas which began with a Negro partner in construction, since dead—so a project is named after him in Dallas!!!!! Do, Jesus!. . . . Me, still "smiling through" and taking a nice comfortable orchestra seat every night to watch the real-life dramat-

---

* The owner of the refurbished Little Theatre, on 44th Street near Broadway in New York City, clashed with the stagehands' union and with the producers of *Tambourines to Glory*, by Langston Hughes. The show, a disaster, closed on November 23, 1963, within three weeks of opening. Hughes called the setback part of his "bad-luck-in-theatre season."

ics in the aisles—which are more exciting than even my own on-stage creations. "No biz like . . . etc.

Lang

Added to this—a 2 day stagehands strike against our theatre only.
P.S. All this show news, of course, *confidential* . . .

A bientot,
L.H.

When you know who his friend is, you know who he is.
—*Senegalese proverb*

Being a friend means mastering the art of timing. There is a time for silence. A time to let go and allow people to hurl themselves into their own history. And a time to pick up the pieces when it's all over.

—Gloria Naylor,
The Women of Brewster Place

COMPASSION

Something dreadful happens to a friend or a stranger. Are you just an interested observer or bystander? Or can you relate?

If you can, your heart may grow softer and you may want to reach out and help. Label this feeling compassion. It is a willingness to construct a bridge over someone else's troubled water—to care and understand when something goes wrong. You don't have to love that person deeply to feel his or her pain and suffering. You only need a dash of tenderness, a little sympathy, and a connection—a sort of "moral umbilical cord" to the rest of humanity. If you lack all that, you are probably a cold fish.

Compassion might well be the most humane moral value of all. It has none of the contemptuous sorrow characterized by pity; it is shaped by great concern, sometimes as much for others as for oneself. We feel compassion when we feel a need to help friends who are ill or injured, the homeless and hungry, those subjected to great suffering or tribulation.

Our ability to feel compassion is in some ways a measure of our own basic moral decency and our ties to others. Compassion perhaps springs from human nature as an awareness that we are created alike and that potentially we can suffer similar pain or loss. Essentially, compassion is the recognition that the person suffering "could be me."

The river of compassion, shaped by powerful currents of misery and hope, runs deep and strong through black America. Down it, African Americans and others have sailed many ships, big and small. One of those boaters was a man who remained a slave so he might help many others escape slavery. This chapter includes his story, "Rowboat to Freedom."

Here you will also find many other stories of compassion—people who made medical advances ("Healers"), a woman who tries to steer an inner-city boy away from a life of crime ("Thank You, M'am"), and another woman who establishes an agency to love and care for babies with AIDS ("Mother Hale"). Each piece shows a deep humanity and affection for others.

Can compassion be developed in young minds? It is debatable whether one can break down tenderness to teach it as one would, say, mathematics or science. But human concern certainly can be encouraged. Some of the greatest moral lessons of all are those that teach that we are all bound together by our humanity.

ᙁᙁᙁ

All life is interrelated. The agony of the poor impoverishes the rich; the betterment of the poor enriches the rich. We are inevitably our brother's keeper because we are our brother's brother. Whatever affects one directly affects all indirectly.

—*Martin Luther King Jr.*

ᙁᙁᙁ

WHAT GAUNT WANTED

Every Christmas, widows in a small town in Ohio get a gift, courtesy of a former slave who probably wanted to look out for his neighbors. This Associated Press article, which appeared in 1996, explains.

YELLOW SPRINGS, OHIO —For years, Yellow Springs has been keeping a list and checking it twice. But it's the widows, not the kids, who get the Christmas gift.

Each year this season, every widow in town gets a free 10 pounds of flour and 10 pounds of sugar, part of a century-old bequest from a former slave.

"The first time I got it I didn't know whether to laugh or cry," said Pat Hubbard, whose husband died nine years ago. "So I did both."

The widows' benefactor, Wheeling Gaunt, bought his freedom from a Kentucky slaveholder for $900, moved to Yellow Springs—a stop on the Underground Railroad—in the 1860s and made his fortune as a teamster, carpenter and farmer.

At his death in 1894, he donated nine acres of farmland to the community on the condition it distribute 25 pounds of flour to its "poor worthy widows" every Christmas.

The village, population 4,000, hasn't missed a Christmas since, though it's made some changes. From the start, the flour was given to all widows, apparently in the belief that that's what Gaunt would have wanted.

Moreover, in the early 1950s, the village cut the amount of flour and added sugar because, it was reasoned, women were not baking as much bread anymore and might have use for sugar.

There are now 110 widows on the distribution list, updated by a village administrative assistant who pores over the obituaries in the newspaper.

"A lot of times the widows will have the doors open and are looking out the window waiting for me to show up," said Kelley Fox, one of the city workers who deliver the goods.

Some of the widows even invite the workers to come back and pick up some of the goodies they've baked. "Around Christmastime a batch of cookies are likely to show up at random. It makes you feel good," Fox said.

Gaunt intended that the rent from the land pay for his gift, which cost about $900 this year. The land is now a park, with a swimming pool, baseball diamonds and soccer fields. The pool admission fees pay for the flour and sugar, which the village buys from a grocery store.

No one knows why Gaunt chose this particular legacy, but local historian Phyllis Jackson noted that most women did not hold jobs then and were often left penniless when their husbands died. "Bread is the staff of life. If you had bread, you could survive for a while," she said.

THE ENDLESS CHAIN
LEWIS LATIMER

When Lewis Latimer (1848–1928), who invented an incandescent lamp, wasn't busy tinkering with some electrical wonder, he was composing verse.* This poem, published in 1925, was dedicated to his wife, Mary Wilson Latimer. It encourages simple acts of kindness, which, taken together, can smooth many paths and link millions.

* For more on Lewis Latimer, see "Lamp to the World: Lewis Latimer" on page 411.

Let's form a kind of endless chain,
Of loving kindly deeds;
Alleviating others' pain,
And ministering to their needs.
Let's do a kindness when we can,
And pass the act along;
Let loving thoughts be in each word,
And tender be each song.
The world has great ones full enough;
Let's be the simple kind;
The path of life is often rough;
Let's smooth it for the blind.
Let each one do a simple act
Of kindness every day,
Think loving, kindly, tender thoughts;
And send them on their way.
Let contact with our fellow men
Be marked by tenderness,
So that our epitaph may be,
He lived and, living, blessed.

HEALERS

Since they arrived in chains, blacks have been practicing the art of healing. Africans introduced Americans to innoculations as a medical treatment. A slave named Onesimus taught the practice to Bostonians, who used it as a cure for smallpox during an epidemic in 1721. Africans who knew the curative powers of plants and herbs also made contributions to pharmacology.

Black physicians are part of a long and illustrious tradition. The first black physician in America was Lucas Santomée, a Holland-trained doctor who in 1667 received land in return for his services to the colony of New Amsterdam. James Derham (1762–?) reportedly had the best record of any physician at treating yellow fever during a deadly outbreak in New

Orleans in 1796. He is considered the first American-trained (though unlicensed) black physician. James McCune Smith (1811–65) became the first black American to receive a medical degree—in Glasgow, Scotland, in 1837. Back in the U.S., he proved false a theory that blacks suffered a higher rate of mental illness than whites. David J. Peck was the first black to receive a medical degree in America—from Chicago's Rush Medical College, in 1847.

Here are four trailblazers whose skill and compassion set them apart.

"SEWED UP HIS HEART!": DANIEL HALE WILLIAMS

Daniel Hale Williams (1856–1931) pushed surgery into a new era with a daring procedure that stunned both physicians and the general public—the world's first successful open heart operation. But Dr. Williams's career didn't end there. He founded hospitals, nursing schools, and the National Medical Association. His career was among the most remarkable in medicine.

Daniel Hale Williams changed the course of medicine with a daring operation to mend a man's heart.

Williams was born on January 18, 1856, in Hollidaysburg, Pennsylvania. He called Frederick Douglass his "cousin" because his mother's mother was a slave on the plantation that Douglass fled.

When Daniel was eleven, his father died. Abandoned by his mother, he made his way to Janesville, Wisconsin, where he worked as a barber and as an apprentice to the town physician. After graduating from Chicago Medical College in 1883, he opened an office in Chicago, but no patients called on him in the first three months. He finally got to perform his first procedure in a makeshift operating room—his patient's dining room.

The patient, who needed surgery, feared hospitals. Williams visited her home and told her, "I'll do it here." He took down her lace curtains, scrubbed, fumigated and disinfected her dining room, and sterilized his equipment on her stove. She lay on the dining room table, where he excised her hemorrhoids. Her relief seemed almost magical, and she was so pleased that she told all her friends. Soon, others called on Williams.

On a cold December night in 1890, the young, immaculate physician drove to a pastor's home through heavily falling snow, covered his horse with a blanket, and entered the home of a pastor, who had sent him a note. The pastor's sister, Emma Reynolds, had arrived from Kansas City, hoping to attend a Chicago nursing school, but was refused admission at every school in town: Negroes were not welcome. "Well, here we are, only twenty-six years since Emancipation!" Williams said, shaking his head. He bit his mustache, thought a moment, smiled, and said: "No, I don't think I'll try to get Miss Reynolds into a training course. We'll do something better. We'll start a hospital of our own and we'll train dozens and dozens of nurses." Williams galvanized the community. Just months later, on May 4, 1891, the first hospital in the U.S. operated by blacks opened in a three-story brick building at Dearborn and 29th Streets: twelve-bed Provident Hospital. It was open to all, regardless of race or creed. Reynolds and six other women enrolled in the historic first class of black nurses in America.

Two years later, on a hot summer day, Williams made history at this hospital. James Cornish was rushed to Provident. He had been stabbed in a saloon fight. The wound appeared superficial, but Cornish showed signs of shock. He coughed shrilly and suffered pain over the region of his heart.

At the time, heart wounds were regarded as fatal. The usual treatment was "absolute rest, cold, and opium." In fact, a leading physician of the day had concluded that "surgical interference with the heart is impracticable." Williams risked condemnation by colleagues when he told an intern, "I'll operate."

Six doctors and nine onlookers crowded into a hot room—a bedroom that had been converted into an operating room—where the thirty-seven-year-old surgeon wielded his scalpel, with none of the medical advances commonly used today. No X rays, no blood transfusions, no breathing apparatus to keep the patient's lungs inflated, and only crude anesthesia.

Williams cut open a neat little trapdoor two inches long and one and a half inches wide, no larger than a knothole. He then peered inside to assess the damage to the left internal mammary artery. There, he discovered an inch-and-a-quarter-long wound on the pericardium, the throbbing sac covering the heart itself. He carefully held the wound apart and examined the heart beneath, beating 130 times a minute. There was a small heart wound, no larger than a tenth of an inch, which would not need suturing. But Williams concluded that the pericardium must be repaired, otherwise infection might occur, the patient might be in constant pain in the future, or he could even die.

Williams quickly sutured first the pericardium wound and then the intercostal and subcartilaginous wounds with fine catgut. He used silkworm gut on the cartilages and skin, then he applied dressing, and he was done.

Williams stood on the threshold of becoming the first man to perform successful surgery in the immediate vicinity of a still-fluttering heart. But members of the surgical team simply went about their everyday duties, suspending judgment on the surgery until its effects could be ascertained.

Fifty-one days later, after a follow-up procedure to drain fluid—perhaps the natural result of irritation from an extensive operation—Cornish left the hospital. A note in his medical record summarized his medical condition: "Termination: Cured."

Word of the daring operation spread. One newspaper headline read: SEWED UP HIS HEART!—words that undoubtedly startled readers.

Williams performed several more of these operations (one patient lived for fifty years after his operation). His method is still routinely recommended.

As for Cornish, some time later, he reappeared at Provident after another brawl, begging for medical care. Williams replied: "Well, you have got some nice fancy work in you, Cornish. I guess I can't afford to lose you. You're an important specimen." Williams treated a head wound and released Cornish in a week.

THE FOLLOWING YEAR, Williams left Provident to head Freedmen's Hospital in Washington, D.C. Arriving in February 1894, he discovered a hospital that was a refuge for the thousands who had flocked into the nation's capital. Conditions were horrendous. Surgical patients were carried outside from one building to another, regardless of the weather or their condition. Meals were transported across a courtyard and arrived cold at bedsides. And the nursing staff consisted of a corps of bandannaed mammies, many of whom could not tell time. In the morning, when they learned that the office clock had struck, they stood at the head of long aisles of beds, clapped and shouted:

"All you 'leven-o'clockers, take yo' medicine!"

How much they took, if anything at all, was up to the patients themselves. It was unlike anything Williams had ever seen.

He reorganized the hospital, creating medical and surgical departments, internships, a new nurses' training program, and a horse-drawn ambulance service. He introduced high professional standards and established hospital systems to increase efficiency.

Williams also operated, leading or assisting in 533 procedures, some open to the public. On Sundays at two in the afternoon, spectators sat in the amphitheater and watched African American surgeons at work. The policy helped inspire confidence in the skills of black surgeons.

At the end of his first year there, the hospital saw a 200 percent increase in operative cases. Anyone interested could read the vital statistics he published—"balance sheets" listing how patients fared. Results were no longer hidden, as before. Freedmen's had truly become a national institution for the first time.

Yet its black physicians were still excluded from the all-white District of Columbia Medical Society, which refused to admit Williams to its ranks and never invited him to speak at its meetings.

He and other black doctors also were denied membership in most chapters of another professional organization, the powerful American Medical Association. Membership enabled physicians to admit and treat patients in most American hospitals. Without these privileges, black physicians were forced to refer their patients to white physicians in order to get them admitted to a hospital.

Once again, Williams saw an opportunity to fill a need in the black community. In January 1895, he founded the Medico-Chirurgical (Middle French for "surgical") Society of the District of Columbia. Black physicians in the D.C. area could join. So could white physicians.

He then helped establish the National Medical Association, a national organization for black physicians. It operated as a counterpart to the AMA and for many decades was the only medical association in the nation open to many African American physicians.

In 1898, Williams returned to Chicago. He eventually broadened his medical activities, serving without pay as a visiting professor at Meharry Medical College, where he was called "the bright and morning star in the firmament of surgery." The student population tripled. In 1912, Chicago's large and important St. Luke's Hospital, then an all-white institution, named Williams associate attending surgeon. Sadly, though, envious associates at Provident Hospital turned on him, prompting him to resign from the staff and board of the hospital he had founded twenty-one years earlier. He died in semiretirement on August 4, 1931.

THE FIRST BLACK WOMAN PHYSICIAN: REBECCA LEE

Rebecca Lee (1833–?), born in the South during the era of slavery, was able to overcome adversity and discrimination to earn her medical degree, proving that medicine was neither the sole province of whites nor of men only. She delivered compassionate care to ex-slaves during Reconstruction.

"I early conceived a liking for and sought every opportunity to be in a position to relieve the suffering of others." So said Rebecca Lee, the nation's first African American female physician.

Born a free woman in Richmond, Virginia, in 1833, Lee was raised in Pennsylvania by an aunt whose devotion to medicine as a lay doctor inspired her niece. Young Rebecca began as a nurse and then, in 1859, enrolled in Boston's New England Female Medical College.

But about the time the Civil War broke out, she had to discontinue her schooling, not to resume until several years later. The college readmitted her only because of local abolitionist sentiment and because she possessed a scholarship granted by Senator Benjamin Wade, a powerful abolitionist from Ohio. At that, the institution was reluctant to grant Lee a degree. Sources disagree on whether this reluctance grew out of racism or a concern that her grasp of the material was inadequate. "Some of us have hesitated very seriously in recommending her," read the faculty notes for February 1864, "and we do so only out of deference to the present state of public feeling."

None of that mattered greatly to Rebecca Lee. With her "Doctoress of Medicine," she returned to postwar Richmond, where she brought health care to the newly freed slaves in that shattered Confederate capital. After that, she maintained a successful practice for many years in her hometown, then went north again to Boston. There, in 1883, she published A *Book of Medical Discourses,* in which she drew on her wide experience to counsel women on how to care for themselves and their children.

—From African American: Voices of Triumph: Leadership, *by the Editors of Time-Life Books,* © *1993 Time-Life Books, Inc.*

BANKING ON BLOOD: CHARLES R. DREW

With his significant contribution to blood preservation, Charles R. Drew (1904–50) saved the lives of countless soldiers in World War II. But because of racism in the armed forces, government officials who selected him to head a U.S. blood collection program considered his blood— and that of any Negro—too "impure" for donation to white soldiers. Drew, a world-renowned researcher, surgeon, and administrator, went on to become one of the most influential educators in modern medicine.

Charles Richard Drew was born on June 3, 1904, in Washington, D.C. The eldest of five sons, he grew up comfortably, in a middle-class, interracial neighborhood and attended Dunbar High School, where he was a four-letter athlete. He was called "Big Red," both for his well-built six-foot-one-inch, 195-pound frame and his reddish-brown hair.

Drew attended Amherst College, where he became an All-America halfback in 1925. But he let his grades slip, obliging the dean to offer him what may have been the shortest lecture he ever heard: "Mr. Drew, Negro athletes are a dime a dozen. Good day." Drew did continue his athletic career, but he studied harder, getting better grades and graduating in 1926.

Though he had decided on a career in medicine, he could not afford medical school. So after graduation, he took a coaching job at Morgan College in Baltimore, where he also taught biology and chemistry for two years. He then applied to Howard Medical School but was denied admission because Howard required eight credits of English. He had only six.

In 1928, Drew entered McGill University's medical school in Montreal, Canada. While there, he won Canadian national track and field championships in the high hurdles, low hurdles, high jump, and long jump.

Drew also studied diligently and made lifelong friendships with whites. One friend, John Beattie, a British bacteriology instructor who was teaching temporarily at McGill, is said to have inspired Drew to delve into blood research. Beattie would influence Drew's career years later.

Drew graduated in 1933 and became an intern at the Royal Victoria Hospital. The following year, he completed a residency in medicine at Montreal General Hospital.

In 1935, at age thirty-one, he headed south to become a pathology instructor at Howard and a resident at Freedmen's Hospital. Then, as one of the Howard dean's brightest stars, he was recommended for a fellowship. He became a surgical resident at one of the world's leading research and teaching facilities, Presbyterian Hospital, which is affiliated with Columbia University's College of Physicians and Surgeons.

While there, he wrote a doctoral dissertation, the first draft of which was described as the "New York telephone directory in size." He had culled and consolidated all that was known at the time about blood banks, from a wide variety of sources, including his own research and

Presbyterian Hospital's blood bank. He completed the dissertation, entitled "Banked Blood," in 1940.

In June of that year, he became the first African American recipient of the coveted doctor of science in medicine degree. His work also earned accolades from his instructor, himself a pioneering blood researcher, who called Drew not only "my most brilliant student, but one of the greatest clinical scientists of the first half of the twentieth century."

Drew then returned to Howard, prepared to train future black physicians. But World War II was now ravaging Europe, and the need for blood transfusions was steadily growing as casualties mounted.

Blood banks were not feasible in cities under aerial bombardment. Blood preservation research was needed. Some blood plasma was sent overseas.

Drew's British friend, John Beattie, now chief of the Royal Air Force's transfusion service, sent a cable to the Blood for Britain program in New York, requesting an impossibly large supply of dried plasma—more than the world's entire inventory. Beattie sent another cable to the blood-collection agency's board of medical directors recommending Drew as the one man capable of filling the order.

Howard granted leave to Drew, who was regarded as one of the world's leading experts in blood plasma and the preservation of whole blood. He was appointed medical supervisor of the Blood for Britain program. He reorganized the program, and his recommendations were adopted, improving the quality of plasma.

Blood was collected using uniform procedures, and all plasma underwent final processing in a central laboratory, where rigorous standards were maintained, ensuring high-quality, sterile plasma. He also came up with the idea of using refrigerated mobile units in blood collection.

Drew's effort ended the British crisis.

Never before had a black American physician been called on to serve the wartime needs of a foreign nation in quite the same way. Britain's desperation had given Drew and his European colleagues an unprecedented opportunity to test the effectiveness of a large-scale blood collection program. Drew served as the program's focal point, and what pushed him into the international spotlight was a January 1941 medical report he wrote on the lessons learned.

Almost overnight, he became a celebrity outside of the scientific community. He was wrongly credited as the man who developed blood plasma for transfusions. Actually, Drew had compiled and synthesized often-contradictory findings from laboratories on both sides of the Atlantic, organized the data, and developed a blueprint for using this knowledge in wartime conditions.

The job of saving thousands of lives had fallen to a black man, a scientist of the highest caliber in his day.

Medical leaders and U.S. government officials carefully noted Drew's successes and asked him to develop a national blood collection program for the military—Jim Crow–style. Authorities wanted rigid segregation to rule—even with blood. Incredibly, racist whites considered "Negro blood" impure, but held that "white blood" would not contaminate or pollute as "Negro blood" might. Thus, the blood of white people would be collected for use by either white or black soldiers. This meant that Drew himself, who was to head the program, would not be allowed to donate blood.

These outrageous beliefs angered Drew. Furthermore, even though the scientific community had irrefutable proof that all human blood is essentially the same—it is classifiable only by type, not by race—many scientists apparently chose to remain silent on the issue, perhaps out of fear that they risked ridicule from racists who assumed Jim Crow dictated laws of nature in addition to laws segregating public restrooms, restaurants, and water fountains.

Drew returned to Howard to teach. There, he wanted to establish a black "school of thought" in medicine. Training Negro surgeons, he believed, would "constitute my greatest contribution to medicine."

In January 1944 he was appointed chief of staff of Freedmen's Hospital and was awarded the NAACP's prestigious Spingarn Medal for his blood preservation work. In 1946 he was named medical director of Freedmen's.

The goal of training surgeons consumed him. He became a taskmaster as well as a "warm, just and understanding but firm" teacher, one of his students recalled.

In December 1948, his first class of trainees took exams for certification by the American Board of Surgery. A call came from the president of Howard, Mordecai Johnson, to inform him that the two top scorers on the examination had been trained by Drew. He breathed a sigh of relief. His dream was coming true. He had wanted his Howard students to compete "with white boys who have had every advantage." The proof that they were doing so was in the test results.

He continued his grinding schedule, mentoring highly skilled surgeons. It has been said that between 1941 and 1950, he trained more than half of the black surgeons certified by the American Board of Surgery. He himself was an examiner for the board, the first black surgeon appointed.

Still, due to racism, the American Medical Association would not admit him to its District of Columbia chapter. The AMA said black physicians had "their own" national organization and could not force its local chapters to admit Negroes. Drew wrote bitter letters accusing the AMA of using self-serving, circuitous reasoning for racist ends. Still, blacks were not admitted into the chapter until two years after his death.

He died in 1950. Myth still surrounds his death.

At 2:15 A.M. on Saturday, April 1, Drew and three other black physicians left Washington for Tuskegee in a 1949 black four-door Buick Roadmaster. Drew was tired and sleepy. He had performed surgery that day, attended a student council meeting, and had only two hours' sleep.

At 7:50 A.M., with Drew behind the wheel, and the other passengers asleep, Drew dozed off. The wheels dropped off the right shoulder of the road, as the car ran off Route 49, two miles north of Haw River, North Carolina.

"Hey, Charlie!" shouted the front-seat passenger, waking Drew, who cut the wheels too sharply. The car crossed the road and ran off the left shoulder into a plowed field, where it rolled over three times.

The passenger in the backseat, on the right, woke, still sitting upright. The passenger to his left was no longer there. He leaned forward. The passenger in front of him was wedged under the dashboard. The backseat passenger freed him—he sustained only cuts on one hand. The other backseat passenger, thrown clear, was sitting on the ground with a broken leg and lacerations—forty feet from the car.

Drew was hanging out of the car, but his right foot was caught under the brake pedal. The car had rolled over him. His left leg was nearly severed, and he sustained internal injuries.

Drew, forty-six, was rushed to Alamance County General Hospital, in Burlington, North Carolina. Three physicians tried to save his life.

Some time afterward, Drew's widow sat down to compose a letter to the hospital's chief surgeon. She wrote: "Though all efforts were futile, there is much comfort derived from knowing that everything was done in his fight for life." The physicians she thanked, through the office of the chief surgeon, were white men.

The facts about his death contradict the myth surrounding it. Somehow the story spread that the "man who invented blood plasma" ironically bled to death on the steps of a white hospital that would not admit him because he was Negro. The creation of such a myth may well extend from Drew's "super Negro" status; from the belief that even "super Negroes" who valiantly fought racism from the upper echelons of science still could not escape a second-class citizenship. But the myth just isn't true.

SAVING BO-BO
BEN CARSON

Ben Carson became world famous for delicate neurosurgery on patients who other surgeons considered too risky to treat. Here Carson tells the story of how he performed lifesaving surgery on a little girl named Bo-Bo, whose case appeared to be hopeless.

The resident flicked off his penlight and straightened up from the bedside of Bo-Bo Valentine. "Don't you think it's time to give up on this little girl?" he asked, nodding toward the four-year-old child.

It was early Monday morning, and I was making rounds. When I came to Bo-Bo, the house officer explained her situation. "Just about the only thing she has left is pupilary response," he said. (That meant that her pupils still responded to light.) The light he shone in her eyes told him that pressure had built inside her head. The doctors had put Bo-Bo in a barbiturate coma and given her hyperventilation but still couldn't keep the pressures down.

Little Bo-Bo was another of the far-too-many children who run out into a street and are hit by a car. A Good Humor truck struck Bo-Bo. She'd lain in the ICU all weekend, comatose and with an *intracranial* pressure monitor in her skull. Her blood pressure gradually worsened, and she was losing what little function, purposeful movement, and response to stimuli she had.

Before answering the resident, I bent over Bo-Bo and lifted her eyelids. Her pupils were fixed and dilated. "I thought you told me the pupils were still working?" I said in astonishment.

"I did," he protested. "They were working just before you came in."

"You're telling me this just happened? That her eyes just now dilated?"

"They must have!"

"Four plus emergency," I called loudly but calmly. "We've got to do something right away!" I turned to the nurse standing behind me. "Call the operating room. We're on our way."

"Four plus emergency!" she called even louder and hurried down the corridor.

Although rare, a plus four—for dire emergency—galvanizes everyone into action. The OR staff clears out a room and starts getting the instruments ready. They work with quiet efficiency, and they're quick. No one argues and no one has time to explain.

Two residents grabbed Bo-Bo's bed and half-ran down the hallway. Fortunately surgery hadn't started on the scheduled patient, so we bumped the case.

On my way to the operating room I ran into another neurosurgeon— senior to me and a man I highly respect because of his work with trauma accidents. While the staff was setting up, I explained to him what had happened and what I was going to do.

"Don't do it," he said, as he walked away from me. "You're wasting your time."

His attitude amazed me, but I didn't dwell on it. Bo-Bo Valentine was still alive. We had a chance—extremely small—but still a chance to save her life. I decided I would go ahead and do surgery anyway.

Bo-Bo was gently positioned on an "egg crate," a soft, flexible pad covering the operating table, and was covered with a pale green sheet. Within minutes the nurses and anesthiologist had her ready for me to begin.

I did a craniectomy. First I opened her head and took off the front portion of her skull. The skull bone was put in a sterile solution. Then I opened up the covering of her brain—the dura. Between the two halves of the brain is an area called the falx. By splitting the falx, the two halves could communicate together and equalize the pressure between her hemispheres. Using cadaveric dura (dura from a dead person), I sewed it over her brain. This gave her brain room to swell, then heal, and still held everything inside her skull in place. Once I covered the area, I closed the scalp. The surgery took about two hours.

Bo-Bo remained comatose for the next few days. It is heartbreaking to watch parents sit by the bedside of a comatose child, and I felt for them. I could only give them hope; I couldn't promise Bo-Bo's recovery. One morning I stopped by her bed and noted that her pupils were starting to work a little bit. I recall thinking, *Maybe something positive is starting to happen.*

After two more days Bo-Bo started moving a little. Sometimes she stretched her legs or shifted her body as if trying to get more comfortable. Over the course of a week she grew alert and responsive. When it became apparent that she was going to recover, we took her back to surgery, and I replaced the portion of her skull that had been removed. Within six weeks Bo-Bo was, once again, a normal four-year-old girl— vivacious, bouncy, and cute.

This is another instance when I'm glad I didn't listen to a critic.

ROWBOAT TO FREEDOM
AS TOLD BY ARNOLD GRAGSTON

*In 1894, residents of Eatonville, a small black town in Florida, wel-
comed Alabama-born Zora Neale Hurston and her family. Hurston later
wrote many stories about Eatonville, immortalizing the words of townsfolk.
Among those she may have known was Arnold Gragston, who was born a
slave in Kentucky in 1840. He was ninety-seven years old when he sat
down to tell this story. From it we see that some people, including Gragston, stayed in slavery, risking their lives to help others—hundreds of
others—escape via the Underground Railroad. Gragston's story is a great
example of compassion for fellow slaves.*

Most of the slaves didn't know when they was born, but I did. You see, I
was born on a Christmas morning—it was in 1840. I was a full-grown
man when I finally got my freedom.

Before I got it, though, I helped a lot of others get theirs. Lord only
knows how many; might have been as much as two-three hundred. It
was 'way more than a hundred, I know.

But that all came after I was a young man—grown enough to know a
pretty girl when I saw one, and to go chasing after her, too. I was born
on a plantation that belonged to Mr. Jack Tabb in Mason County, just
across the river in Kentucky.

Mr. Tabb was a pretty good man. He used to beat us, sure; but not
nearly so much as others did, some of his own kin people, even. But he
was kinda funny sometimes; he used to have a special slave who didn't
have nothing to do but teach the rest of us—we had about ten on the
plantation, and a lot on the other plantations near us—how to read and
write and figure. Mr. Tabb liked us to know how to figure. But sometimes when he would send for us, and we would be a long time coming,
he would ask us where we had been. If we told him we had been
learning to read, he would near beat the daylights out of us—after
getting somebody to teach us! I think he did some of that so that the
other owners wouldn't say he was spoiling his slaves.

He was funny about us marrying, too. He would let us go a-courting
on the other plantations near any time we liked, if we were good, and if
we found somebody we wanted to marry, and she was on a plantation

that belonged to one of his kinfolks or a friend, he would swap a slave so that the husband and wife could be together. Sometimes, when he couldn't do this, he would let a slave work all day on his plantation and live with his wife at night on her plantation. Some of the other owners was always talking about his spoiling us.

He wasn't a Democrat like the rest of 'em in the county; he belonged to the Know Nothing party, and he was a real leader in it. He used to always be making speeches, and sometimes his best friends wouldn't be speaking to him for days at a time.

Mr. Tabb was always specially good to me. He used to let me go all about—I guess he had to; couldn't get too much work out of me even when he kept me right under his eyes. I learned fast, too, and I think he kinda liked that. He used to call Sandy Davis, the slave who taught me, "the smartest nigger in Kentucky."

It was 'cause he used to let me go around in the day and night so much that I came to be the one who carried the running-away slaves over the river. It was funny the way I started it, too.

I didn't have no idea of ever getting mixed up in any sort of business like that until one special night. I hadn't even thought of rowing across the river myself.

But one night I had gone on another plantation courting, and the old woman whose house I went to told me she had a real pretty girl there who wanted to go across the river, and would I take her? I was scared and backed out in a hurry. But then I saw the girl, and she was such a pretty little thing, brown-skinned and kinda rosy, and looking as scared as I was feeling, so it wasn't long before I was listening to the old woman tell me when to take her and where to leave her on the other side.

I didn't have nerve enough to do it that night, though, and I told them to wait for me until tomorrow night. All the next day I kept seeing Mr. Tabb laying a rawhide across my back, or shooting me, and kept seeing that scared little brown girl back at the house, looking at me with her big eyes and asking me if I wouldn't just row her across to Ripley. Me and Mr. Tabb lost, and soon as dusk settled that night, I was at the old lady's house.

I don't know how I ever rowed the boat across the river. The current was strong, and I was trembling. I couldn't see a thing there in the dark, but I felt that girl's eyes. We didn't dare to whisper, so I couldn't tell her how sure I was that Mr. Tabb or some of the others' owners would tear me up when they found out what I had done. I just knew they would find out.

I was worried, too, about where to put her out of the boat. I couldn't ride her across the river all night, and I didn't know a thing about the other side. I had heard a lot about it from other slaves, but I thought it was just about like Mason County, with slaves and masters, overseers and rawhides; and so I just knew that if I pulled the boat up and went to asking people where to take her I would get a beating or get killed.

I don't know whether it seemed like a long time or a short time, now—it's so long ago; I know it was a long time rowing there in the cold and worrying. But it was short, too, 'cause as soon as I did get on the other side the big-eyed, brown-skin girl would be gone. Well, pretty soon I saw a tall light, and I remembered what the old lady had told me about looking for that light and rowing to it. I did; and when I got up to it, two men reached down and grabbed her. I started trembling all over again, and praying. Then, one of the men took my arm and I just felt down inside of me that the Lord had got ready for me. "You hungry, boy?" is what he asked me, and if he hadn't been holding me, I think I would have fell backward into the river.

That was my first trip; it took me a long time to get over my scared feeling, but I finally did, and I soon found myself going back across the river, with two and three people, and sometimes a whole boatload. I got so I used to make three and four trips a month.

What did my passengers look like? I can't tell you any more about it than you can, and you wasn't there. After that first girl—no, I never did see her again—I never saw my passengers. It would have to be the black nights of the moon when I would carry them, and I would meet 'em out in the open or in a house without a single light. The only way I knew who they were was to ask them: "What you say?" And they would answer, "Menare." I don't know what that word meant—it came from the Bible. I only know that that was the password I used, and all of them that I took over told it to me before I took them.

I guess you wonder what I did with them after I got them over the river. Well, there in Ripley was a man named Mr. Rankins; I think the rest of his name was John. He had a regular "station" there on his place for escaping slaves. You see, Ohio was a free state, and once they got over the river from Kentucky or Virginia, Mr. Rankins could strut them all around town, and nobody would bother 'em. The only reason we used to land 'em quietly at night was so that whoever brought 'em could go back for more, and because we had to be careful that none of the owners had followed us. Every once in a while they would follow a boat and catch their slaves back. Sometimes they would shoot at whoever was trying to save the poor devils.

Mr. Rankins had a regular station for the slaves. He had a big light-house in his yard, about thirty feet high, and he kept it burning all night. It always meant freedom for the slave if he could get to this light.

Sometimes Mr. Rankins would have twenty or thirty slaves that had run away on his place at a time. It must have cost him a whole lot to keep 'em and feed 'em, but I think some of his friends helped him.

Those who wanted to stay around that part of Ohio could stay, but didn't many of 'em do it, because there was too much danger that you would be walking along free one night, feel a hand over your mouth, and be back across the river and in slavery again in the morning. And nobody in the world ever got a chance to know as much misery as a slave that had escaped and been caught.

So a whole lot of 'em went on North to other parts of Ohio, or to New York, Chicago, or Canada. Canada was popular then because all of the slaves thought it was the last gate before you got all the way *inside* of heaven. I don't think there was much chance for a slave to make a living in Canada, but didn't many of 'em come back. They seem like they rather starve up there in the cold than to be back in slavery.

The army soon started taking a lot of 'em, too. They could enlist in the Union army and get good wages, more food than they ever had, and have all the little gals waving at 'em when they passed. Them blue uniforms was a nice change, too.

No, I never got anything from a single one of the people I carried over the river to freedom. I didn't want anything; after I had made a few trips I got to like it, and even though I could have been free any night myself, I figured I wasn't getting along so bad so I would stay on Mr. Tabb's place and help the others get free. I did it for four years.

I don't know to this day how he never knew what I was doing. I used to take some awful chances, and he knew I must have been up to something. I wouldn't do much work in the day, would never be in my house at night, and when he would happen to visit the plantation where I had said I was going I wouldn't be there. Sometimes I think he did know and wanted me to get the slaves away that way so he wouldn't have to cause hard feelings by freeing 'em.

I think Mr. Tabb used to talk a lot to Mr. John Fee. Mr. Fee was a man who lived in Kentucky, but Lord! how that man hated slavery! He used to always tell us (we never let our owners see us listening to him though) that God didn't intend for some men to be free and some men be in slavery. He used to talk to the owners, too, when they would listen to him, but mostly they hated the sight of John Fee.

In the night, though, he was a different man. For every slave who came through his place going across the river he had a good word, something to eat and some kind of rags, too, if it was cold. He always knew just what to tell you to do if anything went wrong, and sometimes I think he kept slaves there on his place till they could be rowed across the river. Helped us a lot.

I almost ran the business in the ground after I had been carrying the slaves across for nearly four years. It was in 1863, and one night I carried across about twelve on the same night. Somebody must have seen us, because they set out after me as soon as I stepped out of the boat back on the Kentucky side; from that time on they were after me. Sometimes they would almost catch me. I had to run away from Mr. Tabb's plantation and live in the fields and in the woods. I didn't know what a bed was from one week to another. I would sleep in a cornfield tonight, up in the branches of a tree tomorrow night, and buried in a haypile the next night. The river, where I had carried so many across myself, was no good to me; it was watched too close.

Finally, I saw that I could never do any more good in Mason County, so I decided to take my freedom, too. I had a wife by this time, and one night we quietly slipped across and headed for Mr. Rankins' bell and light. It looked like we had to go almost to China to get across that river. I could hear the bell and see the light on Mr. Rankins' place, but the harder I rowed, the farther away it got, and I knew if I didn't make it I'd get killed. But finally I pulled up by the lighthouse and went on to my freedom—just a few months before all of the slaves got theirs. I didn't stay in Ripley, though; I wasn't taking no chances. I went on to Detroit and still live there with most of ten children and thirty-one grandchildren.

The bigger ones don't care so much about hearing it now, but the little ones never get tired of hearing how their grandpa brought emancipation to loads of slaves he could touch and feel, but never could see.

—SINCERELY, YOUR ESCAPED SLAVE

Frederick Douglass wrote the following letter in England some ten years after he escaped slavery. Letters from former slaves to their old masters were reprinted by abolitionists in hopes of persuading slave owners of the injustice of slavery. Douglass's letter is full of restraint and shows understanding and compassion for the man who once tried to beat him.

LETTER TO MY MASTER
FREDERICK DOUGLASS

Sir—I have selected this day on which to address you, because it is the anniversary of my emancipation; and knowing no better way, I am led to this as the best mode of celebrating that truly important event. Just ten years ago this beautiful September morning, yon bright sun beheld me a slave—a poor degraded chattel—trembling at the sound of your voice, lamenting that I was a man, and wishing myself a brute. The hopes which I had treasured up for weeks of a safe and successful escape from your grasp, were powerfully confronted at this last hour by dark clouds of doubt and fear, making my person shake and my bosom to heave with the heavy contest between hope and fear. I have no words to describe to you the deep agony of soul which I experienced on that never-to-be-forgotten morning—for I left by daylight. I was making a leap in the dark. The probabilities, so far as I could by reason determine them, were stoutly against the undertaking. The preliminaries and precautions I had adopted previously, all worked badly. I was like one going to war without weapons—ten chances of defeat to one of victory. One in whom I had confided, and one who had promised me assistance, appalled by fear at the trial hour, deserted me, thus leaving the responsibility of success or failure solely with myself. You, sir, can never know my feelings. As I look back to them, I can scarcely realize that I have passed through a scene so trying. Trying, however, as they were, and gloomy as was the prospect, thanks be to the Most High, who is ever the God of the oppressed, at the moment which was to determine my whole earthly career, His grace was sufficient; my mind was made up. I embraced the golden opportunity, took the morning tide at the flood, and a free man, young, active, and strong, is the result.

I have often thought I should like to explain to you the grounds upon which I have justified myself in running away from you. I am almost ashamed to do so now, for by this time you may have discovered them yourself. I will, however, glance at them. When yet but a child about six years old, I imbibed the determination to run away. The very first mental effort that I now remember on my part, was an attempt to solve the mystery—why am I a slave? and with this question my youthful mind was troubled for many days, pressing upon me more heavily at times than others. When I saw the slave-driver whip a slave-woman, cut the blood out of her neck, and heard her piteous cries, I went away into the corner of the fence, wept and pondered over the mystery. I had, through some medium, I know not what, got some idea of God, the Creator of all mankind, the black and the white, and that he had made the blacks to serve the whites as slaves. How he could do this and be *good*, I could not tell. I was not satisfied with this theory, which made God responsible for slavery, for it pained me greatly, and I have wept over it long and often. At one time, your first wife, Mrs. Lucretia, heard me sighing and saw me shedding tears, and asked of me the matter, but I was afraid to tell her. I was puzzled with this question, till one night while sitting in the kitchen, I heard some of the old slaves talking of their parents having been stolen from Africa by white men, and were sold here as slaves. The whole mystery was solved at once. Very soon after this, my Aunt Jinny and Uncle Noah ran away, and the great noise made about it by your father-in-law, made me for the first time acquainted with the fact, that there were free states as well as slave states. From that time, I resolved that I would some day run away. The morality of the act I dispose of as follows: I am myself; you are yourself; we are two distinct persons, equal persons. What you are, I am. You are a man, and so am I. God created both, and made us separate beings. I am not by nature bond to you, or you to me. Nature does not make your existence depend upon me, or mine to depend upon yours. I cannot walk upon your legs, or you upon mine. I cannot breathe for you, or you for me; I must breathe for myself, and you for yourself. We are distinct persons, and are each equally provided with faculties necessary to our individual existence. In leaving you, I took nothing but what belonged to me, and in no way lessened your means for obtaining an *honest* living. Your faculties remained yours, and mine became useful to their rightful owner. I therefore see no wrong in any part of the transaction. It is true, I went off secretly; but that was more your fault than mine. Had I let you into the secret, you would have defeated the enterprise entirely; but for this, I should have been really glad to have made you acquainted with my intentions to leave.

You may perhaps want to know how I like my present condition. I am free to say, I greatly prefer it to that which I occupied in Maryland. I am, however, by no means prejudiced against the state as such. Its geography, climate, fertility, and products, are such as to make it a very desirable abode for any man; and but for the existence of slavery there, it is not impossible that I might again take up my abode in that state. It is not that I love Maryland less, but freedom more. You will be surprised to learn that people at the north labor under the strange delusion that if the slaves were emancipated at the south, they would flock to the north. So far from this being the case, in that event, you would see many old and familiar faces back again to the south. The fact is, there are few here who would not return to the south in the event of emancipation. We want to live in the land of our birth, and to lay our bones by the side of our fathers; and nothing short of an intense love of personal freedom keeps us from the south. For the sake of this, most of us would live on a crust of bread and a cup of cold water.

Since I left you, I have had a rich experience. I have occupied stations which I never dreamed of when a slave. Three out of the ten years since

I left you, I spent as a common laborer on the wharves of New Bedford, Massachusetts. It was there I earned my first free dollar. It was mine. I could spend it as I pleased. I could buy hams or herring with it, without asking any odds of anybody. That was a precious dollar to me. You remember when I used to make seven, or eight, or even nine dollars a week in Baltimore, you would take every cent of it from me every Saturday night, saying that I belonged to you, and my earnings also. I never liked this conduct on your part—to say the best, I thought it a little mean. I would not have served you so. But let that pass. I was a little awkward about counting money in New England fashion when I first landed in New Bedford. I came near betraying myself several times. I caught myself saying phip, for fourpence; and at one time a man actually charged me with being a runaway, whereupon I was silly enough to become one by running away from him, for I was greatly afraid he might adopt measures to get me again into slavery, a condition I then dreaded more than death.

I soon learned, however, to count money, as well as to make it, and got on swimmingly. I married soon after leaving you; in fact, I was engaged to be married before I left you; and instead of finding my companion a burden, she was truly a helpmate. She went to live at service, and I to work on the wharf, and though we toiled hard the first winter, we never lived more happily. After remaining in New Bedford for three years, I met with William Lloyd Garrison, a person of whom you have *possibly* heard, as he is pretty generally known among slaveholders. He put it into my head that I might make myself serviceable to the cause of the slave, by devoting a portion of my time to telling my own sorrows, and those of other slaves, which had come under my observation. This was the commencement of a higher state of existence than any to which I had ever aspired. I was thrown into society the most pure, enlightened, and benevolent, that the country affords. Among these I have never forgotten you, but have invariably made you the topic of conversation—thus giving you all the notoriety I could do. I need not tell you that the opinion formed of you in these circles is far from being favorable. They have little respect for your honesty, and less for your religion.

But I was going on to relate to you something of my interesting experience. I had not long enjoyed the excellent society to which I have referred, before the light of its excellence exerted a beneficial influence on my mind and heart. Much of my early dislike of white persons was removed, and their manners, habits, and customs, so entirely unlike what I had been used to in the kitchen-quarters on the plantations of the south, fairly charmed me, and gave me a strong disrelish for the coarse and degrading customs of my former condition. I therefore made an effort so to improve my mind and deportment, as to be somewhat fitted to the station to which I seemed almost providentially called. The transition from degradation to respectability was indeed great, and to get from one to the other without carrying some marks of one's former condition, is truly a difficult matter. I would not have you think that I am now entirely clear of all plantation peculiarities, but my friends here, while they entertain the strongest dislike to them, regard me with that charity to which my past life somewhat entitles me, so that my condition in this respect is exceedingly pleasant. So far as my domestic affairs are concerned, I can boast of as comfortable a dwelling as your own. I have an industrious and neat companion, and four dear children—the oldest a girl of nine years, and three fine boys, the oldest eight, the next six, and the youngest four years old. The three oldest are now going regularly to school—two can read and write, and the other can spell, with tolerable correctness, words of two syllables. Dear fellows! they are all in comfortable beds, and are sound asleep, perfectly secure under my own roof. There are no slaveholders here to rend my heart by snatching them from my arms, or blast a mother's dearest hopes by tearing them from her bosom. These dear children are ours—not to work up into rice, sugar, and tobacco, but to watch over, regard, and protect, and to rear them up in the nurture and admonition of the gospel—to train them up in the paths of wisdom and virtue, and, as far as we can, to make them useful to the world and to themselves. Oh! sir, a slaveholder never appears to me so completely an agent of hell, as when I think of and look upon my dear children. It is then that my feelings rise above my control. I meant to have said more with respect to my own prosperity and happiness, but thoughts and feelings which this recital has quickened, unfits me to proceed further in that direction. The grim horrors of slavery rise in all their ghastly terror before me; the wails of millions pierce my heart and chill my blood. I remember the chain, the gag, the bloody whip; the death-like gloom overshadowing the broken spirit of the fettered bond-man; the appalling liability of his being torn away from wife and children, and sold like a beast in the market. Say not that this is a picture of fancy. You well know that I wear stripes on my back, inflicted by your direction; and that you, while we were brothers in the same church, caused this right hand, with which I am now penning this letter, to be closely tied to my left, and my person dragged, at the pistol's mouth, fifteen miles, from the Bay Side to Easton, to be sold like a beast in the market, for the alleged crime of intending to escape from your possession. All this, and more, you remember, and know to be perfectly true, not only of yourself, but of nearly all of the slaveholders around you.

At this moment, you are probably the guilty holder of at least three of my own dear sisters, and my only brother, in bondage. These you regard as your property. They are recorded on your ledger, or perhaps have been sold to human flesh-mongers, with a view to filling your own ever-hungry purse. Sir, I desire to know how and where these dear sisters are. Have you sold them? or are they still in your possession? What has become of them? are they living or dead? And my dear old grandmother, whom you turned out like an old horse to die in the woods—is she still alive? Write and let me know all about them. If my grandmother be still alive, she is of no service to you, for by this time she must be nearly eighty years old—too old to be cared for by one to whom she has ceased to be of service; send her to me at Rochester, or bring her to Philadelphia, and it shall be the crowning happiness of my life to take care of her in her old age. Oh! she was to me a mother and a father, so far as hard toil for my comfort could make her such. Send me my grandmother! that I may watch over and take care of her in her old age. And my sisters—let me know all about them. I would write to them, and learn all I want to know of them, without disturbing you in any way, but that, through your unrighteous conduct, they have been entirely deprived of the power to read and write. You have kept them in utter ignorance, and have therefore robbed them of the sweet enjoyments of writing or receiving letters from absent friends and relatives. Your wickedness and cruelty, committed in this respect on your fellow-creatures, are greater than all the stripes you have laid upon my back or theirs. It is an outrage upon the soul, a war upon the immortal spirit, and one for which you must give account at the bar of our common Father and Creator.

The responsibility which you have assumed in this regard is truly awful, and how you could stagger under it these many years is marvelous. Your mind must have become darkened, your heart hardened, your conscience seared and petrified, or you would have long since thrown off the accursed load, and sought relief at the hands of a sin-forgiving God. How, let me ask, would you look upon me, were I, some dark night, in company with a band of hardened villains, to enter the precincts of your elegant dwelling, and seize the person of your own lovely daughter, Amanda, and carry her off from your family, friends, and all the loved ones of her youth—make her my slave—compel her to work, and I take her wages—place her name on my ledger as property—disregard her personal rights—fetter the powers of her immortal soul by denying her the right and privilege of learning to read and write—feed her coarsely—clothe her scantily, and whip her on the naked back occasionally; more, and still more horrible, leave her unprotected—a degraded victim to the brutal lust of fiendish overseers, who would pollute, blight, and blast her fair soul—rob her of all dignity—destroy her virtue, and annihilate in her person all the graces that adorn the character of virtuous womanhood? I ask, how would you regard me, if such were my conduct? Oh! the vocabulary of the damned would not afford a word sufficiently infernal to express your idea of my God-provoking wickedness. Yet, sir, your treatment of my beloved sisters is in all essential points precisely like the case I have now supposed. Damning as would be such a deed on my part, it would be no more so than that which you have committed against me and my sisters.

I will now bring this letter to a close; you shall hear from me again unless you let me hear from you. I intend to make use of you as a weapon with which to assail the system of slavery—as a means of concentrating public attention on the system, and deepening the horror of trafficking in the souls and bodies of men. I shall make use of you as a means of exposing the character of the American church and clergy— and as a means of bringing this guilty nation, with yourself, to repentance. In doing this, I entertain no malice toward you personally. There is no roof under which you would be more safe than mine, and there is nothing in my house which you might need for your comfort, which I would not readily grant. Indeed, I should esteem it a privilege to set you an example as to how mankind ought to treat each other.

I am your fellow-man, but not your slave.

HERE'S MY BILL, OLD MASTER
JOURDON ANDERSON

In slavery, African Americans had no choice but to depend on their masters for food, clothing, and shelter. After the Civil War, freed slaves struggled to survive, scratching out a living by raising crops on patches of poor land, depending on skills they had acquired, wandering from place to place in search of work. They survived however they could. So did their former owners, some of whom invited their former slaves back to the plantation. Asked to return "home," Jourdon Anderson, who had fled slavery during the war, mailed the following reply.

Dayton, Ohio, August 7, 1865

To my old Master, Colonel P. H. Anderson, Big Spring Tennessee:

SIR. I got your letter, and was glad to find that you had not forgotten Jourdon, and that you wanted me to come back and live with you again, promising to do better for me than anybody else can. I have often felt uneasy about you. I thought the Yankees would have hung you long before this, for harboring Rebs they found at your house. I suppose they never heard about your going to Colonel Martin's to kill the Union soldier that was left by his company in their stable. Although you shot at me twice before I left you, I did not want to hear of your being hurt, and am glad you are still living. It would do me good to go back to the dear old home again, and see Miss Mary and Miss Martha and Allen, Esther, Green, and Lee. Give my love to them all, and tell them I hope we will meet in the better world, if not in this. I would have gone back to see you all when I was working in the Nashville Hospital, but one of the neighbors told me that Henry intended to shoot me if he ever got a chance.

I want to know particularly what the good chance is you propose to give me. I am doing tolerably well here. I get twenty-five dollars a month, with victuals and clothing; have a comfortable home for Mandy,—the folks call her Mrs. Anderson,—and the children—Milly, Jane, and Grundy—go to school and are learning well. The teacher says Grundy has a head for a preacher. They go to Sunday school, and Mandy and me attend church regularly. We are kindly treated. Sometimes we overhear others saying, "Them colored people were slaves" down in Tennessee. The children feel hurt when they hear such remarks; but I tell them it was no disgrace in Tennessee to belong to Colonel Anderson. Many darkeys would have been proud, as I used to be, to call you master. Now if you will write and say what wages you will give me, I will be better able to decide whether it would be to my advantage to move back again.

As to my freedom, which you say I can have, there is nothing to be gained on that score, as I got my free papers in 1864 from the Provost-Marshal-General of the Department of Nashville. Mandy says she would be afraid to go back without some proof that you were disposed to treat us justly and kindly; and we have concluded to test your sincerity by asking you to send us our wages for the time we served you. This will make us forget and forgive old scores, and rely on your justice and friendship in the future. I served you faithfully for thirty-two years, and Mandy twenty years. At twenty-five dollars a month for me, and two dollars a week for Mandy, our earnings would amount to eleven thousand six hundred and eighty dollars. Add to this the interest for the time our wages have been kept back, and deduct what you paid for our clothing, and three doctor's visits to me, and pulling a tooth for Mandy, and the balance will show what we are in justice entitled to. Please send the money by Adam's Express, in care of V. Winters, Esq., Dayton, Ohio. If you fail to pay us for faithful labors in the past, we can have little faith in your promises in the future. We trust the good Maker has opened your eyes to the wrongs which you and your fathers have done to me and my fathers, in making us toil for you for generations without recompense. Here I draw my wages every Saturday night; but in Tennessee there was never any pay-day for the Negroes any more than for the horses and cows. Surely there will be a day of reckoning for those who defraud the laborer of his hire.

In answering this letter, please state if there would be any safety for my Milly and Jane, who are now grown up, and both good-looking girls. You know how it was with poor Matilda and Catherine. I would rather stay here and starve—and die, if it come to that—than have my girls brought to shame by the violence and wickedness of their young masters. You will also please state if there has been any schools opened for the colored children in your neighborhood. The great desire of my life now is to give my children an education, and have them form virtuous habits.

Say howdy to George Carter, and thank him for taking the pistol from you when you were shooting at me.

From your old servant,
JOURDON ANDERSON

"LIZETTE—THE BEAUTIFUL": A TRUE STORY OF SLAVERY
HALLIE QUINN BROWN

Hallie Quinn Brown (c. 1845–1949) was the daughter of former slaves who gained their freedom before 1865. Her father, Thomas Arthur Brown, worked as a steward and express agent on the riverboat route between Pittsburgh and New Orleans. He helped slaves flee to freedom. Hallie Quinn Brown remembers her father's stories of the Underground Railroad. This tale of compassion is based on a story her father told her.

One blustery March evening in 18— a carriage rolled up and halted at the front entrance of the Old Monongahela House in Pittsburgh, Pennsylvania. I was acting as night porter. The entire force of employees was composed of colored men and women of intelligence and considerable native ability. They deserved better places in life, but this was before the

Civil War, in the dark days of slavery when persons of color were mainly employed as menials. . . . The big Hotel was managed by Mr. and Mrs. Crossan, the proprietor and his wife. They were strong abolitionists and reposed the utmost confidence in their employees who assisted in providing for the comforts of an exacting public.

As I said at the beginning a carriage halted at the main entrance. Two travelers, a man and a woman, alighted and walked rapidly to the door, which I opened to admit them, then hastily closed it against the swirling snow and the biting blast which swept the street.

The arrivals were without baggage except a small leather bag, carried by the man. I directed him to the desk. As he removed his gloves and unbuttoned his overcoat, diamonds flashed from his fingers and bosom. He was below medium height, slender and dark, straight hair fell over his collar. A heavy drooping mustache could not hide the sneering curl of his lip. A wide brimmed black hat shaded small ferret-like eyes which were deep-set and restless. His appearance and manner proclaimed him a Southern planter before he uttered a word. He spoke in an undertone to the clerk who turned to me and said, "Show the gentleman to room 18 second floor. Take the girl to room 40 third floor back. The gentleman will give you further orders." At the word *girl* I looked keenly at the woman who, until now, stood in the shadow of a pillar. The bright light fell upon her fair face. Never shall I forget that lovely young girl! Her tall slender form was enveloped in a long cloak of some dark stuff. The hood which had partly concealed her face was thrown back revealing her wondrous beauty. Her finely chiseled features and clear olive complexion were enhanced by large dark eyes which glowed, but held within their depths both fear and sorrow. Glossy black hair waved from a smooth broad brow and was hidden beneath her cloak which she drew closely about her.

At a glance I comprehended the situation. This girl was a slave: the man her master. That moment I was fired with determination to rescue her from his clutches, no matter what the cost might be. The man snapped his fingers in her direction, signifying she was to follow him. For an instant she recoiled, her face paled, then flushed. With downcast eyes she walked gracefully to the corridor followed by admiring glances from loungers in the lobby. At No. 18 the man bade me halt while he entered the room and deposited his bag; then followed the girl and myself to No. 40, third floor back. I unlocked and opened the door and turned on the light, the man following closely behind. He carefully scrutinized the room; tested the walls; opened and examined the closets; raised the window sash, looked out and down as if measuring the distance to the pavement below; shut and locked the windows. Apparently satisfied with his findings he turned on his heel, walked out of the room without so much as a glance at the girl. He shut and locked the door, and pocketed the key. Although I towered head and shoulders above him and felt myself infinitely his superior as a man, he said, "Boy, are you on watch all night?" [I replied] in the affirmative [and] he continued, "Bring this girl some bread and butter and tea. How soon will dinner be served?" "In half an hour, Sir." "Bring the girl's supper at once," he said, consulting his watch. "Yes Sir," I replied, hastening away. In less than twenty minutes every sympathizer in that Old Monongahela House knew there was a slave girl locked in No. 40 third floor back and indignation ran high. On my return with the tea, I found the planter impatiently pacing the hall. He unlocked the door and we entered. I placed the tray upon a small table which stood in the center of the room. The girl had thrown off her wrap and was seated on a stool at the foot of the bed. Her hands, tensely locked, lay in her lap. Her wavy black hair was unconfined and literally swept the floor, falling like a cloud about her girlish form. She raised a tear-stained face in mute appeal. I dared not look at her again for fear I should say an imprudent word or commit a rash act, so I stepped into the hall where I could observe all without being seen. The girl arose, stood erect with the palms of her shapely hands pressed to her temples. The sight of that stricken girl exasperated the master beyond expression. He advanced toward her with menacing finger, stamped his foot and cried angrily but with suppressed wrath—"Lizette stop this nonsense, eat your supper, then lie down until you are called. Come now, stop that snuffling. Mind what I say and be quick about it, too." From the hall I heard the angry words and saw the look of utter despair on Lizette's face but not a murmur escaped her trembling lips. Again the master locked the door and kept the key. Almost immediately the light in the girl's room went out.

With a muttered imprecation, he commanded me to call the girl at 11 P.M., to order a cab to take them to meet the midnight express South, then strode haughtily downstairs and into the dining room.

Shortly afterward a half dozen determined men held a brief but deci-sive consultation. Mrs. Crossan and the chamber-maid on the third floor were taken into our confidence. Watches were stationed in the several halls and on stairways; a special one was placed to observe the move-ments of the planter. The headwaiter was instructed to delay serving the courses at dinner. With all speed messages were dispatched to friends in the city. The word soon came that a closed carriage would be at the door at 9 P.M. The planter had met some boon companions and every-thing favored our daring scheme. I was given the task of getting the girl out of the room. How was it to be done? The clerk, whom we did not trust, held the pass key, the planter had the other one safe in his pocket. Keys were brought from every part of the house, but the lock [to] No. 40 would not yield. All plans and suggestions failed. Time was flying! We were getting desperate! Finally I called in a low tone through the key hole. "Lizette, Lizette, we are your friends, come nearer. Are you a slave?" "Yes," came the faint answer. "Do you wish to be free?" "Yes, God knows I do." "Will you trust us and do as we tell you?" "Yes, I will," came the prompt response. How were we to get her out? Like a flash the idea came to me. There was but one way, draw her through the transom over the door! "Quick," I cried, "bring a strong rope and ladder!" Then the thought: would she consent? Had she courage for such an ordeal? It was a trying moment! We worked nervously, almost breathlessly. The rope and the ladder were secured. We made a noose, threw it through the transom. The girl put it around her waist as we directed. With great daring and heroism she suffered herself to be drawn through the transom into the hall. We could have shouted for joy, but the battle was yet to be won.

Lizette was hurried into the chamber-maid's room and dressed in male attire. Her shapely head was quickly shorn of its beautiful tresses; green goggles concealed her bright eyes; a wide brimmed hat shaded her face. I threw a gentleman's cape about her shoulders. Leaning on my arm, as an invalid, we passed within a few feet of the master, puffing his after-dinner pipe in great contentment; passed the loungers in the lobby, the clerk at his desk—out into the street and the wintry gale. The poor girl trembled so violently I feared she would fall. I actually carried her from the door to the carriage. A Quaker lady gathered Lizette in her arms as I quickly closed the door. The whip was given to the horses and the vehicle was soon lost in the blinding snow storm. I returned to the lobby just as the clock chimed the hour of *nine*. Our work was accomplished! As we passed, confederates in a holy cause, we silently grasped each other's hands and tears welled to our eyes.

At the home of the Quakeress Lizette told her simple story. She had gone from Virginia to Baltimore, Maryland, as maid to her mistress. Longing for freedom she ran away, but was apprehended. At her third attempt to escape, her master, who was her half brother, decided to sell her to a Georgia Soul Driver, who was to claim her the next day. With the master she was on her way to the place where she was to be turned over to her purchaser when they had halted at Pittsburgh and her rescue had occurred. Kind friends dressed her in a dark travelling suit, gave her a well-filled purse and by 10 P.M., she was on the north bound train speeding to Canada and Freedom.

Not waiting for "Watch" to call the girl, ten minutes to 11 o'clock the master went to No. 40, rapping loudly and saying it was time to be up. Getting no response he unlocked the door and turned on the light, only to find the room empty. *The bird had flown!* He screamed in rage and called, "Lizette, Lizette, where are you, Lizette?" The cry was so loud and insistent that doors were hastily thrown open, while guests and servants alike ran into the corridors, thinking the cry an alarm of fire. It was with great difficulty that he was quieted and only on the promise that a thorough search would be made in the morning. As no one had seen her escape, he was led to believe that she must be in the house.

The planter refused to retire, but sat, the remainder of the night, in the office near the main entrance to watch, and stationed watches at all other exits. By daylight the house was in an uproar. The planter ran here and there calling excitedly and incriminating *everybody*. Detectives searched the premises but without avail. The house watchmen were arraigned. The planter demanded their arrest. They were about to be taken into custody. At that moment all the employees in the house stepped forward and asked for their wages, signifying their intention to quit the service.

With uplifted hands, Mrs. Crossan exclaimed, "For my sake, Brown, don't leave. The guests are at the table and there is no one to serve breakfast." "We are men, madame, and must be treated as such," I replied. Mr. Crossan turned to us and said, "You may resume your work without threat or fear." Then addressing the planter he added with emphasis—"Sir, I have a set of men whom I can trust. If you lay your pocket book down you will get it again, *but I will not vouch for your nigger.*" The planter left immediately, swearing eternal vengeance against the Old Monongahela House and everybody in it, all Pittsburgh and the North generally—*but beautiful Liʒette he never saw again.*

A HUNTER FEEDS THE HUNTED
ERNEST J. GAINES

In the following story—taken from The Autobiography of Miss Jane Pittman *by Ernest J. Gaines—a young girl and boy meet a hunter in the woods while fleeing slavery. The girl, Jane, has taken under her wing young Ned, whose mother was killed by racists. Jane and Ned's encounter with the hunter is a story of generosity and sharing among the destitute. Despite Jane's tough facade, the story illustrates the understanding and humaneness of strangers. It exemplifies how many African Americans helped one another survive the wretched conditions of slavery and the Civil War.*

Night caught us but we kept going, traveling by the North Star all the time. I reckoned it had been dark about three hours when we came in a thicket of pine trees, and I smelled food cooking. I stopped quickly and held out my arms so Ned would be quiet. I turned my head and turned my head, but I couldn't see the fire or the smoke. Now, I didn't know what to do—go back, go forward, or move to one side.

Then somebody spoke: "Now, don't this just beat everything."

I turned around so fast I dropped the bundle on the ground. But I felt much better when I saw another black face standing there looking down on us. He had a green stick about the size and link of a bean pole. He had come on us so quietly he could have killed both of us with that stick before we even saw him.

"What the world y'all doing way out here?" he said. "Y'all by y'all self?"

"Just me and this little boy," I said.

"Lord, have mercy," he said. He was one of the fussin'-est people I had ever seen. "Y'all come on over here," he said.

I picked up my bundle and me and Ned followed him back to his camp. He had a rabbit cooking on the fire. He nodded for me and Ned to sit down. I saw a bow and arrows leaning against one of the trees. The man squatted by the fire and looked at us.

"Now, where the world y'all think y'all going?" he said.

"Ohio," I said.

"My Lord, my Lord," he said. "I done seen things these last few weeks, but if this don't beat everything, I don't know. Coming and going, coming and going, and they don't bit more know what they doing than that rabbit I got cooking on that fire there. I bet y'all hungry."

"We got something to eat," I said.

"What, potatoes and corn y'all done stole?" he said. "Don't have to tell me, I already know. I done met others just like y'all."

He took the rabbit off the fire and laid it on the leaves he had spread out on the ground. Then he took a knife from his belt and cut the rabbit up in three pieces. When it had cooled off good he handed me and Ned a piece. He had seasoned it down good with wild onions that he had found out there in the swamps.

"You going North?" I asked him.

"No, I'm where I'm going right now," he said. "South."

I quit eating. "You got to be crazy," I said.

"I reckoned you got all the sense, dragging that child through the swamps all time of night," he said. "Good thing I'm a friend, not an enemy. I heard y'all long time before you stopped back there listening. I had been leaning on that pole so long I was fixing to fall asleep."

"We was quiet," I said.

"Quiet for you, not for me," he said. "A dog ain't got nothing on these yers. What you think keeping me going, potatoes and corn?"

I didn't answer him. The rabbit was good, but I didn't want show him how much I liked it. Just nibbling here and there like I was particular.

"Who you know in Ohio?" he asked me.

"Just Mr. Brown," I said.

"Mr. Brown who?"

"Mr. Brown, a Yankee soldier," I said.

"Lord, have mercy," the hunter said, shaking his head. "Now, I done heard everything."

"How come you going back South?" I said.

"What?" he said. He wasn't eating, he was thinking about me looking for Brown. "I'm looking for my pappy," he said. But looked like he was still thinking about me looking for Brown.

"Your mama dead?" I asked.

"What?" he said. He looked at me. "No, my mama ain't dead." He just looked at me a good while like he was thinking about me looking for Brown. "I know where she at," he said. "I want find him now."

"Y'all used to stay here in Luzana?" I asked.

"What?" he said.

"Your daddy and y'all?"

"When they sold him he was in Mi'sippi," the hunter said. "I don't know where he at now."

"Then how you know where to look for him?" I asked.

He got mad with me now. "I'm go'n do just what you doing with that child," he said. "Look everywhere. But I got little more sense."

"Well, if you was beat all the time you'd be running away, too," I said.

"I was beat," he said. "Don't go round here bragging like you got all the beating."

I ate and sucked on the bone. I didn't want argue with him no more.

"Who was them other people you seen?" I asked him. "Any of them going to Ohio?"

"They was going everywhere," he said. "Some say Ohio, some say Kansas—some say Canada. Some of them even said Luzana and Mi'sippi."

"Luzana and Mi'sippi ain't North," I said.

"That's right, it ain't North," the hunter said. "But they had left out just like you, a few potatoes and another old dress. No map, no guide, no nothing. Like freedom was a place coming to meet them half way. Well, it ain't coming to meet you. And it might not be there when you get there, either."

"We ain't giving up," I said. "We done gone this far."

"How far?" he asked me. "How long you been traveling?"

"Three days," I said.

"And how far you think you done got in three days?" he said. "You ain't even left that plantation yet. I ought to know. I been going and going and I ain't nowhere, yet, myself. Just searching and searching."

When he said this he looked like he wanted to cry, and I didn't look at him, I looked at Ned. Ned had laid down on the ground and gone to sleep. He still had the flint and iron in his hands.

I told the hunter about the Secesh who had killed Ned's mama and the other people. He told me he had seen some of the Secesh handywork, too. Earlier that same day he had cut a man down and buried him that the Secesh had hung. After hanging him they had gashed out his entrails.

"What they do all that for?" I asked.

"Lesson to other niggers," he said.

We sat there talking and talking. Both of us was glad we had somebody to talk to. I asked him about the bow and arrows. He told me he had made it to shoot rabbits and birds. Sometimes he even got a fish or two. I told him I bet I could use it. He said I didn't have the strength. He said it took a man to pull back on that bow. I asked him what he knowed about my strength. But he kept quiet. After a while he said: "Y'all want me lead y'all back where y'all come from?"

"We didn't come from Ohio," I said.

"You just a pig-headed little old nothing," he told me.

"I didn't ask you for your old rabbit," I said. Now I was full, I got smart. "I don't like no old rabbit nohow," I said.

"How come you ate the bones?" he said.

"I didn't eat no rabbit bones," I said.

"What I ought to do is knock y'all out and take y'all on back," he said.

"I bet you I holler round here and make them Secesh come and kill us, too," I said.

"How can you holler if you knocked out, dried-up nothing?" he said.

I had to think fast.

"I holler when I wake up," I said.

"I don't care about you, but I care about that little fellow there," the hunter said. "Just look at him. He might be dead already."

"He ain't dead, he sleeping," I said. "And I can take care him myself."

"You can't take care you, how can you take care somebody else?" the hunter said. "You can't kill a rabbit, you can't kill a bird. Do you know how to catch a fish?"

"That ain't all you got to eat in this world," I said.

He looked at Ned again.

"If I wasn't looking for my pappy I'd force y'all back," he said. "Or force y'all somewhere so somebody can look after y'all. Two children tramping round in the swamps by themself, I ain't never heard of nothing like this in all my born days."

"We done made it this far, we can make it," I said.

"You ain't go'n make nothing," he said. "Don't you know you ain't go'n make nothing, you little dried-up thing?"

"You should 'a' kept that old rabbit," I said. "I don't like old rabbit meat nohow."

He didn't want argue with me no more.

"Go on to sleep," he said. "I'll stand watch over y'all."

"No, you don't," I said. "You just want take us back."

"Go on to sleep, gnat," he said.

I shook Ned, and he woke up crying. I told him the Secesh was go'n catch him if he kept up that noise. I let him sit there till he had rubbed the sleep out his eyes, then we got up and left. All that time the hunter didn't say a word. We went a little piece, till we couldn't see the camp no more, then we turned around and came on back. I had made up my mind to stay wake all night.

"Well, how was Ohio?" the hunter said.

Ned laid down in the same place and went right back to sleep. I sat beside him watching the hunter. I felt my eyes getting heavy, but I did everything to keep them open. I dugged my heel in the ground, I hummed a song to myself, I poked in the fire with a stick. But nature catch up with you don't care what you do. When I woke up the sun was high in the sky. Something was cooked there for me and Ned—a crow, a hawk, an owl—I don't know what. But there it was, done and cold, and the hunter was gone.

THANK YOU, M'AM
LANGSTON HUGHES

Langston Hughes (1902–67) reminds us that compassion can express itself in unusual ways—in this case, with a powerful, viselike grip. Mrs. Luella Bates Washington Jones admonishes a young man—for his own good. Then she serves him a hearty meal. She's sort of a grandma to every neighborhood kid. People like Mrs. Jones lived in black neighborhoods across the country. They were the respected "village elders" who scolded misbehaving children and who together helped raise local children.

She was a large woman with a large purse that had everything in it but hammer and nails. It had a long strap and she carried it slung across her shoulder. It was about eleven o'clock at night, and she was walking alone, when a boy ran up behind her and tried to snatch her purse. The strap broke with the single tug the boy gave it from behind. But the boy's weight, and the weight of the purse combined caused him to lose his balance so, instead of taking off full blast as he had hoped, the boy fell on his back on the sidewalk, and his legs flew up. The large woman simply turned around and kicked him right square in his blue jeaned sitter. Then she reached down, picked the boy up by his shirt front, and shook him until his teeth rattled.

After that the woman said, "Pick up my pocketbook, boy, and give it here."

She still held him. But she bent down enough to permit him to stoop and pick up her purse. Then she said, "Now ain't you ashamed of yourself?"

Firmly gripped by his shirt front, the boy said, "Yes'm."

The woman said, "What did you want to do it for?"

The boy said, "I didn't aim to."

She said, "You a lie!"

By that time two or three people passed, stopped, turned to look, and some stood watching.

"If I turn you loose, will you run?" asked the woman.

"Yes'm," said the boy.

"Then I won't turn you loose," said the woman. She did not release him.

"I'm very sorry, lady, I'm sorry," whispered the boy.

"Um-hum! And your face is dirty. I got a great mind to wash your face for you. Ain't you got nobody home to tell you to wash your face?"

"No'm," said the boy.

"Then it will get washed this evening," said the large woman starting up the street, dragging the frightened boy behind her.

He looked as if he were fourteen or fifteen, frail and willow-wild, in tennis shoes and blue jeans.

The woman said, "You ought to be my son. I would teach you right from wrong. Least I can do right now is to wash your face. Are you hungry?"

"No'm," said the being-dragged boy. "I just want you to turn me loose."

"Was I bothering *you* when I turned that corner?" asked the woman.

"No'm."

"But you put yourself in contact with *me*, " said the woman. "If you think that that contact is not going to last awhile, you got another thought coming. When I get through with you, sir, you are going to remember Mrs. Luella Bates Washington Jones."

Sweat popped out on the boy's face and he began to struggle. Mrs. Jones stopped, jerked him around in front of her, put a half-nelson about his neck, and continued to drag him up the street. When she got to her door, she dragged the boy inside, down a hall, and into a large kitchen-ette-furnished room at the rear of the house. She switched on the light and left the door open. The boy could hear other roomers laughing and talking in the large house. Some of their doors were open, too, so he knew he and the woman were not alone. The woman still had him by the neck in the middle of her room.

She said, "What is your name?"

"Roger," answered the boy.

"Then, Roger, you go to that sink and wash your face," said the woman, whereupon she turned him loose—at last. Roger looked at the door—looked at the woman—looked at the door—*and went to the sink.*

"Let the water run until it gets warm," she said. "Here's a clean towel."

"You gonna take me to jail?" asked the boy, bending over the sink.

"Not with that face, I would not take you nowhere," said the woman. "Here I am trying to get home to cook me a bite to eat and you snatch my pocketbook! Maybe you ain't been to your supper either, late as it be. Have you?"

"There's nobody home at my house," said the boy.

"Then we'll eat," said the woman. "I believe you're hungry—or been hungry—to try to snatch my pocketbook."

"I wanted a pair of blue suede shoes," said the boy.

"Well, you didn't have to snatch *my* pocketbook to get some suede shoes," said Mrs. Luella Bates Washington Jones. "You could of asked me."

"M'am?"

The water dripping from his face, the boy looked at her. There was a long pause. A very long pause. After he had dried his face and not knowing what else to do dried it again, the boy turned around, wondering what next. The door was open. He could make a dash for it down the hall. He could run, run, run, run, *run!*

The woman was sitting on the day-bed. After awhile she said, "I were young once and I wanted things I could not get."

There was another long pause. The boy's mouth opened. Then he frowned, but not knowing he frowned.

The woman said, "Um-hum! You thought I was going to say *but*, didn't you? You thought I was going to say, *but I didn't snatch people's pocketbooks*. Well, I wasn't going to say that." Pause. Silence. "I have done things, too, which I would not tell you, son—neither tell God, if he didn't already know. So you set down while I fix us something to eat. You might run that comb through your hair so you will look presentable."

In another corner of the room behind a screen was a gas plate and an icebox. Mrs. Jones got up and went behind the screen. The woman did not watch the boy to see if he was going to run now, nor did she watch her purse which she left behind her on the day-bed. But the boy took care to sit on the far side of the room where he thought she could easily see him out of the corner of her eye, if she wanted to. He did not trust the woman *not* to trust him. And he did not want to be mistrusted now.

"Do you need somebody to go to the store," asked the boy, "maybe to get some milk or something?"

"Don't believe I do," said the woman, "unless you just want sweet milk yourself. I was going to make cocoa out of this canned milk I got here."

"That will be fine," said the boy.

She heated some lima beans and ham she had in the icebox, made the cocoa, and set the table. The woman did not ask the boy anything about where he lived, or his folks, or anything else that would embarrass him. Instead, as they ate, she told him about her job in a hotel beauty-shop that stayed open late, what the work was like, and how all kinds of women came in and out, blondes, red-heads, and Spanish. Then she cut him a half of her ten-cent cake.

"Eat some more, son," she said.

When they were finished eating she got up and said, "Now, here, take this ten dollars and buy yourself some blue suede shoes. And next time, do not make the mistake of latching onto *my* pocketbook *nor nobody else's*—because shoes come by devilish like that will burn your feet. I got to get my rest now. But I wish you would behave yourself, son, from here on in."

She led him down the hall to the front door and opened it. "Good-night! Behave yourself, boy!" she said, looking out into the street.

The boy wanted to say something else other than, "Thank you, m'am," to Mrs. Luella Bates Washington Jones, but he couldn't do so as he turned at the barren stoop and looked back at the large woman in the door. He barely managed to say, "Thank you," before she shut the door. And he never saw her again.

MOTHER HALE
CLARA MCBRIDE HALE

Widowed at age twenty-seven Clara McBride Hale (1905–92) raised three children. Then, at nearly sixty-five years old, she started all over again—raising babies born to drug addicts who couldn't cope with motherhood. In 1969, "Mother Hale" founded Hale House in her Harlem apartment. By 1973 Mother Hale and "her family" had outgrown her apartment, so they moved into a Harlem brownstone, where a large staff cared for babies around the clock. An increasing number of hopelessly addicted mothers, it seemed, were giving birth and then abandoning babies. In the 1980s, many of these infants were born infected with HIV.

In 1986, Mother Hale and her babies—primarily African American— got national attention when President Ronald Reagan introduced her to the nation during his State of the Union Address. He called her "an American hero." Her memory serves as a role model for untiring love and compassion.

My mother always had a house full of children. She had four children and all the neighbors' children came to our house.

You couldn't tell that my mother was not white. See, my grandmother, they said she was a beautiful woman. She was a slave and the master gave her my mother. They had some mulattoes that they called "free issues." That's what happened with my mother. She had all the features of the master and she was as fair.

But she was a fair woman, I mean, not only in color. She knew what was happening and she taught this. She kept saying, "I want you to hold your head up and be proud of yourself. We were brought over and we were enslaved all this time, but it's over now. You're supposed to be free, but you aren't free. Remember that."

My husband and I had dreams of what we were going to do with our children. We dreamed that they'd grow up and be what they want to be and have a good life. My first child was Nathan, Nathan Hale. Oh, I was really an American. I wanted them to know.

My husband died when my daughter Lorraine was five and Nathan was six. There was no way under the sun that they would give you any other job except domestic jobs. And that meant being away all day from these poor little children who had nobody.

So I decided to take in other people's children. They were coming for five days and going home Saturday and Sunday. But they got so they didn't want to go home. They wanted to stay with me altogether. So the parents would give me an extra dollar, and that meant I kept them all the time. My daughter said she was at least eleven years old before she realized that these were not her sisters and brothers.

So I raised forty. Every one of them went to college, every one of them graduated, and they have lovely jobs. They're some of the nicest people. Anything they wanted to do, I backed them up. I have singers, dancers, preachers, and things like that. They're schoolteachers, lawyers, doctors, anything else. No big name or anything, but they're happy.

In 1969, I decided I wouldn't take care of no more children. Then my daughter sent me a girl with an addict baby. Inside of two months I had twenty-two babies living in a five-room apartment. My decision to stop didn't mean anything. It seems as though God wanted them. He kept sending them, and He kept opening a way for me to make it. It's been over six hundred addicted babies.

We hold them and rock them. They love you to tell them how great they are, how good they are. Somehow, even at a young age, they understand that. They're happy and they turn out well.

Being black does not stop you. You can sit out in the world and say, "Well, white people kept me back, and I can't do this." Not so. You can have anything you want if you make up your mind and you want it. You don't have to crack nobody across the head, don't have to steal or anything. Don't have to be smart like the men up high stealing all the money. We're good people and we try.

I'm not going to retire again. Until I die, I'm going to keep doing. My people need me. They need somebody that's not taking from them and is giving them something.

We're going to open a place for children with AIDS because there's no cure and these children will die. People shun them and it's not their fault. I want them to live a good life while they can and know someone loves them.

It's back to being very bad for black people now. But I'll live through that, too. If I don't, I have a daughter that will carry on. I have grandchildren and great-grandchildren. They have the same feeling. When I'm gone, somebody else will take it up and do it. This is how we've lived all these years.

I'm hoping that one day there will be no Hale House, that we won't need anybody to look after these children, that the drugs will be gone.

I'm not an American hero. I'm a person that loves children.

Before Mother Hale died in 1992, Hale House had served more than two thousand babies. It has become a model for similar programs in several other cities.

Today, infants arrive from police precincts, prisons, hospitals, welfare offices, churches, and social work programs across the New York metropolitan area. Mothers and babies' relatives still bring infants to Hale House, too.

Hale House runs programs to assist busy moms and provide housing to AIDS-infected mothers with children. It also manages a twenty-eight-apartment halfway house and operates an international education center for instruction in the care of addicted babies. Mother Hale's spirit of compassion lives on in each program.

MOTHER HALE'S PRAYER

This prayer is said almost daily at one of the oldest and most famous child care agencies for addicted and HIV-infected babies—Hale House in Harlem.

(For a baby with AIDS)

Dear Father in Heaven,
This baby will not live long
on this earth, but he will live
forever with you. Grant this
prayer that his remaining days
will be full of the happiness and

joy every infant deserves. Ease his
pain. Calm his fears. Chase away
his loneliness. Let him feel your
eternal love through me. Amen.

ABYSSINIAN SOUP KITCHEN
WIL HAYGOOD

*Adam Clayton Powell Jr. (1908–72) will long be remembered for
many things: preaching and picketing for job opportunities, his helmsman-
ship of the Abyssinian Baptist Church, his newspaper columns, his extraordinary rise and fall as a congressman (Harlem's first), and his civil
rights activities. But before he developed a knack for making headlines,
the young Powell was feeding breadlines at his father's church in Harlem
during the Great Depression. Compassion is often best expressed in concrete, grass-roots form.*

Within months of the [stock market] crash there were breadlines in
Harlem, lines that would last for years. Tired figures stood in long lines,
watched by the police officials who dispensed meal vouchers. Tensions
ran so high that fights broke out. Imaginative out-of-work cooks sold
meals from storefronts for as little as fifteen cents; civic officials pleaded
with churches to feed the hungry; schoolteachers were asked to treat
children with a little more understanding. Illness became prevalent, and
the sick were sent to Harlem Hospital, an institution that lacked the
community's trust and respect. As fall turned to winter and the breadlines lengthened, there were blank stares on the faces of the hungry
children. Figures huddled in alleyways, and people warmed their hands
over the haze of bonfires up and down Harlem's streets.

    The elder Powell knew he had to act. Riding along the streets in his
Packard, with his son conspicuously and often by his side, he grimaced
with pain. The wrenching poverty reminded him of how he had lived as
a boy in West Virginia. When desperate appeals were made to private

citizens and charitable organizations, money came in from the Rockefeller philanthropies, and men like Seward Prosser, the influential banker, and Adam Clayton Powell, Sr., the Abyssinian stalwart, stepped forth. In New York City, charitable donations provided for the creation of an Emergency Work Bureau, which Prosser headed. Workers were to be paid fifteen dollars a week for an assortment of menial jobs. "No man can be moral in Harlem on fifteen dollars a week," Powell feared. But there was opportunity in the Emergency Work Bureau, and he realized it. It was an opportunity for his son.

Young Powell, already named business manager of the church, was appointed to administer the work relief bureau for Harlem, operating out of the basement of the church. Setting up a staff in the basement, he worked with the kind of energy the times demanded. He sent young men, his aides (some of them were older than he was), out to buy discounted food, and when they returned hours later, their arms loaded with sacks of food, they would hand the food over to the church ladies. The ladies would then scurry to empty the contents into big iron pots, and the hungry would be fed; and Mattie Powell would stand there, proud of her son. Every evening, as dark spread over Harlem, the needy would be summoned to the church to eat and to get shoes and clothing, and the young minister would shake hands and pat backs and get to know the men and women who had been raised in his father's church. Word quickly spread about him. "Have you heard about Adam, up in Harlem, feeding the hungry?" a Colgate classmate asked Daniel Crosby. In a few short months, young Powell and his staff had provided 28,500 free meals and given away an estimated 17,000 pieces of clothing and 2,000 pairs of shoes.

The work was like having a government job, but it was more than that, because it did what government was supposed to do and sometimes could not. Powell was just too busy to attend classes at Union Theological Seminary, so he sent church secretaries over to take his class notes. When seminary officials complained about the practice, he quit the seminary in a huff. Directing a staff, feeding the hungry, and appealing to the congregation for collections were so much more vital than sitting at a desk.

SWEET CHARITY
MAYA ANGELOU

Charity improves just about everything and everyone it touches. Maya Angelou reminds us that compassion improves personal lives and the world at large.

The New Testament informs the reader that it is more blessed to give than to receive. I have found that among its other benefits, giving liberates the soul of the giver. The size and substance of the gift should be important to the recipient, but not to the donor save that the best thing one can give is that which is appreciated. The giver is as enriched as is the recipient, and more important, that intangible but very real psychic force of good in the world is increased.

When we cast our bread upon the waters, we can presume that someone downstream whose face we will never know will benefit from our action, as we who are downstream from another will profit from that grantor's gift.

Since time is the one immaterial object which we cannot influence—neither speed up nor slow down, add to nor diminish—it is an imponderably valuable gift. Each of us has a few minutes a day or a few hours a week which we could donate to an old folks' home or a children's hospital ward. The elderly whose pillows we plump or whose water pitchers we refill may or may not thank us for our gift, but the gift is upholding the foundation of the universe. The children to whom we read simple stories may or may not show gratitude, but each boon we give strengthens the pillars of the world.

While our gifts and the recipients should be considered, our bounty, once decided upon, should be without concern, overflowing one minute and forgotten the next.

RECENTLY I WAS asked to speak before a group of philanthropists and was astonished at their self-consciousness. The gathered donors give tens of millions of dollars annually to medical research, educational development, art support, and social reform. Yet to a person they seemed a little, just a little, ashamed of themselves. I pondered their behavior and realized that someone had told someone that not only was it degrading to accept charity but it was equally debasing to give it. And sad to say, someone had believed that statement. Hence, many preferred to have it known that they dispense philanthropy rather than charity.

I like charitable people and like to think of myself as charitable, as being of a generous heart and a giving nature—of being a friend indeed to anyone in need. Why, I pondered, did the benefactors not feel as I?

Some benefactors may desire distance from the recipients of their largess because there is a separation between themselves and the resources they distribute. As inheritors or managers of fortune rather than direct earners, perhaps they feel exiled from the gifts; then it follows that they feel exiled from the recipient.

It is sad when people who give to the needy feel estranged from the objects of their generosity. They can take little, if any, relish from their acts of charity; therefore, are generous out of duty rather than delight.

If we change the way we think of charity, our personal lives will be richer and the larger world will be improved. When we give cheerfully and accept gratefully, everyone is blessed. "Charity . . . is kind; . . . envieth not; . . . vaunteth not itself, is not puffed up."

ⵥⵦⵧ

The best passion is compassion.

—*Jamaican proverb*

ⵥⵦⵧ

RESPONSIBILITY

My mom would walk into a room, see toys strewn on the floor, and ask a question that she could already answer for herself.

Who's responsible for this?

Apparently, she just wanted a confession. And she got one every time. The question was just her way of gently encouraging a child to own up to what he had done—a primary lesson, you might say, in accountability.

This brief lesson was followed closely by another, which came in the form of a simple sentence:

Put your toys away.

And that is how we (her sons, that is) moved from accountability to a closely related concept, responsibility. We quickly learned to be responsible for cleaning our own mess.

Being responsible means being accountable, answerable, dependable, liable, or reliable. It means fulfilling one's obligation or duty.

The older we grow, the more responsibilities we learn to manage. Some people, however, simply refuse to grow with new responsibilities. No matter how light their load, they struggle against being held accountable. Rejecting responsibility or refusing to explore your full potential to manage it is a mark of immaturity. So is not living up to the consequences of your actions.

But irresponsibility is not characteristic of the young alone. Some adults evade responsibility when things go awry, refusing to take the blame for bad planning, mistakes, or misdeeds. Passing the buck like this—not owning up to one's own incompetency—is standard practice in certain spheres. Some elected officials, for example, shirk responsibility for wrong-doings on their watch.

In light of the racial injustices and harm suffered by millions of African Americans over several centuries, many black leaders have held white Americans accountable for not living up to the nation's ideals and official pronouncements, including its formal declaration that "all Men are created equal" and "that they are endowed by their Creator with certain unalienable Rights" such as "Life, Liberty, and the Pursuit of Happiness." In this chapter, nineteenth- and twentieth-century leaders—

including Frederick Douglass and Martin Luther King Jr.—describe the monumental task of setting the nation on the proper course to end racial injustice and create assurances of humane, dignified treatment for every citizen, regardless of race. Other selections focus on becoming a responsible role model (Tavis Smiley) and on teaching youth to excel in education, thus improving their potential in the job market (Bob Moses).

We can teach children to grow with their obligations and duties by giving them charge over small matters at first and slowly increasing their responsibilities. An important lesson might involve holding them accountable for tasks or work they agree to take on or are assigned: putting away toys, school studies, household chores, after-school jobs, summer jobs, and on and on. The better they handle responsibilities as they mature, the better role models they will become for future generations.

❧

Lifting as we climb.

*—Motto of the National
Association of Colored Women*

❧

WHAT TO THE SLAVE IS THE FOURTH OF JULY?

FREDERICK DOUGLASS

*In this excerpt from an address delivered in Rochester, New York, in
1852, Frederick Douglass used the Fourth of July to drive home the irony
and "inhuman mockery" of the national holiday. While whites celebrated
their cherished liberty and freedom from tyranny, blacks mourned American slavery, he said. He called the nation to task for "the great sin and
shame of America."*

FELLOW-CITIZENS—Pardon me, and allow me to ask, why am I called
upon to speak here to-day? What have I, or those I represent, to do with
your national independence? Are the great principles of political freedom and of natural justice, embodied in that Declaration of Independence, extended to us? and am I, therefore, called upon to bring our
humble offering to the national altar, and to confess the benefits, and
express devout gratitude for the blessings, resulting from your independence to us?

Would to God, both for your sakes and ours, that an affirmative
answer could be truthfully returned to these questions! Then would my
task be light, and my burden easy and delightful. For who is there so
cold that a nation's sympathy could not warm him? Who so obdurate
and dead to the claims of gratitude, that would not thankfully acknowledge such priceless benefits? Who so stolid and selfish, that would not
give his voice to swell the hallelujahs of a nation's jubilee, when the
chains of servitude had been torn from his limbs? I am not that man. In
a case like that, the dumb might eloquently speak, and the "lame man
leap as an hart."

But, such is not the state of the case. I say it with a sad sense of the disparity between us. I am not included within the pale of this glorious anniversary! Your high independence only reveals the immeasurable distance between us. The blessings in which you this day rejoice, are not enjoyed in common. The rich inheritance of justice, liberty, prosperity, and independence, bequeathed by your fathers, is shared by you, not by me. The sunlight that brought life and healing to you, has brought stripes and death to me. This Fourth of July is *yours,* not *mine. You* may rejoice, *I* must mourn. To drag a man in fetters into the grand illuminated temple of liberty, and call upon him to join you in joyous anthems, were inhuman mockery and sacrilegious irony. Do you mean, citizens, to mock me, by asking me to speak to-day? If so, there is a parallel to your conduct. And let me warn you that it is dangerous to copy the example of a nation whose crimes, towering up to heaven, were thrown down by the breath of the Almighty, burying that nation in irrecoverable ruin! I can to-day take up the plaintive lament of a peeled and woe-smitten people.

"By the rivers of Babylon, there we sat down. Yea! we wept when we remembered Zion. We hanged our harps upon the willows in the midst thereof. For there, they that carried us away captive, required of us a song; and they who wasted us required of us mirth, saying, Sing us one of the songs of Zion. How can we sing the Lord's song in a strange land? If I forget thee, O Jerusalem, let my right hand forget her cunning. If I do not remember thee, let my tongue cleave to the roof of my mouth."

Fellow-citizens, above your national, tumultuous joy, I hear the mournful wail of millions, whose chains, heavy and grievous yesterday, are to-day rendered more intolerable by the jubilant shouts that reach them. If I do forget, if I do not faithfully remember those bleeding children of sorrow this day, "may my right hand forget her cunning, and may my tongue cleave to the roof of my mouth!" To forget them, to pass lightly over their wrongs, and to chime in with the popular theme, would be treason most scandalous and shocking, and would make me a reproach before God and the world. My subject, then, fellow-citizens, is AMERICAN SLAVERY. I shall see this day and its popular characteristics from the slave's point of view. Standing there, identified with the American bondman, making his wrongs mine, I do not hesitate to declare, with all my soul, that the character and conduct of this nation never looked

blacker to me than on this Fourth of July. Whether we turn to the
declarations of the past, or to the professions of the present, the conduct
of the nation seems equally hideous and revolting. America is false to
the past, false to the present, and solemnly binds herself to be false to
the future. Standing with God and the crushed and bleeding slave on this
occasion, I will, in the name of humanity which is outraged, in the name
of liberty which is fettered, in the name of the constitution and the bible,
which are disregarded and trampled upon, dare to call in question and to
denounce, with all the emphasis I can command, everything that serves
to perpetuate slavery—the great sin and shame of America! "I will not
equivocate; I will not excuse;" I will use the severest language I can
command; and yet not one word shall escape me that any man, whose
judgment is not blinded by prejudice, or who is not at heart a slaveholder, shall not confess to be right and just.

But I fancy I hear some one of my audience say, it is just in this
circumstance that you and your brother abolitionists fail to make a
favorable impression on the public mind. Would you argue more, and
denounce less, would you persuade more and rebuke less, your cause
would be much more likely to succeed. But, I submit, where all is plain
there is nothing to be argued. What point in the anti-slavery creed
would you have me argue? On what branch of the subject do the people
of this country need light? Must I undertake to prove that the slave is a
man? That point is conceded already. Nobody doubts it. The slaveholders themselves acknowledge it in the enactment of laws for their government. They acknowledge it when they punish disobedience on the part
of the slave. There are seventy-two crimes in the state of Virginia,
which, if committed by a black man, (no matter how ignorant he be,)
subject him to the punishment of death; while only two of these same
crimes will subject a white man to the like punishment. What is this but
the acknowledgment that the slave is a moral, intellectual, and responsible being. The manhood of the slave is conceded. It is admitted in the
fact that southern statute books are covered with enactments forbidding,
under severe fines and penalties, the teaching of the slave to read or
write. When you can point to any such laws, in reference to the beasts of
the field, then I may consent to argue the manhood of the slave. When
the dogs in your streets, when the fowls of the air, when the cattle on
your hills, when the fish of the sea, and the reptiles that crawl, shall be

unable to distinguish the slave from a brute, then will I argue with you that the slave is a man!

For the present, it is enough to affirm the equal manhood of the negro race. Is it not astonishing that, while we are plowing, planting, and reaping, using all kinds of mechanical tools, erecting houses, constructing bridges, building ships, working in metals of brass, iron, copper, silver, and gold; that, while we are reading, writing, and cyphering, acting as clerks, merchants, and secretaries, having among us lawyers, doctors, ministers, poets, authors, editors, orators, and teachers; that, while we are engaged in all manner of enterprises common to other men—digging gold in California, capturing the whale in the Pacific, feeding sheep and cattle on the hillside, living, moving, acting, thinking, planning, living in families as husbands, wives, and children, and, above all, confessing and worshiping the christian's God, and looking hopefully for life and immortality beyond the grave,—we are called upon to prove that we are men!

Would you have me argue that man is entitled to liberty? that he is the rightful owner of his own body? You have already declared it. Must I argue the wrongfulness of slavery? Is that a question for republicans? Is it to be settled by the rules of logic and argumentation, as a matter beset with great difficulty, involving a doubtful application of the principle of justice, hard to be understood? How should I look to-day in the presence of Americans, dividing and subdividing a discourse, to show that men have a natural right to freedom, speaking of it relatively and positively, negatively and affirmatively? To do so, would be to make myself ridiculous, and to offer an insult to your understanding. There is not a man beneath the canopy of heaven that does not know that slavery is wrong *for him*.

What! am I to argue that it is wrong to make men brutes, to rob them of their liberty, to work them without wages, to keep them ignorant of their relations to their fellow-men, to beat them with sticks, to flay their flesh with the lash, to load their limbs with irons, to hunt them with dogs, to sell them at auction, to sunder their families, to knock out their teeth, to burn their flesh, to starve them into obedience and submission to their masters? Must I argue that a system, thus marked with blood and stained with pollution, is wrong? No; I will not. I have better employment for my time and strength than such arguments would imply.

What, then, remains to be argued? Is it that slavery is not divine; that God did not establish it; that our doctors of divinity are mistaken? There is blasphemy in the thought. That which is inhuman cannot be divine. Who can reason on such a proposition! They that can, may; I cannot. The time for such argument is past.

At a time like this, scorching irony, not convincing argument, is needed. Oh! had I the ability, and could I reach the nation's ear, I would to-day pour out a fiery stream of biting ridicule, blasting reproach, withering sarcasm, and stern rebuke. For it is not light that is needed, but fire; it is not the gentle shower, but thunder. We need the storm, the whirlwind, and the earthquake. The feeling of the nation must be quickened; the conscience of the nation must be roused; the propriety of the nation must be startled; the hypocrisy of the nation must be exposed; and its crimes against God and man must be proclaimed and denounced.

What to the American slave is your Fourth of July? I answer, a day that reveals to him, more than all other days in the year, the gross injustice and cruelty to which he is the constant victim. To him, your celebration is a sham; your boasted liberty, an unholy license; your national greatness, swelling vanity; your sounds of rejoicing are empty and heartless; your denunciations of tyrants, brass-fronted impudence; your shouts of liberty and equality, hollow mockery; your prayers and hymns, your sermons and thanksgivings, with all your religious parade and solemnity, are to him mere bombast, fraud, deception, impiety, and hypocrisy—a thin veil to cover up crimes which would disgrace a nation of savages. There is not a nation on the earth guilty of practices more shocking and bloody, than are the people of these United States, at this very hour.

Go where you may, search where you will, roam through all the monarchies and despotisms of the old world, travel through South America, search out every abuse, and when you have found the last, lay your facts by the side of the every-day practices of this nation, and you will say with me, that, for revolting barbarity and shameless hypocrisy, America reigns without a rival.

WHO SPEAKS FOR THE NEGRO?

Denied their political rights due to racism in the post–Civil War South, many African American leaders in the late 1800s tried to fulfill their responsibility to their constituents by waging battle from speakers' platforms.

After Congress passed the Reconstruction Act of 1867, blacks became active in the political life of the nation. The former Confederate states held constitutional conventions to draft new constitutions, banning slavery and extending rights to blacks. A number of black leaders emerged and were elected to state legislatures and to Congress. Hiram R. Revels (1822–1901) became the first black U.S. Senator (he filled the seat vacated by Jefferson Davis, who had gone on to become President of the Confederacy). Slave-born Blanche K. Bruce (1841–98) became the second black senator. Robert Smalls served in the U.S. House of Representatives from 1875 to 1887. [See "The Slave Who Stole a Confederate Ship," on page 109, for more on Robert Smalls.]

HENRY MACNEAL TURNER

Among the new black leaders was Henry MacNeal Turner, who was elected to the Georgia legislature. In 1868, the legislature, which was controlled by a white majority, expelled its black members. Turner responded eloquently with these words on September 3, 1868.

Before proceeding to argue this question upon its intrinsic merits, I wish the members of this House to understand the position that I take. I hold that I am a member of this body. Therefore, sir, I shall neither fawn or cringe before any party, nor stoop to beg them for my rights. Some of my colored fellow members, in the course of their remarks, took occasion to appeal to the sympathies of members on the opposite side, and to eulogize their character for magnanimity. It reminds me very much, sir, of slaves begging under the lash. I am here to demand my rights. . . .

The scene presented in this House, to-day, is one unparalleled in the history of the world. . . . Never has a man been arraigned before a body clothed with legislative, judicial or executive functions, charged with the offense of being of a darker hue than his fellowmen . . .

charged with an offense committed by the God of Heaven Himself. Cases may be found where men have been deprived of their rights for crimes and misdemeanors; but it has remained for the State of Georgia, in the very heart of the nineteenth century, to call a man before the bar, and there charge him with an act for which he is no more responsible than for the head which he carries upon his shoulders. . . .

Whose Legislature is this? Is it a white man's Legislature, or is it a black man's Legislature? Who voted for a Constitutional Convention, in obedience to the mandate of the Congress of the United States? Who first rallied around the standard of Reconstruction? Who set the ball of loyalty rolling in the State of Georgia? And whose voice was heard on the hills and in the valleys of his State? It was the voice of the brawny-armed Negro, with the few humanitarian-hearted white men who came to our assistance. I claim the honor, sir, of having been the instrument of convincing hundreds—yea, thousands—of white men, that to reconstruct under the measures of the United States Congress was the safest and the best course for the interest of the State.

Let us look at some facts in connection with this matter. Did half the white men of Georgia vote for this Legislature? Did not the great bulk of them fight, with all their strength, the Constitution under which we are acting? And did they not fight against the organization of this Legislature? And further, sir, did they not vote against it? Yes, sir! And there are persons in this Legislature today, who are ready to spit their poison in my face, while they themselves opposed, with all their power, the ratification of this Constitution. They question my right to a seat in this body, to represent the people whose legal votes elected me. . . . We are told that if black men want to speak, they must speak through white trumpets; if black men want their sentiments expressed, they must be adulterated and sent through white messengers, who will quibble, and equivocate, and evade, as rapidly as the pendulum of a clock. If this be not done, then the black men have committed an outrage, and their Representatives must be denied the right to represent their constituents.

The great question, sir, is this: Am I a man? If I am such, I claim the rights of a man. Am I not a man because I happen to be of a darker hue than honorable gentlemen around me?

We have pioneered civilization here; we have built up your country; we have worked in your fields, and garnered your harvests, for two hundred and fifty years! And what do we ask of you in return? Do we ask you for compensation for the sweat our fathers bore for you—for the tears you have caused, and the hearts you have broken, and the lives you have curtailed, and the blood you have spilled? Do we ask retaliation? We ask it not. We are willing to let the dead past bury its dead; but we ask you now for our rights.

You have all the elements of superiority upon your side; you have our money and your own; you have our education and your own; and you have your land and our own, too. We, who number hundreds of thousands in Georgia, including our wives and families, with not a foot of land to call our own—strangers in the land of our birth; without money, without education, without aid, without a roof to cover us while we live, nor sufficient clay to cover us when we die! . . .

You may expel us, gentlemen, but I firmly believe that you will someday repent it. The black man cannot protect a country, if the country doesn't protect him; and if, tomorrow, a war should arise, I would not raise a musket to defend a country where my manhood is denied. The fashionable way in Georgia when hard work is to be done, is, for the white man to sit at his ease, while the black man does the work; but, sir, I will say this much to the colored men of Georgia, as if I should be killed in this campaign, I may have no opportunity of telling them at any other time: Never lift a finger nor raise a hand in defense of Georgia, unless Georgia acknowledges that you are men, and invests you with the rights pertaining to manhood. . . .

RICHARD CAIN

In 1874, Congressman Richard Cain of South Carolina spoke of his intention to fulfill his duty as a representative of his people. His speech was a reply to a white congressman from North Carolina.

The gentleman wishes that we go to Africa or to the West Indies or somewhere else. I want to enunciate this doctrine upon this floor. We are not going away. We are going to stay here. We propose to stay here and work out the problem. We believe that God Almighty has made of one blood all the nations upon the face of the earth. We believe we are made just like white men are.

Look. I stretch out my arms. See; I have two of them, as you have. Look at our ears; I have two of them. I have two eyes, two nostrils, one mouth, two feet. I stand erect like you. I am clothed with humanity like you. I think, I reason, I talk, I express my views as you do. Is there any difference between us? Not so far as our manhood is concerned, unless it be in this: that our opinions differ and mine are a little higher up than yours. (Laughter)

The gentleman talks about the colored people deteriorating. Sir, who tills your lands now? Who plants your corn? Who raises your cotton? I have traveled over the Southern States and have seen who did this work. Going along, I saw the white men do the smoking, chewing tobacco, riding horses, playing cards, spending money; while the colored men are tilling the soil and bringing the cotton, rice and other products to market.

Sir, we are part and parcel of this nation, which has done more than any other on earth to illustrate the great idea that all races of men may dwell together in harmony. We will take that time-honored flag which has been borne through the heat of a thousand battles. Under its folds Anglo-Saxon and Africo-American can together work out a common destiny, until universal liberty, as announced by this nation, shall be known throughout the world.

LETTER FROM A
BIRMINGHAM CITY JAIL
MARTIN LUTHER KING JR.

Martin Luther King Jr. wrote this letter in April 1963 from an Ala-
bama jail cell after he was arrested for violating an injunction against
marching in Birmingham. He composed the letter over Easter weekend,
first scribbling on scraps of papers and in the margins of a local newspaper

that had published an open letter by eight white clergymen who attacked King's methods, called civil rights demonstrations "unwise and untimely," and urged blacks to claim their rights peacefully through the courts. King's reply, excerpted here, has become a classic protest document. It argued persuasively for social disruption, helped establish a moral framework for civil rights demonstrations, and explained the weapon of choice: nonviolent resistance.

My dear fellow clergymen,

While confined here in the Birmingham city jail, I came across your recent statement calling our present activities "unwise and untimely." Seldom, if ever, do I pause to answer criticism of my work and ideas. . . . But since I feel that you are men of genuine good will and your criticisms are sincerely set forth, I would like to answer your statement in what I hope will be patient and reasonable terms.

I think I should give the reason for my being in Birmingham, since you have been influenced by the argument of "outsiders coming in." I have the honor of serving as president of the Southern Christian Leadership Conference, an organization operating in every southern state, with headquarters in Atlanta, Georgia. We have sought some eighty-five affiliate organizations all across the South. . . . Several months ago our local affiliate here in Birmingham invited us to be on call to engage in a nonviolent direct-action program if such were deemed necessary. We readily consented and when the hour came we lived up to our promises. So I am here, along with several members of my staff, because we were invited here. I am here because I have basic organizational ties here.

Beyond this, I am in Birmingham because injustice is here. . . .

Moreover, I am cognizant of the interrelatedness of all communities and states. I cannot sit idly by in Atlanta and not be concerned about what happens in Birmingham. Injustice anywhere is a threat to justice everywhere. We are caught in an inescapable network of mutuality, tied in a single garment of destiny. Whatever affects one directly affects all indirectly. Never again can we afford to live with the narrow, provincial "outside agitator" idea. Anyone who lives in the United States can never be considered an outsider anywhere in this country.

You deplore the demonstrations that are presently taking place in Birmingham. But I am sorry that your statement did not express a similar concern for the conditions that brought the demonstrations into being. I am sure that each of you would want to go beyond the superficial social analyst who looks merely at effects, and does not grapple with underlying causes. I would not hesitate to say that it is unfortunate that so-called demonstrations are taking place in Birmingham at this time, but I would say in more emphatic terms that it is even more unfortunate that the white power structure of this city left the Negro community with no other alternative.

In any nonviolent campaign there are four basic steps: (1) collection of the facts to determine whether injustices are alive, (2) negotiation, (3) self-purification, and (4) direct action. We have gone through all of these steps in Birmingham. . . .

Birmingham is probably the most thoroughly segregated city in the United States. Its ugly record of police brutality is known in every section of this country. Its injust treatment of Negroes in the courts is a notorious reality. There have been more unsolved bombings of Negro homes and churches in Birmingham than any city in this nation. These are the hard, brutal and unbelievable facts. On the basis of these conditions Negro leaders sought to negotiate with the city fathers. But the political leaders consistently refused to engage in good faith negotiation.

Then came the opportunity last September to talk with some of the leaders of the economic community. In these negotiating sessions certain promises were made by the merchants—such as the promise to remove the humiliating racial signs from the stores. On the basis of these promises, Rev. Shuttlesworth and the leaders of the Alabama Christian Movement for Human Rights agreed to call a moratorium on any type of demonstrations. As the weeks and months unfolded we realized that we were the victims of a broken promise. The signs remained. Like so many experiences of the past we were confronted with blasted hopes, and the dark shadow of a deep disappointment settled upon us. So we had no alternative except that of preparing for direct action, whereby we would present our very bodies as a means of laying our case before the conscience of the local and national community. We were not unmindful of the difficulties involved. So we decided to go through a process of self-purification. We started having workshops on nonviolence and repeatedly asked ourselves the questions, "Are you able to accept blows without retaliating?" "Are you able to endure the ordeals of jail?" . . .

You may well ask, "Why direct action? Why sit-ins, marches, etc.? Isn't negotiation a better path?" You are exactly right in your call for negotiation. Indeed, this is the purpose of direct action. Nonviolent direct action seeks to create such a crisis and establish such creative tension that a community that has constantly refused to negotiate is forced to confront the issue. It seeks so to dramatize the issue that it can no longer be ignored. I just referred to the creation of tension as a part of the work of the nonviolent resister. This may sound rather shocking. But I must confess that I am not afraid of the word tension. I have earnestly worked and preached against violent tension, but there is a type of constructive nonviolent tension that is necessary for growth. Just as Socrates felt that it was necessary to create a tension in the mind so that individuals could rise from the bondage of myths and half-truths to the unfettered realm of creative analysis and objective appraisal, we must see the need of having nonviolent gadflies to create the kind of tension in society that will help men to rise from the dark depths of prejudice and racism to the majestic heights of understanding and brotherhood. So the purpose of the direct action is to create a situation so crisis-packed that it will inevitably open the door to negotiation. We, therefore, concur with you in your call for negotiation. Too long has our beloved Southland been bogged down in the tragic attempt to live in monologue rather than dialogue. . . .

My friends, I must say to you that we have not made a single gain in civil rights without determined legal and nonviolent pressure. History is the long and tragic story of the fact that privileged groups seldom give up their privileges voluntarily. Individuals may see the moral light and voluntarily give up their unjust posture; but as Reinhold Niebuhr has reminded us, groups are more immoral than individuals.

We know through painful experience that freedom is never voluntarily given by the oppressor; it must be demanded by the oppressed. Frankly, I have never yet engaged in a direct action movement that was "well-timed," according to the timetable of those who have not suffered unduly from the disease of segregation. For years now I have heard the word "Wait!" It rings in the ear of every Negro with a piercing familiarity. This "Wait" has almost always meant "Never." It has been a tranquilizing thalidomide, relieving the emotional stress for a moment, only to give birth to an ill-formed infant of frustration. We must come to see with the distinguished jurist of yesterday that "justice too long delayed is justice denied." We have waited for more than 340 years for our constitutional and God-given rights. The nations of Asia and Africa are moving with jetlike speed toward the goal of political independence, and we still creep at horse and buggy pace toward the gaining of a cup of coffee at a lunch counter. I guess it is easy for those who have never felt the stinging darts of segregation to say, "Wait." But when you have seen vicious mobs lynch your mothers and fathers at will and drown your sisters and brothers at whim; when you have seen hate-filled police-men curse, kick, brutalize and even kill your black brothers and sisters with impunity; when you see the vast majority of your twenty million Negro brothers smothering in an airtight cage of poverty in the midst of an affluent society; when you suddenly find your tongue twisted and your speech stammering as you seek to explain to your six-year-old daughter why she can't go to the public amusement park that has just been advertised on television, and see tears welling up in her little eyes when she is told that Funtown is closed to colored children, and see the depressing clouds of inferiority begin to form in her little mental sky, and see her begin to distort her little personality by unconsciously devel-oping a bitterness toward white people; when you have to concoct an answer for a five-year-old son asking in agonizing pathos: "Daddy, why do white people treat colored people so mean?"; when you take a cross-country drive and find it necessary to sleep night after night in the uncomfortable corners of your automobile because no motel will accept you; when you are humiliated day in and day out by nagging signs reading "white" and "colored"; when your first name becomes "nigger" and your middle name becomes "boy" (however old you are) and your last name becomes "John," and when your wife and mother are never given the respected title "Mrs."; when you are harried by day and haunted by night by the fact that you are a Negro, living constantly at tiptoe stance never quite knowing what to expect next, and plagued with inner fears and resentments; when you are forever fighting a degenerat-ing sense of "nobodiness"; then you will understand why we find it difficult to wait. There comes a time when the cup of endurance runs over, and men are no longer willing to be plunged into an abyss of injustice where they experience the blackness of corroding despair. I hope, sirs, you can understand our legitimate and unavoidable impatience.

You express a great deal of anxiety over our willingness to break laws. This is certainly a legitimate concern. Since we so diligently urge people to obey the Supreme Court's decision of 1954 outlawing segregation in the public schools, it is rather strange and paradoxical to find us consciously breaking laws. One may well ask, "How can you advocate breaking some laws and obeying others?" The answer is found in the fact that there are two types of laws: there are *just* and there are *unjust* laws. I would agree with Saint Augustine that "An unjust law is no law at all."

Now what is the difference between the two? How does one determine when a law is just or unjust? A just law is a man-made code that squares with the moral law or the law of God. An unjust law is a code that is out of harmony with the moral law. To put it in the terms of Saint Thomas Aquinas, an unjust law is a human law that is not rooted in eternal and natural law. Any law that uplifts human personality is just. Any law that degrades human personality is unjust. All segregation statutes are unjust because segregation distorts the soul and damages the personality. It gives the segregator a false sense of superiority, and the segregated a false sense of inferiority. To use the words of Martin Buber, the great Jewish philosopher, segregation substitutes an "I-it" relationship for the "I-thou" relationship, and ends up relegating persons to the status of things. So segregation is not only politically, economically and sociologically unsound, but it is morally wrong and sinful. Paul Tillich has said that sin is separation. Isn't segregation an existential expression of man's tragic separation, an expression of his awful estrangement, his terrible sinfulness? So I can urge men to disobey segregation ordinances because they are morally wrong.

Let us turn to a more concrete example of just and unjust laws. An unjust law is a code that a majority inflicts on a minority that is not binding on itself. This is difference made legal. On the other hand a just law is a code that a majority compels a minority to follow that it is willing to follow itself. This is sameness made legal.

Let me give another explanation. An unjust law is a code inflicted upon a minority which that minority had no part in enacting or creating because they did not have the unhampered right to vote. Who can say that the legislature of Alabama which set up the segregation laws was democratically elected? Throughout the state of Alabama all types of conniving methods are used to prevent Negroes from becoming registered voters and there are some counties without a single Negro registered to vote despite the fact that the Negro constitutes a majority of the population. Can any law set up in such a state be considered democratically structured?

These are just a few examples of unjust and just laws. There are some instances when a law is just on its face and unjust on its application. For instance, I was arrested Friday on a charge of parading without a permit. Now there is nothing wrong with an ordinance which requires a permit for a parade, but when the ordinance is used to preserve segregation and to deny citizens the First Amendment privilege of peaceful assembly and peaceful protest, then it becomes unjust.

I hope you can see the distinction I am trying to point out. In no sense do I advocate evading or defying the law as the rabid segregationist would do. This would lead to anarchy. One who breaks an unjust law must do it *openly*, *lovingly* (not hatefully as the white mothers did in New Orleans when they were seen on television screaming, "nigger, nigger, nigger"), and with a willingness to accept the penalty. I submit that an individual who breaks a law that conscience tells him is unjust, and willingly accepts the penalty by staying in jail to arouse the conscience of the community over its injustice, is in reality expressing the very highest respect for law.

Of course, there is nothing new about this kind of civil disobedience. It was seen sublimely in the refusal of Shadrach, Meshach and Abednego to obey the laws of Nebuchadnezzer because a higher moral law was involved. It was practiced superbly by the early Christians who were willing to face hungry lions and the excruciating pain of chopping blocks, before submitting to certain unjust laws of the Roman Empire. To a degree academic freedom is a reality today because Socrates practiced civil disobedience.

We can never forget that everything Hitler did in Germany was "legal" and everything the Hungarian freedom fighters did in Hungary was "illegal." It was "illegal" to aid and comfort a Jew in Hitler's Germany. But I am sure that if I had lived in Germany during that time

I would have aided and comforted my Jewish brothers even though it was illegal. If I lived in a Communist country today where certain principles dear to the Christian faith are suppressed, I believe I would openly advocate disobeying these anti-religious laws. I must make two honest confessions to you, my Christian and Jewish brothers. First I must confess that over the last few years I have been gravely disappointed with the white moderate. I have almost reached the regrettable conclusion that the Negro's great stumbling block in the stride toward freedom is not the White Citizen's Counciler or the Ku Klux Klanner, but the white moderate who is more devoted to "order" than to justice; who prefers a negative peace which is the absence of tension to a positive peace which is the presence of justice; who constantly says, "I agree with you in the goal you seek, but I can't agree with your methods of direct action"; who paternalistically feels that he can set the timetable for another man's freedom; who lives by the myth of time and who constantly advises the Negro to wait until a "more convenient season." Shallow understanding from people of good will is more frustrating than absolute misunderstanding from people of ill will. Lukewarm acceptance is much more bewildering than outright rejection.

I had hoped that the white moderate would understand that law and order exist for the purpose of establishing justice, and that when they fail to do this they become dangerously structured dams that block the flow of social progress. I had hoped that the white moderate would understand that the present tension of the South is merely a necessary phase of the transition from an obnoxious negative peace, where the Negro passively accepted his unjust plight, to a substance-filled positive peace, where all men will respect the dignity and worth of human personality. Actually, we who engage in nonviolent direct action are not the creators of tension. We merely bring to the surface the hidden tension that is already alive. We bring it out in the open where it can be seen and dealt with. Like a boil that can never be cured as long as it is covered up but must be opened with all its pus-flowing ugliness to the natural medicines of air and light, injustice must likewise be exposed, with all of the tension its exposing creates, to the light of human conscience and the air of national opinion before it can be cured.

In your statement you asserted that our actions, even though peaceful, must be condemned because they precipitate violence. But can this assertion be logically made? Isn't this like condemning the robbed man because his possession of money precipitated the evil act of robbery? Isn't this like condemning Socrates because his unswerving commitment to truth and his philosophical delvings precipitated the misguided popular mind to make him drink the hemlock? Isn't this like condemning Jesus because His unique God-consciousness and never-ceasing devotion to his will precipitated the evil act of crucifixion? We must come to see, as federal courts have consistently affirmed, that it is immoral to urge an individual to withdraw his efforts to gain his basic constitutional rights because the quest precipitates violence. Society must protect the robbed and punish the robber.

I had also hoped that the white moderate would reject the myth of time. I received a letter this morning from a white brother in Texas which said: "All Christians know that the colored people will receive equal rights eventually, but it is possible that you are in too great of a religious hurry. It has taken Christianity almost two thousand years to accomplish what it has. The teachings of Christ take time to come to earth." All that is said here grows out of a tragic misconception of time. It is the strangely irrational notion that there is something in the very flow of time that will inevitably cure all ills. Actually time is neutral. It can be used either destructively or constructively. I am coming to feel that the people of ill will have used time much more effectively than the people of good will. We will have to repent in this generation not merely for the vitriolic words and actions of the bad people, but for the appalling silence of the good people. We must come to see that human progress never rolls in on wheels of inevitability. It comes through the tireless efforts and persistent work of men willing to be co-workers with God, and within this hard work time itself becomes an ally of the forces of social stagnation. We must use time creatively, and forever realize that the time is always ripe to do right. Now is the time to make real the promise of democracy, and transform our pending national elegy into a creative psalm of brotherhood. Now is the time to lift our national policy from the quicksand of racial injustice to the solid rock of human dignity.

You spoke of our activity in Birmingham as extreme. At first I was rather disappointed that fellow clergymen would see my nonviolent efforts as those of an extremist. I started thinking about the fact that I stand in the middle of two opposing forces in the Negro community. One is a force of complacency made up of Negroes who, as a result of long years of oppression, have been so completely drained of self-respect and a sense of "somebodiness" that they have adjusted to segregation, and of a few Negroes in the middle class who, because of a degree of academic and economic security, and because at points they profit by segregation, have unconsciously become insensitive to the problems of the masses. The other force is one of bitterness and hatred, and comes perilously close to advocating violence. . . . I have tried to stand between these two forces, saying that we need not follow the "do-nothing-ism" of the complacent or the hatred and despair of the black nationalist. There is the more excellent way of love and nonviolent protest. I'm grateful to God that, through the Negro church, the dimension of nonviolence entered our struggle. If this philosophy had not emerged, I am convinced that by now many streets of the South would be flowing with floods of blood. And I am further convinced that if our white brothers dismiss as "rabble-rousers" and "outside agitators" those of us who are working through the channels of nonviolent direct action and refuse to support our nonviolent efforts, millions of Negroes, out of frustration and despair, will seek solace and security in black nationalist ideologies, a development that will lead inevitably to a frightening racial nightmare.

Oppressed people cannot remain oppressed forever. The urge for freedom will eventually come. This is what happened to the American Negro. Something within has reminded him of his birthright of freedom; something without has reminded him that he can gain it. Consciously and unconsciously, he has been swept in by what the Germans call the *Zeitgeist*, and with his black brothers of Africa, and his brown and yellow brothers of Asia, South America and the Caribbean, he is moving with a sense of cosmic urgency toward the promised land of racial justice. Recognizing this vital urge that has engulfed the Negro community has many pent-up resentments and latent frustrations. He has to get them out. So let him march sometime; let him have his prayer pilgrimages to the city hall; understand why he must have sit-ins and freedom rides. If his repressed emotions do not come out in these nonviolent ways, they will come out in ominous expressions of violence. This is not a threat; it is a fact of history. So I have not said to my people, "Get rid of your discontent." But I have tried to say that this normal and healthy discontent can be channelized through the creative outlet of nonviolent direct action. Now this approach is being dismissed as extremist. I must admit that I was initially disappointed to be so categorized.

But as I continued to think about the matter I gradually gained a bit of satisfaction from being considered an extremist. Was not Jesus an extremist in love—"Love your enemies, bless them that curse you, pray for them that despitefully sue you." Was not Amos an extremist for justice—"Let justice roll down like waters and righteousness like a mighty stream." Was not Paul an extremist for the gospel of Jesus Christ—"I bear in my body the marks of the Lord Jesus." Was not Martin Luther an extremist—"Here I stand; I can do none other so help me God." Was not John Bunyan an extremist—"I will stay in jail to the end of my days before I make a butchery of my conscience." Was not Abraham Lincoln an extremist—"This nation cannot survive half slave and half free." Was not Thomas Jefferson an extremist—"We hold these truths to be self-evident, that all men are created equal." So the question is not whether we will be extremist but what kind of extremist will we be? Will we be extremists for hate or will we be extremists for love? Will we be extremists for the preservation of injustice—or will we be extremists for the cause of justice? In that dramatic scene on Calvary's hill, three men were crucified. We must not forget that all three were crucified for the same crime—the crime of extremism. Two were extremists for immorality, and thusly fell below their environment. The other, Jesus Christ, was an extremist for love, truth and goodness, and thereby rose above his environment. So, after all, maybe the South, the nation and the world are in dire need of creative extremists.

I had hoped that the white moderate would see this. Maybe I was too optimistic. Maybe I expected too much. I guess I should have realized that few members of a race that has oppressed another race can understand or appreciate the deep groans and passionate yearnings of those that have been oppressed and still fewer have the vision to see that injustice must be rooted out by strong, persistent and determined action. I am thankful, however, that some of our white brothers have grasped the meaning of this social revolution and committed themselves to it. They are still too small in quantity, but they are big in quality. . . . They have languished in filthy roach-infested jails, suffering the abuse and brutality of angry policemen who see them as "dirty nigger-lovers." They, unlike so many of their moderate brothers and sisters, have recognized the urgency of the moment and sensed the need for powerful "action" antidotes to combat the disease of segregation. . . .

I had the strange feeling when I was suddenly catapulted into the leadership of the bus protest in Montgomery several years ago that we would have the support of the white church. I felt that the white ministers, priests and rabbis of the South would be some of our strongest allies. Instead, some have been outright opponents, refusing to understand the freedom movement and misrepresenting its leaders; all too many others have been more cautious than courageous and have remained silent behind the anesthetizing security of the stained-glass windows.

In spite of my shattered dreams of the past, I came to Birmingham with the hope that the white religious leadership of this community would see the justice of our cause, and with deep moral concern, serve as the channel through which our just grievances would get to the power structure. I had hoped that each of you would understand. But again I have been disappointed. I have heard numerous religious leaders of the South call upon their worshippers to comply with a desegregation decision because it is the *law,* but I have longed to hear white ministers say, "Follow this decree because integration is morally *right* and the Negro is your brother." In the midst of blatant injustices inflicted upon the Negro, I have watched white churches stand on the sideline and merely mouth pious irrelevancies and sanctimonious trivialities. In the midst of a mighty struggle to rid our nation of racial and economic injustice, I have heard so many ministers say, "Those are social issues with which the gospel has no real concern," and I have watched so many churches commit themselves to a completely other-worldly religion which made a strange distinction between body and soul, the sacred and the secular.

So here we are moving toward the exit of the twentieth century with a religious community largely adjusted to the status quo, standing as a tail light behind other community agencies rather than a headlight leading men to higher levels of justice.

I have traveled the length and breadth of Alabama, Mississippi and all the other Southern states. On sweltering summer days and crisp autumn mornings I have looked at her beautiful churches with their lofty spires pointing heavenward. I have beheld the impressive outlay of her massive religious education buildings. Over and over again I have found myself asking: "What kind of people worship here? Who is their God? Where were their voices when the lips of Governor Barnett dripped with words of interposition and nullification? Where were they when Governor Wallace gave the clarion call for defiance and hatred? Where were their voices of support when tired, bruised and weary Negro men and women decided to rise from the dark dungeons of complacency to the bright hills of creative protest?"

Yes, these questions are still in my mind. In deep disappointment, I have wept over the laxity of the church. But be assured that my tears have been tears of love. There can be no deep disappointment where there is not deep love. Yes, I love the church. I love her sacred walls. How could I do otherwise? I am in the rather unique position of being the son, the grandson and the great-grandson of preachers. Yes, I see the church as the body of Christ. But, oh! How we have blemished and scarred that body through social neglect and fear of being nonconformists.

There was a time when the church was very powerful. It was during that period when the early Christians rejoiced when they were deemed worthy to suffer for what they believed. In those days the church was not merely a thermometer that recorded the ideas and principles of popular opinion; it was a thermostat that transformed the mores of society. Wherever the early Christians entered a town the power structure got disturbed and immediately sought to convict them for being "disturbers of the peace" and "outside agitators." But they went on with the conviction that they were a "colony of heaven," and had to obey God rather than man. They were small in number but big in commitment. They were too God-intoxicated to be "astronomically intimidated." They brought an end to such ancient evils as infanticide and gladiatorial contest.

Things are different now. The contemporary church is often a weak, ineffectual voice with an uncertain sound. It is so often the arch-supporter of the status quo. Far from being disturbed by the presence of the church, the power structure of the average community is consoled by the church's silent and often vocal sanction of things as they are.

But the judgment of God is upon the church as never before. If the church of today does not recapture the sacrificial spirit of the early church, it will lose its authentic ring, forfeit the loyalty of millions, and be dismissed as an irrelevant social club with no meaning for the twentieth century. I am meeting young people every day whose disappointment with the church has risen to outright disgust.

Maybe again I have been too optimistic. Is organized religion too inextricably bound to the status quo to save our nation and the world? Maybe I must turn my faith to the inner spiritual church, the church within the church, as the true *ecclesia* and the hope of the world. But again I am thankful to God that some noble souls from the ranks of organized religion have broken loose from the paralyzing chains of conformity and joined us as active partners in the struggle for freedom. They have left their secure congregations and walked the streets of Albany, Georgia, with us. They have gone through the highways of the South on tortuous rides for freedom. Yes, they have gone to jail with us. Some have been kicked out of their churches, and lost support of their bishops and fellow ministers. But they have gone with the faith that right defeated is stronger than evil triumphant. These men have been the leaven in the lump of the race. Their witness has been the spiritual salt that has preserved the true meaning of the gospel in these troubled times. They have carved a tunnel of hope through the dark mountain of disappointment.

I hope the church as a whole will meet the challenge of this decisive hour. But even if the church does not come to the aid of justice, I have no despair about the future. I have no fear about the outcome of our struggle in Birmingham, even if our motives are presently misunderstood. We will reach the goal of freedom in Birmingham and all over the nation, because the goal of America is freedom. Abused and scorned though we may be, our destiny is tied up with the destiny of America. Before the Pilgrims landed at Plymouth we were here. Before the pen of Jefferson etched across the pages of history the majestic words of the Declaration of Independence, we were here. For more than two centuries our foreparents labored in this country without wages; they made cotton king; and they built the homes of their masters in the midst of brutal injustice and shameful humiliation—and yet out of a bottomless vitality they continued to thrive and develop. If the inexpressible cruelties of slavery could not stop us, the opposition we now face will surely fail. We will win our freedom because the sacred heritage of our nation and the eternal will of God are embodied in our echoing demands. . . .

One day the South will recognize its real heroes. They will be the James Merediths, courageously and with a majestic sense of purpose facing jeering and hostile mobs and the agonizing loneliness that characterizes the life of the pioneer. They will be old, oppressed, battered Negro women, symbolized in a seventy-two-year-old woman of Montgomery, Alabama, who rose up with a sense of dignity and with her people decided not to ride the segregated buses, and responded to one who inquired about her tiredness with ungrammatical profundity: "My feet is tired, but my soul is rested." They will be the young high school and college students, young ministers of the gospel and a host of their elders courageously and nonviolently sitting-in at lunch counters and willingly going to jail for conscience's sake. One day the South will know that when these disinherited children of God sat down at lunch counters they were in reality standing up for the best in the American dream and the most sacred values in our Judeo-Christian heritage, and thusly, carrying our whole nation back to those great wells of democracy which were dug deep by the Founding Fathers in the formulation of the Constitution and the Declaration of Independence. . . .

I hope this letter finds you strong in the faith. I also hope that circumstances will soon make it possible for me to meet each of you, not as an integrationist or a civil rights leader, but as a fellow clergyman and a Christian brother. Let us all hope that the dark clouds of racial prejudice will soon pass away and the deep fog of misunderstanding will be lifted from our feardrenched communities and in some not too distant tomorrow the radiant stars of love and brotherhood will shine over our great nation with all of their scintillating beauty.

Yours for the cause of Peace and Brotherhood,

Martin Luther King Jr.

April 16, 1963

PAUL ROBESON: THE GIANT WHO STOOD UP FOR HIS PEOPLE

SCOTT EHRLICH

The son of a runaway slave, Paul Robeson (1898–1976) was a gifted athlete, scholar, linguist (he spoke some twenty languages), and world-renowned actor and singer. A college All-American and later a professional football player, Robeson graduated from law school and then turned to acting and singing. He starred in eleven films—including the 1933 classic The Emperor Jones—*and in 1943 made theater history, becoming the first black actor to play Othello on Broadway. The play ran 296 performances, setting a Broadway record for a Shakespearean production.*

The immensely talented Robeson toured the world's great concert halls. Singing spirituals such as "Ol' Man River," he overwhelmed audiences with his luscious bass–baritone voice, winning new fans for African American music wherever he sang.

But the U.S. government nearly destroyed Robeson's career because of his controversial political views, which he openly expressed. His admiration for Soviet society gained him many enemies during the McCarthy era. He was harassed, blacklisted, and confined to "internal exile."

Still, Robeson felt a moral obligation to defend the rights of black and oppressed people. One of his most memorable performances took place before a congressional committee. The following story shows his unwavering commitment "to stand up and fight for the rights of his people."

On the morning of June 12, 1956, a panel of grim-faced government officials in Washington, D.C., assembled to review information about a hearing that was about to begin. Members of the House Un-American Activities Committee (HUAC), the officials were part of an investigative body that had been established by Congress in 1939 to look into the affairs of American citizens who were suspected by the government of acting against the interests of their country. Among those called before the committee to testify about their political beliefs were many prominent citizens who had done nothing wrong except to disagree with their government's policies. Some of these people had been sent to prison simply for refusing to disclose their political beliefs before the committee.

On this spring day, the HUAC panel was going to be questioning Paul Robeson, the renowned singer and actor. During his long career on the stages of Europe and the United States, the 58-year-old Robeson had become one of the world's best-known and most beloved black Americans—especially abroad. Yet he had not been content to be only an entertainer. For more than 20 years, he had been using his unforgettable bass voice to speak out about the needs and aspirations of the poor and oppressed people in the United States and around the world.

However, Robeson's ardent support for human rights causes had gained him many enemies. His statements that racism was still rampant within the United States were viewed by some Americans as being unpatriotic. His concerts in support of international peace, workers' rights, and racial tolerance had been picketed by his opponents, and violence had broken out at some of the events. In 1950, the State Department had revoked his passport, and he had since been confined within the United States and subjected to many forms of harassment. He had been blacklisted in the entertainment industry. (His name had been placed on a list of people who should not be hired because of their unpopular political beliefs.) Concert halls, stages, and recording and film studios were closed to him. Although he had continued to speak and sing wherever he could, by the time of his meeting with the HUAC, Robeson's spectacular voice had been virtually silenced because he was believed to be dangerous.

The removal of Robeson from the public stage was a tragedy for the United States. The country needed courageous people who were willing to speak out for international understanding and to propose solutions to America's racial problems. However, since the establishment of the HUAC, the United States had been caught up in a public hunt for traitors, subversives, spies, and members of left-wing organizations such as the Communist party.

During the late 1940s and early 1950s, Senator Joseph McCarthy had been the leader of the crusade to rid the government and American society of the so-called Red Menace, the alleged plot by communist agents to destroy the country. By the time Robeson was called before the HUAC, McCarthy was no longer in power. Yet the campaign against suspected communist sympathizers such as Robeson continued.

It seemed that many Americans wanted to hear Robeson answer only one question: Was he a member of the Communist party? Again and again, he answered the question: No, he was not a party member.

Robeson eventually decided that he would no longer answer this question. By giving any response, he felt that he would be violating the principle of free speech and admitting that holding communist views was illegal. Although he had never belonged to the American Communist party, he sympathized with the communist system in which there is public ownership of all goods. He had stood up for the rights of workers and for labor causes that were unpopular with supporters of America's capitalist system. Robeson and many of his friends were being persecuted for their political beliefs, and he felt that this persecution was clearly illegal according to the U.S. Constitution.

Robeson was a victim of the tensions arising from the global power struggle between the United States and the Soviet Union. These two nations had been allies during World War II, joining forces with other countries to crush Nazi Germany in 1945. Robeson was greatly admired in the Soviet Union and gave concerts there in the 1930s. During World War II, he helped to marshal American aid for the hard-pressed Soviet troops that were trying to turn back the Nazi invasion of the Soviet Union.

After the war ended, the Americans and the Soviets unleashed propaganda attacks against each other in their fight to control strategic global areas. The United States was determined to foster the growth of capitalist economies in other nations; the Soviets were equally committed to foster communist state-run economies. The two countries also began to stockpile powerful arsenals of nuclear weapons, and the terrifying possibility of total destruction of the human race added greatly to the fear and distrust felt between the Americans and the Soviets. Robeson felt that people should speak out against this increase in tension, yet his own voice was not allowed to be heard.

On the day of his hearing before the HUAC, Robeson was determined that his voice would be heard again. Few people had been strong enough to stand up for themselves in the face of the intense public pressure placed upon them by the HUAC and the anticommunist crusaders. But Robeson, who stood 6 feet 3 inches tall and weighed more than 200 pounds, was more than able to take care of himself. He had recently fought a hard battle against the government to regain his legal rights to travel abroad.

Robeson had been told by government officials and spokesmen for the entertainment industry that the blacklisting against him would end if he stopped speaking out on controversial subjects. Yet he had not backed down. As he sat before the HUAC, he knew that his ability to make a living in his chosen profession in the United States might well depend on what happened at the hearing. The chairman of the HUAC was Representative Francis Walter, who had cosponsored the McCarran-Walter Act that allowed the attorney general of the United States to deport from the country any immigrants who were suspected of being sympathetic to communism. Walter and his associates on the committee were determined to show that Robeson was deeply involved in a dangerous network of communist organizers.

The meeting opened with a speech by Walter describing how Americans involved in the "communist conspiracy" against their own country were using their passports to travel abroad and, by some unspecified means, assist the forces seeking to undermine the U.S. government. Although Robeson's lawyer asked that his client not be questioned about his passport troubles because his case was being reviewed in federal court and could be jeopardized by the hearing's discussions, the request was denied. The committee asked Robeson why he would not agree to the State Department's demand that he sign a statement that he was not a communist—an action that would have allowed him to regain his passport. Declaring that such a requirement was unconstitutional, Robeson promised that the Supreme Court would eventually decide that the travel restrictions imposed on him were illegal.

The HUAC then asked the question: Was Robeson a member of the Communist party? Robeson bridled, demanding to know why the communists had less right than the Democrats or Republicans to form a political party. He also asked if his questioner wanted to follow him into the voting booth on election day. Robeson was instructed to give a direct answer to the question. He then invoked the fifth amendment, the constitutional law that gives all citizens appearing in judicial proceedings the right to refuse to answer a question if the answer might incriminate them.

As the hearing proceeded, Robeson responded to the committee's questions in different ways. Asked again whether he was a communist, Robeson praised the bravery of the Russian armies in the recent war against the Nazis. Asked if he was listed under a pseudonym on the membership rolls of the Communist party, Robeson laughed and said the question was ludicrous. Asked if he knew various people whom the committee suspected of being communists, he invoked the fifth amendment after the mention of each name.

Robeson's spirited defense blunted the efforts to trap him. A lawyer himself, he questioned the committee as to whether their hearings were legal. He then attacked the McCarran-Walter Act, saying that it was keeping "all kinds of decent people" out of the country. Walter told Robeson that the law would exclude "only your kind" from America. Robeson responded that by saying "your kind," the congressman meant "black people."

The confrontational hearing continued. Robeson asked to be allowed to read a prepared statement that contained a strong attack on the HUAC, an eloquent appeal for the end to the oppression of blacks and workers, and a list of organizations from around the world that had invited him to speak. When he was told that he could read the statement only if he named the alleged communists who had helped him write it, Robeson exploded. He said that he had agreed to appear at the hearing only because he wanted to discuss the injustices faced by black Americans and oppressed workers.

"I am being tried for fighting for the rights of my people," Robeson said, claiming that nowhere in the United States were blacks treated as full citizens. "That is why I am here," he continued. "You want to shut up every Negro who has the courage to stand up and fight for the rights of his people, for the rights of workers."

Unmoved by Robeson's remarks, the committee members cited some black Americans who had spoken out against him. He countered by listing awards that he had received from numerous respected black organizations. When he was questioned about his visits to the Soviet Union and why, if he liked that country so much, he had not stayed there, Robeson responded, "Because my father was a slave, and my people died to build this country, and I am going to stay here and have a part of it, just like you."

After several more angry exchanges, during which Robeson's allegiance to the United States was attacked, he told the committee members, "You are the nonpatriots, and you are the un-Americans and you ought to be ashamed of yourselves." Finally, upset by the way Robeson was badgering the committee, Walter declared that the meeting was adjourned. Outside the building, Robeson discussed the hearing with members of the press.

By any measure, Robeson's appearance in front of the HUAC was extraordinary—it was one of the most intelligent and courageous performances of his life. The committee had not been able to prove that Robeson was a communist or that he had participated in any conspiracies against the U.S. government. Instead, the hearing had shown that Robeson was a man who would not desert his cause, no matter how intense the pressure. He was still blacklisted and his right to travel abroad had not yet been restored, but for at least one day his voice had been heard loudly and clearly across America.

❧

Service is the rent you pay for room on this earth.
— *Shirley Chisholm*

❧

TWENTY-FIVE LESSONS FOR LIFE
MARIAN WRIGHT EDELMAN

Marian Wright Edelman (b. 1939) became the first black woman to pass the Mississippi state bar examination in 1964. She practiced civil rights law, and in 1973 founded the Children's Defense Fund, an advocacy organization for children at risk. A presidential advisor and a leading voice for the nation's children, Edelman has three grown sons. Many of her lessons for living life read like codes of responsibility.

LESSON 1: *There is no free lunch. Don't feel entitled to anything you don't sweat and struggle for.* Every African American, Latino, Asian American, and Native American youth needs to remember that he or she never can take anything for granted in America—especially now as racial intoler-ance resurges all over our land. Although it may be wrapped up in new euphemisms and better etiquette, as Frederick Douglass warned, it's the same old snake.

Young white people who have been raised to feel entitled to leader-ship by accident of birth need to be reminded that the world they face is already two-thirds nonwhite and poor and that our nation is every day becoming a mosaic of greater diversity.

Each American adult and child must struggle to achieve and not think for a moment that America has got it made. Frederick Douglass re-minded all of us that "men may not get all they pay for in this world, but they must certainly pay for all they get."

While a college degree today may get you in the door, it will not get you to the top of the career ladder or keep you there. You have got to work your way up—hard and continuously. So we need to teach our children—by example—not to be lazy, to do their homework, to pay attention to detail, to take care and pride in work, to be reliable, and not to wobble and jerk through life. Each of us must take the initiative to create our opportunities, not waiting around for favors. We must not assume a door is closed but must push on it. We must not assume if it was closed yesterday that it's closed today.

LESSON 2: *Set goals and work quietly and systematically toward them.* We must all try to resist quick-fix, simplistic answers and easy gains, which often disappear just as quickly as they come. Don't feel compelled to talk if you don't have anything to say that matters. It's all right to feel important if it is not at the expense of doing important deeds. But so many of us talk big and act small.

LESSON 3: *Assign yourself.* My Daddy used to ask us whether the teacher had given us any homework. If we said no, he'd say, "Well, assign yourself." Don't wait around for your boss or your co-worker or spouse to direct you to do what you are able to figure out and do for yourself.

If you see a need, don't ask, "Why doesn't somebody do something?" Ask, "Why don't I do something?" Don't wait around to be told what to do. Hard work, initiative, and persistence are still the nonmagic carpets to success. Let's each commit to help teach the rest of the country how to achieve again by our example.

LESSON 4: *Never work just for money or for power. They won't save your soul or build a decent family or help you sleep at night.* Don't condone or tolerate moral corruption whether it's found in high or low places, whatever its color. It is not okay to push or use drugs even if every person in America is doing it. It is not okay to cheat or lie even if countless corporate or public officials and everybody you know do. Be honest. And demand that those who represent you be honest. Don't confuse legality with morality. Dr. King noted that everything Hitler did in Nazi Germany was legal. Don't give anyone the proxy for your conscience. And don't confuse legality with fairness.

LESSON 5: *Don't be afraid of taking risks or of being criticized.* An anonymous sage said, "If you don't want to be criticized don't say anything, do anything, or be anything." Don't be afraid of failing. It's the way you learn to do things right. It doesn't matter how many times you fall down. What matters is how many times you get up.

LESSON 6: *Take parenting and family life seriously and insist that those you work for and who represent you do.* Our leaders mouth family values they do not practice. As a result, our children lag behind the children of other nations on key child indicators like infant mortality, poverty, and family supports. Seventy nations provide medical care and financial assistance to all pregnant women; we aren't one of them. Seventeen industrialized nations have paid maternity leave programs; we are not one of them.

Men should not father children until they are able and willing to be responsible for the consequences of childbearing. And all men—young and old, rich, middle and lower income, and poor—should be held accountable for supporting their children.

LESSON 7: *Remember that your wife is not your mother or your maid, but your partner and friend.* Learn and practice the sharing of family responsibilities. Let your wife sleep late sometimes just as you want to. If you are lucky enough to be deaf to calling or crying or coughing children at

3:00 A.M., then recognize your wife's added nightly burden and likely exhaustion by taking on some of her responsibilities the next day—without having to be asked or even asking her if she'd like you to. Just do it! Cook breakfast or dinner. Do something thoughtful and unexpected. Rotate and share household chores: cooking, dishes, laundry, garbage. There really is nothing that decrees that only women are capable of cleaning toilets, washing clothes, cleaning up children's vomit, remembering flowers, staying at home from work or having the responsibility for asking you to stay home, any more than it is a given that only you are responsible for meeting all family expenses or for mowing the lawn or cleaning out the garage. What no wife and mother without full-time household help and with a full-time job outside or inside the home wants is to have you assume that she—not you—is responsible for your mess. Clean up your own mess.

LESSON 8: *Forming families is serious business.* It requires a measure of thoughtful planning, economic stability, and commitment, particularly with the downward spiral of wages and job opportunities for young families of all races and with the rising costs of good child care and housing, which often require more than one employed parent.

LESSON 9: *Be honest.* Struggle to live what you say and preach. Call things by their right names. Be moral examples for your children. If you as parents cut corners, your children will too. If you lie, they will too. If you spend all your money on yourselves and tithe no portion of it for charities, colleges, churches, synagogues, and civic causes, your children won't either. And if parents snicker at racial and gender jokes, another generation will pass on the poison adults still have not had the courage to snuff out.

LESSON 10: *Remember and help America remember that the fellowship of human beings is more important than the fellowship of race and class and gender in a democratic society.* Be decent and fair and insist that others be so in your presence. Don't tell, laugh at, or in any way acquiesce to racial, ethnic, religious, or gender jokes or to any practices intended to demean rather than enhance another human being. Walk away from them. Stare them down. Make them unacceptable in your homes, religious congregations, and clubs. Through daily moral consciousness counter the proliferating voices of racial and ethnic and religious division that are gaining respectability over the land, including on college campuses.

LESSON 11: *Sell the shadow for the substance.* Don't confuse style with substance; don't confuse political charm or rhetoric with decency or sound policy. Nobody ever asks what kind of car Ralph Bunche or Reinhold Niebuhr drove or who designed Martin Luther King Jr.'s, or Dorothy Day's clothes or who built Mary McLeod Bethune's or Lloyd Garrison's house. Don't confuse style with meaning. Get your insides in order and your direction clear first and then worry about your clothes and your wheels. You may need them less.

LESSON 12: *Never give up.* Never think life is not worth living. I don't care how hard it gets. An old proverb reminds: "When you get to your wit's end, remember that God lives there."

LESSON 13: *Be confident that you can make a difference.* Don't get overwhelmed. Sometimes when I get frantic about all I have to do and spin my wheels, I try to recall Carlyle's advice: "Our main business is not to see what lies dimly at a distance, but to do what lies clearly at hand." Try to take each day and each task as they come, breaking them down into manageable pieces for action while struggling to see the whole. And don't think you have to "win" immediately or even at all to make a difference.

And do not think that you have to make big waves in order to contribute. My role model, Sojourner Truth, slave woman, could neither read nor write but could not stand slavery and second-class treatment of women. One day during an anti-slavery speech she was heckled by an old man. "Old woman, do you think that your talk about slavery does any good? Why I don't care any more for your talk than I do for the bite of a flea." "Perhaps not, but the Lord willing, I'll keep you scratching," she replied.

LESSON 14: *Don't ever stop learning and improving your mind* or you're going to get left behind. The world is changing like a kaleidoscope right before our eyes. College pays and is a fine investment. It doubles your chance of getting a job over a high school graduate. But don't think you can park there or relegate your mind's and soul's growth to what you have learned or will learn at school. Read. Not just what you have to read for class or work, but to learn from the wisdom and joys and mistakes of others. No time is ever wasted if you have a book along as a companion.

LESSON 15: *Don't be afraid of hard work or of teaching your children to work.* Work is dignity and caring and the foundation for a life with meaning. For all her great accomplishments, Mary McLeod Bethune never forgot the importance of practical work. When asked by a train conductor, "Auntie, do you know how to cook good biscuits?" she responded, "Sir, I am an advisor to presidents, the founder of an accredited four-year college, a nationally known leader of women, and founder of the National Council of Negro Women. And yes, I also cook good biscuits."

LESSON 16: *"Slow Down and Live"* is an African song I sing inside my head when I begin flitting around like a hen with her head wrung off: "Brother slow down and live, brother slow down and live, brother slow down and live, you've got a long way to go. Brothers love one another, brothers love one another, brothers love one another, you've got a long way to go."

LESSON 17: *Choose your friends carefully.* Stay out of the fast lane, and ignore the crowd. You were born God's original. Try not to become someone's copy. Dr. Benjamin Mays used to tell Morehouse and Spelman College students not to give into peer pressure, saying, "Nobody is wise enough, nobody is good enough, and nobody cares enough for you to turn over to them your future and your destiny." You are the person you must compete with and be accountable for.

LESSON 18: *Be a can-do, will-try person.* Focus on what you have and not what you don't have, what you can do rather than what you cannot do. America is being paralyzed by can't-doers with puny vision and punier will.

. . .

LESSON 19: *Try to live in the present;* don't carry around unnecessary burdens from a yesterday you will not live again or a tomorrow that is not guaranteed.

LESSON 20: *Use your political and economic power for the community and others less fortunate.* Vote and hold those you vote for accountable. We get the political leaders we deserve.

America is in urgent need of a band of moral guerrillas who simply decide to do what appears to be right heedless of the immediate consequences. As one anonymous leader said (better than I can): "The world needs more men [and women] who do not have a price at which they can be bought; who do not borrow from integrity to pay for expediency; whose handshake is an ironclad contract; who are not afraid of risk; who are honest in small matters as they are in large ones; whose ambitions are big enough to include others; who know how to win with grace and lose with dignity; who do not believe that shrewdness and cunning and ruthlessness are the three keys to success; who still have friends they made twenty years ago; who are not afraid to go against the grain of popular opinion and do not believe in 'consensus'; who are occasionally wrong and always willing to admit it. In short, the world needs leaders."

LESSON 21: *Listen for "the sound of the genuine" within yourself and others.* Meditate and learn to be alone without being lonely. "There is," Howard Thurman told Spelman College students in 1981, "something in every one of you that waits and listens for the sound of the genuine in yourself." It is "the only true guide you'll ever have. And if you cannot hear it, you will all of your life spend your days on the ends of strings that somebody else pulls."

It is as necessary as it is hard to practice a regular discipline of silence, solitude, or prayer. I have not fully succeeded but I cannot survive long without my moments. A few minutes every hour, a half hour or hour every day, a day a month, a week a year—in dedicated silence—is a goal to pursue.

LESSON 22: *You are in charge of your own attitude*—whatever others do or circumstances you face. The only person you can control is yourself.

It is not what is done to us that matters, but how we take what is done to us, Archbishop Tutu reminds us. Booker T. Washington did not know his father's name, but it did not keep him from becoming a great man.

You didn't have a choice about the parents you inherited, but you do have a choice about the kind of parent you will be. You may not be able to clean up your neighborhood or street but you can clean up your own house or apartment or room.

LESSON 23: *Remember your roots, your history, and the forebears' shoulders on which you stand.* Young people who do not know where they come from and the struggle it took to get them where they are now will not know where they are going or what to do for anyone besides themselves if and when they finally get somewhere. All Black children need to feel the rightful pride of a great people that produced Harriet Tubman and Sojourner Truth and Frederick Douglass from slavery, and Benjamin Mays and Martin Luther King and Mrs. Fannie Lou Hamer from segregation—people second to none in helping transform America from a theoretical to a more living democracy.

I learned the Negro National anthem, "Lift Every Voice and Sing," at the same time I learned "The Star Spangled Banner" and "America the Beautiful" and I love them all.

LESSON 24: *Be reliable. Be faithful. Finish what you start.* America in the 1990s must finish what we started in the Declaration of Independence and Constitution and go all the way until we assure liberty and justice for the millions of children of all races and incomes left behind in our society today despite national leaders who seek to turn us back to the not-so-good old days of race and class and gender divisions.

LESSON 25: *Always remember that you are never alone.* There is nothing you can ever say or do that can take away my or God's love.

Home remains as you go out to serve and conquer the world. And I always follow you wherever you go in spirit, in prayer, and in love. You are *never* alone.

THE PLEDGE

OATH OF A MILLION BLACK MEN

Controversy surrounds the number of people who attended the Million Man March on Washington, D.C., on Monday, October 16, 1995. But many believe it drew the largest crowd to ever attend a demonstration on the Mall. Here is the oath sworn by upwards of one million black men that day.

I *(say your name)* pledge that from this day forward I will strive to love my brother, as I love myself.

I *(say your name)* pledge that from this day forward I will strive to improve myself spiritually, morally, mentally, socially, politically, and economically for the benefit of myself, my family, and my people.

I *(say your name)* pledge that I will strive to build businesses, build houses, build hospitals, build factories, and enter into international trade for the good of myself, my family, and my people.

I *(say your name)* pledge that from this day forward I will never raise my hand with a knife or a gun to beat, cut, or shoot any member of my family, or any human being except in self-defense.

I *(say your name)* pledge that from this day forward I will never abuse my wife by striking her, or disrespecting her, for she is the mother of my children, and the producer of my future.

I *(say your name)* pledge that from this day forward I will never engage in the abuse of children, little boys, or little girls for sexual gratification, but I will let them grow in peace to be strong men and women for the future of our people.

I *(say your name)* will never again use the "B" word to describe any female but particularly my own black sister.

I *(say your name)* pledge that from this day forward I will not poison my body with drugs or that which is destructive to my health or to my well-being.

I *(say your name)* pledge that from this day forward I will support black newspapers, black radio, and black television. I will support black artists who clean up their act, show respect for themselves, respect for their people, and respect for the heirs of the human family.

I *(say your name)* will do all of this, so help me God.

THE PERFECT ROLE MODEL
TAVIS SMILEY

A nationally known television host and radio commentator shares his views on black role models.

Do African American role models have to be perfect?

No.

First of all, most Black athletes and entertainers are *not* role models. Nor is every Black role model an athlete or an entertainer. Talk to most young Black kids and you will discover that typically their role models are people who they know and trust. Parents. Teachers. Clergy. Relatives. And that's the way it should be.

I, for one, was disturbed by the message that was advertised all over the country by Gatorade a few years back with their "Be like Mike" Michael Jordan commercials. The message we must deliver to our youth is not one of trying to be like Michael Jordan, but rather, liking *themselves*, since they will never *be* Michael Jordan. The fact is, a Black child has a one in eight thousand chance of becoming a player in the NBA; and one chance in ten thousand of playing baseball in the major leagues. Why is it then that we make gifted athletes our role models?

A different problem for us created by society at large is the tendency to see any missteps or mistakes by Black celebrities and spokespeople as representative of the race as a whole. Why is it that Elizabeth Taylor can be married nine times, and nobody talks about her many divorces as being indicative of a breakdown in White family values? She's still the queen of Hollywood royalty and her negative qualities are seen as hers alone. Hugh Grant can be caught with his pants down on Sunset Boulevard, but that doesn't mean his actions signify a breakdown in White morality, nor does it prevent him from having a hit movie. But when Michael Jordan, Michael Jackson, or Black politicians from former congressman and now-president of the United Negro College Fund Bill Gray to New York Congressman Floyd Flake are even *accused* of a crime, somehow it's a setback for *our* cause.

Not so. They're human, just like everyone else. I don't know any of these men personally, but what they may or may not do is not a reflection on me or Black Americans generally. We have to stop allowing the media to paint all Black people with this broad brush. And stop feeling guilty when they do. Black role models shouldn't be expected to be any more perfect than White ones are.

Rather than adopting celebrities as role models, each of us would do better to serve as mentors and tutors to Black youth. These are the kind of positive role models our children and our communities need. Mentors and tutors provide the attention and help that our youth are looking for in their lives.

When we get involved with our communities, we take some of the pressure off superstars like Michael Jordan. After all, he's just a very talented athlete. That's it.

❧

Everybody can be great. Because anybody can serve. You don't have to have a college degree to serve. You don't have to make your subject and your verb agree to serve. You don't have to know about Plato and Aristotle to serve. You don't have to know Einstein's theory of relativity to serve. You only need a heart full of grace. A soul generated by love.

—*Martin Luther King Jr.*

❧

Each one teach one.
Each one reach one.

—*Civil Rights Movement*

❧

WE SHALL OVERCOME . . . WITH ALGEBRA
ALEXIS JETTER

In the 1960s Bob Moses, a civil rights legend, barely escaped getting killed in the backwoods of Mississippi for educating and registering black voters. Thirty years later, he returned to Mississippi to continue his fight against racial injustice in the state. This time around, his principal weapon wasn't a voter registration drive, but mathematical literacy— teaching the analytical skills required for many jobs. The following piece, published in the New York Times Magazine, *describes Moses's work to organize the Delta Algebra Project. By empowering others, we fulfill a basic responsibility to the community.*

Deep inside the Mississippi Delta, where he once dodged Klan bullets and sharecropper adulation, Bob Moses has quietly returned to finish the task he started 30 years ago.

It's midnight in Mississippi, and memories stir as Moses walks through the deserted Jackson airport. Black men once feared traversing this state after dark. Tonight, despite the hour, he dials Doc Anderson, a local physician who in the 1960s had a busy sideline stitching up civil rights workers. "Guess what?" Moses says, laughing softly at his own audacity. "I'm here. Can you come get me?"

A call in the night from a man gone almost 30 years doesn't seem to faze people whose bonds were forged in the flames of civil rights era Mississippi. Few here have forgotten the shy, bespectacled math teacher who in 1964 guided Freedom Summer, busing hundreds of college students into backwoods Mississippi to educate and register black voters. "The purpose," Moses says, "was to break open Mississippi as a closed society."

Today he's seeking to open another closed society: the world of educational opportunity denied to poor children, black and white alike. His trademark overalls and baby face are gone, but the curiously unblinking gaze and hushed voice haven't changed at all. And now, in the same Delta towns where he was beaten and jailed three decades ago, Moses has reappeared—retooled for the 90s as director of the Algebra Project, a crusade that experts say could revolutionize math education.

"It's our version of Civil Rights 1992," Moses says. "But this time, we're organizing around literacy—not just reading and writing, but mathematical literacy." The parallels to the past, he says, are clear. "The question we asked then was: What are the skills people have to master to open the doors to citizenship? Now math literacy holds the key."

Labor and education experts agree. According to the Department of Labor, more than half of today's high-school graduates lack the analytic skills required for jobs. And minority groups, which by the year 2000 will constitute a third of all students, are lagging far behind.

Determined to reverse that trend, Moses established the first Algebra Project in Cambridge, Massachusetts, in 1982. The idea was simple: Without algebra, the door to college and most skilled professions is locked. But many black and Hispanic students, if they take algebra at all, learn it too late to get on the college-prep mathematics track. So why not expose every child to algebra in middle school?

The techniques are vintage 1964. Just as Freedom School volunteers used examples from sharecroppers' own experiences to teach history and writing, Algebra Project students learn to think and "speak" mathematically by tackling problems that arise in their daily lives. The philosophical link is universal access: "It wasn't the right to vote for a few people," Moses says. "It was the right to vote for everybody."

The idea struck a deep chord in parents, teachers and school reformers. By its 10th year, the program stretched from Boston to San Francisco, winning accolades from the National Science Foundation and reaching 9,000 inner-city youths. But for Moses, something was missing; call it a matter of the heart. Last year, joined by Dave Dennis, who co-directed Freedom Summer, Moses found his answer: the Delta Algebra Project of Mississippi.

Moses once described Mississippi as "the middle of the iceberg." No other state so defiantly hoisted segregation as its banner; no other state so openly used the sheriff's badge, the lynch mob and the burning cross to enforce it. "Mississippi set itself up to be our destiny," Moses says. "And so it attracted what it eventually got: us."

Raised in the Harlem River Houses in New York, he had been a Harvard Ph.D. candidate in philosophy and was a middle-school math teacher when news of the lunch-counter sit-in movement drew him south in 1960. In Atlanta he met Ella Baker, director of the Southern Christian Leadership Conference, godmother of SNCC (Student Non-violent Coordinating Committee) and a fierce believer in the power of common people to move mountains.

With Baker's backing, Moses set out on a solitary tour of rural Mississippi, written off by most civil rights leaders as too dangerous to organize. By 1961, he was registering blacks to vote in towns where few had dared to claim even their most basic rights. Exhibiting almost mystical calm in the face of terrible violence, the soft-spoken young man quickly became a legend.

When a sheriff's cousin gashed his head open with a knife handle, a badly bleeding Moses still managed to stagger up the courthouse steps to register two black farmers. Seemingly oblivious to danger, he fell asleep in a SNCC office where only hours before workers had leaped out a window to escape an armed mob of local whites. And in Greenwood, when three Klansmen opened fire on his car, Moses grabbed the steering wheel with one hand, cradled the bleeding driver with the other and somehow managed to bring the careening car to a halt.

Arrested and jailed countless times, he resisted his growing "Moses" reputation—going so far as to change his name to Parris, his mother's maiden name. But his exploits fed the legend. "In Mississippi, Bob Moses was the equivalent of Martin Luther King," says Taylor Branch, author of *Parting the Waters,* a Pulitzer Prize-winning account of the early civil rights movement. In 1966, Moses fled to Canada [and then Tanzania].

In 1976, after 10 years in exile, Moses returned. His wife, Janet, entered medical school, and he resumed his doctoral studies at Harvard. But he was soon distracted. Unhappy with the math instruction his eldest daughter, Maisha, was receiving at Martin Luther King Jr. School in Cambridge, Moses insisted on tutoring her at home.

[W]hen her eighth-grade teacher invited Moses to come in and teach algebra, he followed his daughter to school.

It was the end of his doctoral studies and the beginning of the Algebra Project.

Moses noted that children had difficulty moving from an arithmetic understanding of numbers—usually associated with the question "How much?"—to the more flexible algebraic concept, which requires an additional question: "Which way?"

Getting the right answer wasn't the point, Moses realized. Students needed to puzzle their way to the right questions, then chart out a variety of solutions. Watching children distill lessons from concrete experiences, he created a five-step model that reproduced their natural learning process. In an Algebra Project exercise, a child experiences an event, draws or models it, writes and talks about it, translates it into mathematical language and then develops symbols to represent it.

Moses came to believe that even tricky mathematical concepts like negative numbers, which make little sense to children but are critical in algebra, could be more readily explained if linked to everyday applications. He scouted around Cambridge for a simple, vivid example and found one staring him in the face: the Red Line in nearby Central Square.

Herding his students into a subway car, Moses took them inbound to Boston, then back past Central Square to the end of the line in Cambridge. Back in class, armed with magic markers, students assigned a value of zero to the Central Square station. Soon they had transformed the train route into a number line with positive values for inbound stops, negative for outbound.

Students got the point, a fun ride and a chance to make art out of numbers. One boy who used to hide behind a piano during math class emerged. Groans diminished. Resistance ebbed. Soon Moses was experimenting with other ways to teach algebraic concepts: zodiac games to teach multiplication and division and lemonade concentrate to teach ratios.

The best example [of the program's success] is the King School, where the program has been in place for ten years. Before the Algebra Project, few students took the optional advanced-placement qualifying test in ninth grade, and virtually none passed. By 1991, the school's graduates ranked second in Cambridge on the test.

In Chicago, parents emboldened by a citywide school reform movement imported math Moses-style into nineteen elementary schools, beginning in 1990. Several skeptical teachers resisted, but last year many students showed marked improvement in reading and writing as well as in math. And in Louisville, Kentucky, one principal credits the project with nearly doubling the number of students who scored at or above the 50th percentile on a national math achievement test.

News of the project's success spread quickly. Soon schools in Boston, Los Angeles, Milwaukee, Oakland and San Francisco jumped on board. [In rural Mississippi] seeds planted by the Algebra Project are beginning to bear fruit for more than 2,000 Delta schoolchildren in 10 area schools.

Moses wants students to discover their own mathematical thinking. So rather than taking an abstract approach to concepts like equivalency— the idea that one-half is equivalent to five-tenths, even though it doesn't look a thing like it—the Algebra Project asks students to write "make-do" parables that demonstrate equivalencies in real life. In Thelma McGee's classroom, children write about substituting baking soda for toothpaste, flour for pancake mix and liver for fishing bait.

Equivalence, any theoretician will attest, is a fundamental concept of modern mathematics and a stepping stone to higher math. Moses makes it child's play. Using snap-together cubes, Play-Doh, jump ropes and Chinese zodiac restaurant menus, Moses has found ways to introduce even such difficult notions as displacement, integers and vectors. "It gets harder as you go along," confides [a] student. "But it seems like they cover it up by making it fun."

Of course, Mississippi *has* changed since Bob Moses left. Blacks, who constitute 36 percent of the population—the highest concentration in any Southern state—now occupy nearly a quarter of the seats in the

State Legislature. And in the former heartland of the Ku Klux Klan and White Citizens Councils, overt racism is no longer in vogue. Moses, who once slept on the floors of those bold enough to give him shelter, is greeted politely by white clerks at Greenwood's Best Western motel when he comes to town.

But Greenwood's blacks still live apart from whites, separated by the traditional dividing line: railroad tracks. The Magnolia State leads the nation in poverty, infant mortality and illiteracy. And its schools are still segregated.

The educational legacy of Jim Crow still cripples the Delta's black populace. Into the mid-60's, the black school year was substantially shortened by white administrators more concerned with the cotton crop than with educating black children. That shortchange, coupled with agricultural mechanization and a virtually nonexistent industrial base, has mired Delta blacks in illiteracy and unemployment.

For too long, says Howard Sanders, superintendent of schools in Hollandale, black parents have told their children to leave Mississippi and "never look back." The Delta's calcified, semifeudal economy left aspiring young blacks little choice. Now he and local business leaders are looking to the Algebra Project to lay the groundwork for economic revival.

Bob Moses has watched with satisfaction as the Delta Project has grown and flourished. But he never forgets the way things were. "It's interesting to work with teachers who 30 years ago you couldn't talk to," he muses one afternoon. "It's taken a quarter of a century to move through this," he says with a small smile. "But it may be that the times are ready."

〜〜

Treat the world well . . . It was not given to you by your parents . . . It was lent to you by your children.

—Kenyan proverb

〜〜

RESPECT

Any worthwhile discussion of respect must of course begin with the Queen of Soul, Aretha Franklin, who spelled out the word in concerts and on airwaves coast to coast, making certain that no one within listening range misunderstood what it was that she wanted—"R-E-S-P-E-C-T."

The song became the number one record in America in June 1967, perhaps indicating that we all wanted "a little respect." After all, everyone deserves it, regardless of age, race, status, religion, etcetera. But we don't always get it.

Respect is a time-honored moral value in the African American community, a basic human decency easily shared among a people once reviled by others.

In the long-gone past, though respect *for* slaves was virtually nonexistent, respect *among* slaves was deemed essential. While slave owners valued blacks merely as a commodity—one not deserving of kindness and consideration—blacks respected one another as a matter of course. Among African Americans, respect was expected to be given to each other, one's family, extended family, and elders. And it was.

Today, the same old-fashioned respectfulness, which helped blacks survive slavery, is still offered in homes across the land, but not to the same extent. "Voices of Respect," a piece in this chapter, addresses the current trend of "violent self-revulsion and an exploding vulgarity" and the need to adopt a caring attitude in our homes.

What follows are profiles of respect, including stories of two former slaves, Mum Bett, who sued her master and won her freedom, and Sojourner Truth, a towering symbol of strength and integrity who was known to shame audiences into listening attentively.

Other examples are Thurgood Marshall's momentous legal battle in the U.S. Supreme Court battle to desegregate schools and a story of rebellion aboard a slave ship, the *Amistad,* which became a cause célèbre and rallying case for abolitionists. Letters from several proud and defiant Africans involved show the respect and admiration they freely gave their new American friends.

Finally, respect can be a simple matter of the names we chose for ourselves or for others. Some celebrities' names are defined and explained.

How to teach respect is no secret. Children learn to respect others when the adults around them respect others, too. Young people also learn to respect themselves as individuals when adults show that they value themselves and others and take pride in young people and their accomplishments.

〜

R-E-S-P-E-C-T
Find out what it means to me.
> —*Lyrics by Otis Redding.*
> *Sung by Aretha Franklin, 1967*

〜

SOJOURNER TRUTH
ARTHUR HUFF FAUSET

Sojourner Truth (c. 1797–1883) was among the most remarkable and famous African American women of the nineteenth century. She was a symbol of towering strength and unshakable faith. Born a slave in Hurley, Ulster County, New York, she was named Isabella. She grew to be six feet tall and worked as a field hand, milkmaid, cleaning woman, cook, and wet nurse. One morning, before dawn, she walked to freedom, carrying her infant child. She eventually adopted the last name of the family with whom she sought refuge, Van Wagenen. Then, in 1843, after receiving instruction from "voices" she heard, she changed her name once again, this time to become "an instrument of God." Her new name proclaimed her mission: to be a "Sojourner" who spoke only the "Truth." She became one of the abolitionist movement's best "stump" speakers and was among the very few black participants in the early women's rights movement. She quoted long passages from the Bible, most of which she had memorized since she could not read. She used wry humor, assertiveness, and folk wisdom to captivate audiences and silence critics. Through her example, we learn how personal magnetism and self-assuredness can be used to win respect even from one's enemies.

She was a curiosity wherever she went. Her color was both an asset and a liability. People flocked to hear her, because it was such an unusual thing for them to hear a Negro speak; but they were often rude even when they did not mean to be.

One night, after she had spoken in one of the halls in Rochester, she was returning to the home of a friend. A policeman, of small stature, stopped her on the street and demanded her name. This was a surprising request and, coming from this little man, it annoyed her. She paused an instant, then struck the ground firmly with the walking stick she was carrying, and then replied deliberately, in that loud, deep voice which few could imitate, "I am that I am."

Did the policeman really get frightened and imagine that she was some unearthly creature? He hurriedly vanished in the night. Sojourner strode majestically homeward.

She was on one of her many forages into the Middle West. At the close of a meeting in northern Ohio, where she had made some slashing attacks against slave-holding classes, a man approached her and said, "Old woman, do you think that your talk about slavery does any good? Do you suppose that people care what you say? . . . Why," he went on, "I don't care any more for your talk than I do for the bite of a flea."

That was her opening.

"Perhaps not," she replied, "but the Lord willing, I'll keep you scratching!"

Some of her roughest experiences were in Indiana. Here was a state which was undecided about the slave issue, but had strong leanings in favor of the institution. Laws were passed forbidding Negroes to enter the state, much less remain or attempt to speak there. Laws, however, unless they originated in Heaven, had no terror for Sojourner.

A group of ruffians had it all arranged to frustrate her attempts to hold meetings. They spread about the town the rumor that Sojourner was an imposter, and that all her anti-slavery activity was a sham to assist the Republicans, which was anathema in that section. Furthermore, they stated that she was not a woman, but a man disguised in woman's clothing!

Sojourner nevertheless attempted to hold a meeting in the meeting-house of the United Brethren, a sect in Indiana. The atmosphere was quite hostile. In the middle of her attempts to speak, a local physician arose and cried out to her, "Hold on. There is a doubt existing in the minds of many persons present respecting the sex of the speaker. My impression is that the majority of the persons present believe the speaker to be a man. I know that this speaker's friends do not think so, but it really is for the speaker's own benefit that I demand that if she is a woman, she submit her breast to the inspection of some of the ladies present, that the doubt may be removed by their testimony.

The wildest confusion ensued.

Many of the ladies in the house were indignant at such a proposal. It had taken most people by surprise, and enemies of the Negro woman felt as highly incensed as her friends. The suggestion was preposterous.

But Sojourner was in complete control of her emotions. She stood quietly and addressed the group once more.

"Why do you suspect me of being a man?" she asked.

"Your voice is not the voice of a woman. It is the voice of a man, and we believe you are a man." A chorus of voices had responded to her inquiry.

The meeting, thus rudely interrupted, was taken over completely by the physician and his mob.

"Let us have a vote on the proposition," he shouted—as if in a democracy even the sex of an individual could be established by means of a majority vote!

"Aye," was the boisterous response.

"The ayes have it!" and thus Sojourner was voted into the male sex. Sojourner leaped to battle.

"My breasts," she shouted, "have suckled many a white babe, even when they should have been suckling my own. Some of those white babes are now grown men and even though they have suckled my Negro breasts, they are in my opinion far more manly than any of you appear to be."

Then she disrobed her bosom, and showed her breasts to the public gaze.

"I will show my breasts to the entire congregation," she shouted out to them. "It is not my shame but yours that I should do this. Here, then," she cried, "see for yourselves."

And then as a parting thrust at the rude men, she exclaimed with fiery indignation, "Do you wish also to suck!"

SOJOURNER TRUTH MAY have been the direct cause of the change in attitude towards "Jim Crow" in the street cars of Washington.

She was out with a white friend, Mrs. Laura Haviland, who proposed that they ride in the cars. Both of them understood that a Negro and a white person could not ride in the same car; therefore, when Mrs. Haviland signalled for the approaching vehicle, Sojourner stepped over to one side as if she were going to continue walking but when the car stopped, she ran and jumped aboard.

The conductor pushed her back.

"Get out of the way," he yelled at her, "and let the lady come aboard."

"I am a lady, too," remonstrated Sojourner.

The conductor made no reply to this remark, and Sojourner remained on the car.

A little later it was necessary to change cars. A man was coming out of the second car as Sojourner and her friend jumped aboard. He turned to the conductor and asked, "Are niggers allowed to ride?"

The conductor grabbed Sojourner by the shoulder, and jerked her around, at the same time ordering her to get off of the car.

Sojourner said, "I will not."

The conductor started to put her off.

Mrs. Haviland said, "Don't put her out of the car."

"Does she belong to you?" asked the conductor.

"No," replied Sojourner's friend, "she belongs to humanity."

"Then take her and go," the irate official said, as he pushed Sojourner up against the door.

Sojourner was furious.

"I will let you know," she said, "whether you can treat me like a dog."

Then turning to her friend, she continued, "Take the number of this car."

This surprise remark by Sojourner frightened the conductor, and he did not utter another word.

But when Sojourner returned to the hospital, it was discovered that a bone in her shoulder was dislocated as a result of the conductor's rude treatment.

Sojourner made a complaint to the president of the car line, and he advised her to have the conductor arrested. This she did, and the Freedmen's Bureau provided her with a lawyer to argue the case. The conductor was dismissed.

Not long after this incident, the Jim Crow rule was abolished in street cars, and there was a noticeable difference in the attitude of most of the conductors towards Negro riders.

Nevertheless, the possibility of trouble was already present. For instance, not long after the Jim Crow cars were removed, she signalled for a car, but the motorman, observing that she was black, pretended not to see her, and went on. The same thing occurred when a second car approached. By this time the enraged Sojourner with typical ingenuity cried out as loudly as her bellowing voice would carry, "I want to ride! I want to ride!"

At the sound of this unusual noise, all traffic in the very congested street stopped. People blocked the side-walks to see what was happening, and carriages halted in the middle of the street. Before the trolley car could proceed on its way any farther, Sojourner had jumped aboard.

The conductor was furious.

"Go forward with the horses," he shouted at the now gloating woman, "or I will put you out."

Sojourner sat herself calmly down, then replied with all the queenliness of a visitor from heaven, "I am a passenger."

"Go forward where the horses are," the conductor thundered, "or I will throw you out."

The intrepid battler rose in all the proud dignity of a member of one of the first families of New York.

"I am no Marylander," she retorted, "nor Virginian. I am not afraid of your threats. I am from the Empire State of New York and I know the laws as well as you."

The astonished conductor retreated at this display of self-assurance, but some soldiers who were on the car taunted him, and made a point of informing every passenger who entered the car, "You should have heard that old woman talk to the conductor."

Sojourner rode even farther than she needed to, thinking that she might as well make the most of her disputed ride. As she alighted from the car she cried, "Bless God! I have had a ride!"

One day Sojourner was returning from Georgetown with one of the hospital nurses. They boarded an empty car at the station, and waited for it to leave. A little while later two white women came in and sat opposite Sojourner. On observing the Negro couple, they began to whisper to each other, looking scornfully in Sojourner's direction. The nurse, who still entertained illusions about white folks, became frightened, and hung her head almost to her lap; but Sojourner gazed fearlessly in front of her.

A few minutes later, one of the white women faintly called to the conductor and asked, "Conductor, does niggers ride in these cars?"

The conductor looked about him hesitatingly.

"Ye-e-s," he replied.

" 'Tis a shame and a disgrace," the woman said. "They ought to have a nigger car on this track."

Sojourner interrupted at this point, saucily and regally.

"Of course colored people ride in the cars," she said. "Street cars are made for poor white and colored folks. Carriages are for ladies and gentlemen."

Through the window she discerned a carriage. Pointing to it she remarked scornfully, "See those carriages. They will take you three or four miles for six pence—and then you talk of a nigger car!"

The women were more embarrassed than they cared to admit. They abruptly left their seats and alighted from the car.

"Ah," Sojourner shouted at them gleefully, "now they are going to take a carriage. . . . Good bye, ladies!"

"AND AIN'T I A WOMAN?"
SOJOURNER TRUTH

With this speech, Sojourner Truth reportedly saved the day when the crowd at the Women's Rights Convention in Akron, Ohio, on May 29, 1851, became unruly. Male ministers at the meeting used the Bible to uphold their argument that men were superior to women. Sojourner Truth—tall, earnest, and dressed in the Quaker attire typical of abolitionists—approached the speaker's platform. With her unfailing talent for persuasiveness, she took control of the audience, crushing the ministers' contentions and asserting her own equality with any man. A refrain from her speech, "And Ain't I a Woman?," has come to define Sojourner Truth's powerful, womanly persona. Here is one version of what she said.

Well, children, where there is so much racket there must be somethin' out o'kilter. I think that 'twixt the Negroes of the North and the South and the women at the North, all talkin' 'bout rights, the white men will be in a fix pretty soon. But what's all this here talkin' 'bout?

That man over there say that women needs to be helped into carriages, and lifted over ditches, and to have the best place everywhere. Nobody ever helps me into carriages, or over mud-puddles, or give me any best place! And ain't I a woman? Look at me? Look at my arm! I have ploughed, and planted, and gathered into barns, and no man could head me! And ain't I a woman? I could work as much and eat as much as a man—when I could get it—and bear the lash as well! And ain't I a woman? I have borne thirteen children, and seen 'em mos' all sold off to slavery, and when I cried out with my mother's grief, none but Jesus heard me! And ain't I a woman?

Then they talk about this thing in the head; what's this they call it? ["Intellect," whispered some one near.] That's it honey. What's that got to do with women's rights or Negro's rights? If my cup won't hold but a pint and yours holds a quart, wouldn't you be mean not to let me have my little half measure full?

Then that little man in black there, he says women can't have as much rights as men, 'cause Christ wasn't a woman! Where did your Christ come from? Where did your Christ come from? From God and a woman! Man had nothin' to do with Him.

If the first woman God ever made was strong enough to turn the world upside down all alone, these women together ought to be able to turn it back, and get it right side up again. And now they is asking to do it, they better let 'em. 'Bliged to you for hearin' me, and now ole Sojourner hasn't got nothin' more to say.

THE SLAVE WHO SUED
HER MASTER
JON SWAN

Mum Bett (c. 1744–1829) was born a slave but won her freedom in a highly unusual way. Here is how she gained the respect of slave owners and her right to live as she pleased.

Early in 1781, having heard a lot of talk about the "rights of man," a black slave named Mum Bett walked out of her master's house in western Massachusetts to tell a lawyer that she wanted to sue for her freedom. After asking her what had put such an extraordinary idea into her head and being satisfied by her reply, the lawyer agreed to represent her.

Bett and a younger sister, Lizzie, grew up as slave children in Claverack, New York, about twenty miles south of Albany. Their owner was a Dutchman, Pieter Hogeboom. In 1735 his youngest child, Hannah, married John Ashley, the son of one of the original proprietors permitted by the General Court of Massachusetts to organize settlements along the Housatonic River.

The Ashleys had four children. Exactly when they acquired Bett and Lizzie is not known, but Hannah's father died in 1758, when Bett was about fourteen.

By this time John Ashley had become an important figure in Sheffield, Massachusetts, the largest settlement in the western slice of Massachusetts that would later be called Berkshire County. In 1761 he was appointed judge of the Court of Common Pleas, a post he voluntarily resigned twenty years later, when his servant Bett's case came before the court.

In 1773, Sheffield appointed a committee "to take into consideration the grievances which Americans in general and Inhabitants of this Province in particular labor under." Colonel Ashley was appointed chairman.

The meeting of that committee, held in Colonel Ashley's home in early January 1773, very probably was a turning point in the life of Mum Bett. She was now almost thirty years old. The committee's clerk, Theodore Sedgwick, was the lawyer who would ultimately take her case. Sedgwick was only twenty-six. The meeting lasted for several hours, and Mum Bett presumably served refreshments—and perhaps listened in—as the men discussed the evening's business.

The result of that discussion was a document called the Sheffield Declaration. While duly respectful of the crown, it contained a resolution that read: "Resolved that Mankind in a State of Nature are equal, free and independent of each other, and have a right to the undisturbed Enjoyment of their lives, their Liberty and Property."

The first article of the Declaration of Rights of the [Massachusetts] constitution [approved in 1780] stated that "all men are born free and equal, and have certain natural, essential, and inalienable rights." Thus the sentiments expressed by the Sheffield Declaration and the Declaration of Independence were now the law of the state and county in which Mum Bett lived and worked.

A single, but dramatic, domestic scene apparently made her decide that the time had come to put those high-sounding words to the test. Fifty years after the event, Henry Dwight Sedgwick, one of Theodore Sedgwick's ten children, recalled the episode.

"While Mum Bett resided in the family of Col. Ashley, she received a severe wound in a generous attempt to shield her sister. Her mistress in a fit of passion [had] resorted to a degree and mode of violence very uncommon in this country: she struck at the weak and timid [Lizzie] with a heated kitchen shovel: Mum Bett interposed her arm, and received the blow; and she bore the honorable scar it left to the day of her death."

After this incident, according to the lawyer's son, Mum Bett set off to consult Theodore Sedgwick. By now Bett was about thirty-seven years old; Sedgwick was thirty-four. He had seen action in the Revolutionary War and in 1780 had been elected to the first General Court held under the new state constitution.

The conversation between the slave and the lawyer was preserved by Harriet Martineau, a novelist with strong abolitionist views who visited the Berkshires a couple of years after Mum Bett's death in 1829 and who was, for a time, a close friend of the Sedgwicks. According to her account, when the lawyer asked the slave how she had learned "the doctrine and facts on which she proceeded, she replied, 'By keepin' still and mindin' things.'" And when pressed to explain to what things she paid mind, she replied that, "for instance, when she was waiting at table,

she heard gentlemen talking over the Bill of Rights and the new constitution of Massachusetts; and in all they said she never heard but that all
people were born free and equal, and she thought long about it, and
resolved she would try whether she did not come in among them."

A surviving record of the case calls it *Brom & Bett* v. *J. Ashley Esq.*
Brom is described simply as "a Negro Man . . . of Sheffield" and a
"Labourer"; Bett, as "a Negro Woman . . . of Sheffield" and a "Spin-
ster." The case was heard in Great Barrington on August 21, 1781.

Sedgwick pleaded "(1) That no antecedent law had established slavery, and that the laws which seemed to suppose it were the offspring of
error in the legislators," and "(2) That such laws, even if they had
existed, were annulled by the new Constitution."

In any event, the jury was persuaded. Not only did "Jonathan
Holcomb Foreman & His Fellows" find that Brom and Bett "are not and
were not at the time of the purchase of the original Writ the legal Negro
Servants of him the said John Ashley during life," but they ordered
Ashley to pay thirty shillings' damages and the cost of the suit—five
pounds, fourteen shillings, and four pence.

Ashley appealed, but a few months later he dropped the appeal.
Moreover, "he confessed judgment—that is, he assented to the lower
court ruling that Brom and Bett were not slaves." Why? Because in the
intervening months the state's supreme court had ruled, in another case,
that slavery was unconstitutional in Massachusetts. That decision, in
Caldwell v. *Jennison*, was a murky one, and some have argued that
because no legislation banned slavery in the state, it was strictly legal
until 1866—though not practiced.

MUM BETT CHANGED her name to Elizabeth Freeman, and for the rest
of her working life she served as a paid domestic in the household of
Theodore Sedgwick and his second wife, Pamela—first in Sheffield and
then in Stockbridge, where the family moved in 1785.

At what age Mum Bett retired is unknown. But she did have enough
money to buy herself a home.

Elizabeth Freeman died on December 28, 1829. Her supposed age was
85 years. Part of the inscription on her tombstone reads: "She was born
a slave and remained a slave for nearly thirty years. She could neither
read nor write, yet in her own sphere she had no superior nor equal. She

neither wasted time nor property. She never violated a trust, nor failed to perform a duty. In every situation of domestic trial, she was the most efficient helper, and the tenderest friend. *Good mother fare well.*"

When Nat Cole bought a house in a white suburb of Los Angeles, some of the other homeowners in the area drew up a petition against undesirable people moving into the neighborhood, and began passing it around for signatures. When Nat found out about it he went to a neighbor's house and asked if he could sign the petition. He said he didn't want any undesirables moving in, either.

THE *AMISTAD* REBELLION

In the most famous slave rebellion at sea, kidnapped Africans aboard a Spanish slaveship broke free and attempted to sail homeward. Tricked, they ended up in America, but their fate became a cause célèbre and their legal case eventually went before the U.S. Supreme Court. In the end, the thirty-five surviving Mende ('also spelled Mendi) captives won respect across the nation and returned home to Africa. Their struggle to remain free still inspires.

On June 28, 1839, Sengbe Pieh, along with fifty-two other kidnapped Africans, was manacled in the steaming hold of a Spanish schooner, the *Amistad*. A twenty-five-year-old rice farmer and member of a prominent Mende family, Sengbe (whom we know today as Joseph Cinque) had already survived a hellish ordeal—a three day march through the African bush; a fifty-day voyage spent in the hold of a Portugueses slaveship; a trek into the Cuban jungle followed by a two-week stay in a crowded holding pen; a march to Havana; ten days in prison; and finally, auction in a teeming slave market. But once aboard the *Amistad* (which ironically means "friendship" in Spanish), the worst was yet to come.

When he and the other captives were brought up on deck for a breather, Cinque used sign language to ask the cook what the Africans' fate would be. The cook pointed at barrels of salted beef, drew a finger across his throat, and gestured that the crew would salt the Africans and eat them like the barreled beef.

Cinque lost no time plotting an insurrection. He hid a rusty nail in his armpit and used it to pick a padlock, releasing the chain linked to the iron collars around the Africans necks. Under cover of a nighttime storm, they crept up the hatchway with long sugarcane knives, found the ship's captain and cook asleep on deck, and hacked them to death. Alarmed by cries of "Murder!," several crew members jumped overboard.

One African was killed. The slave cabin boy, who begged for mercy, was shackled to the anchor. Two Spaniards—the ones who had bought the Africans at the Havana slave auction—were spared. Cinque ordered them to sail the *Amistad* back to Africa, steering toward sunrise. They did—during the day. But at night the Spaniards steered northwest, toward the United States. After two months of zigzagging across the sea, during which eight Africans died from thirst and illness, the ship finally reached land, anchoring off Culloden Point, Long Island. But only the Spaniards knew where they were.

Cinque and eight Africans rowed ashore. They bought food and drink from stunned islanders, using gold doubloons they had found on the ship. The next morning, before the *Amistad* could head out to open sea, an American naval vessel seized the ship and steered it to New London, Connecticut, where the Africans were imprisoned.

A long legal battle ensued over the fate of the Africans and the *Amistad* and the case caught the public's attention. It touched on complex political, legal, and ethical issues, including national and international law, international treaties, and interpretations of freedom, slavery, and property. And it became a rallying point for abolitionists (among them the descendants of signers of the Declaration of Independence). They raised legal defense funds and used the Africans' plight to publicize abolitionist views.

Even the White House got involved. President Martin Van Buren sided with Cuban and Spanish authorities, who demanded that the Africans be returned in order to stand trial for mutiny and murder. But then he suddenly shifted position. Facing reelection (which he lost to William Henry Harrison), President Van Buren no doubt was swayed by public sympathy for the Africans, who, jailed and emaciated, attracted visitors by the thousands, as if they were a museum attraction.

Meanwhile, the Africans, who could not speak English, faced little prospect for regaining their freedom unless they could communicate with whites. A Yale linguist memorized a few of the Africans' words, then strolled up and down New York City docks uttering them. Incredibly, he found two Mende-speaking Africans, who ended up translating for Cinque and his fellow defendants, enabling them to testify in court and understand the proceedings.

In January 1840, the U.S. District Court ruled in favor of the Africans, but an appeal was filed, and the case eventually was sent to U.S. Supreme Court, where former President John Quincy Adams, seventy-three years old and nearly blind, represented the Africans. In March 1841, the Supreme Court—in which a majority of the justices were Southerners and former slave owners—surprisingly affirmed the original verdict by an eight-to-one margin, and the Africans were freed.

On November 17, 1841, three years after being kidnapped, the thirty-five remaining *Amistad* defendants (others had died in prison), along with their translator, returned to Africa. Cinque, admired by many Americans for his dignity and regal bearing—he was even called a "Black Prince"—returned to Mende, where he died a free man in the late 1870s.

FRIENDLY REBELS
CINQUE, KINNA, AND KALE

*In March 1841, John Quincy Adams (1767–1848) appeared before the
U.S. Supreme Court on behalf of the* Amistad *rebels. He argued that they
should be freed—and they were. Before heading home to Africa, Cinque
and two others from the* Amistad *rebellion wrote this letter of thanks to
their lawyer, the former President.*

Boston, Nov. 6, 1841

To the Hon. John Quincy Adams:

Most Respected Sir,—the Mendi people give you thanks for all your
kindness to them. They will never forget your defence of their rights
before the great Court of Washington. They feel that they owe to you in
a large measure, their delivery from the Spaniards, and from slavery or
death. They will pray for you as long as you live, Mr. Adams. May God
bless and reward you.

We are about to go home to Africa. We go to Sierra Leone first, and
then we reach Mendi very quick. When we get to Mendi we shall tell the
people of your great kindness. Good missionary will go with us. We will
take the Bible with us. It has been a precious book, in prison, and we
love to read it now we are free.—Mr. Adams, we want to make you a
present of a beautiful Bible. Will you please to accept it, and when you
look at it or read it, remember your poor and grateful clients? We read
in this holy book, "if it had not been the Lord who was on our side,
when men rose up against us, then they had swallowed us up quick,
when their wrath was kindled up against us." Blessed be the Lord, who
hath not given us a prey to their teeth. Our soul is escaped as a bird out
of the snare of the fowler—the snare is broken and we are escaped. Our
help is in the name of the Lord who made Heaven and Earth.

For the Mendi people,
CINQUE
KINNA,
KALE

◌◌

I believe in the brotherhood of all men, but I don't believe in wasting brotherhood on anyone who doesn't want to practice it with me. Brotherhood is a two way street.

—*Malcolm X*

◌◌

THE POCKETBOOK GAME
ALICE CHILDRESS

Alice Childress (1916–94), among the most talented playwrights and novelists of the twentieth century, often wrote about poor African Americans and their struggles to maintain their dignity. "I concentrate on portraying have-nots in a have society," she wrote. This piece, in the form of a monologue, reminds us that respect for another person's character may be a telling measure of one's own integrity.

Marge . . . Day's work is an education! Well, I mean workin' in different homes you learn much more than if you was steady in one place. . . . I tell you, it really keeps your mind sharp tryin' to watch for what folks will put over on you.

What? . . . No, Marge, I do not want to help shell no beans, but I'd be more than glad to stay and have supper with you, and I'll wash the dishes after. Is that all right? . . .

Who put anything over on who? . . . Oh yes! It's like this. . . . I been working for Mrs. E . . . one day a week for several months and I notice that she has some peculiar ways. Well, there was only one thing that really bothered me and that was her pocketbook habit. . . . No, not those little novels. . . . I mean her purse—her handbag.

Marge, she's got a big old pocketbook with two long straps on it . . . and whenever I'd go there, she'd be propped up in a chair with her handbag double wrapped tight around her wrist, and from room to room she'd roam with that purse hugged to her bosom . . . yes, girl! This happens every time! No, there's nobody there but me and her. . . . Marge, I couldn't say nothin' to her! It's her purse, ain't it? She can hold onto it if she wants to!

I held my peace for months, tryin' to figure out how I'd make my point. . . . Well, bless Bess! Today was the day! . . . Please, Marge, keep shellin' the beans so we can eat! I know you're listenin', but you listen with your ears, not your hands. . . . Well, anyway, I was almost ready to go home when she steps in the room hangin' onto her bag as usual and says, "Mildred, will you ask the super to come up and fix the kitchen faucet?" "Yes, Mrs. E . . ." I says, "as soon as I leave." "Oh, no," she says, "he may be gone by then. Please go now." "All right," I says, and out the door I went, still wearin' my Hoover apron.

I just went down the hall and stood there a few minutes . . . and then I rushed back to the door and knocked on it as hard and frantic as I could. She flung open the door sayin', "What's the matter? Did you see the super?" . . . "No," I says, gaspin' hard for breath, "I was almost downstairs when I remembered . . . I left my pocketbook!"

With that I dashed in, grabbed my purse and then went down to get the super! Later, when I was leavin' she says real timid-like, "Mildred, I hope that you don't think I distrust you because . . ." I cut her off real quick. . . . "That's all right, Mrs. E . . . , I understand. 'Cause if I paid anybody as little as you pay me, I'd hold my pocketbook too!"

Marge, you fool . . . lookout! . . . You gonna drop the beans on the floor!

JUDGING
ANDY RAZAF

Andy Razaf (1895–1973) gives sound advice to those who would be judgmental about others.

> Seek not to judge thy brother
> He is as good as you;
> Though you may find him lacking,
> For you are lacking too.

No man is wholly evil
No man is wholly good,
The world would be much brighter;
Could this be understood.

It is not yours to censure,
It is not yours to scorn;
Lift up your lower brother,
If you are higher born!

❦

The problem of the twentieth century is the problem of the color-line—the relation of the darker to the lighter races of men in Asia and Africa, in America and the islands of the sea.

—*W. E. B. Du Bois*, The Souls of Black Folk

❦

DEBASING DEBASES
JAMES BALDWIN

James Baldwin (1924–87), a major American writer who helped to define black literature of the last half of the twentieth century, wrote on many themes, one of which was how American democracy had failed the African American. Baldwin's piercing and passionate essays on race earned him acclaim as the "conscience of the nation" during the civil rights era. In this excerpt from his book The Fire Next Time, *published in 1962, he urges blacks to defend their dignity by avoiding the kind of hatefulness that leads to murder. In effect, his words offer a vital lesson in maintaining dignity by respecting people's differences.*

The glorification of one race and the consequent debasement of another—or others—always has been and always will be a recipe for murder. There is no way around this. If one is permitted to treat any group of people with special disfavor because of their race or the color of their skin, there is no limit to what one will force them to endure, and, since the entire race has been mysteriously indicted, no reason not to attempt to destroy it root and branch. This is precisely what the Nazis attempted. Their only originality lay in the means they used. It is scarcely worthwhile to attempt remembering how many times the sun has looked down on the slaughter of the innocents. I am very much concerned that American Negroes achieve their freedom here in the United States. But I am also concerned for their dignity, for the health of their souls, and must oppose any attempt that Negroes may make to do to others what has been done to them. I think I know—we see it around us every day—the spiritual wasteland to which that road leads. It is so simple a fact and one that is so hard, apparently, to grasp: *Whoever debases others is debasing himself.* That is not a mystical statement but a most realistic one, which is proved by the eyes of any Alabama sheriff—and I would not like to see Negroes ever arrive at so wretched a condition.

MARCHING ON JIM CROW
A. PHILIP RANDOLPH

Asa Philip Randolph (1889–1979), founder of the Brotherhood of Sleeping Car Porters, the first black labor union, won key victories in the 1930s, paving the way for civil rights gains in the 1950s and 1960s. He organized the March on Washington Movement, threatening a mass march of 50,000 to 100,000 workers to protest discrimination in hiring in the defense industry, the military, and the government. To head off the march, President Roosevelt issued the first federal decree on race relations since the Emancipation Proclamation—an executive order banning federal discrimination—and the march was canceled. In the article excerpted below, and in five others he published in the Chicago Defender *in 1943, Randolph outlines his basic strategies, which were taken up by future civil rights strategists.*

Is Jim Crow in Washington? What a question! Is water wet? Is fire hot? . . .

Yes "Mr. James H. Crow" has his habitat in Washington. In the capital of our republic, Negro citizens are segregated in life and segregated in death. In the capital of the arsenal of democracy Negro citizens cannot buy a sandwich beyond the Black-Belt except at the railroad station.

Verily, Washington is not only the capital of the nation. It is the capital of Dixie, of 20th Century Copperheaded Confederacy. There, crackerocracy is in the saddle. Ku Klux Klanism runs riot. Here, the alleged headquarters of the democracy of the world, an anti-poll tax bill is filibustered to death by a tiny fraction of "little wilful men"—Southern senators, and an anti-lynching bill cannot survive.

Not only is Jim Crow in Washington. Jim Crow is running Washington. Negroes cannot eat in the restaurant of the Congress. They cannot even sit in the peanut gallery of any cheap theater in downtown Washington.

This is an affront. It is an insult. Here is the Negro's dilemma. They are not first-class citizens because they are jim-crowed and they are jim-crowed because they are not first-class citizens. Thus, to win first class citizenship is to abolish jim-crow and to abolish jim-crow is to win first-class citizenship.

BUT, THE TRAGEDY is not only that Jim Crow is in the District of Columbia, but that the pattern of Washington's Jim Crow is being spread by "official" Washington into areas of our country—North, East and West, where it was hitherto unknown. Our federal government in Washington has become an official carrier of the germ of Jim-Crow throughout the length and breadth of our land, and is infecting the body politic everywhere and poisoning the blood stream of national public opinion. Official Washington is freezing Jim Crow. It is perpetuating the pattern of segregation. It is crystallizing second-class citizenship.

What can be done about it? This question is naturally posed.

Why is Washington such an important center for the Negro to direct his forces upon? In short, why march on Washington? The answer is, Washington is the head and front and nerve center of the world. Washington is the political symbol of the greatest power on earth today. Prime ministers and kings of all of the nations of the earth look to Washington, not so much for ideas as for lend-lease, and they accept America's ideas on race and color. Because of the billions now being appropriated by the Congress in Washington to help the United Nations win the war and for the promotion of plans for the post-war rehabilitation of both the Allies and enemy powers, Washington is the financial and economic powerhouse of the entire world. Upon the well-known theory that politics is a reflex of economics, the political influence of Washington is destined to grow into towering proportions.

Thus, if the Negro people permit Washington to continue and develop as a symbol of color and racial Jim-Crow-ism, the colored and subject peoples everywhere will look with contempt upon the Negro as the classic second-class citizens of all times. . . .

THE FACT IS the Negroes' cause cannot win without the masses. Negroes of talent, genius and ability are about at the end of their ropes. The demonstration of the Negroes' capacity for cultural advancement has been a necessary stage in the evolution of Negro life. And it must continue to go forward. But the Negroes' primary problem now is to survive as an economic, political, social and racial equal.

This involves power, economic, social and political power. The masses alone can supply that power. The masses have numbers. Effective public demonstrations need numbers. The public is always affected by numbers. It is also affected by the purpose for which great masses demonstrate. The public, Negro and white, is affected by large number of people in physical motion. Great mass formations affect all of the physical senses. They stir the feelings of the people. They provoke thought. They cause officials of state to pause and wonder.

Demonstrations of great masses of workers in strikes, on the picket line, is the chief strategy of the trade union movement. It has gotten results and will continue to get results. But the demonstration must be non-violent. The demonstrators must not possess offensive deadly weapons such as knives, razors or guns of any kind. The Negro's most effective weapon is his purpose, cause, moral courage and non-violent mass demonstration.

Thus, it appears that an important part of the future strategy and technique of the Negro must be in the field of demonstration, both non-violent mass activity and disciplined non-violent demonstration of small Negro and white groups for civil and economic justice.

And it does not appear that anything is calculated to awaken both white and black America to the justice and necessity of the Negroes being recognized and accepted as a full-fledged American citizen except some demonstration with the drama of a March on Washington. But when? The answer is: when the people are ready and the times and conditions give such a program strategic power. Even the much talked about Second Front is considered from the point of view of time strategy or its whole point may be lost.

Moreover, the people must not only be ready but they must be prepared and disciplined to march on Washington. And this may have to be done. Such a comprehensive maneuver will require the support and cooperation of Negro leadership from church, labor, business and the people.

But a March on Washington must be the Negroes' last resort.

THURGOOD MARSHALL:
WARRIOR AT THE BAR
MICHAEL D. DAVIS AND HUNTER R. CLARK

Thurgood Marshall (1908–93) perhaps did more to change the social fabric of twentieth-century America than any other man. As head of the NAACP's legal arm, he became the most successful lawyer in U.S. Supreme Court history. Decisions in his cases struck down laws barring blacks from voting and from buying homes in all-white neighborhoods. He successfully argued Brown v. Board of Education, *and in 1954, the Supreme Court overturned the separate-but-equal doctrine of* Plessy v. Ferguson, *which served as the legal foundation for racial segregation. In 1967, President Lyndon Johnson named Marshall to the Supreme Court, where he became one of history's greatest liberal justices. According to his biographers, Marshall "had a panoramic view of American life, from the*

*powerful Oval Office of the White House and the majestic marble corri-
dors of the Supreme Court to the tar-paper and tin-roofed shacks of [the
South], where black Americans lived in fear of night riders and in frustration with a system that denied them the basic decencies of life and at times
life itself. His twenty-four-year tenure [on] the U.S. Supreme Court epitomized the battle of black Americans for equality."*

*Here is how Thurgood Marshall made U.S. legal history, in the second
and final round of arguments of* Brown v. Board of Education.

On December 7, 1953, before a packed Supreme Court chamber, the
Court began hearing three days of reargument in *Brown*.

Marshall stood by his research on the Fourteenth Amendment. He
asserted that the amendment was clearly intended to "strike down all
types of class and caste legislation." Segregation had to be struck down,
he insisted, unless it could be shown that the framers had specifically
intended to exclude segregation in public education from the class- or
caste-based legislation that the amendment was enacted to prohibit.

He reiterated his contention that there is, in effect, no such thing as
race and therefore no rational basis for distinguishing between individuals based on race. "Red things may be associated by reason of their
redness, with disregard of all other resemblances or of distinctions. Such
classification would be logically appropriate," he told the Court. But, he
cautioned, "apply it further: make a rule of conduct depend upon it, and
distinguish in legislation between red-haired men and black-haired men,
and the classification would immediately be seen to be wrong; it would
have only arbitrary relation to the purpose and province of legislation."

From this he concluded that the segregationists "would have to
show—and we have shown to the contrary—they would have to show,
one, that there are differences in race; and, two, that differences in race
have a recognizable relationship to the subject matter being legislated,
namely, public education." He asserted, "That is a rule that has been
uniformly applied by this Court in all other challenges that a classification is unreasonable."

In his closing argument, he drove the point deeper. "The only way
that this Court can decide this case in opposition to our position," he
told the justices, "is that there must be some reason which gives the state
the right to make a classification . . . in regard to Negroes, and we

submit the only way to arrive at this decision is to find that for some reason Negroes are inferior to all other human beings."

He continued, "In order to arrive at the decision that [the segregationists] want us to arrive at, there would have to be some recognition of a reason why of all the multitudinous groups of people in this country you have to single out Negroes and give them this separate treatment."

He asserted, "It can't be because of slavery in the past, because there are very few groups in this country that haven't had slavery some place back in the history of their groups."

He went on, "It can't be color, because there are Negroes as white as the drifted snow, with blue eyes, and they are just as segregated as the colored man."

He concluded, "The only thing it can be is an inherent determination that the people who were formerly in slavery, regardless of anything else, shall be kept as near that stage as is possible, and now is the time, we submit, that this Court should make it clear that that is not what our Constitution stands for."

John W. Davis rose for what was to be his final appearance before the Supreme Court. Now eighty, he had aged visibly in the year since the first round of oral arguments. His memory had failed somewhat, and he referred to notes throughout his presentation. In addition, his voice no longer carried as once it had. He told the Court, "The horn doesn't blow as loud as it used to."

He was compelling nonetheless. Alexander Bickel later recalled, "No one hearing [Davis] emphasize how pervasive and how solidly founded the present order was could fail to be sensible to the difficulties encountered in uprooting it."

As he had in the first round of oral arguments, Davis stressed that the justices should be guided by established precedents and that segregation was a time-honored practice, sanctioned by past decisions of the Court. He insisted, "Somewhere, sometime to every principle comes a moment of repose when it has been so often announced, so confidently relied upon, so long continued, that it passes the limits of judicial discretion and disturbance." It was, in Davis's view, "late indeed in the day" to uproot segregation on any "theoretical or sociological basis."

He urged the Court to consider the practical consequences of a desegregation order. After all, it would not only mean that blacks would attend schools where whites were in the majority; it would also mean that some whites would be forced to attend schools that were predominantly black. Referring specifically to Clarendon County, where black public school children constituted the majority, he asserted, "If it is done on the mathematical basis, with 30 children as a maximum . . . you would have 27 Negro children and 3 whites in one school room." He asked rhetorically, "Would that make the children any happier? Would they learn any more quickly? Would their lives be more serene?"

He refuted Marshall's claim that race was not a reasonable basis for making legislative distinctions. "No man," he declared, quoting the renowned British prime minister Benjamin Disraeli, "will treat with indifference the fact of race. It is the key of history."

In his conclusion Davis assured the Court of South Carolina's intention to create equality of educational opportunity for all its residents, black and white, and implied that a desegregation order would jeopardize progress toward that end. He compared Marshall's position to that of the dog in one of Aesop's fables: "The dog, with a fine piece of meat in its mouth, crossed a bridge and saw the shadow in the stream and plunged for it and lost both substance and shadow."

He went on, echoing what he had told the Court in December 1952, "Here is equal education, not promised, not prophesied, but present. Shall it be thrown away on some fancied question of racial prestige?"

Years later, recalling Davis's performance that day, Justice Stanley Reed observed, "His argument was outstanding beyond its usual excellence." But it was Marshall, his position supported by the Justice Department, who carried the day.

At the December 12, 1953, Saturday conference that followed the reargument of *Brown,* Chief Justice Earl Warren spoke first, making his feelings known unequivocally. In his view segregation was intolerable in a modern, democratic society.

"I don't see how in this day and age we can set any group apart from the rest and say that they are not entitled to exactly the same treatment as all others," he declared. The post–Civil War amendments were, as he interpreted them, "intended to make the slaves equal with all others." Addressing *Brown* specifically, he said, "Personally, I can't see how today we can justify segregation based solely on race."

He went on to assert that the separate-but-equal doctrine was based on "the concept of the inherent inferiority of the colored race." He challenged any fellow justice who believed blacks were inferior to say so openly. If no one was willing to do so, he called for a unanimous opinion to lend weight to the Court's ruling.

At first, it was not at all clear whether the new chief justice would be able to achieve the desired unanimity. Hugo Black, William O. Douglas, Sherman Minton, and Frank Murphy sided with him. Tom C. Clark now leaned toward the NAACP position but, along with Warren and Frank Murphy, wanted to fashion an order that would take into account conditions in different geographic areas, because a desegregation order would surely be met with strong resistance in the South.

Stanley Reed appeared still to favor segregation. Felix Frankfurter was not allowing himself to be pinned down. He seemed to have his own ideas about how the decision should be framed, but he was keeping them to himself.

Justice Robert H. Jackson, like Frankfurter, was inscrutable. A New York aristocrat, he had served as Franklin Roosevelt's attorney general, been appointed to the Court by Roosevelt in 1941, and served as chief prosecutor at the Nuremburg trials. Initially a civil libertarian who aligned himself with Black and Douglas, he was by 1953 considered a judicial conservative.

Somehow Jackson wanted to express his view that in striking down the separate-but-equal doctrine, the Court was making a fundamentally political, rather than judicial, decision. He wrestled with the issue, drafting memorandums that indicated he might be preparing his own separate concurrence. Jackson himself flirted with a concurrence that would have been, if anything, stronger than the position ultimately taken by the Court. . . .

In the end, however, Warren succeeded in marshaling all nine justices behind his draft of a unanimous opinion, which he intended to be "short, readable by the lay public, non-rhetorical, unemotional and, above all, non-accusatory." This is exactly what it was. Warren read it from the bench on Monday, May 17, 1954, to an unsuspecting public and press corps.

It was the practice of the Court to deliver opinions on Mondays, with the author either reading aloud or summarizing the decision from the bench. There were few indications that this particular Monday would be the day for the delivery of *Brown*. Consequently, reporters were caught flat-footed at around one o'clock in the afternoon when Warren announced "the judgment and opinion of the Court in No. 1—*Oliver Brown et al. v. Board of Education of Topeka."* The wire services flashed the news to pressrooms around the country, and hundreds of anxious editors stopped the presses of their editions to await the details of the decision.

Warren read the decision aloud. Much of the text was devoted to a meticulous explanation of the cases' legal and historical background as well as a discussion of the value of public education in a modern society, so no one could be sure which way the Court had decided until he was two-thirds of the way through the fourteen-page opinion. As to the importance of education, he explained:

"Today education is perhaps the most important function of state and local governments. Compulsory school attendance laws and the great expenditures for education both demonstrate our recognition of the importance of education to our democratic society. It is required in the performance of our most basic public responsibilities, even service in the armed forces. It is the very foundation of good citizenship. Today it is a principal instrument in awakening the child to cultural values, in preparing him for later professional training, and in helping him to adjust normally to his environment. In these days, it is doubtful that any child may reasonably be expected to succeed in life if he is denied the opportunity of an education. Such an opportunity, where the state has undertaken to provide it, is a right which must be made available to all on equal terms."

The opinion went on to ask rhetorically, "Does segregation of children in public schools solely on the basis of race, even though the physical facilities and other 'tangible' factors may be equal, deprive the children of the minority group of equal educational opportunities?

"We believe that it does," the Court declared. "To separate [black children] from others of similar age and qualifications solely because of their race generates a feeling of inferiority as to their status in the community that may affect their hearts and minds in a way unlikely ever to be undone."

The decision quoted from the earlier decision of the Kansas court, which, despite its own findings of fact, ruled against the black plaintiffs:

"Segregation of white and colored children in public schools has a detrimental effect upon the colored children. The impact is greater when it has the sanction of the law; for the policy of separating the races is usually interpreted as denoting the inferiority of the negro group. A sense of inferiority affects the motivation of a child to learn. Segregation with the sanction of law, therefore, has a tendency to [retard] the educational and mental development of negro children and to deprive them of some of the benefits they would receive in a racial[ly] integrated school system."

Embracing the sociological perspective argued by Marshall, the Court declared, "Whatever may have been the extent of psychological knowledge at the time of *Plessy v. Ferguson,* [the Kansas court's] finding is amply supported by modern authority."

In a footnote that was to divide generations of legal scholars over the question of how much weight should be accorded authorities that are not, strictly speaking, legalistic, the Court cited as support for its proposition a number of sociological sources, including Kenneth Clark's work and Gunnar Myrdal's *An American Dilemma.*

In conclusion the justices declared, "In the field of public education the doctrine of 'separate but equal' has no place. Separate educational facilities are inherently unequal."

With this much said and done, the Court announced that it would hear reargument of the case in order to determine the appropriate remedy. On May 31, 1955, this would result in a decree that states must abolish segregation in their public education systems "with all deliberate speed."

After the decision Marshall said, "I was so happy I was numb." Not so for John W. Davis. He congratulated Marshall on the afternoon of his victory, although Davis's personal opinion was that the decision was "unworthy of the Supreme Court of the United States." Within a year of the Court's final ruling, Davis was dead. One of his law partners said that the Court's decision in *Brown* killed him.

A BLACK REPORTER described Monday, May 17, 1954, the day the Court delivered the unanimous opinion in *Brown,* as "the day we won; the day we took the white man's law and won our case before an all-white Supreme Court with a Negro lawyer. And we were proud."

Felix Frankfurter, in a personal note to Chief Justice Warren, said it was "a day that will live in glory." He added, "It is also a great day in the history of the Court." Justice Harold Burton, also in a note to Warren, called it "a great day for America and the Court." The justices' law clerks remembered it as a day on which they felt "good—and clean. It was so good."

Marshall himself saw the day as a turning point. The *Brown* decision, he said, "probably did more than anything else to awaken the Negro from his apathy to demanding his right to equality."

VOICES OF RESPECT
MAYA ANGELOU

Even in the cotton fields, slaves, exhausted from grueling work under the hot sun, practiced courtesy. They often addressed one another in gracious tones, creating mellifluous counterpoints to the foul language and hard-heartedness of slave owners and overseers. Such sweet kindness has survived slavery and been passed down through the generations. Today, while many African Americans struggle to control virulent forms of racism, they still abide by time-honored codes of conduct. But some children know only a climate of vulgarity; they lack even basic home training. For their sake, the legacy of respect should be taught. A little tenderness goes a long way.

African Americans as slaves could not even claim to have won the names given to them in haste and given without a care, but they pridefully possessed a quality which modified the barbarism of their lives. They awoke before sunrise to be in the fields at first light and trudged back to floorless cabins in the evening's gloom. They had little chance for amicable exchange in the rows of cotton and the stands of sugarcane; still, they devised ways of keeping their souls robust and spirits alive in that awful atmosphere. They employed formally familial terms when addressing each other. Neither the slaveowner nor the slave overseer was likely to speak to a servant in anything but the cruelest language. But in the slave society Mariah became Aunt Mariah and Joe became Uncle Joe. Young girls were called Sister, Sis, or Tutta. Boys became brother, Bubba, and Bro and Buddy. It is true that those terms used throughout the slave communities had had their roots in the African worlds from which the slaves had been torn, but under bondage they began to have greater meaning and a more powerful impact. As in every society, certain tones of voice were and still are used to establish the quality of communication between the speaker and the person addressed. When African Americans choose to speak sweetly to each other, not only do the voices fall in register, but there is an unconscious increase in music between the speakers. In fact, a conversation between friends can sound as melodic as a scripted song.

We have used these terms to help us survive slavery, its aftermath, and today's crisis of revived racism. However, now, when too many children run mad in the land, and now, when we need courtesy as much as or more than ever, and when a little tenderness between people could make life more bearable, we are losing even the appearance of courtesy. Our youth, finding little or no courtesy at home, make exodus into streets filled with violent self-revulsion and an exploding vulgarity.

We must re-create an attractive and caring attitude in our homes and in our worlds. If our children are to approve of themselves, they must see that we approve of ourselves. If we persist in self-disrespect and then ask our children to respect themselves, it is as if we break all their bones and then insist that they win Olympic gold medals for the hundred-yard dash.

Outrageous.

IN THE COMPANY OF MY FOREMOTHERS
ALICE WALKER

Pulitzer Prize laureate Alice Walker, born in 1944, was the eighth child of a sharecropper and a part-time maid. Poet, novelist, essayist, biographer, and womanist, Walker is credited for beginning, along with Toni Morrison, what has been called a renaissance of black women writers in 1970. Walker considers Zora Neale Hurston her literary foremother. Out of profound respect for and indebtedness to Hurston, whose accomplishments and courageousness had gone unacknowledged for years, Walker visited Florida in 1973 to uncover Hurston's past. Walker discovered Hurston's neglected gravesite and marked it with a headstone. In this excerpt from her essay entitled "Saving the Life That Is Your Own," Walker recalls how she researched material for a short story and found a community of friendly spirits, including Hurston's. From this essay, we can see that respect for others is not bound by the times in which we live.

. . . I don't recall the exact moment I set out to explore the works of black women, mainly those in the past, and certainly, in the beginning, I had no desire to teach them. Teaching being for me, at that time, less rewarding than star-gazing on a frigid night. My discovery of them— most of them out of print, abandoned, discredited, maligned, nearly lost—came about, as many things of value do, almost by accident. As it turned out—and this should not have surprised me—I found I was in need of something that only one of them could provide.

Mindful that throughout my four years at a prestigious black and then a prestigious white college I had heard not one word about early black women writers, one of my first tasks was simply to determine whether they had existed. After this, I could breathe easier, with more assurance about the profession I myself had chosen.

But the incident that started my search began several years ago: I sat down at my desk one day, in a room of my own, with key and lock, and began preparations for a story about voodoo, a subject that had always fascinated me. Many of the elements of this story I had gathered from a story my mother several times told me. She had gone, during the Depression, into town to apply for some government surplus food at the local commissary, and had been turned down, in a particularly humiliating way, by the white woman in charge.

My mother always told this story with a most curious expression on her face. She automatically raised her head higher than ever—it was always high—and there was a look of righteousness, a kind of holy *heat* coming from her eyes. She said she had lived to see this same white woman grow old and senile and so badly crippled she had to get about on *two* sticks.

To her, this was clearly the working of God, who, as in the old spiritual, ". . . may not come when you want him, but he's right on time!" To me, hearing the story for about the fiftieth time, something else was discernible: the possibilities of the story, for fiction.

What, I asked myself, would have happened if, after the crippled old lady died, it was discovered that someone, my mother perhaps (who would have been mortified at the thought, Christian that she is), had voodooed her?

Then, my thoughts sweeping me away into the world of hexes and conjurings of centuries past, I wondered how a larger story could be created out of my mother's story; one that would be true to the magnitude of her humiliation and grief, and to the white woman's lack of sensitivity and compassion.

My third quandary was: How could I find out all I needed to know in order to write a story that used *authentic* black witchcraft?

Which brings me back, almost, to the day I became really interested in black women writers. I say "almost" because one other thing, from my childhood, made the choice of black magic a logical and irresistible one for my story. Aside from my mother's several stories about root doctors she had heard of or known, there was the story I had often heard about my "crazy" Walker aunt.

Many years ago, when my aunt was a meek and obedient girl growing up in a strict, conventionally religious house in the rural South, she had suddenly thrown off her meekness and had run away from home, escorted by a rogue of a man permanently attached elsewhere.

When she was returned home by her father, she was declared quite mad. In the backwoods South at the turn of the century, "madness" of this sort was cured not by psychiatry but by powders and by spells. (One can see Scott Joplin's *Treemonisha* to understand the role voodoo played among black people of that period.) My aunt's madness was treated by the community conjurer, who promised, and delivered, the desired results. His treatment was a bag of white powder, bought for fifty cents, and sprinkled on the ground around her house, with some of it sewed, I believe, into the bodice of her nightgown.

So when I sat down to write my story about voodoo, my crazy Walker aunt was definitely on my mind.

But she had experienced her temporary craziness so long ago that her story had all the excitement of a might-have-been. I needed, instead of family memories, some hard facts about the *craft* of voodoo, as practiced by Southern blacks in the nineteenth century. (It never once, fortunately, occurred to me that voodoo was not worthy of the interest I had in it, or was too ridiculous to study seriously.)

I began reading all I could find on the subject of "The Negro and His Folkways and Superstitions." There were Botkin and Puckett and others, all white, most racist. How was I to believe anything they wrote, since at least one of them, Puckett, was capable of wondering, in his book, if "The Negro" had a large enough brain?

Well, I thought, where are the *black* collectors of folklore? Where is the *black* anthropologist? Where is the *black* person who took the time to travel the back roads of the South and collect the information I need: how to cure heart trouble, treat dropsy, hex somebody to death, lock bowels, cause joints to swell, eyes to fall out, and so on. Where was this black person?

And that is when I first saw, in a *footnote* to the white voices of authority, the name Zora Neale Hurston.

Folklorist, novelist, anthropologist, serious student of voodoo, also all-around black woman, with guts enough to take a slide rule and measure random black heads in Harlem; not to prove their inferiority, but to prove that whatever their size, shape, or present condition of servitude, those heads contained all the intelligence anyone could use to get through this world.

Zora Hurston, who went to Barnard to learn how to study what she really wanted to learn: the ways of her own people, and what ancient rituals, customs, and beliefs had made them unique.

Zora, of the sandy-colored hair and the daredevil eyes, a girl who escaped poverty and parental neglect by hard work and a sharp eye for the main chance.

Zora, who left the South only to return to look at it again. Who went to root doctors from Florida to Louisiana and said, "Here I am. I want to learn your trade."

Zora, who had collected all the black folklore I could ever use.

That Zora.

And having found *that Zora* (like a golden key to a storehouse of varied treasure), I was hooked.

What I had discovered, of course, was a model. A model, who, as it happened, provided more than voodoo for my story, more than one of the greatest novels America had produced—though, being America, it did not realize this. She had provided, as if she knew someday I would come along wandering in the wilderness, a nearly complete record of her life. And though her life sprouted an occasional wart, I am eternally grateful for that life, warts and all.

It is not irrelevant, nor is it bragging (except perhaps to gloat a little on the happy relatedness of Zora, my mother, and me), to mention here that the story I wrote, called "The Revenge of Hannah Kemhuff," based on my mother's experiences during the Depression, and on Zora Hurston's folklore collection of the 1920s, and on my own response to both out of a contemporary existence, was immediately published and was later selected, by a reputable collector of short stories, as one of the *Best Short Stories of 1974.*

I mention it because this story might never have been written, because the very bases of its structure, authentic black folklore, viewed from a black perspective, might have been lost.

Had it been lost, my mother's story would have had no historical underpinning, none I could trust, anyway. I would not have written the story, which I enjoyed writing as much as I've enjoyed writing anything in my life, had I not known that Zora had already done a thorough job of preparing the ground over which I was then moving.

In that story I gathered up the historical and psychological threads of the life my ancestors lived, and in the writing of it I felt joy and strength and my own continuity. I had that wonderful feeling writers get sometimes, not very often, of being *with* a great many people, ancient spirits, all very happy to see me consulting and acknowledging them, and eager to let me know, through the joy of their presence, that, indeed, I am not alone. . . .

NAMING NAMES

Names and nicknames—those given and those taken on—are part of a continuing tradition of creativity and respect in the black community. Some names are traced back to African naming practices. Others are assertions of self-identity. Still others are descriptive of a special talent or attribute. Here are a few names that reflect individual traits or their bearer's approach toward life.

SOME NAME ORIGINS

B. B. King—"B.B." stands for "Blues Boy." It is a shortened form of "Blues Boy from Beale Street," a nickname he took on long ago. B. B. King's birth name is Riley B. King.

Lady Day—Billie Holiday's nickname, Lady Day, was given to her by Lester Young in the 1930s. She was born Eleanora Fagan, but renamed herself after film star Billie Dove and her father, Clarence Holiday.

Duke Ellington—During his youth a friend nicknamed Edward Kennedy Ellington "Duke" because of his personal style and his sophistication. Ralph Ellison wrote that Ellington "proceeded to create for himself a kingdom of sound and rhythm."

Satchel—LeRoy Paige, the baseball great, earned this nickname as a boy while carrying satchel bags at the train station in Mobile, Alabama.

Satchmo—Louis Armstrong's nickname probably came from a few of his early recordings. On the 1930 record of "You're Driving Me Crazy," Armstrong addresses his horn, saying, "Watch it, Satchel-mouth." Satchmo, probably a contraction of Satchel-mouth, was used in advertising and editorial copy.

Ntozake Shange—Born Paulette Williams and reared in a middle-class home in Trenton, New Jersey, the poet, playwright, and novelist adopted the name Ntozake Shange (En-to-za-kee Shong-gay) after two South Africans baptized her in the Pacific Ocean. Ntozake means "She who brings her own things"; Shange means "One who walks with lions."

Sojourner Truth—Named Isabella, she was born a slave in 1797 and nicknamed Belle. She fled slavery and changed her surname to Van Wagenen to conceal her true identity from slave catchers. In 1843, she changed her name again, to Sojourner Truth, after undergoing a spiritual transformation. She believed her mission was a "sojourn" through the land to speak only God's "truth."

Tiger Woods—He was born Eldrick Woods to a Thai mother and an African American father, Earl Woods, a Green Beret who had fought in Indochina. His father nicknamed him after a South Vietnamese named Nguyen Phong, who was known to most people as "Tiger."

Malcolm X—Malcolm X was born Malcolm Little. He adopted X for his surname after joining the Nation of Islam and being awarded his "X" by the organization's leader, Elijah Muhammad. The "X" symbolized the unknown—that is, Malcolm's ancestors' original African name(s).

❦

Duke Ellington never grinned. He smiled. Ellington never shuffled. He strode. It was "Good afternoon, ladies and gentlemen," never "How y'all doin'?" At his performances, we [blacks] sat up high in our seats.

—*Gordon Parks*

❦

LOYALTY

How strong are your allegiances? Are you someone's protégé, closest friend, or trusted companion? If so, you know the world admires and respects an abiding faithfulness to people and duty. Our most steadfast relationships and our finest organizations are built on a bedrock of oaths and allegiances. Like signposts along the roads we travel, our loyalties announce our friendships, concerns, what we really care about, and what we will remain devoted to.

A good friend is, of course, a trusted and loyal companion. But not all loyalties stem from solid friendships. Some loyalties are merely ceremonial. However, a person of high moral character will uphold a sworn allegiance regardless of whether it involves people who are likable or unlikable, friendly or unfriendly.

African American history provides wonderful stories of loyalty, some of which are included here. Black soldiers and sailors fought bravely for America right from the start, remaining loyal to the cause of liberty in spite of being denied liberty for themselves.

Sports has served as another proving ground for black loyalty. Joe Louis's fans—particularly his black fans—felt every blow he ever received in the ring. Maya Angelou recalls the loyalty of fans during the "radio days" of the 1930s.

African Americans causes are represented here, too, including a story with all of the drama you might expect in a mystery about spying behind enemy lines—the report of a black man who investigated white lynchers in the South. Finally, no chapter of African American loyalty would be complete without the lyrics of "Lift Every Voice and Sing," the song called the "Negro national anthem."

ᏹᏽᏹ

We have a wonderful history behind us . . . It reads like the history of a people in a heroic age . . . We are going back to that beautiful history and it is going to inspire us to greater achievements.

—*Carter G. Woodson*

ᏹᏽᏹ

FREEDOM'S JOURNAL

In New York City, John Russwurm and Samuel E. Cornish began publishing Freedom's Journal, *the first African American–owned newspaper, on March 16, 1827, the same year slavery was officially abolished in New York.* The black press would eventually become one of the most important institutions in the black community, serving as an outlet for black expression and reporting on events that were significant to blacks but ignored by the white press. The following piece is an open letter to the readers of* Freedom's Journal, *published in its first edition.*

To Our Patrons

In presenting our first number to our Patrons, we feel all the diffidence of persons entering upon a new and untried line of business. But a moment's reflection upon the noble objects, which we have in view by the publication of this Journal; the expediency of its appearance at this time, when so many schemes are in action concerning our people—encourage us to come boldly before an enlightened publick. For we believe, that a paper devoted to the dissemination of useful knowledge

---

* The newspaper's offices were located at 6 Varick Street and later were moved to 152 Church Street in Manhattan. At the time, black New Yorkers lived in the area where City Hall is now located. (The African Burial Ground, where as many as 20,000 Africans were buried, covered more than five acres in this vicinity—about five city blocks. The cemetery, closed in 1794 and then forgotten, was rediscovered in 1991, when a construction crew unearthed remains. The cemetery has been designated a historic site and is protected by the city's Landmarks Preservation Commission.)

Russwurm was the second black man to graduate from an American college (Bowdoin College). Cornish was a militant minister. They geared *Freedom's Journal* toward ex-slaves and free blacks. The last edition was printed on March 28, 1829, but Cornish resurrected the paper on May 29, 1829, with a new name, the *Rights of All*.

among our brethren, and to their moral and religious improvement, must meet with the cordial approbation of every friend to humanity.

The peculiarities of this Journal, renders [sic] it important that we should advertise to the world our motives by which we are actuated, and the objects which we contemplate.

We wish to plead our own cause. Too long have others spoken for us. Too long has the publick been deceived by misrepresentations, in things which concern us dearly, though in the estimation of some mere trifles; for though there are many in society who exercise towards us benevolent feelings; still (with sorrow we confess it) there are others who make it their business to enlarge upon the least trifle, which tends to the discredit of any person of colour; and pronounce anathemas and denounce our whole body for the misconduct of this guilty one. We are aware that there are many instances of vice among us, but we avow that it is because no one has taught its subjects to be virtuous; many instances of poverty, because no sufficient efforts accommodated to minds contracted by slavery, and deprived of early education have been made, to teach them how to husband their hard earnings, and to secure to themselves comfort.

Education being an object of the highest importance to the welfare of society, we shall endeavour to present just and adequate views of it, and to urge upon our brethren the necessity and expediency of training their children, while young, to habits of industry, and thus forming them for becoming useful members of society. It is surely time that we should awake from this lethargy of years, and make a concentrated effort for the education of our youth. We form a spoke in the human wheel, and it is necessary that we should understand our pendence on the different parts, and theirs on us, in order to perform our part with propriety.

Though not desiring of dictating, we shall feel it our incumbent duty to dwell occasionally upon the general principles and rules of economy. The world has grown too enlightened, to estimate any man's character by his personal appearance. Though all men acknowledge the excellency of Franklin's maxims, yet comparatively few practise upon them. We may deplore when it is too late, the neglect of these self-evident truths, but it avails little to mourn. Ours will be the task of admonishing our brethren on these points.

The civil rights of a people being of the greatest value, it shall ever be our duty to vindicate our brethren, when oppressed; and to lay the case before the publick. We shall also urge upon our brethren, (who are qualified by the laws of the different states) the expediency of using their elective franchise; and of making an independent use of the same. We wish them not to become the tools of party.

And as much time is frequently lost, and wrong principles instilled, by the perusal of works of trivial importance, we shall consider it a part of our duty to recommend to our young readers, such authors as will not only enlarge their stock of useful knowledge, but such as will also serve to stimulate them to higher attainments in science.

We trust also, that through the columns of the FREEDOM'S JOURNAL, many practical pieces, having for their bases, the improvement of our brethren, will be presented to them, from the pens of many of our respected friends, who have kindly promised their assistance.

It is our earnest wish to make our Journal a medium of intercourse between our brethren in the different states of this great confederacy: that through its columns an expression of our sentiments, on many interesting subjects which concern us, may be offered to the publick: that plans which apparently are beneficial may be candidly discussed and properly weighed; if worth, receive our cordial approbation; if not, our marked disapprobation.

Useful knowledge of every kind, and everything that relates to Africa, shall find a ready admission into our columns; and as that vast continent becomes daily more known, we trust that many things will come to light, proving that the natives of it are neither so ignorant nor stupid as they have generally been supposed to be.

And while these important subjects shall occupy the columns of the FREEDOM'S JOURNAL, we would not be unmindful of our brethren who are still in the iron fetters of bondage. They are our kindred by all the times of nature; and though but little can be effected by us, still let our sympathies be poured forth, and our prayers in their behalf, ascend to Him who is able to succour them.

From the press and the pulpit we have suffered much by being incorrectly represented. Men whom we equally love and admire have not hesitated to represent us disadvantageously, without becoming personally acquainted with the true state of things, nor discerning between virtue and vice among us. The virtuous part of our people feel themselves sorely aggrieved under the existing state of things—they are not appreciated.

Our vices and our degradation are ever arrayed against us, but our virtues are passed by unnoticed. And what is still more lamentable, our friends, to whom we concede all the principles of humanity and religion, from these very causes seem to have fallen into the current of popular feeling and are imperceptibly floating on the stream—actually living in the practice of prejudice, while they abjure it in theory, and feel it not in their hearts. Is it not very desirable that such should know more of our actual condition; and of our efforts and feelings, that in forming or advocating plans for our amelioration, they may do it more understandingly? In the spirit of candor and humility we intend by a simple representation of facts to lay our case before the public, with a view to arrest the progress of prejudice, and to shield ourselves against the consequent evils. We wish to conciliate all and to irritate none, yet we must be firm and unwavering in our principles, and persevering in our efforts.

If ignorance, poverty and degradation have hitherto been our unhappy lot; has the Eternal decree gone forth, that our race alone are to remain in this state, while knowledge and civilization are shedding their enlivening rays over the rest of the human family? The recent travels of Denham and Clapperton in the interior of Africa, and the interesting narrative which they have published; the establishment of the republic of Hayti after years of sanguinary warfare; its subsequent progress in all the arts of civilization; and the advancement of liberal ideas in South America, where despotism has given place to free governments, and where many of our brethren now fill important civil and military stations, prove the contrary.

The interesting fact that there are FIVE HUNDRED THOUSAND free persons of colour, one half of whom might peruse, and the whole be benefitted by the publication of the Journal; that no publication, as yet, has been devoted exclusively to their improvement—that many selections from approved standard authors, which are within the reach of few, may occasionally be made—and more important still, that this large body of our citizens have no public channel—all serve to prove the real necessity, at present, for the appearance of the FREEDOM'S JOURNAL.

It shall ever be our desire so to conduct the editorial department of our paper as to give offence to none of our patrons; as nothing is farther from us than to make it the advocate of any partial views, either in politics or religion. What few days we can number, have been devoted to the improvement of our brethren; and it is our earnest wish that the remainder may be spent in the same delightful service.

In conclusion, whatever concerns us as a people, will ever find a ready admission into the FREEDOM'S JOURNAL, interwoven with all the principal news of the day.

And while every thing in our power shall be performed to support the character of our Journal, we would respectfully invite our numerous friends to assist by their communications, and our coloured brethren to strengthen our hands by their subscriptions, as our labour is one of common cause, and worthy of their consideration and support. And we most earnestly solicit the latter, that if at any time we should seem to be zealous, or too pointed in the inculcation of any important lesson, they will remember, that they are equally interested in the cause in which we are engaged, and attribute our zeal to the peculiarities of our situation; and our earnest engagedness in their well-being.

New York, March 16, 1827

THE NEGRO DIGS UP HIS PAST
ARTHUR A. SCHOMBURG

History as a collective enterprise gives people a sense of value, affirming their contributions to civilization. Providing sound evidence of these contributions takes years of dedication and the accumulation of a wealth of materials. Bibliophile Arthur A. Schomburg (1874–1938) helped to establish one of the world's finest resources for studying the history and culture of people of African descent. His vast private collection is now part of the Schomburg Center for Research in Black Culture, formerly the 135th Street branch of the New York Public Library.

Schomburg was born on St. Thomas, U.S. Virgin Islands, and raised in Puerto Rico. In 1891, he moved to New York City, where he began collecting materials on black culture. In 1926, he sold his private collec-

tion—approximately 10,000 books, manuscripts, prints, and pieces of memorabilia—to the New York Public Library. Six years later, he was named curator of his former collection. Located in Harlem, the Schomburg Center now has 5.2 million items, including documents, books, art and artifacts, and audiovisual material. The center, an international hub of black culture, serves as a testament of his loyalty to his people.

Here is what Schomburg had to say about researching the past.

The American Negro must remake his past in order to make his future. Though it is orthodox to think of America as the one country where it is unnecessary to have a past, what is a luxury for the nation as a whole becomes a prime social necessity for the Negro. For him, a group tradition must supply compensation for persecution, and pride of race the antidote for prejudice. History must restore what slavery took away, for it is the social damage of slavery that the present generations must repair and offset. So among the rising democratic millions we find the Negro thinking more collectively, more retrospectively than the rest, and apt out of the very pressure of the present to become the most enthusiastic antiquarian of them all.

Vindicating evidences of individual achievement have as a matter of fact been gathered and treasured for over a century: Abbé Gregoire's liberal-minded book on Negro notables in 1808 was the pioneer effort; it has been followed at intervals by less known and often less discriminating compendiums of exceptional men and women of African stock. But this sort of thing was on the whole pathetically over-corrective, ridiculously over-laudatory; it was apologetics turned into biography. A true historical sense develops slowly and with difficulty under such circumstances. But to-day, even if for the ultimate purpose of group justification, history has become less a matter of argument and more a matter of record. There is the definite desire and determination to have a history, well documented, widely known at least within race circles, and administered as a stimulating and inspiring tradition for the coming generations.

Gradually as the study of the Negro's past has come out of the vagaries of rhetoric and propaganda and become systematic and scientific, three outstanding conclusions have been established:

First, that the Negro has been throughout the centuries of controversy an active collaborator, and often a pioneer, in the struggle for his own freedom and advancement. This is true to a degree which makes it the more surprising that it has not been recognized earlier.

Second, that by virtue of their being regarded as something "exceptional," even by friends and well-wishers, Negroes of attainment and genius have been unfairly disassociated from the group, and group credit lost accordingly.

Third, that the remote racial origins of the Negro, far from being what the race and the world have been given to understand, offer a record of credible group achievement when scientifically viewed, and more important still, that they are of vital general interest because of their bearing upon the beginnings and early development of human culture.

With such crucial truths to document and establish, an ounce of fact is worth a pound of controversy. So the Negro historian to-day digs under the spot where his predecessor stood and argued. Not long ago, the Public Library of Harlem housed a special exhibition of books, pamphlets, prints and old engravings, that simply said, to skeptic and believer alike, to scholar and school-child, to proud black and astonished white, "Here is the evidence." Assembled from the rapidly growing collections of the leading Negro book-collectors and research societies, there were in these cases, materials not only for the first true writing of Negro history, but for the rewriting of many important paragraphs of our common American history. Slow though it be, historical truth is no exception to the proverb.

Here among the rarities of early Negro Americana was Jupiter Hammon's Address to the Negroes of the State of New York, edition of 1787, with the first American Negro poet's famous "If we should ever get to Heaven, we shall find nobody to reproach us for being black, or for being slaves." Here was Phyllis Wheatley's Mss. poem of 1767 addressed to the students of Harvard, her spirited encomiums upon George Washington and the Revolutionary Cause, and John Marrant's St. John's Day eulogy to the "Brothers of African Lodge No. 459" delivered at Boston in 1789. Here too were Lemuel Haynes' Vermont commentaries on the American Revolution and his learned sermons to his white congregation in Rutland, Vermont, and the sermons of the year 1808 by the Rev. Absalom Jones of St. Thomas Church, Philadelphia, and Peter Williams of St. Philip's, New York, pioneer Episcopal rectors who spoke out in daring and influential ways on the Abolition of the Slave Trade. Such things and many others are more than mere items of curiosity: they educate any receptive mind.

Reinforcing these were still rarer items of Africana and foreign Negro interest, the volumes of Juan Latino, the best Latinist of Spain in the reign of Philip V, incumbent of the chair of Poetry at the University of Granada, and author of Poems printed there in 1573 and a book on the Escurial published 1576; the Latin and Dutch treatises of Jacobus Eliza Capitein, a native of West Coast Africa and graduate of the University of Leyden, Gustavus Vassa's celebrated autobiography that supplied so much of the evidence in 1796 for Granville Sharpe's attack on slavery in the British colonies, Julien Raymond's Paris exposé of the disabilities of the free people of color in the then (1791) French colony of Hayti, and Baron de Vastey's *Cry of the Fatherland*, the famous polemic by the secretary of Christophe that precipitated the Haytian struggle for independence. The cumulative effect of such evidences of scholarship and moral prowess is too weighty to be dismissed as exceptional.

But weightier surely than any evidence of individual talent and scholarship could ever be, is the evidence of important collaboration and significant pioneer initiative in social service and reform, in the efforts toward race emancipation, colonization and race betterment. From neglected and rust-spotted pages comes testimony to the black men and women who stood shoulder to shoulder in courage and zeal, and often on a parity of intelligence and talent, with their notable white benefactors. There was the already cited work of Vassa that aided so materially the efforts of Granville Sharpe, the record of Paul Cuffee, the Negro colonization pioneer, associated so importantly with the establishment of Sierra Leone as a British colony for the occupancy of free people of color in West Africa; the dramatic and history-making exposé of John Baptist Phillips, African graduate of Edinburgh, who compelled through Lord Bathhurst in 1824 the enforcement of the articles of capitulation guaranteeing freedom to the blacks of Trinidad. There is the record of the pioneer colonization project of Rev. Daniel Coker in conducting a voyage of ninety expatriates to West Africa in 1820, of the missionary efforts of Samuel Crowther in Sierra Leone, first Anglican bishop of his diocese, and that of the work of John Russwurm, a leader in the work and foundation of the American Colonization Society.

When we consider the facts, certain chapters of American history will have to be reopened. Just as black men were influential factors in the campaign against the slave trade, so they were among the earliest instigators of the abolition movement. Indeed there was a dangerous calm between the agitation for the suppression of the slave trade and the beginning of the campaign for emancipation. During that interval colored men were very influential in arousing the attention of public men who in turn aroused the conscience of the country. Continuously between 1808 and 1845, men like Prince Saunders, Peter Williams, Absalom Jones, Nathaniel Paul, and Bishops Varick and Richard Allen, the founders of the two wings of African Methodism, spoke out with force and initiative, and men like Denmark Vesey (1822), David Walker (1828) and Nat Turner (1831) advocated and organized schemes for direct action. This culminated in the generally ignored but important conventions of Free People of Color in New York, Philadelphia and other centers, whose platforms and efforts are to the Negro of as great significance as the nationally cherished memories of Faneuil and Independence Halls. Then with Abolition comes the better documented and more recognized collaboration of Samuel R. Ward, William Wells Brown, Henry Highland Garnett, Martin Delaney, Harriet Tubman, Sojourner Truth, and Frederick Douglass with their great colleagues, Tappan, Phillips, Sumner, Mott, Stowe and Garrison.

But even this latter group who came within the limelight of national and international notice, and thus into open comparison with the best minds of their generation, the public too often regards as a group of inspired illiterates, eloquent echoes of their Abolitionist sponsors. For a true estimate of their ability and scholarship, however, one must go with the antiquarian to the files of the *Anglo-African Magazine*, where page by page comparisons may be made. Their writings show Douglass, McCune Smith, Wells Brown, Delaney, Wilmot Blyden and Alexander Crummell to have been as scholarly and versatile as any of the noted publicists with whom they were associated. All of them labored internationally in the cause of their fellows; to Scotland, England, France, Germany and Africa, they carried their brilliant offensive of debate and propaganda, and with this came instance upon instance of signal foreign recognition, from academic, scientific, public and official sources. Delaney's *Principia of Ethnology* won public reception from learned societies, Pennington's discourses an honorary doctorate from Heidelberg, Wells Brown's three year mission the entrée of the salons of London and Paris, and the tours of Frederick Douglass, receptions second only to Henry Ward Beecher's.

After this great era of public interest and discussion, it was Alexander Crummell, who, with the reaction already setting in, first organized Negro brains defensively through the founding of the American Negro Academy in 1897 at Washington. A New York boy whose zeal for education had suffered a rude shock when refused admission to the Episcopal Seminary by Bishop Onderdonk, he had been befriended by John Jay and sent to Cambridge University, England, for his education and ordination. On his return, he was beset with the idea of promoting race scholarship, and the Academy was the final result. It has continued ever since to be one of the bulwarks of our intellectual life, though unfortunately its members have had to spend too much of their energy and effort answering detractors and disproving popular fallacies. Only gradually have the men of this group been able to work toward pure scholarship. Taking a slightly different start, The Negro Society for Historical Research was later organized in New York, and has succeeded in stimulating the collection from all parts of the world of books and documents dealing with the Negro. It has also brought together for the first time co-operatively in a single society African, West Indian and Afro-American scholars. Direct offshoots of this same effort are the extensive private collections of Henry P. Slaughter of Washington, the Rev. Charles D. Martin of Harlem, of Arthur Schomburg of Brooklyn, and of the late John E. Bruce, who was the enthusiastic and far-seeing pioneer of this movement. Finally and more recently, the Association for the Study of Negro Life and History has extended these efforts into a scientific research project of great achievement and promise. Under the direction of Dr. Carter G. Woodson, it has continuously maintained for nine years the publication of the learned quarterly, *The Journal of Negro History,* and with the assistance and recognition of two large educational foundations has maintained research and published valuable monographs in Negro history. Almost keeping pace with the work of scholarship has been the effort to popularize the results, and to place before Negro youth in the schools the true story of race vicissitude, struggle and accomplishment. So that quite largely now the ambition of Negro youth can be nourished on its own milk.

Such work is a far cry from the puerile controversy and petty braggadocio with which the effort for race history first started. But a general as well as a racial lesson has been learned. We seem lately to have come at last to realize what the truly scientific attitude requires, and to see that the race issue has been a plague on both our historical houses, and that history cannot be properly written with either bias or counter-bias. The blatant Caucasian racialist with his theories and assumptions of race superiority and dominance has in turn bred his Ethiopian counterpart— the rash and rabid amateur who has glibly tried to prove half of the world's geniuses to have been Negroes and to trace the pedigree of nineteenth century Americans from the Queen of Sheba. But fortunately to-day there is on both sides of a really common cause less of the sand of controversy and more of the dust of digging.

Of course, a racial motive remains—legitimately compatible with scientific method and aim. The work our race students now regard as important, they undertake very naturally to overcome in part certain handicaps of disparagement and omission too well-known to particularize. But they do so not merely that we may not wrongfully be deprived of the spiritual nourishment of our cultural past, but also that the full story of human collaboration and interdependence may be told and realized. Especially is this likely to be the effect of the latest and most fascinating of all the attempts to open up the closed Negro past, namely the important study of African cultural origins and sources. The bigotry of civilization which is the taproot of intellectual prejudice begins far back and must be corrected at its source. Fundamentally it has come about from that depreciation of Africa which has sprung up from ignorance of her true rôle and position in human history and the early development of culture. The Negro has been a man without a history because he has been considered a man without a worthy culture. But a new notion of the cultural attainment and potentialities of the African stocks has recently come about, partly through the corrective influence of the more scientific study of African institutions and early cultural history, partly through growing appreciation of the skill and beauty and in many cases the historical priority of the African native crafts, and finally through the signal recognition which first in France and Germany, but now very generally, the astonishing art of the African sculptures has received. Into these fascinating new vistas, with limited horizons lifting in all directions, the mind of the Negro has leapt forward faster than the slow clearings of scholarship will yet safely permit. But there is no doubt that here is a field full of the most intriguing and inspiring possibilities. Already the Negro sees himself against a reclaimed background, in a perspective that will give pride and self-respect ample scope, and make history yield for him the same values that the treasured past of any people affords.

REFLECTIONS IN A PUBLIC LIBRARY
ANDY RAZAF

Libraries are so much more than simply repositories for books.
Songwriter Andy Raẓaf (1895–1973), who was self-taught, spent many hours in the 135th Street branch of the New York Public Library, now the Schomburg Center for Research in Black Culture. His time there motivated him to write this poem.

Libraries ever seem to me
True symbols of Democracy,
Where folks of every race and creed,
Both rich and poor, may go and read.

And they are like a treasure chest
Where anyone can seek and find;
Gems from the North, South, East and West,
The riches of the human mind.

Librarians, they are to me
Like beacons on life's stormy sea,
They guard the books, the precious light
Forever there to guide me right.

WASHINGTON'S BLACK PATRIOT

On the eve of the American Revolution, the population of the colonies was two and a half million people. A half million were black—some free, most slaves. It has been estimated that during the war years, five thousand blacks served on the patriot side, including Oliver Cromwell, who crossed the Delaware with George Washington and his troops on Christmas night in 1776 to attack the British in New Jersey. Cromwell's exploits were reported in a New Jersey newspaper when he reached his one hundredth birthday.

The attention of many of our citizens has, doubtless, been arrested by the appearance of an old colored man who might have been seen, sitting in front of his residence, in East Union Street, respectfully raising his hat to those who might be passing by. His attenuated frame, his silvered head, his feeble movements, combine to prove that he was very aged; and yet, comparatively few are aware that he is among the survivors of the gallant army who fought for the liberties of our country "in the days which tried men's souls."

On Monday last, we stopped to speak to him, and asked him how old he was. He asked the day of the month, and . . . replied with trembling lips, "I am very old—I am a hundred years old today."

His name is Oliver Cromwell. . . . He enlisted in a company commanded by Capt. Lowery, attached to the Second New Jersey Regiment, under the command of Col. Israel Shreve. He was at the battles of Trenton, Princeton, Brandywine, Monmouth, and Yorktown, at which latter place, he told us, he saw the last man killed. Although his faculties are failing, yet he relates many interesting reminiscences of the Revolution. He was with the army at the retreat of the Delaware, on the memorable crossing of the 25th of December, 1776, and relates the story of the battles of the succeeding days with enthusiasm. He gives the details of the march from Trenton to Princeton, and told us, with much humor, that they "knocked the British about lively" at the latter place. . . .

—Burlington Gazette, *1852*

Cromwell, who was raised as a farmer, served for six years and nine months under the immediate command of George Washington. Cromwell's honorable discharge with Badge of Merit, dated June 5, 1783, is reportedly in Washington's own handwriting.

FIGHTING FOR AMERICA

For more than 200 years, black soldiers and sailors have fought bravely in America's fighting forces. Black warriors saw combat in the Continental army and navy in the War of Independence and have played a crucial role in every major military operation and war the nation has fought. The loyalty and gallantry of African American fighters, who figure prominently among the nation's most highly decorated military heroes, is clear.

Negroes have been an integral part of American military history from its very inception. Serving first under the Spanish and then French flags, they fought under the British colors and served with valor and distinction in the Continental army and navy of the thirteen colonies. Since then, Negroes have participated in every war in which this country has been engaged.

The War of Independence: Some 5,000 blacks served in the Revolutionary War. All were in integrated units until ten months after the Battles of Lexington and Concord, in 1775, when a policy of exclusion developed in Georgia and South Carolina. Nevertheless, they fought in all of the major battles of the war, including those of Brandywine, Yorktown, Monmouth, White Plains, Stillwater, Bennington, Saratoga, Trenton, Rhode Island, Savannah and others.

First to fall in the War of Independence was the Negro patriot, Crispus Attucks, believed by many historians to have been the same man who was advertised as a runaway slave from Framingham, Massachusetts, in 1750. Little is known of his life, other than that he was a seaman and laborer. In an account of his burial, the *Boston Gazette and Country* described him as a "stranger, being six feet two inches in height, and a mulatto." At approximately nine o'clock, on the night of March 5, 1770, Attucks and some 50 patriots converged on the British garrison on King Street, where they were met with a volley of musket fire. Crispus Attucks, standing defiantly in the front rank and most easily distinguishable because of his color, fell dead—the first man, black or white, to die for the concept of freedom which his own people were not to share until the end of the Civil War, a century later. Thus, the Boston Massacre, as the skirmish was called, not only commemorates the beginning of open hostilities between the colonists and England, but honors the black man, Crispus Attucks, the first American symbol of resistance to tyranny.

The War of 1812: Upon the advent of the War of 1812, peacetime militia enlistments were restricted to "able-bodied white males" by an Act of Congress. In some states, however (e.g. Georgia, North Carolina and Louisiana), "certain free men of color" were accepted in the state militia. Despite the exclusions, they nevertheless acquitted themselves nobly; particularly the two battalions of black soldiers who served under General Andrew Jackson when he defeated the British in the decisive Battle of New Orleans.

Many Negroes also saw naval service during the War of 1812, on the high seas and especially in the Great Lakes region where they played an important and heroic role in the Battles of Lake Erie and Lake Champlain (as well as other naval engagements) which were factors bearing on the successful conclusion of the war.

On December 18, 1814, General Jackson issued a proclamation to

Negro troops following the Battle of New Orleans in which he lauded "the men of color":

"Soldiers!

. . . You surpassed my hopes. I have found in you that noble enthusiasm which impels to great deeds."

On February 18, 1820, the Adjutant and Inspector General's Office of the United States Army expressed its "thanks" to the black Americans for their military contributions by issuing the following order:

"No Negro or Mulatto will be received as a recruit of the Army."

The Civil War: At the outbreak of the War between the States, President Abraham Lincoln and his military advisors were confident that the armies of the secessionist states would be forced to surrender within a few months. This confidence quickly evaporated with the disastrous defeat of the Union forces in the Battle of Bull Run. Until then, Lincoln had sought to woo the border states to the Union cause by refraining from arming Negroes. Now, however, it became apparent that the South would not crumble with the first onslaught and that a protracted conflict could be expected. Fifty thousand slaves were enlisted for "volunteer labor" and assigned to the Quartermaster Department of the Union Army.

In less than a year after Bull Run, in May 1862, the First South Carolina Regiment was organized by Major General David Hunter. A month later, the *Corps d'Afrique,* comprising the 1st, 2nd and 3rd Native Guards, was brought into action. These were the first Negro *combat* troops of the war. By January 1, 1863, the date of the Emancipation Proclamation, the exclusion of Negroes as combat troops came to an end. Frederick Douglass, who had been urging Lincoln to free the slaves and arm them for combat, did yeoman service in the recruitment of Negroes for the Union armies, among them his own sons.

Of the 186,000 blacks who served during the war, some 30,000 saw action in the Union Navy—roughly 25 percent of the Navy's personnel. They were aboard the *Kearsage* when she defeated the *Alabama,* the *Monitor* in its engagement with the *Merrimac,* and Farragut's flagship in the Battle of Mobile Bay.

The contribution of the Negroes to the preservation of the Union is self evident: They fought in over 449 battles, produced 16 Medal of Honor recipients, and earned the praise of every commanding officer under whom they served. At the close of the war, more than 38,000 black soldiers had sacrificed their lives for the right of their people to stand as equals among men.

The Indian Wars (1870–1890): The United States Colored Troops, during the Indian Wars, comprised only two regiments of cavalry (the 9th and the 10th) and two of infantry (the 24th and the 25th). These regiments were assigned to isolated posts in hostile Indian territory covering Texas, New Mexico, Colorado, Arizona and Mexico. The Apache, Sioux and other Indian tribes whom they met in combat referred to the black fighters as "Buffalo Soldiers," and under that nomenclature they earned a well-merited place in history. The 9th U.S. Cavalry produced 12 Medal of Honor winners; the 24th Infantry, two.

The Spanish-American War: As with their white fellow citizens, a patriotic fervor seized American Negroes and 16 full regiments of black volunteers were raised during the Spanish-American War. Of these, four regular Negro regiments distinguished themselves in the Battle of San Juan Hill, together with Teddy Roosevelt's "Rough Riders"—a fact appearing in all too few text books. Particularly notable, in addition, was the key Battle of Santiago and the Battle of El Caney, in which the 10th Cavalry made its famous charge. It was his all-Negro 10th Cavalry— Troops H, M, and G—which produced five Medal of Honor winners.

World War I: Of the 370,000 Negroes who participated in World War I, about 135,000 were assigned to the 92nd and 93rd combat divisions. Regiments within the 92nd, after initial training in the United States, were sent to France where they served as all-Negro units in the French army. Members of the four infantry regiments of the 93rd, however, were deployed as individuals in fully integrated units in the French command. Most of these black soldiers, for the first time in their lives, finally knew the meaning of equality, being regarded by their comrades-in-arms as *men* rather than as *black* men.

The "brothers" proved to be valiant fighters. The first Americans to be decorated in France for bravery, Henry Johnson and Needham Roberts, both Negroes, received the celebrated *Croix de Guerre*. Of the all-black regiments, two of the units themselves were awarded the coveted medal by the government of France for courage above and beyond the call of duty. One of them, the illustrious 369th, was the first American regiment of either race to reach the Rhine River, opening the floodgates which led to the collapse of Germany's military capacity and to the Armistice.

World War II: The involvement of Negroes in World War II began in the very first hours of the conflict. On December 7, 1941, the Japanese struck at Pearl Harbor in wave after wave of devastating aerial attacks aimed at American naval installations. In the holocaust that ensued, Dorie Miller of Waco, Texas, a messman aboard the *U.S.S. Arizona,* distinguished himself by manning a machinegun and bringing down four enemy planes. For his act of heroism he was awarded the Navy Cross. Miller was killed in action in the South Pacific in December 1943, at the age of 24. A number of other Negroes were also cited for heroism, including Leonard Roy Harmon, of the *U.S.S. San Francisco,* and William Pinckney, of the *U.S.S. Enterprise,* both of whom were awarded the Navy Cross, and Elbert H. Oliver of the *U.S.S. Intrepid,* who received the Silver Star.

A number of "firsts" occurred during the war. On June 18, 1942, Bernard W. Robinson was made an ensign in the Navy, becoming the first Negro to win a commission in this branch of the service. In 1943, the 99th Pursuit Squadron—the first Negro flying unit—flew its first combat mission in the Mediterranean theater. In Italy, an all-Negro squadron of the 332nd Fighter Group attached to the 15th Air Force was commanded by a Negro captain, Andrew O. Tanner. This was the group which was later placed under the command of Col. Benjamin O. Davis Jr., son of the highest-ranking Negro in the European theater, Brigadier General Benjamin O. Davis Sr. In 1945, Davis Jr.—later a general in his own right—was given command of Godman Field in Kentucky. On March 8, 1945, Phyllis Mae Dailey was sworn into the Navy Nurse Corps in New York City, to become the first Negro nurse to serve in that branch of the service.

All told, more than a million blacks were inducted into the armed forces during the war years. These troops were assigned to posts in such countries as Italy, France, England, Wales, Scotland, Germany, Algeria, Morocco, Liberia, Holland, Egypt, Belgium and Luxembourg. The 92nd Division, one of the first units to be sent overseas, received 753 Bronze

Stars, 95 Silver Stars, 16 Legion of Merit awards, two Distinguished Service crosses, and one Distinguished Service medal and nearly 1,100 Purple Hearts—a thrilling record indeed!*

Korean War (1950–1953): On July 26, 1948, Executive Order 9981 was issued by President Harry Truman ending segregation in the Armed Forces. Troop integration progressed to a point where, during the Korean conflict, only a few scattered units could be identified as racially segregated. There remained, however, the 24th Infantry, an all-Negro regiment which had been part of the Regular Army for over 80 years. Upon the outbreak of the war, the 24th was flown to the combat area from its base in Japan and, only three weeks after the North Korean army invaded South Korea, met the enemy in battle. The victory won by the fighting 24th Infantry at the railhead city of Yech'on represented the first for the United Nations forces in Korea.

Two Medal of Honor recipients were named, both New Yorkers: Pfc. William Thompson, Company M, and Sergeant Cornelius Charlton, Company C, 24th Infantry. Thompson, it should be noted, was the first Negro to be awarded the Medal of Honor since the Spanish-American War. He was killed on August 6, 1950, after fighting off an entire enemy regiment singlehanded. Charlton was the second black soldier to win the Medal of Honor in Korea. He lost his life on June 2, 1951, while leading a platoon attack on a ridge held by the North Koreans.

Despite President Truman's Executive Order, mistreatment and discrimination of Negro troops continued. Future Supreme Court Justice Thurgood Marshall, then representing the NAACP, investigated the court-martial procedures of one case which involved the sentencing of 39 black soldiers. As a result, most were released or given less severe sentences.

Vietnam: From its beginning, the Vietnam War was the most integrated conflict in American history. During the decade following the Korean War, blacks had enlisted in all the services, making the military the most integrated institution in American society. Black soldiers, airmen, sailors, and marines served in Vietnam in every specialty and in every rank.

---

* In 1997, President Clinton awarded the Medal of Honor to seven black veterans for heroism during World War II. The postponement of the awards, which they had earned more than 50 years earlier, was due to racial discrimination. [See "Black Valor," page 149.]

While the military had ignored or downplayed the valor of black soldiers in the previous wars of the twentieth century, it did not do so now. African Americans were among the first to receive Medals of Honor in Vietnam. On October 22, 1965, Chicago native Pfc. Milton Olive, of Company B, Second Battalion, 503rd Infantry, 173rd Airborne Brigade, earned his country's highest award for bravery by sacrificing his life when he fell on a grenade to save the lives of his comrades in the midst of battle.

Specialist Sixth Class Lawrence Joel, a New York City-born medic assigned to Headquarters Company, First Battalion, 503rd Infantry, 173rd Airborne Brigade, earned his Medal of Honor for repeatedly exposing himself to enemy fire to treat his unit's wounded. Struck several times by bullets and shrapnel, Joel bandaged his own wounds and continued to dispense aid during a fight that lasted for more than twenty-four hours.

Olive and Joel were only the first of many blacks who exhibited great bravery and dedication for the rest of the long war. Of 237 Medals of Honor awarded during the Vietnam War, blacks received twenty—fifteen of them soldiers; five, marines.

As the war progressed, blacks as a whole realized that they were paying a higher price in casualties than were whites. As one black soldier remarked about the military in Vietnam, "It's the kind of integration that could kill you."

The military also recognized the disparity and in 1967 began to shift more blacks to support positions. Completion of tours also decreased the number of African Americans in the air cavalry, airborne, and marine divisions that had arrived in Vietnam with a high percentage of minority soldiers. By the end of the year, black casualties decreased to 13 percent and grew smaller during each remaining year of the war. At the conclusion of the conflict, a total of 58,151 Americans had been killed in Vietnam, 7,115 of whom were black. The 12.2 percent equaled the proportion of blacks in the total U.S. population.

As the United States approaches the twenty-first century, African Americans serve in every specialty and in every rank in defense of their country. Their long struggle is not yet over, but African Americans have indeed proved that they, too, are Americans in every sense of the word.

Grenada, Panama, the Persian Gulf, and Beyond: The biggest news in respect to both Grenada and Panama regarding black military history was that neither conflict generated press coverage about white and black personnel but rather about American servicemen and women performing their jobs and doing them well. After two centuries of warfare, blacks were full and equal partners in the defense of their country and the world's democracies.

In its first challenge of the post–cold war era, the United States established a coalition of thirty-eight countries to remove Iraqis from Kuwait after their August 1, 1990, invasion. Assembled as an overwhelming force, the U.S.-led coalition engaged in forty-three days of aerial operations, followed by a hundred hours of ground combat in Operation Desert Storm, totally routing Saddam Hussein's army and freeing Kuwait. Once again blacks played a role in every aspect of the liberation, with Gen. Colin Powell as the chairman of the Joint Chiefs of Staff and Lt. Gen. Cal Waller, a graduate of Prairie View A&M, serving as Desert Storm's second in command.

With the defeat of Saddam Hussein and no longer facing a global threat from the fragmented Soviet Union, the U.S. military resumed the reduction in forces that had begun before the invasion of Kuwait.

Despite these reductions, African Americans continue to be attracted to the military in numbers that exceed their proportion of the population. At the beginning of 1996 blacks made up 22 percent of the total enlisted force—30 percent of the army, 17 percent of the air force, 18 percent of the navy, and 17 percent of the Marine Corps.

The number of black officers has substantially risen since 1981. In 1996, 8 percent of the total number of armed forces' officers were black—11 percent, army; 6 percent, air force; 5 percent, navy; and 6 percent, Marine Corps.

Women, particularly blacks, have also thrived in the all-volunteer force. In 1996 women made up 12 percent of the total enlisted numbers and 13 percent of the officers. Black women constituted a large portion of those percentages. In the army 20 percent of the female officers and 48 percent of the enlisted women were black; in the air force 10 percent of the female officers and 25 percent of the enlisted women were black; in the navy 9 percent of the female officers and 29 percent of the enlisted women were black; and in the marines 8 percent of the officers and 25 percent of the enlisted force were black.

RADIO DAYS
MAYA ANGELOU

Maya Angelou spent most of her childhood in the small segregated town of Stamps, Arkansas, where she was raised by her grandmother, the owner of a general store, and her uncle. In her first autobiographical book, I Know Why the Caged Bird Sings, *Angelou re-creates the scene in the store on June 25, 1935, when blacks gathered to hear the broadcast of the Joe Louis–Primo Carnera bout. The scene was duplicated across black America whenever Louis fought. Millions were loyal fans of the "Brown Bomber," who demolished the myth of white superiority and carried the hope of his people into the ring.**

The last inch of space was filled, yet people continued to wedge themselves along the walls of the Store. Uncle Willie had turned the radio up to its last notch so that youngsters on the porch wouldn't miss a word. Women sat on kitchen chairs, dining-room chairs, stools and upturned wooden boxes. Small children and babies perched on every lap available and men leaned on the shelves or on each other.

The apprehensive mood was shot through with shafts of gaiety, as a black sky is streaked with lightning.

"I ain't worried 'bout this fight. Joe's gonna whip that cracker like it's open season."

"He gone whip him till that white boy call him Momma."

---

* Joe Louis's victories were accompanied by mass jubilation in black communities. One Joe Louis biographer wrote: "The revelry in Memphis after the [Max] Baer fight lasted until dawn, prompting the press to say that Joe had 'driven the blues from Beale Street.' In Baltimore, four men were arrested and fined between five and twenty-five dollars for 'assault with tomatoes.' In Detroit, fire trucks chased after false alarms while reporters remarked about the number of young black boys suddenly seen throwing phantom punches on street corners." In Harlem, 150,000 blacks stopped traffic on Seventh Avenue from 130th to 150th Street.

At last the talking was finished and the string-along songs about razor blades were over and the fight began.

"A quick jab to the head." In the Store the crowd grunted. "A left to the head and a right and another left." One of the listeners cackled like a hen and was quieted.

"They're in a clench, Louis is trying to fight his way out."

Some bitter comedian on the porch said, "That white man don't mind hugging that niggah now, I betcha."

"The referee is moving in to break them up, but Louis finally pushed the contender away and it's an uppercut to the chin. The contender is hanging on, now he's backing away. Louis catches him with a short left to the jaw."

A tide of murmuring assent poured out the doors and into the yard.

"Another left and another left. Louis is saving that mighty right . . ." The mutter in the Store had grown into a baby roar and it was pierced by the clang of a bell and the announcer's "That's the bell for round three, ladies and gentlemen."

As I pushed my way into the Store I wondered if the announcer gave any thought to the fact that he was addressing as "ladies and gentlemen" all the Negroes around the world who sat sweating and praying, glued to their "master's voice."

There were only a few calls for R.C. Colas, Dr. Peppers, and Hire's root beer. The real festivities would begin after the fight. Then even the old Christian ladies who taught their children and tried themselves to practice turning the other cheek would buy soft drinks, and if the Brown Bomber's victory was a particularly bloody one they would order peanut patties and Baby Ruths also.

Bailey and I lay the coins on top of the cash register. Uncle Willie didn't allow us to ring up sales during a fight. It was too noisy and might shake up the atmosphere. When the gong rang for the next round we pushed through the near-sacred quiet to the herd of children outside.

"He's got Louis against the ropes and now it's a left to the body and a right to the ribs. Another right to the body, it looks like it was low . . . Yes, ladies and gentlemen, the referee is signaling but the contender keeps raining the blows on Louis. It's another to the body, and it looks like Louis is going down."

My race groaned. It was our people falling. It was another lynching, yet another Black man hanging on a tree. One more woman ambushed and raped. A Black boy whipped and maimed. It was hounds on the trail of a man running through slimy swamps. It was a white woman slapping her maid for being forgetful.

The men in the Store stood away from the walls and at attention. Women greedily clutched the babes on their laps while on the porch the shufflings and smiles, flirtings and pinching of a few minutes before were gone. This might be the end of the world. If Joe lost we were back in slavery and beyond help. It would all be true, the accusations that we were lower types of human beings. Only a little higher than the apes. True that we were stupid and ugly and lazy and dirty and, unlucky and worst of all, that God Himself hated us and ordained us to be hewers of wood and drawers of water, forever and ever, world without end.

We didn't breathe. We didn't hope. We waited.

"He's off the ropes, ladies and gentlemen. He's moving towards the center of the ring." There was no time to be relieved. The worst might still happen.

"And now it looks like Joe is mad. He's caught Carnera with a left hook to the head and a right to the head. It's a left jab to the body and another left to the head. There's a left cross and a right to the head. The contender's right eye is bleeding and he can't seem to keep his block up. Louis is penetrating every block. The referee is moving in, but Louis sends a left to the body and it's the uppercut to the chin and the contender is dropping. He's on the canvas, ladies and gentlemen."

Babies slid to the floor as women stood up and men leaned toward the radio.

"Here's the referee. He's counting. One, two, three, four, five, six, seven . . . Is the contender trying to get up again?"

All the men in the store shouted, "NO."

"—eight, nine, ten." There were a few sounds from the audience, but they seemed to be holding themselves in against tremendous pressure.

"The fight is all over, ladies and gentlemen. Let's get the microphone over to the referee . . . Here he is. He's got the Brown Bomber's hand, he's holding it up . . . Here he is . . ."

Then the voice, husky and familiar, came to wash over us—"The winnah, and still heavyweight champeen of the world . . . Joe Louis."

Champion of the world. A Black boy. Some Black mother's son. He was the strongest man in the world. People drank Coca-Colas like ambrosia and ate candy bars like Christmas. Some of the men went behind the Store and poured white lightning in their soft-drink bottles, and a few of the bigger boys followed them. Those who were not chased away came back blowing their breath in front of themselves like proud smokers.

It would take an hour or more before the people would leave the Store and head for home. Those who lived too far had made arrangements to stay in town. It wouldn't do for a Black man and his family to be caught on a lonely country road on a night when Joe Louis had proved that we were the strongest people in the world.

BRING THAT COLLEGE HOME
ANONYMOUS

Many men and women feel that, after attending college, they cannot return home for long. They might think they have outgrown their old way of life or that book learning has made them too sophisticated to return.

Here is advice to get a college degree and become "a light in your own village." It's a reminder not to get too highfalutin and to remain loyal to one's parents, who may have devoted years of labor to finance that degree.

This anonymous poem was found on Alex Haley's farm in Clinton, Tennessee. It was given to Haley by Miller Boyd of Morristown College.

I's been sending you to college now for six or seven years,
Since the mornin' dat you lef' me I's been sheddin' bitter tears.
But I thought of dat ole sayin' "sunshine comes behin' de storm,"
So my young man, when you finish, you jes bring dat college home.

I's been scrubbin' by the washtub, I's been sweatin' in de fiel,
Many times I had to borry, an I almost had to steal.
But I hold on to my patience, beat dem soap suds into foam,
All de time my heart was sayin' he's gwine bring dat college home.

Folks here say you gwine be nothin', you jes foolin' time away,
But I shake my finger an' tell dem "wait until some future day."
So nex' June when dogwoods blossom and de bees begin to swarm,
I'll be waitin' for to see you when you bring dat college home.

Don't you min' dese folks here talkin', dey ain't half as good as you,
And deys bound to nag at good folks, dat's all dey know how to do.
I's got wood enough for winter, plenty clothes to keep me warm,
So you trot off to college, then nex' June you bring dat college home.

I don't mean bring home the buildings or to wreck dem good
   folks' place,
Bring home Christian education and dat high tone college grace.
You jes grab dem fessor's habits, hole 'em tight thru win' an' storm,
Den when you get your diploma, take 'em all and light for home.

Show dese folks dat you got 'em by the speeches dat you make,
By the spec's dat you'll be wearin' an' de way your coattail shake.
But don't git above de people, settle down, and cease to roam,
Be a light in your own village, be a college right here at home.

OUR ECONOMIC BLUEPRINT
ELIJAH MUHAMMAD

As leader of the Nation of Islam, Elijah Muhammad (1897–1975) built what was reputedly the largest black-owned and -operated business empire in his day, with assets totaling more than $45 million. His "do for self" philosophy included a plan for economic cooperation among blacks nationwide. At one point, his empire included bakeries, a chain of restaurants, supermarkets, farms, a fish-importing business, a meat-packing operation, a twin-engine private jet, a Chicago bank, real estate in cities nationwide, and a weekly newspaper with a circulation of 900,000 copies.

The Georgia-born son of former slaves, Elijah Muhammad amassed a personal fortune estimated at $25 million, making him one of the country's wealthiest black men. Here is his blueprint for building a "black nation" within the United States.

The Black man in America faces a serious economic problem today. You, the so-called American Negro, with the help of Allah can solve your own problem. The truth must be recognized by the black man. He, himself, has assisted greatly in creating this serious problem of unemployment, insecurity and lack. Before the black man can begin to gain economic security, he must be awakened from the dead and gain knowledge, understanding and wisdom . . .

Know thyself and be yourself. . . . Acknowledge and recognize that you are a member of the Creator's nation and act accordingly. . . . This requires action and deeds, not words and lip service.

The following blueprint shows the way:

1. Recognize the necessity for unity and group operation (activities).
2. Pool your resources, physically as well as financially.
3. Stop wanton criticisms of everything that is black-owned and black-operated.
4. Keep in mind—jealousy destroys from within.
5. Observe the operations of the white man. He is successful. He makes no excuses for his failures. He works hard in a collective manner. You do the same.

If there are six or eight Muslims with knowledge and experience of the grocery business—pool your knowledge, open a grocery store—and you work collectively and harmoniously, Allah will bless you with success.

If there are those with knowledge of dressmaking, merchandising, trades, maintenance—pool such knowledge. Do not be ashamed to seek guidance and instructions from the brother or sister who has more experience, education and training than you have had. Accept his or her assistance.

The white man spends his money with his own kind, which is natural. You, too, must do this. Help to make jobs for your own kind. Take a lesson from the Chinese and Japanese and go give employment and assistance to your own kind when they are in need. This is the first law of nature. Defend and support your own kind. True Muslims do this. . . .

LYNCHED IN FLORIDA

A lynching is a killing by several who are seeking to punish someone by taking the law into their own hands. From 1882 to 1968, 4,743 people were reported lynched in the United States—3,446, or slightly more than 72 percent, of them black. In 1901, 105 black victims were reported lynched. Here is the short, horrible story of two of those victims.

Will Wright and Sam Williams, charged with being implicated in a murder, were lynched without trial in jail at Dade City, by a mob of thirty or more men. Sheriff Griffin refused to give up the keys and they broke down the outer door. Unable to break down the steel doors of the cells, they opened fire through the steel bars, shooting both the Negroes to death.

The Coroner's jury found that they came to their death at the hands of "parties unknown."

—New York Tribune, *February 7, 1901*

I INVESTIGATE LYNCHINGS
WALTER WHITE

One's loyalties, fortunately, are not always readily apparent. Blond-haired and blue-eyed Walter White (1893–1955) could easily pass for white—and sometimes he did, so he could investigate lynchings in the South, a ritual of racial terror. On more than one occasion White himself narrowly escaped being lynched.

In the 1920s and 1930s, White lobbied for federal antilynching legislation. In 1931, he was named executive secretary of the National Association for the Advancement of Colored People. He led the organization through some of its most turbulent years, including 1954, when its legal division won the landmark Brown v. Board of Education *desegregation decision in the U.S. Supreme Court.*

White was called by some people a "voluntary" Negro, because he could cross the color line. The following investigative report makes his loyalties abundantly clear.

In 1918 a Negro woman, about to give birth to a child, was lynched with almost unmentionable brutality along with ten men in Georgia. I reached the scene shortly after the butchery and while excitement yet ran high. It was a prosperous community. Forests of pine trees gave rich returns in turpentine, tar and pitch. The small towns where the farmers and turpentine hands traded were fat and rich. The main streets of the largest of these towns were well paved and lighted. The stores were well stocked. The white inhabitants belonged to the class of Georgia crackers—lanky, slow of movement and of speech, long-necked, with small eyes set close together, and skin tanned by the hot sun to a reddish-yellow hue.

As I was born in Georgia and spent twenty years of my life there, my accent is sufficiently Southern to enable me to talk with Southerners and not arouse their suspicion that I am an outsider. (In the rural South hatred of Yankees is not much less than hatred of Negroes.) On the morning of my arrival in the town I casually dropped into the store of one of the general merchants who, I had been informed, had been one of the leaders of the mob. After making a small purchase I engaged the merchant in conversation. There was, at the time, no other customer in the store. We spoke of the weather, the possibility of good crops in the Fall, the political situation, the latest news from the war in Europe. As his manner became more and more friendly I ventured to mention guardedly the recent lynchings.

Instantly he became cautious—until I hinted that I had great admiration for the manly spirit the men of the town had exhibited. I mentioned the newspaper accounts I had read and confessed that I had never been so fortunate as to see a lynching. My words or tone seemed to disarm his suspicion. He offered me a box on which to sit, drew up another one for himself, and gave me a bottle of Coca-Cola.

"You'll pardon me, Mister," he began, "for seeming suspicious but we have to be careful. In ordinary times we wouldn't have anything to worry about, but with the war there's been some talk of the Federal government looking into lynchings. It seems there's some sort of law during wartime making it treason to lower the man power of the country."

"In that case I don't blame you for being careful," I assured him. "But couldn't the Federal government do something if it wanted to when a lynching takes place, even if no war is going on at the moment?"

"Naw," he said, confidently, obviously proud of the opportunity of displaying his store of information to one whom he assumed knew nothing whatever about the subject. "There's no such law, in spite of all the agitation by a lot of fools who don't know the niggers as we do. States' rights won't permit Congress to meddle in lynching in peace time."

"But what about your State government—your Governor, your sheriff, your police officers?"

"Humph! Them? We elected them to office, didn't we? And the niggers, we've got them disfranchised, ain't we? Sheriffs and police and Governors and prosecuting attorneys have got too much sense to mix in lynching-bees. If they do they know they might as well give up all idea of running for office any more—if something worse don't happen to them—" This last with a tightening of the lips and a hard look in the eyes.

I sought to lead the conversation into less dangerous channels. "Who was the white man who was killed—whose killing caused the lynchings?" I asked.

"Oh, he was a hard one, all right. Never paid his debts to white men or niggers and wasn't liked much around here. He was a mean 'un, all right, all right."

"Why, then, did you lynch the niggers for killing such a man?"

"It's a matter of safety—we gotta show niggers that they mustn't touch a white man, no matter how low-down and ornery he is."

Little by little he revealed the whole story. When he told of the manner in which the pregnant woman had been killed he chuckled and slapped his thigh and declared it to be "the best show, Mister, I ever did see. You ought to have heard the wench howl when we strung her up."

Covering the nausea the story caused me as best I could, I slowly gained the whole story, with the names of the other participants. Among them were prosperous farmers, business men, bankers, newspaper reporters and editors, and several law enforcement officers.

My several days of discreet inquiry began to arouse suspicions in the town. On the third day of my stay I went once more into the store of the man with whom I had first talked. He asked me to wait until he had finished serving the sole customer. When she had gone he came from behind the counter and with secretive manner and lowered voice he asked, "You're a government man, ain't you?" (An agent of the Federal Department of Justice was what he meant.)

"Who said so?" I countered.

"Never mind who told me; I know one when I see him," he replied, with a shrewd harshness in his face and voice.

Ignorant of what might have taken place since last I had talked with him, I thought it wise to learn all I could and say nothing which might commit me. "Don't you tell anyone I am a government man; if I *am* one, you're the only one in town who knows it," I told him cryptically. I knew that within an hour everybody in town would share his "information."

An hour or so later I went at nightfall to the little but not uncomfortable hotel where I was staying. As I was about to enter a Negro approached me and, with an air of great mystery, told me that he had just heard a group of white men discussing me and declaring that if I remained in the town overnight "something would happen" to me.

The thought raced through my mind before I replied that it was hardly likely that, following so terrible a series of lynchings, a Negro would voluntarily approach a supposedly white man whom he did not know and deliver such a message. He had been sent, and no doubt the persons who sent him were white and for some reason did not dare tackle me themselves. Had they dared there would have been no warning in advance—simply an attack. Though I had no weapon with me, it occurred to me that there was no reason why two should not play at the game of bluffing. I looked straight into my informant's eyes and said, in as convincing a tone as I could muster: "You go back to the ones who sent you and tell them this: that I have a damned good automatic and I know how to use it. If anybody attempts to molest me tonight or any other time, somebody is going to get hurt."

That night I did not take off my clothes nor did I sleep. Ordinarily in such small Southern towns everyone is snoring by nine o'clock. That night, however, there was much passing and re-passing of the hotel. I learned afterward that the merchant had, as I expected, told generally that I was an agent of the Department of Justice, and my empty threat had served to reinforce his assertion. The Negro had been sent to me in the hope that I might be frightened enough to leave before I had secured evidence against the members of the mob. I remained in the town two more days. My every movement was watched, but I was not molested. But when, later, it became known that not only was I not an agent of the Department of Justice but a Negro, the fury of the inhabitants of the region was unlimited—particularly when it was found that evidence I gathered had been placed in the hands of the Governor of Georgia. It happened that he was a man genuinely eager to stop lynching—but restrictive laws against which he had appealed in vain effectively prevented him from acting upon the evidence. And the Federal government declared itself unable to proceed against the lynchers.

IN 1926 I WENT to a Southern State for a New York newspaper to inquire into the lynching of two colored boys and a colored woman. Shortly after reaching the town I learned that a certain lawyer knew something about the lynchers. He proved to be the only specimen I have ever encountered in much travelling in the South of the Southern gentleman so beloved by fiction writers of the older school. He had heard of the lynching before it occurred and, fruitlessly, had warned the judge and the prosecutor. He talked frankly about the affair and gave me the names of certain men who knew more about it than he did. Several of them lived in a small town nearby where the only industry was a large cotton mill. When I asked him if he would go with me to call on these people he peered out of the window at the descending sun and said, somewhat anxiously, I thought, "I will go with you if you will promise to get back to town before sundown."

I asked why there was need of such haste. "No one would harm a respectable and well-known person like yourself, would they?" I asked him.

"Those mill hands out there would harm anybody," he answered.

I promised him we would be back before sundown—a promise that was not hard to make, for if they would harm this man I could imagine what they would do to a stranger!

When we reached the little mill town we passed through it and, ascending a steep hill, our car stopped in front of a house perched perilously on the side of the hill. In the yard stood a man with iron gray hair and eyes which seemed strong enough to bore through concrete. The old lawyer introduced me and we were invited into the house. As it was a cold afternoon in late Autumn the gray-haired man called a boy to build a fire.

I told him frankly I was seeking information about the lynching. He said nothing but left the room. Perhaps two minutes later, hearing a sound at the door through which he had gone, I looked up and there stood a figure clad in the full regalia of the Ku Klux Klan. I looked at the figure and the figure looked at me. The hood was then removed and, as I suspected, it was the owner of the house."

"I show you this," he told me, "so you will know that what I tell you is true."

This man, I learned, had been the organizer and kleagle of the local Klan. He had been quite honest in his activities as a Kluxer, for corrupt officials and widespread criminal activities had caused him and other local men to believe that the only cure rested in a secret extra-legal organization. But he had not long been engaged in promoting the plan before he had the experience of other believers in Klan methods. The very people whose misdeeds the organization was designed to correct gained control of it. This man then resigned and ever since had been living in fear of his life. He took me into an adjoining room after removing his Klan robe and there showed me a considerable collection of revolvers, shot guns, rifles and ammunition.

We then sat down and I listened to as hair-raising a tale of Nordic moral endeavor as it has ever been my lot to hear. Among the choice bits were stories such as this: The sheriff of an adjoining county the year before had been a candidate for reelection. A certain man of considerable wealth had contributed largely to his campaign fund, providing the margin by which he was reelected. Shortly afterwards a married woman with whom the sheriff's supporter had been intimate quarreled one night with her husband. When the cuckold charged his wife with infidelity, the gentle creature waited until he was asleep, got a large butcher knife, and then artistically carved him up. Bleeding more profusely than a pig in the stock yards, the man dragged himself to the home of a neighbor several hundred yards distant and there died on the door-step. The facts were notorious, but the sheriff effectively blocked even interrogation of the widow!

I spent some days in the region and found that the three Negroes who had been lynched were about as guilty of the murder of which they were charged as I was. Convicted in a court thronged with armed Klansmen and sentenced to death, their case had been appealed to the State Supreme Court, which promptly reversed the conviction, remanded the appellants for new trials, and severely criticized the judge before whom they had been tried. At the new trial the evidence against one of the defendants so clearly showed his innocence that the judge granted a motion to dismiss, and the other two defendants were obviously as little guilty as he. But as soon as the motion to dismiss was granted the defendant was rearrested on a trivial charge and once again lodged in jail. That night the mob took the prisoners to the outskirts of the town, and told them to run, and as they set out pumped bullets into their backs. The two boys died instantly. The woman was shot in several places, but was not immediately killed. One of the lynchers afterwards laughingly told me that "we had to waste fifty bullets on the wench before one of them stopped her howling."

Evidence in affidavit form indicated rather clearly that various law enforcement officials, including the sheriff, his deputies, various jailers and policemen, three relatives of the then Governor of the State, a member of the State Legislature and sundry individuals prominent in business, political and social life of the vicinity, were members of the mob.

The revelation of these findings after I had returned to New York did not add to my popularity in the lynching region. Public sentiment in the State itself, stirred up by several courageous newspapers, began to make it uncomfortable for the lynchers.

ON ANOTHER OCCASION a serious race riot occurred in Tulsa, Oklahoma, a bustling town of 100,000 inhabitants. In the early days Tulsa had been a lifeless and unimportant village of not more than five thousand people, and its Negro residents had been forced to live in what was considered the least desirable section of the village, down near the railroad. Then oil was discovered nearby and almost overnight the village grew into a prosperous town. The Negroes prospered along with the whites, and began to erect comfortable homes, business establishments, a hotel, two cinemas and other enterprises, all of these springing up in the section to which they had been relegated. This was, as I have said, down near the railroad tracks. The swift growth of the town made this hitherto disregarded land of great value for business purposes. Efforts to purchase the land from the Negro owners at prices far below its value were unavailing. Having built up the neighborhood and knowing its value, the owners refused to be victimized.

One afternoon in 1921 a Negro messenger boy went to deliver a package in an office building on the main street of Tulsa. His errand done, he rang the bell for the elevator in order that he might descend. The operator, a young white girl, on finding that she had been summoned by a Negro, opened the door of the car ungraciously. Two versions there are of what happened then. The boy declared that she started the car on its downward plunge when he was only halfway in, and that to save himself from being killed he had to throw himself into the car, stepping on the girl's foot in doing so. The girl, on the other hand, asserted that the boy attempted to rape her in the elevator. The latter story, at best, seemed highly dubious—that an attempted criminal assault would be made by any person in an open elevator of a crowded office building on the main street of a town of 100,000 inhabitants—and in open daylight!

Whatever the truth, the local press, with scant investigation, published lurid accounts of the alleged assault. That night a mob started to the jail to lynch the Negro boy. A group of Negroes offered their services to the jailer and sheriff in protecting the prisoner. The offer was declined, and when the Negroes started to leave the sheriff's office a clash occurred between them and the mob. Instantly the mob swung into action.

The Negroes, outnumbered, were forced back to their own neighborhood. Rapidly the news spread of the clash and the numbers of mobbers grew hourly. By daybreak of the following day the mob numbered around five thousand, and was armed with machine-guns, dynamite, rifles, revolvers and shotguns, cans of gasoline and kerosene, and—such are the blessings of invention!—airplanes. Surrounding the Negro section, it attacked, led by men who had been officers in the American army in France. Outnumbered and out-equipped, the plight of the Negroes was a hopeless one from the beginning. Driven further and further back, many of them were killed or wounded, among them an aged man and his wife, who were slain as they knelt at prayer for deliverance. Forty-four blocks of property were burned after homes and stores had been pillaged.

I arrived in Tulsa while the excitement was at its peak. Within a few hours I met a commercial photographer who had worked for five years on a New York newspaper and he welcomed me with open arms when he found that I represented a New York paper. From him I learned that special deputy sheriffs were being sworn in to guard the town from a rumored counter attack by the Negroes. It occurred to me that I could get myself sworn in as one of these deputies.

It was even easier to do this than I had expected. That evening in the City Hall I had to answer only three questions—name, age, and address. I might have been a thug, a murderer, an escaped convict, a member of the mob itself which had laid waste a large area of the city—none of these mattered; my skin was apparently white, and that was enough. After we—some fifty or sixty of us—had been sworn in, solemnly declaring we would do our utmost to uphold the laws and constitutions of the United States and the State of Oklahoma, a villainous-looking man next to me turned and remarked casually, even with a note of happiness in his voice: "Now you can go out and shoot any nigger you see and the law'll be behind you."

As we stood in the wide marble corridor of the not unimposing City Hall waiting to be assigned to automobiles which were to patrol the city during the night, I noticed a man, clad in the uniform of a captain of the United States Army, watching me closely. I imagined I saw in his very swarthy face (he was much darker than I, but was classed as a white man while I am deemed a Negro) mingled inquiry and hostility. I kept my eye on him without appearing to do so. Tulsa would not have been a very healthy place for me that night had my race or my previous investigations of other race riots been known there. At last the man seemed certain he knew me and started toward me.

He drew me aside into a deserted corner on the excuse that he had something he wished to ask me, and I noticed that four other men with whom he had been talking detached themselves from the crowd and followed us.

Without further introduction or apology my dark-skinned newly made acquaintance, putting his face close to mine and looking into my eyes with a steely, unfriendly glance, demanded challengingly:

"You say that your name is White?"

I answered affirmatively.

"You say you're a newspaper man?"

"Yes, I represent the *New York*————. Would you care to see my credentials?"

"No, but I want to tell you something. There's an organization in the South that doesn't love niggers. It has branches everywhere. You needn't ask me the name—I can't tell you. But it has come back into existence to fight this damned nigger Advancement Association. We watch every movement of the officers of this nigger society and we're out to get them for putting notions of equality into the heads of our niggers down South here."

There could be no question that he referred to the Ku Klux Klan on the one hand and the National Association for the Advancement of Colored People on the other. As coolly as I could, the circumstances being what they were, I took a cigarette from my case and lighted it, trying to keep my hand from betraying my nervousness. When he finished speaking I asked him:

"All this is very interesting, but what, if anything, has it to do with the story of the race riot here which I've come to get?"

For a full minute we looked straight into each other's eyes, his four companions meanwhile crowding close about us. At length his eyes fell. With a shrug of his shoulders and a half-apologetic smile, he replied as he turned away, "Oh, nothing except I wanted you to know what's back of the trouble here."

It is hardly necessary to add that all that night, assigned to the same car with this man and his four companions, I maintained a considerable vigilance. When the news stories I wrote about the riot (the boy accused of attempted assault was acquitted in the magistrate's court after nearly one million dollars of property and a number of lives had been destroyed) revealed my identity—that I was a Negro and an officer of the Advancement Society—more than a hundred anonymous letters threatening my life came to me. I was also threatened with a suit for criminal libel by a local paper, but nothing came of it after my willingness to defend it was indicated.

SILENT PROTEST PARADE
CARRIE WILLIAMS CLIFFORD

A 1917 race riot in East St. Louis, Illinois, killed dozens, if not hundreds of blacks (the toll was variously estimated at between 40 and 200 people), and martial law had to be declared to stop the spread of further violence. Deeply disturbed by the riot, more than 10,000 blacks protested lynchings and other racial violence by marching silently down Fifth Avenue in New York City on July 28, 1917. Here is a poem by one of the protestors, Carrie Williams Clifford (1862–1934), a spokesperson for women's rights.

(On Fifth Avenue, New York, Saturday, July 28, 1917, protesting against the St. Louis riots)

Were you there? Did you see? Gods! wasn't it fine!
Did you notice how straight we kept the line,

As we marched down the famous avenue,
Silent, dogged and dusky of hue,
Keeping step to the sound of the muffled drum,
With its constantly recurring *tum—tum, tum—*
Tum—Tum—Tum—Tum—Tum;
Ten thousand of us, if there was one!
As goodly a sight as this ancient sun
Has ever looked upon!

Youth and maid
Father, mother—not one afraid
Or ashamed to let the whole world know
What he thought of the hellish East St. Louis "show,"
Orgy—riot—mob—what you will,
Where men and e'en women struggled to kill
Poor black workers, who'd fled in distress from the South
To find themselves murdered and mobbed in the North.

We marched as a protest—we carried our banner,
On which had been boldly inscribed every manner
Of sentiment—all, to be sure, within reason—
But no flag—not that we meant any treason—
Only who'd have the heart to carry Old Glory,
After hearing all of the horrible story,
Of East St. Louis? and never a word,
From the nation's head, as if he'd not heard
The groans of the dying ones here at home,
Though 'tis plain he can hear even farther than Rome.

Oh, yes, I was there in the Silent Parade,
And a man (he was white) I heard when he said,
"If they had music now, 'twould be great!"—
"We march not, sir, with hearts elate,
But sad; we grieve for our dark brothers
Murdered, and we hope that others

Will heed our protest against wrong,
Will help to make our protest strong."

Were you there? Ah, brothers, wasn't it fine!
The children—God bless 'em—headed the line;
Then came the mothers dressed in white,
And some—my word! 'twas a thrilling sight—
Carried their babies upon their breast,
Face tense and eager as forward they pressed,
With never a laugh and never a word,
But ever and always, the thing they heard
Was the *tum—tum—, tum, tum,*
Of the muffled drum—*tum, tum, tum!*

And last the black-coated men swung by,
Head up, chest firm, determined eye—
I was so happy, I wanted to cry.
As I watched the long lines striding by,
(Ten thousand souls if there was one)
And I knew that "to turn, the worm had begun,"
As we marched down Fifth Avenue unafraid
And calm, in our first Silent Protest Parade!

THE LAST SUPPER
INTERPRETED BY P. K. MCCARY

Here is one of the most famous stories of betrayal, from "The Word According to Matthew," interpreted with slang-style words. Judas Iscariot betrayed Jesus for thirty pieces of silver; Peter, out of fear for his life, denied ever knowing him, despite having vowed he could never do so. Peter betrayed Jesus to save his own skin, whereas Judas double-crossed Jesus in order to profit. While both were disloyal, Judas's act seems the more treacherous and unforgivable.

Jesus and his disciples sat 'round the table eating and drinking according to the way the Feast was done up. Things were pretty quiet until Jesus told them, *"One of you will betray Me."*

And everybody, including Judas, asked if he was the one. Jesus told Judas, *"Remember, you said it."* Jesus then took bread and broke it up, handing some to everybody.

"Take this and eat it 'cuz this is My body."

Then He took some wine and blessed it before handing it over to each of the boys. *"Drink, this is My blood. This means that we've got a pack, a deal—that I'm dying 'cuz of you so that things will be right between folks and the Almighty. This is the last time I'm drinking 'til I come back and drink again with each of you."*

Then He told them, *"After tonight everybody's gonna scatter to the wind, 'cuz it was written that when the big boys bring Me down, you all will scatter.* But when I come back after three days, you'll see Me in Galilee."*

But Peter was positive that even if everything went down like Jesus said, he, Peter, would stand and fight for Him. Jesus shook his head. *"Peter. Peter. Peter. I'm tellin' you as sure as My name is Jesus, before the rooster crows, you'll tell folks you never even knew Me. You'll do it three times."*

Peter was adamant. "No I won't. I'll die with you. I'm not gonna diss you that way." Everybody else said the same thing.

AFTER DINNER, JESUS and the disciples went up to a place called Gethsemane and Jesus asked the boys to wait over on the other side while He went up to pray. He took Peter, James and John with Him.

"Ya'll don't know. This is a terrible burden and I've got some mighty powerful praying to do. Stay here and watch with Me."

So, Jesus went up to say His prayers. He fell on His face and called up to the Almighty. *"Father, I wish it were possible not to have to go through with this, but whatever You want done, that's the way it's gonna be."*

Later when Jesus finished praying He walked over to the brothers and they were fast asleep. *"What's the matter? You can't stay up one hour?*

---

* See Zechariah, Chapter 13, verse 7.

Come on, watch and pray with Me or you might be tempted to do something wrong. I know your spirit is willing. Why must your flesh be so weak?"

He went up again and started praying. When He took a break a second time, He found the brothers asleep again. And He did this a third time, and He still came down to find the brothers cutting some Zs.

"You guys are pitiful. It's time and you've slept most of our time away. Come on. Let's get this over with."

WHILE HE SPOKE about these things to His boys, Judas came over with a bunch of brothers carrying weapons. These brothers worked for the big-time preachers in town, and Judas told them, "Whoever I kiss on the cheek, take Him. He's yours." He then walked up to Jesus and said, "Hey, Teacher," and kissed Him.

Jesus asked Judas, *"What's up yourself, Judas?"*

Then the police came and started to take Jesus away when one of the brothers with Jesus took out his sword and cut off the ear of the brother holding him.

"You live by the sword, you die by the sword. Put it away. Don't you know I could get out of this if I wanted. My Father is more powerful than steel. It's gotta be this way 'cuz that's what was told a long time ago. You didn't have to do it this way, sneaking 'round in the dark. I sat in the broad daylight and you didn't touch Me, you cowards. This was done 'cuz that's what the Almighty told the prophets." And then just like Jesus had said, the disciples took off in every direction.

SO THE POLICE took Jesus to stand before Rev. Caiaphas. The other bad honchos were there, too. Peter followed and lay low, trying to see what was going down.

Now inside the brothers tried to find an excuse for wasting Jesus. They asked folks to testify against Him, but found nobody willing to do it. Finally, they found two liars to testify against Jesus.

"Yep, He's the one," the brother was saying. "I heard Him say that He could destroy the church of the Almighty and put it back together again in three days."

The preacher looked over at Jesus. "Got anything to say?"

Jesus said nothing to these trumped-up charges. So the preacher got frustrated and asked Him, "Just tell us. Are you the living Almighty? Are you the Christ, the Son of the Almighty?"

"It's just like that. One day you'll see this Son of the Almighty coming on a cloud with all the power."

So then the preacher went, "Ah ha! I got you! This is blasphemy. What more proof do you need? He deserves to die."

And murmuring like you never heard went up. "Yeah, waste the brother." Then they spit on Him and hit Him, mocking Him to tell them, "Which one of us did it, you know so much?"

OUTSIDE PETER SAT around trying to listen to what was going down, but couldn't hear anything. A young sister saw him, and yelled to everybody, "He was with this Jesus of Galilee."

Peter shook his head. "Uh uh. I don't know what you're talking 'bout." He hung his head and tried to slide away.

"Yeah. Yeah, you are. I saw you," said another sister.

"Hush. You don't know what you're talking 'bout."

Then a brother agreed. "You're right. He was with Jesus."

Peter was outdone. He yelled at them. "I don't know this Jesus. Why do you keep saying that?" Immediately a rooster crowed and Peter felt lower than low. He remembered that Jesus had said, *"Before the rooster crows, you'll say three times you never knew Me."* Peter sat down and cried his heart out 'cuz what Jesus said was true. He had denied Christ.

◈◈

The New Negro
Breaks the icons of his detractors,
Wipes out the conspiracy of silence,
Speaks to *his* America . . .

—From "Dark Symphony" by Melvin B. Tolson
◈◈

LIFT EVERY VOICE AND SING
JAMES WELDON JOHNSON
AND J. ROSAMOND JOHNSON

This song, written in 1900, is considered the unofficial "Negro National Anthem." James Weldon Johnson (1871–1938) and his brother, John Rosamond Johnson (1873–1954), wrote it for a celebration of Abraham Lincoln's birthday in Jacksonville, Florida, their hometown. James wrote the lyrics.

The five hundred schoolchildren who were first taught the song continued to sing it after the celebration, and it spread to churches across the South and elsewhere. The National Association for the Advancement of Colored People adopted the song as its unofficial anthem, bringing it to a wide range of meetings and gatherings.

LIFT EVERY VOICE AND SING

Lift ev'ry voice and sing,
Till earth and heaven ring,
Ring with the harmonies of liberty;
Let our rejoicing rise,
High as the list'ning skies,
Let it resound loud as the rolling sea.
Sing a song full of the faith that the dark past has taught us,
Sing a song full of the hope that the present has brought us;
Facing the rising sun of our new day begun,
Let us march on till victory is won.

Stony the road we trod,
Bitter the chast'ning rod,
Felt in the days when hope unborn had died;
Yet with a steady beat,
Have not our weary feet,
Come to the place for which our fathers sighed?
We have come over a way that with tears has been watered,
We have come, treading our path thro' the blood of the slaughtered,

Out from the gloomy past,
Till now we stand at last
Where the white gleam of our bright star is cast.

God of our weary years,
God of our silent tears,
Thou who hast brought us thus far on the way;
Thou who hast by Thy might,
Led us into the light,
Keep us forever in the path, we pray.
Lest our feet stray from the places, our God, where we met Thee,
Lest our hearts, drunk with the wine of the world, we forget Thee;
Shadowed beneath Thy hand,
May we forever stand,
True to our God,
True to our native land.

༺ৡ৵

It was necessary, as a black historian, to have a personal agenda.
                                              —*John Hope Franklin*
༺ৡ৵

SURVIVAL HUMOR

Funny is an attitude.

—*Flip Wilson*

❦

Humor has played more than just a funny role in the affairs of black folks. Truth is, for African Americans, humor has always been serious business. It has served its purpose well as a survival mechanism, used to defend, attack, counterattack, and guide people through life's rougher spots.

Dynamic, complex, and not easy to pin down, African American humor causes as much head-shaking disbelief as spine-tickling laughter and brings on as much antagonism as joy. In short, African American humor is perhaps more easily described than defined. It is the stories of slaves who outwitted their masters, the tricksterism of animal fables, the "signifying" (fun-poking verbal games) of friends as they displace aggression, the antics of happy-go-lucky black-faced minstrels, the popular routines of the great vaudevillians, the "chitlin' circuit" performances of comedians such as Pigmeat (Here Come De Judge) Markham, the raucous jokes of toothless Jackie (Moms) Mabley, the wise and witty social commentary of Dick Gregory, the raceless humor of Bill Cosby, and the no-holds-barred acts of Richard Pryor.

Ironically, African American humor traces its origins to terrible times: to slavery, when blacks had precious little to laugh about. But after toiling in the fields or in the big house, they returned to the slave quarters and, among themselves, mocked the master and mistress. Slaves masked their intelligence, feigning ignorance so the master would dismiss them as harmless fools. Since smart blacks were deemed "trouble" or a threat to the master's ability to control slaves, this "dumbing-down" served as a defensive measure, a form of subterfuge and deceit that abetted survival. Many blacks used it to save themselves from beatings.

When blacks left the slave shack, humor traveled with them, continuing to conceal their true intelligence. Meanwhile, white artists tried to allay white audiences fears about emancipation by popularizing caricatures of comic darkies. Stereotypes were created, the most basic of which was a caricature of the contented, slow-motion, childlike, dance-crazed, chicken-grubbing, watermelon-loving coon who would sell his soul to keep whites laughing and happy. These vile images persisted for many years.

Blacks also practiced a self-reflexive humor, telling jokes on one another. Some of this intraracial comedy focused on their frustrations in dealing with white society, according to Langston Hughes, and was best exemplified in jokes about blacks who were habitually late, because they operated on "CP Time"—or Colored People's Time.

Gradually, comics grew more daring, using material that skewered everyone. They impersonated and ridiculed—often cruelly—women, dark-skinned African Americans, West Indians, Asians, Mexicans, Native Americans, and other ethnic groups.

Today, no subject is sacred for black humorists, and no medium is off-limits. Whether on Broadway, Hollywood films, or television, their material can still be construed as "survival humor" if it makes someone laugh at the funnier aspects of struggling to get by.

Seeing humor in life has been known to improve a person's whole outlook. So here is a little survival humor to help you sail smoothly along.

❧

A Note on Humor

Humor is laughing at what you haven't got when you ought to have it. Of course, you laugh by proxy. You're really laughing at the other guy's lacks, not your own. That's what makes it funny—the fact that you don't know you are laughing at yourself. Humor is when the joke is on you but hits the other fellow first—because it boomerangs. Humor is what you wish in your secret heart were not funny, but it is, and you must laugh. Humor is your own unconscious therapy.

What does this book mean? Simply that humor can be like a dropped brick or the roar of Niagara Falls. Humor maintains its distance while at the same time keeping you company so long as you are capable of meeting it halfway. Humor does not force itself on you (in fact, cannot) because it has none of the qualities of a bad joke, none of the vulgarity of the wisecrack, or the pushiness of the gag. Humor is a forgotten "Good morning" remembered tomorrow, a lent dime returned in needy time, a gesture from across the room better than a handshake, a friend who looks like a stranger but isn't because you realize you have known him all your life. Humor is your own smile surprising you in the mirror. . . . Like a welcome summer rain, humor may suddenly cleanse and cool the earth, the air, and you.

—*Langston Hughes*

❧

REASON VS. 'RITHMETIC
WILLIAM PICKENS

Reason should be taught in schools, alongside mathematics and writing and other academic subjects. In life, a person needs a solid foundation of common sense. Without it, book learning may be rendered useless. In this story, common sense becomes a prime factor in rewriting the laws of arithmetic.

There should be four "R's": Reading, 'Riting, 'Rithmetic, and Reason.

Just after the Civil War, when Negro children were first allowed to be taught in the Southern states, the little blacks were naturally proud of their learning day by day, and especially of their ability to deal in "figgers" and " 'rithmetic."

Two such little Negro boys sat on a fence in 1866, testing each other's knowledge of the mysteries of mathematics, when finally one put to the other this problem:

"See dem three birds settin' on dat limb dere? S'posin' I takes a gun an' shoots one uv 'em,—how many will be left dere?"

"None," said the other coolly.

"You don't know nuthin'," said the maker of the problem. "Ain't you got 'nough learnin' to figger whut *three* minus *one* eekals?"

"Yass," said the other, "but ain't I also got 'nough sense to know dat if you shoots one uv dem birds wid a gun, de udder two won't be sich fools ez to keep settin' on dat limb?"

⟨∾⟩

If I'm lying, I'm flying.

—*Traditional*

⟨∾⟩

BIG OL' LIES
COLLECTED BY ZORA NEALE HURSTON

Some folks have made an art of stretching the truth.

Gold spoke up and said, "Now, lemme tell one. Ah know one about a man as black as Gene."

"Whut you always crackin' me for?" Gene wanted to know. "Ah ain't a bit blacker than you."

"Oh, yes you is, Gene. Youse a whole heap blacker than Ah is."

"Aw, go head on, Gold. Youse blacker than me. You jus' look my color cause youse fat. If you wasn't no fatter than me you'd be so black till lightnin' bugs would follow you at twelve o'clock in de day, thinkin' it's midnight."

"Dat's a lie, youse blacker than Ah ever dared to be. Youse lam' black. Youse so black till they have to throw a sheet over yo' head so de sun kin rise every mornin'. Ah know yo' ma cried when she seen *you*."

"Well, anyhow, Gold, youse blacker than me. If Ah was as fat as you Ah'd be a yaller man."

"Youse a liar. Youse as yaller as you ever gointer git. When a person is poor he look bright and de fatter you git de darker you look."

"Is dat yo' excuse for being so black, Gold?"

THIS MORNING WHEN we got to the meeting place, the foreman wasn't there. So the men squatted along the railroad track and waited.

Joe Willard was sitting with me on the end of a cross-tie when he saw Jim Presley coming in a run with his bucket and jumper-jacket.

"Hey, Jim, where the swamp boss? He ain't got here yet."

"He's ill—sick in the bed Ah hope, but Ah bet he'll git here yet."

"Aw, he ain't sick. Ah bet you a fat man he ain't," Joe said.

"How come?" somebody asked him and Joe answered:

"Man, he's too ugly. If a spell of sickness ever tried to slip up on him, he'd skeer it into a three weeks' spasm."

Blue Baby stuck in his oar and said: "He ain't so ugly. Ye all jus' ain't seen no real ugly man. Ah seen a man so ugly till he could get behind a jimpson weed and hatch monkies."

Everybody laughed and moved closer together. Then Officer Richardson said: "Ah seen a man so ugly till they had to spread a sheet over his head at night so sleep could slip up on him."

They laughed some more, then Clifford Ulmer said:

"Ah'm goin' to talk with my mouth wide open. Those men y'all been talkin' 'bout wasn't ugly at all. Those was pretty men. Ah knowed one so ugly till you could throw him in the Mississippi river and skim ugly for six months."

"Give Cliff de little dog," Jim Allen said. "He done tole the biggest lie."

"He ain't lyin'," Joe Martin tole them. "Ah knowed dat same man. He didn't die—he jus' uglied away."

They laughed a great big old kah kah laugh and got closer together.

"Looka here, folkses," Jim Presley exclaimed. "Wese a half hour behind schedule and no swamp boss and no log train here yet. What yo' all reckon is the matter sho' 'nough?"

"Must be something terrible when white folks get slow about putting us to work."

"Yeah," says Good Black. "You know back in slavery Ole Massa was out in de field sort of lookin' things over, when a shower of rain come up. The field hands was glad it rained so they could knock off for a while. So one slave named John says:

"More rain, more rest."

"Ole Massa says, 'What's dat you say?'

"John says, 'More rain, more grass.' "

CLIFF ULMER SAID, "It sho is gittin' hot. Ah'll be glad when we git to de lake so Ah kin find myself some shade."

"Man, youse two miles from dat lake yet, and otherwise it ain't hot today," said Joe Wiley. "He ain't seen it hot, is he Will House?"

"Naw, Joe, when me and you was hoboing down in Texas it was so hot till we saw old stumps and logs crawlin' off in de shade."

Eugene Oliver said, "Aw dat wasn't hot. Ah seen it so hot till two cakes of ice left the ice house and went down the street and fainted."

Arthur Hopkins put in: "Ah knowed two men who went to Tampa all dressed up in new blue serge suits, and it was so hot dat when de train pulled into Tampa two blue suits got off de train. De men had done melted out of 'em."

Will House said, "Dat wasn't hot. Dat was chilly weather. Me and Joe Wiley went fishin' and it was so hot dat before we got to de water, we met de fish, coming swimming up de road in dust."

"Dat's a fact, too," added Joe Wiley. "Ah remember dat day well. It was so hot dat Ah struck a match to light my pipe and set de lake afire. Burnt half of it, den took de water dat was left and put out de fire."

WILL HOUSE SAID, "Ah know a lie on a black gnat. Me and my buddy Joe Wiley was ramshackin' Georgy over when we come to a loggin' camp. So bein' out of work we ast for a job. So de man puts us on and give us some oxes to drive. Ah had a six-yoke team and Joe was drivin' a twelve-yoke team. As we was comin' thru de woods we heard somethin' hummin' and we didn't know what it was. So we got hungry and went in a place to eat and when we come out a gnat had done et up de six-yoke team and de twelve-yoke team, and was sittin' up on de wagon pickin' his teeth wid a ox-horn and cryin' for somethin' to eat."

"Yeah," put in Joe Wiley, "we seen a man tie his cow and calf out to pasture and a mosquito come along and et up de cow and was ringin' de bell for de calf."

"Dat wasn't no full-grown mosquito at dat," said Eugene Oliver. "Ah was travellin' in Texas and laid down and went to sleep. De skee-ters bit me so hard till Ah seen a ole iron washpot, so Ah crawled under it and turned it down over me good so de skeeters couldn't git to me. But you know dem skeeters bored right thru dat iron pot. So I up wid a hatchet and bradded their bills into de pot. So they flew on off 'cross Galveston bay wid de wash pot on their bills."

"Look," said Black Baby, "on de Indian River we went to bed and heard de mosquitoes singin' like bull alligators. So we got under four blankets. Shucks! dat wasn't nothin'. Dem mosquitoes just screwed off dem short bills, reached back in they hip-pocket and took out they long bills and screwed 'em on and come right on through dem blankets and got us."

"Is dat de biggest mosquito you all ever seen? Shucks! Dey was li'l baby mosquitoes! One day my ole man took some men and went out into de woods to cut some fence posts. And a big rain come up so they went up under a great big ole tree. It was so big it would take six men to meet around it. De other men set down on de roots but my ole man stood up and leaned against de tree. Well, sir, a big old skeeter come up on de other side of dat tree and bored right thru it and got blood out of my ole man's back. Dat made him so mad till he up wid his ax and bradded dat mosquito's bill into dat tree. By dat time de rain stopped and they all went home.

"Next day when they come out, dat mosquito had done cleaned up ten acres dying. And two or three weeks after dat my ole man got enough bones from dat skeeter to fence in dat ten acres."

Everybody liked to hear about the mosquito. They laughed all over themselves.

"Yeah," said Sack Daddy, "you sho is tellin' de truth 'bout dat big old mosquito 'cause my ole man bought dat same piece of land and raised a crop of pumpkins on it and lemme tell y'all right now—mosquito dust is de finest fertilizer in de world. Dat land was so rich and we raised pumpkins so big dat we et five miles up in one of 'em and five miles down and ten miles acrost one and we ain't never found out how far it went. . . .

"Dat was rich land but my ole man had some rich land too," put in Will House. "My ole man planted cucumbers and he went along droppin' de seeds and befo' he could git out de way he'd have ripe cucumbers in his pockets. What is the richest land you ever seen?"

"Well," replied Joe Wiley, "my ole man had some land dat was so rich dat our mule died and we buried him down in our bottom-land and de next mornin' he had done sprouted li'l jackasses."

"Aw, dat land wasn't so rich," objected Ulmer. "My ole man had some land and it was so rich dat he drove a stob* in de ground at de end of a corn-row for a landmark and next morning there was ten ears of corn on de corn stalk and four ears growin' on de stob."

"Dat lan' y'all talkin' 'bout might do, if you give it plenty commercial-nal† but my ole man wouldn't farm no po' land like dat," said Joe Wiley. "Now, one year we was kinda late puttin' in our crops. Everybody else had corn a foot high when papa said, 'Well, chillun, Ah reckon we better plant some corn.' So Ah was droppin' and my brother was hillin' up behind me. We had done planted 'bout a dozen rows when Ah looked back and seen de corn comin' up. Ah didn't want it to grow too fast 'cause it would make all fodder and no roastin' ears so Ah hollered to my brother to sit down on some of it to stunt de growth. So he did, and de next day he dropped me back a note—says: "passed thru Heben yesterday at twelve o'clock sellin' roastin' ears to de angels."

"Yeah," says Larkins White, "dat was some pretty rich ground, but whut is de poorest ground you ever seen?"

Arthur Hopkins spoke right up and said:

"Ah seen some land so poor dat it took nine partridges to holler 'Bob White.' "

"Dat was rich land, boy," declared Larkins. "Ah seen land so poor dat de people come together and 'cided dat it was too poor to raise

---

* Stake.
† Commercial fertilizer.

anything on, so they give it to de church, so de congregation built de church and called a pastor and held de meetin'. But de land was so poor they had to wire up to Jacksonville for ten sacks of commercial-nal before dey could raise a tune on dat land."

⟡

Who you gonna believe—me or your lying eyes?

—*Richard Pryor*

⟡

A LAUGH THAT MEANT FREEDOM
COLLECTED BY J. MASON BREWER

Cleverness wins the day.

There were some slaves who had a reputation for keeping out of work because of their wit and humor. These slaves kept their masters laughing most of the time, and were able, if not to keep from working altogether, at least to draw the lighter tasks.

Nehemiah was a clever slave, and no master who had owned him had ever been able to keep him at work, or succeeded in getting him to do heavy work. He would always have some funny story to tell or some humorous remark to make in response to the master's question, or scolding. Because of this faculty for avoiding work, Nehemiah was constantly being transferred from one master to another. As soon as an owner found out that Nehemiah was outwitting him, he sold Nehemiah to some other slaveholder. One day David Wharton, known as the most cruel slave master in Southwest Texas, heard about him.

"I bet I can make that rascal work," said David Wharton, and he went to Nehemiah's master and bargained to buy him.

The morning of the first day after his purchase, David Wharton walked over to where Nehemiah was standing and said, "Now you are going to work, you understand. You are going to pick four hundred pounds of cotton today."

"Wal, Massa, dat's aw right," answered Nehemiah, "but ef Ah meks yuh laff, won' yuh lemme off fo' terday?"

"Well," said David Wharton, who had never been known to laugh, "if you make me laugh, I won't only let you off for today, but I'll give you your freedom."

"Ah decla', Boss," said Nehemiah, "yuh sho' is uh goodlookin' man."

"I am sorry I can't say the same thing about you," retorted David Wharton.

"Oh, yes, Boss, yuh could," Nehemiah laughed out, "yuh could, ef yuh tole ez big uh lie ez Ah did."

David Wharton could not help laughing at this; he laughed before he thought. Nehemiah got his freedom.

HONEST FOOL
RETOLD BY STEVE SANFIELD

To some, High John the Conqueror is a term associated with the conjuring powers of plants or root medicine. But to others, High John the Conqueror is a legendary trickster, a cunning slave who outwitted his master and came to symbolize the unconquerable spirit of slaves.

According to author and folklorist Zora Neale Hurston, High John came from Africa, walking the "very winds that filled the sails" of slave vessels. White people did not know he existed because Africans did not let on about him. Slave masters met him, but did not know him by his right name. Although he was a slave, he caused headaches and setbacks for the master. If John was sent to fetch a tool, the tool shed would suddenly go up in flames—accidentally. The slave master couldn't determine whether John was helping him or pushing him closer to wit's end.

Like King Arthur of England, wrote Hurston, "he has served his people and gone back into mystery again. And, like King Arthur, he is not dead. . . . [He] went back to Africa, but he left his power here, and placed his American dwelling in the root of a certian plant. Only possess that root, and he can be summoned at any time."

Here, John teaches a lesson to a tattler—a "house slave" named

George, who had a bad habit of informing Old Master of what the other slaves were doing, planning, or saying among themselves. A loose tongue often ends up getting its owner into a world of trouble.

One of the house slaves, George, was always going back to Old Master with stories about the rest of the slaves, stories about who was taking what, about who was only pretending to be too sick to work, all sorts of things no one wanted Master to know about.

Naturally, High John wasn't particularly fond of George, and he decided to teach him a lesson for his tattling ways. One evening he greeted George in the slave quarters. John was smiling that big smile of his and strutting like a rooster stepping in high mud.

"What are you so happy about?" asked George.

"Why, you'll never guess what I did today."

"No, what'd you do today?"

"Why," said John, beaming like a full moon in August, "I cussed out Old Massa."

"You cussed him out?" George asked in surprise. "What'd he do to you?"

"Nothing. He didn't do nothing, and he ain't going to do nothing either. I cussed him out just as much as I pleased. I called him every name a body could think of. I cussed him frontways, backways, sideways, up and down, and you know what, George? He didn't say nothing, and he ain't never going to say nothing."

George turned that over in his mind for a minute or two and said, "Well, the next time he fusses with me I'm going to cuss him out too."

He didn't have to wait long for his chance. The very next day George dropped a tray while he was serving Old Master and Missy a mid-afternoon snack. Master turned on him and started cursing him something terrible. "You stupid, clumsy, no-good—"

But George cut him off in the middle of his anger. "Massa," he said, "you've got no right to talk to me that way. You're no better than a hog wallowing in the mud. You're so dumb that—"

Of course, George didn't get to finish. Master grabbed him by the ear, dragged him out, and gave him a slavery-time whipping. He was in such terrible shape he had to crawl back to the slave quarters, and there was John waiting for him.

"Why George," he said, "what happened to you?"

"What happened to me?" George moaned. "I cussed out Old Massa, and he did this to me. How come he didn't do anything to you?"

"George, you didn't cuss him out to his face, did you?"

"Of course I did. Isn't that what you did?"

"Oh George, what a fool you are," chuckled John. "When I cussed him out, he was up at the Big House and I was way down by the creek. George, some fools' tongues are long enough to cut their throats. You'd best be careful, George. You'd best be careful."

George was very careful after that. It seemed as if he learned his lesson. He even stopped his tale-bearing.

AN EPIDEMIC OF DUCKS
RETOLD BY STEVE SANFIELD

After the Civil War, ex-slaves had few opportunities open to them. Often, they had no choice but to remain on plantations and continue farming the land of their former masters, who took advantage of them at every turn—by renting out the former slave quarters, overcharging for the use of farm implements, and collecting more than their fair share of profits from crops. High John the Conqueror used a little creativity to keep what he figured was rightly his in the first place. "Ducks" helped him out of a bad situation.

John had been sharecropping a piece of land with Old Boss. Boss would supply the seed, the tools, and whatever else was needed. John would then prepare the land and plant, grow, hoe, harvest, and chop the cotton. After it was sold and the expenses taken out, Boss and John were supposed to share the profits.

It never seemed to work out that way for John, though. Oh, he would grow a fine crop of cotton all right. No one could do more work than John when he wanted to. And he usually got a pretty good price for it, but every time he'd come back from town with the money there'd be Old Boss waiting for him.

"John," he'd say, "it's time to settle up. How much did you get for the cotton?"

"I got a hundred dollars."

Then Old Boss would take out his pencil and a pad of paper and start making little black marks. All the time he'd be talking to himself, so softly John could hardly make out what he was saying. "Let's see, the seed cost such and such, and the hoes cost such and such, and the such and such cost such and such." He'd go on that way for a while and finally announce, "John, I figure you owe me one hundred and eight dollars and eight cents. Why don't you just give me that hundred dollars and we'll call it being settled up."

This went on year after year. John would work the cotton and sell it, but when it came time to settle up John always ended up with the same he had when he started—nothing.

One year John decided that this time it was going to be different. He brought in a bigger crop than ever before, and as he was taking it to town to sell, there was Old Boss waiting to see him off.

"That looks like a fine wagonload of cotton you've got there. What do you think it'll bring?"

"Well, Boss," said John, shaking his head, "it's mighty hard to say, because I hear tell there's an epidemic of ducks this year."

"An epidemic of ducks? What are you talking about, John?"

"I'm talking about an epidemic of ducks, and I hear them ducks are terrible on cotton prices." With that John just rode off into town leaving Boss standing there by the side of the road, wondering what John could be talking about this time.

John sold the cotton for more money than ever before. He went to the store and treated himself to some sugar, some coffee, and a few other victuals and then headed on home.

Sure enough, there was Old Boss waiting for him with his pencil and pad of paper ready.

"It's time to settle up, John," he said. "How'd we make out this year?"

"Oh Boss, you're going to be pleased to hear that I got a better price than I ever did get before, but like I told you, there was this epidemic of ducks."

"John, there you go talking about those ducks again. What does an epidemic of ducks have to do with anything? Just tell me how much you got so we can settle up."

"I sold the cotton for two hundred dollars. I had the money right here in my hand, but before I could blink twice the ducks got it all."

"John, you're driving me crazy with all this talk about ducks."

"I know, Boss, I know, but let me be more particular. First they deducks for the rotten cotton bolls, and then they deducks for their commission. They deducks for taxes. They deducks for the victuals I got. They deducks for this and they deducks for that, and by the time the ducks were through the ducks got it all—so I guess we'll have to wait until next year to settle up."

John rode on to his cabin while Old Boss just stood there with his mouth hanging open trying to figure out what had happened.

John put away his sugar and his coffee and hid the cotton money. He sat down at his table and said to himself, "All Boss ever wants to do is settle up, when all I want is just a little bit of settling down."

MASTER'S WALKING STICK
RETOLD BY STEVE SANFIELD

High John the Conqueror cut his master down to size by proving his brand-new cane had three ends. Wisdom can outshine flashiness.

High John was, among other things, a fine fisherman. He knew where the fish lay, and he knew what had to be done to catch them.

Even Old Master liked to go fishing with John now and then. They'd go down to the big pond under the live oaks, and Master would try to catch a few catfish himself.

John and Master had planned to meet early one bright summer morning. John was already there behind the barn when along came Master.

Of course he had his fishing pole with him, but he was also carrying a brand-new walking stick. The stick was polished almost as bright as a mirror. It had a shiny silver handle on one end and a shiny silver tip on the other.

From the way he was swinging and flashing it about, you could tell Master was very proud of his new stick. John, however, didn't make any mention of it, at least not until they were settled on the bank of the pond with their lines in the water.

"Say Massa," said John, "that's a mighty fine looking walking stick you've got there."

"Why thank you, John. I was beginning to wonder if you were going to take any notice of it."

"Oh Massa, I noticed it right off. I mean it's the only walking stick I've ever seen with three ends."

"Three ends?" asked Master. "What are you talking about, John?"

"Well, I ain't talking about anything but the three ends of that stick," John answered.

"John, are you drunk or have you gone crazy?"

"I'm not drunk and I'm not crazy, Massa, but I can see as clear as the nose on my face that your stick's got three ends."

"John, no stick's got three ends."

"Well, that one does," said John, "and I'd be willing to bet you a big, fat hen that it does."

Old Master took a careful look at his walking stick just to be sure. After all, John had been playing tricks on him for years. This time, though, he was certain John was wrong.

"Agreed," he said. "I'll bet you a hen that this stick has only two ends."

With that, John took the stick and held it out in front of him. He pointed to the silver handle and said, "That's one end, right?"

"Right," answered Master.

He pointed to the silver tip and said, "That's two ends, right?"

"Right," answered Master again.

Then John raised the stick over his head and threw it directly into the center of the pond, where it sank without a trace.

"And that's the third end of that stick, right?" said John with a twinkle in his eye.

Old Master didn't answer this time. He knew John had fooled him again, and that when they got back home he'd have to give him a nice plump hen.

ᝍᝍ

God don't like ugly.

—*Traditional*

ᝍᝍ

ITS AND IFS
AS TOLD BY HAROLD LEE

What's worse—the ifs *or the* its?

Two colored men were talking to themselves. One was a farmer, the other had quit. He said he wasn't going to farm any more, there were too many its and ifs. The ifs were, *if* the boll weevils don't eat it up, *if* the worms don't eat it up, *if* the drouth don't come, he'll make a good crop, for the man to take with the pencil and pad.

The its were: to plow *it*, to plant *it*, to chop *it*, to poison *it*, to pick *it*, to weigh *it*, haul *it* to the gin, sell *it*, and the man behind the desk take *it*.

THE FARMER AND G.P.C.
COLLECTED BY RAY B. BROWNE

Hard work can create powerful visions of what a man was meant to do with his life. But these visions are subject to very different interpretations.

One time dere was a man what was a farmer. One year he had a real good crop. But dis man was kinda lazy, and when it come time to gather de crop he tole ole lady dat he could not he'p gather de crop cause he felt de Lord was callin' him to go preach. He tole her to look up in de sky, and he pointed out de letters G P C, which he say meant, "Go Preach Christ" and he had to go.

But de ole lady she was too much fer him. "Dose letters don' mean, 'Go Preach Christ,' " she said. "Dey mean, 'Go Pick Cotton.' "

TWO LAZY MEN
AS TOLD BY JAMES D. SUGGS

Lazier men than these two are hard to find.

This man was so lazy he wouldn't work, he wouldn't do nothing. He just lay down side of the road. Everybody heard about him being lazy. Fellow said, "Hey, Bill, come over here; here's twenty dollars I'll give you." Bill says, "No, no, bring it over here." "No, but if you be laying there still when I come back I'll give you one hundred dollars." Bill was laying in the shade, you see; sun was mighty hot and he'd have to come into the sun to get the twenty-dollar bill. When the fellow came back Bill was still laying there. "All right, here's the hundred dollars—come and get it." Bill told him, "No—you bring it over here." "No, I won't—you'll have to come and get it." So Bill said, "Well, just lay it down over there—a puff of wind might blow it over."

Another one was even lazier. He wouldn't work, and they were going to bury him alive. They put him in the hearse, and started for the cemetery. An old lady come along and said, "Where you going with Tom?" (His name was Lazy Tom.) "Well, he's so lazy he won't work to get something to eat and we're going to bury him alive." She said, "Don't do that; I got some meat and bread for him." Tom said, "Madam, is it cooked?" "No, it's not cooked." "Well, drive on, boys."

They went on and another lady stopped the hearse, and asked where they were going with Lazy Tom. When they told her she said: "Don't bury him for that. I'll give him a chicken already cooked." He wanted to know was it chewed up. She told him, no, it wasn't chewed up, but she had run it through a sausage mill. He asked her, "Was it swallowed?" "No." Lazy Tom told 'em, "Drive on, boys." So they buried him alive.

ETERNITY
AS TOLD BY HENRY LOUIS GATES JR.

A get-rich-quick scheme that'll take forever.

A man is talking to the Lord, trying to fathom His infinitude. "Lord," he asks, "what's a million years to you?" "A million years is a second to me," the Lord explains. "And a million dollars?" A penny, the Lord replies. "Lord," the man proceeds to ask, emboldened, "would you give me a million dollars?" "Sure," the Lord replies. "Just a second."

AN EXCLUSIVE CHURCH
WILLIAM PICKENS

In some lily-white churches, blacks are not the only ones who are unwelcome.

A Negro in a northern community went to church one Sunday. It was a church of white people, and the minister was speaking from the text: "Come all ye that labor and are heavy laden." In the exaltation of feelings and rhetoric the minister had cried out: "Come! The Gospel is free! Free to all alike! Salvation is free, absolutely free, free to all, to all mankind, to every race, every class, every individual! Come! The church, this church is a brotherhood of men!"

Being a fundamentalist, the Negro interpreted this rhetoric literally, and went up to join. The preacher quietly whispered to the Negro that he would see him in his study, after services. In the study the Negro was asked: "Are you sure the Lord wants you to join this church? Don't you think it best to go and consult the Lord about the matter, and let him direct you?"

The black man thought this a bit strange, as the Lord had already given an urgent, general and unqualified invitation—through this same preacher. But he left the pastor's study resolved to test the matter to the end. He therefore paid another visit to the preacher, indicating that the Lord was willing, and the white man said a little more fervently than before: "Consult the Lord a little further—put the whole matter into the hands of the Lord—and ask him whether you might not serve him better in some other church."

For a third time the Negro went. The pastor was chagrined, and became impatient: "My brother, you are not trusting in the Lord. I have put the matter before the Lord myself, and he has told me" . . .

"Wait a minute," said the black man, anticipating the white man, "cause I done seen de Lord, too, an' he tol' me all about it."

"Well, wh-what?" asked the anxious white man.

"I axed de Lord if I mus' keep tryin' to jine dis-yere church, an' he sez to me, sez he: 'Well, I hates awfully to discourage you, but I mus' tell you de trufe, fer you'se jes' wastin' yo' time on dat pertic'lar church. Fer de las' twenty years,' sez de Lord, sez he, 'dat is, since de 'cumbency o' de present paster-in-charge, I'se tried repeatedly to git into dat church myself, an' I ain't made it yet!' "

TWO FRIENDS AND THE BEAR
RETOLD BY HAROLD COURLANDER

True friends have the courage to stand by one another when the going gets rough.

Two friends, they were on a journey together. They had to go through a thick swamp that was full of bear and other varmints. They promised to stand for one another, and to help one another out if the varmints should attack them. They didn't get halfway through the swamp when a big black bear jumped out of the bushes and made for them. Instead of standing by his friend, one of the men left and climbed a tree. The other man had heard that bears wouldn't eat dead people, so he lay down on the ground and held his breath and shut his eyes, and made out that he was dead.

The bear came up to him, and smelled him, and turned him over, trying to find out if he was breathing. When he found out the man wasn't breathing, he went off a little way and watched him. Then he turned back and smelled him again and looked at him closely. At length he made up his mind, said the man was really dead, and with that he left for good and went off in the woods.

All this time the other friend who was squinched up in the tree was watching what was going on. He was so scared he wouldn't do anything to help his friend, or try to run the bear off. When he saw that the bear was gone for sure, he hollered to his friend on the ground, said, "What the bear been telling you? Him and you seemed like you were having a close conversation."

Then his friend down below answered, "He been telling me never to trust anyone who calls himself a friend, and who runs like a coward as soon as trouble comes."

BIG MOUNTAIN AND
LITTLE MOUNTAIN
COLLECTED BY J. MASON BREWER

Courage isn't a trait limited to just big or extra-large people. To match one's abilities against an adversary of equal stature takes great courage, no matter how big or small you are. Courageous people, then, come in all shapes and sizes, even pint-size.

In a mountain town of North Carolina there lived a man about eight feet tall. One day a little fellow about five feet four walked up to him and said, "Man, if I was as big as you I would go up the mountain and grab a big bear and whup him to death."

The big man looked down on him and said, "There's some little bears up there too!"

LET'S YOU AND HIM FIGHT

Not all black men wanted to fight valiantly for the Union in the Civil War. In this vignette, an escaped slave discusses his view of the black man's true role in the War Between the States.

Samuel Hart, who was later to distinguish himself in the famed 54th Massachusetts Negro Regiment during the Civil War, recalled in his memoirs that he was not so militant in his early youth. He was about fourteen years old when he and his family escaped from slavery in Maryland. His rescuing angel was Harriet Tubman, who guided the family to Auburn, New York, in the year 1855.

Upon reaching safety, young Samuel found himself to be the center of interest among persons who were curious to know "if slavery was all that bad." At a recruiting center in Auburn, a number of young officers were discussing the role of the black man in the conflict between the states. One of them turned to Mr. Hart. "Is it true that the Negroes in the south are doing nothing to help the Union cause?"

Samuel Hart considered the plight of the slave and replied, "Does the turkey arm himself at Thanksgiving?"

"But," persisted the junior officer, "what is the Negro doing about the war in the North? Surely he knows what all the fighting is about."

"My dear friend," replied Mr. Hart, "as an ex-slave, permit me to introduce you to the black man's philosophy. You have undoubtedly seen two dogs fighting over a bone."

"Yes, many times."

"Then tell me," concluded Hart, "have you ever seen the bone participate in any of the fighting?"

BR'ER RABBIT WINS THE REWARD
JULIA PRICE BURRELL

Br'er Rabbit is a trickster animal in African American folk literature. His enemies are Br'er Fox, Br'er Wolf, and Br'er Bear. They are constantly scheming to humiliate him or kill him. But Br'er Rabbit always manages to survive their schemes by outwitting them. This folktale shows just how clever he is. *

* This folktale appeared in *The Brownies' Book*, a children's magazine published in the early 1920s by the editors of *The Crisis*, the NAACP's official publication. The editors—who called *Brownies' Book* readers "Children of the Sun" or "Brownies"—printed articles and stories on black achievement and culture, presenting African Americans in a positive light during a time

Br'er Rabbit, Br'er Fox and Br'er Wolf were hired by the King to work in a certain field. Now because the mosquitoes were so many and stung so hard in this hay field the King had had great difficulty in securing workers, so as a spur to the laborers he promised to him who should work longest without heeding the mosquitoes a special reward.

All three, Br'er Rabbit, Br'er Fox, Br'er Wolf, set to work, each determined to win the reward. How those mosquitoes did bite! Every half minute Br'er Wolf stopped to slap one! Every five minutes Br'er Fox stopped to swat at the troublesome pests!

What of Br'er Rabbit? Oh, they were not sparing him either, but that little animal is a "schemy" creature! He worked away, and as he worked he talked. Said he, "My old Dad, he haves a plough horse; he black here and here," and as he said "here" each time he slapped his stinging legs where the mosquitoes were biting—"and," he went on, "he white all here"—slapping again at the enemy!

So he continued talking and slapping and working. It never occurred to the King that Br'er Rabbit was killing mosquitoes. It appeared to those who looked that Br'er Rabbit was not bothered.

He won the reward.

THE FOX AND THE GOOSE

A crafty plot is revealed in the nick of time.

One day a Fox was going down the road and saw a Goose. "Good-morning, Goose," he said; and the Goose flew up on a limb and said, "Good-morning, Fox."

Then the Fox said, "You ain't afraid of me, is you? Haven't you heard of the meeting up at the hall the other night?"

when many publications printed derogatory and racist material. The magazine is credited with starting African American children's literature.

"No, Fox. What was that?"

"You haven't heard about all the animals meeting up at the hall! Why, they passed a law that no animal must hurt any other animal. Come down and let me tell you about it. The hawk mustn't catch the chicken, and the dog mustn't chase the rabbit, and the lion mustn't hurt the lamb. No animal must hurt any other animal."

"Is that so!"

"Yes, all live friendly together. Come down, and don't be afraid."

As the Goose was about to fly down, way off in the woods they heard a "Woo-wooh! woo-wooh!" and the Fox looked around.

"Come down, Goose," he said.

And the Dog got closer. "Woo-wooh!"

Then the Fox started to sneak off; and the Goose said, "Fox, you ain't scared of the Dog, is you? Didn't all the animals pass a law at the meeting not to bother each other any more?"

"Yes," replied the Fox as he trotted away quickly, "the animals passed the law; but some of the animals round here ain't got much respec' for the law."

BUH LION AND BUH GOAT
RETOLD BY HAROLD COURLANDER

This moralizing animal tale, reminiscent of some African stories, teaches how cleverness can be used as a powerful and decisive weapon against the strong. Though humorous, this tale, first published in 1888, carries a serious message.

Buh Lion was out hunting, and he spied Buh Goat lying on top of a big rock. Buh Goat was working his mouth and chewing. Buh Lion crept up to catch him. When he got close he noticed Buh Goat good. Buh Goat kept on chewing. Buh Lion tried to figure out what Buh Goat was chewing. He didn't see anything but the naked rock that Buh Goat was lying on. Buh Lion was astonished. Buh Goat kept on chewing, chewing, chewing. But Lion couldn't make it out. He came close and said, "Hey, Buh Goat, what are you eating?" Buh Goat was scared when Buh Lion rose up before him, but he kept a bold heart, and he answered, "I'm chewing on this rock, and if you don't get out of here, when I'm through I'm going to eat you." When Buh Lion heard that he said to himself, "If Buh Goat can chew rock what can he do to me?" And he departed. Buh Goat's big words saved him. He was a bold man. A bold man gets out of his difficulties, a coward loses his life.

BEAT THE BULLET
A. W. EDDINS

Here is creative testimony from a man who didn't stick around long enough to become the victim of a bullet. If we cannot be as fast as he was in escaping danger, we should be wise enough to avoid it in the first place.

In the trial of a Negro for shooting at another, a lawyer examining one of the parties said, "You say that when the defendant pulled his gun you began to run. How did you know that he was shooting at you?"

"I heard de gun fire, en I heard de bullet when it passed me."

"Are you absolutely sure that you heard the bullet pass you?"

"Yes, I'm sure I heard dat bullet pass me, 'cause I heard it twice."

"You say you heard the bullet *twice.* How could that be possible?"

"Well, it was jes lack dis—I heard de bullet when it passed me, en I heard it again when I passed it."

❧

Aesop and Uncle Remus have taught us that comedy is a disguised form of philosophical instruction; and especially when it allows us to glimpse the animal instincts operating beneath the surface of our civilized affectations. For by allowing us to laugh at that which is normally unlaughable, comedy provides an otherwise unavailable clarification of vision that calms the clammy trembling which ensues whenever we pierce the veil of conventions that guard us from the basic absurdity of the human condition. During such moments the world of appearances is turned upside down.

—*Ralph Ellison*

❧

Every dog has its day.

—*Traditional*

❧

THE COLORED ZOO
BERT WILLIAMS

The great vaudeville comic Bert Williams (1876–1922) was articulate and cultivated offstage. But onstage, he portrayed hard-luck characters who shuffled and spoke in dialect. Trapped by the racism of the late nineteenth and early twentieth centuries, Williams appeared in blackface in all of his stage appearances. Here, he tells the story of a desperate black man who survived, ironically, by becoming "The King of the Jungles." The story shows that no matter how desperate you may be, chances are you just might meet someone equally desperate.

One time I was stranded in a town an' a circus come along so I went an' told the manager that I was desperate an' jus' *had* to have work. He said, "Well one of our best lions died last week and as we saved the skin, if you want to you can git in it and be a lion till somethin' better comes along."

Naturally I grabbed it and that same afternoon I made my first 'ppearance as "The King of the Jungles." Then here comes the man what does the stunts inside of the animals' cages. He come in my cage first an' after 'splaining 'bout what a fine specimen I was and how much trouble they had ketchin' me in Africa, he say, "Now ladies and gent'men to show you how much we have tamed and trained him, I am goin' to turn him into this next cage with this large and f'rocious Bengal Tagger."

I *imeegitly* backed into the furthest corner of my cage. The man opened up the door between the two cages, drawed out a big pistol an' say, "Git in thare or I'll blow yo' head off." An' kinder under his breath he say to me, "And that *goes* too." And then he took and fired the gun off once up over his head to show me that it would shoot and I looked up and seen the hole it made in the roof of the cage so I jus' went on in the nex' cage and got right down on my knees and commence prayin'. And this big Bengal Tagger leaped todes me and jus' as my heart was gittin' ready to stop for good, that Tagger took and leaned over and I heard him whisper right in my ear, "Don't be skeered pal; I'm colored same as you."

HOW THE LION MET THE KING
OF THE WORLD
ZORA NEALE HURSTON

Zora Neale Hurston collected many folktales in her travels. Here's one about the lion and John. And you thought the lion was king . . .

"Y'all been tellin' and lyin' 'bout all dese varmints but you ain't yet spoke about de high chief boss of all de world which is de lion," Sack Daddy commented.

"He's de King of de Beasts, but he ain't no King of de World, now Sack," Dad Boykin spoke up. "He *thought* he was de King till John give him a straightenin'."

"Don't put dat lie out!" Sack Daddy contended. "De lion won't stand no straightenin'."

"Course I 'gree wid you dat everybody can't show de lion no deep point, but John showed it to him. Oh, yeah, John not only straightened him out, he showed dat ole lion where in."

"When did he do all of dis, Dad? Ah ain't never heard tell of it." Dad spoke up:

Oh, dis was way befo' yo' time. Ah don't recolleck myself. De old folks told me about John and de lion. Well, John was ridin' long one day straddle of his horse when de grizzly bear come pranchin' out in de middle of de road and hollered: "Hold on a minute! They tell me you goin' 'round strowin' it dat youse de King of de World."

John stopped his horse: "Whoa! Yeah, Ah'm de King of de World, don't you b'lieve it?" John told him.

"Naw, you ain't no King. Ah'm de King of de World. You can't be no King till you whip me. Git down and fight."

John hit de ground and de fight started. First, John grabbed him a rough-dried brick and started to work de fat offa de bear's head. De bear just fumbled 'round till he got a good holt, then he begin to squeeze and squeeze. John knowed he couldn't stand dat much longer, do he'd be jus' another man wid his breath done give out. So he reached into his pocket and got out his razor and slipped it between dat bear's ribs. De bear turnt loose and reeled on over in de bushes to lay down. He had enough of dat fight.

John got back on his horse and rode on off.

De lion smelt de bear's blood and come runnin' to where de grizzly was layin' and started to lappin' his blood.

De bear was skeered de lion was gointer eat him while he was all cut and bleedin' nearly to death, so he hollered and said: "*Please* don't touch me, Brer Lion. Ah done met de King of de World and he done cut me all up."

De lion got his bristles all up and clashed down at de bear: "Don't you lay there and tell me you done met de King of de World and not be talkin' 'bout me! Ah'll tear you to pieces!"

"Oh, don't tetch me, Brer Lion! Please lemme alone so Ah kin git well."

"Well, don't you call nobody no King of de World but me."

"But Brer Lion, Ah done *met* de King sho' nuff. Wait till you see him and you'll say Ah'm right."

"Naw, Ah won't, neither. Show him to me and Ah'll show you how much King he is."

"All right, Brer Lion, you jus' have a seat right behind dese bushes. He'll be by here befo' long."

Lion squatted down by de bear and waited. Fust person he saw goin' up de road was a old man. Lion jumped up and ast de bear, "Is dat him?"

Bear say, "Naw, dat's Uncle Yistiddy, he's a useter-be!"

After while a li'l boy passed down de road. De lion seen him and jumped up agin. "Is dat him?" he ast de bear.

Bear told him, "Naw, dat's li'l tomorrow, he's a gointer-be, you jus' lay quiet. Ah'll let you know when he gits here."

Sho nuff after while here come John on his horse but he had done got his gun. Lion jumped up agin and ast, "Is dat him?"

Bear say: "Yeah, dat's him! Dat's de King of de World."

Lion reared up and cracked his tail back and forwards like a bullwhip. He 'lowed, "You wait till Ah git thru wid him and you won't be callin' him no King no mo'."

He took and galloped out in de middle of de road right in front of John's horse and laid his years back. His tail was crackin' like torpedoes.

"Stop!" de lion hollered at John. "They tell me you goes for de King of de World!"

John looked him dead in de ball of his eye and told him, "Yeah, Ah'm de King. Don't you like it, don't you take it. Here's mah collar, come and shake it!"

De lion and John eye-balled one another for a minute or two, den de lion sprung on John.

Talk about fightin'! Man, you ain't seen no sich fightin' and wrasslin' since de mornin' stars sung together. De lion clawed and bit John and John bit him right back.

Way after while John got to his rifle and he up wid de muzzle right in ole lion's face and pulled de trigger. Long, slim black feller, snatch 'er back and hear 'er beller! Dog damn! Dat was too much for de lion. He turnt go of John and wheeled to run to de woods. John levelled down on him agin and let him have another load, right in his hindquarters.

Dat ole lion give John de book; de bookity book.* He hauled de fast mail back into de woods where de bear was laid up.

"Move over," he told de bear. "Ah wants lay down too."

"How come?" de bear ast him.

"Ah done met de King of de World, and he done ruint me."

"Brer Lion, how you know you done met de King?"

" 'Cause he made lightnin' in my face and thunder in my hips. Ah know Ah done met de King, move over."

ADVENTURE
LANGSTON HUGHES

Jesse B. Semple (or Simple) offers a unique vacation idea: Visit the Savage South and get a firsthand view of rednecks in action. Undoubtedly, his plan to expose Northern whites to hostile Southerners would encourage empathy for blacks' experiences in Dixieland. If just witnessing racism is no picnic, imagine living it.

"Adventure is a great thing," said Simple, "which should be in everybody's life. According to 'The Late Late Show' on TV, in the old days when Americans headed West in covered wagons, they was almost sure to run into adventure—at the very least a battle with the Red Skins. Nowadays, if you want to run into adventure, go to Alabama or Mississippi, where you can battle with the White Skins."

" 'Go West, young man, go West,' is what they used to say," I said. " '*Pioneers! O pioneers!*' cried Whitman."

" 'Go South, young man, go South,' is what I would say today," declared Simple. "If I had a son I wanted to make a man out of, I would send him to Jackson, Mississippi, or Selma, Alabama—and not in a covered wagon, but on a bus. Especially if he was a white boy, I would say, 'Go, son, go, and return to your father's house when you have

* The lion ran.

conquered. The White Skins is on the rampage below the Mason-Dixon Line, defying the government, denying free Americans their rights. Go see what you can do about it. Go face the enemy.' "

"You would send your son into the maelstrom of Dixie to get his head beaten by a white cracker or his legs bitten by police dogs?"

"For freedom's sake—and adventure—I might even go South myself," said Simple, "if I was white. I think it is more important for white folks to have them kind of adventures than it is for colored. Negroes have been fighting one way or another all our lives—but it is somewhat new to whites. Until lately, they did not even know what a COLORED ONLY sign meant. White folks have always thought they could go anywhere in the world they wanted to go. They are just now finding out that they cannot go into a COLORED WAITING ROOM in the Jim Crow South. They cannot even go into a WHITE WAITING ROOM if they are with colored folks. They never knew before that if you want adventure, all you have to do is cross the color line in the South."

"Then, according to you," I said, "the Wild West can't hold a candle to the Savage South any more."

"Not even on TV," said Simple. "The Savage South has got the Wild West beat a mile. In the old days adventures was beyond the Great Divide. Today they is below the Color Line. Such adventures is much better than 'The Late Late Show' with Hollywood Indians. But in the South, nobody gets scalped. They just get cold-cocked. Of course, them robes the Klan sports around in is not as pretty as the feathers Indians used to wear, but they is more scary. And though a Klan holler is not as loud as a Indian war whoop, the Klan is just as sneaky. In cars, not on horseback, they comes under cover of night. If the young people of the North really want excitement, let them go face the Klan and stand up to it.

" 'That is why the South will make a man of you, my son,' I would say. 'Go South, baby, go South. Let a fiery cross singe the beard off your beatnik chin. Let Mississippi make a man out of you.' "

"Don't you think white adults as well as white youth should be exposed to this thing?" I asked.

"Of course," said Simple. "If the white young folks go as Freedom Riders, let the white old folks go as sight-seers—because no sooner than they got down there, they would be Freedom Riders anyhow. If I owned one of these white travel bureaus arranging sight-seeing tours next summer to Niagara Falls, Yellowstone Park, the Grand Canyon, and Pikes Peak, I would also start advertising sight-seeing tours to Montgomery with the National Guard as guides, to Jackson with leather leggings as protection against police dogs, to the Mississippi Prison Farms with picnic lunches supplied by Howard Johnson's, and to the Governor's Mansion with a magnolia for all the ladies taking the tour—and a night in jail without extra charge.

"Negroes would be guaranteed as passengers on all tours, so that there would be sure adventures for everybody. My ads would read:

SPECIAL RATES FOR A WEEKEND
IN A TYPICAL MISSISSIPPI JAIL

Get arrested now, pay later. Bail money not included. Have the time of your lives living the life of your times among the Dixie White Skins. Excitement guaranteed. For full details contact the Savage South Tours, Inc., Jesse B. Semple, your host, wishing you hell."

BUS STOP BEAUTIES
BILL COSBY

Entertainer Bill Cosby grew up in Philadelphia. Here he explains why he spent much of his youth watching traffic.

Young men no longer stand at drugstores and make plaintive cries to young women in this age of the equal female; but what memories I have of those boyhood evenings at a bus stop named desire.

I remember the acceleration of my heart one night when a particular object of my fancy came by. She had already rejected every other guy, but I still dreamed she would fall for me; I dreamed that maybe her weakness was a man with a zit on the bridge of his nose. She was aloof and elusive, this beauty, a girl who walked as erectly as a Marine, was always well dressed, and never went to parties because at parties you met guys like us. The problem was that she would have to fall for me without my encouragement because whenever I saw her, I was transfixed, afraid to make a move or utter a word. Sometimes one of the guys would walk one of the girls into the drugstore, but I never had the nerve to approach this princess. What could I have said?

Does your mother have gas again?

Guess how many buses stop here every hour.

Did you like the way World War II came out?

Like that famous tree in the forest without people, when Cosby fell for a girl, did he make any sound?

ON CERTAIN NIGHTS, we drugstore dreamers remained at our watch so long that our parents felt we must have been misbehaving.

"What were you *doing* till after midnight?" my father said early one morning when I returned from another plunge into unrequited love.

"Nothing," I replied.

"Well, tonight you can do it in the house."

"But it's better to do nothing *outdoors*. You see, a lot of my friends also like to do nothing and we do it *together.*"

"Then have 'em come here."

"It's not the same kind of nothing."

"Exactly what kind of nothing do you do outdoors?"

"We stand at the bus stop."

"And do what? Make change?"

"No, we just watch the traffic."

"Okay, suppose I gave you a job and paid you two bucks an hour to stand on that corner and just watch people get on and off the bus. You wouldn't stand there an hour."

"I would if I could have my *friends* with me."

"But they wouldn't be with you because they have a little mental problem. They're terrified of work."

"Dad, you don't understand. What I'm looking for on that corner is the woman of my life."

"You don't know any girls who walk around anyplace else? You gotta meet buses?"

"I go to an all-boys' school and it's got no girls for me to carry their books. I always thought I could get a girl from the way I play basketball, but they never watch me play because they never come out in the daytime. Dad, do *you* know where girls go in the daytime?"

He frowned and was silent for a few seconds.

"Maybe they leave Philadelphia," he said.

"That's why I'm watching the buses."

❧

One monkey don't stop no show.

—*Anonymous*

❧

THE SIGNIFYING MONKEY

The term "signifying" refers to African American games involving insult and parody. This verbal artform is a way to express ideas and feelings indirectly—and a means to criticize and insult without causing harm or injury. Perhaps the first really skillful signifier was the "Signifying Monkey." He instigated a fight by telling the Lion that the Elephant had insulted his family. Here is a Harlem version of the ballad that probably got signifying (and its various forms of verbal play, including "the dozens") started among African Americans.

The Monkey and the Lion
Got to talking one day.
Monkey looked down and said, Lion,
I hear you's king in every way.
But I know somebody
Who do not think that is true—
He told me he could whip
The living daylights out of you.
Lion said, Who?
Monkey said, Lion,
He talked about your mama

And talked about your grandma, too,
And I'm too polite to tell you
What he said about you.
Lion said, Who said what? Who?
Monkey in the tree,
Lion on the ground.
Monkey kept on signifying
But he didn't come down.
Monkey said, His name is Elephant—
He stone sure is not your friend.
Lion said, He don't need to be
Because today will be his end.
Lion took off through the jungle
Lickity-split,
Meaning to grab Elephant
And tear him bit to bit. Period!
He come across Elephant copping a righteous nod
Under a fine cool shady tree.
Lion said, You big old no-good so-and-so,
It's either you or me.
Lion let out a solid roar
And bopped Elephant with his paw.
Elephant just took his trunk
And busted old Lion's jaw.
Lion let out another roar,
Reared up six feet tall.
Elephant just kicked him in the belly
And laughed to see him drop and fall.
Lion rolled over,
Copped Elephant by the throat.
Elephant just shook him loose
And butted him like a goat,
Then he tromped him and he stomped him
Till the Lion yelled, Oh, no!
And it was near-nigh sunset
When Elephant let Lion go.
The signifying Monkey

Was still setting in his tree
When he looked down and saw the Lion.
Said, Why, Lion, who can that there be?
Lion said, It's me.
Monkey rapped, Why, Lion,
You look more dead than alive!
Lion said, Monkey, I don't want
To hear your jive-end jive.
Monkey just kept on signifying,
Lion, you for sure caught hell—
Mister Elephant's done whipped you
To a fare-thee-well!
Why, Lion, you look like to me
You been in the precinct station
And had the third-degree,
Else you look like
You been high on gage
And done got caught
In a monkey cage!
You ain't no king to me.
Facts, I don't think that you
Can even as much as roar—
And if you try I'm liable
To come down out of this tree and
Whip your tail some more.
The Monkey started laughing
And jumping up and down.
But he jumped so hard the limb broke
And he landed—*bam!*—on the ground.
When he went to run, his foot slipped
And he fell flat down.
Grrr-rrr-rr-r! The Lion was on him
With his front feet and his hind.
Monkey hollered, Ow!
I didn't mean it, Mister Lion!
Lion said, You little flea-bag you!
Why, I'll eat you up alive.

I wouldn't a-been in this fix a-tall
Wasn't for your signifying jive.
Please, said Monkey, Mister Lion,
If you'll just let me go,
I got something to tell you, *please,*
I think you ought to know.
Lion let the Monkey loose
To see what his tale could be—
And Monkey jumped right back on up
Into his tree.
What I was gonna tell you, said Monkey,
Is you square old so-and-so,
If you fool with me I'll get
Elephant to whip your head some more.
Monkey, said the Lion,
Beat to his unbooted knees,
You and all your signifying children
Better stay up in them trees.
Which is why today
Monkey does his signifying
A-way-up out of the way.

Act your age and not your shoe size.

—Traditional

HOW TO TREAT A CHICKEN
DICK GREGORY

Dick Gregory gives a lesson in proper table etiquette.

Good evening, ladies and gentlemen. I understand there are a good many Southerners in the room tonight. I know the South very well. I spent twenty years there one night. . . .

It's dangerous for me to go back.

Last time I was down South I walked into this restaurant, and this white waitress came up to me and said: "We don't serve colored people here."

I said: "That's all right, I don't eat colored people. Bring me a whole fried chicken."

About that time these three cousins come in, you know the ones I mean, Klu, Kluck, and Klan, and they say: "Boy, we're givin' you fair warnin'. Anything you do to that chicken, we're gonna do to you." About then the waitress brought me my chicken. "Remember, boy, anything you do to that chicken, we're gonna do to you." So I put down my knife and fork, and I picked up that chicken, and I kissed it.

TALL TALES
COLLECTED BY J. MASON BREWER

QUESTION: What de lowest person you ever saw?
ANSWER: De lowest person Ah done ever saw kin sit on a dime
             wid his feet hangin' down.

QUESTION: What de bowleggedest man you ever done see?
ANSWER: A man so bowlegged that he was goin' across de rail-
             road an' he step so wide until one of his foot went in
             his back pocket.

PLANTATION PROVERBS

*Slaves produced a large body of proverbs—gems of wit and wisdom
that are as true today as they were in the nineteenth century.*

Crow an' corn can't grow in de same fiel'.

•

You can hide de fire, but w'at you gwine do wid de smoke?

•

Ef your coat-tail catch a-fire, don't wait till you kin see de blaze 'fo'
you put it out.

•

De price of your hat ain't de measure of your brain.

•

Buyin' on credit is robbin' next year's crop.

•

In God we trust, all others cash.

•

Dirt show de quickest on de cleanest cotton.

•

Blind horse knows when de trough is empty.

•

Ain't no use askin' the cow to pour you a glass of milk.

•

Last year's hot spell cools off mighty fast.

•

Little hole in your pocket is worse than a big one at de knee.

•

Appetite don't regulate de time of day.

•

Man who gits hurt working oughta show de scars.

•

One person can thread a needle better than two.

•

De point of de pin is de easiest end to find.

•

Sharp ax bettern' big muscle.

•

Little flakes make de deepest snow.

•

Deep snow tell heap o' tales on de rabbit.

•

De cowbell can't keep a secret.

•

Jest countin' stumps don't clear the field.

•

Wagon makes the loudest noise when it's goin' out empty.

•

Talkin' 'bout fire doesn't boil the pot.

•

Old Used-to-Do-It-This-Way don't help none today.

•

Death don't see no difference 'tween the big house and the cabin.

•

Can't break the plow point twice.

•

Hand plow can't make furrows by itself.

•

Dog don't get mad when you says he's a dog.

•

Buzzard ain't circle in the air jest for fun.

•

Can't sit on the bucket and draw water at the same time.

•

If you want to see how much folks is goin' to miss you, just stick your finger in de pond den pull it out and look at the hole.

PERMISSIONS

Reasonable efforts have been made to trace the ownership of all copy-righted material included in this volume. Any errors that may have occurred are inadvertent and will be corrected in subsequent editions provided notification is sent to the publisher.

Grateful acknowledgment is made to the following for permission to reprint copyrighted material:

Index of Names and Titles

ABOUT THE AUTHOR

STEVEN BARBOZA is the author of *American Jihad* and a professional journalist who has written for many magazines and newspapers, including *Smithsonian, Essence,* the *New York Times Magazine,* the *Washington Post,* and *USA Today.* He lives in New York City.